SCHAUM'S OUTLINE OF

THEORY AND PROBLEMS

of

QUANTITATIVE METHODS IN MANAGEMENT

•

by

JOHN E. ULLMANN, Ph.D.

Professor of Management
Hofstra University

SCHAUM'S OUTLINE SERIES

McGRAW-HILL BOOK COMPANY

New York   St. Louis   San Francisco   Auckland   Bogotá   Düsseldorf   Johannesburg
London   Madrid   Mexico   Montreal   New Delhi   Panama   Paris
São Paulo   Singapore   Sydney   Tokyo   Toronto

0-07-065742-4

3 4 5 6 7 8 9 10 11 12 13 14 15 16 17 18 19 20   SH SH 8 7 6 5 4 3 2 1

Library of Congress Cataloging in Publication Data

Ullmann, John E

   Theory and problems of quantitative methods in
management, including solved problems.
    (Schaum's outline series)
   Includes index.
    1. Decision-making—Mathematical models.
I. Title.

HD69.D4U54   658.4'033   76-12621

ISBN 0-07-065742-4

Preface

This Outline is intended as a supplement to current texts in quantitative methods, management science, operations research and applied statistics; as a text in its own right; or as a book of reference. Out of the multitude of possible topics, it focuses on those that are practically useful and of wide application. Further, it emphasizes techniques which lead to solutions with no more than a hand calculator. All ideas are developed through numerous examples and solved problems. An unusually complete set of statistical and other tables is provided in the Appendixes.

The book is informally divided into deterministic models (Chapters 1–7) and probabilistic ones (Chapters 8–19). The mathematical preparation required is essentially college algebra. Some formulas are derived by using elementary calculus, but, except in Chapter 3, none of the problem solutions themselves require calculus. Matrix methods are used implicitly in Chapter 7 and also in Chapter 10; but in the former a set of instructions is given which anyone unacquainted with matrices should be able to follow, while in Chapter 10 matrix methods are one of two alternatives presented. I have, therefore, tried to keep mathematical barriers to a minimum.

It is my pleasure to record my appreciation to Professor James A. Cashin of Hofstra University for his encouragement and to my students who first worked with the material in this book. The presentation of reliability profiles in Chapter 18 owes a great deal to my late friend and colleague, Professor E. J. Gumbel of Columbia University. My particular thanks go to David Beckwith for his truly outstanding editorship. This book is affectionately dedicated to Eva, Jim and Kitty Ullmann who, during the time it was being written, had to contend with substantially more than the writer's usual professorial preoccupation.

JOHN E. ULLMANN

Hofstra University
July 1976

CONTENTS

CONTENTS

CONTENTS

CONTENTS

Chapter 1

Elementary Cost Calculations

COSTS AS DECISION INPUTS

Business costs frequently consist of a fixed component plus a variable cost which varies with sales volume or physical output. *Fixed cost* would include fixed charges for equipment and other overhead; *variable costs per unit* consist mainly of direct labor, direct materials and other directly allocable inputs like power. Let F = fixed cost, v = variable cost per unit and X = number of items produced. The cost C for an output X is then

$$C = F + vX \qquad (1.1)$$

EXAMPLE 1.1. What are the costs for 100,000 items when the fixed costs are $10,000 and the variable costs 60¢ per unit?

Here, $F = 10,000$, $v = 0.60$, $X = 100,000$. From (1.1)

$$C = 10,000 + (0.60)(100,000) = \$70,000 \quad Ans.$$

The variable cost v is the slope of C. Differentiating C with respect to X gives $dC/dX = v$.

Sometimes F and v are not known explicitly and have to be computed from two values of C; i.e. we know total cost C_1 for quantity X_1 and C_2 for X_2. Assuming a straight-line relationship, the cost function looks like Fig. 1-1. Then F is the intercept on the vertical (C) axis and v is the slope. From the geometry,

$$v = \frac{C_2 - C_1}{X_2 - X_1} \qquad (1.2)$$

and

$$F = C_1 - vX_1 = C_2 - vX_2 \qquad (1.3)$$

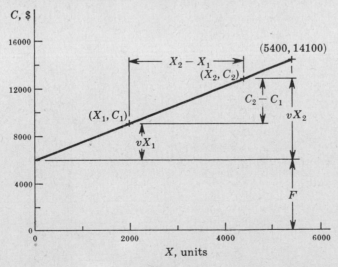

Fig. 1-1

EXAMPLE 1.2. A cost function is linear: when 2000 items are made, total costs are $9000; when 4400 items are made, they are $12,600. (a) Find the fixed cost and the variable cost per unit. (b) Find the cost for 5400 units.

(a) From (1.2) or Fig. 1-1:

$$v = \frac{12,600 - 9000}{4400 - 2000} = \$1.50 \text{ per unit} \quad Ans.$$

From (1.3):

$$F = 9000 - (1.50)(2000) = \$6000 \quad Ans.$$

(b) From (1.1):

$$C = 6000 + (1.50)(5400) = \$14,100 \quad Ans.$$

BREAKEVEN ANALYSIS
Profit Calculations.

When an item is sold for an amount r each, the total revenues R are

$$R = rX \tag{1.4}$$

and the profit is

$$P = R - C \tag{1.5}$$

Plotting R and C on the same graph (Fig. 1-2) shows a crossover or *breakeven* point for which $P = R - C = 0$; i.e. $R = C$. From (1.1) and (1.4), this breakeven point X_b is given by

$$rX_b = F + vX_b \quad \text{or} \quad X_b = \frac{F}{r - v} \tag{1.6}$$

For $X > X_b$ there is a profit; for $X < X_b$, profit is negative, i.e. there is a loss. The quantity $r - v$ is called the *profit contribution*.

EXAMPLE 1.3. In a manufacturing process, fixed cost is $10,000. The variable cost per unit is 40¢ and the item is sold for 60¢ each. Find (a) the breakeven point, (b) the breakeven volume.

(a) $F = 10,000$, $v = 0.4$, $r = 0.6$; from (1.6)

$$X_b = \frac{10,000}{0.6 - 0.4} = 50,000 \text{ units} \quad Ans.$$

(b) The corresponding volume R_b is obtained by substituting $X = X_b$ in either (1.1) or (1.4):

$$R_b = (0.6)(50,000) = \$30,000 \quad Ans.$$

or

$$R_b = 10,000 + (0.4)(50,000) = \$30,000 \quad Ans.$$

The results are plotted in Fig. 1-2.

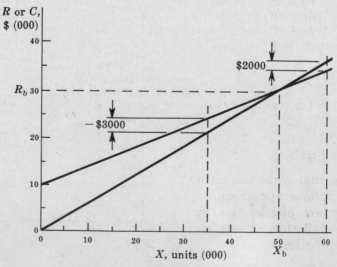

Fig. 1-2

EXAMPLE 1.4. In Example 1.3, find the profit (loss) for volumes of (a) 60,000, (b) 35,000 units.

From (*1.5*):

(a) $$P = R - C = (0.6)(60,000) - [10,000 + (0.4)(60,000)] = \$2000 \quad Ans.$$

(b) $$P = (0.6)(35,000) - [10,000 + (0.4)(35,000)] = -\$3000 \text{ (a loss)} \quad Ans.$$

Assessing Two Alternatives.

Given two processes, 1 and 2, with fixed costs F_1 and F_2 and variable costs per unit v_1 and v_2, breakeven analysis can be used to determine at what volume X it pays to shift from one process to the other, or whether it pays at all. The breakeven point X_b is given by equating the two cost functions (*1.1*):

$$F_1 + v_1 X_b = F_2 + v_2 X_b$$

$$X_b = \frac{F_1 - F_2}{v_2 - v_1} \tag{1.7}$$

If X_b is to be positive, $F_1 > F_2$ and $v_1 < v_2$; this is the typical case which arises from the use of a more expensive automatic machine which, however, saves on direct labor. If $F_1 > F_2$ and $v_1 > v_2$, the cost lines would diverge and process 1 would never be economically justified.

EXAMPLE 1.5. A factory has two machines with the following costs:

	Machine A	Machine B
Fixed Costs, $	1200	2000
Variable Costs per Piece, $/unit	0.75	0.50

Find (a) the breakeven point and (b) the production cost at breakeven.

(a) From (*1.7*): $$X_b = \frac{2000 - 1200}{0.75 - 0.50} = 3200 \text{ pieces} \quad Ans.$$

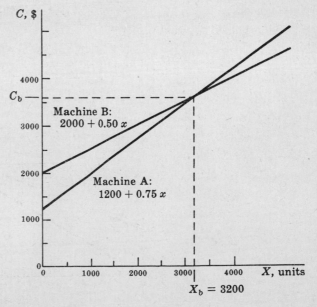

If the order quantity $Q < 3200$, use machine A; if $Q > 3200$, use machine B.

(b) The cost C_b of the 3200 pieces at breakeven is obtained by substituting either the data for machine A or B into (*1.1*):

$$C_b = 2000 + 0.50(3200) = \$3600 \quad Ans.$$

or

$$C_b = 1200 + 0.75(3200) = \$3600 \quad Ans.$$

Figure 1-3 is drawn to scale for this example.

Machine B: $2000 + 0.50\,x$

Machine A: $1200 + 0.75\,x$

$X_b = 3200$

Fig. 1-3

ECONOMY OF SCALE

It has been found that when the costs of many business functions and of equipment and machinery are plotted against the capacity of the installation, an empirical relationship results, given by

$$C = aK^b \tag{1.8}$$

where C is the cost, K the capacity and a and b are constants. When $0 < b < 1$, the cost function looks like Fig. 1-4(b), i.e. the cost goes up more slowly than the capacity. This is called *economy of scale*. Cases in which $b > 1$ exhibit *diseconomy of scale*. Taking logarithms of both sides of (1.8),

$$\log C = \log a + b \log K \tag{1.9}$$

Thus, using logarithmic scales on both axes of the graph paper (log-log paper), (1.8) can be directly represented as a straight line, as in Fig. 1-4(a).

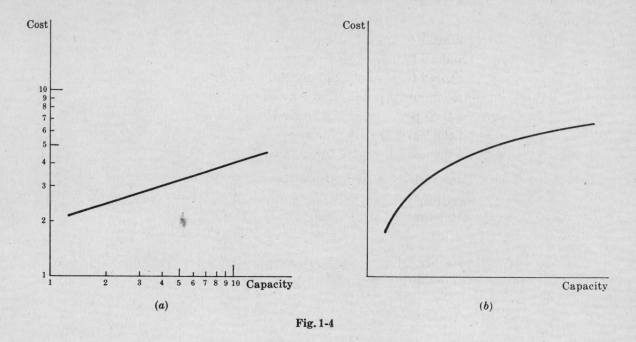

Fig. 1-4

EXAMPLE 1.6. A portion of an electric power plant has the cost function $C = 1.3\,K^{0.7}$ where C is cost in \$ million and K is capacity in megawatts. Find the cost of an 800-MW plant.

From (1.8), $C = (1.3)(800)^{0.7}$. This may be worked out directly using a calculator with an X^Y feature or by the logarithmic method of (1.9):

$$\log C = \log 1.3 + (0.7)(\log 800) = 0.1139 + (0.7)(2.9031) = 2.1461$$

$$C = \text{antilog}\,2.1461 = 140, \text{ i.e. \$140 million} \quad Ans.$$

Given the cost of one plant, (1.8) may be used to "scale up" to another. If there are two plants, 1 and 2, then

$$\frac{C_1}{C_2} = \left(\frac{K_1}{K_2}\right)^b \tag{1.10}$$

EXAMPLE 1.7. Given $b = 0.7$ and the cost of an 800-MW plant as \$140 million, what is the estimated cost of an 1100-MW plant?

Denote the 1100-MW plant as plant 1. Then from (1.10),

$$C_1 = C_2\left(\frac{K_1}{K_2}\right)^b = 140\left(\frac{1100}{800}\right)^{0.7} = 140(1.375)^{0.7} = 140(1.250)$$

$$= 175, \text{ i.e. \$175 million} \quad Ans.$$

A method of estimating a and b from a set of data on cost and capacity is given in Problem 17.2. See also Problem 1.9 for a physical justification of economy of scale.

THE LEARNING CURVE

When a repetitive job is being done, it has been found empirically that as the production run proceeds, the time taken for each item decreases. Specifically, it has been shown that when the average time over a certain number of units is plotted against the serial number of items produced, the result is a straight line on a log-log grid (Fig. 1-5). In practice the rate of learning (which is given by the slope) must be derived from actual operating results (Problem 17.15). However, in estimating a new job, past learning rates for similar work are taken as given and the analysis proceeds as indicated here.

Notation

x = serial number of units

t_1 = time required for first unit

u_x = time required for unit no. x (*marginal time* for x)

T_x = total time required for the first x units

a_x = average time per unit for the first x units

k = slope of the learning curve for a_x

p = slope of the learning curve for a_x in percent notation

The above definitions yield certain basic relationships:

1. The time required for the xth unit is given by the total time taken for the first x units less the total time taken for the first $(x-1)$ units, i.e.

$$u_x = T_x - T_{x-1} \qquad (1.11)$$

2. The average time per unit for the first x units is given by the total time taken for the first x units, divided by x; i.e.

$$a_x = \frac{T_x}{x} \qquad (1.12)$$

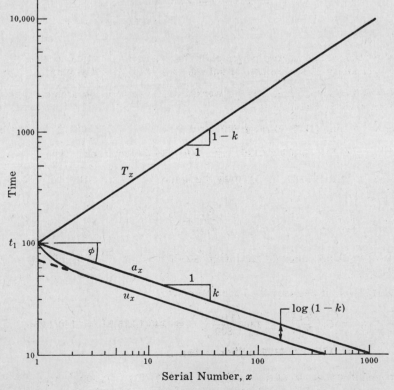

Fig. 1-5

In Fig. 1-5 the line for a_x has an intercept at $x = 1$ (i.e. at $\log x = 0$) of $\log t_1$. Its slope is $-k$, downward slopes being negative. Since we have a straight line on log-log paper, it follows by analogy with (1.9) and (1.8) that

$$\log a_x = \log t_1 - k \log x \tag{1.13}$$

and, taking antilogs,

$$a_x = t_1 x^{-k} \tag{1.14}$$

From (1.12) and (1.14)

$$T_x = x(t_1 x^{-k}) = t_1 x^{1-k} \tag{1.15}$$

The line for T_x is shown in the upper part of Fig. 1-5; usually we do not trouble to plot it.

We obtain u_x by substituting (1.15) in (1.11):

$$u_x = t_1 x^{1-k} - t_1 (x-1)^{1-k} = t_1 [x^{1-k} - (x-1)^{1-k}] \tag{1.16}$$

The function u_x, as shown in Fig. 1-5, first deviates from a_x and then becomes parallel to it. This can be shown by expanding the second term in (1.16) by the binomial theorem:

$$u_x = t_1 [x^{1-k} - x^{1-k} + (1-k)x^{-k} - \text{terms in higher negative powers of } x]$$

When $x > 10$, the last terms may be neglected so that

$$u_x \approx t_1 x^{-k}(1-k) = a_x(1-k) \qquad x > 10 \tag{1.17}$$

On the log-log grid of Fig. 1-5 this is a straight line parallel to a_x and a distance $\log(1-k)$ from it.

Another useful formula is that for the total time $T_{a,b}$ needed to make units numbered a through b ($b > a$). Since $T_{a,b} = T_b - T_{a-1}$, (1.15) gives

$$T_{a,b} = t_1 [b^{1-k} - (a-1)^{1-k}] \tag{1.18}$$

By convention, a learning curve is often designated by its *learning percentage p*, which is another way of measuring its slope. Every doubling of the serial number reduces a_x to p percent of what it was. For example,

$$p = \frac{a_2}{a_1} = \frac{a_4}{a_2} = \frac{a_{60}}{a_{30}} = \frac{a_{4000}}{a_{2000}}$$

or, in general,

$$p = \frac{a_{2x}}{a_x} \tag{1.19}$$

When $x > 10$, it is also approximately true that

$$p = \frac{u_{2x}}{u_x} \tag{1.20}$$

The relationship between p and k is obtained by substituting (1.14) in (1.19):

$$p = \frac{(2x)^{-k}}{x^{-k}} \tag{1.21}$$

or

$$k = \frac{-\log p}{\log 2} = (-3.32) \log p \tag{1.22}$$

In order to draw the a_x line conveniently, it is useful to have the following relation for the angle ϕ:

$$k = \tan \phi \tag{1.23}$$

Figure 1-6 is a complete conversion chart for k, p and ϕ.

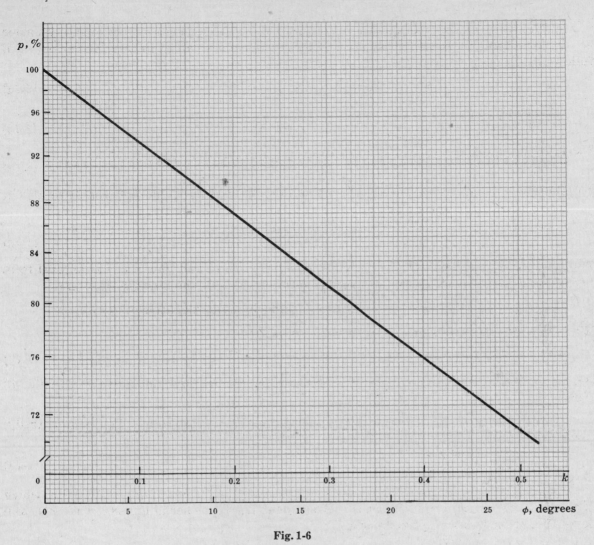

p, %

Fig. 1-6

EXAMPLE 1.8. The first of a batch of 90 machines takes 100 hours to assemble. Given an 80 percent learning rate, find (a) the average time for the batch; (b) the total time for the batch; (c) the time for the last unit; (d) the total time for the last 10 units; (e) the time for the 64th machine; (f) the average time for the first 32 machines.

(a) From (1.22) or Fig. 1-6:

$$k = (-3.32)\log(0.8) = (-3.32)(\bar{1}.9031) = (-3.32)(-0.0969) = 0.322$$

From (1.14):

$$a_{90} = 100(90)^{-0.322} = 23.48 \text{ hr per unit} \quad Ans.$$

(b) From (1.12):

$$T_{90} = 90(23.48) = 2113.2 \text{ hr} \quad Ans.$$

(c) From (1.17), since $x > 10$,

$$u_{90} = a_{90}(1 - k) = 23.48(1 - 0.322) = 15.92 \text{ hr} \quad Ans.$$

(d) From (1.18):

$$T_{80,90} = 100(90^{1-0.322} - 80^{1-0.322}) = 100(21.1337 - 19.5117) = 162.2 \text{ hr} \quad Ans.$$

(e) From (1.17):

$$u_{64} = 100(64)^{-0.322}(1 - 0.322) = 17.77 \text{ hr} \quad Ans.$$

(f) This can be determined as in (a), but we can also use (1.19) and successively multiply the previous a_x by $p = 0.8$ every time x doubles:

x	1	2	4	8	16	32
a_x	100	80	64	51.2	40.96	32.77 hr per unit *Ans.*

Solved Problems

BREAKEVEN ANALYSIS

1.1. Cost functions do not have to be linear. For the nonlinear function

$$C = a + bX + cX^2$$

three pairs of points are known:

Quantity X, units (00)	$X_1 = 6$	$X_2 = 10$	$X_3 = 20$
Total Cost, C, \$ (000)	$C_1 = 104$	$C_2 = 160$	$C_3 = 370$

(a) Find the coefficients a, b and c. (b) Find the marginal or unit incremental cost.

(a) The task is to solve the equations

$$y_1 = a + bx_1 + cx_1^2$$
$$y_2 = a + bx_2 + cx_2^2$$
$$y_3 = a + bx_3 + cx_3^2$$

for a, b and c which also satisfy the general equation $y = a + bx + cx^2$. It can be shown, by the method of *Lagrange interpolation*, that

$$y = y_1 \frac{(x-x_2)(x-x_3)}{(x_1-x_2)(x_1-x_3)} + y_2 \frac{(x-x_1)(x-x_3)}{(x_2-x_1)(x_2-x_3)} + y_3 \frac{(x-x_1)(x-x_2)}{(x_3-x_1)(x_3-x_2)} \quad (1.24)$$

which gives directly the required equation. Writing C for y and X for x in (1.24) and putting in the data,

$$C = 104 \frac{(X-10)(X-20)}{(6-10)(6-20)} + 160 \frac{(X-6)(X-20)}{(10-6)(10-20)} + 370 \frac{(X-6)(X-10)}{(20-6)(20-10)}$$

$$= \frac{13}{7}(X^2 - 30X + 200) - 4(X^2 - 26X + 120) + \frac{37}{14}(X^2 - 16X + 60)$$

$$= \left[\frac{13}{7}(200) - 4(120) + \frac{37}{14}(60)\right] + X\left[\frac{13}{7}(-30) + 4(26) + \frac{37}{14}(-16)\right] + X^2\left(\frac{13}{7} - 4 + \frac{37}{14}\right)$$

$$= \frac{13(200) - 28(120) + 37(30)}{7} + X\frac{13(-30) + 28(26) - 37(8)}{7} + X^2\frac{26 - 56 + 37}{14}$$

$$= 50 + 6X + \tfrac{1}{2}X^2 \quad Ans.$$

(b) The *marginal* or *unit incremental cost* is that which arises from adding one unit to the production. It is given by the rate of change of C, i.e. by

$$\frac{dC}{dX} = b + 2cX = 6 + X \quad Ans.$$

Cost functions of the above type are sometimes fitted when it is desired to have an approximate continuous function take the place of two or more discontinuous ones. The above function is plotted in Fig. 1-7, which shows three tangential straight lines which it fits approximately; such characteristics may arise in practice from overtime, extra shifts, the use of more expensive materials when cheaper sources are exhausted, and so on. (For another approach see Problem 1.4.)

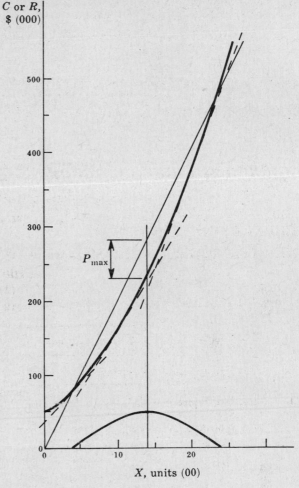

1.2. In Problem 1.1 the sales price is set at \$200 per unit. (*a*) Determine the profit function. (*b*) Show that there are two values for which it is zero. (*c*) Find its maximum.

(*a*) In the units of Problem 1.1

$$r = \frac{200(100)}{1000} = 20$$

From (*1.5*)

$$P = R - C$$
$$= 20X - (50 + 6X + \tfrac{1}{2}X^2)$$
$$= -\tfrac{1}{2}X^2 + 14X - 50 \quad Ans.$$

(*b*) The revenue line $R = 20X$ is shown in Fig. 1-7 as well and indicates that there are two points at which $P = 0$. These are the roots of

Fig. 1-7

$$-\tfrac{1}{2}X^2 + 14X - 50 = 0$$

or

$$X = \frac{-14 \pm \sqrt{196 - 100}}{-1} = 4.2, 23.8$$

i.e. 420 and 2380 units. *Ans.*

The lower point is the breakeven point, the upper one the *profit limit point*.

(*c*) The value of X for which profit is a maximum is determined by setting

$$\frac{dP}{dX} = -X + 14 = 0 \quad \text{or} \quad X = 14$$

Substituting in P, the maximum profit is

$$P_{max} = -\tfrac{1}{2}(14)^2 + 14(14) - 50 = 48, \quad \text{i.e. \$48,000} \quad Ans.$$

The profit function plotted by itself appears at the bottom of Fig. 1-7.

1.3. Breakeven points may also be expressed directly in dollars without reference to units. (*a*) Find V_b in terms of R, C and F. (*b*) What is the breakeven volume if, when revenues are \$42,000, total variable costs are \$28,000 and fixed costs \$10,000?

(*a*) Consider Fig. 1-8. Draw the cost line from F to C and then the revenue line at $45°$ (if scales are the same on both axes, as they usually are). V_b can be read off directly or calculated from the similar triangles $FF'V_b$ and $FF''C$. Hence

$$\frac{V_b}{V_b - F} = \frac{R}{C - F}$$

$$V_b(C - F) = RV_b - RF$$

$$V_b = \frac{RF}{R - C + F} \quad Ans. \tag{1.25}$$

If we denote $P = R - C$ as the profit,

$$V_b = \frac{RF}{P + F} \tag{1.26}$$

(Note that other pairs of similar triangles, e.g. V_bCR and V_bFO, give the same result.)

(*b*) Substituting in (*1.25*), where $C - F = \$28{,}000$,

$$V_b = \frac{42{,}000(10{,}000)}{42{,}000 - 28{,}000} = \$30{,}000 \quad Ans.$$

This is the same result which was expressed in both units and dollars in Example 1.3.

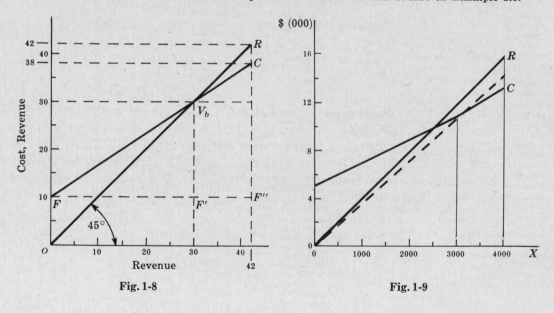

Fig. 1-8   Fig. 1-9

1.4. The fixed cost for a manufacturing process is \$5000 a year. Revenues per piece are \$4. When 3000 or fewer items are being made, the variable cost can be held to \$2 each, but when volume rises above this level, there is overtime and the cost rises to \$2.40 each. Find (*a*) the breakeven point, (*b*) the profit at 4000 pieces.

The problem is illustrated in Fig. 1-9; note the kink in the cost line at $X = 3000$.

(*a*) From (*1.6*):

$$X_b = \frac{5000}{4 - 2} = 2500 \text{ pieces} \quad Ans.$$

(*b*) From (*1.4*), $R = 4000(4) = \$16{,}000$, and

$$C = 5000 + 3000(2) + (4000 - 3000)(2.40) = \$13{,}400$$

where the first term is the fixed cost, the second the variable cost for the first 3000 items and the third the variable cost for the 1000 items beyond the 3000-item breakpoint. Hence

$$P = R - C = 16{,}000 - 13{,}400 = \$2600 \quad Ans.$$

1.5. Recompute the breakeven point for the data of Example 1.4 except that revenues are changed to $3.50 each.

The new revenue line, shown dashed in Fig. 1-9, now passes through the cost line at a point above $X = 3000$ pieces. This changes the cost function used in calculating the breakeven point X_b.

Revenues	Costs

$$3.50 X_b = 5000 + 3000(2) + (X_b - 3000)(2.40)$$

Solving,
$$1.1 X_b = 11,000 - 7200 - 3800$$

$$X_b = 3455 \text{ pieces} \quad Ans.$$

1.6. An ore body contains 15 million tons and can be bought for $12 million plus a royalty of $20 per ton. There is an additional smelting cost of $40 per ton. When refined the metal sells for 50 cents per lb. Find the breakeven grade of the ore.

Let the breakeven grade be p. The total variable cost is $20 + 40 = 60/ton. Applying (1.1) and (1.4),

Costs	Revenues

$$12,000,000 + 60(15,000,000) = (15,000,000p)(0.50)(2000)$$

$$p = \frac{912,000,000}{15,000,000,000} = 6.1 \text{ percent} \quad Ans.$$

1.7. A manufacturer has an order for 100,000 circuit boards. With his present equipment, they cost 80 cents each to make and there is a 6 percent fraction defective. However, he may install special controls which, together with their cost of development, cost $18,000. His variable cost per item then falls to 60 cents each, but the process may be less reliable. How much less reliable can the process be before he should reject the special controls?

We require the breakeven fraction defective, p. To get 100,000 good items, $100,000/(1-p)$ would have to be made.

Cost (old)	Cost (new)

$$(0.80)\frac{100,000}{1 - 0.06} = 18,000 + (0.60)\frac{100,000}{1 - p}$$

$$1 - p = \frac{60,000}{85,106 - 18,000} = 0.894 \quad \text{or} \quad p = 10.6 \text{ percent} \quad Ans.$$

1.8. A household chemical consists of four parts of ingredient Q to one of ingredient P. Fixed costs, variable costs and revenues are as in Table 1-1. Find the breakeven point of the plant.

Table 1-1

Item	P	Q
Fixed Costs F, $/yr	12,000	4,000
Variable Costs v, $/gal	15	6
Revenues r, $/gal	21	10

We first determine the combined effects, taking 5 gal as the volume unit:

Fixed $\qquad F_P + F_Q = 12,000 + 4,000 = 16,000$

Variable $\quad v_P + 4v_Q = 15 + 4(6) = 39$

Revenues $\quad r_P + 4r_Q = 21 + 4(10) = 61$

Then $\qquad\qquad\qquad X_b = \dfrac{16,000}{61 - 39} = 727 \text{ batches} = 3635 \text{ gal} \quad Ans.$

ECONOMY OF SCALE

1.9. Show that cubical tanks may be expected to have an economy of scale index b of about 2/3.

Let one side of the tank be s. The capacity of the tank is s^3, i.e. $K = s^3$ or $K^{1/3} = s$. Its cost is proportional to its surface area, i.e. to s^2. Therefore $C \propto s^2$ and, substituting for s, $C \propto K^{2/3}$. (This index is realistic in practice. It is also affected by the amount of welding, which, being proportional to s, would tend to reduce b below 2/3, and by the cost of connections, which usually does not bear a direct relationship to the size of the tank; this introduces a slight diseconomy, leaving b at about 2/3.)

LEARNING CURVE

1.10. The first unit in a batch of 90 took 40 minutes to complete. The whole run took 30 hours. Find the percent learning rate.

From (1.15) with $T_{90} = 30 \text{ hr} = 1800 \text{ min}$

$$1800 = 40(90)^{1-k}$$

$$\log 1800 = \log 40 + (1-k) \log 90$$

$$3.2553 = 1.6021 + (1-k)(1.9542)$$

$$1 - k = 0.846; \quad k = 0.154$$

From (1.21): $\qquad p = 2^{-0.154} = 0.899, \text{ i.e. } 89.9 \text{ percent} \quad Ans.$

Supplementary Problems

BREAKEVEN ANALYSIS

1.11. A machine makes parts in batches of 2000 each, with a certain fraction defective. If one of the bad parts is installed in the final assembly, it costs $1.20 to fix. The machine can be checked out exactly for an extra $36 in machinist's time and then there are no defective parts. Find the breakeven value of the fraction defective. *Ans.* 1.5 percent

1.12. A publisher plans a reference volume which, he believes, would be of interest to 25,000 public and university libraries. It is expected to have 500 pages which cost $15 each for offset camera copy and plates and 2 cents each to print. The book will sell for $15 a copy less 20 percent discount. (a) What is the breakeven sales volume and (b) what market penetration would that represent?

Ans. (a) 3750 books for $56,250 gross, $45,000 net; (b) 15 percent

1.13. In Problem 1.7, suppose more expensive versions of the equipment are available which, while keeping variable costs at 60¢ each, also keep the fraction defective at (a) 6 percent, (b) 0 percent. How much could the manufacturer spend for such equipment and break even on it?

Ans. (a) $21,277; (b) $25,106

1.14. A manufacturer faces a make-or-buy decision. He can buy a part for $4.50 each; he needs 3000 a year. He could also make the parts for a fixed investment for tooling, etc., of $9000 and a variable cost for labor and materials of $2 each. (a) Should he make or buy? (b) What is the breakeven volume?   *Ans.* (a) buy, (b) 3600

1.15. Based on the data of Table 1-2, draw up a schedule of machine choice depending on production quantities (*Hint.* Draw graphs of the cost functions so as to see the breakeven relationships.)

Table 1-2

Machine	Fixed Cost p.a., $	Variable Cost Each, $
A	5,000	6.00
B	10,000	4.00
C	13,000	2.50
D	18,000	1.25

Ans. Machine A for fewer than 2285 pieces; Machine C between 2285 and 4000 pieces; Machine D above that. Machine B is economically inadvisable.

ECONOMY OF SCALE

1.16. The annual payroll of a chemical firm is given by $W = 43K^{1/4}$ where K is the capacity in thousands of tons and W the payroll in millions of dollars. Find the payroll at (a) 250,000, (b) 350,000 tons a year. Is there an operational reason why the index is as low as 1/4?

Ans. (a) $171 million, (b) $186 million. Chemical plants are generally highly automated and no more manpower is required in operating controls for a large valve, conveyor, etc., than for a small one.

1.17. A certain machine has a cost function of $C = 4500K^{0.8}$ where K is capacity in horsepower. What would a 50-h.p. machine cost?   *Ans.* $102,893.64

1.18. A machine has a cost function of $C = 95K^{0.65}$ where K is the capacity in pounds per day. How much would a 0.78-lb/day machine cost?   *Ans.* $80.83

1.19. An office machine that prints 100 copies per minute costs $5000. How much would a machine with an output of 110 copies per minute cost? The economy of scale index is 2/3.   *Ans.* $5328.01

THE LEARNING CURVE

The following problems relate to a series of 200 assemblies of which the first takes 80 minutes, with learning at 90 percent.

1.20. Find k.   *Ans.* 0.152

1.21. The average time for the whole run.   *Ans.* 35.75 min

1.22. The time for the last item.   *Ans.* 30.32 min

1.23. The total time for the run.   *Ans.* 7150.94 min

1.24. The time for the first 100 items.   *Ans.* 3972.74 min

1.25. The time for the second 100 items. (Check by subtraction.)   *Ans.* 3178.20 min

1.26. The average time for the first 100 items.   *Ans.* 39.72 min

1.27. The time for the 100th unit.   *Ans.* 33.68 min

1.28. The total time for the first ten items.   *Ans.* 563.75 min

Chapter 2

Deterministic Inventory Models

THE TWO KINDS OF MODELS

A *deterministic* model of a business process or operation is a mathematical representation of it in which all input variables are assumed to be known exactly. The opposite is a *probabilistic* model in which at least one major variable is of a random nature. A deterministic model sometimes takes as exactly known the results of a previous analysis that had some elements of uncertainty in it. While this is not strictly correct, much inventory planning is done by departments which have to take at least near-term forecasts as fixed. Errors in such forecasts are usually not expected to be so grave that one cannot "live with them" even for a short time. Also, as shown in Chapter 17, there are methods for compensating for past errors in future periods. Accordingly, the deterministic models of this chapter are probably still the ones most often used.

Probabilistic models are discussed in Chapters 13 and 14.

ECONOMIC LOT SIZE: INSTANTANEOUS REPLENISHMENT, NO SHORTAGES

The problem is to set production quantities (batch sizes) for products which are continuously required. When stock has run out, we assume that it is instantaneously replenished. Usage levels are known with certainty. The quantities are then as shown in the "sawtooth diagram" in Fig. 2-1(a).

The objective is to carry on such an inventory policy at minimum cost, i.e. in such a way that the total of all costs remains a minimum. To do this, we must derive a *total cost function* and obtain that value of the *decision variable*, in this case the production quantity, which will make it a minimum.

Notation

A = cost of one setup, purchase order, etc.

u = usage, units per unit of time

c = carrying or holding cost per unit of product per unit of time

q = production or order quantity, units

t = length of one inventory cycle, units of time (i.e. $t = q/u$)

C = total cost per unit of time

The total cost has two components. First, it is required to set up the machine or place the order, the cost being independent of the order quantity. Clearly, however, the more ordered at one time, the fewer such orders will have to be placed in a year or other fixed time unit, and the smaller will be the setup cost within the time period concerned. On the other hand, ordering a greater quantity at one time means that there is more in stock, on the average, over any period and this involves an increased carrying charge (storage, interest, insurance, etc.). At one value of the batch size the joint effect of the increasing carrying charge and the decreasing setup cost produces a minimum total cost.

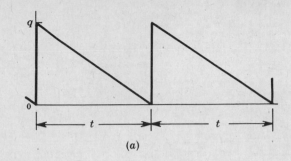

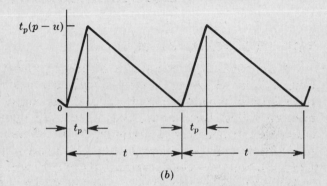

Setup cost. There are u/q setups per unit of time and their cost is Au/q.

Carrying cost. As indicated in Fig. 2-1(a), the inventory on hand varies linearly from q at the beginning of a cycle to 0 at the end. The average on hand is therefore $q/2$, and the cost of carrying it is $cq/2$.

We further assume that the remaining cost of the item does not vary with q. Hence the total cost which is influenced by the choice of q is just the sum of the carrying cost and setup cost. Thus

$$C = \frac{Au}{q} + \frac{cq}{2} \qquad (2.1)$$

To get a minimum, we differentiate with respect to q and set the result equal to zero.

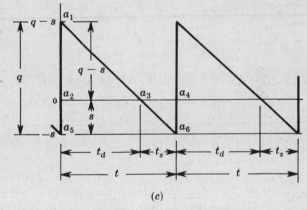

Fig. 2-1

$$\frac{dC}{dq} = -\frac{Au}{q^2} + \frac{c}{2} = 0 \qquad (2.2)$$

$$q^{*2} = \frac{2Au}{c} \quad \text{or} \quad q^* = \sqrt{\frac{2Au}{c}} \qquad (2.3)$$

$$C^* = Au\sqrt{\frac{c}{2Au}} + \frac{c}{2}\sqrt{\frac{2Au}{c}} = \sqrt{2Auc} \qquad (2.4)$$

The cost function and its components are shown in Fig. 2-2. Note that the minimum occurs at the value of q where the two cost components intersect. Therefore q^* can also be obtained by setting the setup and carrying costs equal to each other and solving for q. The quantity q^* is called the *economic order quantity* (EOQ) or *economic lot size*.

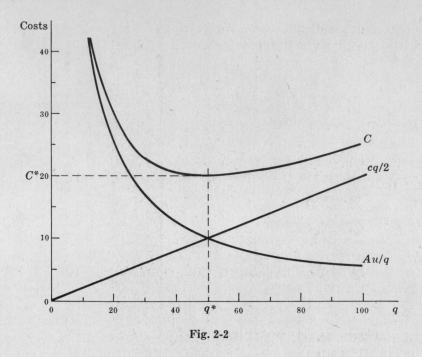

Fig. 2-2

EXAMPLE 2.1. Find the EOQ and minimum cost if

$$\text{Usage} = 100 \text{ items per month}$$

$$\text{Setup} = \$5 \text{ each}$$

$$\text{Carrying charge} = 40¢ \text{ per month per item}$$

Here $u = 100$, $A = 5$, $c = 0.40$. From (2.3) and (2.4), respectively:

$$q^* = \sqrt{\frac{2(5)(100)}{0.40}} = 50 \text{ items} \quad Ans.$$

$$C^* = \sqrt{2(5)(100)(0.40)} = \$20/\text{month} \quad Ans.$$

Note that the C curve (Fig. 2-2) is quite flat at the optimal level.

ECONOMIC LOT SIZE: PRODUCTION CYCLE, NO SHORTAGES

In this case, we discard the assumption of instantaneous replenishment and assume that it takes time t_p to produce q. Production takes place at a rate of p units per unit of time. It is again required to find the minimizing q.

In the cost function C for this problem, the setup cost term is the same as before. The carrying cost term must be changed, however, to reflect the revised average inventory in stock. As shown in Fig. 2-1(b), in every unit of time t_p, p units are produced and u units consumed, so that there is a net increase of $p - u$ per unit of time. This stage reaches a peak at the end of t_p when there are $t_p(p-u)$ items in inventory. But during t_p we have produced q, so that $pt_p = q$ and $t_p = q/p$. Therefore the maximum inventory is

$$\frac{q}{p}(p-u) = q\left(1 - \frac{u}{p}\right)$$

The average in stock is again half the maximum, so that

$$C = \frac{Au}{q} + \frac{cq}{2}\left(1 - \frac{u}{p}\right) \tag{2.5}$$

The simplest way to proceed is to treat the expression in parentheses as simply a multiplier of c and to carry it right through the previous results. It then follows from (2.3) and (2.4) that

$$q^* = \sqrt{\frac{2Au}{c}} \frac{1}{\sqrt{1-(u/p)}} \qquad (2.6)$$

$$C^* = \sqrt{2Auc}\sqrt{1-(u/p)} \qquad (2.7)$$

EXAMPLE 2.2. As in Example 2.1, $u = 100$ units per month, $A = \$5$, $c = 40¢$ per unit per month, and, additionally, production is at the rate of 500 units per month. Find q^* and C^*.

From (2.6) and (2.7), respectively:

$$q^* = \sqrt{\frac{2(5)(100)}{0.40}} \frac{1}{\sqrt{1-(100/500)}} = 56 \text{ items} \quad Ans.$$

$$C^* = \sqrt{2(5)(100)(0.40)}\sqrt{1-(100/500)} = \$17.89 \quad Ans.$$

ECONOMIC LOT SIZE: INSTANTANEOUS REPLENISHMENT, SHORTAGES PERMITTED

If customers are patient up to a point, a stockout need not be deleterious. If the only damage suffered is a small backorder cost b per unit per unit of time (e.g. merely a logging of future requirements and not a complete individual order) and no business is lost beyond that, it may be advantageous to have shortages in each cycle as a matter of deliberate policy. The resulting changes in inventory are shown in Fig. 2-1(c). To derive an optimal policy in such a model, it is necessary to have two decision variables, q and s, where s is the maximum amount of shortage in each cycle. Note that when q is delivered, an amount s is already earmarked, so that the maximum in stock at the beginning of the cycle is $q-s$.

Setup cost. This is Au/q, as before.

Carrying cost. The average number in inventory is $\frac{1}{2}(q-s)$, but this is held only during a part of the cycle given by the ratio t_d/t. From similar triangles $a_1a_5a_6$ and $a_1a_2a_3$

$$\frac{t_d}{t} = \frac{q-s}{q}$$

The carrying cost is therefore

$$\left(c\frac{q-s}{2}\right)\left(\frac{q-s}{q}\right) = \frac{c(q-s)^2}{2q}$$

Shortage cost. The average number short is $s/2$, but there is a shortage only in the portion of the cycle defined by t_s/t. From the similar triangles $a_1a_5a_6$ and $a_3a_4a_6$

$$\frac{t_s}{t} = \frac{s}{q}$$

The shortage cost is therefore

$$\left(b\frac{s}{2}\right)\left(\frac{s}{q}\right) = \frac{bs^2}{2q}$$

Therefore

$$C = \frac{Au}{q} + \frac{c(q-s)^2}{2q} + \frac{bs^2}{2q} = \frac{Au}{q} + \frac{cq}{2} - cs + \frac{cs^2+bs^2}{2q}$$

To get a minimum we have to do partial differentiations with respect to q and s and equate to zero.

$$\frac{\partial C}{\partial s} = -c + (b+c)\frac{s}{q} = 0 \qquad \frac{\partial C}{\partial q} = -\frac{Au}{q^2} + \frac{c}{2} - \frac{cs^2}{2q^2} - \frac{bs^2}{2q^2} = 0$$

The first equation yields

$$s^* = \frac{c}{b+c}\,q^* \qquad (2.8)$$

Multiplying the second equation by 2, rearranging and substituting for s/q from (2.8) gives

$$\frac{2Au}{q^{*2}} = c - (b+c)\frac{c^2}{(b+c)^2} = \frac{bc}{b+c}$$

or

$$q^* = \sqrt{\frac{2Au}{c}}\sqrt{\frac{b+c}{b}} \qquad (2.9)$$

Note that this formula differs from (2.3) only in that c has a multiplier $b/(b+c)$. Hence

$$C^* = \sqrt{2Auc}\sqrt{\frac{b}{b+c}} \qquad (2.10)$$

and substituting (2.9) in (2.8),

$$s^* = \sqrt{\frac{2Au}{b}}\sqrt{\frac{c}{b+c}} \qquad (2.11)$$

Note that $s^* = C^*/b$.

EXAMPLE 2.3. All data are as in Example 2.1, except there is a shortage charge of 15¢/unit/month. Find q^*, C^* and s^*.

From (2.9), (2.10) and (2.11), respectively:

$$q^* = \sqrt{\frac{2(5)(100)}{0.40}}\sqrt{\frac{0.40+0.15}{0.15}} = 50\sqrt{\frac{1}{0.273}} = 96 \text{ units} \quad Ans.$$

$$C^* = \sqrt{2(5)(100)(0.40)}\sqrt{\frac{0.15}{0.15+0.40}} = 20\sqrt{0.273} = \$10.46 \quad Ans.$$

$$s^* = \sqrt{\frac{2(5)(100)}{0.15}}\sqrt{\frac{0.40}{0.15+0.40}} = 70 \text{ units} \quad Ans.$$

This result shows that when stockout costs are low, it becomes possible to run an inventory almost on a special-order basis; here, whenever a lot of 96 items is delivered, 70 of them are already reserved. On the other hand, if no shortages are permitted, i.e. if the stockout cost is made infinite, (2.9) and (2.10) become equal to (2.3) and (2.4), and s^* tends towards zero. More formally,

$$\lim_{b\to\infty}\frac{b}{b+c} = 1 \qquad \lim_{b\to\infty}\frac{c}{b+c} = 0$$

As b is made very small, s^* and q^* become infinite together. In practical terms this means that when there is little or no penalty for being short of inventory, it is best to place individual back orders only and keep no inventory.

ECONOMIC LOT SIZE: PRODUCTION CYCLE, SHORTAGES PERMITTED

The formulas of the last two sections may be combined to cover the case where there is both a finite production period and shortages are permitted as part of the inventory policy. For q^* and C^*, it is only necessary to treat both $1-(u/p)$ and $b/(b+c)$ as multipliers of c. The result is

$$q^* = \sqrt{\frac{2Au}{c}} \frac{1}{\sqrt{1-(u/p)}} \sqrt{\frac{b+c}{b}} \qquad (2.12)$$

$$C^* = \sqrt{2Auc} \sqrt{1-\frac{u}{p}} \sqrt{\frac{b}{b+c}} \qquad (2.13)$$

By similar reasoning, s^* becomes

$$s^* = \sqrt{\frac{2Au}{b}} \sqrt{\frac{c}{b+c}} \sqrt{1-\frac{u}{p}} \qquad (2.14)$$

EXAMPLE 2.4.   Combining the data of Examples 2.2 and 2.3, find q^*, C^* and s^*.

Given $u = 100$/month, $A = \$5$, $c = \$0.40$/unit/month, $b = \$0.15$/unit/month, $p = 500$ units/month. Then from (2.12), (2.13) and (2.14). respectively:

$$q^* = \sqrt{\frac{2(5)(100)}{0.40}} \frac{1}{\sqrt{1-(100/500)}} \sqrt{\frac{0.15+0.40}{0.15}} = 50\frac{1}{\sqrt{0.8}}\sqrt{\frac{1}{0.273}} = 107 \text{ items} \quad Ans.$$

$$C^* = \sqrt{2(5)(100)(0.40)(0.8)(0.273)} = 20\sqrt{(0.8)(0.273)} = \$9.35 \quad Ans.$$

$$s^* = \sqrt{\frac{2(5)(100)}{0.15}} \sqrt{\frac{0.40}{0.15+0.40}} \sqrt{0.8} = 63 \text{ items} \quad Ans.$$

ECONOMIC LOT SIZE: PRICE BREAKS

So far we have assumed that the price of the item remains the same no matter what the value of the order quantity q. It can happen, however, that at and above an order quantity q' there is a discount D from the original price k; i.e. when $q \geqq q'$, the price becomes $(1-D)k$ each. When the price break is granted at a level above the EOQ, i.e. when $q' > q^*$, the question is whether it is worthwhile to buy an extra $q' - q^*$ items and take advantage of the price break.

When a price break is offered we have:

1. **Savings due to the break itself.** These amount to Dku per unit of time (ku being the total value of items consumed in the time period).

2. **Savings due to a reduced setup cost.** Since $q' > q^*$, setups have to be done less frequently. Savings are given by $(Au/q^*) - (Au/q')$.

3. **Extra cost due to keeping a greater inventory.** In the simplest case of instantaneous replenishment and no shortages, this cost is $ik(q' - q^*)/2$, where $i = c/k$ is the carrying charge expressed as a fraction of the unit cost.

It is worthwhile buying the quantity q' whenever the savings are greater than the extra costs, i.e. when

$$Dku + Au\left(\frac{1}{q^*} - \frac{1}{q'}\right) > \frac{ik}{2}(q' - q^*)$$

or

$$Dku > \frac{ik}{2}(q' - q^*) - Au\left(\frac{1}{q^*} - \frac{1}{q'}\right) \qquad (2.15)$$

EXAMPLE 2.5. Let $u = 100$/year, $A = \$5$, $k = \$2.50$ each, $i = 16\%$/year.   The manufacturer offers discounts of (a) 5% when 100 items are bought and (b) 10% if 300 are bought. Which, if any, discounts should be taken?

The EOQ is

$$q^* = \sqrt{\frac{2(5)(100)}{(0.16)(2.50)}} = 50 \text{ items}$$

(a) We compute each side of (2.15) for $D = 0.05$ and $q' = 100$:

$$\text{Savings from discount} = (0.05)(2.50)(100) = \$12.50$$

$$\text{Increased costs} = \frac{(0.16)(2.50)}{2}(100 - 50) - 5(100)\left(\frac{1}{50} - \frac{1}{100}\right) = 10 - 5 = \$5$$

Since savings are greater than extra costs, take the discount.

(b) For $D = 0.10$ and $q' = 300$:

$$\text{Savings from discount} = 0.10(2.50)(100) = \$25$$

$$\text{Increased costs} = \frac{0.16(2.50)}{2}(300 - 50) - 5(100)\left(\frac{1}{50} - \frac{1}{300}\right) = 50 - 8.33 = \$41.67$$

Since extra costs are greater than savings, do not take discount. (Note that if 10% at $q' = 300$ were the only price break offered, the decision would be to buy the economic lot size at full price.)

LEAD TIME AND ORDER POINT

Even if demand is known with certainty, as in the previous models, it is usually necessary to place the order some set time in advance. We will also assume this *lead time* to be known with certainty. It is then clear that the order must be placed when there is enough inventory left to last the lead time at a rate of usage specified in the model. Denoting the lead time by L and the critical inventory level, or *order point*, by R, we have

$$R = Lu \tag{2.16}$$

EXAMPLE 2.6. Given usage of 100 items a month and a lead time of 5 business days, find the order point. What is actually done under the conditions of Examples 2.1, 2.2 and 2.3?

From (2.16), taking 5 days as $\frac{1}{4}$ month, $R = \frac{1}{4}(100) = 25$. Thus, in the model of Example 2.1 (no shortage), order $q^* = 50$ when inventory falls to 25 items.

For Examples 2.2 and 2.3 (with shortages) order $q^* = 96$ and 107 respectively when the shortage allowed is within 25 units of s^*, i.e. when back orders have reached 45 and 38 units respectively.

ECONOMIC LOT SIZE FOR SEVERAL PRODUCTS

When several products are manufactured, a scheduling problem often arises if each one is considered separately. It happens mainly because a large lot of an individual product takes up machine time long enough so that in the meanwhile supplies of another product run out. One remedy is to schedule certain runs more often than originally intended, but this is often awkward and not easy to do systematically.

A better procedure is to schedule jobs as part of a grand cycle, with each product taking a constant share of each cycle. The basis of the analysis is to determine a fraction, f, of annual demand which applied to the demand for each product gives the quantity to be produced as part of each cycle. If q_j is the quantity for the jth product and u_j the usage, then

$$q_j = fu_j \qquad j = 1, 2, \ldots, n \tag{2.17}$$

and f is found by pooling the costs of all n products according to the formula

$$f = \sqrt{\frac{2\Sigma A_j}{\Sigma u_j c_j [1 - (u_j/p_j)]}} \tag{2.18}$$

The summation is over the n items.

EXAMPLE 2.7. Table 2-1 gives the setup cost and the annual usage rate, production rate and carrying charge for a group of five products. Establish lot sizes and details of a production cycle for this group of products.

Table 2-1

Product No.	A	u	p	c
101	10	3,000	25,000	3
102	20	2,000	8,000	6
103	17	4,000	20,000	5
104	13	5,000	15,000	4
105	5	2,000	12,000	2

The computations are presented in Table 2-2. The result is a cycle of 109.5 machine hours, allocated among the five products as shown in Col. 6 and resulting in the quantities shown in Col. 4. *Ans.*

Table 2-2

Product No.	A Col. (1)	$1 - (u/p)$ Col. (2)	$uc[1-(u/p)]$ Col. (3)	Units per Cycle, fu Col. (4)	Units per Hour, $p/2000$ Col. (5)	Hours per Cycle, $2000fu/p$ Col. (6)
101	10	0.88	7,920	154	12.5	12.3
102	20	0.75	9,000	102	4.0	25.5
103	17	0.80	16,000	205	10.0	20.5
104	13	0.67	13,333	256	7.5	34.2
105	5	0.83	3,333	102	6.0	17.0
TOTALS	65		49,583			109.5

NOTES

Col. (4): $f = \sqrt{2(65)/49{,}583} = 0.0512$

Col. (5): output p per year divided by 2000 production hours per year

Col. (6): Col. (4) divided by Col. (5)

Table 2-3

Product No.	Individual EOQ from (2.6)	Units per Cycle from Col. (4)
101	151	154
102	133	102
103	184	205
104	221	256
105	110	102

A comparison between the above results and the individual EOQ's is given in Table 2-3. The differences are substantial in some cases but, as is shown in Problem 2.5, C is not very sensitive to variations in q in the region of its optimal value C^*.

Solved Problems

2.1. Usage for a certain product is 2000 units a week; setups cost $15 each and carrying charges are 30¢ per unit per week. Find the EOQ and minimum cost.

From *(2.3)* and *(2.4)*, respectively:

$$q^* = \sqrt{\frac{2(15)(2000)}{0.30}} = 447 \text{ units} \quad Ans.$$

$$C^* = \sqrt{2(15)(2000)(0.30)} = \$134.16 \quad Ans.$$

2.2. Repeat Problem 2.1 with a production rate given as 12,000 units per week.

In this case it is best to compute $1 - (u/p)$ and use it as a multiplier for the previous results. Thus,

$$1 - \frac{2000}{12,000} = 0.833$$

From *(2.6)*:

$$q^* = 447 \frac{1}{\sqrt{0.833}} = 490 \text{ units} \quad Ans.$$

From *(2.7)*:

$$C^* = (134.16)\sqrt{0.833} = \$122.47 \quad Ans.$$

2.3. Repeat Problem 2.2 with permitted shortages charged at $1.10 per unit per week. Also determine the maximum shortage level.

Here too a stepwise solution is best, using the results of Problem 2.2 as starting point. First obtain

$$\frac{b}{b+c} = \frac{1.10}{1.10 + 0.30} = 0.786$$

Then, from *(2.12)*, *(2.13)* and the relation $s^* = C^*/b$, respectively:

$$q^* = 490 \frac{1}{\sqrt{0.786}} = 553 \text{ units} \quad Ans.$$

$$C^* = (122.47)\sqrt{0.786} = \$108.56 \quad Ans.$$

$$s^* = \frac{108.56}{1.10} = 99 \text{ units} \quad Ans.$$

2.4. In Example 2.5(*b*) a discount of 10 percent was found to be uneconomical when the price break point was set at 300 items. What is the break quantity which would just make it economical?

From Example 2.5, $u = 100$/year, $A = \$5$, $k = \$2.50$ per item, $i = 0.16$/year and $q^* = 50$ items. To find the "breakeven" value of q', turn the inequality *(2.15)* into an equation and solve for q':

$$(0.10)(2.50)(100) = \frac{(0.16)(2.50)}{2}(q' - 50) - 5(100)\left(\frac{1}{50} - \frac{1}{q'}\right)$$

$$25 = (0.20)q' - 10 - 10 + \frac{500}{q'}$$

$$(0.20)q'^2 - 45q' + 500 = 0$$

$$q' = \frac{45 + \sqrt{2025 - 400}}{0.40} = 213 \text{ items} \quad Ans.$$

The critical quantity q' is called the *economic purchase quantity* (EPQ), as distinct from the *economic order quantity* (EOQ, $q*$). In large operations, tables of q' are sometimes prepared for use by the purchasing or inventory control departments. The purchasing rules are then as follows, where q_b is the price break point actually given by the supplier:

(i)   If $p_b <$ EOQ, buy EOQ at discounted price.

(ii) If EOQ $< p_b <$ EPQ, buy p_b at the discounted price.

(iii) If $p_b >$ EPQ, buy EOQ at full price.

Note that EPQ as such is never bought; if p_b turns out to be very near it, it is safer to buy EOQ at full price. In the second rule, the best policy is clearly to buy as little above EOQ as possible, i.e. p_b rather than EPQ, which, being a breakeven value, would not produce a cost reduction.

2.5. In Fig. 2-2, observe that the total cost curve C has an almost flat character around the minimum level. Thus, changing q from $q*$ by an appreciable amount may not make much difference to the total cost C. Show that a change of ± 14 percent in q from $q*$ produces an increase of only about 1 percent in C.

What we are seeking is sometimes called the *production range*, i.e. a range of values for q which produces something close to a minimum cost. Let r be the allowed increase in C relative to $C*$. The new C will then equal $(1+r)C* = (1+r)\sqrt{2Auc}$. To get the corresponding q, we make use of (2.1):

$$(1+r)\sqrt{2Auc} = \frac{Au}{q} + \frac{cq}{2}$$

This is a quadratic equation in q; multiplying by q and dividing by $\sqrt{2Auc}$ gives

$$\frac{q^2}{2}\sqrt{\frac{c}{2Au}} - q(1+r) + \sqrt{\frac{Au}{2c}} = 0$$

The first radical is seen from (2.3) to be $1/q*$; the second one is $q*/2$. Thus

$$\frac{q^2}{2q*} - q(1+r) + \frac{q*}{2} = 0 \qquad \text{or} \qquad q^2 - 2q*(1+r)q + q*^2 = 0$$

Solving in the usual manner,

$$q = q*[(1+r) \pm \sqrt{2r + r^2}]$$

When r is small, we may write $1 + r \approx 1$ and r^2 may be neglected. Then

$$q \approx q*(1 \pm \sqrt{2r}) = q*(1 \pm 1.414\sqrt{r})$$

When $r = 0.01$, $q \approx q*(1 \pm 0.1414)$, which was to have been shown. *Ans.*

Supplementary Problems

2.6. A certain product is used at the rate of 4 units a month. It costs \$50 to set up and carrying charges are \$8 a month. Find the economic order quantity and the minimum cost associated with it.

Ans.   7; \$56.57

2.7. In Problem 2.6 suppose manufacture takes place at the rate of 10 units a month. Find the economic order quantity and the minimum cost.   *Ans.* 9; \$43.82

2.8. A machine part is required at the rate of 2000 a month. It costs \$150 each and the carrying charges are computed at the rate of 16 percent per annum of the cost. A purchase order costs \$100 to process. Find the EOQ and minimum cost.   *Ans.* 447; \$894.43

2.9. In Problem 2.8 shortages are permitted but their cost is $5 a month each. Find the EOQ, minimum cost and maximum shortage level.   *Ans.* 529; $755.93; 151

2.10. In Problem 2.9 production takes place at the rate of 6000 pieces a month. Other data remaining the same, find the EOQ, minimum cost and maximum shortage level.

Ans. 647; $617.22; 123

2.11. Fifty pieces a week of a certain purchased machine part are bought by a manufacturer. It costs $4 to process the order and holding charges are 36¢ a week per piece. (*a*) Find the EOQ. (*b*) The manufacturer has a working capital problem and so wishes to reduce the amount of inventory carried to a minimum. He decides that he would be willing to accept a total cost of his inventory policy 4 percent higher than the optimum. What should his new EOQ be?

Ans. (*a*) 33; (*b*) 24

2.12. Show that if the cost of producing a quantity q of a certain product is given by $A + kq$, where A is the setup cost and k the variable cost per unit, the EOQ is given by $\sqrt{2Au/ik}$, where i is the carrying charge expressed as a fraction of the cost of the item and u is the usage rate in units per unit of time.

2.13. The production cost of a certain product is given by $200 + 35q$, where q is the production quantity. Forty items a year are used and the production capacity if fully used would be 160 a year. Find the economic lot size and the corresponding annual cost. (Take the carrying charge to be 18 percent of the cost.)   *Ans.* 58 items; $275

2.14. Given A and c for a product and a total annual demand of ku, compare the C^*'s for the cases (1) demand is ku for a single product, and (2) demand is u for each of k different types of the product.   *Ans.* $C_2^*/C_1^* = \sqrt{k}$ (it pays to standardize)

Chapter 3

Other Deterministic Models

FUNCTIONS OF SEVERAL VARIABLES

In this chapter we present more far-ranging deterministic models of business operations and include the problem of constraints on resources. A major preliminary task is to define the relationship between various business inputs and outputs. At times, this may be inferred from the physical nature of the process, as in Example 3.1 below. Most often, however, statistical techniques of regression and correlation (see Chapter 17) must be applied.

EXAMPLE 3.1. Let x be the number of components in an assembly of which a number y is required. The components are all different (i.e. one for each assembly) but they are made on the same machines with different tooling and cost differences between them may be neglected. By choosing suitable constants, form a total cost function. Extend the analysis to include revenue and profit functions.

There are various possibilities but the following is plausible. Assume a linear cost function for each component:

$$C_c = a + by$$

because y of each component are needed. The total cost of the components is then xC_c. The cost of assemblage depends on the number of assemblies, y; on the total number, xy, of components handled; and on a setup cost for the assembly job. Thus it can be written in the linear form

$$C_a = c + dy + exy$$

Combining costs of components and assemblage,

$$C = xC_c + C_a = x(a + by) + c + dy + exy = c + ax + dy + (b + e)xy \quad Ans.$$

Proceeding similarly on the revenue side, the price might be expected to be of the form $r = f + gx$, i.e. it depends on the number of components and a fixed part. Revenues are then

$$R = ry = fy + gxy \quad Ans.$$

and, as before, the profit is given by

$$P = R - C = -c - ax + (f - d)y + (g - b - e)xy \quad Ans.$$

A function of the above type might fit an assembly of electrical components or a book (individual pages and then binding), etc. If some of the component cost functions are non-linear, one might obtain the *generalized second-degree model*

$$f(x,y) = ax^2 + by^2 + cxy + dx + ey + f \tag{3.1}$$

Another possibility is the *exponential model*

$$f(x,y,z) = ax^b y^c z^d \tag{3.2}$$

Such a model may be fitted to data by taking logarithms of both sides:

$$\log f(x,y,z) = \log a + b \log x + c \log y + d \log z$$

Writing U for the left side, and $X = \log x$, $Y = \log y$ and $Z = \log z$, gives the linear relationship

$$U = a + bX + cY + dZ \tag{3.3}$$

OPTIMIZATION WITHOUT CONSTRAINTS

When cost or profit functions have one or more variables, they may be minimized or maximized as required by a suitable optimal choice of the variables. Several one-variable models were considered in Chapter 2. A similar procedure is indicated for a function of, say, two variables, $f(x, y)$, except that here we must have simultaneously

$$\frac{\partial f}{\partial x} = 0 \qquad \frac{\partial f}{\partial y} = 0 \tag{3.4}$$

in order to obtain the optimal values x^* and y^*.

It is next necessary to test whether these values give a maximum or a minimum of the function. At times, as in the simple examples of Chapter 2, the answer is clear from inspection of the plotted function or otherwise. In the case of two variables we must have, for a minimum,

$$\frac{\partial^2 f}{\partial x^2} > 0 \qquad \frac{\partial^2 f}{\partial y^2} > 0 \tag{3.5}$$

and, for a maximum,

$$\frac{\partial^2 f}{\partial x^2} < 0 \qquad \frac{\partial^2 f}{\partial y^2} < 0 \tag{3.6}$$

Similar conditions must be added for functions of more than two variables.

EXAMPLE 3.2. A public utility sells both gas and electricity and also sometimes uses gas as fuel. Its cost function has been found to be

$$C = \tfrac{1}{2}x^2 + \tfrac{3}{4}y^2 - 7xy + 134x + 12y + 250$$

where C is cost per month in $\$ \times 10^4$; x = gas sales, cu. ft. $\times 10^9$, and y = electricity sales, kWh $\times 10^8$. Find the mix of gas and electricity sales which will minimize costs.

We make use of (3.4):

$$\frac{\partial C}{\partial x} = x - 7y + 134 = 0$$

$$\frac{\partial C}{\partial y} = \frac{3}{2}y - 7x + 12 = 0$$

Solving simultaneously (multiply the first equation by 7 and add to the second):

$$-\frac{95}{2}y + 950 = 0$$

$$y = 20; \quad x = 6$$

These are the optimal values; i.e. $x^* = 6$, $y^* = 20$. *Ans.*

To test if this represents a minimum,

$$\frac{\partial^2 C}{\partial x^2} = 1 \qquad \frac{\partial^2 C}{\partial y^2} = \frac{3}{2}$$

Thus (3.5) holds and the function is minimized. The optimal cost is

$$C^* = \tfrac{1}{2}(6)^2 + \tfrac{3}{4}(20)^2 - 7(6)(20) + 134(6) + 12(20) + 250 = 772 \quad Ans.$$

EXAMPLE 3.3. A certain product has a demand function $X = 200{,}000r^{-1.5}A^{0.1}S^{0.3}$. In this exponential model X = sales, units; r = price per unit; A = advertising expense; S = cost of sales force; and the constants -1.5, 0.1 and 0.3 are called the *elasticities* of their respective variables. Fixed costs exclusive of sales and advertising expense are $\$80{,}000$ and there is a variable cost of $\$25$ per unit. Find the price, advertising expense and sales expense which will maximize profit.

Combining (1.1), (1.4) and (1.5),

$$(1) \qquad P = R - C = rX - F - vX = (r - v)X - F$$

Substituting for X and noting that the *total* fixed expense is $\$80,000 + A + S$, *(1)* becomes

$$P = (r - 25)(200,000r^{-1.5}A^{0.1}S^{0.3}) - 80,000 - A - S$$

$$= 200,000r^{-0.5}A^{0.1}S^{0.3} - 5,000,000r^{-1.5}A^{0.1}S^{0.3} - 80,000 - A - S$$

To obtain the values of r, A and S which will make this a maximum we set the derivative with respect to each equal to zero:

(2)
$$\frac{\partial P}{\partial r} = -100,000r^{-1.5}A^{0.1}S^{0.3} + 7,500,000r^{-2.5}A^{0.1}S^{0.3} = 0$$

(3)
$$\frac{\partial P}{\partial A} = 20,000r^{-0.5}A^{-0.9}S^{0.3} - 500,000r^{-1.5}A^{-0.9}S^{0.3} - 1 = 0$$

(4)
$$\frac{\partial P}{\partial S} = 60,000r^{-0.5}A^{0.1}S^{-0.7} - 1,500,000r^{-1.5}A^{0.1}S^{-0.7} - 1 = 0$$

Divide *(2)* through by $100,000A^{0.1}S^{0.3}$:

$$r^{-1.5} = 75r^{-2.5}$$

$$r^* = 75, \quad \text{i.e. } \$75 \text{ each} \quad Ans.$$

Equate *(3)* and *(4)*:

$$20,000r^{-0.5}A^{-0.9}S^{0.3} - 500,000r^{-1.5}A^{-0.9}S^{0.3} - 1 = 60,000r^{-0.5}A^{0.1}S^{-0.7} - 1,500,000r^{-1.5}A^{0.1}S^{-0.7} - 1$$

Add 1 to both sides and then multiply through by $r^{1.5}A^{0.9}S^{0.7}/20,000$:

$$rS - 25S = 3rA - 75A$$

Substituting $r = 75$,

$$75S - 25S = 225A - 75A \quad \text{or} \quad S = 3A$$

Substitute this result in *(3)*:

$$20,000(75)^{-0.5}A^{-0.9}(3A)^{0.3} - 500,000(75)^{-1.5}A^{-0.9}(3A)^{0.3} - 1 = 0$$

$$20,000(75)^{-0.5}A^{-0.6}(3)^{0.3}[1 - 25(75)^{-1}] = 1$$

$$A^{0.6} = 20,000(0.11547)(1.39)(0.667) = 2140$$

$$A^* = \$355,400; \quad S^* = \$1,066,200 \quad Ans.$$

The volume X^* at maximum profit is

$$X^* = 200,000(75)^{-1.5}(355,400)^{0.1}(1,066,200)^{0.3}$$

$$= 200,000(0.00154)(3.59)(64.33) = 71,131 \text{ units} \quad Ans.$$

The maximum profit is now obtained from *(1)*:

$$P^* = (75 - 25)(71,131) - 80,000 - 355,400 - 1,066,200 = \$2,054,950 \quad Ans.$$

EXAMPLE 3.4. Find the breakeven point for the operation in Example 3.3.

From *(1.6)*,

$$X_b = \frac{80,000 + 355,400 + 1,066,200}{75 - 25} = 30,032 \text{ units} \quad Ans.$$

In practical terms, the results of Examples 3.3 and 3.4 not only give the optimal advertising and selling expense, but also show that raising the price above $75 will generate enough price resistance to diminish total profits.

CONSTRAINTS

There are many cases in which one or more resources in a demand or production function are limited. In the foregoing examples, we optimized the conditions of operations, arriving at optimal values of the variables. Suppose, however, that these values violate a constraint, e.g. too much money is being spent. Then the constraint has to be brought into the analysis. (The following work is *unnecessary* if the optimal conditions previously determined happen to satisfy all constraints.)

Consider a function of two variables

$$C = f(x, y)$$

in which the two variables x and y are constrained by

$$g(x, y) = a$$

In some cases, the problem may be worked out by simple substitution.

EXAMPLE 3.5. Plant constraints in Example 3.2 make it necessary that $4x + y = 36$. Revise the optimal values of x and y accordingly.

The solution to Example 3.2 was $x^* = 6$, $y^* = 20$, which violates the restriction. To work out the new values, substitute $y = 36 - 4x$ in the original cost function:

$$C = \tfrac{1}{2}x^2 + \tfrac{3}{4}(1296 - 288x + 16x^2) - 7x(36 - 4x) + 134x + 12(36 - 4x) + 250$$

$$= x^2(\tfrac{1}{2} + 12 + 28) - x(216 + 252 - 134 + 48) + 972 + 432 + 250$$

$$= 40.5\,x^2 - 382x + 1654$$

This is a function of one variable and its minimum is given by

$$\frac{dC}{dx} = 81x - 382 = 0$$

$$x^* = 4.72 \quad Ans.$$

$$\frac{d^2C}{dx^2} = 81; \quad \text{hence this is a minimum}$$

$$y^* = 36 - 4(4.72) = 17.12 \quad Ans.$$

The new minimum cost is

$$C^* = (40.5)(4.72)^2 - 382(4.72) + 1654 = \$753.24 \quad Ans.$$

When substitution is not workable, we first write the constraint as

$$g(x, y) - a = 0$$

Next, define the *Lagrangian function*

$$\ell(x, y, \lambda) = f(x, y) + \lambda[g(x, y) - a]$$

where $\lambda \neq 0$ if the x^* and y^* computed without the restriction violate $g(x, y) = a$. λ is called the *Lagrange multiplier*. Then the new optimal values of x and y are obtained by solving simultaneously

$$\frac{\partial \ell}{\partial x} = 0 \qquad \frac{\partial \ell}{\partial y} = 0 \qquad \frac{\partial \ell}{\partial \lambda} = 0$$

EXAMPLE 3.6. In Example 3.3 the total budget for sales and advertising expense is set at \$1,000,000. Find the revised advertising and sales expense and the optimal volume and profit.

The constraint is expressed as

$$A + S = 1,000,000 \quad \text{or} \quad A + S - 1,000,000 = 0$$

so that the Lagrangian function has the form

$$\ell(P) = (r - 25)(200,000r^{-1.5}A^{0.1}S^{0.3}) - 80,000 - A - S + \lambda(A + S - 1,000,000)$$

Because $\partial\ell/\partial r$ does not involve the restriction, equation (2) of Example 3.3 does not change and $r^* = 75$, as before.

$$\frac{\partial\ell}{\partial A} = 20,000r^{-0.5}A^{-0.9}S^{0.3} - 500,000r^{-1.5}A^{-0.9}S^{0.3} - 1 + \lambda = 0$$

$$\frac{\partial\ell}{\partial S} = 60,000r^{-0.5}A^{0.1}A^{-0.7} - 1,500,000r^{-1.5}A^{0.1}S^{-0.7} - 1 + \lambda = 0$$

Again, equating the last two equations brings the same result as for (3) and (4) of Example 3.3, so that once more, $S = 3A$.

Taking the last partial derivative,

$$\frac{\partial\ell}{\partial\lambda} = A + S - 1,000,000 = 0$$

i.e. the constraint itself. Substituting $S = 3A$ gives $A^* = \$250,000$; $S^* = \$750,000$. *Ans.*

Now substituting r^*, A^* and S^* into the volume and profit functions gives

$$X^* = 200,000(75)^{-1.5}(250,000)^{0.1}(750,000)^{0.3}$$

$$= 200,000(0.00154)(3.465)(57.88) = 61,771 \quad Ans.$$

$$P^* = 50(61,771) - 80,000 - 1,000,000 = \$2,008,550 \quad Ans.$$

Solved Problems

3.1. Find the economic lot sizes for the products in Table 3-1 (a) under no constraint, (b) given that total manufacturing capacity for all three products is 2800 units.

Table 3-1

	Product 1	Product 2	Product 3
Demand per year	1200	2000	900
Setup cost, $	80	150	90
Carrying charge per year per unit, ¢	15	20	20

(a) From (2.3) the economic lot sizes are

$$q_1^* = \sqrt{\frac{2(80)(1200)}{0.15}} = 1131, \qquad q_2^* = \sqrt{\frac{2(150)(2000)}{0.20}} = 1732,$$

$$q_3^* = \sqrt{\frac{2(90)(900)}{0.20}} = 900 \quad Ans.$$

(b) The total in (a) is $1131 + 1732 + 900 > 2800$; therefore the problem must be worked out again with the restriction

$$q_1 + q_2 + q_3 = 2800$$

The cost function is derived from (2.1) by adding the Lagrange term:

$$\ell(C) = \frac{80(1200)}{q_1} + \frac{(0.15)q_1}{2} + \frac{150(2000)}{q_2} + \frac{(0.2)q_2}{2} + \frac{90(900)}{q_3} + \frac{(0.2)q_3}{2} + \lambda(q_1 + q_2 + q_3 - 2800)$$

Differentiating with respect to q_1, q_2, q_3 and λ

(1) $$\frac{\partial\ell}{\partial q_1} = -\frac{96,000}{q_1^2} + 0.075 + \lambda = 0$$

$$(2) \qquad \frac{\partial \ell}{\partial q_2} = -\frac{300,000}{q_2^2} + 0.1 + \lambda = 0$$

$$(3) \qquad \frac{\partial \ell}{\partial q_3} = -\frac{81,000}{q_3^3} + 0.1 + \lambda = 0$$

$$(4) \qquad \frac{\partial \ell}{\partial \lambda} = q_1 + q_2 + q_3 - 2800 = 0$$

In this particular case, it is convenient to equate (2) and (3), obtaining

$$\frac{81,000}{q_3^2} = \frac{300,000}{q_2^2} \qquad \text{or} \qquad q_2 = 1.9245\, q_3$$

Equation (4) can now be written

$$(5) \qquad q_1 + 2.9245\, q_3 = 2800$$

When the expressions

$$q_1 = \sqrt{\frac{96,000}{0.075 + \lambda}} \qquad q_3 = \sqrt{\frac{81,000}{0.1 + \lambda}}$$

found from (1) and (3) are substituted in (5), an equation in λ is obtained. This must be solved by trial:

λ	q_1	q_3	$q_1 + (2.9245)q_3$
0.1	741	636	2601
0.07	814	690	2832

We set $q_1^* = 806$, $q_3^* = 682$, $q_2^* = (1.9245)(682) = 1312$. *Ans.*

3.2. Find the optimal cost for Problem 3.1, under (a) no constraint, (b) constraint.

(a) Applying (2.4) to the three products,

$$C^* = \sqrt{2(80)(1200)(0.15)} + \sqrt{2(150)(2000)(0.2)} + \sqrt{2(90)(900)(0.2)}$$

$$= 169.71 + 346.41 + 180 = \$696.12 \quad \textit{Ans.}$$

(b) We work from $\ell(C)$, noting that at the optimum the term in λ is zero.

$$C^* = \frac{96,000}{806} + (0.075)(806) + \frac{300,000}{1312} + (0.1)(1312) + \frac{81,000}{682} + (0.1)(682) = \$726.38 \quad \textit{Ans.}$$

3.3. A certain machine is subject to economy of scale, its cost being $C = aK^b$ $(0 < b < 1)$. It is intended to buy several machines, with one always kept as spare in case another one breaks down. Find the optimal number of machines to buy for a given b.

Review the discussion of economy of scale in Chapter 1. If n machines are to operate at one time, each one will have capacity K/n and $n+1$ machines will have to be bought; each machine purchased will cost $a(K/n)^b$ and the total cost is

$$C = (n+1)a(K/n)^b = aK^b(n+1)(n^{-b}) = aK^b(n^{1-b} + n^{-b})$$

Then

$$\frac{dC}{dn} = aK^b[(1-b)n^{-b} - bn^{-b-1}] = 0$$

$$n^* = b/(1-b) \quad \textit{Ans.}$$

This leads to the following set of values of b for which n^* is an integer:

$$b = \quad 1/2 \quad 2/3 \quad 3/4 \quad 4/5 \quad 5/6 \ \text{etc.}$$
$$n^* = \quad 1 \quad\ \ 2 \quad\ \ 3 \quad\ \ 4 \quad\ \ 5 \ \text{etc.}$$
$$n^* + 1 = \quad 2 \quad\ \ 3 \quad\ \ 4 \quad\ \ 5 \quad\ \ 6 \ \text{etc. (Buy this number.)} \quad \textit{Ans.}$$

3.4. A *marginal cost* is the rate of change of a cost with the quantity produced, i.e. it is the unit cost expressed as a function of the quantity produced, or the first derivative of the total cost function (see Example 1.1). (*a*) If for a given product the marginal cost is $c_m(X) = v$ (a constant), show that the total cost is $C = F + vX$, where F is the cost when $X = 0$. (*b*) The *marginal revenue*, $r_m(X)$, is analogously defined. If $r_m(X) = r$ (a constant), and if the total revenue R equals zero when $X = 0$, show that $R = rX$.

(*a*) This is the same as proving (*1.1*). In general, for a marginal cost $c_m(X)$, the cost function is

$$C = \int c_m(X)\, dX + c \qquad (3.7)$$

where c is a constant of integration which must be determined from given conditions. Here

$$C = \int v\, dX + c = vX + c$$

When $X = 0$, $C = F$; hence $c = F$ and $C = F + vX$. *Ans.*

(*b*) Marginal revenues $r_m(X)$ are the exact equivalent on the revenue side:

$$R = \int r_m(X)\, dX + c \qquad (3.8)$$

In the present case

$$R = \int r\, dX + c = rX + c$$

When $X = 0$, $R = 0$; hence $c = 0$ and $R = rX$. *Ans.*

3.5. The marginal cost of a certain product is $160X^{-1/3}$, where X is the number made. It costs \$17,000 to make 500 pieces. Find a general expression for the cost.

This marginal cost function resembles that due to a learning process, see (*1.14*). From (*3.7*)

$$C = \int 160X^{-1/3}\, dX + c = 160\left(\frac{3}{2}\right)X^{2/3} + c = 240X^{2/3} + c$$

From the initial conditions

$$17{,}000 = 240(500)^{2/3} + c = 15{,}120 + c$$

$$c = 17{,}000 - 15{,}120 = 1880$$

Therefore
$$C = 240X^{2/3} + 1880 \quad Ans.$$

3.6. The marginal revenues for a certain product are given by

$$r_m(X) = 150 + 80e^{-0.8X}$$

where X is the number, in thousands, of units sold. When 5000 items are sold, the total revenues realized are \$1000. Find the total revenue function.

The marginal revenue function is shown in Fig. 3-1. As the quantity increases, the marginal revenue decreases asymptotically to \$150 per thousand units. From (*3.8*)

$$R = \int (150 + 80e^{-0.8X})\, dX + c = 150X + 80\left(\frac{1}{-0.8}\right)e^{-0.8X} + c$$

From the given conditions, using the table of e^x in Appendix A,

$$1000 \; = \; 150(5) - 100e^{-(0.8)(5)} + c \; = \; 750 - \frac{100}{e^4} + c$$

$$= \; 750 - \frac{100}{54.598} + c \; = \; 748.17 + c$$

$$c \; = \; 251.83$$

$$R \; = \; 150X - 100e^{-0.8X} + 251.83 \qquad Ans.$$

This function indicates revenues of \$151.83 when $X = 0$, which does not appear to make much sense. However, in practice, such revenue or cost functions are not meant to be valid within the total range $X \geqq 0$, but only within the limits of variation of production. Such functions are usually fitted empirically within that range. The expression for $r_m(X)$ is *a modified exponential curve*.

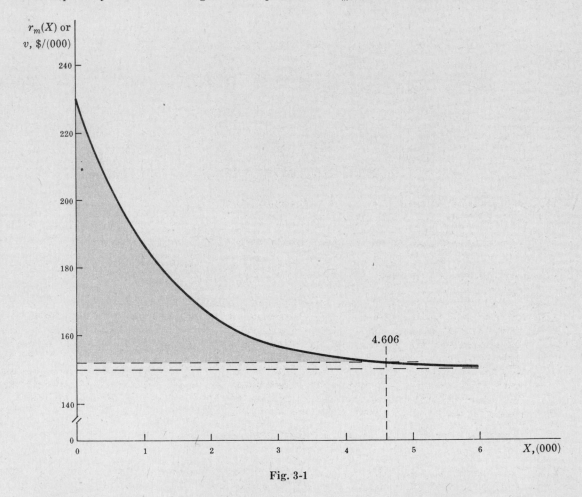

Fig. 3-1

3.7. Consider the revenue function developed in Problem 3.6. In addition, there is a variable cost of \$152 per thousand units and a fixed cost of \$60. (*a*) Show that there is a point beyond which manufacture becomes unprofitable and find that quantity. (*b*) Determine the corresponding net profit.

(*a*) The product ceases to be profitable as soon as the marginal revenues decline below the marginal costs, which are here given as \$152. The value of X at which this occurs may be calculated from $r_m(X) = c_m(X)$, i.e. from

$$150 + 80e^{-0.8X} \; = \; 152 \qquad \text{or} \qquad e^{0.8X} \; = \; 40$$

Using Appendix A in reverse and interpolating,

$$0.8\,X = 3.689 \quad \text{or} \quad X = 4.611$$

i.e. 4611 units.   *Ans.*

Note that for $v < 150$ there would be no quantity above which manufacture is unprofitable, because the line representing v would not intersect the graph of $r_m(X)$.

(b) The profit contribution (revenues less variable costs) is given by the shaded area in Fig. 3-1, which is the area under the function

$$(150 - 152) + 80e^{-0.8\,X}$$

up to $X = 4.611$. Thus it is given by the definite integral

$$P = \int_0^{4.611} (-2 + 80e^{-0.8\,X})\,dX = -2X - 100e^{-0.8\,X}\Big|_0^{4.611}$$

$$= -2(4.611) - 100e^{-3.689} + 100 = -9.22 - \frac{100}{40} + 100 = \$88.28$$

The net profit is obtained by deducting the fixed cost from the profit contribution, i.e. it is $88.28 - 60 = \$28.28$.   *Ans.*

Supplementary Problems

3.8. Show that r^*, A^* and S^* as found in Example 3.3 actually maximize profit P.

3.9. Verify that q^* as given by (*2.3*) leads to a minimum C.

3.10. Verify that n^* as determined in Problem 3.3 leads to a minimum cost for the machines.

3.11. A newsstand operates at a commuter rail station. It does most of its business during the morning rush hour. It has been observed that its marginal rate of profit contribution (i.e. of the difference between sales revenues and direct costs of the items sold) is given by $8 + 3X - \frac{1}{2}X^2$ where X is the time since opening that day, measured in half-hour periods. In addition, there are time-dependent costs (labor, lighting) of \$10 per hour (i.e. \$5 per half hour). (a) How long does the operation stay profitable? (b) What is the maximum instantaneous rate of profit contribution? (c) Assuming that the operation is terminated as soon as it becomes unprofitable, what is the total net profit? (*Hint*: Integrate the *net* profit function.)

Ans.   (a) 3 hr 26 min;   (b) \$12.50 per half hour;   (c) \$37.37

3.12. In a manufacturing process, labor costs \$25 per unit and materials \$16 per unit. The production function is $Q = 30LM$, where $Q =$ quantity produced, $L =$ units of labor used, $M =$ units of materials used. The total cost of labor and materials is not to exceed \$5000. Find the optimal mix of labor and materials and the optimal production quantity, both by substitution and the Lagrange multiplier method.   *Ans.* $M^* = 156.25$; $L^* = 100$; $Q^* = 468{,}750$

3.13. A production function is given by $Q = 650L^{1/2}C^{1/2}$, where Q and L have the meanings given in Problem 3.12 and C is capital input. A unit of capital costs \$5 and a unit of labor costs \$3. No more than \$200 is to be spent for the job. Find the optimal mix of labor and capital, using a Lagrange multiplier, and check your work by means of substitution. For the latter, note that if u and v are both functions of x,

$$\frac{d(uv)}{dx} = u\frac{dv}{dx} + v\frac{du}{dx}$$

Ans. $L^* = 33.3$; $C^* = 20$; $Q^* = 16{,}783$

3.14.   A total cost function often met with in practice (after empirical fitting) is the cubic parabola, because, if the coefficients are suitably chosen, it fits the situation in which costs per unit are relatively high when production is low (poor economy of scale, partial idleness of workers) and when it is at its highest range (overtime, shift premium, etc.).   A cost function of this sort (with x in thousands of units) is given by

$$C \;=\; 2x^3 - 12x^2 + 30x + 27$$

The price per thousand is $32.   Draw the cost and revenue functions and the profit curve.   Find (a) the approximate breakeven and profit limit points, (b) the volume for which the profit is a maximum, (c) the maximum profit.

   Ans.   (a) 1650 units, 5770 units;   (b) 4082 units;   (c) $45.08

Chapter 4

Equipment Selection and Replacement

BASIC FORMULAS

Selection and replacement studies must take interest or the cost of money into account.

Notation

A = amount n periods hence

P = present value of an amount A payable n periods hence

r = rate of interest

For compound interest, when compounding takes place once per period,

$$A = P(1+r)^n \tag{4.1}$$

$$P = A(1+r)^{-n} \tag{4.2}$$

Suppose interest is compounded m times per period. From (4.1),

$$A = P\left(1 + \frac{r}{m}\right)^{nm}$$

As $m \to \infty$, the expression multiplying P approaches e^{rn}, where $e = 2.71828\ldots$. This is the method of *continuous compounding* which is generally used at present; it will be used throughout this chapter. [If the periodic method is preferred, e^{rn} in the following formulas need only be replaced by $(1+r)^n$.] Equations (4.1) and (4.2) thus become

$$A = Pe^{rn} \tag{4.3}$$

$$P = Ae^{-rn} = \frac{A}{e^{rn}} \tag{4.4}$$

The factor e^{rn} is tabulated as a function of $x = rn$ in Appendix A. We call e^{rn} the *compound amount factor*; e^{-rn} is the *present worth factor* for a single payment or receipt.

EXAMPLE 4.1. What is the amount of $1000 compounded continuously at 6% p.a. for 20 years?

$x = rn = (0.06)(20) = 1.2$; from Appendix A, $e^{1.2} = 3.3201$; from (4.3),

$$A = 1000(3.3201) = \$3320.10 \quad Ans.$$

EXAMPLE 4.2. What amount must now be invested at 6.5% to yield $1200 16 years from now?

$x = (0.065)(16) = 1.04$; from Appendix A, $e^{1.04} = 2.8292$; from (4.4),

$$P = \frac{1200}{2.8292} = \$424.15 \quad Ans.$$

UNIFORM FLOW

It often happens that, instead of a single amount, there is a *uniform flow* of costs or revenues at a constant rate of a per period. The present worth of such a flow is the amount P which, when invested at time 0 at an interest rate r, will produce a flow of a per period for n periods. To find P, consider the small time interval from t to $t + \delta t$ during which an amount $a\,\delta t$ will flow (i.e. either be received or paid). The present worth of this element, obtained from (4.4), is $a\,\delta t\,e^{-rt}$. The present worth of the entire flow is obtained by integration as

$$P = \int_0^n ae^{-rt}\,dt = -\frac{a}{r}e^{-rt}\Big|_0^n = a\frac{1-e^{-rn}}{r} = an\frac{1-e^{-rn}}{rn} = anf_u \qquad (4.5)$$

The term $f_u = (1-e^{-rn})/rn$, which is tabulated as a function of $x = rn$ in Appendix L, is called the *present worth factor for uniform flow*; f_u may also be computed from Appendix A by writing

$$f_u = \frac{e^{rn}-1}{rne^{rn}} \qquad (4.6)$$

EXAMPLE 4.3. Find the present value of an annual maintenance charge of $350 for 15 years, assuming a cost of money of 12%.

Here, $x = rn = 15(0.12) = 1.8$; and for $x = 1.8$, Appendix L gives $f_u = 0.46372$. Then, from (4.5),

$$P = 350(15)(0.46372) = \$2434.53 \quad Ans.$$

In the above solution the maintenance charge is considered to be paid out continuously over the year.

EXAMPLE 4.4. An amount of $10,000 is to be invested for 10 years in hope of realizing an annual income of $2000. At what continuously compounded interest rate would this investment have to be made?

Here we reverse (4.5) and obtain

$$f_u = \frac{P}{an} = \frac{10,000}{20,000} = 0.5$$

In Appendix L, x for $f_u = 0.5$ is 1.6; thus

$$rn = 10r = 1.6 \quad \text{or} \quad r = 16 \text{ percent} \quad Ans.$$

EXAMPLE 4.5. Find f_u for 15 years and an interest rate of 12%, using (4.6).

As in Example 4.3, $x = 1.8$. From Appendix A, $e^{1.8} = 6.0496$. From (4.6),

$$f_u = \frac{6.0496 - 1}{(1.8)(6.0496)} = 0.46372 \quad Ans.$$

It also follows from (4.5) that

$$a = \frac{P}{n}\frac{1}{f_u} \qquad (4.7)$$

i.e. the uniform periodic amount is obtained, given the initial investment P and the term n. The quantity $1/f_u$ is the *capital recovery factor*, i.e. the total amount paid over the life of the loan for each dollar of loan. Therefore the total *interest* is $(1/f_u) - 1$ for each dollar.

EXAMPLE 4.6. What is the monthly payment for a 25-year, 9% mortgage for $35,000? How much total interest is paid?

Assume a monthly interest rate of $\frac{1}{12}(9\%) = 0.75\%$ for $25(12) = 300$ months. $x = 0.0075(300) = 2.25$. From Appendix L, $f_u = 0.39760$. From (4.7)

$$a = \frac{35,000}{300(0.39760)} = \$293.43 \quad Ans.$$

The total paid in interest is

$$35,000\left(\frac{1}{0.39760} - 1\right) = \$53,028.17 \quad Ans.$$

EXAMPLE 4.7. Should a machine be rented for \$500 a month or purchased for \$40,000? Either way, its useful life is 10 years, and money is worth 14%.

We may use (4.5) or (4.7). First, using (4.5) to get the present value of the rental: $x = (0.14)(10) = 1.4$ and from Appendix L, $f_u = 0.53815$. Then, with $a = \$6000/\text{yr}$,

$$P = 6000(10)(0.53815) = \$32,289$$

It is more advantageous to rent the machine. *Ans.*

From (4.7), the equivalent annual cost of owning the machine is

$$a = \frac{40,000}{10(0.53815)} = \$7432.87$$

Again, it is more advantageous to rent. Note that

$$\frac{40,000}{32,289} = \frac{7432.87}{6000} = 1.239$$

i.e. the ratios of the present values and of the annual costs for purchase and rental are equal.

CAPITALIZED COST

Capitalized cost is the present value of a series of services or equipment purchases scheduled to be repeated every n periods to perpetuity. It serves to compare equipment with different service lives, or services rendered at different intervals, by reducing them all to their present values. If P is the amount which must be paid every n periods, where n is the life of the machine or the service interval, then the capitalized cost is given by

$$K = P + Pe^{-rn} + Pe^{-2rn} + Pe^{-3rn} + \cdots$$

The first term is the cost of the initial installation, the second the present value of the first replacement, and so on. Summing the geometric series, we obtain

$$K = P\frac{1}{1 - e^{-rn}} = P\frac{e^{rn}}{e^{rn} - 1} = P\frac{1}{rnf_u} \tag{4.8}$$

Comparing (4.7) and (4.8) it follows that

$$K = \frac{a}{r} \quad \text{or} \quad a = Kr \tag{4.9}$$

The latter is actually the formula for simple interest or for a permanent income of a from an investment K, if a is withdrawn at the end of each period.

EXAMPLE 4.8. A steel bridge costs \$380,000 to build, needs painting every 10 years at a cost of \$40,000, and is expected to last 40 years; a wooden bridge has an expected life of 15 years and a first cost of \$200,000, and it needs painting every two years at a cost of \$20,000 each time. Which type of bridge is the more economical? Interest is at 10%.

For the series of steel bridges

First cost: $x = (0.1)(40) = 4$; $f_u = 0.24542$ (from Appendix L); from (4.8)

$$K = \frac{380,000}{4(0.24542)} = \$387,091.51$$

Cost of painting: $x = (0.1)(10) = 1$; $f_u = 0.63212$; from (4.8)

$$K = \frac{40,000}{0.63212} = \$63,279.12$$

Total K: $387,091.51 + 63,279.12 = \$450,370.63$

For the series of wooden bridges

First cost: $x = (0.1)(15) = 1.5$; $f_u = 0.51791$; from (4.8)

$$K = \frac{200,000}{(1.5)(0.51791)} = \$257,444.98$$

Cost of painting: $x = (0.1)(2) = 0.2$; $f_u = 0.90635$; from (4.8)

$$K = \frac{20,000}{(0.2)(0.90635)} = \$110,332.65$$

Total K: $257,444.98 + 110,332.65 = \$367,777.63$

The wooden bridge is preferable. *Ans.*

DEPRECIATION AND TAXES

Assets in the private sector are subject to annual depreciation over a period n' set by law. Depreciation expense is in turn tax deductible, so that a cash flow is generated each year given by τ times the depreciation expense, where τ is the tax rate expressed as a decimal fraction. Denoting by P_a the cost after taxes and by P_b the cost before taxes, it follows that

$$P_a = P_b(1 - \tau D) \tag{4.10}$$

where D is a factor depending on the method of depreciation.

There are two of these of interest. The *straight-line* method calls for a deduction every year of P_b/n', which produces a cash flow of constant rate $a = \tau P_b/n'$ over $n = n'$ periods. The present worth of this flow is, by (4.5), $\tau P_b f_u$; hence

$$P_a = P_b - \tau P_b f_u = P_b(1 - \tau f_u)$$

Comparing with (4.10) we see that for the straight-line method

$$D_l = f_u \tag{4.11}$$

(where the added subscript stands for "linear").

EXAMPLE 4.9. A machine costs \$8000 and will be depreciated by the straight-line method over 10 years although its service life is expected to be 15 years. Find (*a*) the investment after taxes, (*b*) the equivalent annual cost before and after taxes. Assume that money is worth 12% and the tax rate is 52%.

(*a*) For the ten years of depreciation, $x = rn' = (0.12)(10) = 1.2$; $f_u = 0.58234 = D_l$. From (4.10)

$$P_a = 8000[1 - (0.52)(0.58234)] = \$5577.47 \quad Ans.$$

(*b*) The equivalent annual cost *after taxes*, a_l, is obtained by taking the result in (*a*) as the initial investment for substitution in (4.7). For the 15 years of service, $x = (0.12)(15) = 1.8$; $f_u = 0.46372$. Thus

$$a_l = \frac{5577.47}{15(0.46372)} = \$801.84 \quad Ans.$$

Since this is a tax deductible expense, the amount a before taxes is given by

$$a_l = a(1 - \tau) = a(1 - 0.52) = 0.48a$$

Therefore, $a = 801.84/0.48 = \$1670.50$ *Ans.*

The second method of depreciation is the *sum-of-the-years'-digits* (SYD) method. It is designed to produce high deductions in the initial years, falling off uniformly to a small deduction for the last year. The annual percentages are derived as follows:

1. Add the ordinal numbers of the years, i.e.

$$1 + 2 + 3 + \cdots + n' = \frac{n'(n'+1)}{2} = S_n$$

2. Write the numbers of the years in *reverse order*, i.e. $n', n'-1, n'-2, \ldots, 3, 2, 1$.

3. The annual fractions d are then

$$\frac{n'}{S_n}, \quad \frac{n'-1}{S_n}, \quad \frac{n'-2}{S_n}, \quad \ldots, \quad \frac{3}{S_n}, \quad \frac{2}{S_n}, \quad \frac{1}{S_n}$$

EXAMPLE 4.10. Prepare a schedule of depreciation expense rates for a tax life of 10 years, using SYD.

Here $S_n = 10(10+1)/2 = 55$, giving:

Year	1	2	3	4	5	6	7	8	9	10	TOTAL
Rate d	10/55 or 0.182	9/55 or 0.164	8/55 or 0.145	7/55 or 0.127	6/55 or 0.109	5/55 or 0.091	4/55 or 0.073	3/55 or 0.055	2/55 or 0.036	1/55 or 0.018	1 or 1.000

It can be shown that the depreciation factor corresponding to the sum-of-the-years'-digits method is given approximately by

$$D_s = \frac{2}{rn'}(1 - f_u) \tag{4.12}$$

EXAMPLE 4.11. Rework Example 4.9 using SYD.

(a) For the depreciation period, $x = 1.2$ and $f_u = 0.58234$, as in Example 4.9. From (*4.12*)

$$D_s = \frac{2}{1.2}(1 - 0.58234) = 0.6961$$

and then from (*4.10*)

$$P_a = 8000[1 - (0.52)(0.6961)] = \$5104.22 \quad Ans.$$

(b) From (*4.7*), the equivalent annual cost after taxes, a_s, is

$$a_s = \frac{5104.22}{15(0.46372)} = \$733.81 \quad Ans.$$

$$a = \frac{a_s}{0.48} = \$1528.77 \quad Ans.$$

INFLATION

Suppose prices increase at a rate of i per year. Then, if a certain service or item costs P_0 now, it will cost

$$A_n = P_0 e^{in}$$

n years from now, according to (*4.3*). The present value is then given by (*4.4*) as

$$P_n = A_n e^{-rn} = P_0 e^{-(r-i)n} \tag{4.13}$$

This means that, in the case of inflation, all previous formulas remain valid if r is replaced by $r - i$. In particular, we set $x = (r - i)n$ in order to get f_u from Appendix L.

EXAMPLE 4.12. A major overhaul of a machine must be carried out 4, 8 and 12 years from now. The overhaul currently costs $500. What is the present value of the job (a) without inflation? (b) with inflation at 8% a year? Money is worth 12%.

(a)   For 4 years: $x = (0.12)(4) = 0.48$; $e^x = 1.6161$; $P = 500/1.6161 = \$309.39$

   For 8 years: $x = (0.12)(8) = 0.96$; $e^x = 2.6117$; $P = 500/2.6117 =$ 191.45

   For 12 years: $x = (0.12)(12) = 1.44$; $e^x = 4.2207$; $P = 500/4.2207 =$ 118.46

$$\underline{\hspace{2cm}}$$
   $\$619.30$ *Ans.*

(b) The interest rate is reduced to $0.12 - 0.08 = 0.04$.

   For 4 years: $x = (0.04)(4) = 0.16$; $e^x = 1.1735$; $P_n = 500/1.1735 = \$ \ 426.08$

   For 8 years: $x = (0.04)(8) = 0.32$; $e^x = 1.3771$; $P_n = 500/1.3771 =$ 363.08

   For 12 years: $x = (0.04)(12) = 0.48$; $e^x = 1.6161$; $P_n = 500/1.6161 =$ 309.39

$$\underline{\hspace{2cm}}$$
   $\$1098.55$ *Ans.*

EXAMPLE 4.13. Rework Example 4.8 with a 7 percent inflation rate.

The only change necessary is to replace the original interest rate of 0.1 with $0.1 - 0.07 = 0.03$.

For the series of steel bridges

First cost: $x = (0.03)(40) = 1.2$; $f_u = 0.58234$; from (4.8)

$$K = \frac{380,000}{(1.2)(0.58234)} = \$543,783.11$$

Cost of painting: $x = (0.03)(10) = 0.3$; $f_u = 0.86394$; from (4.8)

$$K = \frac{40,000}{(0.3)(0.86394)} = \$154,331.70$$

Total K: $543,783.11 + 154,331.70 = \$698,114.81$

For the series of wooden bridges

First cost: $x = (0.03)(15) = 0.45$; $f_u = 0.80527$; from (4.8)

$$K = \frac{200,000}{(0.45)(0.80527)} = \$551,919.77$$

Cost of painting: $x = (0.03)(2) = 0.06$; $f_u = 0.97059$; from (4.8)

$$K = \frac{20,000}{(0.06)(0.97059)} = \$343,433.71$$

Total K: $551,919.77 + 343,433.71 = \$895,353.48$

The steel bridge is preferable.   *Ans.*

Note that the inclusion of inflation in the calculations has led to a reversal of the previous choice.

DISCOUNTED CASH FLOW

This method is also known as *interest rate of return, investor's method* or *internal rate of return*. It makes it possible to compare the profitability of investments of various kinds by finding the interest rate which, when applied to the proposed investment, would yield the expected schedule of paybacks. In Example 4.4 we considered the simple case of equal expected annual cash flows. Unequal flows, such as occur in many practical cases, require a trial-and-error technique.

EXAMPLE 4.14. A certain improvement is expected to result in the following savings during the next 5 years:

Year	1	2	3	4	5
Savings R, $	20,000	60,000	60,000	40,000	30,000

The first three columns of Table 4-1 show the required investment, broken down by categories having different tax lives for depreciation (SYD) purposes. Find the interest rate of return. (Combined federal and state tax rate is 0.55.)

Table 4-1

Investment Category	Investment P, $	Tax Life n'	Depreciation Ratio d for Year No.				
			1	2	3	4	5
Building	6,000	40	0.049	0.048	0.046	0.045	0.044
Machinery	25,000	15	0.125	0.117	0.108	0.100	0.092
Tooling	8,000	4	0.400	0.300	0.200	0.100	..
Development Expenses	30,000	1	1.000	..	..	..	..

TOTAL $\Sigma P = 69,000$

Table 4-1 includes the multipliers d for SYD depreciation, computed as in Example 4-10, for the given values of n'. Development expenses are written off entirely the first year. The rest of the computation appears in Table 4-2.

Table 4-2

	Category	Year 1	Year 2	Year 3	Year 4	Year 5	SUMMATIONS
(1)	Building	162	158	152	149	145	
(2)	Machinery	1,719	1,609	1,485	1,375	1,265	
(3)	Tooling	1,760	1,320	880	440	..	
(4)	Expenses	16,500	..	..	..	..	
(5)	Savings after taxes	13,500	27,000	27,000	18,000	13,500	
(6)	a_n	33,641	30,087	29,517	19,964	14,910	128,119
(7)	$x - 0.28\,n$	0.28	0.56	0.84	1.12	1.40	
(8)	e^x	1.3231	1.7507	2.3164	3.0649	4.0552	
(9)	a_n/e^x	25,426	17,186	12,743	6,514	3,676	65,545
(10)	$x = 0.26\,n$	0.26	0.52	0.78	1.04	1.30	
(11)	e^x	1.2969	1.6820	2.1815	2.8292	3.6693	
(12)	a_n/e^x	25,940	17,888	13,531	7,056	4,063	68,478

Lines (1) through (4) show the cash flow from the depreciation allowances. They are τdP, i.e. the tax rate times the depreciation factor times the investment concerned; e.g. for the second year, the cash flow for the building is $(0.55)(0.048)(6000) = \$158$. Line (5) is the after-tax income $(1 - \tau)R$, e.g. for the 4th year, the entry is $(1 - 0.55)(40,000) = \$18,000$.

Line (6) is the total of Lines (1) through (5), i.e. the annual returns a_n after taxes. The total of these is Σa_n, which may also be written $5\bar{a}$, where $\bar{a}$ is the average annual return. Since the total initial investment is $\Sigma P = 69,000$, we obtain, as in Example 4.4,

$$f_u = \frac{\Sigma P}{5\bar{a}} = \frac{69,000}{128,116} = 0.53857$$

From Appendix L, the value $f_u = 0.53857$ corresponds to

$$x = \bar{r}(5) = 1.4 \quad \text{or} \quad \bar{r} = \tfrac{1}{5}(1.4) = 0.28$$

This average value of the interest rate $\bar{r}$ is only a first estimate. To complete the problem, the rate has to be checked. Line (7) of Table 4-2 gives $x = 0.28\,n$ and Line (8) the corresponding e^x from Appendix A. The present value of each a_n is then given by (4.4) and appears in Line (9). The total is seen to be $65,545, which is too low. We try $r = 0.26$ in the next three lines and get a revised total of $68,478, which is within less than 1 percent of $69,000. Thus $r = 26\%$.   *Ans.*

In using discounted cash flows to choose between alternative projects, it is best to arrange all the projects in declining order of rate of return and to add up the corresponding total investments (ΣP). When the sum has reached the total budgeted for new plant and equipment, then the rate of return for the last project picked becomes the "passing grade." Usually a standard period is picked (such as 5 years in Example 4.14) for comparing all projects; returns much further in the future tend to become more and more conjectural (see Chapter 17).

Solved Problems

4.1.   Rework Example 4.9, with an inflation rate of 10 percent.

We follow Example 4.9, except that $r - i = 0.12 - 0.10 = 0.02$ is the new effective interest rate.

(a) $x = 0.02\,n' = (0.02)(10) = 0.2$; $f_u = 0.90635 = D_l$.   From (4.10)

$$P_a = 8000[1 - (0.52)(0.90635)] = \$4229.58 \quad Ans.$$

(b) $x = (0.02)(15) = 0.3$; $f_u = 0.86394$.   From (4.7)

$$a_l = \frac{4229.58}{15(0.86394)} = \$326.38 \quad Ans.$$

and

$$a = \frac{a_l}{0.48} = \$679.96 \quad Ans.$$

4.2.   Rework Example 4.11, with an inflation rate of 10 percent.

We follow Example 4.11, except for the new effective rate $r - i = 0.02$.

(a) $x = 0.2$, $f_u = 0.90635$, as in Problem 4.1.   From (4.12)

$$D_s = \frac{2}{0.2}(1 - 0.90635) = 0.9365$$

and then from (4.10)

$$P_a = 8000[1 - (0.52)(0.9365)] = \$4104.16 \quad Ans.$$

(b)   From (4.7),

$$a_s = \frac{4104.16}{15(0.86394)} = \$316.70 \quad Ans.$$

and

$$a = \frac{316.70}{0.48} = \$659.79 \quad Ans.$$

4.3.   In Example 4.6, we calculated that a 25-year, 9% mortgage for $35,000 called for monthly payments of $293.43. Assuming further that there was a $10,000 down payment, what would be the owner's equity in the property after 14 years?

Equity = First Cost — Debt Remaining

The first cost is $35,000 + 10,000 = \$45,000$. After 14 years, $14(12) = 168$ payments have been made, leaving $300 - 168 = 132$ payments. The present value of those remaining 132 payments *at that time* is given by *(4.5)* with

$$x = \frac{0.09}{12}(132) = 0.99$$

From Appendix L, $f_u = 0.63477$. Thus

$$P = (293.43)(132)(0.63477) = \$24,586.39$$

and $\qquad$ Equity $= 45,000 - 24,586.39 = \$20,413.61$ $\quad$ *Ans.*

4.4. What will be the amount A n periods from now of an amount a paid every period at an interest rate r? What will be the amount 15 years from now of \$2000 a year, with interest at 7.5% compounded continuously?

The general solution is obtained by converting the uniform flow to its *present value* and then finding the *compound amount* of that present value n periods from now. Substituting *(4.5)* in *(4.3)*

$$A = Pe^{rn} = e^{rn}an\frac{1 - e^{-rn}}{rn} = an\frac{e^{rn} - 1}{rn} = ane^{rn}f_u \qquad (4.14)$$

Either form may be used to solve the numerical problem. Thus

$$e^x = e^{(0.075)(15)} = e^{1.125} = 3.0803$$

and $\qquad$ $A = 2000(15)\dfrac{3.0803 - 1}{1.125} = \$55,474$ $\quad$ *Ans.*

Alternatively, f_u for $x = 1.125$ is 0.60031 and $A = 2000(15)(3.0803)(0.60031) = \$55,474$.

The foregoing is an *endowment* problem.

4.5. What would have to be the annual payment at 8% interest which will amount to \$20,000 14 years from now?

This reverses *(4.14)*:

$$a = \frac{A}{n}\frac{rn}{e^{rn} - 1} = \frac{A}{ne^{rn}f_u} \qquad (4.15)$$

Applying *(4.15)*, $x = (0.08)(14) = 1.12$; $e^x - 3.0649$; and

$$a = \frac{(20,000)(1.12)}{14(3.0649 - 1)} = \$774.86 \quad Ans.$$

The amount a is called the *sinking fund payment*.

4.6. An investor wishes to buy a mine. He thinks he can get an initial income of \$40,000 a year after taxes from it, but realizes that, as the mine is depleted over its 25-year life, the income will decline at the rate of 6% a year. At the same time, inflation is likely to increase both costs and price of the ore mined by 8% per year. He would like his overall yield to reflect a 16% return before depletion and inflation. What is the maximum present amount he could pay for the property?

Depletion at a rate ℓ is treated like inflation, only with a negative sign. The effective interest rate becomes

$$r - i - (-\ell) = 0.16 - 0.08 + 0.06 = 0.14$$

From *(4.5)*, with $x = (0.14)(25) = 3.5$ and $f_u = 0.27709$,

$$P = (40,000)(25)(0.27709) = \$277,090 \quad Ans.$$

4.7. A company borrows $200,000 in the form of a 25-year bond with a 10% annual coupon (i.e. the interest is payable annually). The principal is payable in a single payment at the end of the 25 years. In order to be able to retire the bond then, the company sets up a sinking fund at 8% a year compounded continuously. What are the total annual payments for servicing this debt?

An amount $(0.10)(200,000) = \$20,000$ a year is payable in interest on the bond. The principal is amortized in a sinking fund, for which the annual payment a is given by (*4.15*) with $x = (0.08)(25) = 2$; $e^x = 7.3891$:

$$a = \frac{(200,000)(2)}{25(7.3891-1)} = \$2504.27$$

The total annual payment is $20,000 + 2504.27 = \$22,504.27$.　*Ans.*

Supplementary Problems

4.8. Find the present value of $500 a year at 8% for 10 years.　*Ans.* $3441.70

4.9. What is the amount after 10 years of $500 a year at 8% p.a.?　*Ans.* $7659.50

4.10. A fund of $40,000 is to be accumulated in 16 years at 7% interest. Find (*a*) the present value, (*b*) the annual payment.　*Ans.* (*a*) $13,051.20; (*b*) $1356.00

4.11. Rework Example 4.7 with depreciation for the "buy" alternative, with the rent charged as expense right away. Find the present value of renting and of buying. Use straight-line depreciation with a tax rate of 52 percent and a tax life of 10 years.　*Ans.* rent: $15,498.72; buy: $28,806.48

4.12. Repeat Problem 4.11 with sum-of-the-years'-digits depreciation.

Ans.　rent: $15,498.72; buy: $26,276.46

4.13. There are three cases of net cash flow after taxes in a discounted cash flow problem. All three yield the same total payout over 5 years for an initial investment of $60,000 (see Table 4-3). Find the interest rate of return in each case.　*Ans.* (*a*) 45.3%; (*b*) 34%; (*c*) 26.5%

Table 4-3

Case	Cash Flow, $ (000)				
	Year 1	Year 2	Year 3	Year 4	Year 5
(*a*)	50	40	30	20	10
(*b*)	30	30	30	30	30
(*c*)	10	20	30	40	50

Chapter 5

Network Analysis

CRITICAL PATH MODELS

Critical path models provide a system whereby it is possible to plan large and complex projects in detail, estimate the time required and, as the most characteristic feature, show where bottlenecks are likely to develop.

Several such techniques are available, the two best known being PERT (Program Evaluation and Review Technique) and CPM (Critical Path Method). A PERT diagram of a certain project appears in Fig. 5-1. The numbers in circles denote *events* such as "finish part A, go on to part B" or "choice between designs completed." The lines between events or nodes are *activities*; they represent time periods, e.g. "manufacture part A" or "run tests on assemblies." The direction of increasing time is indicated by an arrow along each activity. Thus the whole project is represented by a set of linked, continuously directed *paths* running from the starting node to the final node. *All* paths must be gone through to complete the project.

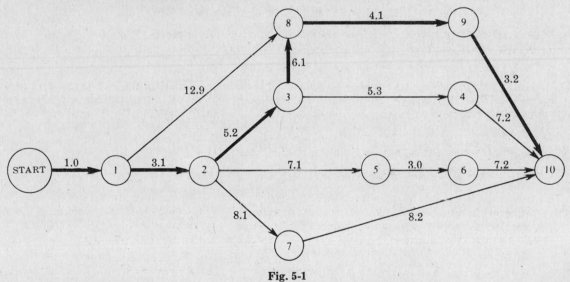

Fig. 5-1

In Fig. 5-1, the events are shown numbered. The numbers are usually chosen such that they increase as one moves along any path to the completion of the project. The numbers shown along the activities are estimates of expected time for each. Some critical path methods use a single estimate resulting from conventional studies or an average of many similar tasks. The PERT scheme calls for three estimates, which might be the judgments of three individuals or reflect the range of time judged proper by a single estimator. The lowest time estimate, a, is called *optimistic*; the highest one, b, is *pessimistic*; and m, the one in between, is called the *most likely*. The expected time t_e is then given by a weighted average:

$$t_e = \frac{1}{6}(a + 4m + b) \tag{5.1}$$

45

EXAMPLE 5.1.   Under what conditions does $t_e = m$?

If
$$\frac{1}{6}(a + 4m + b) = m$$

then $m = (a + b)/2$, i.e. the midpoint. This would be the case if the task were estimated to take "anywhere from a to b" time units with equal likelihood.

CRITICAL PATH AND SLACK

Having determined the times, the network may be constructed. The *critical path* is the path from start to finish which takes the *most* time.

Consider a path from one given node to another. The expected time for this path is $T = \Sigma t_e$, in which the summation is over the activities composing the path. The *slack* for this path is defined as $T_m - T$, where T_m is the maximum time over all paths connecting the given nodes. If T_m is assumed for a part of the critical path, then the slack shows the amount of slippage that may be allowed without affecting the completion time of the whole project.

EXAMPLE 5.2.   Find the critical path and the path with the most slack for the PERT network of Fig. 5-1.

The solution consists in a systematic enumeration of the allowable paths.

(i)   Try S-1-8-9-10: $\Sigma t_e = 1.0 + 12.9 + 4.1 + 3.2 = 21.2$

(ii)   Check 1-2-3-8: $\Sigma t_e = 3.1 + 5.2 + 6.1 = 14.4$

This is greater than the direct route 1-8, which is 12.9; therefore, 1-8 has slack $= 14.4 - 12.9 = 1.5$ and a more critical path is

S-1-2-3-8-9-10: $\Sigma t_e = 1.0 + 14.4 + 4.1 + 3.2 = 22.7$

(iii)   Check 3-4-10: $\Sigma t_e = 5.3 + 7.2 = 12.5$

This is less than 3-8-9-10: $\Sigma t_e = 6.1 + 4.1 + 3.2 = 13.4$

No new critical path has been found; 3-4-10 has slack $= 13.4 - 12.5 = 0.9$.

(iv)   Check 2-5-6-10: $\Sigma t_e = 7.1 + 3.0 + 7.2 = 17.3$

2-7-10: $\Sigma t_e = 8.1 + 8.2 = 16.3$

2-3-4-10: $\Sigma t_e = 5.2 + 5.3 + 7.2 = 17.7$

and compare to

2-3-8-9-10: $\Sigma t_e = 5.2 + 6.1 + 4.1 + 3.2 = 18.6$

The latter remains part of the critical path; slack for the other paths is

Path	2-5-6-10	2-7-10	2-3-4-10
Slack	$18.6 - 17.3 = 1.3$	$18.6 - 16.3 = 2.3$	$18.6 - 17.7 = 0.9$

(v)   This exhausts the choices. The critical path is S-1-2-3-8-9-10: $\Sigma t_e = 22.7$ *Ans.*

Greatest slack is on S-1-2-7-10 (or 1-2-7-10 or 2-7-10): slack $= 2.3$ *Ans.*

The critical path is shown as a heavy line in Fig. 5-1.

Once the project is underway, it is necessary to monitor the duration of each activity carefully and check it against the original estimate t_e. When there has been a deviation, the PERT network must be reevaluated; whether there has been a gain (taking less time than expected) or a slippage (taking longer), it is possible that a new critical path has been created.

EXAMPLE 5.3. The project of Example 5.2 is started and it is found that the activity 3-4 has slipped 2 units of time. Reevaluate the network and find the critical path, as well as the one with the most slack.

For activity 3-4, t_e is now $5.3 + 2.0 = 7.3$. The new Σt_e for 3-4-10 is $7.3 + 7.2 = 14.5$, which exceeds the value 13.4 found in Example 5.2 for 3-8-9-10. The critical path is thus superseded by S-1-2-3-4-10 with

$$\Sigma t_e = 1.0 + 3.1 + 5.2 + 14.5 = 23.8 \quad Ans.$$

Path S-1-2-7-10 remains the one with maximum slack, which is

$$23.8 - (1.0 + 3.1 + 8.1 + 8.2) = 3.4 \quad Ans.$$

It happens in many projects that it may not be possible to proceed beyond a specific event along one path before an event on another path has taken place. For example, it may not be possible to proceed with the manufacture of components until the design of the entire system has been checked out. To allow for such restrictions, dashed lines are used to connect the events affected; they are called *dummy activities* and take no time themselves ($t_e = 0$), but their presence may change the whole project characteristics as well as the critical path.

EXAMPLE 5.4. Figure 5-2 shows a PERT network which is the same as that in Fig. 5-1 except for the dummy activity connecting events 4 and 5. Find the critical path and the one with the most slack.

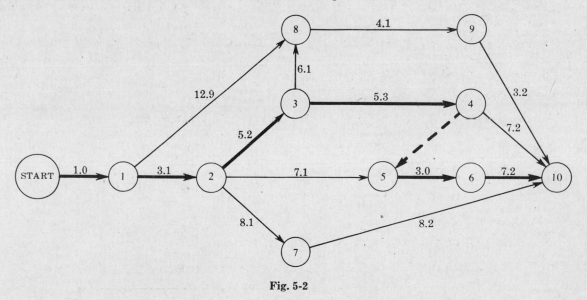

Fig. 5-2

In addition to the paths evaluated in Example 5-2, there is now

$$2\text{-}3\text{-}4\text{-}5\text{-}6\text{-}10: \quad \Sigma t_e = 5.2 + 5.3 + 0 + 3.0 + 7.2 = 20.7$$

Compare this to

2-3-8-9-10: $\Sigma t_e = 18.6$. Slack $= 20.7 - 18.6 = 2.1$

2-3-4-10: $\Sigma t_e = 17.7$. Slack $= 20.7 - 17.7 = 3.0$

2-5-6-10: $\Sigma t_e = 17.3.$ Slack $= 20.7 - 17.3 = 3.4$

2-7-10: $\Sigma t_e = 16.3.$ Slack $= 20.7 - 16.3 = 4.4$

Thus 2-3-4-5-6-10 is a new critical portion and the whole critical path is

$$\text{S-1-2-3-4-5-6-10 with } \Sigma t_e = 1.0 + 3.1 + 20.7 = 24.8 \quad Ans.$$

The slackest path is S-1-2-7-10, with slack 4.4.   *Ans.*

THE SHORTEST ROUTE. GROUPING BY STAGES

A problem closely related to that of the critical path is the one in which a traveler must go from origin to destination through a network of alternate routes. Such a network is shown in Fig. 5-3. It has the characteristic that there are three *stages* or, as they are sometimes called, *districts* which must be traversed, but only one stop in each stage is required. Traveling times or distances between the nodes or stops are also given in the figure. The analysis presented below consists in a systematic enumeration of possibilities. This is done so that, while we actually require the optimization over several stages of decision-making, we reduce the problem so that a set of optima is created at each stage. We may then proceed to the next one, secure in the knowledge that we need not backtrack. This methodology is the essential feature of *dynamic programming*.

EXAMPLE 5.5. Find the shortest distance between start and finish in the network of Fig. 5-3, where the numbers represent distances.

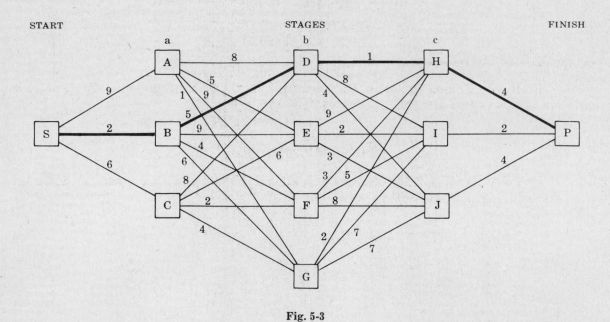

Fig. 5-3

We start with destination P and work backwards, as shown in Table 5-1. Column (1) presents no choice, since, having arrived at H, I or J there is only one route from each to P. Column (2) enumerates the choices in going from Stage b via Stage c to P. Here we pick the smallest distance from each node of Stage b; it is starred in each case. Two entries from F tie and are both starred. In Column (3), we proceed from Stage a to P. Each node in Stage a is combined with one of the starred entries from Column (2). In Column (4) the task is carried back to start S, again by combining the distances from S with the starred entries forward of Stage a. The final answer is SBDHP with distance 12 units.   *Ans.*

Table 5-1
Route and Distances to P from

Stage c		Stage b		Stage a		Start S	
HP	4	DHP	$1 + 4 = 5*$	A(DHP)	$8 + 5 = 13$	S(AGHP)	$9 + 7 = 16$
IP	2	DIP	$8 + 2 = 10$	A(EIP)	$5 + 4 = 9$	S(BDHP)	$2 + 10 = 12*$
JP	4	DJP	$4 + 4 = 8$	A(FHP)	$9 + 7 = 16$	S(CFHP)	$6 + 9 = 15$
				A(FIP)	$9 + 7 = 16$	S(CFIP)	$6 + 9 = 15$
		EHP	$9 + 4 = 13$	A(GHP)	$1 + 6 = 7*$		
		EIP	$2 + 2 = 4*$				
		EJP	$3 + 4 = 7$	B(DHP)	$5 + 5 = 10*$		
				B(EIP)	$9 + 4 = 13$		
		FHP	$3 + 4 = 7*$	B(FHP)	$4 + 7 = 11$		
		FIP	$5 + 2 = 7*$	B(FIP)	$4 + 7 = 11$		
		FJP	$8 + 4 = 12$	B(GHP)	$6 + 6 = 12$		
		GHP	$2 + 4 = 6*$	C(DHP)	$8 + 5 = 13$		
		GIP	$7 + 2 = 9$	C(EIP)	$6 + 4 = 10$		
		GJP	$7 + 4 = 11$	C(FHP)	$2 + 7 = 9*$		
				C(FIP)	$2 + 7 = 9*$		
				C(GHP)	$4 + 6 = 10$		

EXAMPLE 5.6. To show that the shortest route need not be unique, make $SB = 6$ and $SC = 2$ in Fig. 5-3. Then Column (4) of Table 5-1 is changed to

$$S(AGHP) \quad 9 + 7 = 16$$
$$S(BDHP) \quad 6 + 10 = 16$$
$$S(CFHP) \quad 2 + 9 = 11*$$
$$S(CFIP) \quad 2 + 9 = 11*$$

Both SCFHP and SCFIP are optimal at 11 units.   *Ans.*

Problems of this kind occur in the planning of transportation networks, materials handling routes within a factory and communication systems.

Solved Problems

5.1. Figure 5-4 shows a PERT network together with the expected times t_e. Find the critical path and the earliest and latest times for each event.

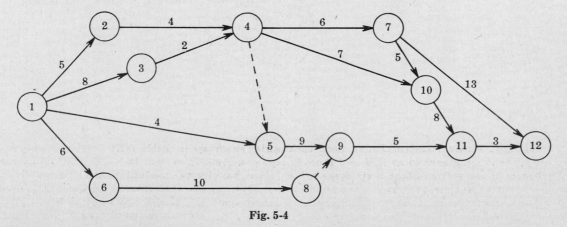

Fig. 5-4

Consider any event in the network. The earliest time it can be reached after the first event at time 0 is given by the *longest* path to it. We can, therefore, find the earliest times by successively getting these longest paths, proceeding one event at a time and identifying the *longest* time it took to get to the event from the one immediately preceding it. We thus work forward along the network. To obtain the latest times, we work backwards. Taking the last event first, we successively identify the *minimum* times it takes to get to the one immediately following it. The work is carried out in Tables 5-2 and 5-3.

Table 5-2

Event	Preceding Event	T_E	t_e	Max $(T_E + t_e)$	Min $(T_L - t_e)$ (from Table 5-3)	Slack
1	..	..	..	0	0	0
2	1	0	5	5	6	1
3	1	0	8	8	8	0
4	2	5	4	..	..	..
4	3	8	2	10	10	0
5	1	0	4	..	..	..
5	4	10	0	10	15	5
6	1	0	6	6	14	8
7	4	10	6	16	16	0
8	6	6	10	16	24	8
9	5	10	9	19	24	5
9	8	16	0	..	..	..
10	4	10	7	..	..	..
10	7	16	5	21	21	0
11	9	19	5	..	..	..
11	10	21	8	29	29	0
12	7	16	13	..	..	..
12	11	29	3	32	32	0

The first two columns of Table 5-2 give each event and the one or more events that precede it. Column t_e is the activity time from the preceding to the present event, taken from Fig. 5-4. Column T_E is the earliest time of the preceding event, and the next column, headed Max $(T_E + t_e)$, gives the earliest time of the event in the first column. We start at $t = 0$ for event 1. The earliest time for 2 is clearly $0 + 5 = 5$ and for 3 it is $0 + 8 = 8$. Event 4, however, can be reached from 2 as well as 3. The path 1-3-4 is the longer one; specifically, going via 1-2-4 takes $5 + 4 = 9$ units, whereas 1-3-4 takes $8 + 2 = 10$ units. Thus the latter is selected for the entry in the Max $(T_E + t_e)$ column. The column labeled T_E thus consists of the entry under Max $(T_E + t_e)$ for the *preceding* event. Unless two or more paths happen to be identical only one entry per event appears in the Max $(T_E + t_e)$ column.

Table 5-3 is laid out in the opposite direction. Starting with a time of 32 units for reaching activity 12 in minimum time, we work backwards through the network. Event 11 is 3 units earlier, i.e. 29 units from $t = 0$, etc. The latest times are given as Min $(T_L - t_e)$, i.e. if an event has more than one immediate successor, the minimum path shows the latest time the event can take place. The column T_L is the entry under Min $(T_L - t_e)$ for the previously computed *next* event, e.g. whenever an event in the first column is succeeded by event 4, the entry Min $(T_L - t_e) = 10$ appears in column T_L.

Table 5-3

Event	Next Event	T_L	t_e	Min $(T_L - t_e)$
12	..	..	..	32
11	12	32	3	29
10	11	29	8	21
9	11	29	5	24
8	9	24	0	24
7	10	21	5	16
7	12	32	13	..
6	8	24	10	14
5	9	24	9	15
4	5	15	0	..
4	7	16	6	10
4	10	21	7	..
3	4	10	2	8
2	4	10	4	6
1	2	6	5	..
1	3	8	8	0
1	5	15	4	..
1	6	14	6	..

Finally, the results of Table 5-3 are transferred to Table 5-2. The difference between earliest and latest times in each case is the slack for that event. It will be noted that the slack is zero for certain events. These, by definition, make up the critical path, which in this example is 1-3-4-7-10-11-12 with a length of 32 time units. For the noncritical events, the earliest and latest times appear in the table. For instance, the earliest time for event 6 is 6 units, the latest 14 units.

5.2.   Consider again the network illustrated in Fig. 5-1. Given that the total of the activity times remains constant, find the minimum time required to do the job, if resources can be diverted from one activity to another at will.

The network has the characteristic that we must go from *source* 0 to *sink* 10, using several partially identical paths and carrying out every activity specified in the network. The network is shown in Fig. 5-5. The problem is solved by making a *cut* of the network such that each path leading from source to sink is cut only once. Furthermore, the cut is made in such a way that the maximum possible number of branches, i.e. activities, is cut. One possible way is indicated by the curved line *AB* in Fig. 5-5 which cuts 5 activities. No greater number of branches is possible in this network, but the solution is not unique. All cuts through 1-8, 3-8, 3-4 *or* 4-10, 2-5 *or* 5-6 *or* 6-10 and 2-7 *or* 7-10 cut the maximum of 5 branches. Since each choice within the three sets from which we must choose is possible, there are $2 \times 3 \times 2 = 12$ optimal cuts.

Having determined the optimal cut or cuts, it remains to divide X, the total time taken for all activities, equally among the n^* branches in an optimal cut. This results in an *optimal distribution* given by $t^* = X/n^*$. In this example, the total time for all activities is 81.7 units (see Fig. 5-1). Thus

$$t^* = \frac{X}{n^*} = \frac{81.7}{5} = 16.34 \text{ units} \quad Ans.$$

The network may thus be redesigned by allocating 16.34 units to each of the activities cut and 0 to all the others. The distribution is shown in Fig. 5-5. The most general solution would be to spread the 81.7 units over all 12 optimal cuts, subject only to the condition that the 5 branches of each cut get equal assignments. This would again produce the minimum time of 16.34 units.

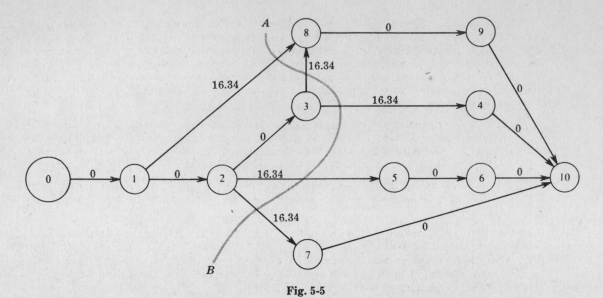

Fig. 5-5

5.3. Table 5-4 first shows the normal values of the t_e's in the network of Fig. 5-1. It is possible, however, to shorten these activities up to a certain point; these shorter times, known as *crash times*, are also shown in the table, followed by the differences between the two times, i.e. the amount of time which could be saved for each activity. Crash times are achieved at the cost of overtime and other charges, which are also listed in the table. By using the extra resources available, shorten the critical path so as to produce minimum elapsed time.

Table 5-4

Activity	Time, t_e			Crash Cost, $		Revisions					
	Normal	Crash	Difference	Total	Per Time Unit Saved	1	2	3	4	5	6
0-1	1.0	1.0	..	..	..						
1-2	3.1*	2.3	0.8	120	150					0.8	
1-8	12.9	10.0	2.9	203	70			0.5		0.8	
2-3	5.2*	4.0	1.2	96	80	1.2					
2-5	7.1	5.8	1.3	325	250						
2-7	8.1	6.9	1.2	204	170						0.3
3-4	5.3	4.0	1.3	169	130						
3-8	6.1*	5.3	0.8	80	100		0.3	0.5			
4-10	7.2	5.7	1.5	120	80				0.2		1.0
5-6	3.0	2.1	0.9	126	140						0.4
6-10	7.2	5.6	1.6	192	120			0.7	0.3		0.6
7-10	8.2	7.5	0.7	112	160						0.7
8-9	4.1*	3.0	1.1	121	110				0.1		1.0
9-10	3.2*	3.0	0.2	18	90				0.2		
Time units shortened						1.2	0.3	0.5	0.3	0.8	1.0
Cost increment, $						96	30	169	81	176	481
Cumulative extra cost, $						96	126	295	376	552	1033
Critical path, time units						21.5	21.2	20.7	20.4	19.6	18.6

The method used generally follows CPM, although a PERT modification called PERT/cost has a similar purpose. First, we add to Table 5-4 a column headed "cost per unit of time saved," e.g. in activity 1-2, saving 0.8 units at a cost of $120 means a cost of $150 per unit. The remaining columns are reserved for modifications of the original network. These are made by successively picking the activity along the critical path with the lowest cost per unit of time saved. Reductions in time are made subject to the condition that once a path becomes critical it stays critical. Six steps are needed here.

1. In Fig. 5-6(a), reduce 2-3 by the maximum "crash" amount, 1.2 units (shown in parentheses). Nothing else is changed. Note that this is along the critical path S-1-2-3-8-9-10, as in Example 5.2. Activity 2-3 is now "fully crashed," as indicated by the italic type; it is also starred in Table 5-4. The critical path is shortened by the 1.2 units to 21.5 units.

2. Shorten 3-8 by 0.3 units. This makes path S-1-8-9-10 likewise a critical path. The time along a critical path has now been shortened by 0.3 units to $21.5 - 0.3 = 21.2$ units. See Fig. 5-6(b).

3. In Fig. 5-6(c), reduce 3-8 by a further 0.5 units, which uses up the available 0.8 units. To keep S-1-2-3-8-9-10 critical it is necessary to reduce 1-8 by 0.5 units as well. These two operations, however, would promote S-1-2-5-6-10 to the path of maximum time. To keep S-1-2-5-6-10 to $21.2 - 0.5 = 20.7$ units, which is the new time along S-1-2-3-8-9-10 or S-1-8-9-10, it is necessary to shorten it by

$$1.0 + 3.1 + 7.1 + 3.0 + 7.2 - 20.7 = 0.7 \text{ units}$$

Table 5-4 shows that the activity along this path with the lowest cost per unit saved is 6-10, which is therefore reduced by 0.7.

4. Now all paths are to be reduced to the time for S-1-2-7-10, which is 20.4 units. This involves the changes shown in Fig. 5-6(d). Note that the 0.3 reduction along 8-9-10 must be split between 8-9 and 9-10 because the latter can be cut by only 0.2 units; it is now at its lower limit.

5. In Fig. 5-6(e) reduce 1-2 by 0.8 units to its lower limit. The only other change needed is to reduce 1-8 to 11.6 units. All paths are now of equal length at 19.6 units.

6. To finish the job, it is necessary to have at least one path consisting only of fully crashed activities. The easiest way to do this [Fig. 5-6(f)] is to start at 8-9 and reduce it by 1 unit to its minimum. The other adjustments follow, with due regard to starting with the lowest cost per unit saved along each path and observing the lower limits. The final result is a balanced network with all paths critical at 18.6 units. *Ans.*

The successive revisions are listed in the right-hand portion of Table 5-4. The cost of each revision is given by the sum of all the reductions multiplied by their costs per unit saved. Thus, revision 3 costs

$$(0.5)(70) + (0.5)(100) + (0.7)(120) = \$169$$

The cumulative costs and critical times are also shown.

5.4. Assuming that times in Problem 5.3 represent days and that there are indirect costs of $100 a day which can be saved if the days are saved, find the net costs of the successive reductions in critical time.

The final results of Table 5-4 are continued in Table 5-5. Revision 1 would be the optimum change to make here (since revision 2 gains nothing further and succeeding revisions lose money). However, decisions on how quickly to complete a project are often made for reasons other than purely financial ones.

Table 5-5

Revision	1	2	3	4	5	6
Cumulative Time Saved, days	1.2	1.5	2.0	2.3	3.1	4.1
Cumulative Crash Cost, $	96	126	295	376	552	1033
Indirect Cost @ $100 per Day	120	150	200	230	310	410
Cumulative Net Saving or Cost (−), $	24	24	−95	−146	−242	−623

Ans.

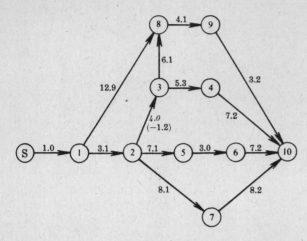

(a) CP = 21.5

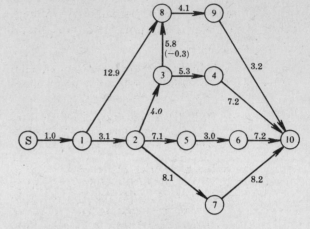

(b) CP = 21.2

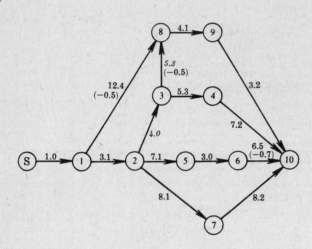

(c) CP = 20.7

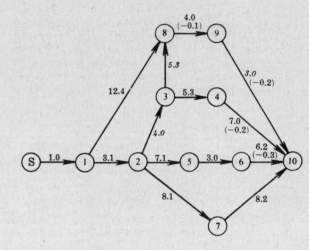

(d) CP = 20.4

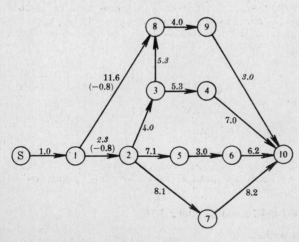

(e) CP = 19.6

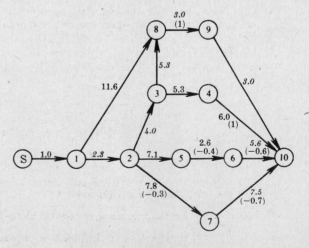

(f) CP = 18.6

Fig. 5-6

5.5. Figure 5-7 depicts a general network together with the times taken for the allowable routes between the nodes. Find the minimum time for travel from A to J.

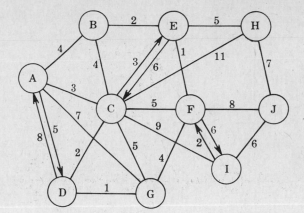

Fig. 5-7

This is a different problem from Example 5.5 or 5.6 because there are no "stages". A graphical step-by-step method is used:

1. In Fig. 5-8 first draw A and then the links between A and all *directly* reachable points, i.e. B, C, G and D.

2. Put in all links between B, C, G and D. Note that ACB, ABC, ADC, AGC, ACG, ADG, ACD and AGD are indirect ways of getting from A to one of the nodes drawn in Step 1. Compare the times taken for these indirect routes with those for the direct routes. Any links which are nonoptimal, i.e. longer, are shown as dashed lines, i.e. AG, CG and BC. Both ACD and AD take 5 units, so both are left as full lines. Steps 1 and 2 take us as far as the area marked off by the irregular line.

3. Starting from B, C and G, repeat Steps 1 and 2.

4. Starting from E, F and I, repeat Steps 1 and 2.

5. Figure 5-8 now shows the optimal routes from A to *all* points by means of the remaining solid lines. There are two optimal paths from A to J:

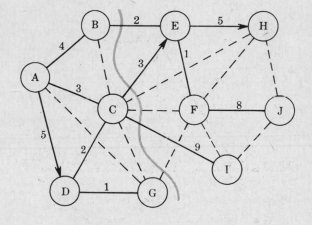

Fig. 5-8

ABEFJ: 4 + 2 + 1 + 8 = 15 units   *Ans.*

ACEFJ: 3 + 3 + 1 + 8 = 15 units   *Ans.*

Note that this method may be used to take into account differences in travel time or costs according to direction (because of road gradients, currents in rivers, prevailing winds, etc.).

Supplementary Problems

5.6. Refer back to Fig. 5-1. Dummy activities are introduced between the events specified. In each case state whether a new critical path is established and how the path of maximum slack is affected.
(a) 5 ← 7;   (b) 4 → 6;   (c) 4 ← 9.

Ans.   (a) No change; slack is now 0.3 along S-1-2-7-5-6-10 and 2.0 along 7-10.

    (b) No effect on critical path or on slackest path.

    (c) New critical path is S-1-2-3-8-9-4-10 for 26.7 units; slackest path is S-1-2-7-10 with slack 6.3 units.

5.7. Rework Example 5.5 (Fig. 5-3) except that travel is from P to S and the paths HE, JG and EB are not available.   *Ans.*   PHDBS is optimal at 12 units.

5.8. Rework Problem 5.5 (Fig. 5-7) in the opposite direction (from J to A).

Ans.   JIFCA and JFCA are both optimal at 16 units.

5.9. Figure 5-9 shows a network with distances marked. Find the shortest routes (*a*) from A and (*b*) from I, to all other points.

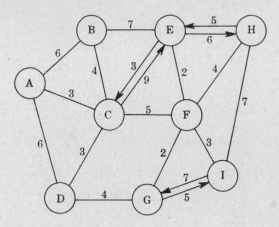

Fig. 5-9

Ans.   (*a*) AB 6, AC 3, AD or ACD 6, ACE 12, ACF 8, ACFG or ADG 10, ACFH 12, ACFI 11.

(*b*) IH or IHF 7, IF 3, IFG 5, IFE 5, IFC or IFEC 8, IFCD or IGD 11, IFECB or IFEB 12, IFCA 11.

5.10. Find the slack, earliest and latest times for the events in Fig. 5-1.   *Ans.*   See Table 5-6.

Table 5-6

Event	S	1	2	3	4	5	6	7	8	9	10
Earliest	0	1.0	4.1	9.3	14.6	11.2	14.2	12.2	15.4	19.5	22.7
Latest	0	1.0	4.1	9.3	15.5	12.5	15.5	14.5	15.4	19.5	22.7
Slack	0	0	0	0	0.9	1.3	1.3	2.3	0	0	0

5.11. In Fig. 5-4, make the optimal distribution and thus find the minimum time, if resources can be shifted at will.

Ans.   Optimal cut goes through 7-12, 7-10, 4-10, 1-5 or 5-9, 1-6 or 6-8 (no resources can be allocated to dummy activity 4-5); 19 units.

Chapter 6

Allocation

THE ASSIGNMENT PROBLEM

The general problem is to take n resources (e.g. workers) and assign them to n recipients (e.g. machines or jobs), knowing what the cost of each choice is; the times taken might also be used. The task is to minimize the total cost of the assignment. This is a task which cannot conveniently be done by enumeration; for example, a mere 5 workers can be assigned to 5 machines in $5 \times 4 \times 3 \times 2 = 120$ ways. The so-called *Hungarian method*, demonstrated in Example 6.1, quickly solves the problem.

EXAMPLE 6.1. Four workers are to be assigned to 4 jobs, it being known that the time taken by each on each job would be as in Fig. 6-1(a). Find an assignment which would minimize the sum of the times taken. (Assume that all workers are paid at the same rate; if not, costs should be used instead.)

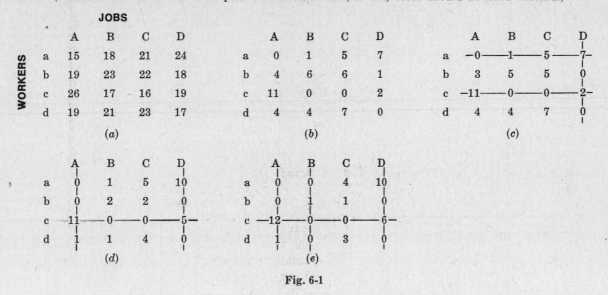

Fig. 6-1

1. First modify the time (cost) matrix, Fig. 6-1(a). Deduct the smallest (nonzero) time in each column from all entries in that column, obtaining at least one zero in each column [Fig. 6-1(b)].

2. In each row of positive entries deduct the smallest time from all entries in that row. In Fig. 6-1(b) this applies only to the second row because all the others already have zeros. The result is Fig. 6-1(c). If Step 1 had produced at least one zero in each *row* as well, the present step would be omitted.

3. Now draw the *minimum* number of lines which will cover all the zeros. In Fig. 6-1(c) three lines suffice. If there are as many such lines as there are rows or columns, an optimal assignment is possible. If not, the matrix must be changed. Here there are three lines instead of four, so the next step is necessary.

4. In Fig. 6-1(c) subtract the smallest uncovered entry (which is 3) from all uncovered entries. Enter the results in Fig. 6-1(d). Then *add* the same number to the elements at which the lines of Fig. 6-1(c) cross (7 in line a and 2 in line c), obtaining 10 and 5 respectively. Enter these results in Fig. 6-1(e), and complete the figure by entering the other covered elements without change.

5. Repeat Step 3. In Fig. 6-1(d) it is again possible to cover all zeros with only three lines. Therefore repeat Step 4, obtaining Fig. 6-1(e) in which four lines are necessary. Thus it is an optimal matrix.

6. Make the actual assignments, starting with the zero which is unique in its row or column. (If no such zero exists, start with any zero.) Here this is cC. Complete the assignment; as may happen, there is more than one. The two solutions are

$$cC,\ aA,\ bD,\ dB;\quad \text{Time} = 16 + 15 + 18 + 21 = 70\quad Ans.$$

$$cC,\ aB,\ bA,\ dD;\quad \text{Time} = 16 + 18 + 19 + 17 = 70\quad Ans.$$

THE TRANSPORTATION PROBLEM

The transportation problem is similar to the assignment problem except that 1 *or more* items may be assigned to any given cell. For example, we may have 4 warehouses being supplied by 3 plants. Given the transportation costs from each plant to each warehouse per unit of output, how should the production of each plant be allocated among the warehouses so that total transportation costs are minimized? Or, if there are 6 machines doing 4 different jobs, how, given the time taken for each job on each machine, should the work be distributed to minimize total time? The method used is sometimes considered a special case of *linear programming* (Chapter 7), but the technique of solution is rather different. It is best explained by means of an example.

EXAMPLE 6.2. The body of Fig. 6-2(a) gives the transportation costs per unit between 3 plants and 4 warehouses, e.g. it costs $10 to ship one unit from plant I to warehouse C. Plant output and warehouse requirements are listed in the margins. How should the output of each plant be distributed in order to minimize transportation costs?

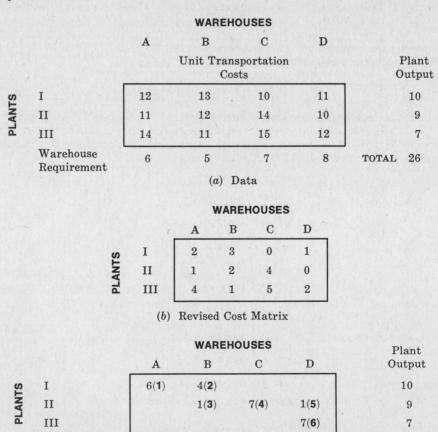

WAREHOUSES

	A	B	C	D	Plant Output
	Unit Transportation Costs				
I	12	13	10	11	10
II	11	12	14	10	9
III	14	11	15	12	7
Warehouse Requirement	6	5	7	8	TOTAL 26

(a) Data

WAREHOUSES

	A	B	C	D
I	2	3	0	1
II	1	2	4	0
III	4	1	5	2

(b) Revised Cost Matrix

WAREHOUSES

	A	B	C	D	Plant Output
I	6(**1**)	4(**2**)			10
II		1(**3**)	7(**4**)	1(**5**)	9
III				7(**6**)	7
Warehouse Requirement	6	5	7	8	TOTAL 26

(c) Northwest Corner Assignment

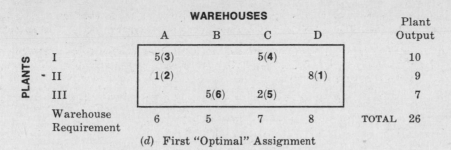

(d) First "Optimal" Assignment

Fig. 6-2

Step 1.   The smallest unit cost is \$10. Since what has to be minimized is the *excess* over this cost, we modify the cost matrix by deducting \$10 from each entry [Fig. 6-2(*b*)].

Step 2.   Find *any* feasible arrangement. One method is to start in the *northwest corner*, making a maximal assignment of 6 units and continuing as shown in Fig. 6-2(*c*). The numbers in parentheses show the order in which the assignments are made. This procedure is simple but may lead to an answer which is much too large. It is therefore usually better to try to come closer to the correct solution by allocating the maximum possible to the lowest-cost cell and to continue in this way until the requisite number of assignments has been made. The result is shown in Fig. 6-2(*d*), with the order of assignment again shown in parentheses. There are $n = r + c - 1$ assignments, where r and c are the numbers of rows and columns, respectively. It is possible to have fewer, but there cannot be more if the maximum amounts have been assigned at every step, as specified.

Step 3.   Enter the costs from the revised matrix, Fig. 6-2(*b*), in every cell in which an assignment has been made; they are italicized in Fig. 6-3(*a*).

Step 4.   Compute the "values" of the assignment. This is done by arbitrarily setting a row or column marginal entry at 0 and computing the other marginals from

$$p_{ij} = r_i + c_j \qquad\qquad (6.1)$$

where p_{ij} is the cell entry, r_i the marginal entry in the row and c_j the marginal entry in the column concerned. After the marginals have been computed, (*6.1*) is used to find values for the remaining cells (i.e. those without the values put in in Step 3). In the following calculations, each cost or value is followed by its cell or marginal position.

Set 0(I)

0(C, I) − 0(I) = 0(C)

5(C, III) − 0(C) = 5(III)

1(B, III) − 5(III) = −4(B)

2(A, I) − 0(I) = 2(A)

1(A, II) − 2(A) = −1(II)

0(D, II) − (−1)(II) = 1(D)

This completes the marginals.   Now the remaining cell entries are computed.

0(I) + (−4)(B) = −4(B, I)

0(I) + 1(D) = 1(I, D)

−1(II) + (−4)(B) = −5(II, B)

−1(II) + 0(C) = −1(II, C)

5(III) + 2(A) = 7(III, A)

5(III) + 1(D) = 6(III, D)

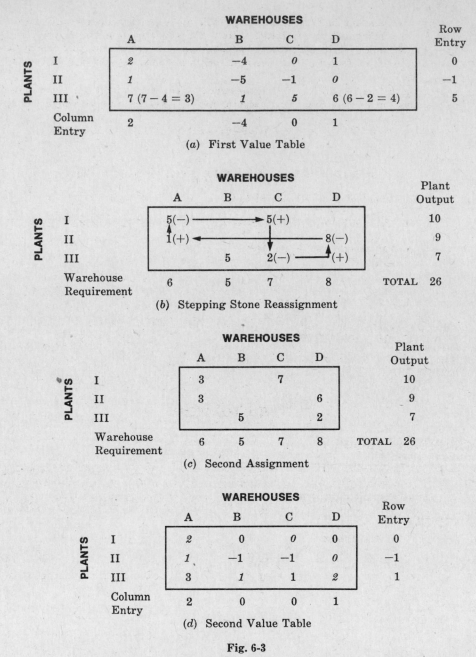

(a) First Value Table

(b) Stepping Stone Reassignment

(c) Second Assignment

(d) Second Value Table

Fig. 6-3

Step 5. Subtract each entry in the cost matrix, Fig. 6-2(b), from the corresponding entry in the value matrix, Fig. 6-3(a). We are looking only for differences which are greater than zero; hence we do not need to write down the subtractions from the italicized numbers (which lead to a difference of 0) or from negative or zero cell values (which lead to negative differences). This leaves only cells (III, A) and (III, D); subtraction shows both differences positive [Fig. 6-3(a)].

Step 6. It follows that making an assignment at (III, D), the site of the largest positive value, would reduce costs. This is done by the *stepping stone method*, in which a maximal assignment is made to the cell selected, (III, D), while adjusting the other cells so that the marginal totals of the assignments are not affected. As shown in Fig. 6-3(b), a path is laid out: start by putting a (+) into cell (III, D), then proceed horizontally or vertically to any cell where an assignment has already been made in Fig. 6-2(d), provided that cell is on a "corner," i.e. to continue the path we would have to make a right-angle turn. Put a (−) in that corner, (II, D). Continue by the same rule to (II, A) and put in a (+); then a (−) at (I, A), a (+) at (I, C) and a (−) at (III, C). The effect of this procedure is to make sure that an amount is reassigned which will make the lowest cell with a (−) equal zero while leaving all the marginal values intact. Here the effect is to put a 2 into (III, D), leaving (III, C) empty. Note that (III, B) is outside the path; not all entries are affected by a change of this sort, but a minimum of four will be. The resultant assignment is shown in Fig. 6-3(c).

Step 7. Repeat Steps 4 and 5 with the new arrangement. The new value table appears in Fig. 6-3(d). Since all subtractions involved in Step 5 give zero or negative results, this assignment is optimal. Its cost, Z^*, is

$$Z^* = 3(12) + 7(10) + 3(11) + 6(10) + 5(11) + 2(12) = \$278 \quad Ans.$$

This compares to

$$Z = 5(12) + 5(10) + 1(11) + 8(10) + 5(11) + 2(15) = \$286$$

for the original assignment of Fig. 6-2(d), and to

$$Z = 6(12) + 4(13) + 1(12) + 7(14) + 1(10) + 7(12) = \$328$$

for the northwest corner assignment, Fig. 6-2(c).

Solved Problems

THE ASSIGNMENT PROBLEM

6.1. Figure 6-4(a) shows the possible assignments of 5 jobs to 5 machines, and gives the relative cost for each job on each machine. Since some of the machines cannot do certain jobs, three entries are marked M, i.e. not permissible. Find the minimum-cost assignment.

MACHINES

	A	B	C	D	E		A	B	C	D	E
a	5	4	2	1	M	a	4	3	1	0	M
b	6	4	M	3	2	b	4	2	M	1	0
c	4	8	M	6	7	c	0	4	M	2	3
d	3	2	4	2	2	d	1	0	2	0	0
e	2	1	1	3	5	e	1	0	0	2	4

JOBS

(a)   (b)

Fig. 6-4

The cost M of the impossible assignments is understood to be a very large number, so that if any other number is added to or subtracted from it, the result is still approximately M. In this case we have chosen to do Step 2 first, which is quite permissible. Step 1 turns out to be unnecessary. The result is shown in Fig. 6-4(b). Here 5 lines are required in order to cover all zeros. Thus the table is optimal and the assignment is

aD, bE, cA, dB, eC;   Cost = 1 + 2 + 4 + 2 + 1 = 10   *Ans.*

6.2. Five jobs are to be assigned to 4 machines, subject to the cost matrix shown in Fig. 6-5(a). Make a minimum-cost assignment.

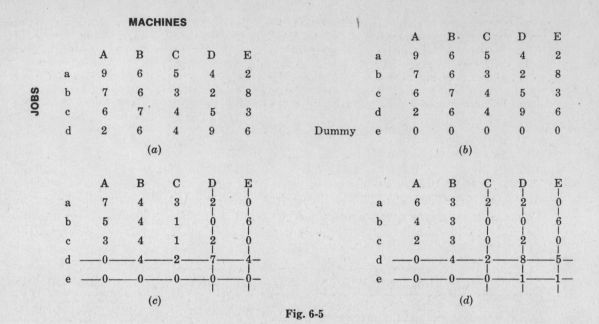

Fig. 6-5

To have a square matrix as required, a 5th row, known as a *dummy* machine or row, must be added. The dummy costs are all zero because no cost is incurred when a job is assigned to the dummy machine, i.e. when the job is not performed. (Conversely, if there were 4 jobs and 5 machines, one machine would remain idle and we would have to add a dummy *job* to make the matrix square.) The matrix changes as shown in Fig. 6-5(b). The matrix is then modified according to Step 2 (adding the dummy machine has accomplished Step 1). The result is Fig. 6-5(c). Four lines cover all the zeros (Step 3), so Steps 4 and 5 are required to produce the optimal scheme of Fig. 6-5(d). The assignment is

$$aE, bD, cC, dA, eB; \quad \text{Cost} = 2 + 2 + 4 + 2 + 0 = 10 \quad Ans.$$

6.3. A sales manager has to assign salesmen to four territories. He has four candidates of varying experience and capabilities and assesses the possible profit for each salesman in each territory as shown in Fig. 6-6(a). Find the assignment which maximizes profit.

TERRITORIES

SALESMEN

	A	B	C	D
a	35	27	28	37
b	28	34	29	40
c	35	24	32	33
d	24	32	25	28

(a)

	A	B	C	D
a	2	10	9	0
b	12	6	11	0
c	0	11	3	2
d	8	0	7	4

(b)

	A	B	C	D
a	2	10	6	0
b	12	6	8	0
c	0	11	0	2
d	8	0	4	4

(c)

	A	B	C	D
a	0	8	4	0
b	10	4	6	0
c	0	11	0	4
d	8	0	4	6

(d)

Fig. 6-6

Here we want to maximize profits rather than minimize costs. To apply the method, we transform the profits into *opportunity losses*, i.e. into losses which result from *not* using each salesman in the territory which yields maximum profit. In each row, therefore, we *subtract* each entry from the *largest* one, e.g. we lose $37 - 28 = \$9$ by putting salesman a into C rather than D. The result is shown in Fig. 6-6(*b*). This operation takes the place of Step 2. We next carry out Step 1, i.e. modifying the columns [Fig. 6-6(*c*)]. Three lines cover all zeros. Follow Steps 3, 4 and 5; now 4 lines are needed to cover the zeros [Fig. 6-6(*d*)], so the assignment is optimal. The allocation is

$$dB, cC, bD, aA; \quad Profit = 32 + 32 + 40 + 35 = \$139 \quad Ans.$$

6.4. A group of 8 workers turns out 48 units of a certain product each 8-hour day. If necessary, they can work 2 hours overtime each day, at time and a half, and make 12 more units. Each worker earns $3.60 per hour. The following is a schedule of work days per month and of monthly demand.

	Jan.	Feb.	Mar.	Apr.	May	June	July	Aug.	Sept.	Oct.	Nov.	Dec.
Work Days	22	19	21	21	22	20	22	12	20	23	19	21
Demand, units	600	500	600	800	900	1100	1200	1500	1600	1300	900	700

If a unit is made earlier than needed, there is a $1 carrying charge per month. Determine a minimum-cost production schedule.

This is another version of the allocation problem. It calls for a simple tabular solution in which units to be manufactured are allocated to the various months. The objective is to find a schedule which gives the overtime needed and also specifies how much is to be made in advance each month for later use, all subject to the minimum-cost criterion.

In Fig. 6-7 it is first necessary to compute the monthly capacities in regular time (R) and overtime (OT). The regular capacity is $48 \times$ work days, and the overtime capacity is $12 \times$ work days. Each entry in the body of the table consists of capacity available (A), unit cost (C) and production schedule (P). Capacity available derives initially from the column heading; e.g. it is 1056 units (R) for January. The unit cost is an *incremental* one and therefore is zero when the work is done in regular time and in satisfaction of the current month's requirement. If we work a month in advance, $C = \$1$; 2 months, $2; etc.; and the cost of each unit is increased by those amounts. For overtime, each worker has a $1.80 premium per hour, i.e. $3.60 per day. There are 8 workers turning out 12 units, so the extra cost per unit is $8(3.60)/12 = \$2.40$. If the unit is made in overtime in previous months, the cost is $3.40 for the previous month, $4.40 for the one before that, etc.

The method is then to fill each month's demand as far as possible out of current regular capacity and then to draw on current overtime capacity and/or unused capacity from previous months, in the order of ascending costs. We start with January and move rightwards in Fig. 6-7. From January to May, there is some capacity left over, but from March onwards the amounts left over are used up in production for later months. In completing this table, it is only necessary to put in the numbers actually needed. Once the capacity available is down to zero, no further attention is paid to the column. In March, for instance, 600 is used for all the March needs, leaving 408 units; a further 196 are made for August, leaving 212 which are used up in September. All 1008 units for which there is capacity in March are thus manufactured. On the other hand, in January, February, November and December, there is unused capacity. Other work should be found for the workers during those months.

The cost of the allocation made in Fig. 6-7 is

$$Z = 140(1.00) + 16(2.00) + 128(2.40) + 196(5.00) + 208(4.00) + 240(4.40) + 136(3.40)$$

$$+ 144(2.40) + 212(6.00) + 188(6.40) + 240(2.40) + 196(2.40)$$

$$= \$7676.80$$

MONTHS PRODUCED IN

MONTHS PRODUCED FOR

Months produced for	A/C/P	J R	J OT	F R	F OT	M R	M OT	A R	A OT	M R	M OT	J R	J OT	J R	J OT	A R	A OT	S R	S OT	O R	O OT	N R	N OT	D R	D OT
Capacities in		1056	264	912	228	1008	252	1008	252	1056	264	960	240	1056	264	576	144	960	240	1104	276	912	228	1008	252
Demand J 600	A	1056																							
	C	0																							
	P	600																							
F 500	A	456		912																					
	C			0																					
	P			500																					
M 600	A			412		1008																			
	C					0																			
	P					600																			
A 800	A					408		1008																	
	C							0																	
	P							800																	
M 900	A							208		1056															
	C									0															
	P									900															
J 1100	A									156		960													
	C									1.00		0													
	P									140		960													
J 1200	A									16		0		1056	264										
	C									2.00					2.40										
	P									16				1056	128										
A 1500	A					408		208		0			240	0	136	576	144								
	C					5.00		4.00					4.40		3.40	0	2.40								
	P					196		208					240		136	576	144								
S 1600	A					212		0			264	0				0	0	960	240						
	C					6.00					6.40								2.40						
	P					212					188							960	240						
O 1300	A					0					76							0	0	1104	276				
	C																			0	2.40				
	P																			1104	196				
N 900	A																			0	80	912			
	C																					0			
	P																					900			
D 700	A																					12		1008	
	C																							0	
	P																							700	
Total demand 11700 — Total production R		600		500		1008		1008		1056		960		1056		576		960		1104		900		700	
OT											188		240		264		144		240		196				

R 10428
OT 1272
11700

Fig. 6-7

THE TRANSPORTATION METHOD

6.5. In Example 6.2, change the requirement for warehouse A to 3 units and rework the example.

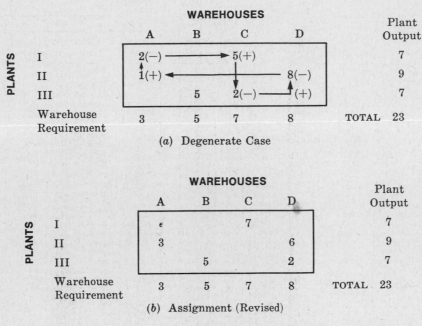

Fig. 6-8

The first assignment is as in Fig. 6-2(d), except that the entry for (I, A) is 2 units. The value table again requires putting an assignment into (III, D), and the stepping stone sequence is shown in Fig. 6-8(a). Now a problem arises in that *two* cells are reduced to zero, i.e. (III, C), as expected, and (I, A). While such an assignment to only 5 cells meets the output and warehouse conditions, it will be found that the marginals in the value table cannot be computed. Accordingly we assign a small amount ϵ to the empty cell (I, A) so that the corresponding cost [2 units, from Fig. 6-2(b)] can be entered into the value table and the task can be completed. Since there have been no changes in the costs from Example 6.2, the value table computed from Fig. 6-8(b) is the same as Fig. 6-3(d) and the assignment is optimal, with the same cost minus the 3 units previously in the cell (I, A), i.e. $Z = 278 - 3(12) = \$242$. *Ans.*

The above is an example of the so-called *degenerate* case.

6.6. A machine shop has to turn out 150 parts in a certain period, 48 of A, 29 of B, 40 of C and 33 of D. In that period, three machines may be used to produce them: machine a can make 28 units; machine b, 32 units; and machine c, 60 units. Figure 6-9 gives the times for each part and each machine. Machine a cannot make C and machine b cannot make D. Find a minimum-time assignment.

	A	B	C	D
a	5	9	n.a.	4
b	6	10	3	n.a.
c	4	2	5	7

Fig. 6-9

The combined capacity of the three machines is only 120 units, whereas 150 are required. Thus it is necessary to add a dummy machine (row d) which, in this context, represents material to be drawn from inventory. (If there were more machine capacity than requirements, some machine time would remain unused. There would be a dummy job.) The impossible assignments are treated by assigning a very large time, M, to them. The total cost and requirements matrix is thus as shown in Fig. 6-10(a). In Fig. 6-10(b) an assignment is made on the basis of putting the maximum into the lowest-cost cells; the sequence is given by the numbers in parentheses. The value table, Fig. 6-10(c), shows only negative results from the required subtractions; hence the assignment is optimal. Its cost is

$$Z = 28(4) + 32(3) + 31(4) + 29(2) + (17 + 8 + 5)(0) = \$390 \quad Ans.$$

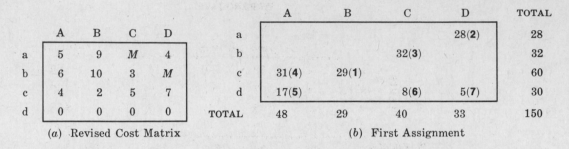

	A	B	C	D
a	5	9	M	4
b	6	10	3	M
c	4	2	5	7
d	0	0	0	0

(a) Revised Cost Matrix

	A	B	C	D	TOTAL
a				28(**2**)	28
b			32(**3**)		32
c	31(**4**)	29(**1**)			60
d	17(**5**)		8(**6**)	5(**7**)	30
TOTAL	48	29	40	33	150

(b) First Assignment

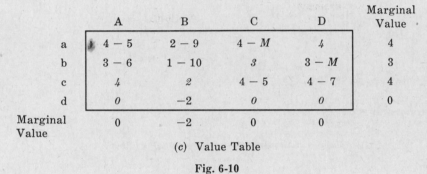

	A	B	C	D	Marginal Value
a	4 − 5	2 − 9	4 − M	4	4
b	3 − 6	1 − 10	3	3 − M	3
c	4	2	4 − 5	4 − 7	4
d	0	−2	0	0	0
Marginal Value	0	−2	0	0	

(c) Value Table

Fig. 6-10

Supplementary Problems

6.7. Figure 6-11 represents the costs in an assignment problem. Find the optimal allocation. (The cells marked n.a. are impermissible.)   *Ans.*   aD, bF, cA, dB, eC, fE; cost $44

JOBS

		A	B	C	D	E	F
WORKERS	a	18	15	14	13	16	17
	b	11	14	13	12	17	10
	c	8	n.a.	12	14	13	n.a.
	d	9	7	6	10	11	12
	e	8	12	6	8	9	13

Fig. 6-11

6.8. In Problem 6.4 the process is such that the firm could hire an extra two workers at the same wages and productivity for the period June through October. Find a minimum-cost schedule and the minimum cost, given the same costs for carrying inventory and working overtime.

Ans.   June 1200 R, 150 OT; July 1320 R, 330 OT; August 720 R, 180 OT;
September 1200 R, 300 OT; October 1300 R; other months unchanged; cost $3354

6.9. In Example 6.2, suppose there were no plant III, i.e. its "output" would have to be furnished from existing inventory. Find the optimal allocation by the transportation method, and find the minimum cost.

Ans.   (I, A) = 3, (I, C) = 7, (II, A) = 1, (II, D) = 8, (dummy, A) = 2, (dummy, B) = 5; cost $197

6.10. Figure 6-12 is a requirements matrix for a transportation problem. Find the optimal allocation and the minimum cost. *Ans.* aD 90, bB 180, cA 60, cC 130, cD 20, dA 90, dB 10; cost $2140

6.11. Solve Problem 6.3 by first subtracting each entry in Fig. 6-6(a) from the largest of all the entries.

WAREHOUSES

		A	B	C	D		Plant Output
			Costs per unit				
PLANTS	a	14	12	9	8		90
	b	4	0	8	6		180
	c	10	8	1	6		210
	d	6	3	7	8		100
Warehouse Requirement		150	190	130	110	TOTAL	580

Fig. 6-12

Chapter 7

Linear Programming

THE STRUCTURE OF LINEAR PROGRAMMING PROBLEMS

Linear programming problems are, for the most part, of the following form: There are two or more products that are formed out of mixtures of two or more ingredients. There are machines or other facilities which are used in the manufacture of the various products, and whose capacities are limited. Alternatively, the quantities of the ingredients are limited. There is, finally, a profit function based on the profit contribution (see Chapter 1) of each unit of each product; it is required to find the production quantities of each product that will maximize the profit function.

Another version of the mixture problem sets minimum quantities for each ingredient and minimizes the costs; the two versions are essentially equivalent.

Let two products be made in quantities X_1 and X_2. The requirements, restrictions and profit contributions are set out in Fig. 7-1. Here a_{ij} denotes the amount of ingredient i in one unit of product j.

	Product 1	Product 2	Amount Available
Ingredient 1	a_{11}	a_{12}	b_1
Ingredient 2	a_{21}	a_{22}	b_2
Profit Contribution Per Unit	c_1	c_2	

Fig. 7-1

First, quantities must be nonnegative. Therefore

$$X_1 \geqq 0, \quad X_2 \geqq 0 \tag{7.1}$$

The two restrictions may also be expressed as inequalities:

$$a_{11}X_1 + a_{12}X_2 \leqq b_1$$
$$a_{21}X_1 + a_{22}X_2 \leqq b_2 \tag{7.2}$$

Actually, there may be only one restriction or more than two. A third one would be written

$$a_{31}X_1 + a_{32}X_2 \leqq b_3$$

However, as will be shown, except in cases of mathematical coincidence rarely met with in practice, *no more than* two restrictions determine the final result in a two-product case. The task is to choose X_1 and X_2 which will maximize the *profit function* or *objective function*

$$Z = c_1X_1 + c_2X_2 \tag{7.3}$$

Objective Function

Several methods are available for solving two-product problems. By far the easiest are the graphical method and the method of enumeration which is based on it. A version of the method of enumeration may also be used for three products with two restrictions. For more products and more restrictions, the simplex method is the one of choice. In the last part of this chapter, we shall demonstrate the simplex method for a three-product, three-constraint problem.

THE GRAPHICAL METHOD

The graphical method is best demonstrated by means of an example.

EXAMPLE 7.1. Figure 7-2 gives the numbers of pounds of each of two ingredients in one unit of each of two chemical compounds. How many units X_1 and X_2 of the two compounds should be produced? (Note that we ask for "units" of the compounds. Materials A and B are the only ones with constraints. A unit of compound 1 may consist of 8 lb of A and 2 lb of B, but it may also have A and B as only the "active" ingredients in a mass of "excipient.")

	Compound 1	Compound 2	Amount Available, lb
Material A	8	4	160
Material B	2	6	60
Profit Contribution, $/unit	3	4	

Fig. 7-2

From (*7.2*) the constraint inequations are

$$\text{For A:}\quad 8X_1 + 4X_2 \leq 160 \quad \text{or} \quad 2X_1 + X_2 \leq 40$$

$$\text{For B:}\quad 2X_1 + 6X_2 \leq 60 \quad \text{or} \quad X_1 + 3X_2 \leq 30$$

These now have to be represented graphically. The graph is restricted to the northeast quadrant, thus satisfying (*7.1*). Now turn the inequations into equations:

$$2X_1 + X_2 = 40 \qquad X_1 + 3X_2 = 30$$

The equation on the left is plotted in Fig. 7-3(*a*). When $X_1 = 0$, $X_2 = 40$ and when $X_2 = 0$, $X_1 = 20$. Thus the restriction on A is *bounded* by the line running from $(0, 40)$ to $(20, 0)$ and the *shaded area* represents all the points which satisfy the original *inequation*.

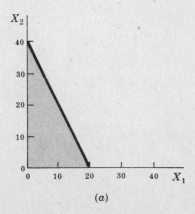

(a)

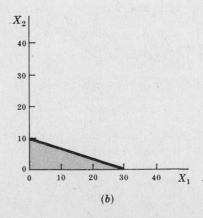

(b)

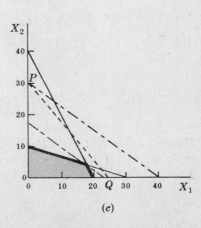

(c)

Fig. 7-3

Likewise the second restriction is the area bounded by the X_1- and X_2-axes and by the line $X_1 + 3X_2 = 30$, i.e. again the inequality becomes an equality at its boundary. When $X_1 = 0$, $X_2 = 10$; when $X_2 = 0$, $X_1 = 30$. Thus the restriction on B is bounded by the line $(0, 10)$ to $(30, 0)$. It is shown in Fig. 7-3(b); again the shaded area represents the original inequation.

In Fig. 7-3(c) both restrictions are shown together; the quadrilateral shown shaded is the part which satisfies *both* restrictions. Now consider the objective function; from (*7.3*)

$$Z = 3X_1 + 4X_2$$

For any fixed value of Z, $X_2 = \frac{1}{4}(Z - 3X_1)$. The slope of this line is

$$\frac{dX_2}{dX_1} = -\frac{3}{4}$$

or, in general, the slope of the objective function (*7.3*) is $-c_1/c_2$. Now draw any line with slope $-3/4$; for instance, the line running from $(0, 30)$ to $(40, 0)$, which is shown dashed in Fig. 7-3(c). Then move a parallel line (using triangle and straight edge) until it *first touches a corner* of the shaded (i.e. feasible) area. The corner of first contact represents the solution: read off the coordinates of that point and the problem is solved. Here it is the corner where the two boundaries of the constraints intersect. Its coordinates are $X_1^* = 18$, $X_2^* = 4$. Thus 18 units of X_1 and 4 of X_2 should be produced.   *Ans.*

The corresponding maximum profit is $Z^* = 3(18) + 4(4) = \$70$.   *Ans.*

In this case, all resources are used. This is not a necessary condition, however. If the profit function were such that the point $(20, 0)$ were optimal, all of A, but only 40 lb of B out of the 60 lb available, would have been used.

EXAMPLE 7.2. The compounds of Example 7.1 also use a third material, C, the supply of which is constrained by $6X_1 + 5X_2 \leqq 150$. Rework Example 7.1 to take this into account.

The boundary is $6X_1 + 5X_2 = 150$. When $X_1 = 0$, $X_2 = 30$; when $X_2 = 0$, $X_1 = 25$. The line, PQ, is shown in Fig. 7-3(c). It is seen to pass outside of the shaded area and thus does not affect the solution. However, this indicates that some of material C is not used. We need only $6(18) + 5(4) = 128$ lbs.   *Ans.*

It is possible to formulate linear programming problems in such a way that there is no solution. For example, if the restriction of Example 7.2 were $6X_1 + 5X_2 \geqq 150$, the area satisfying this condition would be the one *above* the line PQ. Clearly there is no part of the diagram in which all constraints are satisfied. Equally inappropriate formulations can lead to an infinity of solutions.

In Example 7.1 the coordinates of the optimal corner were read off the graph. This may not be accurate enough. It is better to calculate them from the equations of the two lines forming the corner.

EXAMPLE 7.3. In Example 7.1 verify that the coordinates of the optimal corner are $(18, 4)$.

The method is to solve simultaneously:

$$2X_1 + X_2 = 40 \qquad X_1 + 3X_2 = 30$$

Multiply the second equation by -2 and add to the first:

$$
\begin{aligned}
2X_1 + X_2 &= 40 \\
-2X_1 - 6X_2 &= -60 \\
\hline
-5X_2 &= -20
\end{aligned}
$$

whence $X_2 = 4$, $X_1 = 30 - 3(4) = 18$.   *Ans.*

(**ENUMERATION**)

The enumeration method consists in finding the coordinates of all the corner points, substituting them in the objective function and thus finding the optimum result.   When there are two products, it is convenient to sketch out the graphical solution as a first step. For three products (or if preferred, for two products as well) a purely algebraic approach can be used.

EXAMPLE 7.4. Two products have the following production system. There is a machine shop which at most can make either 200 of product 1 or 100 of product 2 per day. There is a paint shop which at most can finish either 120 of product 1 or 160 of product 2 per day. There is also a heat treatment shop which can process no more than 90 of product 2 per day; product 1 does not need heat treatment. Product 1 has a profit contribution of $4 each; that for product 2 is $6 per unit. Find the optimal combination of products 1 and 2 and the corresponding profit.

As always, $X_1 \geqq 0$, $X_2 \geqq 0$. For the machine shop: when $X_1 = 0$, $X_2 = 100$; when $X_2 = 0$, $X_1 = 200$. Using elementary geometry or (1.2), the equation of the boundary line is

$$X_2 = 100 - \frac{100}{200}X_1$$

and the constraint, obtained by multiplying out and simplifying, is

(i) $X_1 + 2X_2 \leqq 200$

For the paint shop: when $X_1 = 0$, $X_2 = 160$; when $X_2 = 0$, $X_1 = 120$. Therefore, the boundary line is given by

$$X_2 = 160 - \frac{160}{120}X_1$$

so that the constraint is

(ii) $4X_1 + 3X_2 \leqq 480$

For the heat treatment shop:

(iii) $X_2 \leqq 90$

The feasible area is shown in Fig. 7-4. To complete the listing of corner points, the coordinates of A and B must be worked out. For A we solve simultaneously (i) and (iii) above, using them as equations:

(i') $X_1 + 2X_2 = 200$

(iii') $X_2 = 90$

Therefore $X_1 = 20$

For B, we solve simultaneously (i) and (ii), again as equations:

(i') $X_1 + 2X_2 = 200$

(ii') $4X_1 + 3X_2 = 480$

From (i'), $X_1 = 200 - 2X_2$. Substituting in (ii'):

$$4(200 - 2X_2) + 3X_2 = 480$$
$$320 - 5X_2 = 0$$
$$X_2 = 64$$
$$X_1 = 72$$

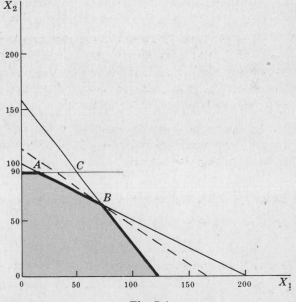

Fig. 7-4

It remains to tabulate the coordinates of the corner points and to compute the objective function $Z = 4X_1 + 6X_2$ for each. The point $(0,0)$ is obviously not a best solution and can be omitted. It is also unnecessary to consider point C, which lies outside the feasible area. However, when a diagram is not available, it would have to be tested. Table 7-1 shows the point $X_1 = 72$, $X_2 = 64$ to be optimal, so that 72 of product 1 and 64 of product 2 should be made, for a profit of $672. *Ans.*

Table 7-1

X_1	X_2	$Z = 4X_1 + 6X_2$
0	90	540
20	90	620
72	64	672*
120	0	480

Example 7.4 shows that unless, by coincidence, three or more restriction boundaries all run through one corner which also gives the optimum objective function, only one or two restrictions determine the solution to a two-product problem. If the point $X_1 = 0$, $X_2 = 90$ were optimal, for instance, only restriction (iii) would determine the solution.

Example 7.5 shows the procedure for a three-product case with two restrictions. Although the feasible domain could be represented by a solid, or a perspective or isometric drawing, this would be of little value in deriving a result. A purely algebraic solution is best.

EXAMPLE 7.5. Figure 7-5 gives requirements per unit for three products, together with the restrictions and profit contributions. Solve this linear programming problem by enumeration.

	Products			Amount
	1	2	3	Available,
		lb/unit		lb
Ingredient A	6	4	8	1000
Ingredient B	3	7	2	600
Profit contribution, $/unit	3	4	5	

Fig. 7-5

The profit function is $Z = 3X_1 + 4X_2 + 5X_3$. The restrictions are

(a) $$6X_1 + 4X_2 + 8X_3 \le 1000$$

(b) $$3X_1 + 7X_2 + 2X_3 \le 600$$

(c) $$X_1 \ge 0$$

(d) $$X_2 \ge 0$$

(e) $$X_3 \ge 0$$

These inequalities are now treated as equations and solved three at a time. There are 10 ways of picking sets of 3 equations out of the total of 5 equations which define the problem [see (8.28)]. In Table 7-2, the equation sets are listed in Col. (1); the solutions X_1, X_2 and X_3 in Cols. (2), (3) and (4); and the corresponding values of the objective function in Col. (5). In three cases Z is meaningless because, though the equations in Col. (1) are satisfied, the solutions violate one of the other *inequations*. For example, the solution to the equation set *abd* includes a negative X_3 and thus violates constraint (e). The equation sets are solved conventionally. For example, consider set *abc*. From (c), $X_1 = 0$. Then

From (a): $X_2 + 2X_3 = 250$

From (b): $\dfrac{-7X_2 - 2X_3 = -600}{}$

$-6X_2 = -350$

$X_2 = 58.3$

and

$$X_3 = \frac{250 - 58.3}{2} = 95.9$$

Table 7-2

Equation Set	X_1	X_2	X_3	Z	Violates Inequation
abc	0	58.3	95.9	713	
abd	233.3	0	−50	..	(e)
abe	153.3	20	0	539	
acd	0	0	125	625	
ace	0	250	0	..	(b)
ade	168.7	0	0	500	
bcd	0	0	300	..	(a)
bce	0	85.7	0	343	
bde	200	0	0	600	
cde	0	0	0	0	

The optimal arrangement is to make 58 of product 2 and 96 of product 3 and no product 1. For three products and two restrictions the result is always that only one or two products are to be made for maximum profit. The corresponding profit is $713. *Ans.*

(**THE SIMPLEX METHOD**)

Simplex Method

The *simplex method* is the most general one for solving linear programming problems; it can be used for any reasonable number of products and constraints and, in addition to the optimal arrangement, it gives certain other information which is sometimes useful. On the other hand, it is a laborious and repetitive procedure which is best suited to the computer.

The following presentation is based on an example with three variables and three constraints. The method is shown in the form of an *algorithm*, i.e. a set of instructions. Readers familiar with linear algebra will recognize the process as essentially one of matrix inversion.

EXAMPLE 7.6. Figure 7-6 gives the processing times of three products in three departments, together with the departmental capacities and the profit contributions. Find the product mix which will give maximum profit.

	Products			
	A	B	C	Capacity
Department I	10	2	1	100
Department II	3	13	4	150
Department III	2	3	12	120
Profit contribution	5	7	6	

Fig. 7-6

Step 1. The restrictions may be written:

$$10X_1 + 2X_2 + X_3 \leq 100$$

$$3X_1 + 13X_2 + 4X_3 \leq 150$$

$$2X_1 + 3X_2 + 12X_3 \leq 120$$

The first step is to reduce them to equations by adding *slack variables* S_1, S_2 and S_3:

$$10X_1 + 2X_2 + X_3 + S_1 + 0 + 0 = 100$$

$$3X_1 + 13X_2 + 4X_3 + 0 + S_2 + 0 = 150$$

$$2X_1 + 3X_2 + 12X_3 + 0 + 0 + S_3 = 120$$

All variables are constrained to be nonnegative.

Step. 2. Write the initial *simplex tableau*, Fig. 7-7(a). The body of the table simply consists of the coefficients of the three restriction equations. The column headings are the coefficients of the profit function, which, after inclusion of the slack variables, becomes

$$Z = 5X_1 + 7X_2 + 6X_3 + 0S_1 + 0S_2 + 0S_3$$

Since slack variables represent unused capacity, their c-values, see (7.3), are zero. The column headed b initially consists of the constants from the restriction equations.

Step 3. Start with a feasible initial solution. In this, only the slack variables are positive; therefore these are the ones listed in the Active column. The first column, c_i, gives their c-values, which are zero. At this stage, $X_1 = X_2 = X_3 = 0$.

c_i	Active	b	c_j 5 X_1	7 X_2	6 X_3	0 S_1	0 S_2	0 S_3	θ
0	S_1	100	10	2	1	1	0	0	50
0	S_2	150	3	13	4	0	1	0	11.538 OUT
0	S_2	120	2	3	12	0	0	1	40
	Z_j	0	0	0	0	0	0	0	
	$c_j - Z_j$		5	7	6	0	0	0	
				IN					

(a) Initial Tableau

c_i	Active	b	c_j 5 X_1	7 X_2	6 X_3	0 S_1	0 S_2	0 S_3	θ
0	S_1	76.924	9.538	0	0.384	1	−0.154	0	200.3
7	X_2	11.538	0.231	1	0.308	0	0.077	0	37.5
0	S_3	85.386	1.307	0	11.076	0	−0.231	1	7.709 OUT
	Z_j	80.766	1.617	7	2.156	0	0.539	0	
	$c_j - Z_j$		3.383	0	3.844	0	−0.539	0	
					IN				

(b) Second Tableau

c_i	Active	b	c_j 5 X_1	7 X_2	6 X_3	0 S_1	0 S_2	0 S_3	θ
0	S_1	73.964	9.493	0	0	1	−0.146	−0.035	7.791 OUT
7	X_2	9.164	0.195	1	0	0	0.083	−0.028	47.0
6	X_3	7.709	0.118	0	1	0	−0.021	0.090	65.3
	Z_j	110.402	2.073	7	6	0	0.455	0.344	
	$c_j - Z_j$		2.927	0	0	0	−0.455	−0.344	
				IN					

(c) Third Tableau

c_i	Active	b	c_j 5 X_1	7 X_2	6 X_3	0 S_1	0 S_2	0 S_3
5	X_1	7.791	1	0	0	0.105	−0.015	−0.004
7	X_2	7.645	0	1	0	−0.020	0.086	−0.027
6	X_3	6.790	0	0	1	−0.012	−0.019	0.090
	Z_j	133.21	5	7	6	0.313	0.413	0.331
	$c_j - Z_j$		0	0	0	−0.313	−0.413	−0.331

(d) Fourth (Optimal) Tableau

Fig. 7-7

Step 4.   Compute the row marked Z_j from

$$Z_j = \sum a_{ij} c_i \qquad (7.4)$$

Thus, for the b-column

$$Z_j = 100(0) + 150(0) + 120(0) = 0$$

for the X_1-column

$$Z_j = 10(0) + 3(0) + 2(0) = 0$$

and so on for the whole row. The Z_j-value in the b-column gives the profit realized from the solution of Step 3.

Step 5.   The row $c_j - Z_j$ shows the benefit to be derived from adding a unit of that variable. Thus, for the first three columns, the values are $5 - 0 = 5$, $7 - 0 = 7$ and $6 - 0 = 6$. Therefore the best thing to do next is to bring in variable X_2, because every unit added also adds \$7 to the profit function. Therefore the X_2-column is marked IN; it is referred to as the *pivot column*, i.e. the column with the highest $c_j - Z_j$.

Step 6.   Determine the row to be removed from the solution, i.e. the row with the lowest contribution. For this, the θ-column on the right is used: θ equals the value of b for each row divided by the entry in the pivot column for that row.   Here

$$\theta_1 = \frac{100}{2} = 50 \qquad \theta_2 = \frac{150}{13} = 11.538 \qquad \theta_3 = \frac{120}{3} = 40$$

The *pivot row*, the one with the *lowest* value of θ, is marked OUT; it is the one which leaves the solution and is replaced by a new row representing the variable of the pivot column, in this case X_2.

Step 7.   Calculate the rows and columns of the *second* simplex tableau.

(a) New X_2-row replaces S_2-row. It is obtained by dividing each element in the old S_2-row by the pivot element in that row, which is the element in the pivot *column*, i.e. dividing by 13. Thus, in the new row, the old pivot element is replaced by a 1; the new row is:

| 7 | X_2 | 11.538 | 0.231 | 1 | 0.308 | 0 | 0.077 | 0 |

Note that the first column must now have the c_i for X_2, which is \$7.

(b) The new S_1-row is obtained from the old one by deducting from it, element by element, the new X_2-row, multiplied by the pivot element of the *old* row (circled):

Old S_1	100	10	②	1	1	0	0
$-2\{X_2\}$	−23.076	−0.462	−2	−0.616	0	−0.154	0
New S_1	76.924	9.538	0	0.384	1	−0.154	0

(c) The new S_3-row is obtained in the same way:

Old S_3	120	2	③	12	0	0	1
$-3\{X_2\}$	−34.614	−0.693	−3	−0.924	0	−0.231	0
New S_3	85.386	1.307	0	11.076	0	−0.231	1

The effect of steps **(a)**, **(b)** and **(c)** is to replace the *intersectional element (key element)* of the pivot row and column (here 13) by 1, and all other elements in the pivot column by 0. On the other hand, the new S_2-column no longer reads 0 1 0 but has other numbers in it. Thus the interchange of X_2 and S_2 is completed.

Step 8.   Construct the second tableau, Fig. 7-7(*b*), using the rows computed in Step 7. The Z_j are next computed. They are 7 times the entries in the new X_2-row, the other rows having $c_i = 0$ as in the first tableau; e.g. $7(11.538) = 80.766$, $7(0.231) = 1.617$, etc. Subtracting the Z_j from the c_j at the top of each column shows that once more there are positive values. The largest one is marked IN; it is seen to be X_3, each unit of which will improve profits by \$3.844 if it is added. Now work out the θ's:

$$\theta_1 = \frac{76.924}{0.384} = 200.3 \qquad \theta_2 = \frac{11.538}{0.308} = 37.5 \qquad \theta_3 = \frac{85.386}{11.076} = 7.709$$

Thus row S_3 is the pivot row and is marked OUT. So far the profit has been improved from 0 in the first tableau to $80.766.

Step 9. Repeat Step 7 for the second tableau.

(a) New X_3-row, denoted $\{X_3\}$, replaces S_3-row; divide S_3-row by 11.076 to obtain:

$\{X_3\}$	7.709	0.118	0	1	0	-0.021	0.090

(b) Subtract $(0.384)\{X_3\}$ from old S_1 to get new S_1:

Old S_1	76.924	9.538	0	(0.384)	1	-0.154	0
$-(0.384)\{X_3\}$	-2.960	-0.045	0	-0.384	0	0.008	-0.035
New S_1	73.964	9.493	0	0	1	-0.146	-0.035

(c) Subtract $(0.308)\{X_3\}$ from old X_2 to get new X_2:

Old X_2	11.538	0.231	1	(0.308)	0	0.077	0
$-(0.308)\{X_3\}$	-2.374	-0.036	0	-0.308	0	0.006	-0.028
New X_2	9.164	0.195	1	0	0	0.083	-0.028

Step 10. Construct the third tableau, Fig. 7-7(c), using the results of Step 9. Compute the Z_j; the profit function is now further improved to

$$(73.964)(0) + (9.164)(7) + (7.709)(6) = \$110.402$$

the next entry in the Z_j-row is $(0.195)(7) + (0.118)(6) = 2.073$ and so on for the other terms. In the $(c_j - Z_j)$-row, all entries are now 0 or negative, except for the X_1-column, where the value of $c_j - Z_j$ indicates that every unit of X_1 which can be brought in would increase profits by $2.927. Column X_1 is thus the pivot column and is marked IN. Also $\theta_1 = 7.791$ is the lowest value of θ, so that row S_1 is the pivot row and marked OUT.

Step 11. Revise the matrix as in Step 7.

(a) New X_1-row, denoted $\{X_1\}$, replaces S_1; divide S_1-row by 9.493 to obtain:

$\{X_1\}$	7.791	1	0	0	0.105	-0.015	-0.004

(b) Subtract $(0.195)\{X_1\}$ from old X_2 to get new X_2:

Old X_2	9.164	0.195	1	0	0	0.083	-0.028
$-(0.195)\{X_1\}$	-1.519	-0.195	0	0	-0.020	0.003	0.001
New X_2	7.645	0	1	0	-0.020	0.086	-0.027

(c) Subtract $(0.118)\{X_1\}$ from old X_3 to get new X_3:

Old X_3	7.709	0.118	0	1	0	-0.021	0.090
$-(0.118)\{X_1\}$	-0.919	-0.118	0	0	-0.012	0.002	0.000
New X_3	6.790	0	0	1	-0.012	-0.019	0.090

Step 12. Complete the fourth tableau, Fig. 7-7(d). All $c_j - Z_j$ are now zero or negative and so the solution is optimal. The optimal profit is

$$Z = (7.791)(5) + (7.645)(7) + (6.790)(6) = \$133.21$$

when making 7.791 units of A, 7.645 of B and 6.790 of C. *Ans.*

Step 13. To check the work, substitute in the constraints:

$$10(7.791) + 2(7.645) + 1(6.790) = \quad 99.99$$
$$3(7.791) + 13(7.645) + 4(6.790) = 149.95$$
$$2(7.791) + 3(7.645) + 12(6.790) = 120.00$$

Thus, within rounding errors, the restrictions are satisfied and, in this case, all resources are used.

The final tableau gives important additional information. In column S_1,

$$Z_j \;=\; 0.105(5) - (0.020)(7) - (0.012)(6) \;=\; 0.313$$

and $c_j - Z_j = 0 - 0.313 = -0.313$. This may be interpreted as follows: slack variable S_1 is part of the constraint on Department I. Increasing the capacity of Department I by 1 unit, i.e. increasing b_1 to $b_1 + 1$, would lead to an increase in profit of \$0.313, provided an additional 0.105 units of X_1 were made and the quantities of X_2 and X_3 were reduced by 0.020 and 0.012 units respectively. S_2 and S_3 are interpreted similarly.

Solved Problems

7.1. In Example 7.1 all data remain the same except that the profit contribution of compound 1 is increased to \$8 per unit. Rework the example.

The feasible area remains as in Fig. 7-3(c), but the objective function is now $Z = 8X_1 + 4X_2$. The profit line thus has a slope of $-8/4 = -40/20$. The line is thus parallel to the boundary of the constraint on material A. Therefore the maximum-profit line would be congruent with it. This problem therefore has an infinite number of solutions lying between the points $X_1 = 18$, $X_2 = 4$ and $X_1 = 20$, $X_2 = 0$. The profit is

$$18(8) + 4(4) \;=\; 160 \qquad \text{or} \qquad 20(8) \;=\; 160$$

at the ends of the line segment and along it as well. *Ans.*

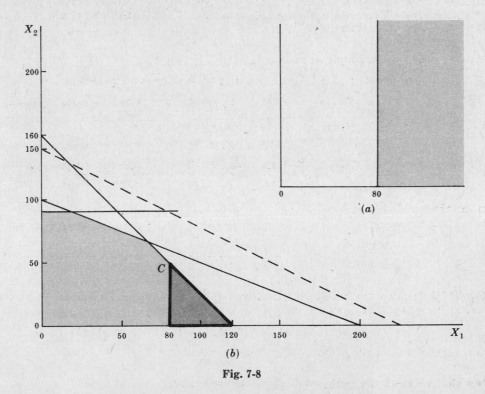

Fig. 7-8

7.2. In Example 7.4 the restrictions remain, but additionally there is a firm order for 80 of product 1, so that at least that number must be produced. Rework the example.

The new restriction is $X_2 \geqq 80$, which would be represented as shown in Fig. 7-8(a). Accordingly, this must be superimposed on the previous diagram in Fig. 7-4. The remaining feasible area is then the dark triangle in Fig. 7-8(b). The profit line (dashed) first hits vertex C, whose coordinates are given by

$$4X_1 + 3X_2 = 480 \qquad X_1 = 80$$

Thus, $X_2 = 53.3$ and the maximum profit is

$$Z = 4(80) + 6(53.3) = \$640$$

if fractional units are allowed. Otherwise use $X_2 = 53$ for a profit of \$638. *Ans.*

7.3. Two chemical compounds are produced in a mixing system which requires that a combined total of 100 barrels be filled. Raw materials are on hand for a maximum of 55 barrels of compound B. Each barrel of compound A further contains 2 lb of a certain ingredient and each barrel of B requires 1 lb; 180 lb of that ingredient is available. Find the optimal mix of A and B under the following conditions: (a) profit contributions are \$7 per barrel for A and \$2 for B. (b) Profit contributions are \$3 per barrel for A and \$8 for B. (c) The production restriction is changed so that *no more than* 100 barrels of A and B combined may be made; profit contributions are \$7 per barrel for A and \$2 for B.

We make X_1 barrels of A and X_2 barrels of B; for cases (a) and (b) the restrictions are

$$X_1 + X_2 = 100$$
$$X_2 \leq 55$$
$$2X_1 + X_2 \leq 180$$
$$X_1 \geq 0; \quad X_2 \geq 0$$

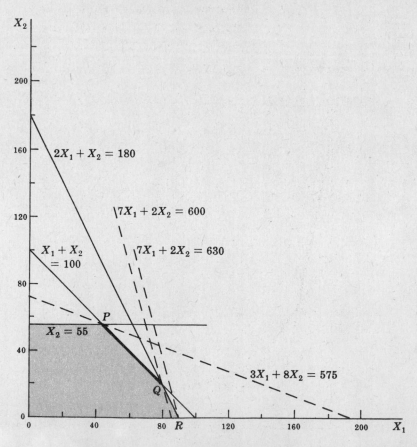

Fig. 7-9

The problem is shown graphically in Fig. 7-9. For (a) and (b) the solution must lie at an end of the line segment PQ. The coordinates are $P(45, 55)$ and $Q(80, 20)$. The profit lines have slopes $-7/2$ and $-3/8$ for (a) and (b), respectively. The answers are therefore:

(a) Point Q: 80 barrels of A, 20 of B. Profit $= 7(80) + 2(20) = \$600$. *Ans.*

(b) Point P: 45 barrels of A, 55 of B. Profit $= 3(45) + 8(55) = \$575$. *Ans.*

(c) The first restriction now becomes $X_1 + X_2 \leqq 100$ and the feasible area is the shaded portion of Fig. 7-9. The profit line with slope $-7/2$ now touches the corner R of the feasible area first, leading to a production of 90 barrels of A only, for a profit of $90(7) = \$630$. *Ans.*

7.4. The contents of vitamins, starch and protein of two foods, as well as the minimum requirements of each ingredient, are given in Fig. 7-10. Food A costs \$1.20 per lb, food B costs \$1.90 per lb. What combination of A and B will give an adequate diet at minimum cost?

	Units per lb of A	Units per lb of B	Minimum Requirement, units
Vitamins	1	3	90
Starch	5	1	100
Protein	3	2	120

Fig. 7-10

This is the "classical" version of the cost minimization problem. It is quite similar to profit maximization, except that the feasible region is unbounded outwards. The constraints are, with quantity of food A as X_1 and of food B as X_2,

$$\text{Vitamins:} \quad X_1 + 3X_2 \geqq 90$$
$$\text{Starch:} \quad 5X_1 + X_2 \geqq 100$$
$$\text{Protein:} \quad 3X_1 + 2X_2 \geqq 120$$

The objective function is $Z = 1.2\,X_1 + 1.9\,X_2$.

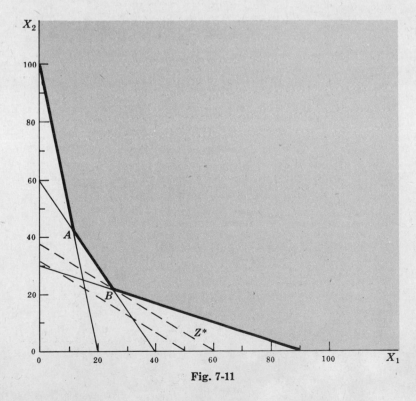

Fig. 7-11

The feasible region is shown in Fig. 7-11. Again Z is plotted, with a slope of $-1.2/1.9$, and moved parallel to touch point B. The coordinates of B are given by the solution of

$$X_1 + 3X_2 = 90$$

$$3X_1 + 2X_2 = 120$$

Multiplying the first equation by 3 and subtracting from the second gives

$$-7X_2 = -150$$

$$X_2 = 21.4 \quad Ans.$$

$$X_1 = 90 - 3(21.4) = 25.8$$

$$Z = (1.2)(25.8) + (1.9)(21.4) = \$71.62 \quad Ans.$$

This solution is based on the vitamin and protein constraints. The amount of starch provided is

$$5(25.8) + 1(21.4) = 150.4$$

i.e. $150.4 - 100 = 50.4$ more units than required.

7.5. Figure 7-12 gives the units of ingredients C and D per pound of compounds A and B, as well as minimum requirements of C and D and costs per lb of A and B. Using the simplex method, find the quantities of A and B which would give a supply of C and D at minimum cost.

	Compound A	Compound B	Minimum Requirement, units
Ingredient C	1	2	80
Ingredient D	3	1	75
Cost per lb, $	4	6	

Fig. 7-12

METHOD 1.

If X_1 and X_2 are the quantities, in pounds, of A and B respectively, the problem can be stated as

$$\text{Minimize} \quad Z = 4X_1 + 6X_2, \quad \text{subject to}$$

$$X_1 + 2X_2 \geqq 80$$

$$3X_1 + X_2 \geqq 75$$

$$X_1 \geqq 0; \quad X_2 \geqq 0$$

To turn the first constraint into an equality, one would normally write

$$X_1 + 2X_2 - S_1 = 80$$

but merely introducing a slack variable S_1 is not sufficient. For a certain range of values of X_1 and X_2, S_1 would be negative in order for the equality to hold, and this is not acceptable. Therefore we must also *add* an *artificial variable* A_1, leading to the new equality

$$X_1 + 2X_2 - S_1 + A_1 = 80$$

and similarly,

$$3X_1 + X_2 - S_2 + A_2 = 75$$

where now the X's, S's and A's are all nonnegative. However, the A's must not appear in the final solution and therefore are given a very high cost, denoted M, a number much greater than any other in the problem. The simplex solution is shown in Fig. 7-13.

Tableau 1

c_j			4	6	0	0	M	M	
	Active	b_j	X_1	X_2	S_1	S_2	A_1	A_2	θ
M	A_1	80	1	2	-1	0	1	0	80
M	A_2	75	3	1	0	-1	0	1	25 OUT
	Z_j	$155M$	$4M$	$3M$	$-M$	$-M$	M	M	
	$c_j - Z_j$		$4-4M$	$6-3M$	M	M	0	0	
			IN						

Tableau 2

M	A_1	55	0	$\frac{5}{3}$	-1	$\frac{1}{3}$	1	$-\frac{1}{3}$	33 OUT
4	X_1	25	1	$\frac{1}{3}$	0	$-\frac{1}{3}$	0	$\frac{1}{3}$	75
	Z_j	$100+55M$	4	$\frac{4}{3}+\frac{5}{3}M$	$-M$	$-\frac{4}{3}+\frac{1}{3}M$	M	$\frac{4}{3}-\frac{1}{3}M$	
	$c_j - Z_j$		0	$-\frac{4}{3}-\frac{5}{3}M$	M	$\frac{4}{3}-\frac{1}{3}M$	0	$-\frac{4}{3}+\frac{4}{3}M$	
				IN					

Tableau 3

6	X_2	33	0	1	$-\frac{3}{5}$	$\frac{1}{5}$	$\frac{3}{5}$	$-\frac{1}{5}$
4	X_1	14	1	0	$\frac{1}{5}$	$-\frac{2}{5}$	$-\frac{1}{5}$	$\frac{2}{5}$
		254	4	6	$-\frac{14}{5}$	$-\frac{2}{5}$	$\frac{14}{5}$	$\frac{2}{5}$
			0	0	$\frac{14}{5}$	$\frac{2}{5}$	$M-\frac{14}{5}$	$M-\frac{2}{5}$

Fig. 7-13

The initial tableau is set up as in Example 7.6. M must be treated like any other cost, e.g. the initial value of the objective function is $80M + 75M = 155M$. In minimization problems, however, variables having *negative* values of $c_j - Z_j$ are brought into the solution, because the negative values are the *savings* which could be realized by introducing 1 unit of that variable. The solution is terminal when all the $c_j - Z_j \geqq 0$. Below are the calculations for the two tableau changes:

Initial to second tableau

New row $\{X_1\}$ is obtained by dividing the old A_2-row by 3:

$\{X_1\}$	25	1	$\frac{1}{3}$	0	$-\frac{1}{3}$	0	$\frac{1}{3}$
Old A_1	80	1	2	-1	0	1	0
$-1\{X_1\}$	-25	-1	$-\frac{1}{3}$	0	$\frac{1}{3}$	0	$-\frac{1}{3}$
New A_1	55	0	$\frac{5}{3}$	-1	$\frac{1}{3}$	1	$-\frac{1}{3}$

Second to third (terminal) tableau

New row $\{X_2\}$ is obtained by dividing the old A_1-row by 5/3:

$\{X_2\}$	33	0	1	$-\frac{3}{5}$	$\frac{1}{5}$	$\frac{3}{5}$	$-\frac{1}{5}$
Old $\{X_1\}$	25	1	$\frac{1}{3}$	0	$-\frac{1}{3}$	0	$\frac{1}{3}$
$-\frac{1}{3}\{X_2\}$	-11	0	$-\frac{1}{3}$	$\frac{1}{5}$	$-\frac{1}{15}$	$-\frac{1}{5}$	$\frac{1}{15}$
New $\{X_1\}$	14	1	0	$\frac{1}{5}$	$-\frac{2}{5}$	$-\frac{1}{5}$	$\frac{2}{5}$

The result is: 33 lb of B, 14 lb of A, for a minimum cost of \$254. *Ans.*

METHOD 2.

An alternative solution employs the *dual* of the problem. If the earlier problem, called the *primal*, is written

$$Y_1: \quad X_1 + 2X_2 \geqq 80$$
$$Y_2: \quad 3X_1 + X_2 \geqq 75$$
$$\text{Minimize} \quad Z = 4X_1 + 6X_2$$

then, using the coefficients along the vertical lines and interchanging $\geqq$ and $\leqq$, the problem can be rewritten in terms of the new variables Y_1 and Y_2 as:

$$Y_1 + 3Y_2 \leqq 4$$
$$2Y_1 + Y_2 \leqq 6$$
$$\text{Maximize} \quad Z = 80Y_1 + 75Y_2$$

This is a conventional maximization problem and thus the simplex method can be used without the artificial variables. The economic significance of Y_1 is that it is the worth to the producer of providing 1 unit of ingredient C; Y_2 is the worth per unit of D. The objective function $80Y_1 + 75Y_2$ thus represents the worth to the producer of meeting the needs, and its optimal value must be identical to the original (least-cost) optimum.

Tableau 1

c_j			80	75	0	0	
	Active	b_j	Y_1	Y_2	S_1	S_2	θ
0	S_1	4	1	3	1	0	4
0	S_2	6	2	1	0	1	3 OUT
Z_j		0	0	0	0	0	
$c_j - Z_j$			80	75	0	0	
			IN				

Tableau 2

0	S_1	1	0	$\frac{5}{2}$	1	$-\frac{1}{2}$	$\frac{2}{5}$ OUT
80	Y_1	3	1	$\frac{1}{2}$	0	$\frac{1}{2}$	6
Z_j		240	80	40	0	40	
			0	35	0	-40	
				IN			

Tableau 3

75	Y_2	$\frac{2}{5}$	0	1	$\frac{2}{5}$	$-\frac{1}{5}$	
80	Y_1	$\frac{14}{5}$	1	0	$-\frac{1}{5}$	$\frac{2}{5}$	
		254	80	75	14	33	
			0	0	-14	-33	

Fig. 7-14

The simplex solution to the dual is given in Fig. 7-14. The solution is for optimal values of Y_1 and Y_2, but actually, the optimal values of X_1 and X_2 appear (to within sign) as the $(c_j - Z_j)$-entries for S_1 and S_2 respectively. Thus optimal X_1 and X_2 also can be obtained from the dual solution. The converse also holds; in Fig. 7-13 the optimal $Y_1 = 14/5$ and $Y_2 = 2/5$ appear as the $(c_j - Z_j)$-entries for S_1 and S_2 respectively. The value of Z, \$254, is the same in both cases.

Supplementary Problems

Use the simplex method to check the results of:

7.6.   Example 7.1.

7.7.   Example 7.2.

7.8.   Example 7.3.

7.9.   Example 7.4.

7.10.   In Problem 7.3 the process is such that a combined total of *at least* 100 barrels of A and B must be produced. The restriction on the key ingredient and the maximum of 55 barrels of B remain in effect. Find the optimal mix, given the following profit contributions per barrel: (*a*) $7 for A, $2 for B; (*b*) $6 for A, $4 for B.

 Ans.   (*a*) 80 bbl of A, 20 bbl of B; $600.   (*b*) 62.5 of A, 55 of B; $595.

7.11.   In Problem 7.4 the prices are changed to $1.90 per lb of A and $1.20 per lb of B. Minimize the cost of the diet.   *Ans.* 11.4 lb of A, 42.9 lb of B; $73.14

7.12.   Two products, A and B, are made in a manufacturing department with 120 available hours; 4 hours are required per unit of A and 3 hours per unit of B. In addition, 4 lb of a certain ingredient is required for 1 unit of A and 5 lb per unit of B. In order to get rid of an excess inventory of the material, it is desired that *at least* 200 lb be used up. (*a*) Show graphically that, regardless of profit contributions, 40 units of B should be made and none of A. (*b*) Show that if it were desired in addition to make at least 45 units of B, the problem has no feasible solution.

7.13.   Figure 7-15 represents the compositions (in units/lb) of two fertilizers, A and B. (*a*) What quantities of A and B should be bought in order to minimize the cost? (*b*) What is the minimum cost? (*c*) What component is available in quantities greater than minimum and by how much? Use the graphical method.   *Ans.* (*a*) 25 lb of A, 10 lb of B; (*b*) $205; (*c*) potash (by 10 units)

7.14.   Check the result of Problem 7.13 by means of the simplex method, employing (*a*) artificial variables, (*b*) the dual.

7.15.   When a constraint is given as an equality, it must be transformed by adding an artificial variable before the simplex method may be used, e.g. $X_1 + X_2 = b_1$ is transformed into $X_1 + X_2 + A_1 = b_1$. The variable A_1 is forced to vanish in the final solution by the device described in Method 1 of Problem 7.5. Use this modification of the simplex method to check the result of Problem 7.3.

	A	B	Minimum Need, units
Nitrate (N)	10	5	300
Phosphorus (P_2O_5)	6	10	250
Potash (K_2O)	4	5	100
Price, $/lb	5	8	

Fig. 7-15

Chapter 8

Fundamentals of Probability

BASIC CONCEPTS

In Fig. 8-1 we have a *sample space* S drawn from a larger population or *opportunity space*. It contains the set A, which contains $n(A)$ elements. Such a representation is called a *Venn diagram*. If $n(S)$ is the number of elements in S, then we define the *probability of A*, $P(A)$, as

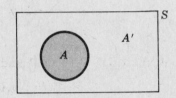

Fig. 8-1

$$P(A) = \frac{n(A)}{n(S)} \qquad (8.1)$$

We let A' (read "non-A") denote the set of elements of S that are not elements of A. Then

$$n(A) + n(A') = n(S)$$

and, dividing by $n(S)$,

$$P(A) + P(A') = 1 \qquad (8.2)$$

i.e. the probabilities of all possible events must sum to 1.

EXAMPLE 8.1. In a group of 200 sample respondents, 75 turn out to be automobile owners. Find the probability that an individual selected at random from the group is (*a*) a car owner, (*b*) a non-owner.

$$P(\text{owner}) = \frac{75}{200} = 0.375 \quad Ans.$$

$$P(\text{non-owner}) = 1 - 0.375 = 0.625 \quad Ans.$$

Figure 8-2 shows two possible configurations of two sets A and B. They enable us to define:

(1) $A \cup B$ ("A-union-B") as the set which contains all elements in A, in B or in both.

(2) $A \cap B$ ("A-intersection-B") as the set which contains all elements in *both* A and B.

(3) $A \setminus B = A \cap B'$, or those elements in A which do not belong to B.

(4) $\emptyset$ as the *null* or *empty set*, which contains no elements. If $A \cap B = \emptyset$, the sets are called *disjoint*.

84

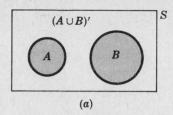 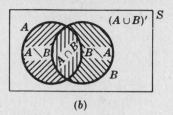

Fig. 8-2

In Fig. 8-2(a)

$$A \cap B = \emptyset \quad \text{and} \quad P(A \cup B) = P(A) + P(B) \tag{8.3}$$

In Fig. 8-2(b), A and B are not disjoint. However, A, B and $A \cup B$ can be expressed as unions of disjoint sets, as follows:

$$A = (A \setminus B) \cup (A \cap B) \qquad B = (B \setminus A) \cup (A \cap B) \tag{8.4}$$

and

$$A \cup B = (A \setminus B) \cup (B \setminus A) \cup (A \cap B) \tag{8.5}$$

Applying (8.3) to (8.4) and (8.5) gives

$$P(A) = P(A \setminus B) + P(A \cap B) \qquad P(B) = P(B \setminus A) + P(A \cap B) \tag{8.6}$$

and

$$P(A \cup B) = P(A \setminus B) + P(B \setminus A) + P(A \cap B) \tag{8.7}$$

Together, (8.6) and (8.7) give

$$P(A \cup B) = P(A) + P(B) - P(A \cap B) \tag{8.8}$$

The formulation of (8.8) ensures that the elements of $A \cap B$ are not counted twice.

EXAMPLE 8.2. In a sample space which consists of 180 individuals who bought one car each, 27 bought Chryslers and 72 bought Fords. Find the probability that a member of the sample space (a) bought a Ford, (b) bought a Ford or a Chrysler, (c) bought neither, (d) bought *only* a Ford.

Since nobody bought more than one car, $A \cap B = \emptyset$. Hence use (8.3).

(a)
$$P(\text{Ford}) = \frac{72}{180} = 0.4 \quad Ans.$$

(b)
$$P(\text{Ford} \cup \text{Chrysler}) = \frac{72}{180} + \frac{27}{180} = 0.55 \quad Ans.$$

(c)
$$P(\text{Ford}' \cap \text{Chrysler}') = 1 - 0.55 = 0.45 \quad Ans.$$

(d)
$$P(\text{Ford} \setminus \text{Chrysler}) = \frac{72}{180} = 0.4 \quad Ans.$$

EXAMPLE 8.3. In another group of 200 car buyers, 34 bought Chryslers, 78 bought GM cars and 7 bought both. Find the probability that a member of the group (a) bought a Chrysler and/or a GM car, (b) did not buy a GM car, (c) bought only a GM car.

(a) If A is the set of GM buyers and B is the set of Chrysler buyers, then $n(A \cap B) = 7$ and, from (8.8),

$$P(A \cup B) = \frac{78}{200} + \frac{34}{200} - \frac{7}{200} = 0.525 \quad Ans.$$

(b)
$$1 - P(A) = 1 - \frac{78}{200} = 0.61 \quad Ans.$$

(c) From (8.6)

$$P(A \setminus B) = P(A) - P(A \cap B) = \frac{78}{200} - \frac{7}{200} = 0.355 \quad Ans.$$

MARGINAL PROBABILITIES

Consider the sample space in Fig. 8-3. It is a grid divided into $r \times c$ cells, corresponding to r row-categories and c column-categories. A total of n points is scattered over the grid, as shown. In a typical cell (A_i, B_j) there are $n(A_i, B_j)$ points, and the column and row totals are $n(B_j)$ and $n(A_i)$ respectively. As in (8.1), we divide all cell values and row and column totals by n to get probabilities. The cell entries become the *joint probabilities*,

$$P(A_i \cap B_j) = \frac{n(A_i, B_j)}{n} \qquad (8.9)$$

The row totals,

$$P(A_i) = \frac{n(A_i)}{n} = \sum_{j=1}^{c} P(A_i \cap B_j) \qquad (8.10)$$

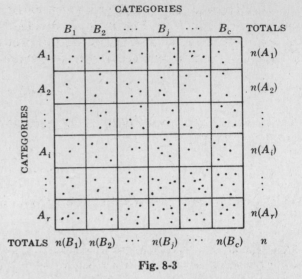

Fig. 8-3

are called the *marginal probabilities* of the A's because they are the marginal totals of the joint probabilities, summed over the columns. See Fig. 8-4(a). Similarly, the column totals,

$$P(B_j) = \frac{n(B_j)}{n} = \sum_{i=1}^{r} P(A_i \cap B_j) \qquad (8.11)$$

are the marginal probabilities of the B's; they are the marginal totals of the joint probabilities, summed vertically over the rows. These too are shown in Fig. 8-4(a).

Categories	B_1	B_2	...	B_j	...	B_c	TOTALS
A_1	$P(A_1 \cap B_1)$	$P(A_1 \cap B_2)$	...	$P(A_1 \cap B_j)$	...	$P(A_1 \cap B_c)$	$P(A_1)$
A_2	$P(A_2 \cap B_1)$	$P(A_2 \cap B_2)$	...	$P(A_2 \cap B_j)$	...	$P(A_2 \cap B_c)$	$P(A_2)$
...	...	...	...	...	...	...	...
A_i	$P(A_i \cap B_1)$	$P(A_i \cap B_2)$	...	$P(A_i \cap B_j)$	...	$P(A_i \cap B_c)$	$P(A_i)$
...	...	...	...	...	...	...	...
A_r	$P(A_r \cap B_1)$	$P(A_r \cap B_2)$	...	$P(A_r \cap B_j)$	...	$P(A_r \cap B_c)$	$P(A_r)$
TOTALS	$P(B_1)$	$P(B_2)$	...	$P(B_j)$	...	$P(B_c)$	1

(a) Joint Probabilities $P(A \cap B)$

	B_1	B_2	...	B_j	...	B_c	
A_1	$P(A_1 \mid B_1)$	$P(A_1 \mid B_2)$	...	$P(A_1 \mid B_j)$	...	$P(A_1 \mid B_c)$	
A_2	$P(A_2 \mid B_1)$	$P(A_2 \mid B_2)$	...	$P(A_2 \mid B_j)$	...	$P(A_2 \mid B_c)$	
...	...	...	...	...	...	...	
A_i	$P(A_i \mid B_1)$	$P(A_i \mid B_2)$	...	$P(A_i \mid B_j)$	...	$P(A_i \mid B_c)$	
...	...	...	...	...	...	...	
A_r	$P(A_r \mid B_1)$	$P(A_r \mid B_2)$	...	$P(A_r \mid B_j)$	...	$P(A_r \mid B_c)$	
TOTALS	1	1	...	1	...	1	

(b) Conditional Probabilities $P(A \mid B)$

	B_1	B_2	...	B_j	...	B_c	
A_1	$P(B_1 \mid A_1)$	$P(B_2 \mid A_1)$	...	$P(B_j \mid A_1)$	...	$P(B_c \mid A_1)$	1
A_2	$P(B_1 \mid A_2)$	$P(B_2 \mid A_2)$	...	$P(B_j \mid A_2)$	...	$P(B_c \mid A_2)$	1
...	...	...	...	...	...	...	
A_i	$P(B_1 \mid A_i)$	$P(B_2 \mid A_i)$	...	$P(B_j \mid A_i)$	...	$P(B_c \mid A_i)$	1
...	...	...	...	...	...	...	
A_r	$P(B_1 \mid A_r)$	$P(B_2 \mid A_r)$	...	$P(B_j \mid A_r)$	...	$P(B_c \mid A_r)$	1

(c) Conditional Probabilities $P(B \mid A)$

Fig. 8-4

CONDITIONAL PROBABILITIES

It is often useful to look at a given category (event) as a sample space in itself. If, for instance, column B_j in Fig. 8-4(a) is divided by $P(B_j)$, we obtain the corresponding column in Fig. 8-4(b). The new entries are the probabilities of $A_1, A_2, \ldots, A_r$, *given that* category B_j applies (event B_j has occurred). We therefore write

$$P(A_i \,|\, B_j) = \frac{P(A_i \cap B_j)}{P(B_j)} \tag{8.12}$$

as the *conditional probability of A_i given B_j*. Similarly, when A_i is taken as the sample space we obtain

$$P(B_j \,|\, A_i) = \frac{P(A_i \cap B_j)}{P(A_i)} \tag{8.13}$$

as the conditional probability of B_j given A_i. These numbers are given by the rows of Fig. 8-4(c).

EXAMPLE 8.4. A sample of 300 is taken from a population which is distributed over three census tracts. Each respondent is asked his or her educational level, with the results shown in Fig. 8-5.

	Tract B_1	Tract B_2	Tract B_3
Level A_1: Below High School	18	24	66
Level A_2: High School Graduate	24	60	48
Level A_3: Beyond High School	33	21	6

Fig. 8-5

Find the complete set of joint and conditional probabilities.

The joint probabilities $P(A \cap B)$ are obtained by dividing the data by $n = 300$, and the marginal probabilities as the row and column sums; see Fig. 8-6(a). The conditional probabilities are then obtained by dividing through by the column sums, see Fig. 8-6(b), or the row sums, see Fig. 8-6(c).

	B_1	B_2	B_3	TOTALS, $P(A)$
A_1	0.06	0.08	0.22	0.36
A_2	0.08	0.20	0.16	0.44
A_3	0.11	0.07	0.02	0.20
TOTALS, $P(B)$	0.25	0.35	0.40	1.00

(a) $P(A \cap B)$

A_1	0.240	0.229	0.550
A_2	0.320	0.571	0.400
A_3	0.440	0.200	0.050
TOTALS	1.000	1.000	1.000

(b) $P(A \,|\, B)$

A_1	0.167	0.222	0.611	1.000
A_2	0.182	0.454	0.364	1.000
A_3	0.550	0.350	0.100	1.000

(c) $P(B \,|\, A)$

Fig. 8-6

The practical interpretation of the conditional probabilities is that when, for example, one meets someone of whom it is known that he is a resident of tract B_2, there is a 57.1 percent chance of his being a high school graduate. Conversely, if one knows that the person is a high school graduate, one can be 45.4 percent certain that he lives in census tract B_2.

STATISTICAL INDEPENDENCE

Two events A and B are said to be *independent* when the probability of either one does not depend on whether or not the other has occurred, i.e. when

$$P(A\,|\,B) \;=\; P(A) \qquad P(B\,|\,A) \;=\; P(B) \tag{8.14}$$

Equivalently, from (8.12) and (8.13),

$$P(A \cap B) \;=\; P(A)\,P(B) \tag{8.15}$$

EXAMPLE 8.5. (a) Examine the data of Example 8.4 to see if tract residence and educational level are independent. (b) What would the data have to look like for independence to be evident?

(a) The data are not independent because (8.15) does not hold. For instance,

$$P(A_2 \cap B_2) \;=\; 0.20 \quad \text{but} \quad P(A_2)\,P(B_2) \;=\; (0.44)(0.35) \;=\; 0.154$$

(b) Equation (8.15) would have to hold for every cell, yielding Fig. 8-7 (assuming that the marginal probabilities stay the same).

	B_1	B_2	B_3	TOTALS
A_1	0.090	0.126	0.144	0.360
A_2	0.110	0.154	0.176	0.440
A_3	0.050	0.070	0.080	0.200
TOTALS	0.250	0.350	0.400	1.000

Fig. 8-7

EXAMPLE 8.6. Given that the probability of a sale being made is p and that successes or failures in sales calls occur independently. Find (a) the probability of a sequence of alternate sales and no-sales in six sales calls, with the first call a sale; (b) the probability of sale, no-sale, no-sale, sale, sale, sale; (c) the probability of no-sale, sale, sale, sale, sale, no-sale.

We have $P(\text{sale}) = p$, $P(\text{no-sale}) = 1 - p = q$.

(a) By (8.15) the probability of the sequence is the product of the probabilities of the individual events, i.e.

$$P \;=\; pqpqpq \;=\; p^3 q^3$$

(b)
$$P \;=\; pqqppp \;=\; p^4 q^2$$

(c)
$$P \;=\; qppppq \;=\; p^4 q^2$$

BAYES' RULE

The two sets of conditional probabilities are related in ways important to modern decision analysis. Equations (8.12) and (8.13) may be combined as the *multiplication rule*

$$P(A_i \cap B_j) \;=\; P(A_i\,|\,B_j)\,P(B_j) \;=\; P(B_j\,|\,A_i)\,P(A_i) \tag{8.16}$$

from which

$$P(A_i\,|\,B_j) \;=\; \frac{P(B_j\,|\,A_i)\,P(A_i)}{P(B_j)} \tag{8.17}$$

and

$$P(B_j\,|\,A_i) \;=\; \frac{P(A_i\,|\,B_j)\,P(B_j)}{P(A_i)} \tag{8.18}$$

Substituting (8.16) for the joint probability in (8.10) and (8.11), we have the *addition rule*

$$P(B_j) = \sum_{i=1}^{r} P(A_i)\,P(B_j\,|\,A_i) \tag{8.19}$$

$$P(A_i) = \sum_{j=1}^{c} P(B_j)\,P(A_i\,|\,B_j) \tag{8.20}$$

Substituting (8.19) in (8.17) and (8.20) in (8.18) gives, respectively,

$$P(A_i\,|\,B_j) = \frac{P(B_j\,|\,A_i)\,P(A_i)}{\sum_{i=1}^{r} P(B_j\,|\,A_i)\,P(A_i)} \tag{8.21}$$

$$P(B_j\,|\,A_i) = \frac{P(A_i\,|\,B_j)\,P(B_j)}{\sum_{j=1}^{c} P(A_i\,|\,B_j)\,P(B_j)} \tag{8.22}$$

Expressions (8.17) and (8.21), and (8.18) and (8.22), are the common forms of *Bayes' rule*, which allows us to compute one kind of conditional probability from the other one and the marginal probabilities. The marginal probabilities can often be obtained only through (8.19) and (8.20). Bayes' rule is useful in cases where a prior tentative assessment of probabilities is revised in the light of subsequent information. Thus in Example 8.7 we use a known conditional probability to obtain a revised probability. The former is also known as *likelihood* and the latter as *posterior probability*.

EXAMPLE 8.7. The market of a certain product consists of two segments, in one of which the probability of making a sale is 0.10 and in the other it is 0.40. A salesman about to call on a prospect rates the probability of the bad segment as 60 percent. He proposes to test this view by trying the sales prospect and then revising his prior judgment in the light of the outcome. What are the revised probabilities if (a) he makes a sale, (b) he does not make a sale?

(a) The calculations are best arranged as in Table 8-1, in which B, G and S respectively denote the events "prospect belongs to bad segment," "prospect belongs to good segment" and "sale is made." Columns

Table 8-1

Segment (1)	Prior Probability of Segment (2)	Conditional Probability of Sale (3)	Joint Probability (4)	Revised Probability of Segment (5)
B	$P(B) = 0.60$	$P(S\,|\,B) = 0.10$	$P(S \cap B)$	$P(B\,|\,S)$
G	$P(G) = 0.40$	$P(S\,|\,G) = 0.40$	$P(S \cap G)$	$P(G\,|\,S)$
TOTALS	1		$P(S)$	1

(2) and (3) are given. By (8.16), Col. (4) is the product of Cols. (2) and (3). The sum of the joint probabilities is the marginal probability of sale, $P(S)$; see (8.10). Column (5) is given by Bayes' rule, (8.18), as the quotient of Col. (4) by $P(S)$. The numbers are computed in Table 8-2.

Table 8-2

(1)	(2)	(3)	(4)	(5)
B	0.60	0.10	0.06	0.273 *Ans.*
G	0.40	0.40	0.16	0.727 *Ans.*
TOTALS	1.00		0.22	1.000

(b) We use the scheme of (a), with the event S replaced by the event N = "no-sale." See Table 8-3.

Table 8-3

Segment	Prior Probability of Segment	Conditional Probability of No-Sale	Joint Probability	Revised Probability of Segment
B	0.60	$P(N \mid B) = 1 - P(S \mid B) = 0.90$	0.54	0.692 *Ans.*
G	0.40	$P(N \mid G) = 1 - P(S \mid G) = 0.60$	0.24	0.308 *Ans.*
TOTALS	1.00		0.78	1.000

Note that Tables 8-2 and 8-3 give for the marginal probabilities:

$$P(S) + P(N) = 0.22 + 0.78 = 1.00$$

EXAMPLE 8.8. In Example 8.7 suppose that the salesman decides to make his judgment on the basis of two sales tries. Find the revised probabilities of the bad and good segments given (a) 2 sales; (b) 2 no-sales; (c) exactly 1 sale. (d) Check the result (c) by considering a single sample of sale and one of no-sale separately.

First, obtain conditional probabilities (Table 8-4), assuming that the outcomes of the two sales tries are independent events. Note that the probability of exactly 1 sale must be the sum of the probabilities of

Table 8-4

		Bad Segment	Good Segment
(a)	$P(2\ \text{sales})$	$0.1 \times 0.1 = 0.01$	$0.4 \times 0.4 = 0.16$
(b)	$P(2\ \text{no-sales})$	$0.9 \times 0.9 = 0.81$	$0.6 \times 0.6 = 0.36$
(c)	$P(\text{sale, no-sale})$ $P(\text{no-sale, sale})$	$\left.\begin{array}{c}0.1 \times 0.9 \\ 0.9 \times 0.1\end{array}\right\} = 0.18$	$\left.\begin{array}{c}0.4 \times 0.6 \\ 0.6 \times 0.4\end{array}\right\} = 0.48$
	TOTALS	1.00	1.00

the two sequences in which one sale and one no-sale may be ordered. We are not concerned with whether the sale is made on the first or second try. Now compute Table 8-5.

Table 8-5

	Segment	Prior Probability	Conditional Probability	Joint Probability	Revised Probability
(a)	B	0.60	0.01	0.006	0.0857 *Ans.*
	G	0.40	0.16	0.064	0.9143 *Ans.*
	TOTALS	1.00		0.070	1.0000
(b)	B	0.60	0.81	0.486	0.7714 *Ans.*
	G	0.40	0.36	0.144	0.2286 *Ans.*
	TOTALS	1.00		0.630	1.0000
(c)	B	0.60	0.18	0.108	0.36 *Ans.*
	G	0.40	0.48	0.192	0.64 *Ans.*
	TOTALS	1.00		0.300	1.00

(d) First, condition on the event "sale," obtaining probabilities 0.273 and 0.727 as in Table 8-2. Then, taking these as prior probabilities, condition on the event "no-sale" as in Table 8-6. The results coincide with those of (c) above, illustrating the important point that the total sample taken in order to revise a prior distribution may be partitioned in any way without affecting the result. (See also Problem 12.1.)

Table 8-6

Segment	Prior Probability	Conditional Probability	Joint Probability	Revised Probability
B	0.273	0.90	0.246	0.36
G	0.727	0.60	0.436	0.64
TOTALS	1.000		0.682	1.00

FACTORIAL NUMBERS, PERMUTATIONS AND COMBINATIONS

The analysis of probability problems is much facilitated by systematic methods of counting groups and arrangements. These require attention to factorial numbers, permutations and combinations. A *factorial number* is the product of the positive integers up to the number required, i.e. $k!$ (k-factorial) is given by

$$k! = 1 \cdot 2 \cdot 3 \cdots (k-2)(k-1)k \qquad (8.23)$$

The identity $k! \equiv k(k-1)!$ holds for all values of k. By definition, $0! = 1$.

Factorial numbers become very large as k increases; for example, $10! = 3,628,800$. It is therefore convenient to have available a table of log-factorials (Appendix J). When a table of log-factorials is not available, or for analytic work, there is an excellent approximation which holds as the number increases and lies within 1.7 percent of the true value even for as low a number as $5!$. It is *Stirling's formula*:

$$M! \approx (2\pi M)^{1/2} M^M e^{-M}$$

from which

$$\log M! \approx \tfrac{1}{2} \log 2\pi + (M + \tfrac{1}{2}) \log M - M \log e$$
$$= 0.39908 + (M + \tfrac{1}{2}) \log M - 0.43429 M \qquad (8.24)$$

EXAMPLE 8.9. Compute $\log 10!$ and $\log 100!$ by means of Stirling's formula and check the results in Appendix J.

$$\log 10! = 0.39908 + (10 + 0.5)(1) - (0.43429)(10) = 6.5561$$

From Appendix J, $\log 10! = 6.5598$ (within 0.06 percent). *Ans.*

$$\log 100! = 0.39908 + (100 + 0.5)(2) - (0.43429)(100) = 157.9700$$

From Appendix J, $\log 100! = 157.9700$. *Ans.*

Each of the *arrangements* which can be made by taking some or all of a number of things is called a *permutation*. The number of arrangements which can be made out of n elements taken X at a time is denoted P_X^n [other notations are $_nP_X$, $P(n, X)$, ^nP_X and $(n)_X$]. It is obtained by noting that the first place in the arrangement may be filled in n ways, the second in $n-1$ ways, the third in $n-2$ ways, and so on for X terms. Since each selection can be associated with all the others,

$$P_X^n = n(n-1)(n-2) \cdots (n-X+2)(n-X+1) \qquad (8.25)$$

Multiplying (8.25) by $(n-X)!/(n-X)!$ transforms the numerator into $n!$ and thus

$$P_X^n = \frac{n!}{(n-X)!} \qquad (8.26)$$

EXAMPLE 8.10. List the permutations which can be made out of the numbers $1, 2, 3, 4$, taking the elements two at a time. Check by calculation.

The permutations are:

$$1, 2 \quad 1, 3 \quad 1, 4 \quad 2, 3 \quad 2, 4 \quad 3, 4$$

$$2, 1 \quad 3, 1 \quad 4, 1 \quad 3, 2 \quad 4, 2 \quad 4, 3$$

Thus $P_2^4 = 12$ _Ans._   **Check:** $P_2^4 = 4 \cdot 3 = 12$.

EXAMPLE 8.11. An airline assigns 8 planes to its Megalopolitan Shuttle. It also decides to paint each one a different color. How many different color arrangements could one encounter on a round trip if (a) planes may not be used twice, (b) planes may be used twice.

(a)
$$P_2^8 = 8 \cdot 7 = 56 \quad Ans.$$

(b)
$$P_2^8 + 8 = 64 = 8 \times 8 \quad Ans.$$

An important special case of permutations is the one in which all elements have to be chosen. Then $X = n$ and (8.25) gives

$$P_n^n = n! \qquad (8.27)$$

EXAMPLE 8.12. In how many ways can 6 machinists be assigned to 6 machines?

$$P_6^6 = 6! = 6 \cdot 5 \cdot 4 \cdot 3 \cdot 2 \cdot 1 = 720 \quad Ans.$$

Each of the _groups_ or _selections_ which can be made by taking all or some of a number of things is called a _combination_. Note that, while in a permutation the order of the elements counts, it does not count in a combination. From (8.27) it follows that each combination of size X has $P_X^X = X!$ permutations within it, i.e. the X members of the group can be arranged $X!$ ways. Thus the number of combinations of n things taken X at a time, C_X^n [also written $\binom{n}{X}$, $_nC_X$, $C(n, X)$ or ^nC_X], is given by dividing the expression for P_X^n by P_X^X, i.e.

$$C_X^n = \frac{n!}{X!(n-X)!} \qquad (8.28)$$

Note the special cases $C_0^n = C_n^n = 1$ and $C_1^n = C_{n-1}^n = n$.

EXAMPLE 8.13. In Example 8.11(a) suppose we are interested only in different color _combinations_, i.e. we are not particular about which leg of the trip a particular color appears in. How many such combinations are there?

$$C_2^8 = \frac{8!}{2!\,6!} = \frac{8 \cdot 7}{2} = 28 \quad Ans.$$

EXAMPLE 8.14. In how many ways may a sample of 20 items be picked out of a population of 60?

The answer is $C_{20}^{60} = 60!/20!\,40!$, which is most conveniently worked out by the log-factorials in Appendix J.

$$\begin{aligned}
\log 60! &= 81.9202 \\
-\log 20! &= -18.3861 \\
-\log 40! &= -47.9116 \\
\hline
\log C_{20}^{60} &= 15.6225
\end{aligned}$$

$$C_{20}^{60} = \text{antilog } 15.6225 = 4.193 \times 10^{15}$$

EXAMPLE 8.15. Suppose that the population of 60 in Example 8.14 consists of eggs, of which 1/6 are extra large, 1/3 large and the rest medium. In how many ways can we pick a sample of 20 in which there are 5 extra large, 8 large and 7 medium?

We can only pick the 5 extra large eggs out of the $60/6 = 10$ in the population, the 8 large out of the $60/3 = 20$ in the population and the 7 medium eggs out of the 30 in the population. Thus the number required is $C_5^{10} C_8^{20} C_7^{30}$. Again, Appendix J is used.

$$
\begin{aligned}
\log 10! &= 6.5598 \\
-\log 5! &= -2.0792 \\
-\log 5! &= -2.0792 \\
\log 20! &= 18.3861 \\
-\log 8! &= -4.6055 \\
-\log 12! &= -8.6803 \\
\log 30! &= 32.4237 \\
-\log 7! &= -3.7024 \\
-\log 23! &= -22.4125 \\
\hline
\log C_5^{10} C_8^{20} C_7^{30} &= 13.8105
\end{aligned}
$$

$$C_5^{10} C_8^{20} C_7^{30} = \text{antilog } 13.8105 = 6.465 \times 10^{13}$$

Examples 8.14 and 8.15 lead to an important result. The ratio

$$\frac{\text{number of possible samples with desired characteristics}}{\text{number of all possible samples}}$$

is seen by virtue of the basic definition of probability, (8.1), to be the *probability* of that particular kind of sample. Thus

$$
\begin{aligned}
P(\text{5 extra large, 8 large, 7 medium}) &= \frac{C_5^{10} C_8^{20} C_7^{30}}{C_{20}^{60}} \\
&= \text{antilog } (13.8105 - 15.6225) = \text{antilog } (-1.8120) \\
&= \text{antilog } \overline{2}.1880 = 0.01542
\end{aligned}
$$

When such probabilities are desired, the tabulations in Examples 8.14 and 8.15 are combined and the answer obtained directly.

In general, if a population of size N consists of g groups of size D_i ($i = 1, 2, \ldots, g$), so that $\Sigma D_i = N$, and a sample of size n is taken such that X_i is taken from D_i, where $\Sigma X_i = n$, then the probability of the sample is given by

$$f(X_1, X_2, \ldots, X_g \mid D_1, D_2, \ldots, D_g) = \frac{C_{X_1}^{D_1} C_{X_2}^{D_2} \cdots C_{X_g}^{D_g}}{C_n^N} \tag{8.29}$$

When there are two groups ($g = 2$), this formula leads directly to the hypergeometric distribution (see Chapter 9).

EXAMPLE 8.16. In Example 8.6 we obtained the probabilities of getting 3 sales in 6 tries in one particular sequence, and 4 sales in 6 tries in two particular sequences. Find the probabilities of (a) 3 sales in 6 tries and (b) 4 sales in 6 tries, given p as the probability of each sale, and that sales are independent of each other.

(a) Each sequence containing exactly 3 sales has the same probability, $p^3 q^3$. The desired probability is obtained by adding the probabilities of all such sequences, i.e. by multiplying $p^3 q^3$ by the number of ways in which 3 sales can be picked out of 6 tries. There are C_3^6 such ways. Therefore

$$f(3 \mid 6, p) = C_3^6 p^3 q^3 = \frac{6!}{3! \, 3!} p^3 q^3 = 20 p^3 q^3$$

(b) Similarly,

$$f(4 \mid 6, p) = C_4^6 p^4 q^2 = \frac{6!}{4! \, 2!} p^4 q^2 = 15 p^4 q^2$$

We may generalize the above results to

$$f(X \mid n, p) = C_X^n p^X q^{n-X} \qquad (8.30)$$

This formula gives the binomial density function (see Chapter 9), derived from first principles.

Solved Problems

BASIC CONCEPTS

8.1. In a group of 200 appliance owners, 70 have washing machines, 50 have clothes driers and 30 have both. Find the probability that a given owner has a washer and/or drier.

If owners of driers are denoted B and owners of washers A, we require

$$P(A \cup B) = P(A) + P(B) - P(A \cap B) = \frac{70}{200} + \frac{50}{200} - \frac{30}{200} = 0.45 \quad Ans.$$

8.2. A group of 200 appliance owners has the following distribution of washing machines, driers and dishwashers:

Washers	110	Washers and driers	40
Driers	50	Dishwashers and driers	25
Dishwashers	60	Washers and dishwashers	35
		All three	20

Find the probability that an owner (a) has a washer and/or drier and/or dishwasher, (b) has only a washer, (c) who has a washer also has the other two appliances.

(a) This extends Problem 8.1 to three different sets. Figure 8-8 gives a Venn diagram in which owners of washers are A, owners of driers B and owners of dishwashers C. By inspection, and by analogy with (8.8), we again avoid multiple counting by writing

$$P(A \cup B \cup C) = P(A) + P(B) + P(C) - P(A \cap B) - P(A \cap C) - P(B \cap C) + P(A \cap B \cap C) \qquad (8.31)$$

Substituting,

$$P(A \cup B \cup C) = \frac{110 + 50 + 60 - 40 - 35 - 25 + 20}{200} = 0.7 \quad Ans.$$

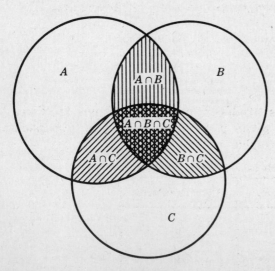

Fig. 8-8

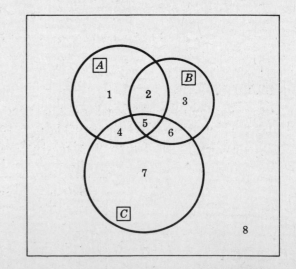

Fig. 8-9

(b) This problem extends (8.6) to three sets. By inspection of Fig. 8-8, the probability of having only a washer is

$$P(A \setminus B \setminus C) = P(A) - P(A \cap B) - P(A \cap C) + P(A \cap B \cap C) \qquad (8.32)$$

the last term being added to avoid double counting. Substituting,

$$P(A \setminus B \setminus C) = \frac{110 - 40 - 35 + 20}{200} = 0.275 \quad Ans.$$

(c)
$$P(B \cap C \,|\, A) = \frac{P(A \cap B \cap C)}{P(A)} = \frac{20}{110} = 0.1818 \quad Ans.$$

8.3. Using the data of Problem 8.2, show that the probability of someone owning neither a washer nor a dishwasher nor a drier can be obtained from either side of the identity

$$(A \cup B \cup C)' = A' \cap B' \cap C' \qquad (8.33)$$

and that the probability of not owning the three machines together can be obtained from either side of the identity

$$(A \cap B \cap C)' = A' \cup B' \cup C' \qquad (8.34)$$

Figure 8-9 is a Venn diagram for this problem, in which disjoint area elements are shown numbered. In the following statements numbers within braces { } denote a set whose elements are the numbered subsets specified. From Fig. 8-9,

$$A \cup B \cup C = \{1,2,3,4,5,6,7\} \qquad (A \cup B \cup C)' = \{8\}$$

Also $A' = \{3,6,7,8\}$; $B' = \{1,4,7,8\}$; $C' = \{1,2,3,8\}$. The common element is $\{8\}$. Therefore

$$A' \cap B' \cap C' = \{8\} = (A \cup B \cup C)'$$

which verifies (8.33). From the result of Problem 8.2(a), $P(A \cup B \cup C) = 0.7$, so that by (8.2)

$$P[(A \cup B \cup C)'] = 1 - 0.7 = 0.3 \quad Ans.$$

Continuing, $A \cap B \cap C = \{5\}$; hence its complement consists of all other elements:

$$(A \cap B \cap C)' = \{1,2,3,4,6,7,8\}$$

Identifying the elements appearing in one or more of A', B' and C', as given above, we find:

$$A' \cup B' \cup C' = \{1,2,3,4,6,7,8\} = (A \cap B \cap C)'$$

which verifies (8.34). From the data

$$P(A \cap B \cap C) = \frac{20}{200} = 0.1 \quad \text{and} \quad P[(A \cap B \cap C)'] = 1 - 0.1 = 0.9 \quad Ans.$$

Equations (8.33) and (8.34) constitute *De Morgan's theorem* for three sets.

BAYES' RULE

8.4. The numbers of good and defective parts produced by three machines are given in Table 8-7. Find the probabilities that a given part comes from a certain machine, given that it is good or given that it is defective.

Table 8-7

Machine	Good Parts	Defective Parts
A	17	8
B	12	6
C	10	2

We first obtain row and column totals as in Table 8-8.

Table 8-8

Machine	Good Parts	Defective Parts	TOTALS
A	17	8	25
B	12	6	18
C	10	2	12
TOTALS	39	16	55

Next divide all entries in Table 8-8 by 55 to obtain the joint probabilities $P(G \cap M)$ and $P(D \cap M)$ as shown in Table 8-9.

Table 8-9

Machine	$P(G \cap M)$	$P(D \cap M)$	$P(M)$
A	0.309	0.146	$0.455 = P(A)$
B	0.218	0.109	$0.327 = P(B)$
C	0.182	0.036	$0.218 = P(C)$
	$P(G) = 0.709$	$P(D) = 0.291$	1.000

Table 8-10

Machine	$P(M \mid G)$	$P(M \mid D)$
A	0.436	0.502
B	0.307	0.374
C	0.257	0.124
TOTALS	1.000	1.000

Finally, divide the columns of Table 8-9 by $P(G)$ and $P(D)$, respectively, to get $P(M \mid G)$ and $P(M \mid D)$. See Table 8-10.

8.5. Construct a table of original data for Problem 8.4 which would lead to the finding that product quality is independent of the machines.

If product quality and machines were independent, a proportion given by $P(G)$ of the output of each machine would be good and a proportion $P(D)$ would be defective. Then, from the totals in Tables 8-8 and 8-9, we construct Table 8-11.

Table 8-11

Machine	Good Parts	Defective Parts	TOTALS
A	25(0.709) = 17.725	7.275	25
B	18(0.709) = 12.762	5.238	18
C	12(0.709) = 8.508	3.492	12

8.6. Consider the salesman of Examples 8.7 and 8.8. How would the prior probability estimate have to be revised if he made (a) 5 calls and (b) 10 calls, all without making a sale?

(a) The conditional probabilities of 5 no-sales in the two segments are

$$[1 - P(S \mid B)]^5 = (0.9)^5 = 0.5905$$

and

$$[1 - P(S \mid G)]^5 = (0.6)^5 = 0.0778$$

The computation now proceeds as in Table 8-12.

Table 8-12

Segment	Prior Probability	Conditional Probability	Joint Probability	Revised Probability
B	0.60	0.5905	0.3543	0.9193 *Ans.*
G	0.40	0.0778	0.0311	0.0807 *Ans.*
TOTALS	1.00		0.3854	1.0000

(*b*) Using conditional probabilities of $(0.9)^{10}$ and $(0.6)^{10}$, we obtain Table 8-13.

Table 8-13

Segment	Prior Probability	Conditional Probability	Joint Probability	Revised Probability
B	0.60	0.3487	0.2092	0.9887 *Ans.*
G	0.40	0.0060	0.0024	0.0113 *Ans.*
TOTALS	1.00		0.2116	1.0000

In comparing the above results with those of Examples 8.7 and 8.8, it is clear that as there are, successively, 1, 2, 5 and 10 sales calls without success, the proportion of customers likely to be in the bad market segment increases too. From a prior value of 0.60, it is revised, respectively, to 0.6920, 0.7714, 0.9193 and 0.9887.

8.7. During month 0 a certain product, *A*, has 60% of a market, with several others sharing the remainder. The customers in the market buy once a month. If anyone buys product *A* one month, the probability is 75% that he will buy it the following month and 25% that he will switch. If a customer buys a competing product one month, the probability is 45% that he will switch to product *A* in the next month and 55% that he will stick with a competing brand. Find the expected market share of *A* at the end of month 3.

In this problem it is assumed that the purchase decision in one month depends *solely* on that in the previous month. Thus the probability of a given event depends exclusively on the outcome of the previous event. This is a *Markov process* and the successive calculations represent a *Markov chain*, whose fixed *transition probabilities* are the probabilities of retaining and losing a customer from one month to the next. Since only the last previous event is involved, this problem is a *first-order* Markov process.

The solution may best be visualized by employing a simple *tree diagram*. Figure 8-10 shows all the possible outcomes of the decisions of customers. In month 1, 75% of the customers who had started with *A* continue with *A* and 25% switch to the other brands, denoted *B*. Among those who stayed with *A*, the same happens in month 2; while among those who switched to *B*, 45% come back to *A* and 55% continue with *B* in month 2. The same happens in month 3.

Let us denote by A_i ($i = 0, 1, 2, 3$) the event "customer holds brand *A* at end of month *i*," and let B_j be defined analogously. Then $P(A_3 \mid A_0)$ stands for the probability that a customer ends with *A* (at the close of month 3) given that he started with *A* (at the close of month 0). We compute

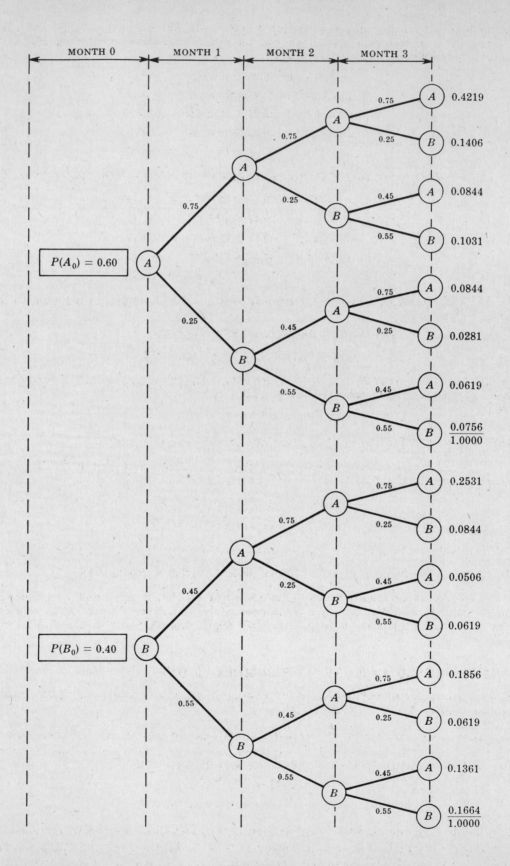

Fig. 8-10

this probability by finding all paths of length 3 in Fig. 8-10 that start with an A and end with an A. The probability of each path is the product of the probabilities along its branches, and the sum of the path probabilities is $P(A_3 \mid A_0)$.   Thus:

$$P(AAAA) \ = \ (0.75)(0.75)(0.75) \ = \ 0.4219$$
$$P(AABA) \ = \ (0.75)(0.25)(0.45) \ = \ 0.0844$$
$$P(ABAA) \ = \ (0.25)(0.45)(0.75) \ = \ 0.0844$$
$$P(ABBA) \ = \ (0.25)(0.55)(0.45) \ = \ \underline{0.0619}$$
$$P(A_3 \mid A_0) \ = \ 0.6526$$

In similar fashion we compute $P(A_3 \mid B_0)$, the probability of ending with A, having started with B:

$$P(BAAA) \ = \ (0.45)(0.75)(0.75) \ = \ 0.2531$$
$$P(BABA) \ = \ (0.45)(0.25)(0.45) \ = \ 0.0506$$
$$P(BBAA) \ = \ (0.55)(0.45)(0.75) \ = \ 0.1856$$
$$P(BBBA) \ = \ (0.55)(0.55)(0.45) \ = \ \underline{0.1361}$$
$$P(A_3 \mid B_0) \ = \ 0.6254$$

The final market share of A, $P(A_3)$, can now be obtained by applying the addition rule for conditional probabilities:

$$P(A_3) \ = \ P(A_0)\,P(A_3 \mid A_0) + P(B_0)\,P(A_3 \mid B_0)$$
$$= \ (0.60)(0.6526) + (0.40)(0.6254) \ = \ 0.6417 \quad Ans.$$

The final market share of B is, of course, $1 - 0.6417 = 0.3583$, which also might have been obtained directly by considering all paths in Fig. 8-10 ending in a B.

8.8.   In Problem 8.7, find the market share of A at the end of month 6.

Since all other conditions are unchanged, the combined transition probabilities for any three months in succession are the same, i.e.

$$P(A_6 \mid A_3) \ = \ P(A_3 \mid A_0) \ = \ 0.6526$$
$$P(A_6 \mid B_3) \ = \ P(A_3 \mid B_0) \ = \ 0.6254$$

The new initial probabilities are $P(A_3) = 0.6417$ and $P(B_3) = 0.3583$.   Hence,

$$P(A_6) \ = \ (0.6417)(0.6526) + (0.3583)(0.6254) \ = \ 0.6429 \quad Ans.$$

The difference between the shares in month 3 and month 6 is very small, thus indicating the emergence of a "steady state"; however, in practice, transition probabilities seldom stay constant long enough for this analysis to be anything other than a preliminary estimate.

FACTORIALS, PERMUTATIONS AND COMBINATIONS

8.9.   Find the number of permutations of n things X at a time when each element may be repeated once, twice, ..., up to X times.

We will denote the number of permutations with repeated elements R_X^n.   The first place may be filled in n ways.   The second and following places may also be filled in n ways, however, because we may use each element up to X times.   Thus [see also Example 8.11(b)]

$$R_X^n \ = \ n^X \quad Ans.$$

8.10.   A typical telephone number in the United States and Canada consists of a three-digit area code, in which the second number is 0 or 1 and the first and third are neither 0 nor 1, followed by a three-digit exchange number in which the first two digits are neither 0 nor 1, and a four-digit number. (*a*) How many individual telephone numbers can be assigned under this system? (*b*) How many exchanges can be assigned to each area code? (*c*) How many area codes can there be?

(*a*) The arrangement is as follows:

Number of available digits   8 2 8   8 8 10   10 10 10 10
                               Area code   Exchange   Number

There are thus four 8-digit places, one 2-digit place and five 10-digit places. From the formula in Problem 8.9:

$$N = 8^4 \times 2^1 \times 10^5 = 819{,}200{,}000 \quad Ans.$$

(*b*) By similar reasoning,

$$N = 8^2 \times 10 = 640 \quad Ans.$$

(*c*)

$$N = 8^2 \times 2 = 128 \quad Ans.$$

8.11. A tasting panel is to rate 9 products. In how many different ways may first, second and third places be assigned?

This is given by $P_3^9 = 9 \cdot 8 \cdot 7 = 504.$ *Ans.*

8.12. Suppose that in Problem 8.11 it were only necessary to pick three superior products without distinguishing between them. In how many ways can that be done?

Here the order does not matter; hence

$$C_3^9 = \frac{9!}{3!\,6!} = 84 \quad Ans.$$

8.13. A board of directors consists of 7 outside directors and 4 officers. In how many ways can an executive committee of 6 be selected when it is to have (*a*) exactly 2 officers, (*b*) at least 2 officers.

(*a*) The 2 officers can be chosen out of the 4 on the board in C_2^4 ways; the 4 non-officers are chosen in C_4^7 ways from among the 7 outside directors. Each set can be combined with any other. Thus the total is given by

$$C_2^4 C_4^7 = \frac{4!}{2!\,2!}\,\frac{7!}{4!\,3!} = \frac{7 \cdot 6 \cdot 5 \cdot 4}{2 \cdot 2} = 210 \quad Ans.$$

(*b*) There are three possible compositions: 2 officers and 4 outsiders, 3 officers and 3 outsiders and 4 officers and 2 outsiders. The total number of ways is obtained by adding the number of ways for each composition:

$$C_2^4 C_4^7 + C_3^4 C_3^7 + C_4^4 C_2^7 = 210 + 4\frac{7!}{3!\,4!} + 1\frac{7!}{2!\,5!}$$

$$= 210 + 140 + 21 = 371 \quad Ans.$$

8.14. Ten jobs are to be allocated among 5 turret lathes and 5 center lathes. One job cannot be done on the turret lathes and two cannot be done on the center lathes. The rest can be done on either. In how many ways can the jobs be scheduled?

The job which cannot be done on the turret lathes can be assigned in 5 ways. The jobs which cannot be done on the center lathes can be assigned in $P_2^5 = 5 \cdot 4 = 20$ ways. The other 7 jobs can be assigned in $P_7^7 = 7! = 5040$ ways. Each assignment can be associated with any of the others, so that the total number of ways is

$$5 \times 20 \times 5040 = 504{,}000 \quad Ans.$$

8.15. Twenty books are to be put on display. Six are of one title, 5 of another, 3 of a third and the rest all different. How many different arrangements can be made of these books?

This is a case of permutations in which not all elements are different. In general, we have n items, of which p are of one kind, q of another, r of a third, s of a fourth, and the rest are all different. Let the number required be X. If the p elements were all different, they could be arranged in $P_p^p = p!$ ways and the number of permutations would be increased from X to $Xp!$. Similarly, if the q elements were made all different, the number of arrangements could be increased still more to $Xp! q!$; and so on for r and s, so that, if all elements were to be made different from each other, there would be $Xp! q! r! s!$ permutations. But then there would be n different items taken all together, which could be arranged in $P_n^n = n!$ ways. Thus

$$Xp! q! r! s! = n! \quad \text{or} \quad X = \frac{n!}{p! q! r! s!}$$

The formula can, of course, be extended to more subgroups, as needed.

For the data,

$$X = \frac{20!}{6! 5! 3!}$$

This is best worked out by logs; using Appendix J:

$$\log X = \log 20! - \log 6! - \log 5! - \log 3!$$
$$= 18.3861 - 2.8573 - 2.0792 - 0.7782 = 12.6714$$
$$X = \text{antilog } 12.6714 = 4.692 \times 10^{12}$$

8.16. A pharmaceutical company wants to use a computer to generate trade names with 5 different letters, taking 3 consonants and 2 vowels from an alphabet of 5 vowels and 20 consonants (q is omitted). How many words could be formed, in the absence of other restrictions?

The 3 consonants may be taken from the 20 in C_3^{20} ways; the 2 vowels from the 5 in C_2^5 ways. Once the 5 letters have been chosen, they may be arranged among themselves in P_5^5 ways. Thus the answer is

$$C_3^{20} C_2^5 P_5^5 = \frac{20!}{3! 17!} \frac{5!}{2! 3!} 5! = 1140 \times 10 \times 120 = 1,368,000 \quad Ans.$$

8.17. Suppose that in Problem 8.16 it were decided that the consonants were always to be in the odd places and the vowels in the even ones. How many words could then be formed?

There would still be 1140×10 ways to pick the five letters, but they could be arranged among themselves only in $3! \times 2! = 12$ ways. Thus there could be $1140 \times 10 \times 12 = 136,800$ words. *Ans.*

Supplementary Problems

8.18. In a group of 1400 employees, 30 had accidents and 50 had to take one or more days of sick leave in a certain period. Of those with accidents, 15 had to take one or more days off. Find (*a*) the probability that an employee had an accident or was off work on sick leave, (*b*) the probability that an employee was sick for reasons unconnected with an accident, (*c*) the probability that a worker had no accident. *Ans.* (*a*) 0.0464; (*b*) 0.025; (*c*) 0.9786

8.19. The probability that a customer in a service station will buy gas is 0.71; that he will buy oil, 0.09; and that he will buy both, 0.04. Find the probability that a customer (*a*) will buy oil or gas, (*b*) will not buy gas, (*c*) will buy only gas, (*d*) who buys oil will also buy gas, (*e*) who buys gas will also buy oil. *Ans.* (*a*) 0.76; (*b*) 0.29; (*c*) 0.67; (*d*) 0.444; (*e*) 0.0563

8.20. In a group of 250 car buyers, 207 buy automatic transmission, air conditioning or power steering. These purchases are broken down as follows:

Automatic transmission	158	Automatic transmission and air conditioning	73
Air conditioning	96	Automatic transmission and power steering	34
Power steering	79	Air conditioning and power steering	35

Find the probability that a customer (*a*) buys all three options; (*b*) buys only (i) automatic transmission, (ii) air conditioning, (iii) power steering; (*c*) buys neither air conditioning nor power steering; (*d*) who buys air conditioning buys the other two options as well; (*e*) who buys an automatic transmission buys air conditioning as well.

Ans. (*a*) 0.064; (*b*) (i) 0.268, (ii) 0.016, (iii) 0.104; (*c*) 0.44; (*d*) 0.167; (*e*) 0.462

8.21. In a group of 80 first-level supervisors, 48 work in the plant and the rest in the office; 60 have had some college work and the rest have not. If college work is independent of where the supervisors work, what is the probability that a supervisor works in the office and has had some college?

Ans. 0.30

8.22. Given the marginal totals in Problem 8.21, suppose it were found that there are 28 office supervisors who have had some college work. Determine the probability that (*a*) an office supervisor has had no college, (*b*) someone without college is a plant supervisor, (*c*) out of all 80 supervisors, a plant supervisor who has done college work is selected at random.

Ans. (*a*) 0.125; (*b*) 0.800; (*c*) 0.4

8.23. In how many ways may 11 machinists be assigned to (*a*) 4 machines, (*b*) 11 machines?
Ans. (*a*) 7920; (*b*) 39,916,800

8.24. How many different automobile license plates may be made up using 3 numerals preceded by (*a*) 2, (*b*) 3 and (*c*) 4 letters? *Ans.* (*a*) 676,000; (*b*) 17,576,000; (*c*) 456,976,000

8.25. Suppose that among license plates with 3 letters followed by 3 numerals it were decided to eliminate plates with (*a*) the number 000; (*b*) the number 000 or a letter group of the same letter, i.e. AAA, BBB, etc. How many plates could be issued in each case?

Ans. (*a*) 17,558,424; (*b*) 17,532,450

8.26. A group of 18 workers is equally divided between drill press operators, lathe operators and assemblers. In a sample of 6 workers, what is the probability of getting (*a*) 2 of each; (*b*) 3 drill press operators, 1 lathe operator and 2 assemblers; (*c*) 5 drill press operators and 1 lathe operator?

Ans. (*a*) 0.1818; (*b*) 0.09696; (*c*) 0.001939

8.27. Out of 26 courses in a university, two are required. In how many ways can one make up (*a*) a five-course schedule (i.e. sequence), (*b*) a five-course program (ignoring time constraints in both cases)?

Ans. (*a*) 242,880; (*b*) 2024

Chapter 9

Statistical Distributions

BASIC CHARACTERISTICS

A statistical distribution is a way of expressing the probability of a variable attaining a certain value as a function of that variable. It may be a matter of judgment (arbitrary) or based on past experience (empirical), as in the following example in which it is assumed that the variable X can take on only the values 100, 200, 300 and 400:

X	$P(X)$
100	0.10
200	0.55
300	0.30
400	0.05
	1.00

Note that the probabilities of all possible events must sum to 1. Arbitrary or empirical distributions have their uses, especially in the kinds of decision problems described in Chapter 10, but, in general, probabilistic models in quantitative methods are based on a mathematical function $f(X)$, which is called the *probability density function* (p.d.f.) or *frequency function*. It gives the probability of X when its desired value is substituted into it. The choice of $f(X)$ depends on the physical circumstances of the problem.

Statistical distributions may be represented in three ways. Figure 9-1(a) shows a *discrete* distribution in which the variable takes on only separated values between a and b. Figure 9-1(b) shows a *histogram*. Here X takes on many values, but they have been put into class intervals of width u (which do not have to be equal). The ith interval contains f_i values of X, and if there is a population of N items, then

$$f(X) = \frac{f_i}{N} \qquad (9.1)$$

i.e. $f(X)$ is simply the proportion of the N values of X contained in interval i.

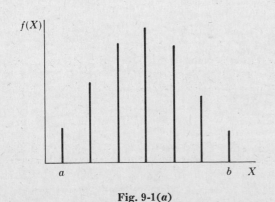

Fig. 9-1(a)

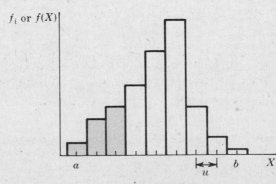

Fig. 9-1(b)

EXAMPLE 9.1. Table 9-1 shows the incomes X of 250 families in a certain community in 10 class intervals. Find $f(X)$.

The values of $f(X)$ are computed in the third column of Table 9-1. The principal convenience of the histogram presentation is that for further work all f_i items in a given class interval are assumed to have the value of their corresponding class midpoint X; e.g. instead of 76 incomes located anywhere between \$8000 and \$9999.99, all are now represented by the midpoint $X = \$9000$.

Table 9-1

Class Interval, dollars	f_i	$f(X) = f_i/250$
0– 1,999.99	3	0.012
2,000– 3,999.99	2	0.008
4,000– 5,999.99	13	0.052
6,000– 7,999.99	26	0.104
8,000– 9,999.99	76	0.304
10,000–11,999.99	53	0.212
12,000–13,999.99	40	0.160
14,000–15,999.99	25	0.100
16,000–17,999.99	10	0.040
18,000–19,999.99	2	0.008
TOTALS	250	1.000

Fig. 9-1(c)

The third type is the *continuous* distribution [Fig. 9-1(c)]. Here all X-values are different (or would be, if they could be measured with sufficient accuracy) and thus each is its own "class interval." A continuous distribution results when the width u of the class interval in the histogram is reduced to $\delta X \to dX$. The probability of X falling between, say, X_1 and X_2 is given by the shaded area between the two points.

Since all values of $f(X)$ must, in a given case, add to 1,

$$\sum f(X) = 1 \tag{9.2}$$

for a discrete distribution over the range a to b or for a histogram. For a continuous distribution, the area under the entire distribution curve must equal 1; hence

$$\int_a^b f(X)\,dX = 1 \tag{9.3}$$

EXAMPLE 9.2. Find $f(X)$ for a rectangular distribution within the limits $a \leq X \leq b$.

In a rectangular distribution, $f(X)$ has the same value over the whole domain. To satisfy the condition that the area under the distribution equal 1 we must have (Fig. 9-2)

$$f(X) = \begin{cases} \dfrac{1}{b-a} & \text{for } a \leq X \leq b \\ \\ 0 & \text{otherwise} \end{cases}$$

This could be checked by substituting for $f(X)$ in (9.3).

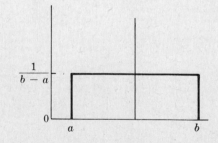

Fig. 9-2

We further define $F(X_0)$, the *cumulative distribution function*, which is the probability of X falling between a, the lower limit, and X_0. For a discrete distribution or histogram

$$F(X_0) = \sum_{X=a}^{X_0} f(X) \tag{9.4}$$

For a continuous distribution

$$F(X_0) = \int_a^{X_0} f(X)\, dX \qquad (9.5)$$

[see Fig. 9-1(c)]. In practically useful distributions, tables of the integral (9.5) are available.

The function $F(X_0)$ thus gives the probability of the variable being X_0 *or less*. The probability of the variable being X_0 *or more* is denoted $R(X_0)$.

$$F(X_0) = P(X \leqq X_0)$$
$$R(X_0) = P(X \geqq X_0) \qquad (9.6)$$

For a continuous distribution,

$$R(X_0) = 1 - F(X_0) \qquad (9.7)$$

i.e. the probability of the variable being more than a certain value is one minus the probability of it being less than that value. For a discrete distribution with X-values 1 unit apart,

$$R(X_0) = 1 - F(X_0 - 1)$$
$$F(X_0) = 1 - R(X_0 + 1) \qquad (9.8)$$

EXAMPLE 9.3. In the histogram of Example 9.1, find the probability that an income in the group is less than $10,000.

　　The range required encompasses the first five class intervals.

$$F(X) = 0.012 + 0.008 + 0.052 + 0.104 + 0.304 = 0.480 \quad Ans.$$

The cumulative distribution function may also be graphically represented. In Figs. 9-1(b) and (c) it is shown as the shaded areas on the left. It may also be shown directly, as in Fig. 9-3(a) for a discrete distribution and in Fig. 9-3(b) for a continuous one.

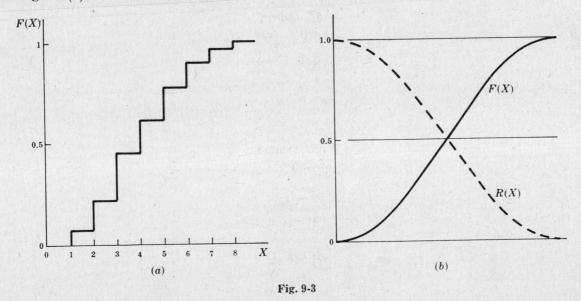

(a)　　　　　　　　　　　　　　　　　　　　(b)

Fig. 9-3

DESCRIPTIVE STATISTICS: MEAN AND VARIANCE

　　A statistical distribution is specified first of all by its p.d.f. The density function in turn is a function not only of the variable but also of one or more *parameters*, which are constants pertaining to the particular problem. Population size and the number in a sample having a desired characteristic are typical parameters and, as will be noted below, parameters and variables may interchange their roles in different distributions, i.e. a parameter in one may be the variable in another.

Aside from the p.d.f. itself, descriptive measures exist which serve to describe the *central tendency* and *dispersion* of the distribution. These are the most commonly used descriptive statistics. The most common measure of central tendency is the *mean*, or *expected value*, denoted μ or $E(X)$, where X is the variable and $E(\ )$ is the *expectation operator*; and the most common measure of dispersion is the *variance* σ^2, whose square root is the *standard deviation* σ. Formulas for the computation of μ and σ^2 are given in Table 9-2; they differ for the various data forms, but basically the mean is the *first* moment about the *origin* of $f(X)$ and the variance is the *second* moment about the *mean*. This explains the recurrence of the term $(X-\mu)^2$ in the formulas for the latter. Note also that the conceptual formulas, while important in defining the nature of the variance, are less convenient for calculations than the computational forms. The conceptual forms are obtained by substituting $(X-\mu)^2$ for X in the corresponding formulas for the mean. We can therefore also write the variance as the expectation of $(X-\mu)^2$, or $\sigma^2 = E[(X-\mu)^2]$. Note that the summations or integrations are taken over the total range of X, i.e. from a to b.

Table 9-2

Form of Data	Mean $\mu = E(X)$	Variance $\sigma^2 = E[(X-\mu)^2]$	
		Conceptual Formula	Computational Formula
Discrete	$\sum_{X=a}^{b} X f(X)$	$\sum_{X=a}^{b} (X-\mu)^2 f(X)$	$\sum_{X=a}^{b} X^2 f(X) - \mu^2$
Grouped (histogram)	$\dfrac{\sum_{X=a}^{b} Xf}{N}$	$\dfrac{\sum_{X=a}^{b} (X-\mu)^2 f}{N}$	$\dfrac{\sum_{X=a}^{b} X^2 f}{N} - \mu^2$
Ungrouped	$\dfrac{\sum_{X=a}^{b} X}{N}$	$\dfrac{\sum_{X=a}^{b} (X-\mu)^2}{N}$	$\dfrac{\sum_{X=a}^{b} X^2}{N} - \mu^2$
Continuous	$\int_a^b X f(X)\, dX$	$\int_a^b (X-\mu)^2 f(X)\, dX$	$\int_a^b X^2 f(X)\, dX - \mu^2$

EXAMPLE 9.4. Find the mean, variance and standard deviation of the discrete distribution given on page 103.

The computation may be arranged as in Table 9-3.

Table 9-3

X	$f(X)$	$X f(X)$	$X^2 f(X)$
100	0.10	10	1,000
200	0.55	110	22,000
300	0.30	90	27,000
400	0.05	20	8,000
TOTALS	1.00	$\mu = 230$ *Ans.*	$\sum X^2 f(X) = 58,000$

$$\sigma^2 = 58,000 - (230)^2 = 5100 \quad Ans.$$

$$\sigma = \sqrt{5100} = 71.414 \quad Ans.$$

EXAMPLE 9.5. Find the mean, variance and standard deviation for the grouped data of Table 9-1.

For calculations of ΣXf and ΣX^2f see Table 9-4, in which the midpoints (the X's) have been coded in thousands of dollars.

Table 9-4

Class Interval, dollars	X	f	Xf	X^2f
0– 1,999.99	1	3	3	3
2,000– 3,999.99	3	2	6	18
4,000– 5,999.99	5	13	65	325
6,000– 7,999.99	7	26	182	1,274
8,000– 9,999.99	9	76	684	6,156
10,000–11,999.99	11	53	583	6,413
12,000–13,999.99	13	40	520	6,760
14,000–15,999.99	15	25	375	5,625
16,000–17,999.99	17	10	170	2,890
18,000–19,999.99	19	2	38	722
TOTALS		$N = 250$	$\Sigma Xf = 2626$	$\Sigma X^2f = 30,186$

$$\mu = \frac{\Sigma Xf}{N} = \frac{2626}{250} = 10.504$$

$$\sigma^2 = \frac{\Sigma X^2f}{N} - \mu^2 = \frac{30,186}{250} - (10.504)^2 = 10.41$$

$$\sigma = \sqrt{10.41} = 3.226$$

Removing the coding, the results are

$$\mu = \$10,504 \quad Ans.$$
$$\sigma^2 = 10,410,000 \text{ (in } \$^2) \quad Ans.$$
$$\sigma = \$3226 \quad Ans.$$

It is also possible to code the X's by simply counting class intervals, *provided* these are equal.

EXAMPLE 9.6. Recompute Example 9.5 by coding the data in class intervals.

1. Pick a central class interval X_e and code it as 0.

2. Code the X's as $1, 2, 3, \ldots$ for class intervals greater than X_e and as $-1, -2, -3, \ldots$ for class intervals less than X_e.

3. Compute Σuf and Σu^2f, where u is the number of class intervals from X_e (see Table 9-5).

4. Compute

$$\mu = X_e + i\frac{\Sigma uf}{N} \tag{9.9}$$

$$\sigma^2 = i^2\left[\frac{\Sigma u^2f}{N} - \left(\frac{\Sigma uf}{N}\right)^2\right] \tag{9.10}$$

where $i =$ width of each class interval in original units.

From Table 9-5:

$$X_e = 11,000, \quad i = 2000$$

$$\mu = 11,000 + 2000\frac{-62}{250} = 10,504 \quad Ans.$$

$$\sigma^2 = (2000)^2\left[\frac{666}{250} - \left(\frac{-62}{250}\right)^2\right] = 10,410,000 \quad Ans.$$

$$\sigma = \$3226 \quad Ans.$$

Table 9-5

Class Interval, dollars	u	f	uf	u^2f
0– 1,999.99	−5	3	−15	75
2,000– 3,999.99	−4	2	−8	32
4,000– 5,999.99	−3	13	−39	117
6,000– 7,999.99	−2	26	−52	104
8,000– 9,999.99	−1	76	−76	76
10,000–11,999.99	0	53	0	0
12,000–13,999.99	1	40	40	40
14,000–15,999.99	2	25	50	100
16,000–17,999.99	3	10	30	90
18,000–19,999.99	4	2	8	32
TOTALS		$N = 250$	$\Sigma uf = -62$	$\Sigma u^2f = 666$

EXAMPLE 9.7. A certain product had the following sales on 15 consecutive days: 15, 14, 12, 13, 17, 18, 19, 22, 16, 12, 18, 16, 20, 13, 15. Find the mean, variance and standard deviation.

These are ungrouped data. Adding the given sales figures, $\Sigma X = 240$ and

$$\mu = \frac{240}{15} = 16 \quad Ans.$$

Squaring the data and adding:

$$\Sigma X^2 = 225 + 196 + 144 + 169 + 289 + 324 + 361$$
$$+ 484 + 256 + 144 + 324 + 256 + 400 + 169 + 225 = 3966$$

$$\sigma^2 = \frac{3966}{15} - (16)^2 = 8.4 \quad Ans.$$

$$\sigma = \sqrt{8.4} = 2.898 \quad Ans.$$

RANDOM SAMPLING

Unless otherwise stated, all discussion of sampling in the following chapters assumes *random* sampling, i.e. a process in which every item in the population has equal probability of being picked for the sample.

SPECIFIC STATISTICAL DISTRIBUTIONS

The characteristics of certain important statistical distributions are given in Table 9-6. The use of the formulas and the physical circumstances in which the distributions apply are explained below.

The Hypergeometric Distribution.

If we have a population of size N with D elements in it having a certain property, and a sample of size n is taken, the probability that exactly X elements in the *sample* have the property is given by the hypergeometric distribution. The formula for $f_H(X \mid N, D, n)$ follows from the reasoning that led to (8.29); this p.d.f. can also be written

$$f_H(X \mid N, Np, n) = \frac{C_X^{Np} C_{n-X}^{Nq}}{C_n^N} \tag{9.11}$$

in which p and q are the respective proportions of the population that have and do not have the specified property.

Table 9-6

Distribution	Variable and Range	Parameters	Probability Density Function	Mean	Variance
Hypergeometric	$X = 0, 1, 2, \ldots, n$	N, D, n $\left(p = 1 - q = \dfrac{D}{N}\right)$	$f_H(X\mid N,D,n) = \dfrac{C_X^D C_{n-X}^{N-D}}{C_n^N}$	np	$npq\,\dfrac{N-n}{N-1}$
Binomial	$X = 0, 1, 2, \ldots, n$	n, p	$f_B(X\mid n,p) = C_X^n p^X q^{n-X}$ $= \dfrac{n!}{X!(n-X)!}\, p^X q^{n-X}$	np	npq
Beta	$p\ (0 \le p \le 1)$	n, X	$f_\beta(p\mid n,X) = \dfrac{(n-1)!}{(X-1)!\,(n-X-1)!}\, p^{X-1} q^{n-X-1}$	$\dfrac{X}{n}$	$\dfrac{X(n-X)}{n^2(n+1)}$
Rectangular*	$p\ (0 \le p \le 1)$	$0, 1$	$f_R(p\mid 0,1) = f_\beta(p\mid 2,1) = 1$	$\dfrac{1}{2}$	$\dfrac{1}{12}$
Rectangular**	$X\ (a \le X \le b)$	a, b	$f_R(X\mid a,b) = \dfrac{1}{b-a}$	$\dfrac{a+b}{2}$	$\dfrac{(b-a)^2}{12}$
Pascal	$n = X, X+1, X+2, \ldots$	X, p	$f_{Pa}(n\mid X,p) = C_{X-1}^{n-1} p^X q^{n-X}$	$\dfrac{X}{p}$	$\dfrac{Xq}{p^2}$
Geometric	$n = 1, 2, 3, \ldots$	p	$f_G(n\mid p) = f_{Pa}(n\mid 1,p) = pq^{n-1}$	$\dfrac{1}{p}$	$\dfrac{q}{p^2}$
Poisson	$X = 0, 1, 2, \ldots$	m	$f_P(X\mid m) = \dfrac{e^{-m} m^X}{X!}$	m	m
Gamma	$m \ge 0$	X	$f_\gamma(m\mid X) = \dfrac{e^{-m} m^{X-1}}{(X-1)!}$	X	X
	$t \ge 0,\ m = t/T$	X, T	$f_\gamma(t\mid X,T) = \dfrac{e^{-t/T}(t/T)^{X-1}}{T(X-1)!}$	XT	XT^2
Exponential	$t \ge 0$	T	$f_e(t\mid T) = f_\gamma(t\mid 1,T) = \dfrac{1}{T}\, e^{-t/T}$	T	T^2
Normal	$-\infty \le X \le \infty$	μ, σ	$f_N(X\mid \mu,\sigma) = \dfrac{1}{\sigma\sqrt{2\pi}}\, e^{-[(X-\mu)/\sigma]^2/2}$	μ	σ^2
	$-\infty \le z \le \infty,\ z = \dfrac{X-\mu}{\sigma}$		$f_N(z) = \dfrac{1}{\sqrt{2\pi}}\, e^{-z^2/2}$	0	1

*Derived as special case of beta distribution.   **General version.

EXAMPLE 9.8. A lot of 20 parts is known to contain 5 defectives. If a sample of 4 parts is drawn from the lot, what are the probabilities of there being 0, 1, 2, 3 and 4 defectives in the sample? Also find the mean, variance and standard deviation.

This requires the computation of $f_H(X \mid 20, 5, 4)$ for $X = 0, 1, 2, 3, 4$. The calculation is carried out in Table 9-7. Note that the results sum to 1 because $X = 0, 1, 2, 3, 4$ exhausts all possibilities in a sample of size 4. We further compute

$$\text{Mean:} \quad \mu = E(X) = np = \frac{nD}{N} = \frac{(4)(5)}{20} = 1 \quad Ans.$$

$$\text{Variance:} \quad \sigma^2 = np(1-p)\frac{N-n}{N-1} = 4\left(\frac{5}{20}\right)\left(1 - \frac{5}{20}\right)\left(\frac{20-4}{20-1}\right) = 0.6316 \quad Ans.$$

$$\text{Standard deviation:} \quad \sigma = 0.7947 \quad Ans.$$

Table 9-7

X	C_X^D	C_{n-X}^{N-D}	$C_X^D C_{n-X}^{N-D}$	$f(X \mid N, D, n) = C_X^D C_{n-X}^{N-D}/C_n^N$ where $C_n^N = C_4^{20} = 4845$
0	$C_0^5 = 1$	$C_4^{15} = 1365$	1365	0.2817
1	$C_1^5 = 5$	$C_3^{15} = 455$	2275	0.4696
2	$C_2^5 = 10$	$C_2^{15} = 105$	1050	0.2167
3	$C_3^5 = 10$	$C_1^{15} = 15$	150	0.0310
4	$C_4^5 = 5$	$C_0^{15} = 1$	5	0.0010
		TOTALS	4845	1.0000

Such computations become laborious for any but small values of the parameters. Fortunately, the hypergeometric distribution can be approximated by other and more convenient ones under a variety of frequently encountered special conditions. Thus, while the hypergeometric distribution is, in important respects, the most basic and general one in sampling, it is not indispensable.

The Binomial Distribution.

The p.d.f. of the binomial distribution was derived from first principles in (8.30). It is distinguished from the hypergeometric in being based on an infinite population N. This condition may be realized in practice by sampling from a finite population *with* replacement (rather than *without* replacement, which leads to the hypergeometric). However, if we write $p = D/N$ and if the sampling fraction $n/N < 0.10$ and N is large, it can be shown that the hypergeometric p.d.f. tends to the binomial. The condition under which binomial sampling takes place is also called a *Bernouilli process*.

EXAMPLE 9.9. A salesman calls on a population of customers in which the proportion placing an order is 1/4. Use Table 9-6 to determine the probability of making 0, 1, 2, 3 and 4 sales in 4 calls. Also find mean, variance and standard deviation.

Substitute in the formula for $f_B(X \mid n, p)$: $X = 0, 1, 2, 3, 4$; $n = 4$; $p = \frac{1}{4}$ and $q = 1 - p = \frac{3}{4}$. The results are shown in Table 9-8.

Table 9-8

X	C_X^n	p^X	q^{n-X}	$f_B(X \mid n, p) \times 4^4$	$f_B(X \mid n, p)$
0	1	1	$(3/4)^4$	81	0.3164
1	4	$1/4$	$(3/4)^3$	108	0.4219
2	6	$(1/4)^2$	$(3/4)^2$	54	0.2109
3	4	$(1/4)^3$	$3/4$	12	0.0469
4	1	$(1/4)^4$	1	1	0.0039
			TOTALS	256	1.0000

$$\mu = E(X) = 4(1/4) = 1; \quad \sigma^2 = 4(1/4)(3/4) = 0.75; \quad \sigma = 0.8660 \quad Ans.$$

The usual method of working out examples in the binomial distribution is to apply Appendix C. It gives the *cumulative* distribution. For $p \leq 0.5$, using the left column (X) and inner columns (p) gives

$$R_B(X \mid n, p) = \sum_{x=X}^{n} C_x^n p^x q^{n-x} = P(x \geq X \mid n, p)$$

i.e. the probability that the variable x is equal to or greater than X, given n and p. For $p \geq 0.5$, using the right-hand column, which gives $n - X$, and the inner columns, which now represent $q = 1 - p$, provides

$$F_B(X \mid n, p) = \sum_{x=0}^{X} C_x^n p^x q^{n-x} = P(x \leq X \mid n, p)$$

i.e. the probability that the variable x is equal to or less than X, given n and p.

EXAMPLE 9.10. A sample of 20 items is drawn from a population which is 15 percent defective. Find the probability that the sample contains (a) 4 or more, (b) less than 2, (c) exactly 5, (d) no, defectives.

(a)
$$R_B(4 \mid 20, 0.15) = 0.3523 \quad Ans.$$

(b)
$$P(x < 2) = 1 - P(x \geq 2) = 1 - R(2 \mid 20, 0.15)$$
$$= 1 - 0.8244 = 0.1756 \quad Ans.$$

(c)
$$f_B(5 \mid 20, 0.15) = P(x \geq 5) - P(x \geq 6) = R_B(5 \mid 20, 0.15) - R_B(6 \mid 20, 0.15)$$
$$= 0.1702 - 0.0673 = 0.1029 \quad Ans.$$

(d)
$$f_B(0 \mid 20, 0.15) = 1 - P(x \geq 1) = 1 - R_B(1 \mid 20, 0.15)$$
$$= 1 - 0.9612 = 0.0388 \quad Ans.$$

EXAMPLE 9.11. A sample of 18 is drawn from a population of which 30 percent are considered prospects for the purchase of a certain product. What is the probability in the sample of (a) 5 or fewer, (b) 5 or more, (c) exactly 8, (d) more than 5, sales? (e) Find the mean, variance and standard deviation.

(a)
$$F_B(5 \mid 18, 0.30) = 1 - R_B(6 \mid 18, 0.30) = 1 - 0.4656 = 0.5346 \quad Ans.$$

(b)
$$R_B(5 \mid 18, 0.30) = 0.6673 \quad Ans.$$

(c)
$$f_B(8 \mid 18, 0.30) = R_B(8 \mid 18, 0.30) - R_B(9 \mid 18, 0.30)$$
$$= 0.1407 - 0.0596 = 0.0811 \quad Ans.$$

(d)
$$R_B(6 \mid 18, 0.30) = 0.4656 \quad Ans.$$

(e)
$$\mu = 18(0.30) = 5.4; \quad \sigma^2 = 18(0.30)(0.70) = 3.78; \quad \sigma = 1.944 \quad Ans.$$

EXAMPLE 9.12. A sample of 18 is drawn from a population of which 70 percent are *not* considered prospects for the purchase of a certain product. What is the probability in the sample of (*a*) 13 or more, (*b*) 13 or less, (*c*) exactly 10, (*d*) less than 13, no-sales? (*e*) Find the mean, variance and standard deviation. (*f*) Compare the results with those of Example 9.11.

Note that here $p > 0.5$; therefore use the $(n - X)$-column at the right of Appendix C, and use the column for $1 - p = 1 - 0.70 = 0.30$ in the table.

(*a*) $$R_B(13 \mid 18, 0.70) = 1 - F_B(12 \mid 18, 0.70) = 1 - 0.4656 = 0.5346 \quad Ans.$$

(*b*) $$F_B(13 \mid 18, 0.70) = 0.6673 \quad Ans.$$

(*c*) $$f_B(10 \mid 18, 0.70) = F_B(10 \mid 18, 0.70) - F_B(9 \mid 18, 0.70) = 0.1407 - 0.0596 = 0.0811 \quad Ans.$$

(*d*) $$F_B(12 \mid 18, 0.70) = 0.4656 \quad Ans.$$

(*e*) $$\mu = 18(0.70) = 12.6; \quad \sigma^2 = 18(0.70)(0.30) = 3.78; \quad \sigma = 1.944 \quad Ans.$$

(*f*) Results (*a*), (*b*), (*c*) and (*d*) are identical to those in Example 9.11 because in both examples we dealt with the same population and the same events. Mathematically, the equivalence of X sales to $n - X$ no-sales is expressed by the identity

$$f_B(X \mid n, p) = f_B(n - X \mid n, 1 - p)$$

The means in the two examples add up to the sample size: $5.4 + 12.6 = 18$; the variances are equal $(npq = nqp)$.

EXAMPLE 9.13. A sample of size 50 is drawn from a population which is 23 percent defective. What is the probability of getting 14, 15 or 16 defectives in the sample? Also find the mean, variance and standard deviation.

$$P(x \geq 14) - P(x \geq 17) = R_B(14 \mid 50, 0.23) - R_B(17 \mid 50, 0.23)$$
$$= 0.2456 - 0.0508 = 0.1948 \quad Ans.$$

$$\mu = 50(0.23) = 11.5; \quad \sigma^2 = 50(0.23)(0.77) = 8.855; \quad \sigma = 2.9757 \quad Ans.$$

The Beta Distribution.

The beta distribution is closely related to the binomial; it results when the binomial parameter p is turned into the variable and the binomial variable X becomes one of the two parameters of the beta distribution. The other parameter is n, as in the binomial distribution. The beta distribution is thus a continuous one; it is especially useful when the variable represents a fraction of some entity, since, as shown in Table 9-6, $0 \leq p \leq 1$.

The parameters X and n need not be integers. However, when they are, cumulative beta probabilities may be obtained directly from the tables of the cumulative binomial distribution (Appendix C):

$$F_\beta (p \mid n, X) = R_B(X \mid n - 1, p) \quad \text{for} \quad p \leq 0.5 \qquad (9.12)$$

$$F_\beta (p \mid n, X) = 1 - R_B(n - X \mid n - 1, 1 - p) \quad \text{for} \quad p \geq 0.5 \qquad (9.13)$$

Most problems involving the beta distribution call for it in the cumulative form.

EXAMPLE 9.14. A sample of 11 parts is chosen and 3 parts are found defective. Taking this result as parameters of a beta distribution, find the probability that $p \leq 0.25$ and the mean, variance and standard deviation of the distribution.

Using (*9.12*):
$$F_\beta(0.25 \mid 11, 3) = R_B(3 \mid 10, 0.25) = 0.4744 \quad Ans.$$

From Table 9-6:
$$\mu = \frac{3}{11} = 0.2727 \quad Ans.$$

$$\sigma^2 = \frac{3(11 - 3)}{(11)^2(11 + 1)} = 0.01653; \quad \sigma = 0.1286 \quad Ans.$$

The beta distribution can take on a wide variety of shapes, including reverse J, skewed, bell-shaped and U-shaped. For several of these it is necessary that n and X be other than integers, although always $n > 1$, $X > 0$ and $n > X$. The cumulative beta distribution has been tabulated for this wider range of values in K. Pearson, *Tables of the Incomplete Beta-Function* (London: Biometrika, 1948). In Pearson's notation

$$F_\beta(p \mid n, X) = I_p(X, n - X) \quad \text{when} \quad X \geqq n - X$$

$$R_\beta(p \mid n, X) = I_{1-p}(n - X, X) \quad \text{when} \quad X \leqq n - X$$

The Rectangular Distribution.

The cumulative distribution function for the rectangular distribution may be obtained from a simple formula:

EXAMPLE 9.15. Show that the cumulative distribution function for the rectangular distribution from a to b is a straight line from $(a, 0)$ to $(b, 1)$.

From (9.5) and Table 9-6, we have for $a \leqq X \leqq b$:

$$F(X) = \int_a^X f(x)\, dx = \int_a^X \frac{dx}{b - a} = \frac{X - a}{b - a} \qquad (9.14)$$

This represents a straight line; when $X = a$, $F(X) = 0$; when $X = b$, $F(X) = 1$.

EXAMPLE 9.16. A distribution is rectangular between 9 and 25. Find (a) $f(X)$, (b) $F(14)$, (c) $R(21)$.

(a)
$$f(X) = \frac{1}{25 - 9} = \frac{1}{16} \quad (9 \leqq X \leqq 25) \quad Ans.$$

(b)
$$F(14) = \frac{14 - 9}{25 - 9} = \frac{5}{16} \quad Ans.$$

(c)
$$R(21) = 1 - F(21) = 1 - \frac{21 - 9}{25 - 9} = \frac{1}{4} \quad Ans.$$

The Pascal Distribution.

The Pascal distribution is also closely related to the binomial; it is sometimes called the *negative binomial* distribution. In this case, it is n which becomes the variable, and X and p the parameters. Again, most practical problems require the cumulative distribution, which is obtained from the cumulative binomial by means of the relationships:

$$F_{Pa}(n \mid X, p) = R_B(X \mid n, p)$$
$$R_{Pa}(n \mid X, p) = F_B(X \mid n, p) \qquad (9.15)$$

In words: Given the proportion p of (for example) trainees passing a course, the probability of requiring n or fewer students to get exactly X good ones is the same as the probability of getting X or more good students in a class of n. Conversely, the probability of needing n or more trainees to have exactly X successes is the same as the probability of having at most X successes in a class of n entrants.

EXAMPLE 9.17. A manufacturing process runs at a rate of 10 percent defective. What is the probability of needing 100 or fewer pieces in a batch in order to have exactly 85 good pieces? Find the mean and variance of the batch size.

Using $p = 0.9$, the percentage *good*, in (9.15) gives

$$F_{Pa}(100 \mid 85, 0.9) = R_B(85 \mid 100, 0.9) = 1 - 0.0399 = 0.9601 \quad Ans.$$

Because $p > 0.5$, we use the right side of the binomial table and the $1 - p = 0.10$ column, noting further that

$$P(85 \text{ or more}) = 1 - P(84 \text{ or less})$$

The last term is given in the table.

$$\mu = \frac{85}{0.9} = 94.44 \qquad \sigma^2 = \frac{85(0.1)}{(0.9)^2} = 10.494 \quad Ans.$$

EXAMPLE 9.18. Given a 30 percent failure rate in a training course, what is the probability of needing exactly 12 entering trainees to have 8 successes?

Method 1. Using the binomial conversion,

$$P(12) = P(12 \text{ or less}) - P(11 \text{ or less})$$

and so:

$$f_{Pa}(12 \mid 8, 0.7) = F_{Pa}(12 \mid 8, 0.7) - F_{Pa}(11 \mid 8, 0.7) = R_B(8 \mid 12, 0.7) - R_B(8 \mid 11, 0.7)$$

$$= [1 - F_B(7 \mid 12, 0.7)] - [1 - F_B(7 \mid 11, 0.7)]$$

$$= (1 - 0.2763) - (1 - 0.4304) = 0.1541 \quad Ans.$$

Method 2. Using the formula for f_{Pa} in Table 9-6,

$$f_{Pa}(12 \mid 8, 0.7) = C_7^{11}(0.7)^8(0.3)^4 = \frac{11!}{7!\,4!}(0.7)^8(0.3)^4 = 0.1541 \quad Ans.$$

The Geometric Distribution.

The geometric distribution is the special case of the Pascal distribution for which $X = 1$, i.e. it describes the numbers of trials in a Bernoulli process required to get one "success," given p, the proportion of successes. It is therefore possible to calculate the cumulative distribution using Pascal methods. However, it is simpler to observe that n or more trials will be needed if and only if the first $n-1$ trials result in "failures." Thus,

$$R_G(n \mid p) = q^{n-1} \qquad (9.16)$$

EXAMPLE 9.19. A machine turns out a product with a scrap rate of 0.07. What is the probability of requiring $1, 2, 3, \ldots$, trials to get a good part? Check by means of the direct formula the probability of needing 2 or more, and 3 or more, trials.

The calculation of $f_G(n \mid 0.93)$ is shown in Table 9-9.

Table 9-9

n	pq^{n-1}
1	0.93000
2	0.06510
3	0.00456
4	0.00032
5	0.00002
$\geqq 6$	0.00000
TOTAL	1.00000

From Table 9-9

$$R_G(2 \mid 0.93) = 1 - 0.93 = 0.07$$

$$R_G(3 \mid 0.93) = 1 - 0.93 - 0.0651 = 0.0049$$

From (9.16)

$$R_G(2 \mid 0.93) = 0.07$$

$$R_G(3 \mid 0.93) = (0.07)^2 = 0.0049$$

The Poisson Distribution.

The Poisson distribution is derived from the binomial by letting $n \to \infty$ and $p \to 0$, in such a way that $np \to m > 0$. It thus has to do with the occurrences of a "rare event" $(p \to 0)$ in a large number or continuum of independent trials $(n \to \infty)$, given that the expected number of occurrences is m. Such occurrences are said to be generated by a *Poisson process*. The Poisson distribution is very important, with applications to quality control and acceptance sampling, queueing theory and other quantitative problems and, like the binomial, it serves to approximate other distributions which likewise have wide applications.

It is generally most convenient to make use of the cumulative Poisson distribution and the tables are usually provided in that form. Appendix D gives $F_P(X \mid m)$, which is the probability of X or fewer occurrences when the average number of occurrences is $m = np$.

EXAMPLE 9.20. A sample of 150 parts is taken from a production lot which is 2.4 percent defective. (*a*) What is the probability of getting 4 or fewer defectives in the sample? (*b*) What is the probability of getting exactly 4 defectives? (*c*) more than 3 defectives? (*d*) 3 or more defectives?

First, compute $m = np = 150(0.024) = 3.6$.

(*a*) From Appendix D

$$F_P(4 \mid 3.6) = 0.706 \quad Ans.$$

(*b*)
$$P(4) = P(4 \text{ or less}) - P(3 \text{ or less}) = F_P(4 \mid 3.6) - F_P(3 \mid 3.6)$$
$$= 0.706 - 0.515 = 0.191 \quad Ans.$$

(*c*)
$$P(\text{more than } 3) = 1 - P(3 \text{ or less}) = 1 - F_P(3 \mid 3.6)$$
$$= 1 - 0.515 = 0.485 \quad Ans.$$

(*d*)
$$P(3 \text{ or more}) = 1 - P(2 \text{ or less}) = 1 - F_P(2 \mid 3.6) = 1 - 0.303 = 0.697 \quad Ans.$$

EXAMPLE 9.21. Consider the following three sample sizes and population proportions: $n = 4$, $p = 0.25$; $n = 20$, $p = 0.05$; $n = 100$, $p = 0.01$. Find the values of $f_B(X \mid n, p)$ from the binomial tables and compare them with the Poisson approximation.

Note that $np = m = 1$ for all these samples. The entries in Table 9-10 are obtained by the method of Example 9.20(*b*) for the Poisson and Example 9.10(*c*) for the binomial. Note that, for the fixed value of np, the Poisson approximation gets better as n becomes larger.

Table 9-10

X	Binomial, $f_B(X \mid n, p)$			Poisson, $f_P(X \mid np)$
	$n = 4, \ p = 0.25$	$n = 20, \ p = 0.05$	$n = 100, \ p = 0.01$	
0	0.3164	0.3585	0.3660	0.368
1	0.4219	0.3773	0.3698	0.368
2	0.2109	0.1887	0.1848	0.184
3	0.0469	0.0596	0.0610	0.061
4	0.0039	0.0173	0.0150	0.015
5	..	0.0023	0.0029	0.003
6	..	0.0003	0.0004	0.001
7	..	0.0000	0.0001	0.000
TOTALS	1.0000	1.0000	1.0000	1.000

The Gamma Distribution.

The gamma distribution bears the same relationship to the Poisson distribution as the Pascal to the binomial: it is obtained by interchanging variable and parameter. It is a continuous distribution and may take on a great variety of shapes. It is therefore possible to fit empirical gamma distributions to many observed sets of data and benefit from the relative ease with which subsequent work involving the gamma distribution may be carried out.

When the parameter X is an integer, the cumulative gamma distribution may be readily obtained from tables of the cumulative Poisson distribution (Appendix D), using

$$F_\gamma(m \mid X) = R_P(X \mid m) = 1 - F_P(X - 1 \mid m) \qquad (9.17)$$

EXAMPLE 9.22.   In a transmission line, there is a fault in the insulation every 2.5 miles, on the average. What is the probability of having 2 faults in less than 6 miles?

We use the second form of the gamma distribution shown in Table 9-6.   Here

$$X = \text{number of faults} = 2$$

$$t = \text{distance in miles out to the } X\text{th fault}$$

$$1/T = \text{average number of faults per mile} = 1/2.5$$

The required probability is

$$P(t < 6) = P(t \le 6) = F_\gamma(6 \mid 2, 2.5)$$

since $P(t = 6) = 0$ for a continuous distribution.   Changing the variable to

$$m = \frac{t}{T} = \text{expected number of faults in distance } t$$

we have from (9.17)

$$F_\gamma(6 \mid 2, 2.5) = F_\gamma(6/2.5 \mid 2) = F_\gamma(2.4 \mid 2) = R_P(2 \mid 2.4)$$
$$= 1 - F_P(1 \mid 2.4) = 1 - 0.308 = 0.692 \quad Ans.$$

The problem may also be reasoned out directly from the Poisson by observing that having 2 faults in *less than* 6 miles is the same as having 2 *or more* faults in the 6 miles.   But

$$P(2 \text{ or more faults}) = R_P(2 \mid 2.4)$$

which gives the previous solution.

EXAMPLE 9.23.   A truck dock has an average interval between arrivals of 1.25 hours.   What are the probabilities that 10, 9, 8, 7 and 6 trucks arrive in less than an 8-hour shift?

The reasoning is like that in Example 9.22.   In this case,

$$m = \frac{8}{1.25} = 6.4 \text{ (average number of trucks per shift)}$$

and

$$F_\gamma(6.4 \mid X) = 1 - F_P(X - 1 \mid 6.4)$$

The computation is shown in Table 9-11.

Table 9-11

X	$F_P(X - 1 \mid 6.4)$	$F_\gamma(6.4 \mid X)$
6	0.384	0.616
7	0.542	0.458
8	0.687	0.313
9	0.803	0.197
10	0.886	0.114

When a gamma distribution is fitted to empirical data, it often happens that X is not an integer.   Numerical values can then be obtained from K. Pearson, *Tables of the Incomplete* Γ-*Function* (London: Biometrika, 1934), which give

$$I(u, p) = F_\gamma(m \mid X)$$

where $u = m/\sqrt{X}$ and $p = X - 1$.

The Exponential Distribution.

The exponential distribution is the special case of the gamma distribution in which $X = 1$, and the gamma procedure may be used to work out problems concerning it. However, convenient formulas for the cumulative exponential distribution may be derived:

$$F_e(t \mid T) = 1 - e^{-t/T}$$
$$R_e(t \mid T) = e^{-t/T} \tag{9.18}$$

The exponential distribution is often used in problems concerning product life, even though it is not as a rule a good representation of the actual life characteristics (see Chapter 19).

EXAMPLE 9.24. A component has an average life of 90 hours. Assuming exponential failure distribution, what is the probability of running at least 180 hours before failing?

From (9.18)

$$R_e(180 \mid 90) = e^{-180/90} = e^{-2} = 0.135 \quad Ans.$$

This result may also be obtained from Appendix A, which covers less convenient values of t/T as well. In reliability problems of this kind, T is called the *mean time before failure* (MTBF).

Using the gamma-Poisson approach, $m = 180/90 = 2$ and

$$R_\gamma(180 \mid 1, 90) = R_\gamma(2 \mid 1) = 1 - F_\gamma(2 \mid 1) = 1 - [1 - F_P(0 \mid 2)] = 0.135$$

Alternatively, we may simply argue that the answer is the probability of no event (i.e. of no failure) in a period twice the MTBF, and use the Poisson table directly, i.e.

$$F_P(0 \mid 2) = 0.135$$

The Normal Distribution.

The normal distribution may well be considered the most important one in probability and statistics, for three reasons:

1. A bell-shaped density function empirically fits many observed phenomena.

2. It is an approximation, limit or special case of many other statistical distributions. (See next section.)

3. It plays a central role in sampling theory, which in turn is an essential part of probabilistic decision problems. (See Chapter 11.)

The normal distribution will be applied extensively in later work. This introduction first focuses on the use of the table in Appendix B. This table gives the area, $A(z)$, under the normal curve between 0 and positive values of z, where $z = (X - \mu)/\sigma$ is the deviation of X from the mean, expressed in units of the standard deviation. By symmetry, the area from $-\infty$ to 0 is 1/2; hence

$$\text{For } z \geq 0: \quad F_N(z) = \frac{1}{2} + A(z)$$
$$\text{For } z \leq 0: \quad F_N(z) = \frac{1}{2} - A(-z) \tag{9.19}$$

To find the probabilities of various X-values we convert to the variable z and then use (9.19).

EXAMPLE 9.25. A chemical is packed in bags whose weights are known to be normally distributed with mean 50 lb and standard deviation 2 lb. Find the probability of getting a bag containing (a) less than 51 lb, (b) less than 47 lb, (c) from 48 to 52 lb, (d) from 46 to 53 lb, (e) from 48 to 49 lb.

For this distribution $\mu = 50$ and $\sigma = 2$, so that

$$z = \frac{X - 50}{2}$$

(a) $X = 51$ corresponds to

$$z = \frac{51 - 50}{2} = 0.5$$

and $X < 51$ corresponds to $z < 0.5$. From Appendix B,

Area between 0 and 0.5 $= A(0.5) = 0.1915$

[see Fig. 9-4(a)], to which must be added the area 0.5 to the left of 0. Thus,

$$P(z < 0.5) = F_N(0.5) = 0.5 + 0.1915 = 0.6915 \quad Ans.$$

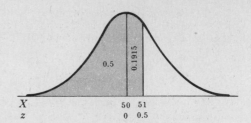

Fig. 9-4(a)

(b) $X = 47$ corresponds to

$$z = \frac{47 - 50}{2} = -1.5$$

and $X < 47$ corresponds to $z < -1.5$. From Appendix B,

Area between 0 and $+1.5 = A(+1.5) = 0.4332$

which must be subtracted from the area 0.5 to the left of 0 [see Fig. 9.4(b)]. Thus,

$$P(z < -1.5) = F_N(-1.5) = 0.5 - 0.4332$$
$$= 0.0668 \quad Ans.$$

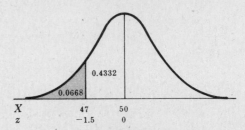

Fig. 9-4(b)

(c) The range $48 < X < 52$ corresponds to the range $-1 < z < 1$. From Appendix B,

Area between 0 and 1 $= A(1) = 0.3413$

and, by symmetry, the area between -1 and 0 is the same [Fig. 9-4(c)]. Thus,

$$P(-1 < z < 1) = F_N(1) - F_N(-1)$$
$$= 0.3413 + 0.3413 = 0.6826 \quad Ans.$$

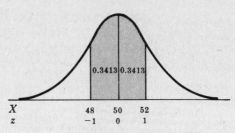

Fig. 9-4(c)

(d) The range $46 < X < 53$ corresponds to the range $-2 < z < 1.5$, which is asymmetrical [Fig. 9-4(d)]. We have:

Area between -2 and 0 $=$ Area between 0 and $+2$
$$= A(2) = 0.4772$$

Area between 0 and 1.5 $= A(1.5) = 0.4332$

Therefore,

$$P(-2 < z < 1.5) = F_N(1.5) - F_N(-2)$$
$$= 0.4772 + 0.4332 = 0.9104 \quad Ans.$$

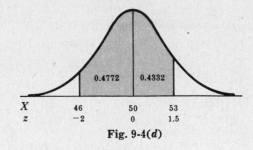

Fig. 9-4(d)

(e) The range $48 < X < 49$ corresponds to the range $-1.0 < z < -0.5$. Here a subtraction of areas is needed [Fig. 9-4(e)].

Area between -1.0 and 0 $=$ Area between 0 and $+1.0$
$$= A(1.0) = 0.3413$$

Area between -0.5 and 0 $=$ Area between 0 and $+0.5$
$$= A(0.5) = 0.1915$$

so that

$$P(-1.0 < z < -0.5) = F_N(-0.5) - F_N(-1.0)$$
$$= 0.3413 - 0.1915 = 0.1498 \quad Ans.$$

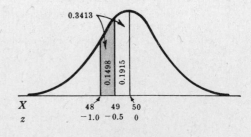

Fig. 9-4(e)

EXAMPLE 9.26. The mean weekly wage of a group of workers is \$150. The wages are believed to be normally distributed with a standard deviation of \$16. Find the wage levels which delimit the middle (a) 68 percent, (b) 75 percent, (c) 90 percent.

In all such problems the area required on either side of the mean is looked up in Appendix B and z is determined from it. Given p, we require X_1 and X_2 such that

$$P(X_1 < X < X_2) \; = \; p$$

where $\mu - X_1 = X_2 - \mu$ (see Fig. 9-5).

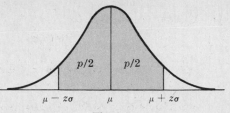

Fig. 9-5

(a) $p = 0.68$; find z corresponding to $p/2 = 0.34$. Appendix B gives it as $z \approx 1$; hence

$$X_1 \; = \; \mu + z\sigma \; = \; 150 + 16 \; = \; 166$$
$$X_2 \; = \; \mu - z\sigma \; = \; 150 - 16 \; = \; 134$$

and $$P(134 < X < 166) \; = \; 0.68$$

(b) $p = 0.75$; z for area 0.375 is 1.15.

$$X_1 \; = \; 150 + 1.15(16) \; = \; 168.4$$
$$X_2 \; = \; 150 - 1.15(16) \; = \; 131.6$$
$$P(131.6 < X < 168.4) \; = \; 0.75$$

(c) $p = 0.90$; z for area 0.45 is 1.645 (requires interpolation).

$$X_1 \; = \; 150 + 1.645(16) \; = \; 176.32$$
$$X_2 \; = \; 150 + 1.645(16) \; = \; 123.68$$
$$P(123.68 < X < 176.32) \; = \; 0.90$$

INTERRELATIONS BETWEEN THE MAJOR STATISTICAL DISTRIBUTIONS

We have previously noted several interconnections between the distributions discussed; it is helpful to summarize them in Fig. 9-6.

Among the relationships not so far referred to in this chapter, by far the most important is the *normal approximation to the binomial*. When n is large and when

$$\frac{1}{n+1} \; < \; p \; < \; \frac{n}{n+1}$$

and the variance $npq > 9$, the binomial distribution may be approximated by a normal distribution with mean $\mu = np$ and variance $\sigma^2 = npq$.

EXAMPLE 9.27. A sample of 50 is taken out of a population of consumers, 30 percent of whom are believed to favor a new product. Use the normal approximation to the binomial distribution to find the probability of having (a) 17 or more, (b) 12 or more, respondents favoring the new product. Check using the tables of the binomial distribution.

(a) We require $R_B(17 \mid 50, 0.3)$. Transforming this to the normal distribution with $\mu = 50(0.3) = 15$ and $\sigma = \sqrt{50(0.3)(0.7)} = 3.24$, we can consider it equivalent to the shaded area in Fig. 9-7(a). Note, however, that this procedure requires us to divide the continuous X-axis into discrete strips one unit wide. The binomial variable $X = 17$ is thus transformed into a normal variable extending from $X = 16.5$ to $X = 17.5$. The normal approximation thus requires the computation of $P(X > 16.5)$, as shown. From the data

$$z \; = \; \frac{16.5 - 15}{3.24} \; = \; 0.463$$

Interpolation in Appendix B then gives

$$P(z > 0.463) \; = \; 0.5 - 0.1783 \; = \; 0.3217 \quad \textit{Ans.}$$

From Appendix C,

$$R_B(17 \mid 50, 0.3) \; = \; 0.3161 \quad \textit{Ans.}$$

The two answers are within 1.8 percent of each other.

(b) See Fig. 9-7(b)

$$P(z > -1.08) \; = \; 0.8599 \quad \textit{Ans.} \qquad R_B(12 \mid 50, 0.3) \; = \; 0.8610 \quad \textit{Ans.}$$

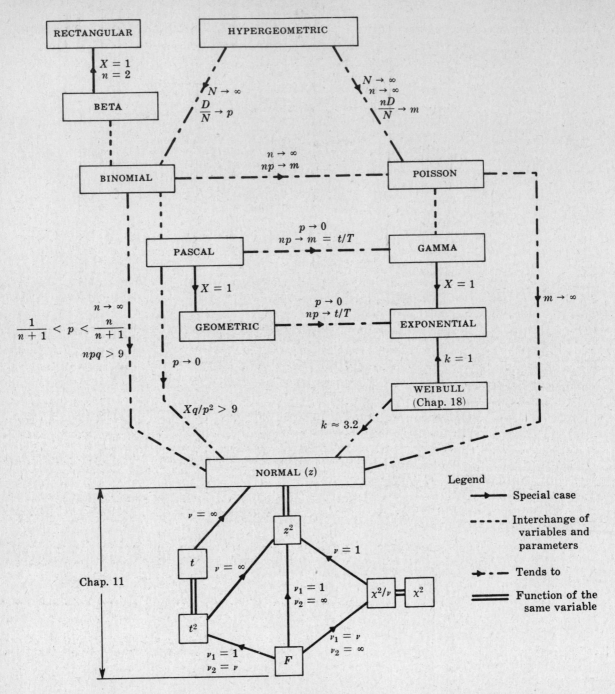

Fig. 9-6

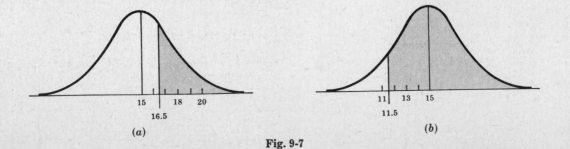

Fig. 9-7

   Similar relationships exist between the Poisson or Pascal and the normal.   Since the Pascal probabilities are obtained directly from the binomial, they approach the normal, with mean X/p and variance Xq/p^2.   (See Problem 13.12.)   For the Poisson, as m becomes large, the distribution tends to a normal one, with mean and variance both equal to m.

EXAMPLE 9.28.   An average of 15 trucks arrive at a certain terminal within each hour.   What is the probability of having fewer than 14 arrive?   Use the normal approximation to the Poisson distribution and check, using the Poisson table.

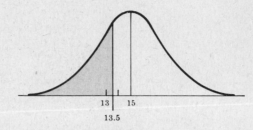

Fig. 9-8

   Here $m = 15$; we require the normal approximation to $F_P(13 \mid 15)$.   Again (Fig. 9-8), we must adjust for the continuous variable.   Therefore, the required area under the normal curve, with parameters $\mu = \sigma^2 = 15$, is $P(X < 13.5)$. We have

$$z = \frac{13.5 - 15}{\sqrt{15}} = 0.387$$

From Appendix B (interpolating),

$$P(z < 0.387) = 0.5 - 0.1506 = 0.3494 \quad Ans.$$

From Appendix D, $F_P(13 \mid 15) = 0.363 \quad Ans.$

GENERAL RESTRICTIONS ON STATISTICAL DISTRIBUTIONS

   In many cases the form of the p.d.f. is not known.   It is then useful to know that all statistical distributions are limited in the amount of the data which can lie more than a specified distance from the mean.   The best-known relationship defining these restrictions is *Chebyshev's inequality*, which states that for $k \geqq 1$ more than $1 - (1/k^2)$ of *any* set of finite numbers must lie within the enclosed range $\mu \pm k\sigma$.   Here, μ and σ are the mean and standard deviation of a variable which takes on the given set of numbers with equal probabilities.   Thus, for *any* variable X, Chebyshev's inequality implies that

$$P(\mu - k\sigma < X < \mu + k\sigma) \; > \; 1 - \frac{1}{k^2} \qquad (9.20)$$

Nothing need be known about the distribution of X, other than that it has mean μ and standard deviation σ.

   If further it is given that the distribution of X has only one mode, which coincides with the mean (i.e. an approximately symmetrical bell-shape), then the *Camp-Meidell extension* of Chebyshev's inequality improves the right-hand side of (9.20) to $1 - (1/2.25 \, k^2)$.

EXAMPLE 9.29.   A set of measurements on a group of parts shows the mean of one dimension as 3.03 inches with a standard deviation of 0.05 inches.   Find the minimum proportion of parts which must lie within ± 0.125 inches of the mean, under (a) general, (b) Camp-Meidell, conditions.   (c) Contrast with the result obtained from the normal distribution.

   Here, $k = 0.125/0.05 = 2.5$.

(a) By Chebyshev's inequality,

$$1 - \frac{1}{k^2} = 1 - \frac{1}{(2.5)^2} = 1 - 0.16 = 0.84 \quad Ans.$$

(b) By Camp-Meidell,

$$1 - \frac{1}{2.25 \, k^2} = 1 - \frac{1}{(2.25)(2.5)^2} = 1 - 0.071 = 0.929 \quad Ans.$$

(c) $$P(\mu - k\sigma < X < \mu + k\sigma) = P(-k < z < k)$$

   From Appendix B, the area under the normal curve between 0 and $k = 2.5$ is 0.4938.   Hence, the desired probability, or proportion, is $2 \times 0.4938 = 0.9876$.   *Ans.*

The Camp-Meidell conditions approximate the normal much better than the more general Chebyshev, but either way, there is a clear limit to the possible error when normality is assumed and does not actually exist.   Thus, for the above data, we are guaranteed that the normal estimate of the fraction of parts in the given range—namely, 98.76%—is in error by at most

$$98.76 - 84 = 14.76\%$$

Solved Problems

DESCRIPTIVE STATISTICS

9.1.   Find the mean, variance and standard deviation for the grouped data in Table 9-12.

Table 9-12.   Number of Establishments, by Number of Employees, Fertilizer Industry (SIC2871)

Number of Employees	Number of Establishments
1–4	8
5–9	7
10–19	14
20–49	55
50–99	71
100–249	40
250–499	14
500–999	3
1000–2499	1

Source: U.S. Census of Manufactures (1967)

In this case the class intervals are unequal; X is set as the average of the two bounds, e.g. for 10–19, $X = \frac{1}{2}(10 + 19) = 14.5$.   For the calculations, see Table 9-13.

Table 9-13

Interval	X	f	Xf	X^2f
1–4	2.5	8	20	50
5–9	7	7	49	343
10–19	14.5	14	203	2,943.5
20–49	34.5	55	1897.5	65,463.75
50–99	74.5	71	5289.5	394,067.75
100–249	174.5	40	6890	1,218,010
250–499	374.5	14	5243	1,963,503.5
500–999	749.5	3	2248.5	1,685,250.75
1000–2499	1749.5	1	1749.5	3,060,750.25
TOTALS		213	23590	8,390,382.5

$$\mu = \frac{\Sigma Xf}{N} = \frac{23,590}{213} = 110.75 \quad Ans.$$

$$\sigma^2 = \frac{\Sigma X^2 f}{N} - \mu^2 = \frac{8,390,382.5}{213} - (110.75)^2 = 27,126 \quad Ans.$$

$$\sigma = 164.7 \quad Ans.$$

THE HYPERGEOMETRIC DISTRIBUTION

9.2. A production lot of 50 pieces has 10 defectives. What is the probability of getting 2 defectives in a sample of 13 pieces?

$$f_H(2 \mid 50, 10, 13) = \frac{C_2^{10} C_{13-2}^{50-10}}{C_{13}^{50}} = \frac{\dfrac{10!}{2! \, 8!} \dfrac{40!}{11! \, 29!}}{\dfrac{50!}{13! \, 37!}}$$

$$= \frac{(10 \cdot 9)(40 \cdot 39 \cdot 38 \cdots 31 \cdot 30)(13 \cdot 12 \cdot 11 \cdots 2 \cdot 1)}{(2 \cdot 1)(11 \cdot 10 \cdot 9 \cdots 2 \cdot 1)(50 \cdot 49 \cdot 48 \cdots 39 \cdot 38)}$$

$$= \frac{37 \cdot 36 \cdot 17 \cdot 3 \cdot 31 \cdot 13}{7 \cdot 47 \cdot 23 \cdot 43 \cdot 7 \cdot 41} = 0.29316 \quad Ans.$$

9.3. A sample of 25 is taken from a production lot of 200 with 40 defectives. What is the probability of getting 8 defectives in the sample?

Since large numbers are involved, it is easier to use logarithms of factorials (Appendix J), noting that $\log 200! = \log 200 + \log 199!$. In Table 9-14 the left-hand column is merely the conversion of the formula for $f_H(X \mid N, D, n)$ into logarithmic terms.

Table 9-14

Term	Number	Log-factorial
$+ \log D!$	40	$+47.9116$
$- \log X!$	8	-4.6055
$- \log (D - X)!$	32	-35.4202
$+ \log (N - D)!$	160	$+284.6735$
$- \log (n - X)!$	17	-14.5511
$- \log (N - D - n + X)!$	143	-247.5860
$- \log N!$	200	-374.8969
$+ \log n!$	25	$+25.1906$
$+ \log (N - n)!$	175	$+318.0509$
TOTALS	$\log f_H(8 \mid 200, 40, 25)$	$-1.2331 = \bar{2}.7669$

$$f_H(8 \mid 200, 40, 25) = \text{antilog } \bar{2}.7669 = 0.05846 \quad Ans.$$

THE BINOMIAL DISTRIBUTION

9.4. Use the binomial approximation to the hypergeometric to recompute the probabilities asked for in Problems 9.2 and 9.3.

In both cases $p = D/N = 0.2$. For Problem 9.2, Appendix C gives

$$f_B(2 \mid 13, 0.2) = R_B(2 \mid 13, 0.2) - R_B(3 \mid 13, 0.2) = 0.7664 - 0.4983 = 0.2681 \quad Ans.$$

This is within 9.6 percent of the hypergeometric value.

For Problem 9.3, Appendix C does not give values for $n = 25$; hence we write

$$f_B(8 \mid 25, 0.2) = \frac{25!}{8! \, 17!} (0.2)^8 (0.8)^{17}$$

and use Appendix J:

$$\begin{aligned}
\log 25! &= 25.1906 \\
- \log 8! &= -4.6055 \\
- \log 17! &= -14.5511 \\
8 \log 0.2 = 8(\bar{1}.3010) &= 2.4080 - 8 \\
17 \log 0.8 = 17(\bar{1}.9031) &= 15.3527 - 17 \\
\hline
\log f_B(8 \mid 25, 0.2) &= 23.7947 - 25 = \bar{2}.7947
\end{aligned}$$

and

$$f_B(8 \mid 25, 0.2) = 0.06233 \quad Ans.$$

This is within 6.5 percent of the hypergeometric value.

9.5. In a sample of 100 respondents to a question, what is the probability that 51 or more will answer in the affirmative, given that the affirmative percentage in the population is 0.40, 0.45, 0.48, 0.49, 0.50, 0.51, 0.52, 0.55 and 0.60?

From Appendix C, working with the right-hand side when $p > 0.5$ and noting that

$$P(51 \text{ or more}) = 1 - P(50 \text{ or less})$$

Table 9-15

p	$R_B(51 \mid 100, p)$
0.40	0.0168
0.45	0.1346
0.48	0.3082
0.49	0.3819
0.50	0.4602
0.51	$1 - 0.4599 = 0.5401$
0.52	$1 - 0.3816 = 0.6184$
0.55	$1 - 0.1827 = 0.8173$
0.60	$1 - 0.0271 = 0.9729$

9.6. A consignment of eggs consists of 1/6 extra large, 1/3 large and the rest medium. What is the probability of getting 5 extra large and 8 large eggs in a sample of 20?

This is an important extension of the binomial distribution which provides for more than two characteristics in the sampled population. It leads to the *multinomial* distribution. By writing $p_i = D_i/N$ and rearranging (8.29), it can be shown that, for large N, the multinomial p.d.f. is given by

$$f_M(X_1, X_2, \ldots, X_g \mid n, p_1, p_2, \ldots, p_g) = \frac{n!}{X_1! \, X_2! \cdots X_g!} \, p_1^{X_1} p_2^{X_2} \cdots p_g^{X_g} \qquad (9.21)$$

where $\Sigma X_i = n$ as before and $\Sigma p_i = 1$. Here $X_1 = 5$, $X_2 = 8$, $X_3 = 7$; $p_1 = 1/6$, $p_2 = 1/3$, $p_3 = 1/2$.

$$f_M(5, 8, 7 \mid 20, 1/6, 1/3, 1/2) = \frac{20!}{5! \, 8! \, 7!} \left(\frac{1}{6}\right)^5 \left(\frac{1}{3}\right)^8 \left(\frac{1}{2}\right)^7$$

This is best evaluated by logarithms, using Appendix J for the factorials:

$$\log 20! \qquad\qquad\qquad\qquad = 18.3861$$
$$-\log 5! \qquad\qquad\qquad\qquad = -2.0792$$
$$-\log 8! \qquad\qquad\qquad\qquad = -4.6055$$
$$-\log 7! \qquad\qquad\qquad\qquad = -3.7024$$
$$5 \log (1/6) = 5(-0.7782) \qquad = -3.8910$$
$$8 \log (1/3) = 8(-0.4771) \qquad = -3.8168$$
$$7 \log (1/2) = 7(-0.3010) \qquad = -2.1070$$
$$\log f_M(5, 8, 7 \mid 20, 1/6, 1/3, 1/2) = \overline{-1.8158} = \bar{2}.1842$$

$$f_M(5, 8, 7 \mid 20, 1/6, 1/3, 1/2) = \text{antilog } \bar{2}.1842 = 0.01529 \quad Ans.$$

Note that, aside from the infinite population, the data are the same as in Examples 8.14 and 8.15. The result agrees quite well with the value 0.01542 obtained there.

Formula (9.21) can also be proved from first principles. The term $p_1^{X_1} p_2^{X_2} \cdots p_g^{X_g}$ is the probability of a single arrangement of n independent events, of which X_1 events each have probability p_1, X_2 have p_2, etc. The term $n!/X_1! \, X_2! \cdots X_g!$ is the number of arrangements which can be made up out of the n events, when $X_1, X_2, \ldots, X_g$ are the required subcategories (see Problem 8.15).

THE BETA DISTRIBUTION

9.7. Consider a beta distribution with parameters $n = 20$, $X = 7$. Find the probability that p is (a) equal to or less than 0.4, (b) less than 0.2, (c) more than 0.7, (d) less than 0.66, (e) less than 0.5.

Using the binomial conversion formulas, (9.12) and (9.13):

(a) $$F_\beta(0.4 \mid 20, 7) = R_B(7 \mid 19, 0.4) = 0.6919 \quad Ans.$$

(b) $$F_\beta(0.2 \mid 20, 7) = R_B(7 \mid 19, 0.2) = 0.0676 \quad Ans.$$

(c) $$R_\beta(0.7 \mid 20, 7) = R_B(13 \mid 19, 0.3) = 0.0006 \quad Ans.$$

(d) $$F_\beta(0.66 \mid 20, 7) = 1 - R_B(13 \mid 19, 0.34) = 1 - 0.0023 = 0.9977 \quad Ans.$$

(e) $$F_\beta(0.5 \mid 20, 7) = R_B(7 \mid 19, 0.5) = 0.9165 \quad Ans.$$

Note that (e) can also be obtained using the right side of Appendix C:

$$F_\beta(0.5 \mid 20, 7) = 1 - R_B(13 \mid 19, 0.5) = 1 - 0.0835 = 0.9165$$

9.8. In a beta distribution with parameters $n = 18$, $X = 7$ find the probability that p lies between 0.25 and 0.75.

$$\begin{aligned} P(0.25 \le p \le 0.75) &= F_\beta(0.75 \mid 18, 7) - F_\beta(0.25 \mid 18, 7) \\ &= [1 - R_B(11 \mid 17, 0.25)] - R_B(7 \mid 17, 0.25) \\ &= 1 - 0.0006 - 0.1071 = 0.8923 \quad Ans. \end{aligned}$$

9.9. A beta distribution is estimated to have a mean of 1/5 and a variance of 1/100. Find the probability that p is less than 1/4.

It is first necessary to find the parameters:

$$\mu = \frac{1}{5} = \frac{X}{n} \quad \text{or} \quad n = 5X$$

$$\sigma^2 = \frac{1}{100} = \frac{X(n-X)}{n^2(n+1)} = \frac{X(5X-X)}{25X^2(5X+1)} = \frac{4}{25(5X+1)}$$

Cross-multiplying the second equation gives

$$5X + 1 = 16$$

whence $X = 3$ and $n = 5(3) = 15$. We require

$$F_\beta(0.25 \mid 15, 3) = R_B(3 \mid 14, 0.25) = 0.7189 \quad Ans.$$

THE RECTANGULAR DISTRIBUTION

9.10. (a) Prove the formulas for mean and variance of the rectangular distribution as given in Table 9-6. (b) Show that $P(\mu - 1.5\sigma < X < \mu + 1.5\sigma)$ satisfies the Camp-Meidell condition.

(a) It was shown in Example 9.2 that the p.d.f. is

$$f(X) = \begin{cases} \dfrac{1}{b-a} & \text{for } a \le X \le b \\ 0 & \text{otherwise} \end{cases}$$

From Table 9-2, using the formulas for continuous distributions,

$$\mu = \int_a^b \frac{X \, dX}{b-a} = \frac{1}{b-a} \frac{X^2}{2}\bigg|_a^b = \frac{b^2 - a^2}{2(b-a)} = \frac{a+b}{2} \quad Ans.$$

$$\sigma^2 = \int_a^b \frac{X^2 \, dX}{b-a} - \left(\frac{a+b}{2}\right)^2 = \frac{1}{b-a} \frac{X^3}{3}\bigg|_a^b - \left(\frac{a+b}{2}\right)^2 = \frac{b^3 - a^3}{3(b-a)} - \left(\frac{a+b}{2}\right)^2$$

$$= \frac{b^2 + ab + a^2}{3} - \left(\frac{a+b}{2}\right)^2 = \frac{(b-a)^2}{12} \quad Ans.$$

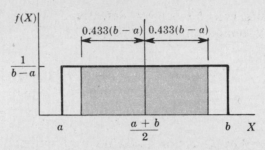

Fig. 9-9

(b) We have

$$1.5 \, \sigma = 1.5 \frac{b-a}{\sqrt{12}} = (0.433)(b-a)$$

The area under the p.d.f. within $\pm(0.433)(b-a)$ of the mean at $(a+b)/2$ is given by (see Fig. 9-9)

$$2[(0.433)(b-a)] \frac{1}{b-a} = 0.866$$

The minimum area, according to the Camp-Meidell condition, is

$$1 - \frac{1}{(2.25)(1.5)^2} = 0.802$$

Since $0.866 > 0.802$ the Camp-Meidell condition is satisfied.

THE PASCAL DISTRIBUTION

9.11. We require 6 good parts from a process which turns out 38 percent good parts. What is the probability of getting this result with an initial batch size of (a) 15 or less, (b) 13 or more, (c) 14, (d) more than 16.

(a) $\qquad F_{Pa}(15 \,|\, 6, 0.38) = R_B(6 \,|\, 15, 0.38) = 0.5335$ (from Appendix C)   *Ans.*

(b) $\qquad R_{Pa}(13 \,|\, 6, 0.38) = F_B(6 \,|\, 13, 0.38) = 1 - R_B(7 \,|\, 13, 0.38)$

$\qquad\qquad\qquad\qquad\qquad\quad = 1 - 0.1853 = 0.8147$ *Ans.*

(c) $\quad f_{Pa}(14 \,|\, 6, 0.38) = F_{Pa}(14 \,|\, 6, 0.38) - F_{Pa}(13 \,|\, 6, 0.38)$

$\qquad\qquad\qquad\quad = R_B(6 \,|\, 14, 0.38) - R_B(6 \,|\, 13, 0.38) = 0.4519 - 0.3673 = 0.0846$ *Ans.*

(d) $\qquad R_{Pa}(17 \,|\, 6, 0.38) = 1 - R_B(7 \,|\, 17, 0.38) = 1 - 0.4839 = 0.5161$ *Ans.*

9.12. We require 12 good parts from a process which has a 20 percent rate of defectives. How big should the initial batch be to be 90 percent certain of getting at least 12 good ones?

We work with 0.8 as the fraction good. We require the solution for n of

$$F_{Pa}(n \,|\, 12, 0.8) = R_B(12 \,|\, n, 0.8) = 0.90$$

Working with the right-hand side of Appendix C, this reduces to

$$1 - F_B(11 \mid n, 0.8) = 0.9 \quad \text{or} \quad F_B(11 \mid n, 0.8) = 0.1$$

Appendix C shows that $F_B(11 \mid 17, 0.8) = 0.1057$, which is near enough; the actual probability of starting with 17 pieces and getting at least 12 good ones is $1 - 0.1057 = 0.8943$. *Ans.*

THE GEOMETRIC DISTRIBUTION

9.13. A certain process runs 18 percent defective. What is the probability of needing three or fewer attempts to get a good part?

Using *(9.16)*,

$$P(3 \text{ or fewer}) = 1 - P(4 \text{ or more}) = 1 - R_G(4 \mid 0.18)$$
$$= 1 - (0.18)^3 = 0.9942 \quad Ans.$$

9.14. The probability that a certain machine part will fail in the next δt hours is $\delta t/T$, where T is the MTBF (in hours). (*a*) Find the probability that the part will last at least t more hours. (*b*) Use the result of (*a*) to verify the connection between the geometric and exponential distributions indicated in Fig. 9-6.

(*a*) We divide the t hours into a large number n of small intervals of length $\delta t = t/n$ (see Fig. 9-10). Each little interval can be considered as a "trial" in a Bernoulli process with parameter $p = \delta t/T$. Then the desired probability is given by *(9.16)* as

$$R_G(n+1 \mid p) = q^n = \left(1 - \frac{\delta t}{T}\right)^n = \left(1 - \frac{t/T}{n}\right)^n$$

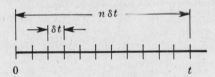

Fig. 9-10

(*b*) From calculus we know that $[1 + (x/n)]^n \to e^x$ as $n \to \infty$. Thus, as $n \to \infty$, i.e. as $\delta t \to 0$, $p \to 0$ and $np \to t/T$, we have

$$\left(1 - \frac{t/T}{n}\right)^n \longrightarrow e^{-t/T} = R_e(t \mid T)$$

See *(9.18)*.

THE POISSON DISTRIBUTION

9.15. A certain machine subassembly is inspected for a variety of mounting dimensions and output characteristics. Inspection reveals an average of 2.8 defects for each dozen parts. Find, for each dozen parts, the probability of having (*a*) 3 or fewer, (*b*) 2, (*c*) 0 and (*d*) more than 4, defects.

Use Appendix D.

(*a*)
$$F_P(3 \mid 2.8) = 0.692 \quad Ans.$$

(*b*)
$$F_P(2 \mid 2.8) - F_P(1 \mid 2.8) = 0.469 - 0.231 = 0.238 \quad Ans.$$

(*c*)
$$F_P(0 \mid 2.8) = 0.061 \quad Ans.$$

(*d*)
$$1 - F_P(4 \mid 2.8) = 1 - 0.848 = 0.152 \quad Ans.$$

9.16. Health statistics for a certain plant indicate that, on the average, 11 injuries occur every week. Use the Poisson distribution and its normal approximation to find the probability of no more than 13 injuries.

Poisson probabilities are obtained from Appendix D as $F_P(13 \mid 11) = 0.781$.   *Ans.*

For the normal approximation, we have to work with strips 1 unit wide for each value of the equivalent discrete variable; thus we desire $P(X \leqq 13.5)$. From the data, $\mu = 11$, $\sigma^2 = 11$ and $\sigma = 3.317$.   Therefore

$$z = \frac{13.5 - 11}{3.317} = 0.754$$

and, as in Example 9.24(*a*), Appendix B gives, after interpolation, $F_N(0.754) = 0.5 + 0.2746 = 0.7746$, which is within 0.8 percent of the Poisson result.   *Ans.*

THE GAMMA DISTRIBUTION

9.17. Orders arrive at an average rate of 0.4 per week for a part that takes 9 weeks to manufacture. At the beginning of manufacture there are 4 parts in inventory. What is the probability of being more than 2 weeks out of stock?

We require the probability that the 4 parts last less than $9 - 2 = 7$ weeks, i.e. that the time till the fourth order is less than 7 weeks. Since the average interval between orders is $1/0.4 = 2.5$ weeks, the required probability is $F_\gamma(7 \mid 4, 2.5)$. Writing $m = 7/2.5 = 2.8$, this becomes

$$F_\gamma(2.8 \mid 4) = R_P(4 \mid 2.8) = 1 - F_P(3 \mid 2.8) = 1 - 0.692 = 0.308   \text{Ans.}$$

9.18. A company wishes to follow a simple procedure in reordering a very slow-moving part: Keep one part in stock and whenever a part is required, ship the one in inventory and start a new one through the shops, a process which takes 13 weeks. An average of one order is placed every 10 weeks. (*a*) What is the probability of running short (i.e. of having zero inventory and at least one request for the part)? (*b*) What is the probability of running short if (i) 2 and (ii) 3 parts are kept in inventory instead?

Measuring time from the moment that a new part is begun, when there are $X - 1$ parts in stock, we want to know the probability that the Xth order arrives within 13 weeks.

(*a*) Here $X = 1$ and $m = 13/10 = 1.3$; hence we require

$$F_\gamma(1.3 \mid 1) = R_P(1 \mid 1.3) = 1 - F_P(0 \mid 1.3) = 1 - 0.273 = 0.727   \text{Ans.}$$

Note that since $X = 1$, the exponential distribution could be used instead:

$$F_\gamma(13 \mid 1, 10) = F_e(13 \mid 10) = 1 - e^{-13/10} = 1 - 0.2725 = 0.7275$$

(from Appendix A).

(*b*) Here $X = 2$ and

$$F_\gamma(1.3 \mid 2) = 1 - F_P(1 \mid 1.3) = 1 - 0.627 = 0.373   \text{Ans.}$$

(*c*) Here $X = 3$ and

$$F_\gamma(1.3 \mid 3) = 1 - F_P(2 \mid 1.3) = 1 - 0.857 = 0.143   \text{Ans.}$$

While it is now possible to decide on the basis of the probabilities whether to have 1, 2 or 3 parts in inventory (e.g. that 0.727 is "bad" and 0.373 "good," or whatever), such decisions are best made on the basis of the economic consequences.

9.19. One workpiece in 300 turns out to be defective. What is the probability of finding (*a*) the first defective among the first 300 pieces, (*b*) the third defective among the first 900 pieces and (*c*) the eighth defective after the 2700th piece.

The relevant distribution is the Pascal, but since p is small and n is large we approximate it by the gamma.

(a) $F_\gamma(300 \mid 1, 300) = F_\gamma(1 \mid 1) = 1 - F_P(0 \mid 1) = 1 - 0.368 = 0.632$ *Ans.*

Note that this is the same as $F_e(1 \mid 1) = 1 - e^{-1} = 0.632$.

(b) $F_\gamma(900 \mid 3, 300) = F_\gamma(3 \mid 3) = 1 - F_p(2 \mid 3) = 1 - 0.423 = 0.577$ *Ans.*

(c) $R_\gamma(2700 \mid 8, 300) = R_\gamma(9 \mid 8) = 1 - F_\gamma(9 \mid 8) = 1 - [1 - F_P(7 \mid 9)] = 0.324$ *Ans.*

THE NORMAL DISTRIBUTION

9.20. Bags of a certain chemical are supposed to contain 50 lb. They are weighed on a scale which can only read to half pounds. What is the probability of the weight being 50 lb, assuming a normal distribution with standard deviation of 0.5 lb?

A nominal weight of 50 lb would be any value within ±0.25 lb of the true 50 lb reading. Therefore
$$0.25 = z\sigma = \frac{z}{2} \quad \text{or} \quad z = 0.5$$

From Appendix B, the area included within ±0.5 is
$$2(0.1915) = 0.3830 \quad \textit{Ans.}$$

Note that unless a range of accuracy is specified, problems of this kind cannot be solved. The height $f(X)$ of a strip of normal (or any other continuous) distribution does not give the probability; it has to be multiplied by an increment δX along the base so that there is an area $f(X)\,\delta X$, which *does* represent a probability.

9.21. An observation of 80-lb bags of a certain chemical yields the result that 50 percent of the bags weigh between 79 and 81 lb. Estimate the standard deviation, assuming a normal distribution.

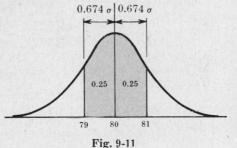

For an area of 0.5 about the mean (0.25 on each side), Appendix B gives $z = 0.674$ (with interpolation). As shown in Fig. 9-11, this means that

$$0.674\,\sigma = 81 - 80 = 1 \quad \text{or} \quad \sigma = 1.484$$

Fig. 9-11

Supplementary Problems

In Problems 9.22–9.24 find the binomial probabilities requested, the mean, variance and standard deviation.

9.22. $n = 20$, $p = 0.70$. Find $P(15 \text{ or more})$ and $P(15)$.   *Ans.* 0.4164; 0.1789; 14; 4.2; 2.049

9.23. $n = 20$, $p = 0.30$. Find $P(5 \text{ or less})$ and $P(5)$.   *Ans.* 0.4164; 0.1789; 6; 4.2; 2.049

9.24. $n = 13$, $p = 0.60$. Find $P(4, 5, 6 \text{ or } 7)$.   *Ans.* 0.4178; 7.8; 3.12; 1.766

9.25. A process has a fraction defective of 0.15; 45 good pieces are required. What is the probability of needing more than 49 pieces in the initial batch?   *Ans.* $R_{Pa}(50 \mid 45, 0.85) = 0.8879$

9.26. A process has a fraction defective of 0.08; 3 good pieces are required. What is the probability of needing $3, 4, 5, \ldots$ pieces for the job? Also find mean and variance.

Ans.

n	3	4	5	6	7	8 or more
$f_{Pa}(n \mid 3, 0.92)$	0.7787	0.1869	0.0299	0.0040	0.0004	0.0001

mean 3.26; variance 0.2836

9.27. In a Bernoulli process, $n = 6$ and $p = 0.32$. Find the probability of getting $0, 1, 2, \ldots, 6$ items having the characteristic of interest.

Ans.

X	0	1	2	3	4	5	6
$f_B(X \mid 6, 0.32)$	0.0989	0.2791	0.3284	0.2061	0.0727	0.0137	0.0011

9.28. In a type of electrical cable there are, on the average, m_i faults per mile in the insulation and m_c faults per mile in the core. Assuming independent Poisson distributions, show that the total number of faults in one mile of the cable has a Poisson distribution with mean $m = m_i + m_c$.

[*Hint*: Use (*8.19*) and the binomial theorem.]

9.29. A batch of 50 pieces is started in a production process which has a 20 percent rate defective. At least how many good pieces can be expected with about 90 percent reliability? Give the actual reliability.   *Ans.* 37 pieces with assurance 0.8894

9.30. A beta probability distribution has parameters $n = 13$, $X = 2$. Find the probability that p is equal to or (*a*) less than 0.15, (*b*) less than 0.47, (*c*) less than 0.64, (*d*) more than 0.52. (*e*) Find the mean and variance.   *Ans.* (*a*) 0.5565; (*b*) 0.9943; (*c*) 0.9999; (*d*) 0.0021; (*e*) 0.1538, 0.0093

9.31. In a beta probability distribution with parameters $n = 18$, $X = 4$, find the probability that p lies between 0.15 and 0.45.   *Ans.* 0.7372

9.32. Forty-five good pieces are required from a production process with a 0.20 defective rate. (*a*) What is the probability of getting this result from a batch of 50? (*b*) What is the expected initial batch size?

Ans.   (*a*) 0.048;   (*b*) 56.25

9.33. We need 15 good parts from a process with a 15 percent defective rate. We want to be 85 percent (approx.) certain of getting at least that many. What would the batch size be?   *Ans.* 19

9.34. A sample of 100 is taken from a population which is believed to be 5 percent defective. Use (*a*) the binomial and (*b*) the Poisson distributions to find the probability of (i) more than 6 defectives, (ii) 6 or more, (iii) 6 and (iv) 4 or fewer.

Ans.   (*a*) (i) 0.2340, (ii) 0.3840, (iii) 0.1500, (iv) 0.436;

(*b*) (i) 0.238, (ii) 0.384, (iii) 0.146, (iv) 0.440

9.35. In a roadbed there is, on the average, a defect once every 250 feet. What is the probability of (*a*) 1 defect within the first 200 feet, (*b*) a defect between 300 feet and 500 feet, (*c*) 3 defects in more than 1000 feet?   *Ans.* (*a*) 0.551: (*b*) 0.166; (*c*) 0.238

9.36. A population of workers has a weekly wage which is normally distributed with mean \$120 and standard deviation \$15. Find the probabilities of an individual wage being (a) greater than \$110, (b) less than \$85, (c) greater than \$150, (d) between \$110 and \$135, (e) between \$125 and \$135.

Ans.   (a) 0.7454; (b) 0.0099; (c) 0.0228; (d) 0.7495; (e) 0.2120

9.37. For the population of Problem 9.36, find the limits which enclose the middle (a) 95, (b) 68, (c) 98 percent.   *Ans.*   (a) \$90.60, \$149.40; (b) \$105, \$135; (c) \$85.11, \$154.89

9.38. Estimate the standard deviation of drums containing an average of 80 lb of material if, in a sampling procedure, it is found that (a) 68 percent of the drums contain between 75 and 85 lb, (b) 95 percent of the drums contain between 68 and 92 lb. Assume a normal distribution.   *Ans.*   (a) 5; (b) 6.122

9.39. A certain population is believed to divide as follows on an issue in a poll: Yes, 40 percent; No, 25 percent; Don't Know, 35 percent. What is the probability that a sample of 10 will contain 5 Yes, 3 No and 2 Don't Know?   *Ans.* 0.04939

9.40. By integrating $f_e(t \mid T)$ prove (9.18).

Chapter 10

Decision Theory Without Sampling

THE NATURE OF THE PROBLEM

This chapter deals with the making of optimal decisions in the presence of uncertainty, or, more exactly, of risk, regarding some determinative physical state (such as product demand or product quality in a manufacturing process). While we do not usually have formal objective functions of the kind met with in linear programming, the objective is still to maximize profits, minimize losses or costs or elapsed time, or in other ways use a resource in the best manner possible given the conditions of the problem. Let us, for simplicity, speak only of "costs."

To solve decision problems of this kind we must first know the costs associated with each possible choice or action, i.e. with each possible value of the *decision variable*. Second —and it is this which identifies the problems as *probabilistic* rather than deterministic— we have to be able to describe the physical states by means of a probability distribution. This means that we must be able to define all outcomes (for instance, the full range of the demand for spark plugs) and the probability of each outcome (the probability of selling 10, 20, 30, . . ., spark plugs).

The solution consists in first working out *conditional costs*, i.e. the cost given that the decision variable has a particular value and that a particular physical state obtains. Multiplying each conditional cost by the probability of the particular physical state gives the *expected cost* (for that choice and that state). The sum of the expected costs over all states is then the *expected monetary value* (EMV) for the given value of the decision variable. Comparing the EMV's for all possible values of the decision variable allows the selection of the optimal EMV, denoted EMV*. One way of doing all this is by a stepwise, tabular procedure. The other is through analytical methods.

This chapter is the first of three dealing with decision analysis based on the above approach. Chapter 12 uses sampling to refine and improve upon the analysis. Chapter 13 employs the distributions of Chapter 9, as well as more advanced statistical concepts, to provide speedier solutions.

STEPWISE OR TABULAR METHODS WITH EMPIRICAL DISTRIBUTIONS

EXAMPLE 10.1. An electronic circuit element is made in lots of 800 on a machine which, when set up by hand, is described by the following probability distribution for the fraction defective, p:

p	0.02	0.05	0.10	0.15	0.20
$P(p)$	0.40	0.30	0.15	0.10	0.05

If a defective element is installed and must be replaced when the complete unit is tested, it costs $1.50 each to correct. It is, however, possible to design a special fixture for $40 per lot such that the quality is always at the 2 percent defective level (i.e. at the best level obtainable with the manual setup). Prepare a complete analysis of whether to use the fixture.

In this *two-action* problem the decision variable has only two values, which may be taken as 0 or DON'T USE FIXTURE and 1 or USE FIXTURE.

Method 1. Payoff Table.

This is given as Table 10-1. "Payoff" here means "cost," which we seek to minimize.

Table 10-1

		DON'T USE FIXTURE		USE FIXTURE		
(1)	(2)	(3)	(4)	(5)	(6)	(7)
p	$P(p)$	CC	EC	CC	EC	ECC
0.02	0.40	24	9.60*	64	25.60	9.60
0.05	0.30	60	18.00*	64	19.20	18.00
0.10	0.15	120	18.00	64	9.60*	9.60
0.15	0.10	180	18.00	64	6.40*	6.40
0.20	0.05	240	12.00	64	3.20*	3.20
TOTALS	1.00		75.60		EMV* = 64.00	46.80

Columns (1) and (2). The physical states are specified by p, with associated probabilities $P(p)$.

Column (3). The conditional costs (CC) under DON'T USE FIXTURE for the various proportions defective in Column (1).

$$CC = 800p \times 1.50 = 1200p$$

or $1200 \times$ Col. (1).

Column (4). The expected costs (EC),

$$EC = CC \times P(p) \tag{10.1}$$

or Col. (2) $\times$ Col. (3). The total is the EMV of DON'T USE FIXTURE.

Column (5). This is the conditional cost under USE FIXTURE. It consists of the $24 for the 2 percent of defectives which cannot be avoided plus the $40 for the fixture: $24 + 40 = 64$. This is the same for all values of p, since using the fixture reduces defectives to the best level specified.

Column (6). The EC is computed similarly to Column (4), i.e.

$$\text{Col. (6)} = \text{Col. (2)} \times \text{Col. (5)}$$

The total is the EMV of USE FIXTURE. Note that it is less than the EMV of DON'T USE FIXTURE, so that it is better to use the fixture. *Ans.*

Column (7). This computes the *expected cost under certainty* (ECC). It is the cost if p were known in advance on each occasion, *given* the prior distribution. It is *not*, therefore, the ultimate "certainty": if the prior distribution is wrong, so is the ECC. But if it is correct and if we know in advance how the product will turn out, we would decide whether or not to use the fixture according to which conditional or expected costs are smaller. These are shown starred in Columns (4) and (6) and added in Column (7), for a total of $46.80.

The result is, therefore, to use the fixture, for a saving of $75.60 - 64.00 = \$11.60$. The difference between the smallest EMV and the ECC, here $64.00 - 46.80 = \$17.20$, is called the *expected value of perfect information* (EVPI). Thus, if we knew in advance what p would turn out to be, we could save the EVPI (also called *regret* and the *cost of uncertainty*).

$$EVPI = EMV^* - ECC \tag{10.2}$$

Method 2. Opportunity Loss Table.

This is shown as Table 10-2. The *conditional opportunity loss* (COL) is a measure of the resources wasted if a wrong decision is made. It is the difference between what was actually used, given a certain

Table 10-2

		DON'T USE FIXTURE		USE FIXTURE	
(1)	(2)	(3)	(4)	(5)	(6)
p	$P(p)$	COL	EOL	COL	EOL
0.02	0.40	0	0	40.00	16.00
0.05	0.30	0	0	4.00	1.20
0.10	0.15	56.00	8.40	0	0
0.15	0.10	116.00	11.60	0	0
0.20	0.05	176.00	8.80	0	0
TOTALS	1.00		28.80		EVPI = 17.20

decision and physical state, and what would have been used if the best decision had been made. There are two ways of obtaining the COL's. We saw in Method 1, Column (3), that the cost of defectives is $1200p$. To find the breakeven fraction, p_b, we set this equal to the cost of using the fixture, $64 [Method 1, Column (5)]:

$$1200p_b = 64 \quad \text{or} \quad p_b = 0.0533$$

When $p < 0.0533$, we should *not* use the fixture, but if we do, we waste an amount $64 - 1200p = $ COL. When $p > 0.0533$, using the fixture is the right decision and *not* using it results in a COL given by $1200p - 64$. Thus, for every p,

$$\text{COL} = |1200p - 64| = |\text{Col. (3)} - \text{Col. 5}|$$

which means that the COL's may be simply found by subtracting the smallest entry in each row of the payoff table from the others; in this case there are only two entries per row but the result applies for any number of entries. Thus the COL for $p = 0.15$, for instance, is $180 - 64 = $116 and, in general, the italicized figures in the payoff table are subtracted from the other CC's to obtain the COL's.

The *expected opportunity losses* (EOL) are obtained from

$$\text{EOL} = \text{COL} \times P(p) \tag{10.3}$$

e.g. $4 \times 0.30 = $1.20. The smaller sum of the EOL's is in Column (6) of Table 10-2 and is seen to be the EVPI. Note also that the difference between the two EOL totals is $11.60, the same as the difference between the two EC totals in the payoff table.

The opportunity losses are sometimes easier to compute, and zeros reduce the labor of finding the expectations. It is still necessary to compute a portion of the payoff table or the ECC if the EMV* is also asked for.

Method 3. Using the Mean of p.

We can also get a decision by comparing the breakeven p_b with the mean of p, denoted $\bar{p}$ and given by

$$\bar{p} = \sum p P(p) \tag{10.4}$$

From the data

$$\bar{p} = (0.02)(0.40) + (0.05)(0.30) + (0.10)(0.15) + (0.15)(0.10) + (0.20)(0.05) = 0.063$$

Since $\bar{p} > p_b$, i.e. $0.063 > 0.0533$, the fixture should be used. The gain from taking the rational action is

$$1200(\bar{p} - p_b) = 1200(0.063 - 0.0533) = 1200(0.00967) = $11.60$$

as before.

For any fraction defective p, there is a COL of $1200(p - p_b)$ when $p > p_b$ and $1200(p_b - p)$ when $p < p_b$. As before, EOL = COL $\times P(p)$. The EVPI again consists of all the EOL's which are incurred from taking the optimal action in the *wrong* circumstances. Here, this means *using* the fixture when the fraction defective is below 0.0533, i.e. at 0.02 and 0.05. Thus

$$\text{EVPI} = 1200(0.0533 - 0.02)(0.40) + 1200(0.0533 - 0.05)(0.30)$$

$$= 40(0.40) + 4(0.30) = \$17.20 \quad Ans.$$

In this case the result can be obtained more conveniently by using Method 2 directly, but Method 3 is the basis for more advanced analysis (Chapter 13).

Next is an example of a *many-action* problem, in which the optimization is over a decision variable with many values.

EXAMPLE 10.2. A certain product has the following demand distribution, recorded over 200 days:

Demand, units	5	6	7	8	9
Number of Days	20	40	80	30	30

The units are bought for \$2 each and sold for \$5; they spoil if not sold. Find the optimal initial inventory, the optimal expected profit and the EVPI. (Note: This is the "newsboy" or "crash sales" problem.)

Method 1. Payoff Table.

This is presented as Table 10-3.

Table 10-3

Event	$P(E)$	ACT 5	6	7	8	9	ACT 5	6	7	8	9	EPC
		CP					EP					
5	0.10	15	13	11	9	7	1.50	1.30	1.10	0.90	0.70	1.50
6	0.20	15	18	16	14	12	3.00	3.60	3.20	2.80	2.40	3.60
7	0.40	15	18	21	19	17	6.00	7.20	8.40	7.60	6.80	8.40
8	0.15	15	18	21	24	22	2.25	2.70	3.15	3.60	3.30	3.60
9	0.15	15	18	21	24	27	2.25	2.70	3.15	3.60	4.05	4.05
TOTALS	1.00						15.00	17.50	19.00*	18.50	17.25	21.15

1. We are given that on 20 of 200 days, 5 units were sold; on 80 days, 7 were sold; and so on. This is turned into a probability distribution $P(E)$ by dividing "number of days" by the total number of days, i.e. 200.

2. The left part of the table lists the conditional payoffs (CP) for "acts," i.e. for decisions to stock 5, 6, 7, 8 or 9 units, and for "events," i.e. for actual demands of 5, 6, 7, 8 or 9 units. Under Act 5, for instance, the 5 units sold have a payoff of $5(5 - 2) = \$15$ and this is the same even if more items should be demanded. For Act 6, if only 5 units are sold, the payoff is $5(5 - 2) - (1 \times 2) = \$13$, because the sixth unit is wasted. If 6 or more are demanded, the payoff is $6(5 - 2) = \$18$.

3. The right part of the table lists the expected payoffs (EP), arranged in the same way. Each row is obtained by multiplying the corresponding CP row by the probability $P(E)$, e.g. for Event 6, 15, 18, 16, 14 and 12 are multiplied in turn by 0.20, giving \$3.00, \$3.60, \$3.20, \$2.80 and \$2.40. All EP's are totaled and the optimal value, EMV*, is seen to be \$19.00 at Act 7, i.e. a decision to stock 7 items. *Ans.*

4. In each row of the EP table, the maximum EP is italicized. This is the amount which would be realized if the demand were known in advance; then 5 items would be stocked for a demand 5, 6 for a demand 6, and so on. The total of these maxima is the *expected profit under certainty* (EPC), which is shown in the right-hand column to be $21.15. From this we have, analogous to (*10.2*),

$$\text{EVPI} = \text{EPC} - \text{EMV*} \qquad\qquad (10.5)$$

Thus, if we knew the demand in advance, we could gain a further $21.15 - 19.00 = \$2.15$. *Ans.*

Method 2. Opportunity Loss Table.

This is presented as Table 10-4.

Table 10-4

Event	P(E)	ACT 5	6	7	8	9	ACT 5	6	7	8	9
		COL					EOL				
5	0.10	0	2	4	6	8	0	0.20	0.40	0.60	0.80
6	0.20	3	0	2	4	6	0.60	0	0.40	0.80	1.20
7	0.40	6	3	0	2	4	2.40	1.20	0	0.80	1.60
8	0.15	9	6	3	0	2	1.35	0.90	0.45	0	0.30
9	0.15	12	9	6	3	0	1.80	1.35	0.90	0.45	0
TOTALS	1.00						6.15	3.65	2.15*	2.65	3.90

1. The left portion of Table 10-4 presents the *conditional opportunity losses* (COL). They can be obtained from Table 10-3 by subtracting each entry in the row from the highest one in that row. Thus, for Event 8, Act 5 is $24 - 15 = 9$, Act 6 is $24 - 18 = 6$, etc., until Act 9 which is $24 - 22 = 2$. One can, however, proceed from first principles. If demand and act are equal, the best possible situation exists and there are no losses; hence the zero diagonal. Above it are the cases of "overage," where $2 is wasted for each item unsold. Thus, for Act 8 and Event 6, 2 items are left over and the loss is $\$2 \times 2 = \$4$. Below the diagonal we have "underage," i.e. for each item which could have been sold, there is a lost profit of $5 - 2 = \$3$. (Note that this assumes that only the one sale is lost, e.g. the customer is not lost permanently.)

2. The *expected opportunity loss* (EOL) is obtained from the COL by multiplying each COL by its respective $P(E)$. The lowest opportunity loss is the EVPI, which is $2.15 as before.

3. The EPC is readily obtained by multiplying the expected sales volume $\bar{n}$ by the profit per item, i.e. by $3. The EPC is thus

$$\text{EPC} = 3[5(0.1) + 6(0.2) + 7(0.4) + 8(0.15) + 9(0.15)] = 3(7.05) = \$21.15$$

as before. The computation of $\bar{n}$ follows the same model as that for $\bar{p}$, see (*10.4*).

In summary, Methods 1 and 2 both give an optimal stock of 7 units, EMV* = $19.00 and EVPI = $2.15.

STEPWISE OR TABULAR METHODS WITH FORMAL DISTRIBUTIONS

It is possible to use the same methods of solution when the prior distribution, rather than being empirical as in Examples 10.1 and 10.2, is one of the formal distributions defined in Chapter 9. It is especially easy to do so in the case of discrete distributions.

EXAMPLE 10.3. A certain machine is bought which has a critical part that occasionally needs replacement. If the part is bought initially with the machine, it costs $10,000. On the other hand, if not enough parts are on hand and one has to be reordered for a later breakdown, what with the need for the supplier to set up his machines and the delay and lost production, the cost of such an incident is $120,000. Based on experience with similar machines, an average of 1.4 parts is believed to be required. How many parts should actually be bought? What is the cost of uncertainty?

It is proper to assume a Poisson distribution for the parts requirements with $m = 1.4$. Appendix D gives:

c	0	1	2	3	4	5	6	7
$P(X \leq c \mid m = 1.4)$	0.247	0.592	0.833	0.946	0.986	0.997	0.999	1.000
$P(X = c \mid m = 1.4)$	0.247	0.345	0.241	0.113	0.040	0.011	0.002	0.001

The probabilities of exactly 0, 1, 2, etc., parts being needed are obtained as the successive differences in the tabulated cumulative Poisson distribution. Table 10-5 is then prepared. Above the zero diagonal we have "overage," i.e. parts bought which are not needed, at $10,000 each. Thus, for Stock 7 and Need 5, the

Table 10-5

Need (c)	$P(c \mid m)$	Stock 0	1	2	3	4	5	6	7
					COL, $ thousands				
0	0.247	0	10	20	30	40	50	60	70
1	0.345	110	0	10	20	30	40	50	60
2	0.241	220	110	0	10	20	30	40	50
3	0.113	330	220	110	0	10	20	30	40
4	0.040	440	330	220	110	0	10	20	30
5	0.011	550	440	330	220	110	0	10	20
6	0.002	660	550	440	330	220	110	0	10
7	0.001	770	660	550	440	330	220	110	0

entry is $10,000 \times 2 = $20,000. Below the diagonal we have "underage," i.e. there are not enough parts and one or more breakdowns occur, for each of which the loss is $120,000 minus the $10,000 for the part which we should have had on hand but did not. The *avoidable* amount is thus $110,000 for each part short; e.g. for Stock 3 and Need 6, the COL is $110,000 \times 3 = $330,000. The EOL is given as Table 10-6 It is seen that three parts should be bought, at an EVPI of $24,640. *Ans.*

Table 10-6

Need	Stock 0	1	2	3	4	5	6	7
				EOL, $ thousands				
0	0	2.47	4.94	7.41	9.88	12.35	14.82	17.29
1	37.95	0	3.45	6.90	10.35	13.80	17.25	20.70
2	53.02	26.51	0	2.41	4.82	7.23	9.64	12.05
3	37.29	24.86	12.43	0	1.13	2.26	3.39	4.52
4	17.60	13.20	8.80	4.40	0	0.40	0.80	1.20
5	6.05	4.84	3.63	2.42	1.21	0	0.11	0.22
6	1.32	1.10	0.88	0.66	0.44	0.22	0	0.02
7	0.77	0.66	0.55	0.44	0.33	0.22	0.11	0
TOTALS	154.00	73.64	34.68	24.64*	28.16	36.48	46.12	56.00

Actually, as shown in Chapter 13, there are shorter methods based on the most important statistical distributions, which enable us to compute the best decision and the various measures associated with it without going through a procedure like the one in Example 10.3.

MORE COMPLEX DECISIONS

Decision Tree Diagrams.

EXAMPLE 10.4. In Example 10.1 it was specified that if the fixture is used, the resulting product is always of the best quality (here 0.02 defective). We might instead have specified that it is always **perfect**, resulting in a conditional cost with fixture of $40 rather than $64. Suppose, however, that the use of the fixture results in another distribution for fraction defective p, as follows:

p	0.02	0.08	0.12
$P(p)$	0.7	0.2	0.1

All other conditions remain the same. Find the best action and the cost of the optimal policy.

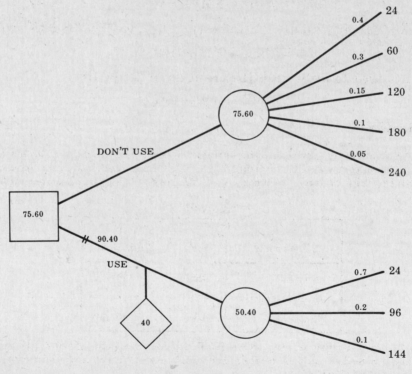

Fig. 10-1

It is helpful to represent the decision process by means of a tree diagram. The square at the junction in Fig. 10-1 indicates that a *decision* must be made there. The circles at the junctions show that an *event* takes place there, i.e. that one of several outcomes is realized, with the probabilities indicated. The diamond shows an *additional input*, in this case the cost of the fixture, or $40.

On the right margin appear all the conditional costs. The ones for the DON'T USE branch are seen to be the same as in the solution to Example 10.1. The expected cost is again $75.60, obtained in Table 10-1. We proceed the same way on the USE branch: The CC's are again ($1200)$p$, which gives $24, $96 and $144 for $p = 0.02$, 0.08 and 0.12 respectively. Then

$$EC = 24(0.7) + 96(0.2) + 144(0.1) = \$50.40$$

Alternatively, $\bar{p} = (0.02)(0.7) + (0.08)(0.2) + (0.12)(0.1) = 0.042$

and $$EC = 1200(0.042) = \$50.40$$

We must add the $40 for the fixture to this expected loss from having defectives even with the fixture, obtaining a total of $90.40 as indicated. We thus have a choice between an expected opportunity loss of $75.60 without the fixture and $90.40 with it. We put a double bar across the USE branch to show that it is a wrong choice; the EMV* is $75.60.

Preposterior Analysis Based on Surveys.

Example 10.5 introduces the concept of purchasing information in order to improve the decision-making process. The example is virtually "standard" of its type. The decision is whether or not to take the survey and, if the survey is taken, how to react to the results it can give, e.g. whether or not to go ahead with the project, given the survey result. Such an evaluation of a survey before it is taken is called *preposterior analysis*.

In problems of this type, the expected payoff associated with the best action will, as usual, be denoted EMV*. Now, if *without* the survey the optimal expected payoff is EMV_n (the n standing for "no survey") and if *with* the survey it is EMV_s, then clearly the EMV* is the *larger* of EMV_n and the excess of EMV_s over the cost of the survey:

$$EMV^* = \max(EMV_n, EMV_s - CS) \tag{10.6}$$

where CS = cost of survey. With EMV* defined by *(10.6)*, the EVPI will be given by *(10.5)* as

$$EVPI_1 = EPC - EMV^*$$

The subscript 1 is used to distinguish the preposterior EVPI from

$$EVPI_0 = EPC - EMV_n$$

which is the prior EVPI.

EXAMPLE 10.5. A company is considering the introduction of a new product. The marketing manager foresees three kinds of outcomes θ of the decision to go ahead, i.e. a good, indifferent or poor market. His estimates of the probabilities of these outcomes and of the corresponding conditional payoffs are shown in Table 10-7.

Table 10-7

Outcome, θ	$P(\theta)$	CP, $ millions
θ_1 (good)	0.25	+15
θ_2 (indifferent)	0.30	+1
θ_3 (poor)	0.45	−6

It is possible to buy a survey for $600,000. While he does not know the predictive accuracy of the survey, he does have a record of its past performance (Table 10-8). What is the best course of action and the expected payoff associated with it?

Table 10-8

	ABOUT PRODUCTS THAT TURNED OUT TO BE		
	θ_1 (good)	θ_2 (indifferent)	θ_3 (poor)
SURVEY HAD CONCLUDED S_1 (good)	0.65	0.25	0.10
S_2 (indifferent)	0.25	0.45	0.15
S_3 (poor)	0.10	0.30	0.75
TOTALS	1.00	1.00	1.00

The probabilities given in Table 10-8 are P(survey result S | product outcome θ). To obtain the expectations of product performance, however, we require $P(\theta \mid S)$, e.g. the probability of getting a good product outcome when the survey result had been good, rather than the chance of having had a good survey result when the product had actually turned out to be good. To convert the given set of conditional probabilities, $P(S \mid \theta)$, into the ones we need, $P(\theta \mid S)$, Bayes' theorem, (8.17), is applied in a tabular form.

1. Obtain the joint probabilities $P(\theta \cap S) = P(S \mid \theta) \, P(\theta)$ as in Table 10-9. Here the first column is 0.25 times the first column of Table 10-8, etc.

Table 10-9

	θ_1 (good)	θ_2 (indifferent)	θ_3 (poor)	Marginal Probability $P(S)$
S_1 (good)	0.1625	0.075	0.0450	0.2825
S_2 (indifferent)	0.0625	0.135	0.0675	0.2650
S_3 (poor)	0.0250	0.090	0.3375	0.4525
Marginal Probability $P(\theta)$	0.2500	0.300	0.4500	1.0000

2. Obtain the other set of conditional probabilities,

$$P(\theta \mid S) = \frac{P(\theta \cap S)}{P(S)}$$

as in Table 10-10. Here the first row is equal to the first row of Table 10-9 divided by 0.2825, etc.

Table 10-10

	θ_1 (good)	θ_2 (indifferent)	θ_3 (poor)	TOTALS
S_1 (good)	0.575	0.266	0.159	1.000
S_2 (indifferent)	0.236	0.509	0.255	1.000
S_3 (poor)	0.055	0.199	0.746	1.000

3. Lay out the decision tree (Fig. 10-2). There are two stages of decisions. The first is whether or not to take the survey (SURVEY or NO SURVEY); the second is whether or not to develop the product (YES or NO). The decision to take the survey is followed by the three outcomes of the survey itself. Each of them in turn has different payoffs, depending on whether a decision is made to develop or not to do so. The decision not to develop is taken to have a payoff of zero. Enter the original conditional payoffs at the extreme right, and the given or computed probabilities where appropriate. Note that the marginal probabilities $P(S)$ computed in Table 10-9 must be used for the total probabilities of getting a specified survey outcome—"good," "indifferent" or "poor."

4. Determine the payoffs and carry them back toward the origin, employing *backward induction*. First obtain expectations for every YES decision. For the YES decision under NO SURVEY,

$$\text{EP} = (15)(0.25) + (1)(0.30) + (-6)(0.45) = 1.35$$

The EP's for the YES decisions under SURVEY are obtained by multiplying each column of Table 10-10 by the CP, i.e.

$$\text{EP} = \text{CP} \times P(\theta \mid S)$$

as shown in Table 10-11. The row sums of Table 10-11 are then the expected payoffs given the three survey results.

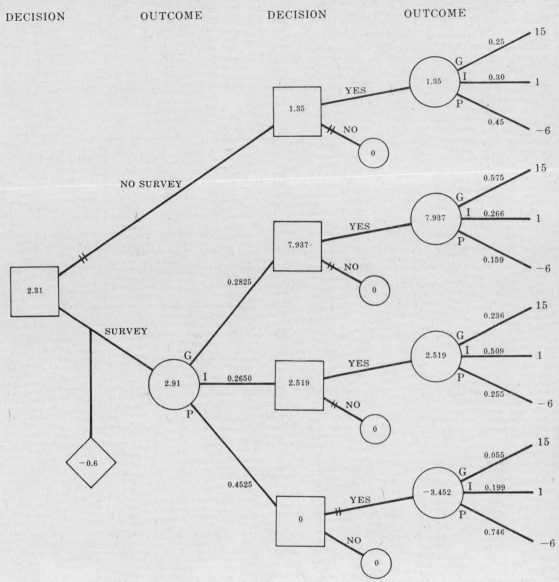

Fig. 10-2

Table 10-11

	θ_1	θ_2	θ_3	EP of YES given S
	CP = 15	CP = 1	CP = −6	
S_1	8.625	0.266	−0.954	7.937
S_2	3.540	0.509	−1.530	2.519
S_3	0.825	0.199	−4.476	−3.452

5. For survey results "good" and "indifferent," bar off the NO branches because the expected YES payoffs are greater than zero. For the result "poor" bar off the YES branch because its expected payoff is negative. Enter the "surviving" payoffs—7.937, 2.519 and 0—in the three squares. Find the expected payoff of SURVEY:

$$\text{EMV}_s = (7.937)(0.2825) + (2.519)(0.2650) + (0)(0.4525) = 2.91$$

6. The net payoff of SURVEY is 2.91 less the cost of the survey: $2.91 - 0.6 = 2.31$. Since this is more than $\text{EMV}_n = 1.35$, bar off the branch NO SURVEY.

7. The result is: Take the survey. If it shows "good" or "indifferent," develop product; if "poor," do not develop. $\text{EMV}^* = \$2,310,000$. *Ans.*

We can also calculate the EPC and use it for an important new concept. If we knew the condition of the market in advance, we would develop if the market were good or indifferent, and not develop if the market were poor. Hence,

$$\text{EPC} = (15)(0.25) + (1)(0.30) + (0)(0.45) = 4.05$$

The difference between the EPC and the optimal expected payoff, either with or without a survey, can be interpreted as the *expected cost of uncertainty* (ECU) in either case. Thus, with no survey,

$$\text{ECU}_n = \text{EPC} - \text{EMV}_n = \text{EVPI}_0$$

while with a survey,

$$\text{ECU}_s = \text{EPC} - \text{EMV}_s$$

The difference between ECU_n and ECU_s represents the amount of uncertainty which has been removed by making the survey; it is also called the *expected value of sampling information* (EVSI). We have:

$$\text{EVSI} = \text{ECU}_n - \text{ECU}_s = \text{EMV}_s - \text{EMV}_n \qquad (10.7)$$

i.e. the EVSI is the difference of the EMV's with and without the survey. In the present case

$$\text{EVSI} = 2.91 - 1.35 = 1.56$$

To obtain the *expected net gain from sampling* (ENGS) we subtract the cost of the sample, CS, from the EVSI:

$$\text{ENGS} = \text{EVSI} - \text{CS} \qquad (10.8)$$

Here $$\text{ENGS} = 1.56 - 0.6 = 0.96$$

In Example 10.5 a tabulation of survey reliability under different conditions was given (Table 10-8). It may happen in two-way decisions (e.g. sales can be "good" or "poor" and the survey can indicate "good" or "poor") that the survey is simply described as being "p percent reliable." In that case, Table 10-8 for $P(S \mid \theta)$ is replaced by Table 10-12, and the rest of the work is carried out as before.

Table 10-12

		ABOUT PRODUCTS THAT TURNED OUT TO BE	
		θ_1 (good)	θ_2 (poor)
SURVEY HAD CONCLUDED	S_1 (good)	p	$1 - p$
	S_2 (poor)	$1 - p$	p
	TOTALS	1	1

Another use of preposterior analysis is in choosing between different kinds of surveys. See Chapter 12.

Matrix Methods.

In Example 10.5 several calculations can be interpreted as matrix and vector multiplications. For example, in Step 4 the EP for NO SURVEY is

$$\overset{P(\theta)}{(0.25 \ \ 0.30 \ \ 0.45)} \overset{\text{CP}}{\begin{pmatrix} 15 \\ 1 \\ -6 \end{pmatrix}} = (0.25)(15) + (0.30)(1) + (0.45)(-6) \overset{\text{EP}}{=} 1.35$$

The EP's for SURVEY can be obtained by multiplying the matrix of $P(\theta \mid S)$ probabilities by the CP vector:

$$
\begin{matrix} P(\theta \mid S) \end{matrix}
\begin{pmatrix} 0.575 & 0.266 & 0.159 \\ 0.236 & 0.509 & 0.255 \\ 0.055 & 0.199 & 0.746 \end{pmatrix}
\begin{matrix} CP \end{matrix}
\begin{pmatrix} 15 \\ 1 \\ -6 \end{pmatrix}
=
\begin{pmatrix} 8.625 + 0.266 - 0.954 \\ 3.540 + 0.509 - 1.530 \\ 0.825 + 0.199 - 4.476 \end{pmatrix}
=
\begin{matrix} EP \end{matrix}
\begin{pmatrix} 7.937 \\ 2.519 \\ -3.452 \end{pmatrix}
$$

The optimal payoff is obtained by replacing the negative entry in the EP vector by zero (i.e. by DON'T DEVELOP), and the final payoff is

$$
\begin{matrix} P(S) \end{matrix}
(0.2825 \quad 0.2650 \quad 0.4525)
\begin{matrix} EP^* \end{matrix}
\begin{pmatrix} 7.937 \\ 2.519 \\ 0 \end{pmatrix}
=
\begin{matrix} EMV_s \end{matrix}
2.91
$$

which is the previous result. This method is especially useful for more complex decisions in which the tree diagram might be awkward.

EXAMPLE 10.6. A company is considering an expansion of its plant in response to the possibility of a substantial increase in sales. But this is not certain; the probabilities of good, fair and poor markets are 0.20, 0.35 and 0.45 respectively. If the firm expands in the face of poor business it will have losses due to operating below the breakeven point of the new plant. If it does not expand and the market increases it will lose profit. The payoffs are given by Table 10-13. The company could decide on the basis of this prior information, but it has available for purchase at \$200,000 a survey which has produced the past results indicated in Table 10-14. Find the optimal decision, the EMV*, the EPC, the $EVPI_1$, the EVSI and the ENGS.

Table 10-13

Market	Expansion, \$ millions		
	A_1 (no)	A_2 (small)	A_3 (large)
θ_1 (good)	5	10	16
θ_2 (fair)	4	6	-3
θ_3 (poor)	3	-2	-9

Table 10-14

	WHEN MARKET TURNED OUT		
	θ_1 (good)	θ_2 (fair)	θ_3 (poor)
S_1 (good)	0.65	0.15	0.10
S_2 (fair)	0.25	0.60	0.20
S_3 (poor)	0.10	0.25	0.70

SURVEY HAD PREDICTED

The first decision is SURVEY or NO SURVEY. If SURVEY, there are three possible results S, for each of which one of three further decisions A must be made. This means a total of nine decisions, each of which can result in three final outcomes, "good," "fair" and "poor." Thus there are 27 possibilities under SURVEY. In addition, if the decision is NO SURVEY, there are nine more outcomes. Thus there would be 36 branches on the right-hand side of the tree diagram. This is somewhat unwieldy and the matrix method is much more compact.

1. Find the prior EP's by multiplying the prior probability vector, $P(\theta)$, by the CP matrix (Table 10-13):

$$(0.20 \quad 0.35 \quad 0.45)\begin{pmatrix} 5 & 10 & 16 \\ 4 & 6 & -3 \\ 3 & -2 & -9 \end{pmatrix} = (3.75 \quad 3.2 \quad -1.9)$$

Note that the computations are the same as in Example 10.2, in spite of the different layout.

2. The prior decision is thus A_1, NO EXPANSION, for a payoff (EMV$_n$) of \$3.75 million. The EPC is given by

$$\text{EPC} = (0.20 \quad 0.35 \quad 0.45)\begin{pmatrix} 16 \\ 6 \\ 3 \end{pmatrix} = (0.2)(16) + (0.35)(6) + (0.45)(3) = 6.65$$

i.e. by multiplying the prior probability vector by a vector of the highest entries in the rows of the CP matrix—again as in previous examples.

3. Find the required $P(\theta \mid S)$ from the given $P(S \mid \theta)$ as in Steps 1 and 2 of Example 10.5. See Tables 10-15 and 10-16.

Table 10-15. $P(\theta \cap S) = P(S \mid \theta)\, P(\theta)$

	θ_1	θ_2	θ_3	$P(S)$
S_1	0.13	0.0525	0.045	0.2275
S_2	0.05	0.2100	0.090	0.3500
S_3	0.02	0.0875	0.315	0.4225
$P(\theta)$	0.20	0.3500	0.450	1.0000

Table 10-16. $P(\theta \mid S) = P(\theta \cap S)/P(S)$

	θ_1	θ_2	θ_3	TOTALS
S_1	0.571	0.231	0.198	1.000
S_2	0.143	0.600	0.257	1.000
S_3	0.047	0.207	0.746	1.000

4. Each row of the conditional probability matrix $P(\theta \mid S)$, Table 10-16, must be used with each column of the conditional payoff matrix, Table 10-13, to get the EP of each combination of three survey results S with each action A. This is done by multiplying the $P(\theta \mid S)$ matrix (of orientation $S \times \theta$) by the CP matrix (of orientation $\theta \times A$), i.e. to be able to multiply the matrices, the θ's must correspond to columns in the first matrix and rows in the second.

$$\begin{pmatrix} 0.571 & 0.231 & 0.198 \\ 0.143 & 0.600 & 0.257 \\ 0.047 & 0.207 & 0.746 \end{pmatrix} \begin{pmatrix} 5 & 10 & 16 \\ 4 & 6 & -3 \\ 3 & -2 & -9 \end{pmatrix}$$

$$= \begin{pmatrix} 2.855 + 0.924 + 0.594 & 5.710 + 1.386 - 0.396 & 9.136 - 0.693 - 1.782 \\ 0.715 + 2.4 + 0.771 & 1.430 + 3.6 - 0.514 & 2.288 - 1.8 - 2.313 \\ 0.235 + 0.828 + 2.238 & 0.470 + 1.242 - 1.492 & 0.752 - 0.621 - 6.714 \end{pmatrix}$$

$$= \begin{matrix} & A_1 & A_2 & A_3 \\ S_1 & 4.373 & 6.700^* & 6.661 \\ S_2 & 3.886 & 4.516^* & -1.825 \\ S_3 & 3.301^* & 0.220 & -6.583 \end{matrix}$$

The S's and A's have been added only to facilitate the interpretation of the product.

5. From the matrix product pick out the highest payoff corresponding to each survey result S and note the corresponding A. These are the starred entries above. Thus we have the following decision rules:

   (i) If survey says "good" or "fair" (S_1 or S_2), make small expansion (A_2).

   (ii) If survey says "poor" (S_3), do not expand (A_1).

6. To find out whether to take the survey at all, form the vector of the optimal payoffs from Step 5 and multiply it by the $P(S)$ vector:

$$(0.2275 \quad 0.3500 \quad 0.4225)\begin{pmatrix}6.700 \\ 4.516 \\ 3.301\end{pmatrix} = 4.50 = EMV_s$$

The net payoff with survey is thus $4.5 - 0.2 = \$4.3$ million, compared to $\$3.75$ million for the prior action without the survey (Step 2). It follows that the survey should be undertaken. We have:

$$EVPI_1 = 6.65 - 4.3 = 2.35$$

$$EVSI = 4.50 - 3.75 = 0.75$$

$$ENGS = 0.75 - 0.2 = 0.55$$

7. Recapitulation of results:

  (a) Take survey.

  (b) If survey results are "good" or "fair," make small expansion.

  (c) If survey result is "poor," do not expand.

  (d) $EMV^* = \$4.3$ million; $EPC = \$6.65$ million; $EVPI_1 = \$2.35$ million; $EVSI = \$750,000$; $ENGS = \$550,000$

Solved Problems

STEPWISE OR TABULAR METHODS

10.1. An investor has $\$100,000$ which he could place in bond, blue chip or high risk portfolios. Depending on the state of the economy, he judges the payoffs to be as shown in Table 10-17. He further judges the probabilities of the states of the economy to be: good, 0.2; stagnant, 0.4; bad, 0.4. What is the best investment to make? What is the EVPI?

Table 10-17

State of Economy	Bonds	Blue Chips	High Risk
Good	+15%	+25%	+150%
Stagnant	+6%	+10%	−20%
Bad	−5%	−30%	−60%

Prepare the payoff table (Table 10-18).

Table 10-18

Event	$P(E)$	Bonds	B. C.	H. R.	Bonds	B. C.	H. R.	EPC
		ACT			ACT			
		CP			EP			EPC
Good	0.2	15,000	25,000	150,000	3,000	5,000	*30,000*	30,000
Stagnant	0.4	6,000	10,000	−20,000	2,400	*4,000*	−8,000	4,000
Bad	0.4	−5,000	−30,000	−60,000	*−2,000*	−12,000	−24,000	−2,000
TOTALS	1.0				3,400*	−3,000	−2,000	32,000

It is seen that the best investment is in bonds, and

$$\text{EVPI} = 32,000 - 3,400 = \$28,600 \quad Ans.$$

Note that this value for EVPI is correct only in the case where one of the three specified choices must be made. In practice, it is usually possible to do nothing, or invest in a savings account, etc. Thus, in computing the EPC we would have no negative items, but then the whole problem would have to be evaluated with four, instead of three, choices.

10.2. A manufacturer has a choice of either making 9000 of a certain part at a setup cost of $50,000 plus $12 each, or buying them at $20 each. Unfortunately, while the bought product is always satisfactory, the product he makes is often defective, having a distribution of the fraction defective p as follows:

p	0	0.10	0.20	0.30	0.40
$P(p)$	0.10	0.20	0.30	0.25	0.15

If a defective part is installed and discovered on final test of the product, it must be corrected at a cost of $10 each. Should the firm decide to make or buy? What is the EVPI?

Method 1. Payoff Table.

This is presented as Table 10-19.

Table 10-19

p	$P(p)$	CC	EC	CC	EC	ECC
		MAKE		BUY		
0	0.10	158,000	15,800*	180,000	18,000	15,800
0.10	0.20	167,000	33,400*	180,000	36,000	33,400
0.20	0.30	176,000	52,800*	180,000	54,000	52,800
0.30	0.25	185,000	46,250	180,000	45,000*	45,000
0.40	0.15	194,000	29,100	180,000	27,000*	27,000
TOTALS	1.00		177,350*		180,000	174,000

Thus the decision is to make, with savings of $180,000 - 177,350 = \$2650$ and

$$\text{EVPI} = 177,350 - 174,000 = \$3350 \quad Ans.$$

Note that the CC for $p = 0$ is $50,000 + 9000(12) = 158,000$; for $p = 0.10$, 10 percent of the parts, or 900, must be replaced at \$10 each. Thus $\text{CC} = 158,000 + 900(10) = 167,000$.

In the BUY column the conditional cost is $9000(20) = \$180,000$ for all values of p. This makes the expected cost \$180,000 times the sum of all p's, or $180,000(1)$.

Method 2. Opportunity Loss Table.

Table 10-20

p	$P(p)$	MAKE COL	MAKE EOL	BUY COL	BUY EOL
0	0.10	0	0	22,000	2,200
0.10	0.20	0	0	13,000	2,600
0.20	0.30	0	0	4,000	1,200
0.30	0.25	5,000	1,250	0	0
0.40	0.15	14,000	2,100	0	0
TOTALS	1.00		EVPI = 3,350		6,000

The result is identical to that of Method 1.

10.3. A manufacturer can make a certain part at a setup cost of \$50,000 plus \$12 each. He needs 9000, but proposes to make more so as to allow for defective product. The distribution of the fraction defective p is given by

p	0	0.1	0.2	0.3	0.4
$P(p)$	0.10	0.20	0.30	0.25	0.15

If a defective part is installed he has to buy a replacement (assumed good). Such a defective part costs \$5 each to remove and the replacement part costs \$25 each. About how many should the manufacturer make, or should he buy them all? What is EVPI?

The minimum number to be made is 9000 and the maximum is 15,000 (which, if 40 percent defective, will yield exactly 9000 good parts). In Table 10-21 we compute the CC's for 9,000, 11,000,

Table 10-21

p	$P(p)$	MAKE 9,000	MAKE 11,000	MAKE 13,000	MAKE 15,000	BUY 9,000
0	0.10	158,000	182,000	206,000	230,000	225,000
0.1	0.20	185,000	182,000	206,000	230,000	225,000
0.2	0.30	212,000	188,000	206,000	230,000	225,000
0.3	0.25	239,000	221,000	206,000	230,000	225,000
0.4	0.15	266,000	254,000	242,000	230,000	225,000

13,000 and 15,000, as well as for the decision BUY 9000. As a sample calculation, consider MAKE 11,000 and $p = 0.2$. There will be

$$(11,000)(1 - 0.2) = 8800$$

good parts, which is 200 short. These 200 must be replaced at $5 + 25 = \$30$ each. Hence

$$CC = 50,000 + (11,000)(12) + (200)(30) = 188,000$$

The EC's are computed in Table 10-22. We see that MAKE 11,000 is optimal and

$$EVPI = 204,350 - 193,850 = \$10,500 \quad Ans.$$

Table 10-22

p	MAKE 9,000	MAKE 11,000	MAKE 13,000	MAKE 15,000	BUY 9,000	ECC
0	15,800*	18,200	20,600	23,000	22,500	15,800
0.1	37,000	36,400*	41,200	46,000	45,000	36,400
0.2	63,600	56,400*	61,800	69,000	67,500	56,400
0.3	59,750	55,250	51,500*	57,500	56,250	51,500
0.4	39,900	38,100	36,300	34,500	33,750*	33,750
TOTALS	216,050	204,350*	211,400	230,000	225,000	193,850

10.4. A business firm requires 12 salesmen and proposes to train them in a course for which fixed costs (e.g. instructor and room rental) are $5000. Not all trainees finish such a course, however, and the numbers n required to yield 12 passing graduates have the following probabilities $P(n)$:

n	12	13	14	15	16	17	18
$P(n)$	0.10	0.15	0.25	0.25	0.15	0.05	0.05

The course takes six weeks and each trainee is paid $180 a week. If not enough pass, the course must be given again. Determine the optimal size of the starting class and the cost of this optimal policy.

We apply the opportunity loss method. For cases where the course must be repeated, we suppose that the first and second courses together contain the number n of trainees that ought to have been chosen for the first course, and that the two courses together produce exactly 12 passing graduates. Under this simplifying assumption the COL's are as shown in Table 10-23 and the EOL's as in Table 10-24. If, for instance, 16 students are needed ($n = 16$), then any entering class

Table 10-23

n	$P(n)$	Chosen Size of Entering Class 12	13	14	15	16	17	18
12	0.10	0	1080	2160	3240	4320	5400	6480
13	0.15	5000	0	1080	2160	3240	4320	5400
14	0.25	5000	5000	0	1080	2160	3240	4320
15	0.25	5000	5000	5000	0	1080	2160	3240
16	0.15	5000	5000	5000	5000	0	1080	2160
17	0.05	5000	5000	5000	5000	5000	0	1080
18	0.05	5000	5000	5000	5000	5000	5000	0

of less than 16 requires us to train the shortage, whatever its size, in a second course, which costs $5000 to set up. If we start with 16, we have done exactly the right thing and the COL is zero. If we start with 18, the training of two men will be wasted, costing $2 \times 6 \times 180 = \$2160$. From Table 10-24 it is seen that the optimal size is 15, with an EVPI of $2168. *Ans.*

Table 10-24

n	Chosen Size of Entering Class						
	12	13	14	15	16	17	18
12	0	108	216	324	432	540	648
13	750	0	162	324	486	648	810
14	1250	1250	0	270	540	810	1080
15	1250	1250	1250	0	270	540	810
16	750	750	750	750	0	162	324
17	250	250	250	250	250	0	54
18	250	250	250	250	250	250	0
TOTALS	4500	3858	2878	2168*	2228	2950	3726

To obtain the cost of this policy we must compute the "size 15" column of the payoff table (Table 10-25). For a chosen class size of 15, the cost for $n \leqq 15$ is $15(1080) + 5000 = \$21,200$. The cost for $n = 16$ is

21,200 (for the first course)

5,000 (to set up the second course)

1,080 (to pay the single student in the second course)

27,280

For each student above 16, add $1080. From Table 10-25, EMV* = $22,882. *Ans.*

Table 10-25

n	$P(n)$	CC	EC
12	0.10	21,200	2120
13	0.15	21,200	3180
14	0.25	21,200	5300
15	0.25	21,200	5300
16	0.15	27,280	4092
17	0.05	28,360	1418
18	0.05	29,440	1472
TOTALS	1.00		22,882

Alternatively, proceeding as in Example 10.2, we can find the mean number $\bar{n}$ of trainees required. The expected cost under certainty, ECC, is then given by

$\text{ECC} = 5000 + 1080\bar{n}$

$= 5000 + 1080[12(0.10) + 13(0.15) + 14(0.25) + 15(0.25) + 16(0.15) + 17(0.05) + 18(0.05)]$

$= 5000 + 1080(14.55) = 20,714$

To obtain the expected cost, EMV*, we add the cost of uncertainty, i.e. the EVPI:

$\text{EMV*} = 20,714 + 2168 = \$22,882$

10.5. Jack Jones and Jill Smith intend to get married. Xanadu Caterers, Inc. has offered to conduct the wedding reception at \$500 for facilities, band, etc., plus \$18 a couple for the refreshments. Before making the final arrangements, Jack and Jill try to see whether they will come out ahead financially. They estimate the distribution of attendance as:

n, couples	60	80	100	120
$P(n)$	0.15	0.25	0.40	0.20

and the distribution of the value of a couple's gift as

V, dollars	10	15	20	25	50	100
$P(V)$	0.10	0.15	0.25	0.30	0.15	0.05

Assuming that the value of a couple's gift is independent of the number attending, find the expected profit or loss from the event.

The expected number of attendees is

$$\bar{n} = \sum n\,P(n)$$
$$= 60(0.15) + 80(0.25) + 100(0.40) + 120(0.20) = 93 \text{ couples}$$

and the expected value of a gift is

$$\bar{V} = \sum V\,P(V)$$
$$= 10(0.10) + 15(0.15) + 20(0.25) + 25(0.30) + 50(0.15) + 100(0.05) = \$28.25$$

Under the assumption of independence, the expected receipts are simply

$$\bar{n}\bar{V} = (93)(28.25) = \$2627.25$$

Then, since the expected costs are $500 + 18\bar{n} = \$2174$, the expected profit is

$$2627.25 - 2174 = \$453.25 \quad Ans.$$

Alternatively, we can work out the breakeven attendance, n_b, using (1.6):

$$500 + 18n_b = (28.25)n_b$$

$$n_b = \frac{500}{28.25 - 18} = 48.78$$

The profit is then the excess over breakeven attendance times the excess of "revenue" per couple over variable cost per couple, i.e.

$$(93 - 48.78)(28.25 - 18) = \$453.25$$

It could be argued that, in an example like this, value of gift and attendance are not likely to be independent, in that a small wedding may mean closer friends and relatives who might be more generous. In that case, each attendance level n would have its own distribution of V, and thus its mean contribution $\bar{V}_n$. The total collected would then be given by $\sum n\,P(n)\,\bar{V}_n$.

10.6. A certain product has the following demand distribution:

n, units	12	14	16	18	20
$P(n)$	0.15	0.40	0.30	0.10	0.05

The product sells for \$100 but, before the season starts, it can be purchased for \$60. After the season is underway, shortages can be made up at the higher cost of \$75 each.

If any product is left over after the season, it can be liquidated for $40 each.   Find the optimal level of initial inventory, the EMV*, the ECC and the EVPI.

We use the opportunity loss method as in Example 10.2 (Method 2), except that here the opportunity cost of shortage for each unit is not the entire profit but is the difference between the profit on goods bought before the season and goods bought later, i.e. the shortage cost is $75 - 60 = \$15$. Table 10-26 shows that the optimal stock level is 14 units, ECC = $600 and EVPI = $25.50.   *Ans.*

Table 10-26

Event, n	$P(n)$	\multicolumn{5}{STOCK} COL, $					\multicolumn{5}{STOCK} EOL, $					CCC	ECC
		12	14	16	18	20	12	14	16	18	20		
12	0.15	0	40	80	120	160	0	6	12	18	24	480	72
14	0.40	30	0	40	80	120	12	0	16	32	48	560	224
16	0.30	60	30	0	40	80	18	9	0	12	24	640	192
18	0.10	90	60	30	0	40	9	6	3	0	4	720	72
20	0.05	120	90	60	30	0	6	4.5	3	1.5	0	800	40
TOTALS	1.00						45	25.5*	34	63.5	100		600

Furthermore, by *(10.2)*,

$$\text{EMV*} = \text{ECC} + \text{EVPI} = 600 + 25.50 = \$625.50 \quad Ans.$$

10.7. A theatrical producer has to spend $320,000 for fixed costs and then $3000 per night for variable costs.   He expects receipts of $7000 per night.   His expectation of the length of run which will produce such an average level of receipts is:

t, nights	10	50	100	200
$P(t)$	0.15	0.30	0.40	0.15

(a) Should he put on the show?   What is the EMV of the best decision?   (b) If another producer offers $30,000 for the complete rights to the run, should he accept the offer? (c) What is the EVPI?

Method 1. Expected Monetary Value.

(a) For every performance, the contribution to overhead is $7000 - 3000 = \$4000$, which yields Table 10-27 for the action PUT ON SHOW.   Because the EMV for DO NOT PUT ON SHOW is zero, he should put on the show, for an expected payoff of $26,000.   *Ans.*

Table 10-27

t, nights	$P(t)$	CP, $ thousands	EP, $ thousands
10	0.15	$4(10) - 320 = -280$	-42
50	0.30	$4(50) - 320 = -120$	-36
100	0.40	$4(100) - 320 = 80$	32
200	0.15	$4(200) - 320 = 480$	72
		EMV*	26

(b) He should accept the offer of $30,000, which is better than $26,000 and is risk-free.

(c) The EVPI can be found in two ways. The expected payoff under certainty is given by

$$EPC = 32 + 72 = 104$$

i.e. by the sum of the outcomes in those cases in which it *pays* to put on the show (100 and 200 nights).   Then

$$EVPI = EPC - EMV^* = 104 - 26 = 78, \text{ or } \$78,000 \quad Ans.$$

The EVPI can also be found directly, by noting that the EOL for the decision to put on the show when that should *not* be done is given by the losses incurred when the show runs only 10 or 50 nights, i.e. by

$$EVPI = 42 + 36 = 78$$

Method 2. Expected Values.

(a) The expected duration of the run is given by

$$\bar{t} = 10(0.15) + 50(0.30) + 100(0.40) + 200(0.15) = 86.5 \text{ nights}$$

The breakeven value of t, t_b, is given by

$$(7000 - 3000)t_b = 320,000 \quad \text{or} \quad t_b = 80$$

Thus $\bar{t} > t_b$ and the show should be put on. Its EMV is given by

$$EMV^* = 4000(86.5 - 80) = \$26,000$$

as before. The answers for (b) and (c) follow as above.

MORE COMPLEX DECISIONS

10.8. Table 10-28 gives the conditional payoffs and prior probabilities for the events "good," "marginal" and "poor" sales.

Table 10-28

Event, θ	Conditional Payoff, units	Prior Probability, $P(\theta)$
θ_1 (good)	120	0.15
θ_2 (marginal)	−20	0.60
θ_3 (poor)	−40	0.25

A survey, obtainable at a cost of 3 units, has a track record given by Table 10-29.

Table 10-29

		ACTUAL EVENT WAS		
		θ_1 (good)	θ_2 (marginal)	θ_3 (poor)
SURVEY HAD READ	S_1 (good)	0.50	0.25	0.15
	S_2 (marginal)	0.35	0.65	0.20
	S_3 (poor)	0.15	0.10	0.65

Find (a) the proper decision procedure, (b) the EMV*, (c) EVPI₁, (d) EVSI and (e) ENGS.

First, the joint probabilities $P(\theta \cap S)$ are obtained as in Table 10-30, and then the conditional probabilities $P(\theta \mid S)$ are computed as in Table 10-31. Multiplying the columns of Table 10-31 by the respective CP's from Table 10-28, we obtain the expected payoffs for the DEVELOP decisions under SURVEY (Table 10-32). Under the decision NO SURVEY, we have from Table 10-28:

Table 10-30

	θ_1	θ_2	θ_3	$P(S)$
S_1	0.0750	0.15	0.0375	0.2625
S_2	0.0525	0.39	0.0500	0.4925
S_3	0.0225	0.06	0.1625	0.2450
$P(\theta)$	0.1500	0.60	0.2500	1.0000

Table 10-31

	θ_1	θ_2	θ_3	TOTALS
S_1	0.2857	0.5714	0.1429	1.0000
S_2	0.1066	0.7919	0.1015	1.0000
S_3	0.0918	0.2449	0.6633	1.0000

Table 10-32

	θ_1	θ_2	θ_3	EP of DEVELOP given S
S_1	34.284	−11.428	−5.716	17.140
S_2	12.792	−15.838	−4.060	−7.106
S_3	11.016	−4.898	−26.532	−20.414

$$\text{EP for DEVELOP} = (120)(0.15) + (-20)(0.60) + (-40)(0.25) = -4$$

$$\text{EP for DO NOT DEVELOP} = 0 = \text{EMV}_n$$

Next draw the tree diagram (Fig. 10-3), barring off branches with inferior payoffs. Under SURVEY, the EMV is

$$\text{EMV}_s = (17.140)(0.2625) + (0)(0.4925) + (0)(0.2450) = 4.499$$

This is entered in Fig. 10-3 and adjusted for the cost of the survey, yielding a net payoff of $4.499 - 3 = 1.499$, as shown. The final results are then:

(a) SURVEY: if the outcome is S_1, DEVELOP; if S_2 or S_3, DO NOT DEVELOP.

(b)
$$\text{EMV}^* = 1.499$$

(c)
$$\text{EPC} = (120)(0.15) + (0)(0.60) + (0)(0.25) = 18$$

$$\text{EVPI}_1 = \text{EPC} - \text{EMV}^* = 18 - 1.499 = 16.501$$

(d)
$$\text{EVSI} = \text{EMV}_s - \text{EMV}_n = 4.499 - 0 = 4.499$$

(e)
$$\text{ENGS} = \text{EVSI} - \text{CS} = 4.499 - 3 = 1.499$$

10.9. A company is considering the purchase of a new machine. There is also the possibility of rebuilding the existing one or of managing with the old machine without rebuilding. The machines perform differently with the two grades in which the raw material can be classified. Because both the rebuilt and new machines work much faster, they damage the product when the input grade is bad, but when it is good, their speed results in a substantially increased payoff compared to the old machine. The payoff table (entries are in units of $1000) is as follows:

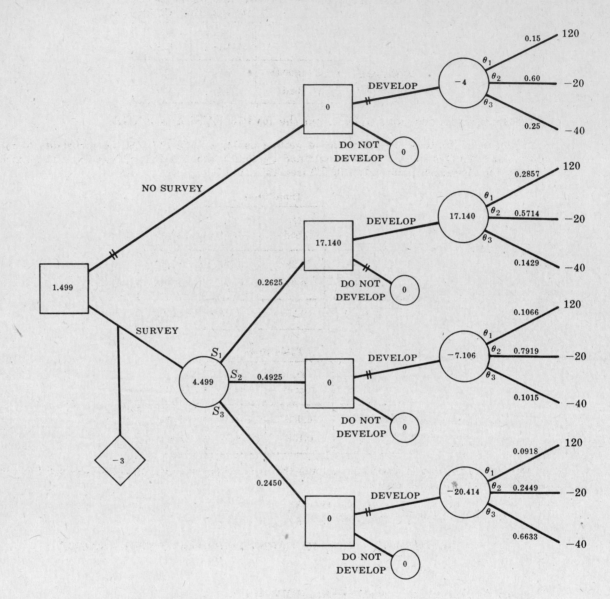

Fig. 10-3

Input Quality	New Machine	Rebuilt Machine	Old Machine
good	30	12	8
bad	−15	3	6

There is a 35 percent chance of getting good raw material. It is also possible to make a preliminary test at a cost of $600 but, unfortunately, it is not infallible. The true quality can be determined only during processing. In the past, the test has been characterized by the conditional probabilities given in Table 10-33.

Table 10-33

		WHEN QUALITY LATER TURNED OUT TO BE	
		Q_1 (good)	Q_2 (bad)
TEST HAD	T_1 (good)	0.8	0.3
INDICATED	T_2 (bad)	0.2	0.7

Find the optimal decision, EMV*, and the EVPI$_1$, EVSI and ENGS.

Given are $P(Q)$, the prior probability of getting quality Q, and $P(T \mid Q)$, the probability of the test result when Q is known. Thus we first find the joint probability $P(T \cap Q)$ (see Table 10-34) and, from it, the conditional probability $P(Q \mid T)$ (see Table 10-35).

Table 10-34

	Q_1 (good)	Q_2 (bad)	$P(T)$
T_1 (good)	0.28	0.195	0.475
T_2 (bad)	0.07	0.455	0.525
$P(Q)$	0.35	0.650	1.000

Table 10-35

	Q_1 (good)	Q_2 (bad)	TOTALS
T_1 (good)	0.589	0.411	1.000
T_2 (bad)	0.133	0.867	1.000

We choose the matrix method to compute the expected payoffs. For no testing, we multiply the $P(Q)$ vector by the payoff matrix:

$$\text{EP} = (0.35 \quad 0.65)\begin{pmatrix} 30 & 12 & 8 \\ -15 & 3 & 6 \end{pmatrix}$$

$$= \big((0.35)(30) + (0.65)(-15) \quad (0.35)(12) + (0.65)(3) \quad (0.35)(8) + (0.65)(6)\big)$$

$$= (0.75 \quad 6.15 \quad 6.7)$$

The prior decision is to use the old machine (EMV$_n = 6.7$).

$$\text{EPC} = (0.35 \quad 0.65)\begin{pmatrix} 30 \\ 6 \end{pmatrix} = (0.35)(30) + (0.65)(6) = 14.4$$

(i.e. if the raw material is good, we use the new machine; if bad, the old one; the rebuilt machine is not optimal).

The EP's with the test are obtained by multiplying the $P(Q \mid T)$ matrix (Table 10-35) by the payoff matrix:

$$\text{EP} = \begin{pmatrix} 0.589 & 0.411 \\ 0.133 & 0.867 \end{pmatrix}\begin{pmatrix} 30 & 12 & 8 \\ -15 & 3 & 6 \end{pmatrix}$$

$$= \begin{pmatrix} (0.589)(30) + (0.411)(-15) & (0.589)(12) + (0.411)(3) & (0.589)(8) + (0.411)(6) \\ (0.133)(30) + (0.867)(-15) & (0.133)(12) + (0.867)(3) & (0.133)(8) + (0.867)(6) \end{pmatrix}$$

$$= \begin{pmatrix} 11.505^* & 8.301 & 7.178 \\ -9.000 & 4.200 & 6.267^* \end{pmatrix}$$

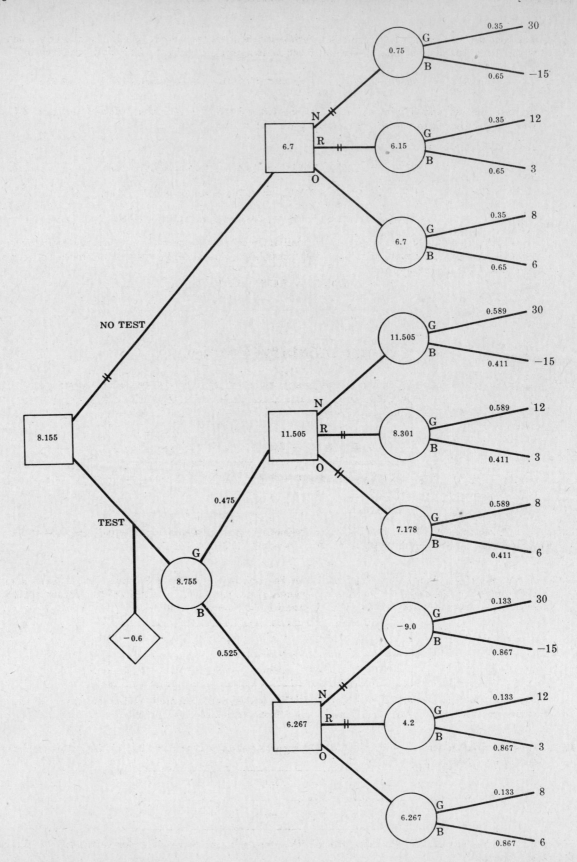

Fig. 10-4

The best action for each test result is asterisked: when the test shows "good," use the new machine; when "bad," the old machine; the rebuilt machine is again not optimal. The EMV_s is given by

$$EMV_s = (0.475 \ 0.525)\begin{pmatrix} 11.505 \\ 6.267 \end{pmatrix} = (0.475)(11.505) + (0.525)(6.267) = 8.755$$

Because the net payoff with the test, $8.755 - 0.6 = 8.155$, exceeds that without the test, 6.7, the rational decision is to use the test, at an EMV* of 8.155. *Ans.*

Furthermore, we find:

$$EVPI_1 = EPC - EMV^* = 14.4 - 8.155 = 6.245 \quad Ans.$$

$$EVSI = EMV_s - EMV_n = 8.755 - 6.7 = 2.055 \quad Ans.$$

$$ENGS = EVSI - CS = 2.055 - 0.6 = 1.455 \quad Ans.$$

Figure 10-4 should enable readers unfamiliar with matrix notation to follow the computation of the expected payoffs. Note that it is also possible to obtain ENGS as the difference between the two final EP's on the left side:

$$ENGS = 8.155 - 6.7 = 1.455$$

Supplementary Problems

10.10. A certain product has a demand characteristic given by the following probability distribution:

D, units	5	6	7	8	9
$P(D)$	0.10	0.20	0.40	0.15	0.15

If profit per unit is $3 and salvage loss per unit $4, find the best action and the EVPI.

Ans.   stock 7; EVPI = $2.95

10.11. Recompute the best action and EVPI in Problem 10.10, if the profit per unit is changed to $6 and the salvage loss per unit to $2.   *Ans.* stock 8; EVPI = $3.10

10.12. A certain product can be bought initially for $4 each and is sold for $7 each. If left over it must be liquidated at $2 each. If there is not enough stock, moreover, it is possible to reorder additional quantities but these then cost $6 each. Demand is distributed as follows:

D, units	5	6	7	8	9
$P(D)$	0.10	0.20	0.35	0.20	0.15

Find (a) the best action, (b) the highest EMV, (c) the expected profit under certainty, (d) the cost of uncertainty.   *Ans.* (a) stock 7; (b) $19.50; (c) $21.30; (d) $1.80

10.13. Given a product with a unit profit of $3, a salvage loss per unit of $2, and the following demand record over 300 days:

Units	5	6	7	8	9
Days	30	60	90	75	45

find (a) the best action, (b) the highest EMV, (c) the expected profit under certainty, (d) the cost of uncertainty.

Ans.   (a) stock either 7 or 8; (b) $19.00 in each case; (c) $21.45; (d) $2.45

10.14. Use the opportunity loss method to check your results in Problem 10.13.

10.15. Use the opportunity loss method to check the results in Problem 10.3.

10.16. Complete the payoff table and check the previous results for Problem 10.4.

10.17. A firm can acquire a spare part for $100 when bought with the machine. If a breakdown occurs later, retooling and delays increase the cost to $1200. On the basis of experience with similar machines, the expected usage is:

Number of Parts, n	0	1	2	3	4
$P(n)$	0.30	0.30	0.20	0.15	0.05

(a) How many parts, if any, should be bought with the machine? (b) What is the expected cost of this policy? (c) What are the costs under certainty and the EVPI? Use the payoff table method and check by means of the opportunity loss method.

Ans. (a) 3 parts; (b) $360; (c) ECC = $135, EVPI = $225

10.18. In Example 10.3, find (a) the expected cost of the optimal policy, (b) the expected cost under certainty. *Ans.* (a) $38,640; (b) $14,000

10.19. A certain part can be produced on two machines. The first is an old machine, which results in the following distribution of fraction defective:

p	0.01	0.05	0.10	0.15	0.20	0.25
$P(p)$	0.30	0.25	0.18	0.15	0.10	0.02

If a defective part is installed in a final assembly, it has to be replaced at a cost of $2.50. The new machine produces parts which are only 1 percent defective, but its cost, allocated over each batch of 1500 parts, adds $250 to the cost. (a) Should the new machine be bought? (b) Find EMV*, ECC and EVPI. *Ans.* (a) yes; (b) $287.50, $187.50, $100

10.20. A machine has a distribution of fraction defective as follows:

p	0.01	0.05	0.10	0.15	0.20
$P(p)$	0.25	0.35	0.18	0.13	0.09

If a defective product is used, it costs $2.50 each to fix. Lot size is 1400. It is possible to install an inspection attachment for $280 per lot which automatically removes all defective product. (a) What is the proper action? Should the inspection attachment be installed? (b) How much is saved by making the least-cost decision? (c) What is the expected cost of the optimal decision? (d) What are the expected cost under certainty and the EVPI?

Ans. (a) do not install; (b) $15.75; (c) $264.25; (d) $182, $82.25

10.21. A lot of 15,000 parts is made on a machine which produces the following fraction defective:

p	0	0.05	0.10	0.15	0.20	0.25
$P(p)$	0.05	0.10	0.20	0.30	0.30	0.05

Each lot costs $80,000 for setup and tooling and each part costs $20 additionally in direct labor and materials. If a defective part is installed, replacement costs a further $15 each. It is possible to buy perfect parts for $28 each. (a) Should one make or buy? (b) How much is saved by making the correct decision? (c) What is the expected cost under certainty? (d) What is the EVPI?

Ans.   (a) make; (b) $7937.50; (c) $409,750; (d) $2315.50

10.22.   A hotel with 60 rooms had the following distribution of occupancy last season:

n	60	55	50	45	40	35
$P(n)$	0.10	0.15	0.32	0.28	0.10	0.05

Its fixed costs are $600 per day and the variable costs are $4 a day per rented room. The rooms rent for $19 a day. A potential lessee offers to pay $140 a day above expenses for the rights to operate the hotel. (a) Should the owner accept the offer? (b) What are his expected net earnings per day?   *Ans.*   (a) yes; (b) $129

10.23.   A bakery has recorded the following sales for rye bread over the last 300 days:

Loaves	25	26	27	28	29	30
Days	15	45	105	90	30	15

Each loaf costs 35¢ to bake. It sells for 50¢ on the day baked and 10¢ thereafter. (a) What is the optimal number of loaves that should be baked? (b) What is the expected monetary value for the optimal number? (c) What is the expected profit under certainty?

Ans.   (a) 27; (b) $3.95; (c) $4.11

10.24.   A certain product can be bought at the beginning of the season at $43 each and is sold at $70. If any shortages develop later, further products can be flown in, but their cost rises to $53 each, with the sales price remaining at $70. If any product is left over at the end of the season it is liquidated at $31 each. The probability distribution of demand is given by

Number Sold, n	10	11	12	13	14
$P(n)$	0.30	0.30	0.20	0.12	0.08

(a) What is the optimal number to stock? (b) What is the EVPI?   *Ans.*   (a) 11; (b) $10.40

10.25.   A certain spare part costs $8000 if bought with the machine and $60,000 if bought later. The probability of needing n spare parts over the life of the machine is

n	0	1	2	3
$P(n)$	0.40	0.35	0.15	0.10

Find (a) the optimal number of spare parts; (b) the expected cost of the optimal policy; (c) the EVPI; (d) the maximum amount which could be charged for a spare part needed later, if there are to be no spare parts bought initially.   *Ans.*   (a) 2; (b) $22,000; (c) $14,400; (d) $13,333

10.26.   In a certain oil drilling project, it is estimated that a successful well will bring in $10 million, while an unsuccessful one would lose $4 million. The chance of a well being successful is estimated at 30 percent. A seismic survey is available for $600,000, whose past accuracy is indicated by the probabilities in Table 10-36.

Table 10-36

		OF WELLS WHICH ACTUALLY WERE	
		gusher	dry
SURVEY HAD SAID	gusher	0.75	0.40
	dry	0.25	0.60

What choices should be made to maximize the return and what is the expected payoff of the optimal decision?   *Ans.*   Take survey; if favorable, drill.   EMV* = $533,000.

10.27.   In Problem 10.26, suppose that the prior probability of success is reduced to 0.20.   All other conditions are the same.   Find the optimal decision and determine its expected payoff.

Ans.   Don't take survey and don't drill; 0.

10.28.   In Problem 10.8, the conditional payoff for a marginal market is changed from −20 to −10 units. All other data are the same.   Find the optimal decison and the EMV*.

Ans.   Take survey; if good or marginal, develop.   EMV* = 3.4 units.

10.29.   A firm must consider the future state (good or bad) of the market for its product when contemplating the purchase of a machine.   The marginal probability of a good market is 0.4, of a bad market 0.6.   The payoffs are given in $(000) as follows:

	new machine	existing machine
good market	20	10
bad market	−6	9

A survey costing $200 is available which has the previous record given in Table 10-37.

Table 10-37

		MARKET TURNED OUT TO HAVE BEEN	
		good	bad
WHEN SURVEY SAID	good	0.60	0.25
	bad	0.40	0.75

Find the best decision sequence and EMV*.

Ans.   Don't take survey; keep existing machine.   EMV* = $9400

10.30.   Suppose that in Problem 10.29 the survey is improved to the extent that its ability to forecast is now given by Table 10-38.

Table 10-38

		MARKET TURNED OUT TO HAVE BEEN	
		good	bad
WHEN SURVEY SAID	good	0.80	0.25
	bad	0.20	0.75

All other data are as before. Find the optimal decision sequence and EMV*.

Ans.   Take survey: if result is good, get new machine; if bad, keep existing machine.
EMV* = $10,152.

10.31. A seismic survey which costs $500,000 can yield any one of five geological findings. Its past accuracy is indicated in Table 10-39.

Table 10-39

	AND THE HOLE HAD TURNED OUT	
	good	dry
I	0.60	0.05
II	0.20	0.10
III	0.10	0.10
IV	0.05	0.25
V	0.05	0.50

SURVEY HAD GIVEN RESULT NUMBER

If the well is dry, there is a loss of $3 million; if there is oil, the profit is $20 million. The prior probability that there will be oil is 0.10. Find the optimal decison and EMV*.

Ans.   Take survey: if result is I or II, drill; otherwise don't drill.   EMV* = $688,000.

10.32. Consider the data for Problem 10.7. The producer has revised his expectations of the run of the show as follows:

t, nights	10	50	100	200
P(t)	0.20	0.40	0.30	0.10

All other data are as before. (a) What is the EMV of the decision PUT ON SHOW? Should he do it?
(b) What is the EVPI?   *Ans.*   (a) −$32,000, no; (b) $72,000

10.33. An operator of a hamburger stand normally clears $65,000 a year but he is in an area liable to be hurt badly if there were to be gasoline rationing. Accordingly, in the Fall of 1973, he postulated four possible forms of rationing and the consequences to his profit, as indicated in Table 10-40.

Table 10-40

Event	Probability	Profit, $(000)
No rationing	0.15	65
1	0.25	40
2	0.30	5
3	0.20	−15
4	0.10	−75

In view of this, he wished to sit out 1974 and lease the place to another operator. One such candidate offered him $12,000 for the year; he would get to keep everything he made above that. Should the owner have accepted this offer? Why?   *Ans.*   Yes, EMV of operation is only $10,750.

Chapter 11

Statistical Estimation and Inference

BASIC PRINCIPLES AND FORMULAS

In this chapter, we deal with the use of samples for the purpose of estimating the characteristics of a population. Further, we present the methods of statistical inference which allow us to quantify errors in terms of specifiable probabilities and to test, again within specifiable probabilities of error, whether a given statement about a variable is true or not.

The basic formulas for estimation appear in Table 11-1. In the first row of the table we deal with the variable X which expresses the characteristic of interest among a certain population. For instance, the population might consist of all electronics firms in New England and the value of X for a firm might be the number of its employees. The mean and variance of X, known as the *population mean* and the *population variance*, are given by the formulas of Col. (2). These measures are generally unknown and must be estimated from the sample, which consists of the X's corresponding to n members picked out at random (see page 108) from the population. The *sample mean* and *sample variance* are computed in Col. (3). Unlike the population mean and variance, these are themselves variables, for they depend upon the sample chosen. Column (4) shows how the sample measures serve to estimate the population measures. Note that for large samples, $\hat{s}^2 \approx s^2$.

The second row of Table 11-1 deals with a special case of the first row—that in which the variable X has the value 1 for πN members of the population and the value 0 for the remaining $(1 - \pi)N$ members. Thus π is the proportion of the population that possess the characteristic of interest (e.g. the proportion defective in a batch of machine parts). Note that in this case the variable X is binomially distributed, with p.d.f. $f_B(X \mid 1, \pi)$. In Col. (3) the sample mean becomes the *sample proportion*, p, and this serves to estimate the population proportion π as shown in Col. (4).

Table 11-1

	Measure (1)	Population (Size N) (2)	Sample (Size n) (3)	Population Estimate Derived from Sample (4)
Variable X	Mean	$\mu = \dfrac{\Sigma X}{N}$	$\overline{X} = \dfrac{\Sigma X}{n}$	$E(\overline{X}) = \mu$ $E(\hat{s}^2) = \sigma^2$
	Variance	$\sigma^2 = \dfrac{\Sigma X^2}{N} - \mu^2$	$s^2 = \dfrac{\Sigma X^2}{n} - \overline{X}^2$	where $\hat{s}^2 = \dfrac{n}{n-1}s^2$
Proportion p where $P(X=1) = \pi$ $P(X=0) = 1 - \pi$	Mean	$\pi = \dfrac{\Sigma X}{N}$	$p = \dfrac{\Sigma X}{n}$	$E(p) = \pi$ $E(\hat{s}^2) = \pi(1-\pi)$
	Variance	$\pi(1-\pi) = \dfrac{\Sigma X^2}{N} - \pi^2$	$s^2 = p(1-p)$	where $\hat{s}^2 = \dfrac{n}{n-1}s^2$

EXAMPLE 11.1. In a survey of spending habits of households in a certain community, a sample of 9 households gives annual expenditures, exclusive of taxes and shelter, as (in thousands of dollars) 4.9, 5.3, 6.5, 5.2, 7.4, 5.4, 6.8, 5.4, 6.3.   Estimate the mean and the variance of these expenditures in the community.

For the sample,

$$\Sigma X = 4.9 + 5.3 + 6.5 + 5.2 + 7.4 + 5.4 + 6.8 + 5.4 + 6.3 = 53.2$$

$$\overline{X} = \frac{53.2}{9} = 5.911 = \$5911 \quad Ans.$$

$$\Sigma X^2 = (4.9)^2 + (5.3)^2 + (6.5)^2 + (5.2)^2 + (7.4)^2 + (5.4)^2 + (6.8)^2 + (5.4)^2 + (6.3)^2 = 320.4$$

$$\hat{s}^2 = \frac{9}{8}\left[\frac{320.4}{9} - (5.911)^2\right] = 0.7425 = 742,500 \text{ dollars}^2 \quad Ans.$$

The results are the best *estimates* of the population measures that can be obtained from the sample results. (Quantities like ΣX^2 may be conveniently obtained by means of the cumulative features of calculators; in future we will not list these computations in detail.)

EXAMPLE 11.2. Distinguish between the *sample variance* and the *variance of the sample mean*. What is the variance of the sample proportion p?

The sample variance, s^2, is computed from the X's composing the sample by means of the formulas given in Table 11-1. On the other hand, the probability distribution of the sample mean, $\overline{X}$, can be derived from the joint distribution of the X's composing the sample, which can in turn be derived from the distribution of the population variable X (even though the form of this last distribution is usually unknown). Relative to its distribution, then, $\overline{X}$ has a variance, $\sigma_{\overline{X}}^2$, and this is the variance of the sample mean. It can be shown that

$$\sigma_{\overline{X}}^2 = \frac{\sigma^2}{n} \tag{11.1}$$

where σ^2 is the population variance. The quantity $\sigma_{\overline{X}} = \sigma/\sqrt{n}$ is called the *standard error* of the sample mean.

In particular, for sampling of proportions, the population variable is binomial, with mean π and variance $\pi(1 - \pi)$. Hence, *(11.1)* gives the variance of p as

$$\sigma_p^2 = \frac{\pi(1 - \pi)}{n} \tag{11.2}$$

THE CENTRAL LIMIT THEOREM

If a sample of size n is taken from a population with finite mean μ and finite variance σ^2 which has *any* statistical distribution, then, as n increases, the distribution of the sample mean $\overline{X}$ tends toward a normal distribution with mean μ and variance $\sigma_{\overline{X}}^2 = \sigma^2/n$. Equivalently, the distribution of $z = (\overline{X} - \mu)/(\sigma/\sqrt{n})$ tends toward the standard normal distribution (mean 0 and variance 1) tabulated in Appendix B.

This is a very important result which serves as the basis of much of statistical inference. While we often work with populations which are either known to be nonnormal in their distribution or whose distribution is unknown, using the sample mean allows us to use the normal distribution. Note, however, that in order to do this, *we must know* σ; if we do not, other measures are called for.

SAMPLING LIMITS FOR THE MEAN: KNOWN σ

Knowing the standard error of the sample mean, and the population mean μ itself, we can establish limits within which a specified proportion of the sample means $\overline{X}$ may be expected to fall.

For a standard normal variable z we define the value z_g by

$$P(0 \leq z \leq z_g) = g$$

Thus, in Appendix B, z_g corresponds to the area g. The central limit theorem then implies that a proportion $1 - \alpha$ of sample means lies within $\pm z_{(1-\alpha)/2}\sigma_{\bar{X}}$ of the expected value μ (the population mean). We call α the *significance level*, $1 - \alpha$ the *confidence level*, and the numbers

$$S_{1-\alpha}(\overline{X}) = \mu \pm z_{(1-\alpha)/2}\sigma_{\bar{X}} \tag{11.3}$$

the *sampling limits*. In summary: we can be $1 - \alpha$ sure that a (large) sample drawn from any population has a mean that lies between the sampling limits (*11.3*).

Looked at the other way round, the above furnishes an inspection criterion: Suppose that a sample mean falls *outside* the sampling limits. Since such an event would occur *by chance* only with probability α, there is a strong likelihood (if α is small) that the sample was *not* drawn from a population with mean μ.

EXAMPLE 11.3. A bulk product is packed in drums holding 70 lb. The filling machine can maintain this, but with a standard deviation of 8 lb. Samples of 25 are taken from the production line. (*a*) Between what limits may we expect to find 95 percent of the sample means? (*b*) If a sample mean is (i) 72 lb, (ii) 68 lb, (iii) 66 lb, can we be 95% sure that the sample has come from a population of 70 lb drums?

(*a*) $\mu = 70$; $\sigma = 8$; $n = 25$; $\sigma_{\bar{X}} = \sigma/\sqrt{n} = 1.6$; from Appendix B, area from 0 to 1.96 is 0.475, so that $z_{0.475} = 1.96$. Then from (*11.3*),

$$S_{0.95}(\overline{X}) = 70 \pm (1.96)(1.6) = 70 \pm 3.136 = 66.864, 73.136 \quad Ans.$$

(*b*) (i) Yes: 72 lb is within limits in (*a*).

   (ii) Yes: 68 lb is within limits in (*a*).

   (iii) No: 66 lb is outside limits in (*a*).

For proportions, (*11.2*) and (*11.3*) give

$$S_{1-\alpha}(p) = \pi \pm z_{(1-\alpha)/2}\sigma_p \tag{11.4}$$

where $\sigma_p = \sqrt{\pi(1-\pi)/n}$.

EXAMPLE 11.4. A politician commissions a poll, believing himself to have 55 percent of the vote. (*a*) If a sample of 196 voters is taken, what would be the 95 percent limits of the sample p? (*b*) What would they be for a sample of 500?

(*a*)
$$\sigma_p = \sqrt{\frac{(0.55)(1-0.55)}{196}} = 0.0355$$

$$S_{0.95}(p) = 0.55 \pm (1.96)(0.0355) = 0.55 \pm 0.0696 = 0.4804, 0.6196 \quad Ans.$$

(*b*)
$$\sigma_p = \sqrt{\frac{(0.55)(1-0.55)}{500}} = 0.0222$$

$$S_{0.95}(p) = 0.55 \pm (1.96)(0.0222) = 0.55 \pm 0.0435 = 0.5065, 0.5935 \quad Ans.$$

These results mean that, in a sample of 196, from $(0.4804)(196) \approx 96$ to $(0.6196)(196) \approx 121$ favorable would be consistent with a 55 percent overall result, with 5 percent probability of error. The figures for the sample of 500 are 253 and 297. Note also that in the smaller sample the lower sampling limit is less than 50 percent, so that there would be a significant chance of predicting the wrong election result. The minimum sample size to avoid such an error may be computed exactly, as described later in this chapter.

In this section we have considered only *two-tailed tests*, i.e. those with limits on both sides of the mean. One-tailed tests are covered in Problems 11.1 and 11.2.

CONFIDENCE LIMITS FOR THE MEAN: KNOWN σ

When the population mean μ is unknown, the limits may be centered on $\overline{X}$ instead. They are then *confidence limits* and represent the limits between which the true (population) value may be expected to lie, within specified probability of error. These limits are given by

$$C_{1-\alpha}(\mu) = \overline{X} \pm z_{(1-\alpha)/2}\, \sigma_{\bar{X}} \qquad (11.5)$$

EXAMPLE 11.5. Suppose that in Example 11.3 the population mean were not known; only the standard deviation of 8 lb and sample size of 25 are given. What are the 95 percent confidence limits for the true value of the population mean, if the sample mean is (a) 68 lb, (b) 66 lb?

(a) $\qquad\qquad C_{0.95}(\mu) = 68 \pm (1.96)(1.6) = 64.864, 71.136 \quad$ *Ans.*

(b) $\qquad\qquad C_{0.95}(\mu) = 66 \pm (1.96)(1.6) = 62.864, 69.136 \quad$ *Ans.*

The relationship between confidence and sampling limits is shown in Fig. 11-1. We may consider the whole process as one of proposing a *null hypothesis* (H_0: $\mu = \mu_0$), i.e. that the population mean is some specified value μ_0. If $\mu_0 = 70$, then we *accept* the hypothesis in Example 11.5(a) and *reject* it in Example 11.5(b), because the value 70 is within and outside the confidence limits respectively. We can, however, equally refer to Example 11.3(b) and say that in (ii), 68 lb is inside the sampling limits and thus H_0 should be accepted, whereas in (iii), 66 lb is outside the sampling limits and thus H_0 should be rejected. As is clear from the two configurations in Fig. 11-1, the verdict is the same in each case: $\overline{X}$ and μ are inside and outside their respective limits by the same amount.

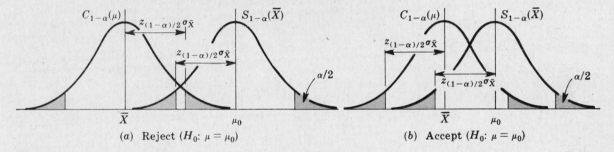

$\qquad\qquad$ (a) Reject (H_0: $\mu = \mu_0$) $\qquad\qquad\qquad\qquad$ (b) Accept (H_0: $\mu = \mu_0$)

Fig. 11-1

HYPOTHESIS TESTING FOR THE MEAN: KNOWN σ

Hypotheses may be tested directly, as well, by establishing $z_{(1-\alpha)/2}$ as a critical value and then calculating the *test statistic*

$$(z)_c = \frac{|\overline{X} - \mu_0|}{\sigma_{\bar{X}}} \qquad (11.6)$$

Reject (H_0: $\mu = \mu_0$) if $(z)_c > z_{(1-\alpha)/2}$.

EXAMPLE 11.6. Formulate Examples 11.3 and 11.5 as exercises in hypothesis testing with $\mu_0 = 70$ and (a) $\overline{X} = 68$, (b) $\overline{X} = 66$.

Here, $z_{(1-\alpha)/2} = 1.96$.

(a) $(z)_c = \dfrac{|68 - 70|}{1.6} = 1.25 < 1.96.$ Accept H_0 (as before). *Ans.*

(b) $(z)_c = \dfrac{|66 - 70|}{1.6} = 2.50 > 1.96.$ Reject H_0 (as before). *Ans.*

OPERATING CHARACTERISTIC CURVES FOR THE MEAN: KNOWN σ

Figure 11-2(a) shows a set of sampling limits. This is a two-tailed test, in that there are both upper and lower limits. By use of (11.3) we have set the upper limit $\overline{X}_u = \mu_0 + z_{(1-\alpha)/2}\,\sigma_{\bar{X}}$ and the lower limit $\overline{X}_\ell = \mu_0 - z_{(1-\alpha)/2}\,\sigma_{\bar{X}}$. Any experimental value $\overline{X}$ lying between these limits in the acceptance region marked serves as confirmation of H_0. However, as we have previously noted, there is a probability α that a value of $\overline{X}$ will fall outside those limits by chance, even though it comes from a population with mean μ_0. Thus α may also be called the probability of *rejecting the truth* or of a *Type I error*. Suppose now we have a *wrong* population, whose mean is μ_1 located as in Fig. 11-2(b). A large proportion of sample means drawn from this wrong population lies within the sampling limits of the correct mean μ_0, so that there is a substantial chance β that we shall think the sample has come from a population of mean μ_0 when in fact it has come from a population with mean μ_1. This represents a second type of error, called *Type II* or *accepting something false*. The following cases may thus arise:

	True	**False**
Accept	Correct	Type II (β)
Reject	Type I (α)	Correct

To compute β in Fig. 11-2(b), i.e. when $\mu_0 < \mu_1 < \overline{X}_u$, we divide it into two areas β' and β'' for which the corresponding z's are given by

$$z_{\beta'} = \frac{\mu_1 - \overline{X}_\ell}{\sigma_{\bar{X}}} \tag{11.7}$$

$$z_{\beta''} = \frac{\overline{X}_u - \mu_1}{\sigma_{\bar{X}}} \tag{11.8}$$

When μ_1 is on the other side, i.e. $\overline{X}_\ell < \mu_1 < \mu_0$, the result is a mirror image of Fig. 11-2(b) and the formulas for $z_{\beta'}$ and $z_{\beta''}$ are interchanged. In the configuration of Fig. 11-2(c), $\mu_1 = \overline{X}_u$ (set arbitrarily). Here $\beta \approx 0.5$ because α is usually small and so the portion to the left of $\overline{X}_\ell$ may be neglected. This holds even more in the general case $\mu_1 > \overline{X}_u$ shown in Fig. 11-2(d), where

$$z_{(1/2)-\beta} = \frac{\mu_1 - \overline{X}_u}{\sigma_{\bar{X}}} \tag{11.9}$$

and for its mirror image when $\mu_1 < \overline{X}_\ell$, where

$$z_{(1/2)-\beta} = \frac{\overline{X}_\ell - \mu_1}{\sigma_{\bar{X}}} \tag{11.10}$$

In a two-tailed test, moreover, the values of β are symmetrical, which simplifies matters when μ_1 on both sides of μ_0 is considered.

EXAMPLE 11.7. A set of measurements is supposed to have a mean of 100 units (the population mean) and it is known that the population standard deviation is 20 units. Assuming that $\alpha = 0.05$ and $n = 16$, find the values of β at intervals of 2 units from 100 to 124.

Here $\mu_0 = 100$, $\sigma_{\bar{X}} = 20/\sqrt{16} = 5$ and

$$S_{0.95}(\overline{X}) = 100 \pm (1.96)(5) = 100 \pm 9.8$$

or

$$\overline{X}_\ell = 90.2 \qquad \overline{X}_u = 109.8$$

The work is best set out in tabular form as in Table 11-2. When $\mu_1 = \mu_0 = 100$, $\beta = 1 - \alpha = 0.95$. For $102 \leqq \mu_1 \leqq 108$ we use (11.7) and (11.8); for larger values we use (11.9).

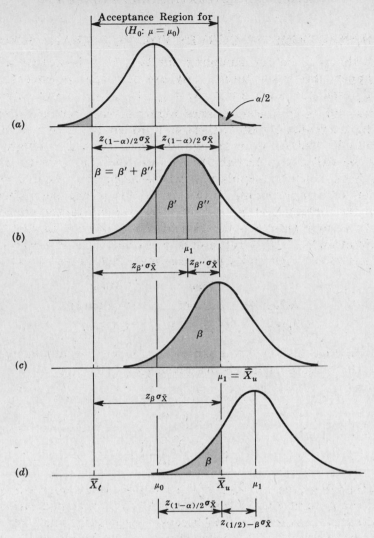

Fig. 11-2

Table 11-2

μ_1	$\mu_1 - \overline{X}_\ell$	$z_{\beta'}$	β'	$\overline{X}_u - \mu_1$	$z_{\beta''}$	β''	β
100							0.9500
102	11.8	2.36	0.4909	7.8	1.56	0.4406	0.9315
104	13.8	2.76	0.4971	5.8	1.16	0.3770	0.8741
106	15.8	3.16	0.4992	3.8	0.76	0.2764	0.7756
108	17.8	3.56	0.4998	1.8	0.36	0.1406	0.6404
				$\mu_1 - \overline{X}_u$	$z_{(1/2)-\beta}$	$(1/2) - \beta$	
110				0.2	0.04	0.0160	0.4840
112				2.2	0.44	0.1700	0.3300
114				4.2	0.84	0.2996	0.2004
116				6.2	1.24	0.3925	0.1075
118				8.2	1.64	0.4495	0.0505
120				10.2	2.04	0.4793	0.0207
122				12.2	2.44	0.4927	0.0073
124				14.2	2.84	0.4977	0.0023

The values of β are shown plotted for different values of μ_1 in Fig. 11-3; this is known as an *operating characteristic curve*. It gives the probability of *accepting* (H_0: $\mu = 100$) for different values of μ_1, including those below μ_0. If the probability of *rejecting* H_0 is of interest instead, $1 - \beta$ has to be plotted instead of β; such a rejection curve is called a *power curve*.

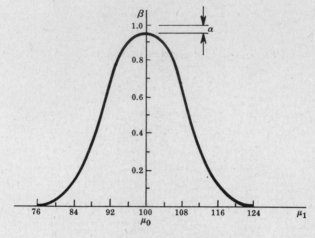

Fig. 11-3

A similar test applies to sample proportions. It starts out with (*11.4*) rather than (*11.3*). See Chapter 15.

SAMPLE SIZE: KNOWN σ

Since $\sigma_{\bar{X}}$ and σ_p are both proportional to $1/\sqrt{n}$, sampling limits can be made narrower or wider by respectively increasing or decreasing the sample size.

EXAMPLE 11.8. In Example 11.3, with mean 70 and standard deviation 8, suppose it were thought necessary that the variation about the mean be no more than ±1.5. Find the new sample size.

Let the variation about the mean be $\pm D$. Then

$$z_{(1-\alpha)/2}\frac{\sigma}{\sqrt{n}} = D$$

Solving for n,

$$n = \left[\frac{z_{(1-\alpha)/2}\sigma}{D}\right]^2 \tag{11.11}$$

From (*11.11*)

$$n = \left[\frac{(1.96)(8)}{1.5}\right]^2 \approx 109 \quad Ans.$$

EXAMPLE 11.9. The Presidential election in 1960 had a margin in the popular vote of 0.1 percent between the two leading candidates. In 1964 and 1972, there was about a 60-40 split. How big would the samples have had to be in an election poll in each year, in order to avoid, with 95 percent assurance, picking the wrong candidate as probable winner?

Since we are only concerned with the confidence limit not crossing the 50 percent mark, a one-tailed test is appropriate. The critical situation is illustrated in Fig. 11-4, where π is the proportion of the population who will vote for the winner. Writing

$$\pi = \frac{1}{2} + \frac{\Delta}{2}$$

where Δ is the margin between the two candidates, we have

$$\sigma_p = \sqrt{\frac{\pi(1-\pi)}{n}} = \frac{1}{2}\sqrt{\frac{1-\Delta^2}{n}}$$

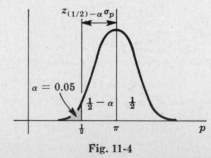

Fig. 11-4

and the critical value of n is given by

$$z_{(1/2)-\alpha} \frac{1}{2} \sqrt{\frac{1-\Delta^2}{n}} = \frac{\Delta}{2}$$

or
$$n = z_{(1/2)-\alpha}^2 \frac{1-\Delta^2}{\Delta^2} \approx \left[\frac{z_{(1/2)-\alpha}}{\Delta} \right]^2 \qquad (11.12)$$

if Δ is reasonably small.

For $\alpha = 0.05$, $z_{0.45} = 1.645$. In the 1960 election, $\Delta = 0.001$ and (11.12) gives

$$n \approx \left(\frac{1.645}{0.001} \right)^2 = 2,706,000 \quad Ans.$$

So large a sample is impractical; hence several pollsters refused to predict the outcome, when their much smaller samples showed a very close result. In 1964 and 1972, $\Delta = 0.2$ and

$$n \approx \left(\frac{1.645}{0.2} \right)^2 = 68 \quad Ans.$$

In determining sample sizes it is also possible to specify both α and β for a given μ_1.

EXAMPLE 11.10. In Example 11.7, it follows that when $\mu_1 = 108$, there is a 64.04 percent chance that we will falsely think that the sample comes from a population with mean $\mu_0 = 100$. Suppose we want to reduce this probability to 0.15. What would have to be the new sample size?

Instead of the configuration of Fig. 11-2(b), the new sample would have to produce that of Fig. 11-2(d). From the geometry, it is seen that

$$z_{(1-\alpha)/2} \sigma_{\bar{X}} + z_{(1/2)-\beta} \sigma_{\bar{X}} = \mu_1 - \mu_0$$

Substituting $\sigma_{\bar{X}} = \sigma/\sqrt{n}$ and simplifying,

$$n = \left[\frac{\sigma(z_{(1-\alpha)/2} + z_{(1/2)-\beta})}{\mu_1 - \mu_0} \right]^2 \qquad (11.13)$$

Here $z_{(1-\alpha)/2} = 1.96$ and $z_{(1/2)-\beta} = z_{0.35} = 1.036$ (from Appendix B); thus, from (11.13),

$$n = \left[\frac{20(1.96 + 1.036)}{108 - 100} \right]^2 \approx 56 \quad Ans.$$

SAMPLING LIMITS FOR MEANS: UNKNOWN σ

In this case, $\hat{s}$ must be used instead of σ, from which $\hat{s}_{\bar{X}} = \hat{s}/\sqrt{n}$. Further, the distribution to be used is no longer normal; instead of z, *Student's t distribution* is used. It is tabulated in Appendix F, which gives the values $t_{g,\nu}$ such that

$$P(0 \leq t \leq t_{g,\nu}) = g$$

Here the additional parameter ν is the number of *degrees of freedom* in the distribution. For a sample of size n, $\nu = n-1$. Thus (11.3) is replaced by

$$S_{1-\alpha}(\overline{X}) = \mu \pm t_{(1-\alpha)/2, n-1} \hat{s}_{\bar{X}} \qquad (11.14)$$

EXAMPLE 11.11. Consider the data of Example 11.1. Use sampling limits to show whether or not this is a population whose mean spending differs significantly ($\alpha = 0.05$) from \$6500 a year.

In Example 11.1 we found $\overline{X} = 5911$ and $\hat{s} = \sqrt{742,500} = 861.7$, from which $\hat{s}_{\bar{X}} = 861.7/\sqrt{9} = 287.2$. From Appendix F, for $\alpha = 0.05$ and $\nu = 9-1 = 8$, $t_{0.475, 8} = 2.31$. Therefore,

$$S_{0.95}(\overline{X}) = 6500 \pm (2.31)(287.2) = 6500 \pm 663 = 5837, 7163$$

Since 5911 is within these limits, (H_0: $\mu = 6500$) is accepted. *Ans.*

CONFIDENCE LIMITS FOR MEANS: UNKNOWN σ

For confidence limits, (11.5) is replaced by

$$C_{1-\alpha}(\mu) = \overline{X} \pm t_{(1-\alpha)/2,\,n-1}\hat{s}_{\overline{X}} \tag{11.15}$$

EXAMPLE 11.12. From the data of Example 11.1 find 95 percent confidence limits for the population mean. Also test whether a mean of \$6500 is compatible with these limits.

Using the results of Example 11.11 in (11.15) gives

$$C_{0.95}(\mu) = 5911 \pm 663 = 5248, 6574 \quad Ans.$$

The value $\mu = 6500$ is within these limits, hence accept $(H_0\colon \mu = 6500)$.

The difference between 6500 and the upper confidence limit is 74, which is the same as the difference between 5911 and the lower sampling limit of 5837. Thus, as was shown for the normal distribution in Fig. 11-1, sampling limits and confidence limits also give the same verdict with the t distribution, since it is also symmetrical.

HYPOTHESIS TESTING FOR MEANS: UNKNOWN σ

Here the test statistic is

$$(t)_c = \frac{|\overline{X} - \mu_0|}{\hat{s}_{\overline{X}}} \tag{11.16}$$

Reject $(H_0\colon \mu = \mu_0)$ if $(t)_c > t_{(1-\alpha)/2,\,n-1}$.

EXAMPLE 11.13. Express the analysis of Examples 11.11 and 11.12 in the form of a statistical test.

$$(t)_c = \frac{|5911 - 6500|}{287.2} = 2.051 < 2.306 = t_{0.475,\,8}$$

Accept $(H_0\colon \mu = 6500)$.

LIMITS AND TESTS FOR THE VARIANCE

Testing the sample estimate of the variance, $\hat{s}^2$, against a set population variance, σ^2, requires the *chi-square* (χ^2) *distribution*. Appendix E tabulates this distribution, giving the values $\chi^2_{g,\nu}$ such that

$$P(0 \leq \chi^2 \leq \chi^2_{g,\nu}) = g$$

where, once more, $\nu = n - 1$ for a sample of size n. The variable χ^2 is always positive and its distribution is unsymmetric. For two-tailed tests we have the sampling limits

$$S_{1-\alpha}(\hat{s}^2)\colon \quad \frac{\chi^2_{\alpha/2,\,n-1}\,\sigma^2}{n-1} < \hat{s}^2 < \frac{\chi^2_{1-(\alpha/2),\,n-1}\,\sigma^2}{n-1} \tag{11.17}$$

and the confidence limits

$$C_{1-\alpha}(\sigma^2)\colon \quad \frac{(n-1)\hat{s}^2}{\chi^2_{1-(\alpha/2),\,n-1}} < \sigma^2 < \frac{(n-1)\hat{s}^2}{\chi^2_{\alpha/2,\,n-1}} \tag{11.18}$$

EXAMPLE 11.14. Given the results of Example 11.1, find 95 percent confidence limits for the variance.

Working in thousands of dollars, $\hat{s}^2 = 0.7425$. From Appendix E, $\chi^2_{0.025,\,8} = 2.18$ and $\chi^2_{0.975,\,8} = 17.5$. Then, from (11.18),

$$C_{0.95}(\sigma^2)\colon \quad \frac{(9-1)(0.7425)}{17.5} < \sigma^2 < \frac{(9-1)(0.7425)}{2.18}$$

or

$$0.339 < \sigma^2 < 2.72$$

EXAMPLE 11.15. Given that $\sigma^2 = 0.3$ for the population in Example 11.1, find the 95 percent sampling limits and test whether the result of Example 11.1 is compatible with them. This is equivalent to asking whether, with 5 percent probability of error, the sample could have come from a population with variance 0.3.

From (*11.17*)

$$S_{0.95}(\hat{s}^2): \quad \frac{(2.18)(0.3)}{8} < \hat{s}^2 < \frac{(17.5)(0.3)}{8}$$

or

$$0.08175 < \hat{s}^2 < 0.6563$$

Since the calculated $\hat{s}^2$ is 0.7425, $(H_0: \sigma^2 = 0.3)$ must be rejected. *Ans.*

Another important test involves the equality of the variances of two populations. Specifically, the null hypothesis is $(H_0: \sigma_1^2 = \sigma_2^2)$. To test it, we form the ratio

$$(F)_c = \hat{s}_1^2/\hat{s}_2^2 \tag{11.19}$$

in which the subscript 1 is assigned to the sample with the larger variance, so that $(F)_c \geqq 1$. This test statistic is compared to the tabulated values of the *F distribution* (Appendix G). For a variable F of the form (*11.19*) the table lists F_{g,ν_1,ν_2}, where

$$P(0 \leqq F \leqq F_{g,\nu_1,\nu_2}) = g$$

Here ν_1 and ν_2 are respectively the number of degrees of freedom in the numerator and denominator of F. The test then is:

$$\text{Reject } (H_0: \sigma_1^2 = \sigma_2^2) \text{ if } (F)_c > F_{1-(\alpha/2),\, n_1-1,\, n_2-1}$$

EXAMPLE 11.16. A sample of 16 lengths of extrusions has a *sample* standard deviation of 11 inches. A second sample of 30 lengths has a sample standard deviation of 8 inches. Test whether the corresponding population variances are equal, with a 10 percent probability of error.

First we convert the given sample standard deviations s into the desired estimates $\hat{s}^2$ by the relation (see Table 11-1)

$$\hat{s}^2 = \frac{n}{n-1} s^2$$

Thus

$$\hat{s}_1^2 = \frac{16}{15}(11)^2 = 129.07 \qquad \hat{s}_2^2 = \frac{30}{29}(8)^2 = 66.21$$

Notice that the subscript 1 has been given to the sample whose variance turned out to be the larger. From Appendix G, $F_{0.95,\,15,\,29} = 2.03$ and

$$(F)_c = \frac{129.07}{66.21} = 1.95 < 2.03$$

Therefore accept $(H_0: \sigma_1^2 = \sigma_2^2)$.

RELATIONSHIPS BETWEEN THE NORMAL, CHI-SQUARE, t AND F DISTRIBUTIONS

1. The normal distribution may be regarded as the distribution of the z values. The χ^2 distribution is the distribution of the sum of all the z^2 in a sample, where $z = (X - \mu)/\sigma$, as usual.

2. The ratio χ^2/ν, called *chi-square over degrees of freedom*, has important relationships to the other distributions. Specifically:

$$t = \frac{z}{\sqrt{\chi^2/\nu}}$$

$$F = \frac{\chi_{\nu_1}^2/\nu_1}{\chi_{\nu_2}^2/\nu_2}$$

3. The F, t and χ^2/ν have the following limiting values (see also Fig. 9-6):

$$t = z \text{ for } \nu = \infty$$

$$\chi^2/\nu = z^2 \text{ for } \nu = 1$$

$$F = t^2 \text{ for } \nu_1 = 1; \quad F = \chi^2/\nu \text{ for } \nu_2 = \infty; \quad F = z^2 \text{ for } \nu_1 = 1, \ \nu_2 = \infty$$

For example, in Appendix G, $F_{0.95,1,\infty} = 3.84$, which is the same as $(z_{0.475})^2 = (1.96)^2$.

It is also possible to have OC curves pertaining to the t, χ^2 or F distribution. Charts for the purpose are included in such texts as A. J. Bowker and G. J. Lieberman, *Engineering Statistics* (Englewood Cliffs, N. J.: Prentice-Hall, 1959).

OC CURVES FOR BINOMIAL SAMPLES

The OC curves for binomial samples are based on the performance of a *sampling plan*, which is defined by the sample size n and an *acceptance number* c. There is also a *rejection number* r which, in a single sample, is $r = c + 1$. The plans thus usually serve some purpose related to *acceptance sampling*, which is discussed in more detail in Chapter 15. They also figure in decision theory (Chapter 12). As before, the OC curve gives the probability of acceptance,

$$P(A) = F_B(c \mid n, p) = 1 - R_B(r \mid n, p) \tag{11.20}$$

The power curve gives the probability of rejection,

$$P(R) = R_B(r \mid n, p) \tag{11.21}$$

obtainable directly from Appendix C.

EXAMPLE 11.17. Draw the OC and power curves for the plan ($n = 18$, $c = 2$).

In Appendix C, go to the field $n = 18$, and, for the power curve, read off $R_B(3 \mid 18, p)$ for various values of p. The OC curve is the complement. The curves are plotted in Fig. 11-5.

p	0	0.04	0.08	0.12	0.16	0.20	0.24	0.28	0.32
$P(R)$	0	0.0333	0.1702	0.3690	0.5673	0.7287	0.8430	0.9158	0.9581
$P(A)$	1	0.9667	0.8298	0.6310	0.4327	0.2713	0.1570	0.0842	0.0419

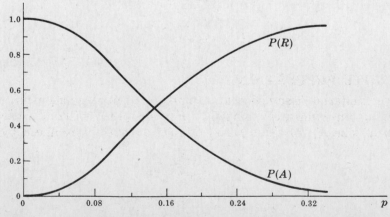

Fig. 11-5

OC CURVES FOR POISSON SAMPLES

When p is small and n large, Poisson sampling provides a versatile simplification of binomial sampling.   Appendix D gives the OC curve directly:

$$P(A) = F_P(c \mid m) \qquad (11.22)$$

where $m = np$.   The power curve is obtained as the complement.

EXAMPLE 11.18.   Find the OC and power curves for a Poisson sampling plan ($n = 75$, $c = 5$).

From Appendix D, we obtain for $m = 75p$ and $c = 5$, $P(A) = F_P(5 \mid m)$ and $P(R) = 1 - P(A)$.   See Table 11-3 and Fig. 11-6.

Table 11-3

p	0	0.02	0.04	0.06	0.08	0.10	0.12	0.14	0.16
m	0	1.5	3.0	4.5	6.0	7.5	9.0	10.5	12.0
$P(A)$	1	0.996	0.916	0.703	0.446	0.242	0.116	0.050	0.020
$P(R)$	0	0.004	0.084	0.297	0.554	0.758	0.884	0.950	0.980

EXAMPLE 11.19.   In Example 11.18, find the value of p for which $P(A) = P(R) = 0.5$.

To find this *indifference point*, we set $F_P(5 \mid m) = 0.5$ and look for a value of 0.500 in column $c = 5$ of Appendix D; we then find the corresponding m.   After interpolation, $m = 5.67$ and

$$p = \frac{m}{n} = \frac{5.67}{75} = 0.0756 \quad Ans.$$

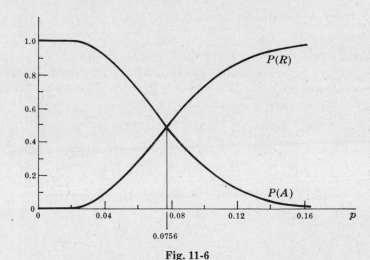

Fig. 11-6

CASE OF A FINITE POPULATION

The foregoing material assumes that sampling is with replacement, which is tantamount to assuming an infinite population.   For sampling without replacement from a finite population of size N, formulas (11.1) and (11.2) must be replaced by

$$\sigma_{\bar{X}}^2 = \frac{\sigma^2}{n}\left(\frac{N-n}{N-1}\right)$$

$$\sigma_p^2 = \frac{\pi(1-\pi)}{n}\left(\frac{N-n}{N-1}\right)$$

When N is large, as it usually is in practical cases,

$$\frac{N-n}{N-1} \approx 1 - \frac{n}{N} = 1 - f \qquad (11.23)$$

where $f = n/N$ is the *sampling fraction*. Its reciprocal, $g = N/n$, is called the *expansion factor*. Thus,

$$\sigma_{\bar{X}}^2 = \frac{\sigma^2}{n}(1-f) \qquad (11.24)$$

$$\sigma_p^2 = \frac{\pi(1-\pi)}{n}(1-f) \qquad (11.25)$$

Provided N and n are large enough to allow application of the central limit theorem, all our previous results for the case of known population variance remain valid if only $\sigma_{\bar{X}}$ as given by (11.24) is used instead of $\sigma_{\bar{X}} = \sigma/\sqrt{n}$. In effect, sampling from a finite population with variance σ^2 is equivalent to sampling from an infinite population with variance $\sigma^2(1-f)$.

EXAMPLE 11.20.   Correct (11.11) for a finite population.

For an infinite population with variance σ^2, (11.11) gives

$$n_i = K\sigma^2$$

For a finite population with variance σ^2, this must be replaced by

$$n_f = K\sigma^2(1-f)$$

Hence $n_f/n_i = 1 - f$. But $f = n_f/N$. Thus,

$$\frac{n_f}{n_i} = 1 - \frac{n_f}{N}$$

or

$$n_f = \frac{n_i}{1 + (n_i/N)} \qquad (11.26)$$

EXAMPLE 11.21.   A population of 900 families is believed to have an average liquor consumption of 2.5 gallons each, with a standard deviation of 1.2 gallons. It is required to devise a sample size which will ensure with 95 percent confidence that the estimate of the mean will be no more than 8 percent in error.

Here $D = (0.08)(2.5) = 0.2$. From (11.11)

$$n_i = \left[\frac{(1.96)(1.2)}{(0.2)}\right]^2 = 138.3$$

and from (11.26)

$$n_f = \frac{138.3}{1 + \frac{138.3}{900}} \approx 120 \text{ families} \quad Ans.$$

The same correction, (11.26), can be applied to the critical values of n found in (11.12) and (11.13).

EXAMPLE 11.22.   Suppose that the sample in Example 11.10 is taken from a population of 500. How would the critical sample size change?

From Example 11.10, $n_i = 56$. Applying (11.26),

$$n_f = \frac{56}{1 + \frac{56}{500}} \approx 50 \quad Ans.$$

When the population variance is unknown, we must use

$$\hat{s}_{\bar{X}}^2 = \frac{\hat{s}^2}{n}(1-f) \qquad (11.27)$$

instead of (11.24) in the tests involving the t distribution—i.e. in (11.14), (11.15) and (11.16).

EXAMPLE 11.23. Assuming that the community of Example 11.1 consists of 100 households, rework Example 11.11.

Now
$$\hat{s}_{\bar{X}} = 287.2\sqrt{1 - \frac{9}{100}} = 274$$

so that
$$S_{0.95}(\bar{X}) = 6500 \pm (2.306)(274) = 6500 \pm 631.8 = 5868.2, 7131.8$$

Since 5911 is still within the limits, $(H_0: \mu = 6500)$ is still accepted. *Ans.*

POPULATION TOTALS

It frequently happens, especially in surveys, that a population total X_t must be estimated. If the mean for the population is μ, then $X_t = N\mu$. If we work from an estimate of μ given by the sample $\bar{X}$, and let Y equal the unbiased estimate of X_t, then

$$E(Y) = E(N\bar{X}) = X_t \qquad (11.28)$$

If we work with the sample total, $x_t = n\bar{X} = \sum_1^n X$, then

$$E(gx_t) = E(gn\bar{X}) = X_t \qquad (11.29)$$

Thus, both $N\bar{X}$ and gx_t give unbiased estimates of X_t.

For the sample variable $Y = N\bar{X}$ we have $\hat{s}_Y^2 = N^2\hat{s}_{\bar{X}}^2$. Then, using (11.27) and $N = n/f$,

$$\hat{s}_Y^2 = N^2\left[\frac{\hat{s}^2}{n}(1-f)\right] = \frac{n(1-f)}{f^2}\hat{s}^2 \qquad (11.30)$$

When the population variance is unknown, (11.30) provides the standard error, $\hat{s}_Y$, of the estimate of X_t.

EXAMPLE 11.24. For the population of 100 households in Example 11.1, find the estimated total expenditures and the standard error of the estimate.

From Example 11.1, $\bar{X} = \$5911$, $\hat{s}^2 = 742{,}500$ dollars^2. Hence

$$Y = 100(5911) = \$591{,}100 \quad Ans.$$

and from (11.30)

$$\hat{s}_Y^2 = \frac{9\left(1 - \dfrac{9}{100}\right)}{\left(\dfrac{9}{100}\right)^2}(742{,}500) = 750{,}750{,}000$$

$$\hat{s}_Y = \sqrt{750{,}750{,}000} = \$27{,}400 \quad Ans.$$

Alternatively, from Example 11.23, $\hat{s}_{\bar{X}} = 274$ and

$$\hat{s}_Y = N\hat{s}_{\bar{X}} = 100(274) = \$27{,}400$$

CONCLUDING NOTE

This chapter has presented the treatment of samples and their use in a variety of analyses which probably still make up the majority of practical applications in business. The methodology is sometimes called "classical" statistics, in contrast to the Bayesian or decision-theoretic approach featured in Chapters 10, 12 and 13. The main difference is that in decision theory, costs of actions are put to the fore, whereas in the classical methods one aims at an optimal result through judicious choice of significance or confidence levels. It follows from Fig. 11-2, for example, that an increase in Type 1 error reduces Type II error and vice versa, by moving the acceptance zone. In many cases, however, it has been found that $\alpha = 0.05$ gives the "best of both worlds"; exceptions will be noted in later chapters, as required.

Solved Problems

11.1. Suppose that in Example 11.7 the mean of the measurements is expected to be *no more than* 100 units. Again assuming that $\sigma = 20$, $n = 16$ and $\alpha = 0.05$, find the probability of Type II errors for values of μ_1 from 94 to 120, at intervals of 2 units.

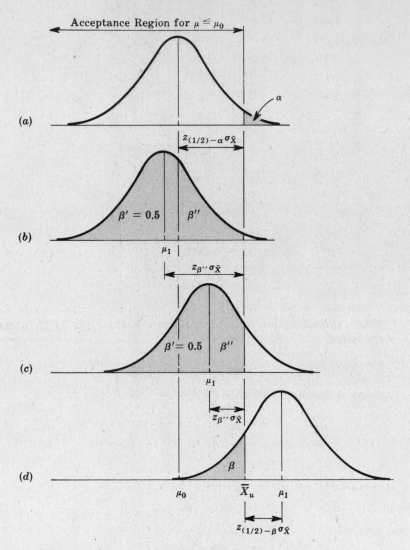

Fig. 11-7

This is a *one-tailed test*, i.e. the null hypothesis is (H_0: $\mu \leqq \mu_0$), or in this example, (H_0: $\mu \leqq 100$). The successive values of μ_1 produce values of β as shown in Fig. 11-7. In Fig. 11-7(a) there is only an upper limit $\overline{X}_u$ which marks off *all* of α to its right. In Fig. 11-7(b), $\mu_1 < \mu_0$; therefore the shaded area $\beta = 0.5 + \beta''$ is greater than $1 - \alpha$. Figure 11-7(c) is similar to Fig. 11-2(b), except that here too $\beta' = 0.5$. Figure 11-7(d) is the same as Fig. 11-2(d).

From Appendix B, $z_{0.45} = 1.645$, and $\sigma_{\overline{X}} = 20/\sqrt{16} = 5$, so that the sampling limit is

$$\overline{X}_u = 100 + (1.645)(5) = 108.225$$

i.e. accept (H_0: $\mu \leqq 100$) if $\overline{X} \leqq 108.225$. The calculations for the OC curve are given in Table 11-4. The OC curve is shown plotted in Fig. 11-8. Note that to the left of $\mu_0 = 100$, β soon becomes asymptotic to 1.

Table 11-4

μ_1	$\overline{X}_u - \mu_1$	$z_{\beta''}$	β''	β
94	14.225	2.845	0.4978	0.9978
96	12.225	2.445	0.4928	0.9928
98	10.225	2.045	0.4796	0.9796
100	8.225	1.645	0.4500	0.9500
102	6.225	1.245	0.3934	0.8934
104	4.225	0.845	0.3009	0.8009
106	2.225	0.445	0.1718	0.6718
108	0.225	0.045	0.0180	0.5180
	$\mu_1 - \overline{X}_u$	$z_{(1/2)-\beta}$	$(1/2) - \beta$	
110	1.775	0.355	0.1387	0.3613
112	3.775	0.755	0.2749	0.2251
114	5.775	1.155	0.3760	0.1240
116	7.775	1.555	0.4400	0.0600
118	9.775	1.955	0.4747	0.0253
120	11.775	2.355	0.4908	0.0092

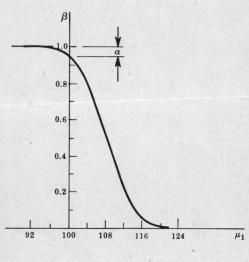

Fig. 11-8

11.2. In Example 11.12 find a one-sided 95 percent confidence limit so as to test for the minimum average spending level. Is that limit compatible with a mean spending level of at least \$5500?

Here we have an unknown σ, so that t must be used. For the lower limit in a *two-tailed* test, (11.15) gives $\overline{X} - t_{(1-\alpha)/2, n-1}\hat{s}_{\overline{X}}$. For a one-tailed test at the same level, we must double α in this expression, since the single tail is twice as big. Hence the desired limit is

$$\mu_\ell = \overline{X} - t_{(1/2)-\alpha, n-1}\hat{s}_{\overline{X}}$$

From Example 11.11 $\hat{s}_{\overline{X}} = 287.2$; from Appendix F $t_{0.45, 8} = 1.860$. **Thus**

$$\mu_\ell = 5911 - (1.86)(287.2) = \$5377 \quad Ans.$$

Since \$5500 is above that limit, we can accept the hypothesis. *Ans.*

If we wished to obtain this result from formal hypothesis testing, we would set

$$(t)_c = \frac{|5500 - 5911|}{287.2} = 1.43$$

Thus $(t)_c < 1.860$; accept $(H_0: \mu \geq 5500)$. *Ans.*

11.3. Assume that a proportion of 63 percent in favor is the expected result from a poll of 120 people. (a) Find the 95 percent sampling limits. (b) Find the Type II error for 57 percent and for 75 percent. Use a two-tailed test.

(a) In this case, the standard error of the sample proportion, $\sigma_p = \sqrt{\pi(1-\pi)/n}$, changes for every value of π_0 or π_1. Corresponding to $\pi_0 = 0.63$,

$$\sigma_{p0} = \sqrt{\frac{(0.63)(1-0.63)}{120}} = 0.04407$$

and $\quad S_{0.05}(p) = 0.63 \pm (1.96)(0.04407) = 0.63 \pm 0.0864 = 0.5436, 0.7164 \quad Ans.$

(b) For $\pi_1 = 0.57$, the standard error is

$$\sigma_{p1} = \sqrt{\frac{(0.57)(1-0.57)}{120}} = 0.04519$$

It is this value which must be used to find $z_{\beta'}$ and $z_{\beta''}$. See Fig. 11-9(a).

$$z_{\beta'} = \frac{0.57 - 0.5436}{0.04519} = 0.5842$$

$$z_{\beta''} = \frac{0.7164 - 0.57}{0.04519} = 3.24$$

From Appendix B, $\beta' = 0.2204$, $\beta'' = 0.4994$;

$$\beta = 0.2204 + 0.4994 = 0.7198 \quad Ans.$$

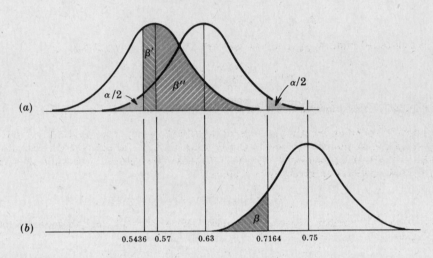

Fig. 11-9

For $\pi_1 = 0.75$, the standard error is

$$\sigma_{p1} = \sqrt{\frac{(0.75)(1-0.75)}{120}} = 0.03953$$

The configuration is that of Fig. 11-9(b).

$$z_{(1/2)-\beta} = \frac{0.75 - 0.7164}{0.03953} = 0.8500$$

From Appendix B, $(1/2) - \beta = 0.3023$, so that

$$\beta = 0.5000 - 0.3023 = 0.1977 \quad Ans.$$

11.4. Two reactors are connected to a single feed line. A set of 15 different feed formulations is run in order to see whether or not the two reactors perform the same way. In each case, the yield per batch is measured; the data are given below (X_1 and X_2). Test for equality of performance of the two reactors at the 0.05 significance level.

Test	1	2	3	4	5	6	7	8	9	10	11	12	13	14	15
X_1	10.0	9.7	9.9	9.8	10.5	9.4	10.7	10.3	10.7	10.4	9.7	9.8	10.7	9.2	10.6
X_2	10.3	10.5	10.0	10.3	10.5	10.3	10.3	10.1	10.4	10.1	9.6	10.2	10.4	10.1	10.6

This is an example of *inherently paired* data, i.e. each X_1 has an X_2 which is linked to it by some physical circumstance. This is solved by working with the differences between each of the number pairs, i.e. we set $d = X_1 - X_2$ and then test the null hypothesis $(H_0: \delta = 0)$, where δ is the population mean of the d's. The following are the values of d:

Test	1	2	3	4	5	6	7	8	9	10	11	12	13	14	15
d	−0.3	−0.8	−0.1	−0.5	0.0	−0.9	0.4	0.2	0.3	0.3	0.1	−0.4	0.3	−0.9	0.0

from which $\Sigma d = -2.3$; $\bar{d} = -2.3/15 = -0.1533$; $\Sigma d^2 = 3.25$;

$$\hat{s}_{\bar{d}}^2 = \frac{\Sigma d^2 - n\bar{d}^2}{(n-1)n} = \frac{3.25 - 15(0.1533)^2}{14(15)} = 0.013797$$

$$\hat{s}_{\bar{d}} = 0.1174$$

For a two-tailed test, $t_{0.475,14} = 2.14$ so that we can compare it to

$$(t)_c = \frac{|\bar{d} - \delta|}{\hat{s}_{\bar{d}}} = \frac{|-0.1533 - 0|}{0.1174} = 1.306$$

Since $1.306 < 2.14$, accept H_0. *Ans.*

There is another way of getting at least an approximate result for problems of this kind. Note the signs of the d's; one would expect that $+$ and $-$ would be equal in number (omitting 0's), i.e. the probability of each would be 0.5. Suppose there are a of the less frequent sign; the probability of a or fewer is given by the binomial

$$F_B(a \mid n', 0.5) = 1 - R_B(a+1 \mid n', 0.5)$$

where n' is the number of nonzero values. Here $n' = 13$ and there are 6 plus signs, so that $a = 6$ and

$$1 - R_B(7 \mid 13, 0.5) = 0.5000$$

which is clearly a good result under the null hypothesis. If there had only been 3 plus signs, however, the result would have been

$$F_B(3 \mid 13, 0.5) = 1 - R_B(4 \mid 13, 0.5) = 0.0461$$

A result which could only arise that rarely by chance would cast doubt on the null hypothesis; H_0 should be rejected. The foregoing is called the *sign test*.

11.5. In a community of 3000, a sample of 150 indicates 42 percent in favor of a certain proposition. (*a*) Find the 95 percent confidence limits for the population proportion. (*b*) What would the sample size have to be so that the upper confidence bound does not exceed 50 percent?

(*a*) This is a case of unknown σ. From (*11.27*) and Table 11-1,

$$\hat{s}_p^2 = \frac{\hat{s}^2}{n}(1-f) = \frac{p(1-p)}{n-1}(1-f) \qquad (11.31)$$

and

$$C_{1-\alpha}(\pi) = p \pm t_{(1-\alpha)/2, n-1}\hat{s}_p \qquad (11.32)$$

Here, $t_{0.475,149} \approx 1.98$. Thus

$$\hat{s}_p^2 = \frac{(0.42)(0.58)}{150 - 1}\left(1 - \frac{150}{3000}\right) = 0.001553 \quad \text{or} \quad \hat{s}_p = 0.0394$$

$$C_{0.95}(\pi) = 0.42 \pm (1.98)(0.0394) = 0.42 \pm 0.078 = 0.342, 0.498 \quad \textit{Ans.}$$

(b) Since $n \approx 150$, use $t_{0.475,149} \approx 1.98$. For an infinite population the critical value of n would be given by

$$0.42 + (1.98)\sqrt{\frac{(0.42)(0.58)}{n_i - 1}} = 0.50$$

or $\qquad n_i - 1 = (0.42)(0.58)\left(\frac{1.98}{0.08}\right)^2 = 149.2$ i.e. $n_i \approx 150$

Then, applying the correction (11.26),

$$n_f = \frac{150.2}{1 + \dfrac{150.2}{3000}} \approx 143 \quad Ans.$$

11.6. In a population of 2000, a sample of 25 indicates 36 percent in favor of a certain proposal. Find the 95 percent confidence limits for the population proportion.

From (11.31),
$$\hat{s}_p^2 = \frac{(0.36)(0.64)}{24}\left(1 - \frac{25}{2000}\right) = 0.00948 \quad \text{or} \quad \hat{s}_p = 0.0974$$

and we use the t distribution for this relatively small sample. Here $t_{0.475,24} = 2.06$ and (11.32) gives

$$C_{0.95}(\pi) = 0.36 \pm (2.06)(0.0974) = 0.36 \pm 0.201 = 0.159, 0.561 \quad Ans.$$

11.7. A product is packed in nominal 300-litre drums, with the actual amount subject to a standard deviation of 18 litres. It is desired to set up a test so that a minimum average of 300 litres is shipped, based on samples of 36 drums. For what alternative quantity is the Type II error 0.25?

This problem has a configuration like the mirror image of Fig. 11-7(d) (which is based on a *maximum* limit). The null hypothesis is $(H_0: \mu_0 \gtrless 300)$. Using $z_{0.45} = 1.645$ and $\sigma_{\bar{X}} = 18/\sqrt{36} = 3$,

$$\bar{X}_\ell = 300 - (1.645)(3) = 295.065, \quad \text{i.e. accept } H_0 \text{ if } \bar{X} > 295.065$$

For a value of $\beta = 0.25$, $z_{(1/2)-\beta} = 0.674$. Thus the value of μ_1 is $(0.674)(3)$ to the left of $\bar{X}_\ell$, i.e.

$$\mu_1 = 295.065 - (0.674)(3) = 293.043 \quad Ans.$$

Supplementary Problems

11.8. Reformulate the test in Problem 11.4 by setting up the appropriate sampling limits.

Ans. $S_{0.95}(\bar{d}) = \pm 0.2512$

11.9. For the data of Example 11.3 draw the operating characteristic curve.

11.10. Change the conditions of Example 11.3 to a *minimum* average weight of 70 lb. Find the lower acceptance limit and draw the operating characteristic curve. *Ans.* $\bar{X}_\ell = 67.368$

11.11. (a) In a survey of 49 people, find a statistical test for the hypothesis that at least 40 percent are in favor. Take $\alpha = 0.05$. (b) What is the Type II error for $\pi_1 = 0.35$?

Ans. (a) Accept H_0 if $p > 0.285$; (b) 0.8238

11.12. A certain electronic component is supposed to last 50 days. Its standard deviation is 8 days. A sample of 16 is chosen and tested. (a) Given that $\alpha = 0.0455$, what are the sampling limits? (b) Find the Type II error for 48 days and 56 days. (c) For what lifetime would the Type II error be 0.20?   *Ans.* (a) 46 and 54 days; (b) 0.8400, 0.1587; (c) 55.68 days

11.13. A set of 9 readings is taken of a certain measurement. From the data it is found that $\Sigma X = 108$ and $\Sigma X^2 = 1584$. Find the confidence limits for the population mean and test the hypothesis that the population mean is 8 units. Take $\alpha = 0.05$.   *Ans.* $C_{0.95}(\mu) = 7.38, 16.62$; accept H_0

11.14. From the data of Problem 11.13, form the confidence limits for the population variance and test whether it differs significantly from a value of 13.   *Ans.* $16.46 < \sigma^2 < 132.11$; reject H_0

11.15. A certain metal is designed to have a breaking strength of 90,000 psi; the standard deviation is known to be 20,000 psi. Find a sample size such that, with a probability of Type I error of 0.05, the probability that a metal with breaking strength 85,000 psi will be accepted is 0.2. The test is to be made by sampling from 1200 specimens. Strengths greater than 90,000 psi may be accepted without limit.   *Ans.* 91

11.16. A firm maintains inventory of several products. The stock of each product consists of several production lots which, because they were manufactured at different times, have different costs and thus there are different valuations for the items in stock. A count shows 18,000 items in stock and the accountants have estimated their value at $3 million. To test the correctness of this value, a sample of 500 items is taken and each one valued exactly. The total value of the audited items is $\Sigma X = \$86,000$ and, corresponding, $\Sigma X^2 = 85,000,000$. (a) What is the estimated total value of the inventory on the basis of the sample? (b) With $\alpha = 0.05$, is the estimate from the sample consistent with the accountants' estimate?   *Ans.* (a) $3,096,000; (b) yes

Chapter 12

Decision Theory with Sampling: Empirical Distributions

INTRODUCTION

In decision theory sampling is resorted to in order to improve the prior distribution. By adding information obtained from sampling, a new distribution is obtained in which prior experience (which, by itself, might be out of date) and sampling information (which, by itself, might not be representative) are combined. There are two kinds of problems to be discussed in this chapter. First, there is the simple task of combining prior with sampling information and then using the resulting revised distribution in a recomputation of the decision and its characteristics, such as EVPI, ECC and EMV*. The second class of problems deals with preposterior analysis, i.e. with the value of various kinds of sampling procedures.

REVISION OF PROBABILITIES

EXAMPLE 12.1. Refer to Example 10.1. All conditions remain the same except that the firm tests the quality of the work without the fixture by running off a sample of 20 elements. One turns out to be defective. Revise the prior probabilities and reassess the decision. Also find EVPI, EMV* and ECC.

We first revise the prior probabilities, using Bayes' theorem and setting up the computation as in Example 8.7. See Table 12-1.

Table 12-1

Fraction Defective, p	Prior Probability, $P_0(p)$	Conditional Probability, $P(X=1 \mid 20, p)$	Joint Probability, $P(X=1 \cap p)$	Revised Probability, $P(p \mid X=1)$
(1)	(2)	(3)	(4)	(5)
0.02	0.40	0.2725	0.10900	0.39030
0.05	0.30	0.3773	0.11319	0.40531
0.10	0.15	0.2701	0.04052	0.14509
0.15	0.10	0.1368	0.01368	0.04899
0.20	0.05	0.0577	0.00288	0.01031
TOTALS	1.00		$0.27927 = P(X=1)$	1.00000

Column (3). This is the probability of getting one defective in a sample of 20, given that p is the quality level of the batch. It is appropriate here to assume a Bernoulli process and use the binomial distribution; for example (using Appendix C and the methods of Chapter 9),

$$P(X=1 \mid 20, 0.05) = f_B(1 \mid 20, 0.05) = R_B(1 \mid 20, 0.05) - R_B(2 \mid 20, 0.05)$$

$$= 0.6415 - 0.2642 = 0.3773$$

Column (4). By (*8.16*), Col. (4) = Col. (2) × Col. (3). The total is the marginal probability of getting one defective in 20.

Column (5). As in (*8.13*), the revised probability is the joint probability divided by the marginal probability:

$$P(p \mid X = 1) = \frac{P(X = 1 \cap p)}{P(X = 1)}$$

For $p = 0.10$,

$$P(0.10 \mid X = 1) = \frac{0.04052}{0.27927} = 0.14509$$

The solution now proceeds exactly as in the case without sampling, except for the use of the revised probability. All three methods will be repeated here; the revised probability is called $P_1(p)$, to simplify notation.

Method 1.   Payoff Table.

Table 12-2

p	$P_1(p)$	DON'T USE FIXTURE		USE FIXTURE		
		CC	EC	CC	EC	ECC
0.02	0.39030	24	9.37	64	24.98	9.37
0.05	0.40531	60	24.32	64	25.94	24.32
0.10	0.14509	120	17.41	64	9.28	9.28
0.15	0.04899	180	8.81	64	3.14	3.14
0.20	0.01031	240	2.47	64	0.66	0.66
TOTALS	1.00000		62.38*		64.00	46.77

See Table 12-2. The decision is *not* to use the fixture. Note that this reverses the decision based on the prior distribution $P_0(p)$. The expected saving is $64 - 62.38 = \$1.62$.

$$\text{EVPI} = 62.38 - 46.77 = \$15.61 \qquad \text{EMV*} = \$62.38 \qquad \text{ECC} = \$46.77 \quad \textit{Ans.}$$

Method 2.   Opportunity Loss Table.

Table 12-3

p	$P_1(p)$	DON'T USE FIXTURE		USE FIXTURE	
		COL	EOL	COL	EOL
0.02	0.39030	0	0	40	15.61
0.05	0.40531	0	0	4	1.62
0.10	0.14509	56	8.13	0	0
0.15	0.04899	116	5.67	0	0
0.20	0.01031	176	1.81	0	0
TOTALS	1.00000		EVPI = 15.61		17.23

See Table 12-3; note that the difference is \$1.62, as before.

Method 3.   Using the Mean of p.

Table 12-4

p	$P_1(p)$	$p\,P_1(p)$
0.02	0.39030	0.00781
0.05	0.40531	0.02027
0.10	0.14509	0.01451
0.15	0.04899	0.00735
0.20	0.01031	0.00206
		$\bar{p} = 0.05199$

As computed in Table 12-4, the mean of p is less than the breakeven percentage, $64/1200 = 0.05333$; therefore, do not use the fixture.   The saving will be

$$1200(0.05333 - 0.05199) = \$1.61$$

which is within roundoff error of previous answers.   The EVPI may be computed as in Example 10.1, except that here the terms under DON'T USE FIXTURE make up the EVPI:

EVPI $= 1200(0.1 - 0.05333)(0.14509) + 1200(0.15 - 0.05333)(0.04899) + 1200(0.2 - 0.05333)(0.01031)$

$\quad = \$15.62$

This is the same result as above, within rounding error.

In most cases, the above method, including binomial sampling, is appropriate.   When the sample constitutes a large proportion of the batch ($n/N > 0.25$ approximately), the hypergeometric distribution gives a better result for the conditional probability.   When p is small, the Poisson approximation to the binomial may be used.   It has the advantage that we are not restricted in practice to the limited group of sample sizes listed in Appendix C.

EXAMPLE 12.2.   A batch of 10,000 parts is made on a machine which turns out perfect work when it uses tooling costing \$300.   When not using it, there is a distribution of fraction defective estimated as:

p	0.02	0.04	0.06	0.08	0.10
$P(p)$	0.20	0.40	0.25	0.10	0.05

When a defective part is installed it costs 50¢ to fix.   (a) On the basis of the prior distribution, find the correct decision and EVPI.   (b) A sample of 130 is put through the machine without the tooling and 9 parts turn out to be defective.   Revise the probability and find the new EVPI.

(a)   This part follows the standard prior analysis, using the opportunity loss table.   The breakeven percentage p_b is given by

$$(10,000)(0.50)p_b = 300 \quad \text{or} \quad p_b = 0.06$$

Therefore,

$$\text{COL} = \begin{cases} 5000(p - 0.06) & p > 0.06 \\ 0 & p = 0.06 \\ 5000(0.06 - p) & p < 0.06 \end{cases}$$

see Table 12-5.

Table 12-5

p	$P_0(p)$	DON'T USE FIXTURE		USE FIXTURE	
		COL	EOL	COL	EOL
0.02	0.20	0	0	200	40
0.04	0.40	0	0	100	40
0.06	0.25	0	0	0	0
0.08	0.10	100	10	0	0
0.10	0.05	200	10	0	0
TOTALS	1.00		EVPI = 20		80

The decision is DON'T USE FIXTURE; EVPI = $20.   *Ans.*

(b) First, revise the prior probabilities using the Poisson distribution (see Table 12-6). Note that from Appendix D, $f_P(9 \mid m) = F_P(9 \mid m) - F_P(8 \mid m)$.

Table 12-6

p	$P_0(p)$	$m = np = 130p$	$f_P(9 \mid m)$	$P(X = 9 \cap p)$	$P_1(p)$
0.02	0.20	2.6	0.001	0.00020	0.0032
0.04	0.40	5.2	0.042	0.01680	0.2690
0.06	0.25	7.8	0.121	0.03025	0.4844
0.08	0.10	10.4	0.119	0.01190	0.1906
0.10	0.05	13.0	0.066	0.00330	0.0528
TOTALS	1.00			$P(X = 9) = 0.06245$	1.0000

To evaluate $f_P(9 \mid 10.4)$ requires interpolation in Appendix D:

m	c = 8	9	$f_P(9 \mid m)$
10.0	333	458	125
10.5	279	397	118
interpolated 10.4			119

Second, make the revised opportunity loss table (Table 12-7).

Table 12-7

p	$P_1(p)$	DON'T USE FIXTURE		USE FIXTURE	
		COL	EOL	COL	EOL
0.02	0.0032	0	0	200	0.64
0.04	0.2690	0	0	100	26.90
0.06	0.4844	0	0	0	0
0.08	0.1906	100	19.06	0	0
0.10	0.0528	200	10.56	0	0
TOTALS	1.0000		29.62		EVPI = 27.54

The decision is USE FIXTURE; EVPI = $27.54.   *Ans.*

PREPOSTERIOR ANALYSIS

Preposterior analysis involves the evaluation of a *sampling plan* which, as in the cases discussed in Chapter 11, consists of a sample size n and an acceptance number c (and a rejection number $r = c + 1$). The value of a sampling plan depends on its ability to lead to a correct decision; conversely, the costs associated with it are due to the errors which it makes. Ideally, a sampling plan in a decision problem should render one decision whenever $p < p_b$ and the opposite one when $p > p_b$. It does not do this, of course; instead, there is a definable probability of error at each value of p. In the fixture problem, for instance, the plan should "accept," i.e. produce the decision DON'T USE FIXTURE, whenever $p < p_b$ and "reject," i.e. produce the decision USE FIXTURE, whenever $p > p_b$. If it rejects when $p < p_b$ or accepts when $p > p_b$, it is in error. The probabilities of such error at each value of p may thus be written as the conditional probability of error, given p, or $P(E \mid p)$. From the above reasoning,

$$P(E \mid p) = \begin{cases} P(R) = 1 - P(A) & \text{when } p < p_b \\ P(A) = 1 - P(R) & \text{when } p > p_b \end{cases} \qquad (12.1)$$

These probabilities can be directly derived from the OC and power curves. At each value of p the cost of an error is then obtained by multiplying the expected opportunity loss by the probability of error. The reasoning is that loss is incurred only if there is an error. The total EOL for the sampling plan concerned, denoted $EOL(n, c)$, is therefore given by

$$EOL(n, c) = \sum_p EOL \times P(E \mid p) = \sum_p COL \times P_0(p) \times P(E \mid p) \qquad (12.2)$$

The quantity $EOL(n, c)$ is the remaining cost of uncertainty after taking the sample and acting on the verdict of the plan. Therefore, the expected value of sampling information is given by the difference between $EVPI_0$, the prior cost of uncertainty, and $EOL(n, c)$:

$$EVSI = EVPI_0 - EOL(n, c) \qquad (12.3)$$

As in (10.8), the expected net gain from sampling is given by

$$ENGS = EVSI - CS \qquad (12.4)$$

where CS is the cost of sampling.

EXAMPLE 12.3. In Example 10.1 a sampling plan is suggested: 20 elements are to be tested, and if 2 or more are defective the fixture will be used. Find the EVSI for this sampling plan and the ENGS, given that the sampling cost is 25¢ per item.

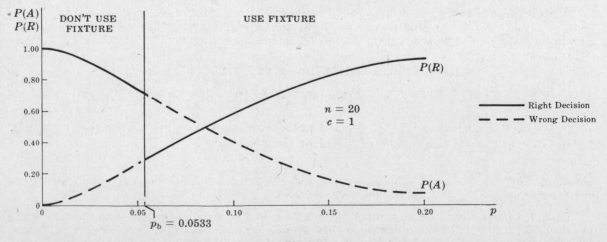

Fig. 12-1

The $EVPI_0$ was found in Table 10-2 to be \$17.20. The first step in the current problem is to calculate the acceptance and rejection characteristics of the sampling plan. The method was presented in Chapter 11. To illustrate the current computation in detail, Fig. 12-1 gives the OC and power curves of the proposed plan. (Normally, examples of this kind may be worked out by the tabular method below without drawing the curves.)

We now use the reasoning of (*12.1*) above; here $p_b = 0.05333$ and when $p < 0.05333$, $P(E \mid p) = P(R)$. Hence the power curve gives the probability of error. Conversely when $p > 0.05333$, the OC curve gives the probability of error and $P(E \mid p) = P(A)$. The "wrong" portions are shown dashed on Fig. 12-1. Between them, these two parts are called the *error curve*. The calculations are set out in Table 12-8.

Table 12-8

(1)	(2)	(3)	(4)	(5)	(6)	(7)	(8)
p	$P_0(p)$	$P(R)$	$P(A)$	$P(E \mid p)$	COL	EOL	$EOL(n, c)$
0.02	0.40	*0.0599*	0.9401	0.0599	40	16.00	0.958
0.05	0.30	*0.2642*	0.7358	0.2642	4	1.20	0.317
0.10	0.15	0.6083	*0.3917*	0.3917	56	8.40	3.290
0.15	0.10	0.8244	*0.1756*	0.1756	116	11.60	2.036
0.20	0.05	0.9308	*0.0692*	0.0692	176	8.80	0.609
TOTALS	1.00						7.210

Columns (1) and (2).   These are from Example 10.1.

Column (3). $P(R) = P(X \geqq 2 \mid 20, p) = R_B(2 \mid 20, p)$, obtained from Appendix C.

Column (4). $P(A) = 1 - P(R)$, i.e. Col. (4) = 1 − Col. (3). In both Columns (3) and (4) the *wrong* decisions are in italics.

Column (5).   The "wrong" entries from Columns (3) and (4).

Columns (6) and (7) are formed respectively of the nonzero entries in Columns (5) and (3) and in Columns (6) and (4) of Table 10-2. The COL's are incurred *if* the physical state p is realized and *if*, in addition, a wrong decision is made with the sample.

Column (8).   These are the components of $EOL(n, c)$ which are derived from (*12.2*).   Hence

$$\text{Col. (8)} = \text{Col. (7)} \times \text{Col. (5)} = \text{Col. (2)} \times \text{Col. (6)} \times \text{Col. (5)}$$

While Table 12-8 includes all detailed steps, in practice the computation may be shortened by omitting Columns (3) and (4), working with Column (5) alone, and omitting Column (7) as well (if it has not been already computed for the prior decision). Column (8) is then obtained directly from Columns (2), (5) and (6), as above.

$$EVSI = EVPI_0 - EOL(20, 1) = 17.20 - 7.21 = \$9.99 \quad \textit{Ans.}$$

$$ENGS = EVSI - CS = 9.99 - 20(0.25) = 9.99 - 5.00 = \$4.99 \quad \textit{Ans.}$$

It is possible to find the EVSI for a Poisson sampling plan in exactly the same way, merely by using the Poisson tables instead of the binomial.

EXAMPLE 12.4.   In Example 12.2 find the EVSI and ENGS for a Poisson sampling plan with $n = 130$ and acceptance number $c = 7$; sampling costs 5¢ per item.

Since EOL has already been determined in Table 12-5, we can use a short version of the opportunity loss table (Table 12-9). Note that $m = np = 130p$ is used here as well. $P(A)$ is obtained directly from Appendix D as $F_P(7 \mid m)$; the entry for $m = 10.4$ requires interpolation. The entries for $P(A)$ when

Table 12-9

p	$m = 130p$	$P(A)$	$P(E \mid p)$	EOL	$\text{EOL}(n, c)$
0.02	2.6	0.995	0.005	40	0.20
0.04	5.2	0.845	0.155	40	6.20
0.06	7.8	*0.481*	0.481	0	0
0.08	10.4	*0.187*	0.187	10	1.87
0.10	13.0	*0.054*	0.054	10	0.54
				$\text{EOL}(130,7)$	8.81

$p = 0.02$ and 0.04 give the probabilities of correct decisions and hence, in the next column, must be changed to $1 - P(A)$. The other entries, in italics, are wrong decisions and so their probabilities are simply transferred to the $P(E \mid p)$ column.

$$\text{EVSI} = \text{EVPI}_0 - \text{EOL}(130, 7) = 20 - 8.81 = \$11.19 \quad Ans.$$

$$\text{ENGS} = \text{EVSI} - \text{CS} = 11.19 - 130(0.05) = \$4.69 \quad Ans.$$

The computation of the EVSI may be extended to yield the marginal probability of getting a wrong decision. Consider the product $P(E \mid p) \times P_0(p)$ in (*12.2*). From (*8.12*) it is clear that this is the joint probability of p and an error, i.e.

$$P(E \cap p) = P(E \mid p) P_0(p) \tag{12.5}$$

and from (*8.10*) the marginal probability, $P(E)$, is given by

$$P(E) = \sum_p P(E \cap p) = \sum_p P(E \mid p) P_0(p) \tag{12.6}$$

EXAMPLE 12.5. Find the marginal probability of error in Example 12.4.

Using the prior distribution from Example 12.2 and the conditional probabilities of error from Table 12-9, we obtain Table 12-10.

Table 12-10

$P_0(p)$	$P(E \mid p)$	$P(E \mid p) P_0(p)$
0.20	0.005	0.0010
0.40	0.155	0.0620
0.25	0.481	0.1203
0.10	0.187	0.0187
0.05	0.054	0.0027
	$P(E) = 0.2047$	*Ans.*

THE OPTIMAL SAMPLING PLAN

The optimal sampling plan for a given problem is the one that maximizes the ENGS. The n and c for such a plan must therefore be determined. In general, this can only be done by trial and error, but there are two characteristics which help to narrow the search:

1. In choosing n, it is found that while the EVSI increases with the sample size, it does so at a declining rate. Meanwhile the cost of sampling usually increases directly with the sample size, so that eventually an increment in sample size brings a reduc-

tion in ENGS; the extra cost of sampling is greater than the gain in EVSI. Thus, as the sample size increases, ENGS reaches a maximum and then declines, eventually becoming negative.

2. The acceptance number c is chosen such that $c/n \approx p_b$, i.e. the acceptance fraction of the sample having the characteristic of interest should approximate as closely as possible to the breakeven fraction.

EXAMPLE 12.6. Find the optimal sampling plan for Example 12.3.

Table 12-11 is a shortened multiple version of the tabular solution to Example 12.3. Equation (12.2) is applied for each n and c. Because $p_b = 0.0533$ the entries in the $P(E \mid p)$ columns for $p = 0.02$ and $p = 0.05$ are given by $R_B(c+1 \mid n, p)$; the remaining entries are given by $F_B(c \mid n, p) = 1 - R_B(c+1 \mid n, p)$.

Table 12-11

		$n = 19, \ c = 1$		$n = 20, \ c = 0$		$n = 20, \ c = 2$	
p	EOL	$P(E \mid p)$	EOL(n, c)	$P(E \mid p)$	EOL(n, c)	$P(E \mid p)$	EOL(n, c)
0.02	16.00	0.0546	0.8736	0.3324	5.3184	0.0071	0.1136
0.05	1.20	0.2453	0.2944	0.6415	0.7698	0.0755	0.0906
0.10	8.40	0.4203	3.5305	0.1216	1.0214	0.6769	5.6860
0.15	11.60	0.1985	2.3026	0.0388	0.4501	0.4049	4.6968
0.20	8.80	0.0829	0.7295	0.0115	0.1012	0.2061	1.8137
EOL(n, c)			7.7306		7.6609		12.4007
EVSI = 17.20 − EOL(n, c)			9.47		9.54		4.80
CS = $(0.25)n$			4.75		5.00		5.00
ENGS = EVSI − CS			4.72		4.54		−0.20

Note that the plan $(n = 20, c = 1)$, which was analyzed in Example 12.3, still gives the best result (ENGS = 4.99). Plan (19, 1) has almost the same c/n ratio (0.0526) as plan (20, 1) ($c/n = 0.05$); in fact it is nearer to $p_b = 0.0533$, but the smaller n gives a lower ENGS. Thus no n smaller than 19 need be considered. As for values of $n > 20$, Appendix C restricts us to $n = 50$ and 100. Table 12-12 gives the results for $n = 50$, $c = 3$.

Table 12-12

p	EOL	$P(E \mid p)$	EOL(n, c)
0.02	16.00	0.0178	0.2848
0.05	1.20	0.2396	0.2875
0.10	8.40	0.2503	2.1025
0.15	11.60	0.0460	0.5336
0.20	8.80	0.0057	0.0502
		EOL(50, 3)	3.2586

$$\text{EVSI} = 17.20 - 3.26 = \$13.94 \qquad \text{ENGS} = 13.94 - 50(0.25) = \$1.44$$

It is clear that while the use of a sample of 50 improves the EVSI, the much greater sampling cost more than counterbalances this advantage. It is almost certain that further improvements can be made by the use of a sample size higher than 20 but much less than 50. A more exact analysis is possible with the Poisson approximation.

EXAMPLE 12.7. Find the optimal sampling plan for Example 12.4.

The solution is again an abbreviated version of the previous table (Table 12-9). Since the EOL for $p = 0.06$ is zero, the row $p = 0.06$ may be omitted. The procedure is again to let n decrease and increase from 130, which was the sample size in Example 12.4, and to set $c/n \approx 0.06$; see Tables 12-13, 12-14 and 12-15.

Table 12-13

(n, c)		(100, 6)			(110, 7)			(115, 7)		
p	EOL	$m = np$	$P(E \mid p)$	$EOL(n, c)$	$m = np$	$P(E \mid p)$	$EOL(n, c)$	$m = np$	$P(E \mid p)$	$EOL(n, c)$
0.02	40	2	0.005	0.20	2.2	0.002	0.08	2.3	0.002	0.08
0.04	40	4	0.111	4.44	4.4	0.079	3.16	4.6	0.095	3.80
0.08	10	8	0.313	3.13	8.8	0.349	3.49	9.2	0.302	3.02
0.10	10	10	0.130	1.30	11.0	0.143	1.43	11.5	0.114	1.14
		$EOL(n, c)$		9.07			8.16			8.04
		EVSI = 20 − EOL(n, c)		10.93			11.84			11.96
		CS = (0.05)n		5.00			5.50			5.75
		ENGS = EVSI − CS		5.93			6.34			6.21

Table 12-14

(n, c)		(115, 8)			(120, 8)			(125, 8)		
p	EOL	$m = np$	$P(E \mid p)$	$EOL(n, c)$	$m = np$	$P(E \mid p)$	$EOL(n, c)$	$m = np$	$P(E \mid p)$	$EOL(n, c)$
0.02	40	2.3	0.000	0.00	2.4	0.001	0.04	2.5	0.001	0.04
0.04	40	4.6	0.045	1.80	4.8	0.056	2.24	5.0	0.068	2.72
0.08	10	9.2	0.429	4.29	9.6	0.380	3.80	10.0	0.333	3.33
0.10	10	11.5	0.191	1.91	12.0	0.155	1.55	12.5	0.125	1.25
		$EOL(n, c)$		8.00			7.63			7.34
		EVSI = 20 − EOL(n, c)		12.00			12.37			12.66
		CS = (0.05)n		5.75			6.00			6.25
		ENGS = EVSI − CS		6.25			6.37			6.41

Table 12-15

(n, c)		(130, 8)			(150, 9)		
p	EOL	$m = np$	$P(E \mid p)$	$EOL(n, c)$	$m = np$	$P(E \mid p)$	$EOL(n, c)$
0.02	40	2.6	0.001	0.04	3	0.001	0.04
0.04	40	5.2	0.082	3.28	6	0.084	3.36
0.08	10	10.4	0.290	2.90	12	0.242	2.42
0.10	10	13.0	0.100	1.00	15	0.070	0.70
		$EOL(n, c)$		7.22			6.52
		EVSI = 20 − EOL(n, c)		12.78			13.48
		CS = (0.05)n		6.50			7.50
		ENG = EVSI − CS		6.28			5.98

The plan (125, 8) gives the highest ENGS. However, there are several other plans almost as good and it would appear logical to assume that any other sample size between 110 and 130, with $c = 7$ when $n < 120$ and $c = 8$ otherwise, would give a result very near the optimum. This is a typical result. In most cases there is a wide optimal range and any sample plan within it may be used.

Solved Problems

REVISION OF PRIOR PROBABILITIES

12.1. Suppose that the sampling process in Example 12.1 instead takes place in two stages. First, a sample of 5 is taken and 1 defective is found. Then a further sample of 15 is taken and 1 more defective is found. Revise the probabilities in two stages and compare with a single revision based on a sample of 20 with 2 defectives.

The two-stage revision is carried out in Tables 12-16 and 12-17, while the single revision is performed in Table 12-18.

Table 12-16

p	$P_0(p)$	$P(X=1 \mid 5, p)$ $= f_B(1 \mid 5, p)$	$P(X=1 \cap p)$	$P(p \mid X=1)$ $= P_r(p)$
0.02	0.40	0.0923	0.03692	0.1785
0.05	0.30	0.2036	0.06108	0.2953
0.10	0.15	0.3280	0.04920	0.2379
0.15	0.10	0.3915	0.03915	0.1893
0.20	0.05	0.4096	0.02048	0.0990
TOTALS	1.00		0.20683	1.0000

Table 12-17

p	$P_r(p)$	$P(X=1 \mid 15, p)$ $= f_B(1 \mid 15, p)$	$P(X=1 \cap p)$	$P_1(p \mid X=1)$
0.02	0.1785	0.2261	0.0403588	0.1407
0.05	0.2953	0.3675	0.1079912	0.3766
0.10	0.2379	0.3431	0.0816234	0.2846
0.15	0.1893	0.2312	0.0437661	0.1526
0.20	0.0990	0.1319	0.0130581	0.0455
TOTALS	1.0000		0.2867976	1.0000

Table 12-18

p	$P_0(p)$	$P(X=2 \mid 20, p)$ $= f_B(2 \mid 20, p)$	$P(X=2 \cap p)$	$P_1(p \mid X=2)$
0.02	0.40	0.0528	0.02112	0.1405
0.05	0.30	0.1887	0.05661	0.3767
0.10	0.15	0.2852	0.04278	0.2847
0.15	0.10	0.2293	0.02293	0.1526
0.20	0.05	0.1369	0.00684	0.0455
TOTALS	1.00		0.15028	1.0000

The results for $P_1(p)$ are identical to within rounding errors. This indicates that a sample taken may be partitioned in any way desired, e.g. if we had first taken a sample of 12 with 2 defectives and then a sample of 8 with none, the result would again have been as above, for a total of 20 in the sample and 2 defectives.

12.2. Use the payoff table and opportunity loss table to find the best decision, EVPI, ECC and EMV* for Problem 12.1, using the conditions in Example 10.1 and the posterior distribution computed in Table 12-17.

Table 12-19. Payoff Table

		DON'T USE FIXTURE		USE FIXTURE		
p	$P_1(p)$	CC	EC	CC	EC	ECC
0.02	0.1407	24	3.38	64	9.00	3.38
0.05	0.3766	60	22.60	64	24.10	22.60
0.10	0.2846	120	34.15	64	18.21	18.21
0.15	0.1526	180	27.47	64	9.77	9.77
0.20	0.0455	240	10.92	64	2.91	2.91
	1.0000		98.52		63.99*	56.87

From Table 12-19, the optimal decision is USE FIXTURE, EMV* = \$64.00 (corrected for rounding error), ECC = \$56.87 and

$$EVPI = EMV* - ECC = 64.00 - 56.87 = \$7.13$$

While the best decision and the EMV* remain unchanged from Example 10.1 (note that EMV* = $64 \times \Sigma P(p) = 64 \times 1$ in both cases), the result of the sampling has been to reduce the EVPI from \$17.20 to \$7.13.

Table 12-20. Opportunity Loss Table

		DON'T USE FIXTURE		USE FIXTURE	
p	$P_1(p)$	COL	EOL	COL	EOL
0.02	0.1407	0	0	40	5.62
0.05	0.3766	0	0	4	1.51
0.10	0.2846	56	15.94	0	0
0.15	0.1526	116	17.70	0	0
0.20	0.0455	176	8.00	0	0
TOTALS	1.0000		41.64		EVPI = 7.13

12.3. Recompute Example 10.1, assuming a sample of 20 results in no defectives. Find the best decision, EVPI, EMV* and ECC. Use the payoff table and check by means of the opportunity loss table and the mean of p.

The revision of probabilities for $n = 20$, $X = 0$ is carried out in Table 12-21. The resulting distribution, $P_1(p)$, is used in Table 12-22.

Table 12-21

p	$P_0(p)$	$P(X=0 \mid 20, p)$ $= f_B(0 \mid 20, p)$	$P(X=0 \cap p)$	$P(p \mid X=0)$ $= P_1(p)$
0.02	0.40	0.6676	0.26704	0.67215
0.05	0.30	0.3585	0.10755	0.27071
0.10	0.15	0.1216	0.01824	0.04591
0.15	0.10	0.0388	0.00388	0.00977
0.20	0.05	0.0115	0.00058	0.00146
TOTALS	1.00		0.39729	1.00000

Table 12-22.   Payoff Table

		DON'T USE FIXTURE		USE FIXTURE		
p	$P_1(p)$	CC	EC	CC	EC	ECC
0.02	0.67215	24	16.13	64	43.02	16.13
0.05	0.27071	60	16.24	64	17.33	16.24
0.10	0.04591	120	5.51	64	2.94	2.94
0.15	0.00977	180	1.75	64	0.62	0.62
0.20	0.00146	240	0.35	64	0.09	0.09
TOTALS	1.00000		39.98*		64.00	36.02

The optimal decision is DON'T USE FIXTURE,   EMV* = \$39.98,   ECC = \$36.02   and

$$EVPI \;=\; EMV^* - ECC \;=\; 39.98 - 36.02 \;=\; \$3.96$$

Table 12-23.   Opportunity Loss Table

		DON'T USE FIXTURE		USE FIXTURE	
p	$P_1(p)$	COL	EOL	COL	EOL
0.02	0.67215	0	0	40	26.89
0.05	0.27071	0	0	4	1.09
0.10	0.04591	56	2.57	0	0
0.15	0.00977	116	1.13	0	0
0.20	0.00146	176	0.26	0	0
TOTALS	1.00000		EVPI = 3.96		27.98

Table 12-24.   Mean of p

p	$P_1(p)$	$p\,P_1(p)$
0.02	0.67215	0.01344
0.05	0.27071	0.01354
0.10	0.04591	0.00459
0.15	0.00977	0.00147
0.20	0.00146	0.00029
TOTALS	1.00000	$\bar{p}_1 = 0.03333$

The mean value, $\bar{p}_1$, is less than the breakeven value, $p_b = 0.05333$; the saving is

$$1200(p_b - \bar{p}_1) \;=\; 1200(0.05333 - 0.03333) \;=\; \$24.00$$

which is (within rounding errors) the same as the difference of the EC's in Table 12-22 or the difference of the EOL's in Table 12-23.

It is useful to recapitulate the results of the various conditions under which this example has been computed:

Conditions	Decision	EVPI	Reference
no sampling	USE	$17.20	Example 10.1
$n = 20$, $X = 1$	DON'T USE	15.61	Example 12.1
$n = 20$, $X = 2$	USE	7.13	Problem 12.2
$n = 20$, $X = 0$	DON'T USE	3.96	Problem 12.3

In this case the addition of the sampling information reduces the EVPI; more is now known and so perfect information is now worth less. Further, when $X = 1$, the proportion defective within the sample is 1/20 or 0.05, which is very near to the breakeven percentage $p_b = 0.05333$. The EVPI is thus relatively high, because there is a greater degree of remaining uncertainty when the result is so close. On the other hand, the other cases give a more "obvious" result and the resulting decision can be accepted with more confidence. Thus the EVPI is again less.

12.4. A manufacturer is contemplating the introduction of an attachment to a machine which requires $156,000 in development costs, has variable costs of $300 and sells for $500. He has 2000 users of the machine who might be interested in buying the attachment and he estimates the probability of different percentages p doing so as follows:

p	0.2	0.3	0.4	0.5	0.6
$P(p)$	0.15	0.30	0.30	0.20	0.05

(a) Find the best prior decision and the EVPI. (b) If an approach is made to a sample of 50 customers and 21 buy the attachment, find the best decision under those conditions and the posterior EVPI.

(a) The profit contribution is $500 - 300 = 200$. At breakeven there will be $2000p_b$ customers, so that

$$2000p_b(200) = 156,000 \quad \text{or} \quad p_b = 0.39$$

Therefore, $\text{COL} = (400,000)|p - p_b|$ and the opportunity loss table may be constructed (Table 12-25).

Table 12-25

p	$P(p)$	DEVELOP COL	DEVELOP EOL	DON'T DEVELOP COL	DON'T DEVELOP EOL
0.2	0.15	76,000	11,400	0	0
0.3	0.30	36,000	10,800	0	0
0.4	0.30	0	0	4,000	1,200
0.5	0.20	0	0	44,000	8,800
0.6	0.05	0	0	84,000	4,200
TOTALS	1.00		22,200		EVPI = 14,200

DON'T DEVELOP; EVPI = $14,200. *Ans.*

(b) Table 12-25 is revised in Table 12-26.

Table 12-26

p	$P(p)$	$f_B(21 \mid 50, p)$	$P(21 \cap p)$	$P_1(p)$	DEVELOP COL	DEVELOP EOL	DON'T DEVELOP COL	DON'T DEVELOP EOL
0.2	0.15	0.0002	0.00003	0.0006	76,000	45.60	0	0
0.3	0.30	0.0227	0.00681	0.1316	36,000	4,737.60	0	0
0.4	0.30	0.1091	0.03273	0.6326	0	0	4,000	2,530.40
0.5	0.20	0.0598	0.01196	0.2312	0	0	44,000	10,172.80
0.6	0.05	0.0042	0.00021	0.0040	0	0	84,000	336.00
TOTALS	1.00		0.05174	1.0000		4,783.20		13,039.20

DEVELOP; EVPI = \$4,783.20.   *Ans.*

Note that when $p = 0.6$, the right-hand side of Appendix C must be used and that

$$f_B(21 \mid 50, 0.6) = F_B(21 \mid 50, 0.6) - F_B(20 \mid 50, 0.6) = 0.0076 - 0.0034 = 0.0042$$

PREPOSTERIOR ANALYSIS AND OPTIMUM SAMPLE SIZE

12.5. In Problem 12.4 find the EVSI and ENGS of the sample plan ($n = 50$, $c = 20$). Sampling cost is \$30 per item.

Table 12-27

p	EOL	$P(E \mid p)$	EOL(n, c)
0.2	11,400	0.0003	3.42
0.3	10,800	0.0478	516.24
0.4	1,200	0.5610	673.20
0.5	8,800	0.1013	891.44
0.6	4,200	0.0034	14.28
EOL(50, 20)			2,098.58
EVSI = 14,200 − EOL(50, 20)			12,101.42 *Ans.*
CS = 50(30)			1,500.00
ENGS = EVSI − CS			10,601.42 *Ans.*

In the $P(E \mid p)$ column of Table 12-27 the entries for $p = 0.2$ and 0.3 are $R_B(21 \mid 50, p)$. For $p = 0.4$ (which is greater than $p_b = 0.39$) and 0.5, the entries are $1 - R_B(21 \mid 50, p) = F_B(20 \mid 50, p)$. The R_B are read directly from the left side of Appendix C when $p \leq 0.5$. For $p = 0.6$, the right side of Appendix C is used and $F_B(20 \mid 50, p)$ is read directly in the $1 - p = 0.4$ column.

12.6. For the manufacturer in Problem 12.4, find the optimal sampling plan from among the values appearing in Appendix C.

For the plan ($n = 50$, $c = 20$) examined in Problem 12.5, $c/n = 0.40$. We will try ($n = 50$, $c = 19$), for which $c/n = 0.38$; when the c/n ratios straddle p_b in this way, one ENGS is always slightly higher than the other. We will also try ($n = 100$, $c = 39$) and ($n = 20$, $c = 8$), given the limitations of Appendix C. Table 12-28 shows that the plan (50, 19) is optimal. *Ans.*

Table 12-28

		($n = 50$, $c = 19$)		($n = 100$, $c = 39$)		($n = 20$, $c = 8$)	
p	EOL	$P(E \mid p)$	EOL(n, c)	$P(E \mid p)$	EOL(n, c)	$P(E \mid p)$	EOL(n, c)
0.2	11,400	0.0009	10.26	0.0000	0	0.0100	114.00
0.3	10,800	0.0848	915.84	0.0210	226.80	0.1133	1,223.64
0.4	1,200	0.4465	535.80	0.4621	554.52	0.5956	714.72
0.5	8,800	0.0595	523.60	0.0176	154.88	0.2517	2,214.96
0.6	4,200	0.0014	5.88	0.0000	0	0.0565	237.30

	EOL(n, c)	1,991.38	936.20	4,504.62
EVSI $= 14,200 -$ EOL(n, c)		12,208.62	13,263.80	9,695.38
CS $= 30n$		1,500.00	3,000.00	600.00
ENGS $=$ EVSI $-$ CS		10,708.62	10,263.80	9,095.38

Supplementary Problems

12.7. For Example 12.2, use both prior and posterior means to check the correctness of the decision and the saving resulting from the correct decision.

12.8. Repeat Problem 12.7 for Problem 12.4.

12.9. In Examples 10.1, 12.3 and 12.6, find the EVSI and ENGS for the sampling plans (a) ($n = 50$, $c = 2$) and (b) ($n = 18$, $c = 1$).   *Ans.*   (a) \$14.28, \$1.78; (b) \$8.88, \$4.38

12.10. In Examples 12.2, 12.4 and 12.7, find the EVSI and ENGS for the following sampling plans:
(a) ($n = 80$, $c = 5$);   (b) ($n = 120$, $c = 7$);   (c) ($n = 110$, $c = 8$).
Ans.   (a) \$9.81, \$5.81;   (b) \$11.87, \$5.87;   (c) \$11.41, \$5.91

12.11. An organization is planning a dinner and conference.   The cost is \$500 for renting the premises plus \$10 per plate for the dinner.   The group wishes to set \$15 as the registration fee.   The organization has 1200 members and the program chairman assesses the probability of a fraction p attending as

p	0.04	0.08	0.12	0.16	0.20	0.24
$P(p)$	0.12	0.18	0.30	0.22	0.15	0.03

(a) Find the prior decision whether or not to run the function and the EVPI.   (b) Assume that a sample of 15 members is canvassed and 1 decides to come.   Revise the probabilities and find the new decision and EVPI.   *Ans.*   (a) RUN DINNER, \$34.80;   (b) RUN DINNER, \$44.75

12.12. As part of finding an optimal sampling plan for Problem 12.11, assume that sampling is done by letters costing 15¢ each and determine the EVSI and ENGS for the following sampling plans:
(a) ($n = 12$, $c = 1$);   (b) ($n = 50$, $c = 4$);   (c) ($n = 100$, $c = 8$);   (d) ($n = 100$, $c = 9$).
Ans.   (a) −\$81.06, −\$82.86;   (b) \$4.04, −\$3.46;   (c) \$21.13, \$6.13;   (d) \$15.25, −\$0.25

12.13. Try to improve on the results of Problem 12.12 by finding the EVSI and ENGS of a better sampling plan, if any.   *Ans.*   ($n = 50$, $c = 3$); \$15.74, \$8.24

Chapter 13

Decision Theory: Partial Expectation Methods

INTRODUCTION

In Chapters 10 and 12, a wide array of problems in decision theory was covered. The underlying probability distributions were either empirical or were treated as if empirical in the various tabular methods by which the optimal decision, EVPI, EVSI, etc., were computed. It is, however, possible to use the most generally relevant formal distributions directly, through special computational techniques which eliminate the tabular procedures and are therefore very much simpler.

Many-Action Problems

GENERAL THEORY

The basic idea is shown in the general solution to the "newsboy" problem (Example 10.2).

Notation

$$I \;=\; \text{initial inventory, units}$$

$$I^* \;=\; \text{optimal initial inventory, units}$$

$$k_o \;=\; \text{overage loss per unit (salvage loss per unit)}$$

$$k_u \;=\; \text{underage loss per unit (lost profit per unit)}$$

$$u \;=\; \text{demand, units}$$

$$f(u), F(u) \;=\; \text{probability density function and cumulative distribution function of the demand } u$$

In the nomenclature of Chapter 10, I is the decision variable (which here can assume many values) and u is the physical state variable. It is required to find I^*, the value of I which will minimize total costs; more exactly, I^* will be set so as to minimize the sum of the expected overage and underage losses. When $I \geqq u$, a conditional quantity $I - u$ will be left over, resulting in a conditional loss of $k_o(I-u)$. The probability of a specific value of u occurring is $f(u)$, so that the expected loss associated with a specific value of u and a specific value of $I \geqq u$ is $k_0(I-u)f(u)$. The total expected overage loss, K_o, is the summation or integral of this element over the range $0 \leqq u \leqq I$:

$$K_o \;=\; k_o \int_0^I (I-u) f(u) \, du \qquad\qquad (13.1)$$

When $I < u$, there is underage of $u - I$ and, reasoning in the same way, the total expected underage loss, K_u, is

$$K_u \;=\; k_u \int_I^\infty (u-I) f(u) \, du \qquad\qquad (13.2)$$

The total expected cost, K_t, is equivalent to the EVPI and is given by

$$\text{EVPI} \;=\; K_t \;=\; K_o + K_u \;=\; k_o \int_0^I (I - u)\,f(u)\,du \;+\; k_u \int_I^\infty (u - I)\,f(u)\,du \qquad (13.3)$$

To find I^* we set

$$\frac{dK_t}{dI} \;=\; k_o \int_0^I (1)\,f(u)\,du + k_u \int_I^\infty (-1)\,f(u)\,du \;=\; k_o F(u)\Big|_0^I - k_u F(u)\Big|_I^\infty \;=\; 0$$

$$k_o F(I^*) - k_u + k_u F(I^*) \;=\; 0$$

$$F(I^*) \;=\; \frac{k_u}{k_o + k_u} \qquad\qquad (13.4)$$

The relationship (13.4) is illustrated in Fig. 13-1. It is clear that optimally it is proper to have enough stock to be able to serve all customers in a proportion of the transactions given by $k_u/(k_o + k_u)$, called the *service level*, and *not* to serve them all, i.e. to have at least some shortage, on $k_o/(k_o + k_u)$ of the occasions. To stock more than I^* is, on the average, to increase overage; to stock less than I^* is to increase underage.

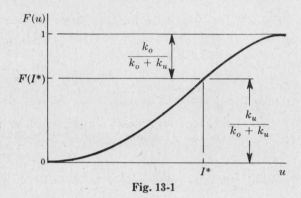

Fig. 13-1

EXAMPLE 13.1. Determine the optimal inventory in Example 10.2.

From the data, $k_o = \$2$, $k_u = 5 - 2 = \$3$. From (13.4),

$$F(I^*) \;=\; \frac{3}{2 + 3} \;=\; 0.6$$

Now rewrite the probabilities of the various demands cumulatively:

Demand, u	5	6	7	8	9
$f(u)$	0.10	0.20	0.40	0.15	0.15
$F(u)$	0.10	0.30	0.70*	0.85	1.00

The value $F(7)$ encompasses the critical value 0.6, so that $I^* = 7$ units.   *Ans.*

To find the EVPI, rewrite (13.1) as

$$K_o \;=\; k_o \int_0^I I\,f(u)\,du - k_o \int_0^I u\,f(u)\,du$$

The first integral is $I\,F(I)$; the second is the so-called *partial expectation* of u from 0 to I, and it is denoted $E_0^I(u)$. The reason for the name is that if the integral $\int u\,f(u)\,du$ were taken over the *entire* range of u (which here would be $0 \leqq u < \infty$) the result would be the expected value of u, $E(u)$. Here the integral is taken over only part of the range. Hence

$$K_o \;=\; k_o [I\,F(I) - E_0^I(u)] \qquad\qquad (13.5)$$

Analogously, from (13.2)

$$K_u \;=\; k_u [E_I^\infty(u) - I\,R(I)] \qquad\qquad (13.6)$$

for continuous distributions. For discrete distributions it is necessary to use

$$K_u \;=\; k_u [E_{I+1}^\infty(u) - I\,R(I + 1)] \qquad\qquad (13.7)$$

in order to avoid overlap with (13.5).

To obtain EVPI in any given case, we substitute I^* for I in (13.5) and in (13.6) or (13.7), obtaining K_o^* and K_u^* respectively. If tabulations for the cumulative functions and partial expectations are available, the formulas can be worked out and EVPI is then given by the sum of K_o^* and K_u^*, as in (13.3). It is also possible to use this method on empirical distributions.

EXAMPLE 13.2. Find the EVPI for Example 13.1 (using the data of Example 10.2) by the partial expectation method.

In Example 13.1 we found $I^* = 7$, $F(I^*) = 0.70$. Furthermore the mean of u is given by

$$E(u) = [5(0.10) + 6(0.20) + 7(0.40)] + [8(0.15) + 9(0.15)] = 4.50 + 2.55$$

in which the right-hand side has been partitioned into $E_5^7(u) = E_0^7(u)$ and $E_8^9(u) = E_8^\infty(u)$. Thus, from (13.5),

$$K_o^* = 2[7(0.70) - 4.50] = 0.80$$

and from (13.7)

$$K_u^* = 3[2.55 - 7(0.30)] = 1.35$$

so that EVPI $= 0.80 + 1.35 = \$2.15$, as before. *Ans.*

It is also possible to complete Example 10.2 by finding the EPC as well. This is given by the unit profit (\$3) times the mean sales, $E(u) = 4.50 + 2.55 = 7.05$. Hence

$$\text{EPC} = 3(7.05) = \$21.15$$

as before. Thus the entire problem can be solved by these simple formulas rather than the tabular methods.

The partition of $E(u)$ in Example 13.2 serves as a reminder that, in general, when $a \leqq u \leqq b$,

$$E(u) = E_a^k(u) + E_k^b(u) \qquad \text{(continuous variable)} \qquad (13.8)$$

$$E(u) = E_a^k(u) + E_{k+1}^b(u) \qquad \text{(discrete variable)} \qquad (13.9)$$

Thus, if one partial expectation is known, its complement can be obtained by subtracting it from the mean.

THE POISSON DISTRIBUTION

Prior distributions following the Poisson form are readily analyzed by the foregoing methods. There is a simple relationship that allows us to obtain partial Poisson expectations from Appendix D. Since, from Table 9-6, $f_P(u \mid m) = e^{-m} m^u / u!$,

$$E_0^I(u) = \sum_{u=0}^{I} u \frac{e^{-m} m^u}{u!} = m \sum_{u-1=0}^{I-1} \frac{e^{-m} m^{u-1}}{(u-1)!} = m F_P(I-1 \mid m) \qquad (13.10)$$

and

$$E_{I+1}^\infty(u) = E(u) - E_0^I(u) = m[1 - F_P(I-1 \mid m)] \qquad (13.11)$$

EXAMPLE 13.3. Rework Example 10.3, using the partial expectation method. Also confirm the answers to Problem 10.18.

If parts are left over, they cost \$10,000 each, i.e. $k_o = \$10,000$. If there are not enough, each such incident costs an extra

$$120,000 - 10,000 = \$110,000 = k_u$$

The prior distribution is Poisson, with $m = 1.4$.

First we find the best decision. From (13.4)

$$F_P(I^* \mid 1.4) = \frac{110,000}{10,000 + 110,000} = 0.917$$

In Appendix D, $F_P(3 \mid 1.4) = 0.946$ and $F_P(2 \mid 1.4) = 0.833$, so that buying 3 parts beforehand is the best policy. *Ans.*

To find EVPI, we use (13.5) and (13.7). From (13.5) and (13.10), omitting thousands,

$$K_o^* = 10[3F_P(3 \mid 1.4) - (1.4)F_P(2 \mid 1.4)] = 10(2.838 - 1.1662) = 16.72$$

From (13.7) and (13.11)

$$K_u^* = 110[(1.4 - 1.1662) - 3(1 - 0.946)] = 7.90$$

and

$$\text{EVPI} = K_o^* + K_u^* = 1000(16.72 + 7.90) = \$24,620 \quad Ans.$$

This is virtually identical to the previous result.

The expected cost under certainty is obtained by multiplying the prior cost by the mean usage, i.e.

$$\text{ECC} = (10,000)(1.4) = \$14,000 \quad Ans.$$

The total expected cost of the optimal action is therefore

$$\text{EMV}^* = 14,000 + 24,620 = \$38,620 \quad Ans.$$

THE NORMAL DISTRIBUTION

It is shown in Problem 13.1 that when the distribution of the demand variable u is normal, the expected costs of overage and underage are

$$K_o = k_o \sigma [z + L(z)] \tag{13.12}$$

$$K_u = k_u \sigma L(z) \tag{13.13}$$

where

σ = standard deviation of u

$$z = \frac{I - \mu}{\sigma} \tag{13.14}$$

$\mu = E(u)$

and $L(z)$, the *unit normal loss integral,* is defined as

$$L(z) = f_N(z) - z R_N(z) \tag{13.15}$$

and tabulated in Appendix I. Using $z^* = (I^* - \mu)/\sigma$ in (13.12) and (13.13) gives $\text{EVPI} = K_o^* + K_u^*$, as usual.

EXAMPLE 13.4. Demand for a certain product is believed to be normally distributed with mean 150 units and standard deviation 18 units. Profit per item is \$25 and salvage loss is \$15 per item. Find the optimal initial inventory level, EVPI, EPC and EMV*.

By (13.4)

$$F_N(I^* \mid \mu, \sigma) = \frac{25}{15 + 25} = 0.625$$

or, equivalently, $F_N(z^*) = 0.625$, where I^* and z^* are connected by (13.14). From Appendix B, the area under the standard normal curve between 0 and 0.32 is 0.1255, so that

$$F_N(0.32) = \tfrac{1}{2} + 0.1255 = 0.6255$$

which is good enough. Thus, $z^* = 0.32$ and

$$I^* = \mu + \sigma z^* = 150 + 18(0.32) \approx 156 \text{ units} \quad Ans.$$

From (13.12) and (13.13) and entering Appendix I with $z^* = 0.32$,

$$K_o^* = (15)(18)(0.32 + 0.2592) = \$156.38$$

$$K_u^* = (25)(18)(0.2592) = \$116.64$$

$$\text{EVPI} = 116.64 + 156.38 = \$273.02 \quad Ans.$$

The expected profit under certainty is the unit profit times the mean sales, i.e.

$$EPC = (25)(150) = \$3750 \quad Ans.$$

and, from (10.5),

$$EMV^* = 3750 - 273.02 = \$3476.98 \quad Ans.$$

In many cases, standard deviations are not known and must be estimated from rather crude prior judgments. The following procedure is used to "assess" a normal distribution for such data.

EXAMPLE 13.5. Sales for a certain product are estimated to have a mean of 400 items, with a 50 percent chance of sales being between 300 and 500 items. Profit per unit is $7 and salvage losses are $10 per unit. Find the optimal initial inventory level, EVPI, EPC and EMV*.

As shown in Fig. 13-2, 25 percent of the data lie on each side of the mean. In Appendix B, it is seen that the value of z corresponding to the area 0.25 is (after some interpolation) 0.674. Thus, from Fig. 13-2,

$$(0.674)\sigma = 100 \quad \text{or} \quad \sigma = 148.4$$

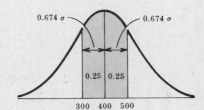

Fig. 13-2

We next find I^* from

$$F_N(I^* \mid 400, 148.4) = \frac{7}{10 + 7} = 0.4118$$

This refers to the area shown in Fig. 13-3(a). In Appendix B, it is necessary to find z^* for the area $0.5 - 0.4118 = 0.0882$. This is found to be 0.223 but being measured to the left of the mean, must be given a *negative* sign. Thus

$$I^* = 400 - (0.223)(148.4) \approx 367 \quad Ans.$$

To find the EVPI, it is necessary to find the values of $L(z)$ and $z + L(z)$ for negative arguments.

$$L(-z) = f(-z) - (-z)R(-z)$$

By inspection of Fig. 13-3(b) it is readily apparent that $f(z) = f(-z)$; this follows from the symmetry of the distribution. Also $R(-z) = 1 - R(z)$; with the negative z the effect is that of a mirror image. Thus

$$L(-z) = f(z) + z - zR(z) = z + L(z)$$

and

$$(-z) + L(-z) = L(z)$$

(13.16)

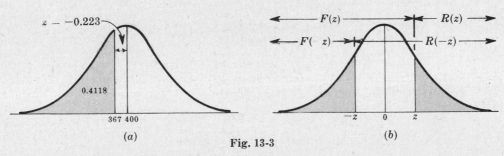

(a)   Fig. 13-3   (b)

The effect is to interchange $L(z)$ and $z + L(z)$ in (13.12) and (13.13). From Appendix I, $L(0.223) = 0.2973$ (after interpolation) and therefore

$$K_o^* = 10(148.4)(0.2973) = \$441.19$$
$$K_u^* = 7(148.4)(0.223 + 0.2973) = \$540.49$$
$$EVPI = 441.19 + 540.49 = \$981.68 \quad Ans.$$
$$EPC = 7(400) = \$2800 \quad Ans.$$
$$EMV^* = 2800 - 981.68 = \$1818.32 \quad Ans.$$

The above method of assuming a normal distribution is reasonable whenever the distribution is of approximately symmetrical character and the data are not in sufficient detail to permit analysis by the previous treatment of empirical distributions.

THE GAMMA DISTRIBUTION

When it is definitely known that the distribution of the demand variable u is markedly skewed, as shown in Fig. 13-4, it is possible to estimate a gamma distribution, $f_\gamma(u \mid X, U)$, which will fit. From Table 9-6, $E(u) = XU$ and Var $(u) = XU^2$, so that the parameters are assigned as

$$X = \frac{[E(u)]^2}{\text{Var}(u)} \qquad U = \frac{\text{Var}(u)}{E(u)} \qquad (13.17)$$

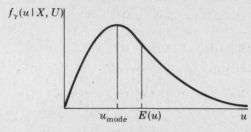

Fig. 13-4

Another possibility, when the distribution looks like Fig. 13-4, is to work with the mean and with the *mode*,

$$u_{\text{mode}} = (X - 1)U$$

which is the value of u with the highest probability. This may lend itself to observation when the variance cannot be readily estimated or computed. We have:

$$X = \frac{E(u)}{E(u) - u_{\text{mode}}} \qquad U = E(u) - u_{\text{mode}} \qquad (13.18)$$

Depending on what is given, therefore, we may use either (*13.17*) or (*13.18*) to estimate the parameters X and U of the gamma distribution.

For the gamma distribution (one-parameter form),

$$E_0^I(u) = XUF_\gamma(m \mid X + 1) \qquad \text{where} \qquad m = \frac{I}{U}$$

which, using (*9.17*), can be written in terms of the Poisson distribution as

$$E_0^I(u) = XU[1 - F_P(X \mid m)]$$

from which

$$E_I^\infty(u) = XUF_P(X \mid m)$$

Equations (*13.5*) and (*13.6*) then become

$$K_o = k_oU\{m[1 - F_P(X - 1 \mid m)] - X[1 - F_P(X \mid m)]\} \qquad (13.19)$$

$$K_u = k_uU[XF_P(X \mid m) - mF_P(X - 1 \mid m)] \qquad (13.20)$$

When m has its optimal value $m^* = I^*/U$, EVPI $= K_o^* + K_u^*$, as before. Note that the above use of the Poisson distribution presumes that X is an integer.

EXAMPLE 13.6. Demand distribution of a certain product is believed to be gamma with mean 45 units and standard deviation 12 units. Profit per unit is \$12 and salvage loss per unit is \$18. Find the optimal initial inventory, EVPI, EPC and EMV*.

From (*13.17*)

$$X = \frac{(45)^2}{(12)^2} \approx 14 \qquad U = \frac{(12)^2}{45} = 3.2$$

so that $m = I/3.2$. From (*13.4*)

$$F_\gamma(m^* \mid 14) = \frac{12}{18 + 12} = 0.4$$

or, working with the Poisson distribution,

$$1 - F_P(13 \mid m^*) = 0.4 \quad \text{or} \quad F_P(13 \mid m^*) = 0.6$$

In Appendix D we now go down the column headed 13.   For $m = 12.5$, $F_P(13 \mid 12.5) = 0.628$ and for $m = 13$, $F_P(13 \mid 13) = 0.573$.   Interpolating gives $m^* = 12.75$, almost exactly.   Therefore

$$I^* = (3.2)m^* \approx 41 \text{ units} \quad Ans.$$

From (13.19)

$$K_o^* = 18(3.2)\{(12.75)[1 - F_P(13 \mid 12.75)] - 14[1 - F_P(14 \mid 12.75)]\}$$

$$= 18(3.2)[(12.75)(1 - 0.600) - 14(1 - 0.700)] = 18(3.2)(0.9) = \$51.84$$

From (13.20)

$$K_u^* = 12(3.2)[14 F_P(14 \mid 12.75) - (12.75)F_P(13 \mid 12.75)]$$

$$= 12(3.2)[14(0.700) - (12.75)(0.600)] = 12(3.2)(2.15) = \$82.56$$

$$\text{EVPI} = 51.84 + 82.56 = \$134.40 \quad Ans.$$

$$\text{EPC} = 45(12) = \$540 \quad Ans.$$

$$\text{EMV}^* = 540 - 134.40 = \$405.60 \quad Ans.$$

Two-Action Problems

GENERAL THEORY

Two-action problems first require us to find the breakeven point of the physical state variable and then to determine the conditional opportunity losses, which depend on whether the breakeven value is more or less than the expected value of the physical state variable. This is essentially the same method used throughout Chapters 10 and 12, except that it will now be put in more succinct mathematical form suitable for methods of partial expectations. The principal two-action problems are, as before, product development and decisions on whether or not to use a certain piece of equipment.

Notation

F = fixed costs or costs of proposed equipment

v = variable cost per unit

r = revenues or sales price per unit

k = profit contribution or net cost of one incident (e.g. fixing a defective part)

N = size of batch, population of customers, etc.

y = number of sales, defectives, etc.

θ = sales volume per customer, cost per item in batch for fixing faults

p = fraction buying, fraction defective, etc.

Note that, for product development problems,

$$k = r - v \tag{13.21}$$

If y is chosen as the state variable, the breakeven point, y_b, is given by

$$y_b = \frac{F}{k} \tag{13.22}$$

see (1.6), and the conditional opportunity loss for any value of y is

$$\text{COL} = k|y_b - y| \tag{13.23}$$

i.e. it is the cost or profit contribution per event times the absolute difference between y and its breakeven value y_b.

If p is chosen as the state variable, then, since $p = y/N$, (13.22) gives

$$p_b = \frac{F}{Nk} \qquad (13.24)$$

and (13.23) gives

$$\text{COL} = Nk|p_b - p| = C|p_b - p| \qquad (13.25)$$

where $C = Nk$.

If θ is chosen as the state variable, then, since

$$\theta = \frac{ky}{N} = kp$$

(13.24) gives

$$\theta_b = \frac{F}{N} \qquad (13.26)$$

and (13.25) gives

$$\text{COL} = N|\theta_b - \theta| \qquad (13.27)$$

The choice of the variable depends on the distribution used. All three may be used with the normal distribution, p is used with the beta, and y and θ with the gamma. In the following general derivation, p is used, but either of the others may be used just as well if C is replaced by k or N.

First, the expected opportunity loss is given, as before, by

$$\text{EOL} = \text{COL} \times P(p) \qquad (13.28)$$

The EOL's are then totaled separately for each decision. As before, the EVPI is the lower of the two sums. It is also seen to be the sum of the EOL's for the cases in which it would have been *wrong* to use the best decision. For instance, in Example 10.1 it was found best to use the fixture, because $E(p) > p_b$. The EVPI then consisted of the EOL's for the events $p \leqq p_b$. Thus, substituting (13.25) into (13.28) and summing (or integrating) gives for the two possible decisions:

$$\text{EVPI} = C \sum_{p=0}^{p_b} (p_b - p) P(p) = C[p_b F(p_b) - E_0^{p_b}(p)] \qquad E(p) \geqq p_b \qquad (13.29)$$

$$\text{EVPI} = C \sum_{p=p_b}^{\infty} (p - p_b) P(p) = C[E_{p_b}^{\infty}(p) - p_b R(p_b)] \qquad E(p) \leqq p_b \qquad (13.30)$$

The remainder of the analysis depends on how the partial expectations of the distribution of p may be worked out. If these lead to simple expressions, all such problems can be solved with dispatch. The following detailed discussions of distributions will encompass their use in finding the right decisions, EVPI, revised EVPI and EVSI.

THE BETA DISTRIBUTION

The most generally useful distribution for p is the beta distribution. Depending on its parameters, it can, as noted in Chapter 9, take on a variety of shapes. Its partial expectations are also given by simple formulas:

$$E_0^{p_b}(p) = E(p) F_\beta(p_b \mid n+1, X+1)$$

$$E_{p_b}^{\infty}(p) = E(p)[1 - F_\beta(p_b \mid n+1, X+1)]$$

where $E(p) = X/n$. Substituting into (13.29) and (13.30) gives

$$\text{EVPI} = C[p_b F_\beta(p_b \mid n, X) - E(p) F_\beta(p_b \mid n+1, X+1)] \qquad E(p) \geqq p_b \qquad (13.31)$$

$$\text{EVPI} = C\{E(p)[1 - F_\beta(p_b \mid n+1, X+1)] - p_b[1 - F_\beta(p_b \mid n, X)]\} \qquad E(p) \leqq p_b$$
$$(13.32)$$

It is also well to recall formulas (9.12) and (9.13) for getting beta cumulative distributions from the binomial tables when n and X are integers:

(A) $\qquad\qquad F_\beta(p_b \mid n, X) = R_B(X \mid n-1, p_b) \quad$ for $\quad p_b \leqq 0.5$

(B) $\qquad\qquad F_\beta(p_b \mid n, X) = 1 - R_B(n-X \mid n-1, 1-p_b) \quad$ for $\quad p_b \geqq 0.5$

In solving a given problem, one therefore has to choose between (13.31) and (13.32) according to whether $E(p) \geqq p_b$ or $E(p) \leqq p_b$, and then between (A) and (B) depending on whether $p_b \leqq 0.5$ or $p_b \geqq 0.5$.

To find the EMV* it is necessary to distinguish between the case where the decision is to go ahead with the project and the alternative of doing nothing. Thus

$$\text{EMV*} = \begin{cases} C[E(p) - p_b] & E(p) \geqq p_b \\ 0 & E(p) \leqq p_b \end{cases} \qquad (13.33)$$

As before, $\text{EPC} = \text{EVPI} + \text{EMV*}$.

Prior Action.

EXAMPLE 13.7. A certain machine has development costs of $200,000. It is to sell for $14,000 each and the variable unit cost is $9000. There are 400 possible customers. The fraction p of customers buying the machine is assumed *a priori* to have a beta distribution with parameters $n_0 = 8$, $X_0 = 1$. Find the prior decision, EVPI and EMV*.

Here $E_0(p) = 1/8 = 0.125$ and from (13.24)

$$p_b = \frac{200,000}{400(14,000 - 9000)} = 0.1$$

Therefore $E_0(p) > p_b$; develop product. *Ans.*

Equation (13.31) applies, and also conversion (A) since $p_b < 0.5$.

$$\text{EVPI}_0 = C[(0.1)F_\beta(0.1 \mid 8, 1) - (0.125)F_\beta(0.1 \mid 9, 2)]$$
$$= C[(0.1)R_B(1 \mid 7, 0.1) - (0.125)R_B(2 \mid 8, 0.1)]$$
$$= C[(0.1)(0.5217) - (0.125)(0.1869)] = C(0.02881)$$

Using $C = Nk = 400(14,000 - 9000) = 400(5000) = 2,000,000$:

$$\text{EVPI}_0 = (2,000,000)(0.02881) = \$57,620 \quad Ans.$$

From (13.33)

$$\text{EMV*} = (2,000,000)(0.125 - 0.1) = \$50,000 \quad Ans.$$

Revised Probabilities.

The revision of beta prior probabilities is particularly simple. If the prior parameters are n_0 and X_0 and a binomial sample of size n_s results in X_s items of interest (sales, defectives, or whatever), then combining them creates a new beta distribution in which the parameters n_1 and X_1 are

$$n_1 = n_0 + n_s \qquad X_1 = X_0 + X_s \qquad (13.34)$$

EXAMPLE 13.8. Before making its final decision, the management in Example 13.7 decides to approach 12 of its customers. No one buys the machine. Revise the probabilities accordingly and find the new decision, EVPI and EMV*.

From *(13.34)*, $n_1 = 8 + 12 = 20$; $X_1 = 1 + 0 = 1$.   Therefore,

$$E_1(p) = \frac{1}{20} = 0.05 < p_b$$

Do not develop.   *Ans.*

Using *(13.32)* with conversion *(A)*:

$$EVPI_1 = C\{(0.05)[1 - F_\beta(0.1 \mid 21, 2)] - (0.1)[1 - F_\beta(0.1 \mid 20, 1)]\}$$

$$= C\{(0.05)[1 - R_B(2 \mid 20, 0.1)] - (0.1)[1 - R_B(1 \mid 19, 0.1)]\}$$

$$= C[(0.05)(1 - 0.6083) - (0.1)(1 - 0.8649)]$$

$$= (2,000,000)(0.006075) = \$12,150 \quad Ans.$$

Here the product is *not* to be developed and so the rational decision, *(13.33)*, indicates $EMV^* = 0$.   *Ans.*

Preposterior Analysis.

The determination of EVSI for a prior beta distribution is not difficult either, although the analysis is restricted by having only limited values of n in Appendix C and most other binomial tables. Thus it cannot be readily used to find optimal sample sizes. The method is first to find new beta parameters, n_e and X_e, given by

$$n_e = \frac{(n_0 + n_s)(n_0 + 1)}{n_s} - 1 \qquad X_e = \frac{n_e X_0}{n_0} \tag{13.35}$$

The rest of the calculation proceeds exactly as before. The values for n_e and X_e are substituted into *(13.31)* or *(13.32)*, which then gives EVSI instead of EVPI.

The formulas *(13.35)* are approximations only, holding whenever n_s is large compared with n_0. When it is not, use the normal distribution (see below).

EXAMPLE 13.9. A product development problem has the following data: Fixed cost, \$37,000; profit contribution, \$250; 400 potential customers; prior distribution is beta with parameters $n_0 = 5$, $X_0 = 2$. Find (*a*) the prior decision and EVPI, (*b*) the EVSI for a sample of 15.

(*a*)
$$p_b = \frac{37,000}{400(250)} = 0.37 \qquad E(p) = \frac{2}{5} = 0.4$$

Develop product.   *Ans.*

Using *(13.31)*, with $C = Nk = 400(250) = 10^5$, and conversion *(A)*:

$$EVPI = 10^5[(0.37)F_\beta(0.37 \mid 5, 2) - (0.4)F_\beta(0.37 \mid 6, 3)]$$

$$= 10^5[(0.37)R_B(2 \mid 4, 0.37) - (0.4)R_B(3 \mid 5, 0.37)]$$

$$= 10^5[(0.37)(0.4724) - (0.4)(0.2670)] = 10^5(0.067988) = \$6798.80 \quad Ans.$$

(*b*) Substituting $n_s = 15$ in *(13.35)*,

$$n_e = \frac{(5 + 15)(5 + 1)}{15} - 1 = 8 - 1 = 7 \qquad X_e = \frac{7(2)}{5} = 2.8 \approx 3$$

(Note that we are restricted to integral values of n_e and X_e if we wish to use binomial tables.) Using these parameters in *(13.31)*, but retaining the prior expectation $E(p) = E_0(p) = 0.4$, we find:

$$EVSI = 10^5[(0.37)F_\beta(0.37 \mid 7, 3) - (0.4)F_\beta(0.37 \mid 8, 4)]$$

$$= 10^5[(0.37)R_B(3 \mid 6, 0.37) - (0.4)R_B(4 \mid 7, 0.37)]$$

$$= 10^5[(0.37)(0.3937) - (0.4)(0.2341)] = 10^5(0.052029) = \$5202.90 \quad Ans.$$

Computation of Beta Parameters.

When the parameters of a beta distribution are not given directly, they may be estimated either from the expected value, $E(p) = X/n$, and the variance,

$$\text{Var}(p) = \frac{X(n - X)}{n^2(n + 1)}$$

or from the expected value and the mode,

$$p_{\text{mode}} = \frac{X-1}{n-2}$$

If the latter procedure is chosen, then

$$n = \frac{1 - 2p_{\text{mode}}}{E(p) - p_{\text{mode}}} \qquad X = \frac{1 - 2p_{\text{mode}}}{E(p) - p_{\text{mode}}} E(p) \qquad (13.36)$$

Note that numerator and denominator of the fraction in (13.36) must have the same sign; i.e. either $p_{\text{mode}} < \frac{1}{2}$ and $p_{\text{mode}} < E(p)$ or $p_{\text{mode}} > \frac{1}{2}$ and $p_{\text{mode}} > E(p)$. It is well to use this method of estimation only when numerator and denominator are not too small. Otherwise small errors in the mean and mode could produce great changes in the values of n and X.

EXAMPLE 13.10. Find the prior parameters for a beta distribution whose mean is estimated at 4/10 and mode at 1/3.

From (13.36)

$$n_0 = \frac{1 - (2/3)}{(4/10) - (1/3)} = \frac{1/3}{2/30} = 5 \qquad X_0 = 5(4/10) = 2 \quad Ans.$$

This method of estimation could, therefore, have been suitable for Example 13.9, in which 5, 2 were the prior parameters.

For estimation making use of the mean and variance, the relevant formulas are

$$n = \frac{E(p)[1 - E(p)]}{\text{Var}(p)} - 1 \qquad X = \left\{\frac{E(p)[1 - E(p)]}{\text{Var}(p)} - 1\right\} E(p) \qquad (13.37)$$

EXAMPLE 13.11. A machine has development costs of $2,800,000, sells for $2000 and has variable costs of $750. There are 8000 customers. The prior distribution of the proportion likely to buy the machine is beta with a mean of 0.3 and a standard deviation of 0.1. Find the prior decision, EVPI and EMV*.

From (13.37), writing $\text{Var}_0(p) = (0.1)^2 = 0.01$ and $E_0(p) = 0.3$,

$$n_0 = \frac{(0.3)(1 - 0.3)}{0.01} - 1 = 21 - 1 = 20 \qquad X_0 = 20(0.3) = 6$$

Because

$$p_b = \frac{2,800,000}{8000(2000 - 750)} = 0.28 < 0.3$$

the decision is to develop. *Ans.*

With $C = 8000(1250) = 10^7$, (13.31) and conversion (A) give

$$\text{EVPI} = 10^7[(0.28)F_\beta(0.28 \mid 20, 6) - (0.3)F_\beta(0.28 \mid 21, 7)]$$

$$= 10^7[(0.28)R_B(6 \mid 19, 0.28) - (0.3)R_B(7 \mid 20, 0.28)]$$

$$= 10^7[(0.28)(0.4484) - (0.3)(0.3169)] = 10^7(0.03048) = \$304,800 \quad Ans.$$

and from (13.33)

$$\text{EMV*} = 10^7(0.3 - 0.28) = \$200,000 \quad Ans.$$

THE NORMAL DISTRIBUTION

Any of the variables y, p, θ may be normally distributed, with respective standard deviations σ_y, σ_p, σ_θ. In fact, because the three variables are linearly related, all are normal when any one is. It is shown in Problem 13.2 that

$$\text{EVPI} = k\sigma_y L(D) \quad \text{or} \quad C\sigma_p L(D) \quad \text{or} \quad N\sigma_\theta L(D) \qquad (13.38)$$

where the function $L(D)$ is defined in (13.15) and

$$D = \frac{|y_b - E(y)|}{\sigma_y} \quad \text{or} \quad \frac{|p_b - E(p)|}{\sigma_p} \quad \text{or} \quad \frac{|\theta_b - E(\theta)|}{\sigma_\theta} \qquad (13.39)$$

Note that (*13.38*) provides a single expression for the EVPI, valid whether the mean of the variable is above or below the breakeven value.

Prior Analysis.

EXAMPLE 13.12. Recompute Example 13.11, assuming that the variable is sales per customer and that it is normally distributed.

From (*13.26*) $\theta_b = 2,800,000/8000 = \$350$. To find $E(\theta)$ and σ_θ, recall that $\theta = kp$. From the data

$$k = 2000 - 750 = \$1250$$

so that

$$E(\theta) = kE(p) = 1250(0.3) = \$375$$

$$\sigma_\theta = k\sigma_p = 1250(0.1) = \$125$$

From (*13.39*)

$$D = \frac{|350 - 375|}{125} = 0.2$$

Then, from (*13.38*) and Appendix I,

$$\text{EVPI} = 8000(125)(0.3069) = \$306,900 \quad Ans.$$

This compares to \$304,800 when the beta assumption is used instead.

$$\text{EMV*} = 8000(375 - 350) = \$200,000 \quad Ans.$$

as before.

EXAMPLE 13.13. Show that using p as the normally distributed variable gives the same EVPI as in Example 13.12.

Working with p, we recall that $E(p) = 0.3$, $p_b = 0.28$, $\sigma_p = 0.1$, so that

$$D = \frac{|0.28 - 0.3|}{0.1} = 0.2$$

as before. The formula for EVPI becomes

$$\text{EVPI} = 8000(1250)(0.1)(0.3069) = \$306,900$$

Revision of Prior Probabilities.

To find the posterior EVPI, the revised mean and standard deviation—$E_1(y)$, σ_{y1} or $E_1(p)$, σ_{p1} or $E_1(\theta)$, $\sigma_{\theta1}$—are used in (*13.39*) and (*13.38*) instead of the prior values $E_0(y)$, σ_{y0} or $E_0(p)$, σ_{p0} or $E_0(\theta)$, $\sigma_{\theta0}$.

One way to find these revised values is to take a sample of size n and record $\bar{p} = (\Sigma X)/n$, where each X is 1 or 0 according as a sale was or was not made (a part was or was not defective, etc.). Thus $\bar{p}$ is the fraction of sales or of defectives in the sample, and assuming that the sample is binomial, it is possible to calculate the revised parameters, using $\bar{p}$ directly or converting to the sample variable $\bar{y}$ or $\bar{\theta}$. The necessary formulas are given in Table 13-1.

The revised means are seen to be the sum of the prior and sample means, weighted by their respective reciprocal variances. The reciprocal of the revised variance is seen to be the sum of the reciprocals of the prior and sample variances.

EXAMPLE 13.14. In Example 13.12, a preliminary survey is taken in which 40 potential customers are approached and 10 buy the product. Find the revised decision, EVPI and EMV*.

The prior parameters are $E_0(\theta) = \$375$ and $\sigma_{\theta0} = \$125$. From Table 13-1,

$$\bar{\theta} = 1250\left(\frac{10}{40}\right) = 312.50$$

$$s_{\bar{\theta}}^2 = (1250)^2 \frac{\frac{10}{40}\left(1 - \frac{10}{40}\right)}{40} = \frac{468,750}{64} = (85.58)^2$$

$$E_1(\theta) = \frac{\dfrac{375}{(125)^2} + \dfrac{312.50}{(85.58)^2}}{\dfrac{1}{(125)^2} + \dfrac{1}{(85.58)^2}} = \frac{0.024 + 0.04267}{0.000064 + 0.0001365} = \$332.52$$

Thus, $E_1(\theta) < \theta_b$; do not develop product, EMV* = 0.   *Ans.*

Further, from Table 13-1,

$$\sigma_{\theta 1} = \frac{125(85.58)}{\sqrt{(125)^2 + (85.58)^2}} = \$70.62$$

From (*13.39*)

$$D_1 = \frac{|350 - 332.52|}{70.62} = 0.2475$$

and from (*13.38*) and Appendix I

$$\text{EVPI} = 8000(70.62)\,L(0.2475) = 8000(70.62)(0.2873) = \$162,300 \quad Ans.$$

Table 13-1

	Variable		
	p	y	θ
Sample Mean	$\bar{p} = \dfrac{\Sigma X}{n}$	$\bar{y} = N\bar{p}$	$\bar{\theta} = k\bar{p}$
Estimated Variance of Sample Mean	$s_{\bar{p}}^2 = \dfrac{\bar{p}(1-\bar{p})}{n}$	$s_{\bar{y}}^2 = N^2 s_{\bar{p}}^2$	$s_{\bar{\theta}}^2 = k^2 s_{\bar{p}}^2$
Revised Mean	$E_1(p) = \dfrac{\dfrac{E_0(p)}{\sigma_{p0}^2} + \dfrac{\bar{p}}{s_{\bar{p}}^2}}{\dfrac{1}{\sigma_{p0}^2} + \dfrac{1}{s_{\bar{p}}^2}}$	$E_1(y) = \dfrac{\dfrac{E_0(y)}{\sigma_{y0}^2} + \dfrac{\bar{y}}{s_{\bar{y}}^2}}{\dfrac{1}{\sigma_{y0}^2} + \dfrac{1}{s_{\bar{y}}^2}}$	$E_1(\theta) = \dfrac{\dfrac{E_0(\theta)}{\sigma_{\theta0}^2} + \dfrac{\bar{\theta}}{s_{\bar{\theta}}^2}}{\dfrac{1}{\sigma_{\theta0}^2} + \dfrac{1}{s_{\bar{\theta}}^2}}$
Revised Variance	$\dfrac{1}{\sigma_{p1}^2} = \dfrac{1}{\sigma_{p0}^2} + \dfrac{1}{s_{\bar{p}}^2}$	$\dfrac{1}{\sigma_{y1}^2} = \dfrac{1}{\sigma_{y0}^2} + \dfrac{1}{s_{\bar{y}}^2}$	$\dfrac{1}{\sigma_{\theta1}^2} = \dfrac{1}{\sigma_{\theta0}^2} + \dfrac{1}{s_{\bar{\theta}}^2}$
Revised Standard Deviation	$\sigma_{p1} = \dfrac{\sigma_{p0} s_{\bar{p}}}{\sqrt{\sigma_{p0}^2 + s_{\bar{p}}^2}}$	$\sigma_{y1} = \dfrac{\sigma_{y0} s_{\bar{y}}}{\sqrt{\sigma_{y0}^2 + s_{\bar{y}}^2}}$	$\sigma_{\theta1} = \dfrac{\sigma_{\theta0} s_{\bar{\theta}}}{\sqrt{\sigma_{\theta0}^2 + s_{\bar{\theta}}^2}}$

Preposterior Analysis.

For preposterior analysis (discussed here in terms of the variable p), it is necessary to estimate in advance what the mean and variance will be after the sample is taken. The prior estimate of the posterior mean is, in the absence of other information, $E_e(p) = E_0(p)$. The prior estimate of σ_{p1}^2 has to be based on the formula in Table 13-1. But that expression contains $s_{\bar{p}}^2$, which in turn was used to approximate the actual variance of the sample mean:

$$s_{\bar{p}}^2 \approx \sigma_{\bar{p}}^2 = \frac{\sigma_X^2}{n}$$

see (*11.1*). Hence, for the proposed sample of size n_s, we may write $s_{\bar{p}}^2 \approx \sigma_X^2/n_s$, where the value of σ_X^2 has been obtained from an earlier similar project, from a guess, or from the results of a pilot sample.

The reduction in variance produced by the proposed sample is

$$\sigma_{pe}^2 = \sigma_{p0}^2 - \sigma_{p1}^2$$

Substituting this, and the above value of $s_{\bar{p}}^2$, into Table 13-1 leads to

$$\sigma_{pe}^2 = \frac{\sigma_{p0}^4}{\sigma_{p0}^2 + (\sigma_X^2/n_s)}$$

Using the parameters $E_e(p)$, σ_{pe} in (13.38) gives the EVSI.

The analysis for the variables y and θ is exactly similar; the results are collected in Table 13-2.

EXAMPLE 13.15. In Example 13.14 consider the sampling result as a means of estimating σ_X^2, i.e. it is a pilot sample. Find the EVSI and the ENGS, assuming that each sales call costs \$40, (a) for $n_s = 100$ and (b) for $n_s = 198$.

In Example 13.14 we found that for $n = 40$,

$$(85.58)^2 = s_{\hat{\theta}}^2 = k^2 s_{\bar{p}}^2 \approx \frac{k^2 \sigma_X^2}{40}$$

Moreover, $E_0(\theta) = \$375$, $\sigma_{\theta0} = \$125$, $N = 8000$ and $\theta_b = \$350$.

(a) For $n_s = 100$, Table 13-2 gives

$$E_e(\theta) = 375 \qquad \sigma_{\theta e} = \frac{(125)^2}{\sqrt{(125)^2 + \frac{40}{100}(85.58)^2}} = 114.71$$

$$D_e = \frac{|350 - 375|}{114.71} = 0.218$$

$$\text{EVSI} = 8000(114.71)\,L(0.218) = 8000(114.71)(0.2994)$$
$$= \$274{,}753 \quad Ans.$$

Hence, ENGS $= 274{,}753 - 100(40) = \$270{,}753$. *Ans.*

(b) For $n_s = 198$, Table 13-2 gives

$$E_e(\theta) = 375 \qquad \sigma_{\theta e} = \frac{(125)^2}{\sqrt{(125)^2 + \frac{40}{198}(85.58)^2}} = 119.47$$

$$D_e = \frac{|350 - 375|}{119.47} = 0.209$$

Table 13-2

	Variable		
	p	y	θ
Prior Parameters	$E_0(p)$ σ_{p0}	$E_0(y)$ σ_{y0}	$E_0(\theta)$ $\sigma_{\theta0}$
Estimated Parameters	$E_e(p) = E_0(p)$ $\sigma_{pe} = \dfrac{\sigma_{p0}^2}{\sqrt{\sigma_{p0}^2 + \frac{\sigma_X^2}{n_s}}}$	$E_e(y) = E_0(y)$ $\sigma_{ye} = \dfrac{\sigma_{y0}^2}{\sqrt{\sigma_{y0}^2 + \frac{N^2\sigma_X^2}{n_s}}}$	$E_e(\theta) = E_0(\theta)$ $\sigma_{\theta e} = \dfrac{\sigma_{\theta0}^2}{\sqrt{\sigma_{\theta0}^2 + \frac{k^2\sigma_X^2}{n_s}}}$
D_e	$\dfrac{|p_b - E_e(p)|}{\sigma_{pe}}$	$\dfrac{|y_b - E_e(y)|}{\sigma_{ye}}$	$\dfrac{|\theta_b - E_e(\theta)|}{\sigma_{\theta e}}$
EVSI	$C\sigma_{pe}L(D_e)$	$k\sigma_{ye}L(D_e)$	$N\sigma_{\theta e}L(D_e)$

$$\text{EVSI} = 8000(119.47)\,L(0.209) = 8000(119.47)(0.3027)$$

$$= \$289{,}308 \quad Ans.$$

Hence, $\text{ENGS} = 289{,}308 - 198(40) = \$281{,}388 \quad Ans.$

From the answers for the two sample sizes it is clear that the difference is not large. Such relative insensitivity to sample size over a wide range is quite typical of normal sampling. A procedure for finding the optimal sample size is given in Problem 13.16.

THE GAMMA DISTRIBUTION

As in the case of many-action problems, it is sometimes useful in two-action problems to have available a prior distribution which can describe a markedly skewed set of prior estimates. The gamma distribution fills the bill here. Substituting the appropriate expressions for the gamma distribution into (13.29) and (13.30), we obtain, for the variable $m = p/P$ and parameter X,

$$\text{EVPI} = C[p_b F_\gamma(m_b \,|\, X) - E_0^{p_b}(p)]$$

$$= C[p_b F_\gamma(m_b \,|\, X) - XP\,F_\gamma(m_b \,|\, X+1)] \qquad E(m) \geqq m_b \qquad (13.40)$$

and

$$\text{EVPI} = C[E_{p_b}^\infty(p) - p_b R_\gamma(m_b \,|\, X)]$$

$$= C[XP\,R_\gamma(m_b \,|\, X+1) - p_b R_\gamma(m_b \,|\, X)] \qquad E(m) \leqq m_b \qquad (13.41)$$

Equations (13.40) and (13.41) hold for the variable y or θ if we replace C by k or N, respectively. When X is an integer the equations may be transformed via (9.17), yielding

$$\text{EVPI} = C\{p_b[1 - F_P(X-1 \,|\, m_b)] - XP[1 - F_P(X \,|\, m_b)]\} \qquad E(m) \geqq m_b \qquad (13.42)$$

$$\text{EVPI} = C[XP\,F_P(X \,|\, m_b) - p_b F_P(X-1 \,|\, m_b)] \qquad E(m) \leqq m_b \qquad (13.43)$$

Prior Analysis.

In the prior distribution the parameters are X_0 and P_0. They must be either given or else computed from the mean and variance via (13.17) or from the mean and mode via (13.18).

EXAMPLE 13.16. Rework Example 13.12 assuming a gamma prior distribution rather than a normal one.

We have $E(\theta) = \$375$, $\sigma_\theta = \$125$ and $\theta_b = \$350$. From (13.17)

$$X_0 = \frac{(375)^2}{(125)^2} = 9 \qquad \Theta_0 = \frac{(125)^2}{375} = 41.67$$

and

$$m_{b0} = \frac{\theta_b}{\Theta_0} = \frac{350}{41.67} = 8.4$$

From Table 9-6, $E(m) = X_0 = 9$; as this exceeds m_{b0}, the decision is to go ahead (as previously). Using (13.42) with C replaced by N, and interpolating in Appendix D,

$$\text{EVPI} = 8000\{350[1 - F_P(8 \,|\, 8.4)] - 375[1 - F_P(9 \,|\, 8.4)]\}$$

$$= 8000[350(1 - 0.537) - 375(1 - 0.666)]$$

$$= 8000(36.8) = \$294{,}400 \quad Ans.$$

Note that this compares with \$306,900 for the normal distribution (Example 13.12) and \$304,800 for the beta distribution (Example 13.11). If the normal and gamma distributions are considered approximations to the beta (which they are), then the former gives a higher and the latter a lower result; the difference is not great, however, and is satisfactory in problems of this kind.

Revision of Prior Probabilities.

Computation of the revised EVPI is done in the same way as the prior analysis, except that X_0 and m_{b0} are replaced by

$$X_1 = X_0 + X_s \qquad m_{b1} = m_{b0} + m_s \tag{13.44}$$

where X_s and m_s are derived from a Poisson sample.

EXAMPLE 13.17.   In Example 13.16, a sample of 24 potential customers is canvassed and 6 buy the product.   Revise the prior analysis on the basis of this information and find the EVPI.

The sample is actually binomial, with (unknown) parameter p.   Approximating the binomial distribution with a Poisson distribution, we have (see Chapter 9)

$$m_s = n_s p \approx n_s p_b = 24(0.28) = 6.72$$

where p_b was computed in Example 13.11.   Then from (13.44)

$$X_1 = 9 + 6 = 15 \qquad m_{b1} = 8.4 + 6.72 = 15.12$$

To accord with the limitations of Appendix D, we will approximate this to $m_{b1} = 15$ when looking up the Poisson probabilities.

The second revised parameter, Θ_1, is obtained as

$$\Theta_1 = \frac{\theta_b}{m_{b1}} = \frac{350}{15.12} = 23.15$$

Because $E_1(m) = X_1 = 15 < 15.12 = m_{b1}$, the decision is revised to DON'T DEVELOP.   *Ans.*

For the computation of EVPI, (13.43) must be used (with N in place of C):

$$\begin{aligned} \text{EVPI} &= 8000[(15)(23.15)F_P(15 \mid 15) - 350F_P(14 \mid 15)] \\ &= 8000[(347.2)(0.568) - 350(0.466)] \\ &= 8000(34.11) = \$272,880 \quad Ans. \end{aligned}$$

Preposterior Analysis.

A simple procedure is available for doing a preposterior analysis with a gamma prior distribution.   It can be used for relatively large sample sizes but is, in practice, also limited by the values of m given in Appendix D or other Poisson tables.

It is required to find the EVSI for a sample of n_s in a Poisson process in which the number of items with the desired characteristic, X_s, is unknown in advance of actual sampling. The first step is to find a parameter n_0 of the prior distribution such that

$$m_{b0} = n_0 p_b \tag{13.45}$$

Using an approximation which applies when n_s is large, we may then find the new parameter

$$n_e = \frac{n_0 + n_s}{n_s} n_0 \tag{13.46}$$

From these,

$$m_{be} = n_e p_b \qquad X_e = \frac{n_e}{n_0} X_0 \tag{13.47}$$

A quicker alternative method is to compute

$$m_s = n_s p_b \tag{13.48}$$

Then $$m_{be} = \frac{m_{b0} + m_s}{m_s} m_{b0} \qquad X_e = \frac{m_{b0} + m_s}{m_s} X_0 \tag{13.49}$$

The formula for EVSI is then identical to that for EVPI—i.e. (13.42) or (13.43)—except that m_{be} is used as the parameter and X_e (rounded to an integer) as the variable.

EXAMPLE 13.18. A product development situation has the following data: Breakeven sales per customer, $250; 3000 customers; sales per customer gamma distributed with mean $300 and variance 30,000; breakeven percentage of market penetration, 12.5. (a) Find the prior decision, EVPI and EMV*. (b) Find the EVSI for a sample of size 60.

(a) From (13.17)

$$X_0 = \frac{(300)^2}{30,000} = 3 \qquad \Theta_0 = \frac{30,000}{300} = 100$$

and

$$m_{b0} = \frac{\theta_b}{\Theta_0} = \frac{250}{100} = 2.5$$

Because $E_0(m) = 3 > 2.5 = m_{b0}$, the prior action is DEVELOP. *Ans.*

From (13.33),

$$\text{EMV*} = N[E_0(\theta) - \theta_{b0}] = 3000(300 - 250) = \$150,000 \quad Ans.$$

Using (13.42),

$$\begin{aligned}
\text{EVPI} &= 3000\{250[1 - F_P(2 \mid 2.5)] - 300[1 - F_P(3 \mid 2.5)]\} \\
&= 3000[250(1 - 0.544) - 300(1 - 0.7575)] \\
&= 3000(41.25) = 123,750 \quad Ans.
\end{aligned}$$

(b) $n_s = 60$; from (13.48), $m_s = 60(0.125) = 7.5$. Then, from (13.49),

$$m_{be} = \frac{2.5 + 7.5}{7.5}(2.5) = 3.33 \qquad X_e = \frac{2.5 + 7.5}{7.5}(3) = 4$$

Since $E_e(m) = X_e = 4 > 3.33 = m_{be}$, we use (13.42) to obtain:

$$\begin{aligned}
\text{EVSI} &= 3000\{250[1 - F_P(3 \mid 3.33)] - 300[1 - F_P(4 \mid 3.33)]\} \\
&= 3000[250(1 - 0.574) - 300(1 - 0.757)] \\
&= 3000(33.6) = \$100,800 \quad Ans.
\end{aligned}$$

Note that in applying (13.42) we have retained the prior value $X\Theta = E_0(\theta) = 300$.

Solved Problems

ADDITIONAL THEORETICAL MATTER

13.1. Prove (13.12) and (13.13).

Let the demand u be normally distributed with mean μ and standard deviation σ. Then, from (13.6),

$$K_u = k_u \int_I^\infty (u - I) f_N(u \mid \mu, \sigma)\, du = k_u \int_I^\infty (u - I) \frac{1}{\sigma\sqrt{2\pi}} e^{-[(u-\mu)/\sigma]^2/2}\, du$$

Make the change of variable $u = \mu + \sigma w$ in the integral, and write $I = \mu + \sigma z$.

$$\begin{aligned}
K_u &= k_u \int_z^\infty \sigma(w - z) \frac{1}{\sigma\sqrt{2\pi}} e^{-w^2/2}\, \sigma\, dw \\
&= k_u \sigma \int_z^\infty \frac{1}{\sqrt{2\pi}} e^{-w^2/2}\, w\, dw - k_u \sigma z \int_z^\infty \frac{1}{\sqrt{2\pi}} e^{-w^2/2}\, dw
\end{aligned}$$

In the first integral on the right, let $t = w^2/2$. The integral becomes

$$\int_{z^2/2}^\infty \frac{1}{\sqrt{2\pi}} e^{-t}\, dt = \frac{1}{\sqrt{2\pi}} e^{-z^2/2} = f_N(z)$$

The second integral on the right is simply $R_N(z)$. Thus,

$$K_u = k_u \sigma f_N(z) - k_u \sigma z R_N(z) = k_u \sigma L(z)$$

which proves (13.13).

From (*13.5*) and (*13.6*) we note that

$$\frac{K_o}{k_o} - \frac{K_u}{k_u} = I[F(I) + R(I)] - [E_0^I(u) + E_I^\infty(u)]$$

$$= I - E_0^\infty(u) = I - \mu = \sigma z$$

Hence, $$K_o = k_o\left(\sigma z + \frac{K_u}{k_u}\right) = k_o\sigma[z + L(z)]$$

which proves (*13.12*). Note that in equating $E_0^\infty(u)$ to μ we have supposed the normal distribution to be such that negative values of u have negligible probabilities.

13.2. Prove (*13.38*).

For the normal variable p, (*13.30*) takes the form

$$\text{EVPI} = C \int_{p_b}^\infty (p - p_b)f_N(p \mid E(p), \sigma_p)\, dp \qquad E(p) \leqq p_b$$

Comparing this to the expression for K_u in Problem 13.1 gives at once

(*1*) $$\text{EVPI} = C\sigma_p L(z) \quad \text{where} \quad z = \frac{p_b - E(p)}{\sigma_p} \geqq 0$$

Similarly, comparing (*13.29*) with the result for K_o in Problem 13.1 gives

(*2*) $$\text{EVPI} = C\sigma_p[z + L(z)]$$
$$= C\sigma_p L(-z) \quad \text{where} \quad z = \frac{p_b - E(p)}{\sigma_p} \leqq 0$$

the second step following from (*13.16*). Now, if we let

$$\frac{|p_b - E(p)|}{\sigma_p} = D$$

we see that in (*1*), $z = D$; while in (*2*), $z = -D$. Hence, in both cases, $\text{EVPI} = C\sigma_p L(D)$.

ADDITIONAL MANY-ACTION MODELS

13.3. In a newsboy-type sales model, it has been observed that sales depend on how long the store is open; after high initial sales, demand slackens. Specifically, sales are normally distributed with means and standard deviations as shown in Table 13-3.

Table 13-3

Time Open, days	Mean Sales, pieces	Standard Deviation, pieces
1	140	20
2	240	34
3	310	44
4	340	49

Profit per item is 70 cents and salvage loss is 40 cents. It costs \$25 per day to keep the sales booth open. Find the optimal time of operation, the optimal initial inventory and the corresponding EMV.

This is an extended version of the standard problem, which is solved for each opening period in turn.

$$F(I^*) = \frac{0.70}{0.40 + 0.70} = 0.6364$$

Entering Appendix B with an area of $0.6364 - 0.5 = 0.1364$, we find $z \approx 0.35$, so that

$$I^* = \mu + (0.35)\sigma$$

From (13.12) and (13.13)

$$K_o^* = (0.40)\sigma[0.35 + L(0.35)]$$
$$= (0.40)\sigma(0.35 + 0.2481) = (0.23924)\sigma$$

$$K_u^* = (0.70)\sigma L(0.35) = (0.70)\sigma(0.2481) = (0.17367)\sigma$$

$$\text{EVPI} = K_o^* + K_u^* = (0.41291)\sigma$$

Also:
$$\text{EPC} = (0.70)\mu$$

$$\text{Gross EMV} = \text{EPC} - \text{EVPI}$$

$$\text{Net EMV} = \text{Gross EMV} - (T \times \$25)$$

where T is the time open.

The foregoing relationships enable us to prepare Table 13-4. The result indicates that the booth should be open 3 days and have an initial inventory of 325 items. The EMV* is \$123.83.

Table 13-4

T	μ	σ	$z\sigma$	I^*	EVPI	EPC	Gross EMV	$T \times \$25$	Net EMV
1	140	20	7.0	147	8.26	98	89.74	25	64.74
2	240	34	11.9	252	14.04	168	153.96	50	103.96
3*	310	44	15.4	325*	18.17	217	198.83	75	123.83*
4	340	49	17.2	357	20.23	238	217.77	100	117.77

13.4. A bank of in-process inventory is to be established at a point in an assembly line. If there is a breakdown, then, for a certain time at least, the machines downstream from the material bank can draw on it and thus avoid breakdown costs. It is not, of course, possible to have unlimited inventories of this kind, due to the carrying charges involved. Assume that if the material bank is depleted, it can be replaced in a short time—say, by running the upstream machines during lunch or after work. Analyze this problem and derive a general expression for the optimal level of the material bank and for the expected cost of the optimal policy.

The following notation will be used:

I = level of material bank, units

I^* = optimal level of material bank, units

c = carrying charge per unit per unit of time (cf. Chapter 2)

k = cost of breakdown per unit of time (cost per unit of idle time)

p = production rate, units per unit of time

b = average number of breakdowns per unit of time

t = duration of breakdown

$f(t), F(t)$ = p.d.f. and c.d.f. of breakdown duration t

The inventory required during a breakdown of duration t is pt. If $I < pt$, an amount of idle time $t - (I/p)$ will be incurred, costing $k[t - (I/p)]$. The expected cost of a single breakdown per unit of time is derived in the same way as K_u and is given by

$$k \int_{I/p}^{\infty} [t - (I/p)] f(t) \, dt$$

Such an event occurs b times per unit time. Further, the inventory used for material banks has a carrying charge of c per unit, or cI total. Thus the total expected cost C is

$$C = cI + bk \int_{I/p}^{\infty} [t - (I/p)] f(t) \, dt$$

To find I^*, set $dC/dI = 0$:

$$c + bk(-1/p) \int_{I/p}^{\infty} f(t)\, dt = 0 \quad \text{or} \quad c - \frac{bk}{p}\left[1 - F\left(\frac{I}{p}\right)\right] = 0$$

Therefore

$$F\left(\frac{I^*}{p}\right) = 1 - \frac{cp}{bk} \tag{13.50}$$

Once this equation has been solved for I^*, the expected cost C^* is given by

$$C^* = cI^* + bkE_{I^*/p}^{\infty}(t) - \frac{I^* bk}{p} R(I^*/p) \tag{13.51}$$

If t is normally distributed with mean $E(t)$ and standard deviation σ_t, then analogy with (13.6) leads to

$$C^* = cI^* + bk\sigma_t L(u) \quad \text{where} \quad u = \frac{(I^*/p) - E(t)}{\sigma_t} \tag{13.52}$$

Note that in practical cases it is possible for $1 - (cp/bk)$ to be negative. This occurs, for example, when the cost of carrying one unit of inventory is greater than the cost of a breakdown per unit time and p and b have suitable values. Then no inventory should be provided.

13.5. In Problem 13.4 there are 8 breakdowns a year, on the average; a breakdown costs $60 per hour; carrying charges per unit of inventory per year are $4; the production rate is 40 units per hour. Find the optimal level of standby inventory and the expected annual cost of that policy. Breakdown times are normally distributed with mean 2.5 hours and standard deviation 1.3 hours.

Here, $b = 8$, $k = 60$, $c = 4$, $p = 40$; note that b and c are per year and k and p per hour; thus consistency of units is safeguarded in (13.50), which gives

$$F_N\left(\frac{I^*}{p}\,\middle|\,2.5, 1.3\right) = 1 - \frac{4(40)}{8(60)} = 0.6667$$

From Appendix B, $u \approx 0.43$ for $F_N(u) = 0.6667$, so that

$$0.43 = \frac{(I^*/p) - 2.5}{1.3}$$

$$\frac{I^*}{p} = 2.5 + (0.43)(1.3) = 3.059$$

$$I^* = (3.059)(40) \approx 122 \text{ units} \quad Ans.$$

From (13.52)

$$C^* = 4(122) + 8(60)(1.3)\,L(0.43)$$

$$= 488 + 480(1.3)(0.2203) = \$625.47 \quad Ans.$$

13.6. The following data apply to a material bank model of the type in Problems 13.4 and 13.5: On the average there are 1.3 breakdowns a year, a breakdown costs $60 per hour, production is at a rate of 10 units per hour and carrying charges for the inventory are $2 per unit per year. Distribution of the breakdown time is exponential with mean 1.4 hours. Find I^* and C^*.

Note that the exponential distribution specified here has a reverse-J shape. This has a certain plausibility in problems of this kind because quite often the shortest breakdowns occur most frequently and longer ones less often.

From (9.18) and (13.50)

$$F_e\left(\frac{I^*}{p}\,\middle|\,T\right) = 1 - e^{-I^*/pT} = 1 - \frac{cp}{bk}$$

or

$$e^{-I^*/pT} = \frac{cp}{bk}$$

Substituting $c = 2$, $p = 10$, $b = 1.3$, $k = 60$ and $T = 1.4$,

$$e^{-I^*/14} = 0.2564 \qquad e^{I^*/14} = 3.9$$

From Appendix A, $e^{1.36} = 3.8962$, which is close enough.   Thus

$$I^* = 14(1.36) \approx 19 \text{ items} \quad Ans.$$

To obtain C^* we substitute the exponential p.d.f. (Table 9-6) into (13.51) and integrate by parts:

$$
\begin{aligned}
C^* &= cI^* + bk \int_{I^*/p}^{\infty} [t - (I^*/p)] \frac{1}{T} e^{-t/T} \, dt \\
&= cI^* + bk \left[-[t - (I^*/p)]e^{-t/T} - Te^{-t/T} \right]_{I^*/p}^{\infty} \\
&= cI^* + bkTe^{-I^*/pT} \qquad\qquad (13.53)
\end{aligned}
$$

The exponential term is again $e^{-1.36} = 0.25666$, so that

$$C^* = 2(19) + (1.3)(60)(1.4)(0.25666) = 38 + 78(0.3593) = \$66.03 \quad Ans.$$

13.7. Deliveries of a certain bulk product are made at regular intervals.   The amount delivered each time is V.   The demand during the period is u, which is a random variable with probability density function $f(u)$.   If the firm runs short before a scheduled delivery date, it can obtain the material on a less-than-carload basis at an extra cost of k_u per unit quantity.   If there is a delivery when there is still a significant amount in storage, it cannot be returned, but rather is wasted at a cost of k_o per unit quantity.   The material must be kept under refrigeration, which costs k_s per unit quantity per cycle, i.e. $k_s V$ altogether.   Find the optimal delivery, V^*, and the corresponding expected cost, C^*.

This is a simple extension of the "newsboy" problem, applied to incoming storage.   When $V > u$, an amount $V - u$ is wasted; when $u > V$, there is a shortage of $u - V$.   The resulting conditional costs are $k_o(V - u)$ and $k_u(u - V)$ respectively.   In addition there is a storage cost of $k_s V$.   Then, similar to (13.3),

$$C = k_o \int_0^V (V - u) f(u) \, du + k_u \int_V^{\infty} (u - V) f(u) \, du + k_s V$$

and V^* is obtained by solving

$$\frac{dC}{dV} = k_o F(V) - k_u[1 - F(V)] + k_s = 0$$

from which

$$F(V^*) = \frac{k_u - k_s}{k_u + k_o} \quad Ans.$$

Clearly, when $k_s > k_u$ no storage of material should be undertaken at all.   The expression for C^* may be written as

$$C^* = K_o^* + K_u^* + k_s V^* \quad Ans.$$

13.8. In an incoming storage situation, the cost per gallon of underage is 40¢, of overage 55¢ and of storage space 15¢.   Demand is normally distributed with mean 600 gallons per cycle and standard deviation 200 gallons.   Find the optimal storage quantity and the corresponding cost.

From Problem 13.7

$$F_N(V^* \mid 600, 200) = \frac{k_u - k_s}{k_u + k_o} = \frac{40 - 15}{40 + 55} = 0.2632$$

From Appendix B (looking up z for $0.5 - 0.2632 = 0.2368$), $z \approx -0.633$ and

$$V^* = 600 - (0.663)(200) \doteq 467 \text{ gallons} \quad Ans.$$

To compute C^*, use (13.12), (13.13) and (13.16), the last because the argument of $L(z)$ is negative here. From Appendix I, $L(0.663) = 0.1625$.

$$K_o^* = (0.55)(200)(0.1625) = 17.88$$

$$K_u^* = (0.40)(200)(0.663 + 0.1625) = 66.04$$

$$k_s V^* = (0.15)(467) = 70.05$$

$$C^* = 17.88 + 66.04 + 70.05 = \$153.97 \qquad Ans.$$

13.9. It is estimated that the number of parts required by a certain model of tractor during its lifetime is normally distributed with mean 9000 and standard deviation 800. If these parts are produced together with the original batch, they cost \$1.80 each; but if ordered later, their cost rises to \$6 each. Find the optimal number to be produced with the tractors and the expected optimal cost.

The analysis of Example 13.3 applies here, except that the normal distribution is used instead of the Poisson. Given that $k_o = \$1.80$ and $k_u = 6 - 1.80 = \$4.20$,

$$F_N(I^* \mid 9000, 800) = \frac{4.20}{1.80 + 4.20} = 0.70$$

From Appendix B, $z = 0.525$ (corresponding to an area of 0.20 in the table). Then

$$I^* = 9000 + (0.525)(800) = 9420 \qquad Ans.$$

From (13.12) and (13.13)

$$K_o^* = (1.8)(800)[0.525 + L(0.525)]$$

$$= (1.8)(800)(0.525 + 0.1902) = 1029.89$$

$$K_u^* = (4.2)(800)(0.1902) = 639.07$$

$$C^* = 1029.89 + 639.07 = \$1668.96 \qquad Ans.$$

13.10. A sales training course is conducted by a company which needs X new salesmen. The time spent by each sales trainee in the course is valued at v and the cost to set up the course, including instruction, room rental, etc., is S. The number of trainees required to produce X is n, which is a random variable with p.d.f. $f(n)$, where $f(n) = 0$ for $n < X$. Find the optimal size Q^* of the entering class and the corresponding optimal cost C^*.

If $n < Q$, we have an excess of $Q - n$ trainees, resulting in a COL of $v(Q - n)$. The expected loss is therefore

$$v \int_0^Q (Q - n) f(n) \, dn$$

If $Q < n$, there is a loss of S since a whole new course must be started, regardless of the actual size of the shortfall. (We are assuming here that the shortfall will be exactly made up in the repeat course.) The expected cost from this source is $S \times P(n > Q)$, i.e. S times the probability of n, the number needed to get X successful candidates, being greater than Q, the number actually entering the class. For a continuous distribution this is $S R(Q) = S[1 - F(Q)]$ and for a discrete distribution, it is $S R(Q + 1) = S[1 - F(Q)]$. Thus the cost function C is

$$C = v \int_0^Q (Q - n) f(n) \, dn + S[1 - F(Q)] \qquad (13.54)$$

Recalling that $F(Q) = \int_0^Q f(n)\, dn$, the function can be minimized by setting

$$\frac{dC}{dQ} = v \int_0^Q f(n)\, dn - S f(Q) = 0$$

$$v F(Q) - S f(Q) = 0$$

whence
$$\frac{f(Q^*)}{F(Q^*)} = \frac{v}{S} \qquad\qquad (13.55)$$

which must be solved for Q^*. C^* is obtained by substituting Q^* in (13.54).

13.11. A business firm requires 12 salesmen and proposes to train them in a class for which the fixed costs are \$5000. The variable cost per student is \$1080. Assume a Pascal distribution for the size of the class, with a probability of success of 0.82. Find the optimal size of the entering class and the EVPI.

This problem is essentially the same as Problem 10.4, except that a Pascal distribution has been substituted for the empirical one. The probability of success is, however, about the same in both cases. (The empirical distribution had mean $\bar{n} = 14.55$. Fitting this by a Pascal distribution with mean $12/p$, see Table 9-6, gives $p = 12/14.55 \approx 0.825$.) The Pascal distribution is clearly the appropriate one to use when successes and failures follow a Bernoulli process.

The critical ratio is given by (13.55) as

$$\frac{f_{Pa}(Q^* \mid 12, 0.82)}{F_{Pa}(Q^* \mid 12, 0.82)} = \frac{v}{S} = \frac{1080}{5000} = 0.216$$

The solution for Q^* is accomplished in Table 13-5, which converts to the binomial distribution by use of (9.15). Because

$$f_{Pa}(Q \mid X, p) = F_{Pa}(Q \mid X, p) - F_{Pa}(Q - 1 \mid X, p)$$

the $f_{Pa}(Q \mid 12, 0.82)$ values may be simply obtained as the first differences of the $F_{Pa}(Q \mid 12, 0.82)$ column. It is seen that $Q = 15$ gives a critical ratio closest to the required value 0.216, so that an entering class of 15 candidates is optimal. *Ans.*

Table 13-5

Q	$F_{Pa}(Q \mid 12, 0.82)$ $= 1 - F_B(11 \mid Q, 0.82)$	$f_{Pa}(Q \mid 12, 0.82)$	$\dfrac{f_{Pa}(Q \mid 12, 0.82)}{F_{Pa}(Q \mid 12, 0.82)}$
12	0.0924	0.0924	1.0000
13	0.2920	0.1996	0.6836
14	0.5256	0.2336	0.4444
15	0.7218	0.1962	0.2718*
16	0.8542	0.1324	0.1550
17	0.9305	0.0763	0.0820

The EVPI is given by C^*; comparing the integral in (13.54) with (13.1), it is seen that it is the loss due to overage, K_o.   Thus

$$\text{EVPI} = K_o^* + S[1 - F_{Pa}(Q^* \mid X, p)]$$

From (13.5)
$$K_o^* = v[Q^* F_{Pa}(Q^* \mid X, p) - E_0^{Q^*}(n)]$$

It can be shown that for the Pascal distribution

$$E_0^{Q^*}(n) = \frac{X}{p} F_{Pa}(Q^* + 1 \mid X + 1, p) = \frac{X}{p}[1 - F_B(X \mid Q^* + 1, p)]$$

Therefore, noting from Table 13-5 that $F_{Pa}(Q^* \mid X, p) = 0.7218$,

$$K_o^* = 1080 \left\{ 15(0.7218) - \frac{12}{0.82} [1 - F_B (12 \mid 16, 0.82)] \right\}$$

$$= 1080[10.8270 - 14.6341(1 - 0.3223)]$$

$$= 1080(0.9094) = \$982.15$$

and $$\text{EVPI} = 982.15 + 5000(1 - 0.7218) = \$2373.15 \quad Ans.$$

This compares reasonably well with the value \$2168 found for the similar empirical distribution of Problem 10.4.

13.12. A certain machining process has a scrap rate of 13 percent. A batch of 8000 pieces is to be manufactured. A setup costs \$900 and each part manufactured in excess costs \$13.50; such parts must be considered wasted. Assuming a normal distribution of the number required to produce the batch, find the optimal initial quantity, Q^*, and the EVPI.

Here we make use of the normal approximation to the Pascal. Under conditions similar to the normal approximation to the binomial, it can be shown that a Pascal distribution can be approximated by a normal one with the same mean (X/p) and variance (Xq/p^2), see Table 9-6. Therefore,

$$\bar{n} = \frac{8000}{1 - 0.13} = 9195.4 \text{ pieces}$$

$$\sigma_n^2 = \frac{8000(0.13)}{(0.87)^2} = 1374.02 \quad \text{and} \quad \sigma_n = 37.07$$

The critical ratio is

$$\frac{f_N(Q^* \mid \bar{n}, \sigma_n)}{F_N(Q^* \mid \bar{n}, \sigma_n)} = \frac{13.50}{900} = 0.015$$

It is convenient to change the variable from n to $z = (n - \bar{n})/\sigma_n$. From Table 9-6

$$f_N(n \mid \bar{n}, \sigma_n) = \frac{1}{\sigma_n} f_N(z) \qquad F_N(n \mid \bar{n}, \sigma_n) = F_N(z)$$

so that the critical ratio becomes, with $z^* = (Q^* - \bar{n})/\sigma_n$,

$$\frac{f_N(z^*)}{F_N(z^*)} = \sigma_n(0.015) = 0.556$$

The function $f_N(z)/F_N(z)$ is plotted in Fig. 13-5. Entering with 0.556 on the vertical axis and dropping down to the z-axis, we obtain $z^* = 0.44$. Hence

$$Q^* = \bar{n} + z^*\sigma_n = 9195.4 + (0.44)(37.07) \approx 9212 \text{ pieces} \quad Ans.$$

To obtain the EVPI we first find K_o, using (13.12) and Appendix I:

$$K_o = v\sigma_n[z^* + L(z^*)] = (13.50)(37.07)[0.44 + L(0.44)]$$

$$= (13.50)(37.07)(0.44 + 0.2169) = \$328.74$$

Then, also using Appendix B,

$$\text{EVPI} = C^* = 328.74 + 900R_N(0.44) = 328.74 + 900(0.3300) = \$625.74 \quad Ans.$$

In scrap allowance problems of this kind, it is assumed that if a second batch has to be started, the amount to be ordered then is $X - Q$ and there is no scrap or wastage the second time around. Clearly, one could treat such a problem approximately and work out a second scrap allowance, but this is not often done in practice; a small arbitrary increase in Q^* is usually sufficient if secondary scrap is a matter of concern.

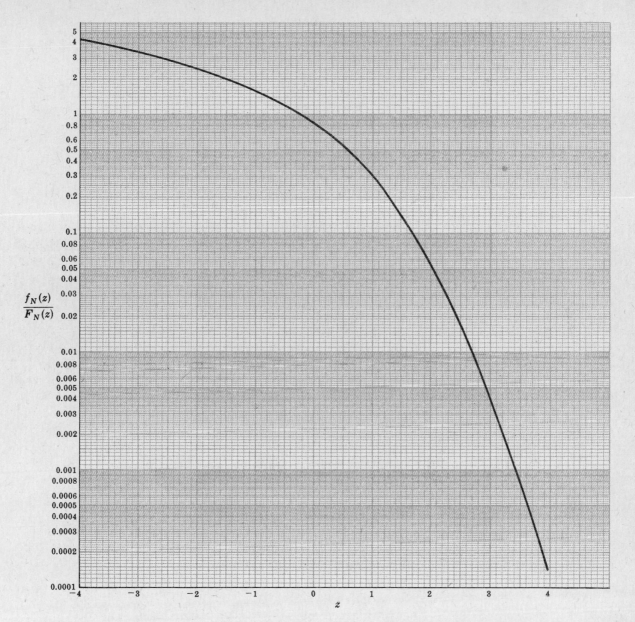

Fig. 13-5   (after R. Schlaifer, *Probability and Statistics for Business Decisions,* New York, McGraw-Hill, 1959)

13.13. Demand in a "newsboy" problem is rectangular between limits a and b. Unit costs of overage and underage are k_o and k_u, as before. Derive formulas for the optimal inventory and EVPI.

Equation *(13.4)* for I^* holds for any distribution. The cumulative rectangular distribution is shown in Fig. 13-6. From similar triangles

$$\frac{F_R(I^* \mid a, b)}{1} = \frac{d^*}{b - a}$$

Substituting for $F_R(I^* \mid a, b)$ from *(13.4)* and noting that $I^* = a + d^*$,

$$I^* = a + \frac{(b - a)k_u}{k_o + k_u} \quad Ans.$$

Fig. 13-6

For a rectangular distribution, Table 9-6 shows that $f_R(u \mid a, b) = 1/(b-a)$. Substituting in (13.2):

$$K_u = \frac{k_u}{b-a} \int_I^b (u-I)\, du = \frac{k_u}{b-a} \left(\frac{u^2}{2} - Iu \right) \Big|_I^b = \frac{k_u}{2(b-a)}(b-I)^2$$

Similarly,

$$K_o = \frac{k_o}{b-a} \int_a^I (I-u)\, du = \frac{k_o}{2(b-a)}(I-a)^2$$

As before,

$$\text{EVPI} = K_o^* + K_u^* = \frac{k_o}{2(b-a)} \frac{(b-a)^2 k_u^2}{(k_o+k_u)^2} + \frac{k_u}{2(b-a)} \frac{(b-a)^2 k_o^2}{(k_o+k_u)^2}$$

$$= \frac{b-a}{2} \frac{k_o k_u}{k_o+k_u} \quad Ans.$$

TWO-ACTION PROBLEMS

13.14. A machine attachment has development costs of \$200,000. It is to sell for \$18,000 and the variable unit cost is \$13,000. There are 50 users of the main machine and it is estimated that most of them will buy the attachment. In fact, the prior expectation is such that a beta distribution with parameters $n_0 = 10$, $X_0 = 9$ is set. Find the prior decision, EVPI and EMV*.

This is similar to Example 13.7, except that now $p_b \geq 0.5$.

From Table 9-6, $E_0(p) = 9/10 = 0.9$ and from (13.24)

$$p_b = \frac{200,000}{50(18,000 - 13,000)} = 0.8$$

Thus $E_0(p) > p_b$; develop product. *Ans.*

Applying (13.31) with $C = Nk = 50(5000) = 250,000$, and using conversion (B),

$$\text{EVPI} = (250,000)[(0.8)F_\beta(0.8 \mid 10, 9) - (0.9)F_\beta(0.8 \mid 11, 10)]$$

$$= (250,000)\{(0.8)[1 - R_B(1 \mid 9, 0.2)] - (0.9)[1 - R_B(1 \mid 10, 0.2)]\}$$

$$= (250,000)[(0.8)(1 - 0.8658) - (0.9)(1 - 0.8926)]$$

$$= (250,000)(0.10736 - 0.09666) = (250,000)(0.01070) = \$2675 \quad Ans.$$

From (13.33)

$$\text{EMV}^* = (250,000)(0.9 - 0.8) = \$25,000 \quad Ans.$$

13.15. In Problem 13.14, 10 customers are approached and 6 decide to buy the attachment. Revise the probabilities on the basis of this result and find the new optimal decision, EVPI and EMV*.

Given $n_s = 10$ and $X_s = 6$; from (13.34), $n_1 = 10 + 10 = 20$; $X_1 = 9 + 6 = 15$. Therefore

$$E_1(p) = \frac{15}{20} = 0.75 < p_b$$

Don't develop; EMV* = 0. *Ans.*

From (13.32) and conversion (B).

$$\text{EVPI}_1 = (250,000)\{(0.75)[1 - F_\beta(0.8 \mid 21, 16)] - (0.8)[1 - F_\beta(0.8 \mid 20, 15)]\}$$

$$= (250,000)[(0.75)R_B(5 \mid 20, 0.2) - (0.8)R_B(5 \mid 19, 0.2)]$$

$$= (250,000)[(0.75)(0.3704) - (0.8)(0.3267)] = (250,000)(0.01644) = \$4110 \quad Ans.$$

13.16. Given the results of Example 13.15, extend the analysis to find the optimal sample size for the sales survey.

This problem may be solved by repeating the calculations for other sample sizes. The work makes use of the following relationships pertaining to these data:

$$\sigma_{\theta e} = \frac{(125)^2}{\sqrt{(125)^2 + \dfrac{40(85.58)^2}{n_s}}}$$

$$D_e = \frac{25}{\sigma_{\theta e}}$$

$$\text{EVSI} = 8000\sigma_{\theta e}L(D_e) \qquad \text{ENGS} = \text{EVSI} - 40n_s$$

The calculations are set out in Table 13-6. A sample size of 300 gives the highest expected net gain from sampling. Testing further values of n_s near 300 could probably refine the result further, but it hardly seems worth the effort.

Table 13-6

n_s	$\sigma_{\theta e}$	D_e	$L(D_e)$	EVSI	$40n_s$	ENGS
100	114.71	0.218	0.2994	274,753	4,000	270,753
198	119.47	0.209	0.3031	289,691	7,920	281,771
300	121.27	0.206	0.3044	295,317	12,000	283,317
500	122.72	0.204	0.3052	299,633	20,000	279,633

13.17. A certain ore deposit is estimated at 2 million tons. The ore is to be subjected to a concentration process. The requisite plant would cost $10 million and there would be a further variable cost of $40 per ton. In addition, a severance tax and royalty of $20 per ton is payable. A prior assay of the ore body indicates that each ton would yield a dollar amount of concentrate which has a normal distribution with mean $69 and standard deviation $28. Find the prior decision and EVPI.

Let θ be the monetary yield per ton. Then the breakeven value θ_b is given by

$$\begin{array}{cc} \textbf{Revenues} & \textbf{Expenses} \\ (2{,}000{,}000)\theta_b = & (2{,}000{,}000)(40+20) + 10{,}000{,}000 \end{array}$$

$$\theta_b = \frac{130{,}000{,}000}{2{,}000{,}000} = 65$$

$$D_0 = \frac{|65-69|}{28} = 0.1429$$

$$\text{EVPI} = (2{,}000{,}000)(28)\,L(0.1429)$$
$$= (2{,}000{,}000)(28)(0.3315) = \$18{,}564{,}000 \quad Ans.$$

The decision is to go ahead, since $E_0(\theta) = 69 > \theta_b$. *Ans.*

13.18. In Problem 13.17, 16 samples of 1 ton each are taken. They result in an average concentrate yield of $61 per ton, with a standard deviation of $25. Revise the decision in the light of this new information and find EMV*.

The 16 1-ton samples are regarded as a sample of 16 items. In the notation of Table 13-1, the sample results are:

$$\bar{\theta} = 61 \qquad s_{\bar{\theta}}^2 = \frac{(25)^2}{16}$$

The revised mean is then

$$E_1(\theta) = \frac{\dfrac{69}{(28)^2} + 61\dfrac{16}{(25)^2}}{\dfrac{1}{(28)^2} + \dfrac{16}{(25)^2}} = 61.37$$

Since $61.37 < \theta_b$, do not develop. EMV* = 0.

13.19. The introduction of a new product is expected to cost $400,000. Variable costs per item are $300 and the expected sales price is $500. The company has 16,000 customers and expects that 2200 will buy the product, with a 50-50 chance of getting between 1000 and 3400 customers to buy the product. Find the prior decision, EVPI and EMV*.

Here it is most convenient to work with y, the number buying, as the variable. We assume it to be normally distributed with mean 2200. From the data (see Example 9.26)

$$P\left(-\frac{1200}{\sigma_y} < z < \frac{1200}{\sigma_y}\right) = 0.50$$

where $z = (y - 2200)/\sigma_y$. Appendix B then gives

$$\frac{1200}{\sigma_y} = 0.674 \quad \text{or} \quad \sigma_y = 1780$$

The breakeven value, y_b, is

$$y_b = \frac{400,000}{500 - 300} = 2000 < 2200$$

The decision therefore is to go ahead. *Ans.*

From (*13.39*) and (*13.38*), with $D = (2200 - 2000)/1780 = 0.1124$,

$$\text{EVPI} = k\sigma_y L(D) = 200(1780)(0.3452) = \$122,891 \quad Ans.$$

and from (*13.33*)

$$\text{EMV*} = 200(2200 - 2000) = \$40,000 \quad Ans.$$

13.20. The following relates to the manufacture of 800 electronic components: Without fixture, fraction defective has beta distribution with parameters $X_0 = 1$, $n_0 = 16$. With a fixture costing $40, fraction defective is always 0.02. If a defective part is installed, it costs $1.50 to fix. Should the fixture be installed? What is the EVPI?

This is Example 10.1, except that the empirical distribution, which has $E(p) = 0.063$, has been replaced by the almost equivalent beta distribution which has an $E(p) = 1/16 = 0.0625$. As in Method 3 of Example 10.1, $p_b = 0.0533$ and, as $E(p) > p_b$, USE FIXTURE. For EVPI, use (*13.31*) along with conversion (*A*) (interpolating in Appendix C):

$$\begin{aligned}
\text{EVPI} &= 800(1.50)[(0.0533)F_\beta(0.0533 \mid 16, 1) - (0.0625)F_\beta(0.0533 \mid 17, 2)] \\
&= 1200[(0.0533)R_B(1 \mid 15, 0.0533) - (0.0625)R_B(2 \mid 16, 0.0533)] \\
&= 1200[(0.0533)(0.5594) - (0.0625)(0.2091)] \\
&= 1200(0.0298344 - 0.0130687) = \$20.12 \quad Ans.
\end{aligned}$$

13.21. An assembly is built in module form and costs $200; if necessary, it can be removed and replaced in 15 minutes. It is also possible to repair it, however. In that case, the cost of the new parts needed is normally distributed with mean $100 and standard deviation $30, and the repair time is normally distributed with mean 5 hours and standard deviation 1.4 hours. Parts cost and repair time are independent. Each hour spent costs $25. Is it worthwhile repairing the module, or should it be replaced? Find the EVPI.

Here there are two random variables, the parts cost, K, and the time taken, h, whenever it is decided to repair instead of replace the module. It is possible to combine K and h into a single variable, C, the cost of repairing, where $C = K + 25h$. The problem is then one of finding the mean (and later the standard deviation) of a new variable which is the sum of two others. This problem is solved in general terms by first considering an arbitrary set of variables $X_1, X_2, \ldots$; the mean of their weighted sum is given by

$$E(a_1 X_1 \pm a_2 X_2 \pm \cdots) = a_1 E(X_1) \pm a_2 E(X_2) \pm \cdots$$

Here, $E(K) = 100$ and $E(h) = 5$, so that

$$E(C) = 100 + 25(5) = \$225$$

When the whole module is replaced, the cost is $200 + 25(0.25) = \$206.25$, which is also the break-even cost, C_b. Since $E(C) > C_b$, REPLACE THE WHOLE MODULE.   *Ans.*

To find EVPI, we must first obtain a pooled standard deviation for C. With the same notation as above, it can be shown that, if $X_1, X_2, \ldots$ are independent,

$$\text{Var}\,(a_1 X_1 \pm a_2 X_2 \pm \cdots) = a_1^2\,\text{Var}\,(X_1) + a_2^2\,\text{Var}\,(X_2) + \cdots$$

so that here

$$\sigma_C^2 = \sigma_K^2 + (25)^2 \sigma_h^2 = (30)^2 + (25)^2(1.4)^2 = 2125 \qquad \text{and} \qquad \sigma_C = 46.1$$

The rest of the procedure is as before for two-action problems:

$$D = \frac{|206.25 - 225|}{46.1} = 0.4067$$

and, from Appendix I, $L(D) = 0.2281$ (after interpolation). Since there is only one machine and all costs are included in the variable cost, $Nk = 1$.   Therefore

$$\text{EVPI} = \sigma_C\,L(D) = (46.1)(0.2281) = \$10.52   \quad \textit{Ans.}$$

Supplementary Problems

MANY-ACTION PROBLEMS

13.22. Demand for a certain product in a "newsboy" model is normal with mean 100 units and standard deviation 25. Lost profit is \$8 per unit and salvage loss is \$12. Find the optimal initial inventory and EVPI.   *Ans.* 94; \$193.15

13.23. Repeat Problem 13.22 with the values of lost profit and salvage loss interchanged.
Ans.   106; \$193.15

13.24. A "newsboy" model including incoming storage costs is arranged so that a single fixed bulk delivery is made. The quantity is thus constant, and the variable is time between deliveries rather than the quantity. Show that this reduces the model to the simple version without considering storage charges.

13.25. Suppose that in the model of Problem 13.24 salvage loss is \$6 per gallon, premium cost for shortages is \$9 per gallon and storage capacity costs \$4 per gallon. The firm uses 1000 gallons a day (at \$6 per gallon). The distribution of the time between deliveries is gamma, with a mean of 75 days and a mode of 60 days. Find the optimal interval between deliveries and the cost of uncertainty.
Ans.   78 days; \$196,605

13.26. In a material bank model, production is at a rate of 20 units per hour; there are 4.5 breakdowns a year, on the average; a breakdown costs \$150 per hour; and carrying charges for inventory are \$5 per unit per year. The duration of breakdown has a gamma distribution with mean of 2 hours and mode of 1 hr 36 min. Find the optimal size of inventory and EVPI.
Ans.   58 items; \$355

13.27. A batch of 500 pieces is to be produced in a process with a scrap rate of 3/8. Each part made unnecessarily costs 80¢; a setup for the process costs \$60. Find the optimal initial batch size and the expected cost of the policy, assuming the normal approximation to the Pascal distribution.
Ans.   822 pieces; \$28.51

TWO-ACTION PROBLEMS

13.28. Consider the data of Problem 13.17. Assume that the concentrate sells for $250 per ton. A further sample of 20 tons is taken and it is found that a concentrate yield of 25 percent is realized. Revise the prior estimates and find the new expected dollar yield, optimal decision and EVPI.

Ans. $65.28 per ton; GO AHEAD; $14,329,000

13.29. Let the samples in Problem 13.28 represent a pilot sample, subsequent to the prior estimate. The sponsors of the mining project are considering taking a further sample of 100 tons at a cost of $750 per ton. Find the EVSI and ENGS.   *Ans.* $17,079,900; $17,004,900

13.30. Return again to the data in Problem 13.17. Everything remains the same, except that a beta prior distribution is assumed, with parameters $n = 15$ and $X = 4$. Find the expected dollar yield per ton, optimal decision, EVPI and EMV*. (*Hint:* The fraction p must be calculated on the basis of $250 per ton, which would be a 100% yield.)   *Ans.* $66.67; GO AHEAD; $20,514,000; $3,333,333

13.31. Suppose in Example 13.17 that the sample had been only of 23 firms and 6 had bought the device. What would then have been the revised average sales per customer, decision and EVPI?

Ans. $353.70; GO AHEAD; $270,640

13.32. A company ($N = 1$) wants to find out if it should rent a new inspection unit for $50,000 a month in the expectation that it will save $55,000 in reduced scrap, with the savings normally distributed with a 50-50 chance of lying between $40,000 and $70,000. (*a*) What is the chance of losing money on the deal? (*b*) Would it pay to install the unit? (*c*) What is the EVPI?

Ans.   (*a*) 0.411; (*b*) yes; (*c*) $6600

13.33. In the product development situation of Problem 13.19, a sample of 50 customers is canvassed and 6 decide to buy. Revise the prior analysis on the basis of this additional information and find the revised expected number of customers buying, the decision, EVPI and EMV*.

Ans.   1961; no; EVPI = $33,640; EMV* = 0

13.34. A production lot of 2000 items has an unknown fraction defective. If a defective part is installed it costs $1.50 to fix. The setup cost for the process is $200 and each part has a variable cost of 25 cents. Rather than make the part, it is possible to buy fully inspected and perfect parts for 50 cents each. A prior beta distribution of product fraction defective may be estimated from a pilot run of 12 pieces of which 1 turns out to be defective. Find the prior decision and EVPI.

Ans.   Make the parts; $69.95

13.35. A further sample of 8 pieces is taken of the product in Problem 13.34. One piece turns out to be defective. Revise the prior decision and find the new decision, EVPI and EMV*.

Ans.   Indifferent (at breakeven); $76.98; 0

13.36. Introduction costs for a new service are $300,000. On each occasion fees are $150 and there is a variable cost of $90. There are 40,000 customers and it is assumed a priori that sales per customer will be normally distributed, with mean $8 and with about 68 percent lying between $6 and $10. Find the right decision, EVP and EMV*.   *Ans.*   GO AHEAD; $22,904; $20,000

13.37. A sample of 25 customers is taken and 3 buy. Find the revised decision, based on the data in Problem 13.36, as well as the new EVPI and EMV*.

Ans.   GO AHEAD; $22,306.96; $13,200

13.38. Taking the result of Problem 13.37 as a pilot sample, find the EVSI for a sample of size 80. If each customer test costs $50, find the ENGS.   *Ans.* $13,028; $9028

13.39. Fixed expenses in a product development situation are \$702,000; sales price, \$190; cost of each item, \$60; 9000 customers. Find the prior decision, EVPI and EMV*, given the following prior beta parameters for the fraction buying, p:

(a) $n = 18$, $X = 11$ (b) $n = 16$, $X = 10$ (c) $n = 17$, $X = 10$ (d) $n = 19$, $X = 12$

Ans.   (a) DEVELOP, \$46,777, \$12,870   (c) DO NOT DEVELOP, \$47,986, 0

          (b) DEVELOP, \$42,611, \$29,250   (d) DEVELOP, \$35,089, \$36,947

13.40. Use the same breakeven conditions as in Problem 13.39, except use sales per customer as the variable. The prior distribution is assumed normal with a mean of \$80 and a probability of lying between \$75 and \$85 of (a) 50%, (b) 68%, (c) 95.45%. Find the prior decision, EVPI and EMV*.

Ans.   (a) DEVELOP, \$18,587, \$18,000   (c) DEVELOP, \$2,704.50, \$18,000

          (b) DEVELOP, \$10,368, \$18,000

13.41. Development costs are \$300,000. Variable cost per unit is \$11,000 and sales price \$17,000. There are 500 customers. Find the decision, EVPI and EMV* for (a) a prior beta distribution for fraction buying with parameters $X_0 = 1$ and $n_0 = 8$; (b) a sample of 0 sales in 7 tries, combined with the prior distribution.

Ans.   (a) DEVELOP, \$86,430, \$75,000;   (b) DON'T DEVELOP, \$41,700, 0

13.42. Development costs are \$300,000. Variable cost per unit is \$11,000 and sales price \$17,000. There are 80 customers. Find the decision, EVPI and EMV* for (a) a prior beta distribution with parameters $X_0 = 7$ and $n_0 = 8$; (b) a sample of 4 sales out of 12 tries, combined with the prior distribution.

Ans.   (a) DEVELOP, \$1404, \$120,000;   (b) DON'T DEVELOP, \$7477, 0

Chapter 14

Selected Probabilistic Inventory Models

INTRODUCTION

In Chapter 13 several of the examples using partial expectations had as their objective the determination of inventory under conditions of risk. The "newsboy" model was the main such analysis presented. Similar approaches may be applied to other inventory problems; in this chapter we deal with several simple models of wide applicability. The subject is actually highly complex and includes many cases beyond our scope.

ORDER POINT–ORDER QUANTITY SYSTEM

This system requires the setting of an order point, i.e. a certain inventory level. When the amount in stock has fallen to the order point, a certain quantity is ordered. The reason for the uncertainty is the existence of lead time. If replenishment were instantaneous, there would be no such problem, because as soon as the inventory was exhausted, a new supply could be instantly procured, i.e. the order point would be zero [see (2.16)].

Notation

$$R = \text{reorder point, units}$$

$$B = \text{buffer stock, units}$$

$$L = \text{lead time, units of time}$$

$$q = \text{order quantity}$$

$$k_u = \text{shortage cost per unit}$$

$$c = \text{carrying charges per unit per unit of time}$$

$$A = \text{cost of one setup}$$

$$u = \text{rate of usage, units per unit of time}$$

$$\bar{u}, \sigma_u, f(u), F(u) = \text{mean, standard deviation, p.d.f. and c.d.f. of } u$$

The scheme is illustrated for one cycle in Fig. 14-1. If consumption is at the rate of $\bar{u}$, there will be a buffer stock B left at the end of the cycle. The stock at the order point will therefore accommodate an increased rate of consumption, as represented by the lower dashed line for which $u = R/L$. If the consumption rate is $u > R/L$, a shortage of

$$Lu - R = L\left(u - \frac{R}{L}\right)$$

will be the result, with conditional cost *for each cycle* in which it occurs of

$$k_u L\left(u - \frac{R}{L}\right)$$

and expected cost given by

$$k_u L \int_{R/L}^{\infty} \left(u - \frac{R}{L}\right) f(u)\, du$$

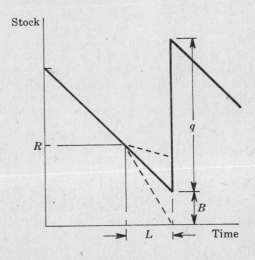

Fig. 14-1

If the product is made q units at a time, then in the long run there will be $\bar{u}/q$ inventory cycles in each period of time. Thus the expected cost of stockouts *per unit of time* is

$$\frac{\bar{u}}{q} k_u L \int_{R/L}^{\infty} \left(u - \frac{R}{L}\right) f(u)\, du$$

To this cost must be added the cost of holding inventory during the lead time period. Here we distinguish two different cases.

Case 1. Order Quantity Independent of Buffer Stock.

We saw in Problem 2.5 that a variation of as much as 14 percent on either side of the economic lot size results in a cost increase of only about 1 percent. Thus, if the buffer stock is small relative to the economic lot size, no significant problem is created if at every reorder point, shortages in the buffer stock created in the *last* cycle are added to the new order or surpluses are deducted. For example, 500 items are ordered at one time with a buffer stock set at 85; last time the buffer stock had been partially depleted so that there were only 42 units in stock by the time the new shipment had arrived. Then $500 + (85 - 42) = 543$ would be the new order quantity.

The total carrying cost is that due to the cycle stock and that due to the buffer stock. The former is simply the quantity q in a deterministic model, as discussed in Chapter 2; in this case it does not enter into the calculations. Because of variations in demand, the actual value of B at the end of a cycle may vary, as shown in the two dashed lines in Fig. 14-1. The average amount of buffer stock is given by $B = R - L\bar{u}$, so that the average carrying cost is $c(R - L\bar{u})$. The total expected buffer cost is therefore

$$C_B = c(R - L\bar{u}) + \frac{\bar{u}}{q} k_u L \int_{R/L}^{\infty} \left(u - \frac{R}{L}\right) f(u)\, du \qquad (14.1)$$

Differentiating to obtain a minimum:

$$\frac{dC_B}{dR} = c + \frac{\bar{u}}{q} k_u L\left(-\frac{1}{L}\right) F(u)\Big|_{R/L}^{\infty} = 0$$

$$c - \frac{\bar{u}}{q} k_u \left[1 - F\left(\frac{R^*}{L}\right)\right] = 0$$

$$F\left(\frac{R^*}{L}\right) = 1 - \frac{cq}{k_u \bar{u}} \qquad (14.2)$$

The order quantity q is determined separately from the economic lot size formula, (2.3):

$$q^* = \sqrt{\frac{2A\bar{u}}{c}}$$

EXAMPLE 14.1. Annual demand is normally distributed with mean of 5000 units and standard deviation of 100 units. Setup charges are \$10 each time. Carrying charges are 10¢ per unit per year and shortage loss is 20¢ per unit. The lead time is two months (1/6 year). Production time may be neglected. Find the order point, order quantity, expected buffer stock and optimal cost.

From above and (2.3)

$$q^* = \sqrt{\frac{2(10)(5000)}{0.1}} = 1000 \text{ units} \quad Ans.$$

From (14.2)

$$F_N(6R^* \mid 5000, 100) = 1 - \frac{(0.1)(1000)}{(0.2)(5000)} = 0.9$$

From Appendix B, $z^* = 1.282$, so that

$$6R^* = \bar{u} + (1.282)\sigma_u = 5000 + (1.282)(100) = 5128.2$$

$$R^* = \frac{5128.2}{6} \approx 855 \text{ units} \quad Ans.$$

$$B = R^* - L\bar{u} = \frac{5128.2 - 5000}{6} \approx 21 \text{ units} \quad Ans.$$

To find C^*, note that for the normal distribution the integral in (14.1) is $\sigma_u L(z^*)$, so that the portion C_B^* which pertains to the buffer stock is

$$C_B^* = c(R^* - L\bar{u}) + \frac{\bar{u}}{q^*}k_u L\sigma_u L(z^*)$$

where $z^* = 1.282$ and $L(z^*)$ from Appendix I is 0.04730.

$$C_B^* = (0.1)(21) + \frac{5000}{1000}(0.2)\frac{1}{6}(100)(0.04730) = 2.10 + 0.79 = \$2.89$$

In addition, the cost of keeping the cycle stock must be considered. From (2.4) this is

$$C_C^* = \sqrt{2A\bar{u}c} = \sqrt{2(10)(5000)(0.1)} = \$100$$

and

$$C^* = C_B^* + C_C^* = 2.89 + 100 = \$102.89 \quad Ans.$$

Case 2.   Joint Model for Order Quantity and Buffer Stock.

When the buffer stock is large relative to the cycle stock, the equation for the total cost C must include the terms for the cycle stock as well and must lead to a simultaneous solution for both q^* and R^*. The setup cost for the cycle stock was shown in Chapter 2 to be $A\bar{u}/q$. The average inventory is now the buffer stock plus half the cycle stock, i.e. $R - L\bar{u} + (q/2)$. Therefore

$$C = c\left(R - L\bar{u} + \frac{q}{2}\right) + \frac{\bar{u}}{q}k_u L \int_{R/L}^{\infty}\left(u - \frac{R}{L}\right)f(u)\,du + \frac{A\bar{u}}{q} \quad (14.3)$$

The optimal values R^* and q^* are obtained from

$$\frac{\partial C}{\partial R} = c - \frac{\bar{u}}{q}k_u\left[1 - F\left(\frac{R^*}{L}\right)\right] = 0$$

which again gives (14.2), and

$$\frac{\partial C}{\partial q} = \frac{c}{2} - \frac{\bar{u}}{q^2}\left[A + k_u L \int_{R/L}^{\infty}\left(u - \frac{R}{L}\right)f(u)\,du\right] = 0 \quad (14.4)$$

EXAMPLE 14.2.   Rework Example 14.1 by simultaneously considering order point and order quantity.

Since the underlying distribution of demand is normal, the integral in (14.4) reduces to $\sigma_u L(z)$, where $z = [(R/L) - \bar{u}]/\sigma_u$, whence

$$q = \left\{ \frac{2\bar{u}}{c} [A + k_u L \sigma_u L(z)] \right\}^{1/2} \tag{14.5}$$

As a first trial we again use (2.3), as in Example 14.1, obtaining $q = 1000$ units and, consequently, $z = 1.282$. The right-hand side of (14.5) then yields

$$\left\{ \frac{2(5000)}{0.1} \left[10 + (0.2)\left(\frac{1}{6}\right)(100)(0.4730) \right] \right\}^{1/2} = 1007.85$$

This does not agree with $q = 1000$; we therefore try $q = 1008$. From (14.2)

$$F\left(\frac{R^*}{L}\right) = \frac{(0.1)(1008)}{(0.2)(5000)} = 0.8992$$

From Appendix B, $z = 1.277$, and (14.5) gives

$$q = \{100{,}000[10 + (3.33)L(z)]\}^{1/2} = \{100{,}000[10 + (3.33)(0.04780)]\}^{1/2} \approx 1008 \text{ units}$$

The agreement is sufficiently good to end the iteration process.

$$q^* = 1008 \text{ units} \qquad z^* = 1.277 \qquad R^* = L(\bar{u} + \sigma_u z^*) = 855 \text{ units} \quad Ans.$$

The buffer stock is $B = 21$ units, as before, since the R's are practically the same.   *Ans.*

To obtain C^*, substitute q^* in (14.4) and then multiply by q^*. Rearranging,

$$\frac{cq^*}{2} - \frac{A\bar{u}}{q^*} = W$$

where W is the integral term of (14.3). Substituting for W in (14.3) gives

$$C^* = c\left(R^* - L\bar{u} + \frac{q^*}{2}\right) + \frac{cq^*}{2} - \frac{A\bar{u}}{q^*} + \frac{A\bar{u}}{q^*} = c(R^* - L\bar{u} + q^*) \tag{14.6}$$

which is distribution-free, i.e. it does not depend on $f(u)$. Substituting,

$$C^* = (0.1)(21 + 1008) = \$102.90 \quad Ans.$$

This is virtually the same as the answer in Example 14.1. It is clear that for these data the separate computation of cycle stock and buffer stock or reorder point is justified. When it is not justified, the iterative method must be used.

RETENTION TIME FOR OBSOLESCENT STOCK

Generally, obsolescent or perishable stock may be dealt with as a "newsboy" situation. We now give a model of another aspect of a probabilistic distribution of spoilage or obsolescence. A population of items in inventory may be conceived as gradually "failing" item by item. Accordingly, this is a process resembling reliability and survivorship, which will be discussed in much greater detail in Chapter 18.

Consider first the conditional probability that an item which has been in stock for a time t will be sold in the next short interval δt. By definition, the probability that the item will be sold in the interval from t to $t + \delta t$ is $f(t)\,\delta t$, where $f(t)$ is the probability density function of the time to sale. Moreover, the probability of the item not having been sold before t is $R(t)$, i.e. 1 minus the probability of having been sold before t. Thus the required conditional probability is

$$\frac{f(t)\,\delta t}{R(t)} = Z(t)\,\delta t \tag{14.7}$$

The ratio $Z(t) = f(t)/R(t)$ is also called the *hazard rate*. For further discussion see Chapter 18.

If the profit per item is denoted p, then the *expected* profit from selling a hitherto unsold item in the interval from t to $t + \delta t$ is $p\,Z(t)\,\delta t$. The cost of carrying the item in the same interval is $c\,\delta t$. If we now assume the plausible condition that the longer an item has remained unsold the less likely it is to be sold in the future [i.e. that $Z(t)$ is monotonically decreasing], then the time beyond which retention in stock is unprofitable is given by

$$p\,Z(t)\,\delta t \;=\; c\,\delta t \quad \text{or} \quad Z(t) \;=\; \frac{c}{p} \tag{14.8}$$

EXAMPLE 14.3. (a) Sales in relation to time for a product result in a hazard rate

$$Z(t) \;=\; \frac{k}{T}\left(\frac{t}{T}\right)^{k-1}$$

where $k < 1$ and T are parameters. Find the optimal retention time. (b) Given $k = 0.6$, $T = 45$ days, storage cost 8¢ per item per day and profit \$3 per item, find the optimal retention time.

(a) From (14.8)

$$\frac{k}{T}\left(\frac{t}{T}\right)^{k-1} \;=\; \frac{c}{p}$$

$$t^* \;=\; T\left(\frac{cT}{pk}\right)^{1/(k-1)} \qquad Ans.$$

(b) Substituting in the last result

$$t^* \;=\; 45\left[\frac{8(45)}{300(0.6)}\right]^{1/(0.6-1)} \;=\; 45(2)^{-2.5} \;\approx\; 8 \text{ days} \quad Ans.$$

This result shows that after 8 days the expected profit no longer is enough to meet storage charges as they accumulate.

SYSTEMS WITH EQUAL REVIEW PERIODS

Systems employing order points and order quantities depend for their proper functioning on accurate maintenance of perpetual inventory records. Particularly when forming part of a suitable data processing system, these may be used to generate virtually continuous, real-time reports on what has to be ordered, or at least often enough to have the same effect. However, when inventories must rely on periodic inspections, it is possible to devise systems geared to that procedure. One of the most useful is the so-called *S,s model*. It operates as follows: Set a maximum inventory level S and a lower level s (i.e. $S - s > 0$). Let y be the amount on hand when a decision is to be made. Then,

If $y \leqq s$, order an amount $S - y$

If $y > s$, order nothing

The model for setting S and s resembles the "newsboy" model with storage costs (Problem 13.7). If $F(u)$ denotes the c.d.f. of the usage, u, then the optimal S is given by

$$F(S^*) \;=\; \frac{r - v}{r + c} \tag{14.9}$$

where r = selling price per item, v = variable cost per item, excluding carrying charges and c = carrying charge, as before, but expressed in dollars per item *per review period* instead of per unit of time. Usage u is also expressed per period. The value of s^* can be shown to satisfy

$$vs^* + K_{us}^* + K_{os}^* \;=\; A + vS^* + K_{uS}^* + K_{oS}^* \tag{14.10}$$

where K_{os}^* and K_{oS}^* are the costs of overage when stocking s^* and S^* respectively, K_{us}^* and K_{uS}^* are the costs of underage when stocking s^* and S^* respectively, and A is the setup cost per period. The value of either side of (14.10) is the optimal expected cost, C^*. The cost relationships are shown in Fig. 14-2.

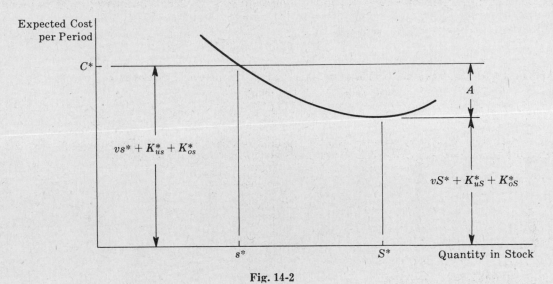

Fig. 14-2

EXAMPLE 14.4. Consumption is normally distributed with mean 40 units per period and standard deviation 8. Setup charges are $16 each time. Selling price per item is $18, variable cost is $2 per item and carrying charges are $4 per item per period. Find the optimal S, s and the corresponding cost.

From (14.9)

$$F_N(S^* \mid 40, 8) = \frac{18 - 2}{18 + 4} = 0.7272$$

From Appendix B, $z^* = 0.605$ and

$$S^* = 40 + (0.605)(8) \approx 45 \quad Ans.$$

Here it is useful to correct z^* for rounding off S^* to 45:

$$z^* = \frac{45 - 40}{8} = 0.625$$

To find K_{uS}^* and K_{oS}^* use (13.12) and (13.13):

$$vS^* + K_{uS}^* + K_{oS}^* = 2(45) + 18(8)L(0.625) + 4(8)[0.625 + L(0.625)]$$
$$= 90 + 144(0.1619) + 32(0.625 + 0.1619) = \$138.49$$

We now require the value of s which will make

$$vs + K_{us} + K_{os} = 138.49 + 16 = \$154.49$$

This must be done by trial and is best arranged as in Table 14-1.

Table 14-1

s	vs	$z = \dfrac{s - 40}{8}$	$L(z)$	$K_{us} = 144\,L(z)$	$z + L(z)$	$K_{os} = 32[z + L(z)]$	$vs + K_{us} + K_{os}$
42	84	0.25	0.2863	41.22	0.5368	17.18	142.40
40	80	0	0.3989	57.44	0.3989	12.76	150.20
39	78	−0.125	0.4646	66.90	0.3396	10.87	155.77*
38	76	−0.25	0.5363	77.23	0.2863	9.16	162.39
36	72	−0.5	0.6978	100.48	0.1978	6.33	178.81

[Note the evaluations of $L(z)$ for negative z; see (13.16).]   Clearly, the entry for total cost for $s = 39$ is nearest to the critical value of \$154.49.   Hence $s^* = 39$ and $C^* \approx \$155$.   *Ans.*

Although the S,s model lends itself to any fixed review period, it is clear that, theoretically, the best policy is to set S, s and the length of the review period so as to make the economic lot size equal to (or close to) $\bar{u}$.   In practice, however, the review period may be determined by other managerial considerations, like location of the items, necessity of blanket inventories, etc.

When the distribution of demand, $f(u)$, is exponential, the foregoing work may be simplified.   From Table 9-6 and (9.18)

$$f_e(u \mid \bar{u}) = \frac{1}{\bar{u}} e^{-u/\bar{u}} \quad \text{and} \quad F_e(u \mid \bar{u}) = 1 - e^{-u/\bar{u}}$$

so that (14.9) gives

$$1 - e^{-S^*/\bar{u}} = \frac{r - v}{r + c}$$

$$e^{-S^*/\bar{u}} = \frac{v + c}{r + c} \tag{14.11}$$

$$S^* = \bar{u} \ln \frac{r + c}{v + c} = (2.3026)\bar{u} \log \frac{r + c}{v + c} \tag{14.12}$$

When the ratio $(S^* - s^*)/\bar{u}$ is small enough so that its powers higher than the second may be neglected, it can be shown that

$$s^* = S^* - \sqrt{\frac{2A\bar{u}}{v + c}} \tag{14.13}$$

By working out the integrals for K_{oS}^* and K_{uS}^* and eliminating the term $e^{-S^*/\bar{u}}$ by using (14.11) it can be further shown that

$$C^* = A + (S^* + \bar{u})(v + c) \tag{14.14}$$

EXAMPLE 14.5.   Rework Example 14.4, except use an exponential distribution for the demand, with mean 40 units per period.

Depending on the availability of tables, (14.11) or (14.12) may be used.   From (14.11)

$$e^{-S^*/\bar{u}} = \frac{2 + 4}{18 + 4} = 0.2727$$

From Appendix A, $S^*/\bar{u} \approx 1.30$, so that

$$S^* = (1.30)(40) = 52 \text{ units} \quad \textit{Ans.}$$

$$s^* = 52 - \sqrt{\frac{2(16)(40)}{2 + 4}} = 52 - 14.6 \approx 37 \text{ units} \quad \textit{Ans.}$$

$$C^* = 16 + (52 + 40)(2 + 4) = \$568 \quad \textit{Ans.}$$

While the above is a very simple procedure, it will be recalled from Table 9-6 that in an exponential distribution, mean and standard deviation are the same.   In a given case, this assumption may be wide of the mark (see Problem 14.8).   Note also that here

$$\left(\frac{S^* - s^*}{\bar{u}}\right)^3 = \left(\frac{14.6}{40}\right)^3 = 0.049$$

which is small enough for the approximations to hold.

THE BASE STOCK SYSTEM

This system starts with B units in stock. Whenever an order of size y is placed, a replenishment order in that amount is also put through. The total on hand and on order is thus always B. If a shortage occurs, this is not lost business but is backlogged at an ordering cost of k_u per unit. The amount in stock incurs a carrying charge of c per unit during the time the material is on order but not yet delivered, i.e. during the lead time L, which is taken as fixed. Since conditional shortage costs are $k_u(x-B)$ and conditional carrying costs are $c(B-x)$, where x is the amount on order during L, the model is seen to be equivalent to the "newsboy" model and

$$F(B^*) = \frac{k_u}{k_u + c} \tag{14.15}$$

EXAMPLE 14.6. Find the base stock level for an inventory system in which the ordering cost is \$0.30 per item, the carrying cost \$1.10 and demand has a gamma distribution with parameters $X = 5$, $T = 18$.

$$F_\gamma(B^* \mid 5, 18) = F_\gamma(m^* \mid 5) = \frac{30}{30 + 110} = 0.2143$$

where $m^* = B^*/18$. Proceeding as in Example 13.6,

$$F_P(5 - 1 \mid m^*) = 1 - 0.2143 = 0.7857$$

From Appendix D, $m^* \approx 3.2$ and $B^* = (3.2)(18) \approx 58$ units.   *Ans.*

The cost may be worked out as in the other "newsboy" problems of Chapter 13.

Solved Problems

ORDER POINT–ORDER QUANTITY SYSTEM

14.1   Rework Example 14.1, except that the distribution is now rectangular with the same mean of 5000 and standard deviation of 100.

Using the methods of Chapter 9, we must first determine the limits a and b. Since the mean is 5000, b and a must be located equal amounts above and below this value. For a rectangular distribution (Table 9-6)

$$\sigma^2 = \frac{(b-a)^2}{12} = (100)^2$$

$$b - a = 100\sqrt{12} = 346.4$$

Hence, $\quad b = 5000 + \dfrac{346.4}{2} \approx 5173 \qquad a = 5000 - \dfrac{346.4}{2} \approx 4827$

Rewriting (*14.2*) for the rectangular distribution (and recalling that $q = 1000$),

$$F_R(R^*/L \mid a, b) = \frac{(R^*/L) - a}{b - a} = 1 - \frac{cq}{k_u \bar{u}}$$

$$\frac{6R^* - 4827}{5173 - 4827} = 0.9$$

$$6R^* = 4827 + (0.9)(5173 - 4827) = 5138.4$$

$$R^* \approx 856 \text{ units} \quad Ans.$$

$$B^* = 856 - \frac{5000}{6} \approx 22 \text{ units} \quad Ans.$$

To find C_B we note that the integral in (14.1) is now

$$\int_{R/L}^{b} \frac{u - R/L}{b - a} \, du = \frac{(u - R/L)^2}{2(b-a)} \Big|_{R/L}^{b} = \frac{(b - R/L)^2}{2(b-a)}$$

so that

$$C_B^* = c(R^* - L\bar{u}) + \frac{\bar{u}}{q} k_u L \frac{(b - R^*/L)^2}{2(b - a)}$$

$$= (0.1)\left(856 - \frac{5000}{6}\right) + \frac{5000}{1000}(0.2)\left(\frac{1}{6}\right)\frac{(5173 - 5138.4)^2}{2(5173 - 4827)}$$

$$= 2.27 + 0.29 = \$2.56$$

Adding to this the cost of the cycle stock, $C_C^* = \$100$, gives $C^* = \$102.56$.   *Ans.*

It is noteworthy that using the rectangular distribution diminishes the cost of uncertainty somewhat, although the results of Example 14.1 are virtually identical. Such correspondence is mainly coincidental.

14.2. Table 14-2 is to be used to estimate order point and order quantity for a single production cycle. Setups cost \$25 each, there is a carrying charge of 20 cents per item per year and a shortage cost of 40 cents per item. The lead time is $1\frac{1}{2}$ months ($\frac{1}{8}$ yr). Assume that buffer and cycle stocks may be computed separately.

Table 14-2

Demand, units/yr	Probability
1000–1999	0.02
2000–2999	0.08
3000–3999	0.10
4000–4999	0.20
5000–5999	0.35
6000–6999	0.25

In this case, the method of Example 14.1 must be applied to an empirical distribution. We first construct Table 14-3, using the midpoints u and adding to obtain the cumulative distribution $F(u)$. From the table we compute the mean:

Table 14-3

u	$f(u)$	$F(u)$
1500	0.02	0.02
2500	0.08	0.10
3500	0.10	0.20
4500	0.20	0.40
5500	0.35	0.75
6500	0.25	1.00

$$\bar{u} = \sum u f(u) = 5030$$

whence

$$q^* = \sqrt{\frac{2(25)(5030)}{0.2}} \approx 1121 \text{ units} \quad Ans.$$

and

$$F(R^*/L) = 1 - \frac{(0.2)(1121)}{(0.4)(5030)} = 0.8886$$

This level of service must be interpolated in what is evidently the highest class interval. It begins at 6000 for which $F(u) = 0.75$. We need a further $(0.8886 - 0.75)$ out of the 0.25 of the data in the class interval. The amount to be added to 6000 is therefore

$$\frac{0.8886 - 0.75}{0.25}(999) \approx 554$$

there being 999 items in the class interval. Thus, $R^*/L = 6554$ and

$$R^* = \frac{6554}{8} \approx 819 \text{ items} \quad Ans.$$

$$B^* = 819 - \frac{5030}{8} \approx 190 \text{ items} \quad Ans.$$

To work out C_B^*, we have to put the integral in (14.1) in finite form; this is

$$\sum_{R^*/L}^{\infty}\left(u - \frac{R^*}{L}\right)f(u) = \sum_{R^*/L}^{\infty} u\, f(u) - \frac{R^*}{L}\sum_{R^*/L}^{\infty} f(u)$$

The first term on the right is the first moment about the origin of all the data lying above $R^*/L = 6554$. As shown in Fig. 14-3, the only area which qualifies is part of the highest class interval. The probability associated with it is $1 - 0.8886 = 0.1114$, and the distance to its centroid is

$$\frac{1}{2}(6554 + 6999) = 6776.5$$

The second term is

$$\frac{R^*}{L}R\left(\frac{R^*}{L}\right) = (6554)(0.1114)$$

The summation is therefore

$$(6776.5)(0.1114) - (6554)(0.1114) = 24.79$$

Therefore, (14.1) gives

$$C_B^* = (0.2)\left(819 - \frac{5030}{8}\right) + \frac{5030}{1121}(0.4)\left(\frac{1}{8}\right)(24.79)$$

$$= 38.05 + 5.56 = \$43.61$$

For the cycle stock, $C_C^* = \sqrt{2(25)(5030)(0.2)} = \$224.28$, so that

$$C^* = 43.61 + 224.28 = \$267.89 \quad Ans.$$

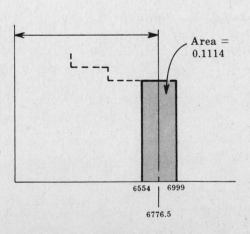

Fig. 14-3

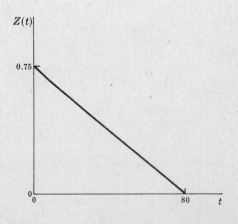

Fig. 14-4

RETENTION TIME FOR OBSOLESCENT STOCK

14.3. A perishable product has a probability density of being sold in the next short time period, given it has remained unsold so far, that is uniformly declining from 0.75 at $t = 0$ to 0 at $t = 80$ days, i.e. after 80 days it must be removed from sale. Neglecting scrap value and given that profit per item is 18 cents and carrying charges 8 cents per item per day, find the optimal retention time.

As shown in Fig. 14-4,

$$Z(t) = (0.75)\left(1 - \frac{t}{80}\right)$$

Also $c/p = 8/18 = 0.4444$. Therefore, from (14.8),

$$(0.75)\left(1 - \frac{t}{80}\right) = 0.4444$$

$$\frac{t}{80} = 0.4075$$

$$t^* = 32.6 \text{ days} \quad Ans.$$

14.4. A certain product has a conditional profit of \$3 per unit and a carrying charge of 8¢ per unit per day. The time to sale is assumed to be exponentially distributed with mean 45 days. What decision rule should be adopted with respect to retention time in inventory?

From Table 9-6 and (9.18),

$$Z(t) = \frac{f_e(t/T)}{R_e(t/T)} = \frac{1}{T}\frac{e^{-t/T}}{e^{-t/T}} = \frac{1}{T}$$

The hazard rate for the exponential distribution is thus a constant and equals the reciprocal of its mean.

To arrive at a decision rule, it is useful to restate (14.8) as: Retain item in inventory so long as $Z(t) \geq c/p$, i.e.

$$\frac{1}{T} \geq \frac{c}{p} \quad \text{or} \quad T \leq \frac{p}{c}$$

This is equivalent to saying: Retain item in inventory if the mean time to sale is less than the time taken for the carrying charges to cancel out the profit. In the present case $T = 45$, $p = 300$ and $c = 8$. We have

$$45 > \frac{300}{8}$$

Therefore, *do not* retain items in inventory. In practice, if needed, they would be ordered specially.

Note that the hazard rate for the exponential distribution is the special case $k = 1$ of the hazard rate used in Example 14.3.

THE S,s MODEL

14.5. Rework Example 14.4, except that the demand has a rectangular distribution with limits 26 and 54 units.

Note that

$$\bar{u} = \frac{54 + 26}{2} = 40 \qquad \sigma_u = \frac{54 - 26}{\sqrt{12}} \approx 8$$

so that this distribution has the same mean and standard deviation as the normal one in Example 14.4.

$$F_R(S^* \mid 26, 54) = \frac{S^* - 26}{54 - 26} = 0.7272$$

$$S^* = 26 + (0.7272)(28) \approx 46 \text{ units} \quad Ans.$$

By working out the integrals as in Problem 14.1, it follows that, for a rectangular distribution with limits a and b,

$$K_{uS} = k_u \frac{(b-S)^2}{2(b-a)} \qquad K_{oS} = k_o \frac{(S-a)^2}{2(b-a)} \qquad (14.16)$$

Thus
$$vS^* + K_{uS}^* + K_{oS}^* = 2(46) + 18\frac{(54-46)^2}{2(54-26)} + 4\frac{(46-26)^2}{2(54-26)}$$

$$= 92 + (0.3214)(54-46)^2 + (0.07143)(46-26)^2 = \$141.14$$

From (14.10)

$$vs^* + K_{us}^* + K_{os}^* = 16 + 141.14 = \$157.14 = C^* \qquad Ans.$$

The left side is worked out by substituting s for S in (14.16) and adding $2s$, i.e.

$$2s + (0.3214)(54-s)^2 + (0.07143)(s-26)^2 = 157.14$$

$$2s + (0.3214)(2916 - 108s + s^2) + (0.07143)(s^2 - 52s + 676) = 157.14$$

$$(0.3928)s^2 - (36.42)s + 828.35 = 0$$

$$s^* = \frac{36.42 \pm \sqrt{(36.42)^2 - 4(0.3928)(828.35)}}{2(0.3928)} = 40.00 \text{ or } 52.71$$

Only the solution $s^* < S^*$ is admissible, hence $s^* = 40$ units.   *Ans.*

Comparing these results with those of Example 14.4, s^*, S^* are within one unit of each other and there is a difference of less than 1 percent in C^*.

Supplementary Problems

14.6. A product is to be managed on an order point–order quantity system. Annual usage has a normal distribution with a mean of 900 units and a standard deviation of 130 units. Cost of a shortage is \$1.20 and carrying charges are \$2.50 per unit per year. There is a lead time of 4 months and a setup costs \$20. Find the reorder point, order quantity, expected buffer stock and expected annual cost of the optimal policy.

Ans. $R^* = 326$ units; $q^* = 120$ units; $B^* = 26$ units; $C^* = \$431.85$

14.7. Plot the hazard rate in Example 14.3 against t and check that it is monotonically decreasing.

14.8. Rework Example 14.4, changing the standard deviation of the usage to 40 units. (Note that this gives the usage the same mean and standard deviation in a normal distribution as it had in the exponential distribution of Example 14.5.)

Ans. $S^* = 62$ units; $s^* = 51$ units; $C^* = \$389$

14.9. Rework Example 14.4, changing the selling price to \$6 per unit.

Ans. $S^* = 38$ units; $s^* = 29$ units; $C^* = \$127$

14.10. A product is to be managed on an order point–order quantity system. Setup costs are \$40; usage is normally distributed with mean 10,000 units a year and standard deviation 300. Shortage cost is \$120 per unit and carrying charges are 80¢ per unit per year. Lead time is 1 month. Find the reorder point, order quantity, expected buffer stock and expected annual cost of the optimal policy.

Ans. $R^* = 871$ units; $q^* = 1000$ units; $B^* = 38$ units; $C^* = \$839.19$

Chapter 15

Quality Control and Acceptance Sampling

CONTROL CHARTS FOR VARIABLES

Control charts are used to monitor the central tendency and variation of a variable in a manufacturing process. The ones most commonly used are those for the means of certain small samples of size n and those for the standard deviation or range of the sample. Control charts for the sample mean are based on the sampling limits defined in (*11.3*) as

$$S_{1-\alpha}(\bar{X}) = \mu \pm z_{(1-\alpha)/2}\sigma_{\bar{X}} = \mu \pm z_{(1-\alpha)/2}\frac{\sigma}{\sqrt{n}}$$

The differences are:

1. The value of α is set by making $z_{(1-\alpha)/2} = 3$, so that, as shown in Appendix B,

$$\frac{1-\alpha}{2} = 0.4987 \quad \text{or} \quad \alpha = 0.0027$$

which corresponds to a confidence level of 99.73 percent. Control limits are thus also called *3-sigma limits*.

2. It is sometimes decided to set μ and σ at specific values μ_0 and σ_0 simply by managerial fiat. Here, the chosen values are known to be within the capabilities of the process by past experience.

3. More often, however, estimates of μ and σ are obtained, not from single sample observations as in Chapter 11, but from a succession of k preliminary samples of size n each. A mean $\bar{X}$ is obtained from each sample, and the estimate of μ is the grand mean

$$\bar{\bar{X}} = \frac{\Sigma\bar{X}}{k} = \frac{\Sigma X}{nk} \tag{15.1}$$

4. The estimate of σ, denoted σ', is also derived from the k preliminary samples. For each sample we compute the sample standard deviation

$$s = \sqrt{\frac{\Sigma X^2}{n} - \bar{X}^2}$$

(see Table 11-1) and then obtain the average $\bar{s}$ of the k values so obtained, i.e.

$$\bar{s} = \frac{\Sigma s}{k} \tag{15.2}$$

Alternatively, and more simply, we derive an estimate σ' by determining the *range* of each of the k samples, i.e. the largest X in the sample minus the smallest,

$$R = X_{\max} - X_{\min} \tag{15.3}$$

and then calculating the mean range

$$\bar{R} = \frac{\Sigma R}{k} \tag{15.4}$$

5. Either $\bar{R}$ or $\bar{s}$ is converted into the estimate σ' by using the coefficient d_2 or c_2 respectively, see Table 15-1. The table further shows how, by using the 3-sigma limits, the coefficients may be presented more simply as A_1 or A_2; the latter is most often used in practice. These and all other coefficients in this section are tabulated against n in Appendix H.

6. Control limits for the sample standard deviation s and the sample range R are likewise 3-sigma limits, with the lower limit $\geqq 0$; $\bar{s}$ or $\bar{R}$ serve as central values and σ_s, σ_R are derived as shown in Table 15-1, using the basic coefficients c_3 and d_3, which are then modified and combined to give B_1, B_2, B_3, B_4 and D_1, D_2, D_3, D_4. The last two are used with $\bar{R}$ and are thus the simplest.

Table 15-1

CONTROL CHART FOR $\bar{X}$	
Using $\sigma' = \bar{s}/c_2$	Using $\sigma' = \bar{R}/d_2$
$\text{UCL}_{\bar{x}} = \bar{\bar{X}} + \dfrac{3\bar{s}}{c_2\sqrt{n}} = \bar{\bar{X}} + A_1\bar{s}$	$\text{UCL}_{\bar{x}} = \bar{\bar{X}} + \dfrac{3\bar{R}}{d_2\sqrt{n}} = \bar{\bar{X}} + A_2\bar{R}$
$\text{LCL}_{\bar{x}} = \bar{\bar{X}} - \dfrac{3\bar{s}}{c_2\sqrt{n}} = \bar{\bar{X}} - A_1\bar{s}$	$\text{LCL}_{\bar{x}} = \bar{\bar{X}} - \dfrac{3\bar{R}}{d_2\sqrt{n}} = \bar{\bar{X}} - A_2\bar{R}$
CONTROL CHART FOR s	
Using $\sigma_s = c_3\bar{s}/c_2$	Using $\bar{s} = c_2\sigma'$, $\sigma_s = c_3\sigma'$
$\text{UCL}_s = \bar{s} + \dfrac{3c_3\bar{s}}{c_2} = B_4\bar{s}$	$\text{UCL}_s = c_2\sigma' + 3c_3\sigma' = B_2\sigma'$
$\text{LCL}_s = \bar{s} - \dfrac{3c_3\bar{s}}{c_2} = B_3\bar{s} \quad (B_3 \geqq 0)$	$\text{LCL}_s = c_2\sigma' - 3c_3\sigma' = B_1\sigma' \quad (B_1 \geqq 0)$
CONTROL CHART FOR R	
Using $\sigma_R = d_3\bar{R}/d_2$	Using $\bar{R} = d_2\sigma'$, $\sigma_R = d_3\sigma'$
$\text{UCL}_R = \bar{R} + \dfrac{3d_3\bar{R}}{d_2} = D_4\bar{R}$	$\text{UCL}_R = d_2\sigma' + 3d_3\sigma' = D_2\sigma'$
$\text{LCL}_R = \bar{R} - \dfrac{3d_3\bar{R}}{d_2} = D_3\bar{R} \quad (D_3 \geqq 0)$	$\text{LCL}_R = d_2\sigma' - 3d_3\sigma' = D_1\sigma' \quad (D_1 \geqq 0)$

EXAMPLE 15.1. The first four columns of Table 15-2 give the results of measuring the output voltage of an electronic device in samples of 4 each. Find control limits for mean, range and standard deviation.

We first complete Table 15-2 by adding columns for $\bar{X}$, R and s. Their totals are divided by $k = 15$, resulting in $\bar{\bar{X}}$, $\bar{R}$ and $\bar{s}$.

Limits for the Mean

Using $\bar{R}$, with $A_2 = 0.729$ for $n = 4$ (from Appendix H),
$$\text{UCL}_{\bar{x}} = 132.30 + (0.729)(21.467) = 147.95$$
$$\text{LCL}_{\bar{x}} = 132.30 - (0.729)(21.467) = 116.65 \quad Ans.$$

Using $\bar{s}$, with $A_1 = 1.88$ for $n = 4$ (from Appendix H),
$$\text{UCL}_{\bar{x}} = 132.30 + (1.88)(8.233) = 147.78$$
$$\text{LCL}_{\bar{x}} = 132.30 - (1.88)(8.233) = 116.82 \quad Ans.$$

Note that the two sets of results are within 0.12 percent for the upper, and 0.15 percent for the lower, limit. In practice the limits based on R would be more convenient.

Table 15-2

X_1	X_2	X_3	X_4	$\bar{X}$	R	s
140	149	138	137	141.00	12	4.7
109	129	121	117	119.00	20	7.2
143	137	114	130	131.00	29	10.8
124	132	129	144	132.25	20	7.4
138	136	132	107	128.25	31	12.5
130	125	139	138	133.00	14	5.8
142	122	134	134	133.00	20	7.1
137	125	137	122	129.25	15	6.0
118	122	133	120	123.25	15	5.8
159	138	128	142	141.75	31	11.2
134	133	134	133	133.50	1	0.5
140	138	127	133	134.50	13	5.0
109	125	139	138	127.75	30	12.2
151	145	113	155	141.00	42	16.6
141	119	136	148	136.00	29	10.7
			TOTALS	1984.50	322	123.5
			÷ 15	132.30	21.467	8.233
				$\bar{\bar{X}}$	$\bar{R}$	$\bar{s}$

Limits for the Range

For $n = 4$, $D_4 = 2.282$; $D_3 = 0$.

$$\text{UCL}_R = (2.282)(21.467) = 48.99 \qquad \text{LCL}_R = 0 \quad Ans.$$

Limits for the Standard Deviation

For $n = 4$, $B_4 = 2.266$; $B_3 = 0$.

$$\text{UCL}_s = (2.266)(8.233) = 18.66 \qquad \text{LCL}_s = 0 \quad Ans.$$

The limits are illustrated in Fig. 15-1; the difference between the two sets derived for $\bar{X}$ does not show up graphically. It is important to distinguish *physically* between the significance of a point beyond the $\bar{X}$ limits and a point beyond those for R or s. For example, in the former case, it may be that tool wear has caused a gradual drift to a higher dimension (for outside diameters, for instance) or to a lower one (for holes). If the dispersion runs out, however, it may mean a destabilizing of the process, e.g. something having worked loose in a setting, etc. The further readings which have been added to Fig. 15-1 show both situations. As shown in Appendix H, in cases of higher n, $B_1, B_3, D_1, D_3 > 0$, so that positive lower control limits exist for R and s. Thus, a runout below the lower limit may occur, indicating an abnormally *stable* process. If this has occurred, perhaps some change has been made by the operator, like increased skill, better tooling, etc. In that case we should study the possibility of tightening the standards.

As long as the subsequent readings of $\bar{X}$ and R (or s) for each sample taken are within the control limits, the process is said to be *in control;* when they fall outside, the process is said to be *out of control*. The value of α is set at the very low level given by the 3-sigma limits so that whenever a runout does occur, the necessary changes, shutdowns or other dislocations are most unlikely to be prompted only by the random fluctuations of the variable. Rather, the wrong readings are almost certain to be the effect of some outside change in the process.

The sample range R embodies less information than the sample standard deviation s, and so its use introduces some inaccuracy. However, the difference is usually small.

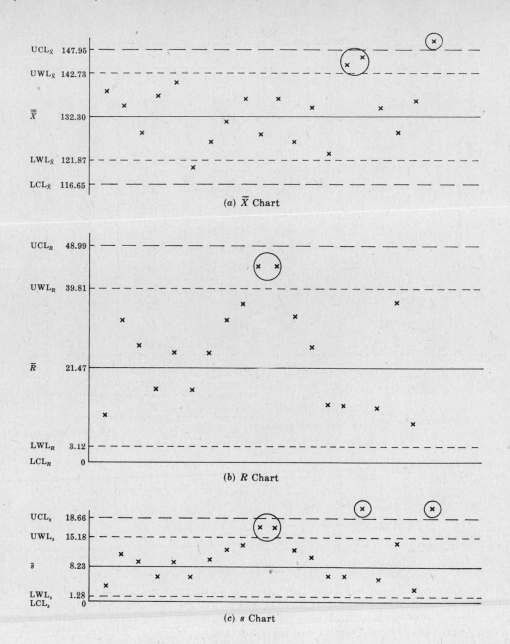

(a) $\bar{X}$ Chart

(b) R Chart

(c) s Chart

Fig. 15-1

EXAMPLE 15.2. Using the data of Example 15.1, calculate σ' both from $\bar{R}$ and from $\bar{s}$.

From Appendix H, for $n = 4$, $d_2 = 2.059$ and $c_2 = 0.7979$, which give

$$\sigma' = \frac{21.467}{2.059} = 10.42 \quad \text{and} \quad \sigma' = \frac{8.223}{0.7979} = 10.32$$

The difference is about 1 percent.

WARNING LIMITS

Occasionally, in practice, it may be desirable to set up *warning limits* at ±2-sigma. When two sample readings in a row are on the same side of the central line in the zone between the 2- and 3-sigma limits, action is taken as if a point had fallen outside the control limits. This is because the probability of a point falling between 2- and 3-sigma limits on the same side is

$$F_N(3) - F_N(2) = 0.4987 - 0.4772 = 0.0215$$

The probability of two points like that in a row is $(0.0215)^2 = 0.00046$, which is certainly a very low value for α. If the event arises, a more likely interpretation is that the process is out of control.

EXAMPLE 15.3. Add 2-sigma warning limits to the control charts of Example 15.1.

This is done by multiplying the deviations from the central line, given in Table 15-1, by 2/3. Thus, for the mean,

$$\text{UWL}_{\bar{X}} = \bar{\bar{X}} + \frac{2}{3}A_2\bar{R}$$

$$\text{LWL}_{\bar{X}} = \bar{\bar{X}} - \frac{2}{3}A_2\bar{R}$$

$$(15.5)$$

or

$$\text{UWL}_{\bar{X}} = \bar{\bar{X}} + \frac{2}{3}A_1\bar{s}$$

$$\text{LWL}_{\bar{X}} = \bar{\bar{X}} - \frac{2}{3}A_1\bar{s}$$

$$(15.6)$$

In the present case

$$\text{UWL}_{\bar{X}} = 132.30 + \frac{2}{3}(0.729)(21.467) = 142.73$$

$$\text{LWL}_{\bar{X}} = 132.30 - \frac{2}{3}(0.729)(21.467) = 121.87$$

or

$$\text{UWL}_{\bar{X}} = 132.30 + \frac{2}{3}(1.88)(8.233) = 142.62$$

$$\text{LWL}_{\bar{X}} = 132.30 - \frac{2}{3}(1.88)(8.233) = 121.98$$

For the range:

$$W(R) = \bar{R} \pm \frac{2}{3}(\text{UCL}_R - \bar{R}) = \bar{R} \pm \frac{2}{3}(D_4 - 1)\bar{R}$$

Simplifying,

$$\text{UWL}_R = \frac{1}{3}(1 + 2D_4)\bar{R}$$

$$\text{LWL}_R = \frac{1}{3}(5 - 2D_4)\bar{R} \text{ or } 0, \text{ whichever is greater}$$

$$(15.7)$$

In the present example

$$\text{UWL}_R = \frac{1}{3}[1 + 2(2.282)](21.467) = 39.81$$

$$\text{LWL}_R = \frac{1}{3}[5 - 2(2.282)](21.467) = 3.12$$

For the standard deviation:

$$\text{UWL}_s = \frac{1}{3}(1 + 2B_4)\bar{s}$$

$$\text{LWL}_s = \frac{1}{3}(5 - 2B_4)\bar{s} \text{ or } 0, \text{ whichever is greater}$$

$$(15.8)$$

In the present example

$$\text{UWL}_s = \frac{1}{3}[1 + 2(2.266)](8.233) = 15.18$$

$$\text{LWL}_s = \frac{1}{3}[5 - 2(2.266)](8.233) = 1.28$$

The warning limits also appear on Fig. 15-1.

RUNS

A further refinement in the analysis of control charts is to examine the length of runs on either side of the center line. If there are k readings taken, one would expect that $k/2$ would be above and $k/2$ below the center line. The latter is here considered as the *median*, i.e. the line with half of all readings above and half below it. As the control limits are based on the normal approximation resulting from the central limit theorem, mean and median are approximately equal.

Let $k_r > (0.5)k$ be the number of readings to one side of the central line. The probability that k_r or more are to one side is binomial and given by $R_{\mathrm{B}}(k_r \,|\, k, 0.5)$; an equal probability exists that k_r or more are on the other side. The total of the two is the probability that such an event occurs purely by chance, so that the significance level is

$$\alpha = 2R_{\mathrm{B}}(k_r \,|\, k, 0.5) \qquad (15.9)$$

Table 15-3 gives the combinations of k and k_r which produce $\alpha \approx 0.013$ and $\alpha \approx 0.002$, the latter being comparable to α for 3-sigma limits. A significant run calls for the same action as a point outside the control limits.

EXAMPLE 15.4. In 3 series of 20 readings, (a) 12, (b) 18, (c) 16 lie on one side of the center line. Which of these runs are significant?

From Table 15-3, (c) is significant at $\alpha = 0.0118$; (b) at $\alpha < 0.0026$; (a) is not significant.   *Ans.*

Table 15-3

k	k_r	α	k	k_r	α
7	7	0.0156	7	..	..
11	10	0.0118	11	11	0.0010
14	12	0.0130	14	13	0.0018
17	14	0.0128	17	15	0.0024
20	16	0.0118	20	17	0.0026

CONTROL CHARTS FOR FRACTION DEFECTIVE

A control chart for fraction defective is based on the sampling limits given by (11.4):

$$S_{1-\alpha}(p) = \pi \pm z_{(1-\alpha)/2}\sigma_p$$

where $\sigma_p = \sqrt{\pi(1-\pi)/n}$. Again:

1. We choose $z_{(1-\alpha)/2} = 3$, making $\alpha = 0.0027$.

2. An estimate of π is obtained from k samples of n each. The ith sample has c_i defectives $(i = 1, 2, \ldots, k)$. These are added, i.e. we obtain Σc, and an estimate p' of π is obtained from

$$p' = \frac{\Sigma c}{nk} \qquad (15.10)$$

and an estimate σ'_p of σ_p is given by

$$\sigma'_p = \sqrt{\frac{p'(1-p')}{n}} \qquad (15.11)$$

The control limits are then:

$$\mathrm{UCL}_p = p' + 3\sigma'_p$$
$$\mathrm{LCL}_p = p' - 3\sigma'_p \text{ or } 0, \text{ whichever is greater} \qquad (15.12)$$

EXAMPLE 15.5. Twenty-five samples of 100 each are taken of a certain electronic component. The numbers of defectives found are 3, 2, 5, 1, 0, 2, 5, 6, 1, 9, 6, 2, 7, 9, 3, 2, 1, 9, 5, 3, 8, 9, 6, 5, 4. Find the control limits for fraction defective and plot the subsequent sample results 5, 7, 4, 9, 11, 3, 7, 4, 6, 4.

Adding the c's,
$$\Sigma c = 3 + 2 + 5 + \cdots + 5 + 4 = 113$$

From (15.10) and (15.11)
$$p' = \frac{113}{(100)(25)} = 0.0452 \qquad \sigma'_p = \sqrt{\frac{(0.0452)(1 - 0.0452)}{100}} = 0.02077$$

and from (15.12)
$$\text{UCL}_p = 0.0452 + 3(0.02077) = 0.1075 \quad \textit{Ans.}$$
$$\text{LCL}_p = 0 \quad \textit{Ans.}$$

The control chart is shown in Fig. 15-2, with the further readings plotted. The point corresponding to $c = 11$, i.e. $p = 0.11$, is above the UCL_p.

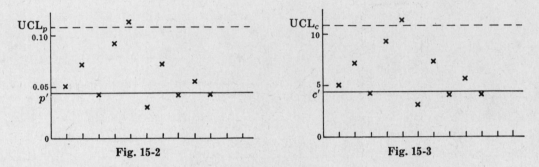

Fig. 15-2   Fig. 15-3

CONTROL CHARTS FOR NUMBER DEFECTIVE

The number of defectives in a sample of size n is $c = np$. Approximating the binomial distribution of c by a Poisson distribution with parameter m, we have for the sampling limits:
$$S_{1-\alpha}(c) = m \pm z_{(1-\alpha)/2}\sigma_c = m \pm z_{(1-\alpha)/2}\sqrt{m}$$

The estimate of m, c', is obtained from k preliminary samples as
$$c' = \frac{\Sigma c}{k}$$

Thus, the 3-sigma control limits are
$$\text{UCL}_c = c' + 3\sqrt{c'}$$
$$\text{LCL}_c = c' - 3\sqrt{c'} \text{ or } 0, \text{ whichever is greater}$$

As would be expected, these limits are almost exactly n-times the limits for the variable p.

EXAMPLE 15.6. Convert the data for Example 15.5 to a control chart for number defective.

Since $\Sigma c = 113$,
$$c' = \frac{113}{25} = 4.52$$
which is the central line.
$$\text{UCL}_c = 4.52 + 3\sqrt{4.52} = 10.9 \qquad \text{LCL}_c = 0$$

Figure 15-3 illustrates this control chart. It is virtually identical in effect to Fig. 15-2.

ACCEPTANCE SAMPLING: OC CURVES FOR SINGLE SAMPLING

The process is based on a simple interpretation of the OC curve for Poisson sampling. A sampling plan (n, c) is selected. If c or fewer are defective, the lot is accepted; if $r = c + 1$ or more are defective, it is rejected. The plan ($n = 75$, $c = 5$) was worked out in

Example 11.18; its OC or $P(A)$ curve is repeated as Fig. 15-4. Consider now two values of the fraction defective, p_1 and p_2; p_1 is a "good" quality level and so its probability of acceptance is high. In Fig. 15-4 it is 0.95; nevertheless, there is a 0.05 chance that a *good* lot like this will be rejected. Clearly, this is a Type I ($\alpha = 0.05$) error, which is known in acceptance sampling as the *producer's risk* (because the producer risks having a good lot unfairly rejected). The value of p_1 corresponding to α is also called the *acceptable quality level* (AQL).

Consider now the "poor" fraction defective, p_2. Here there is still a chance of (in this case) 10 percent that so bad a lot will be accepted. Accordingly, this is the probability of accepting something false, i.e. a Type II or β error, which is here called *consumer's risk*. The value p_2 which corresponds to a given β is also called *lot tolerance percent defective* (LTPD).

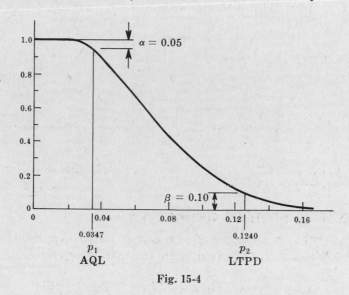

Fig. 15-4

EXAMPLE 15.7. In the sampling plan ($n = 75$, $c = 5$), find AQL if producer's risk is 0.05 and LTPD if consumer's risk is 0.10.

In Appendix D, look down the column $X = 5$ to the entries closest to $1 - \alpha = 0.95$ and $\beta = 0.10$. After interpolation for the latter, the results are

$$m_1 = np_1 = 2.6$$

$$p_1 = \frac{2.6}{75} = 0.0347 \quad Ans.$$

$$m_2 = np_2 = 9.3$$

$$p_2 = \frac{9.3}{75} = 0.1240 \quad Ans.$$

THE AVERAGE OUTGOING QUALITY LIMIT

When it is possible to correct unsatisfactory product, it is possible to use a procedure called *rectifying inspection*. A sampling plan such as the one in the previous section is instituted. If the actual number of defectives is c or less, the lot passes. If there are more than c defectives, the entire lot of N is inspected and any defective items are repaired or replaced. Thus the only time defective items are accepted is in the event that the sample of n is satisfactory, leaving $N - n$ items uninspected that include, on the average, $p(N - n)$ defectives which remain undetected. Now the probability of accepting a lot with a fraction defective p is just $P(A)$ for that p, or $F_P(c\,|\,np)$. The expected number of remaining defectives is thus $p(N-n)F_P(c\,|\,np)$. Dividing this by N gives the expected proportion of remaining defectives in the lot N, called the *average outgoing quality* (AOQ):

$$AOQ = pF_P(c\,|\,np)\frac{N-n}{N} \qquad (15.13)$$

Note that for large N, $(N-n)/N \approx 1$.

As p increases, the AOQ first increases, then peaks and decreases again. The reason is that when p is low, the outgoing p naturally is also low; and when p is high, a higher proportion of the lots will be rejected and therefore rectified, again producing a lower proportion of remaining defectives. We can thus compute a maximum value of AOQ, called the *average outgoing quality limit* (AOQL):

$$AOQL = \max(AOQ) \qquad (15.14)$$

EXAMPLE 15.8. Find the AOQ for the sampling plan $(75,5)$ of Example 15.7, plot it and find AOQL. The lot size is $N = 2000$.

The factor $1 - (n/N)$ has the value $1 - (75/2000) = 0.9625$. In the following table, the second row reproduces

$$P(A) = F_P(c\,|\,np) = F_P(5\,|\,75p)$$

from Example 11.18 and the last row gives

$$AOQ = (0.9625)p\,F_P(5\,|\,75p)$$

p	0	0.02	0.04	0.06	0.08	0.10	0.12	0.14	0.16
$F_P(c\,|\,np)$	1	0.996	0.916	0.703	0.446	0.242	0.116	0.050	0.020
AOQ	0	0.0192	0.0353	0.0406	0.0343	0.0233	0.0134	0.0067	0.0031

The table and Fig. 15-5 indicate that AOQL ≈ 0.0406. *Ans.*

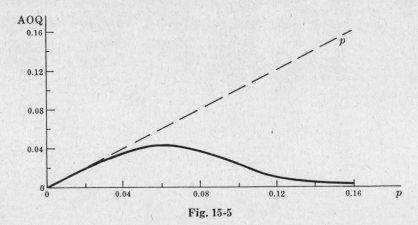

Fig. 15-5

SYSTEMATIC SETS OF PLANS: MIL-STD-105D

It is possible to have sampling plans with virtually any combination of n and c. Moreover, all their OC curves start at $p = 0$, $P(A) = 1$; and if one further point is set, a family of plans can be devised which will very nearly pass through that also. For exam-

n	5	26	55	87	122	158	195	233
c	0	1	2	3	4	5	6	7

ple, the family all pass through the point $(p = 0, P(A) = 1)$ and very near the point $(p = 0.02, P(A) = 0.90)$, which can be interpreted as $AQL = 0.02$ for a producer's risk of 0.10. Using tables devised by J. M. Cameron (*Industrial Quality Control*, July 1952, p. 39) we can in fact find n and c for a plan the OC curve of which will pass as nearly as possible through given $(AQL, 1 - \alpha)$ and $(LTPD, \beta)$.

However, it is more customary to employ a systematically arranged set of plans of which the most commonly used is MIL-STD-105D, published by the U.S. Department of Defense and also known as the ABC standard. For a single sampling plan we first choose a sample size code letter from Table 15-4. Unless otherwise provided in the purchase transaction, use level II. With the code letter we enter Table 15-5 and proceed across to the appropriate AQL, which here is given as number of *defects* per 100 *items* inspected. (This definition of the AQL permits sampling for several attributes at once; for single-attribute sampling it reduces to the percentage defective, or 100 times the AQL as we have previously defined it.) The acceptance and rejection numbers are given for each plan.

Table 15-4

Lot or Batch Size	Special Inspection Levels				General Inspection Levels		
	S-1	S-2	S-3	S-4	I	II	III
2–8	A	A	A	A	A	A	B
9–15	A	A	A	A	A	B	C
16–25	A	A	B	B	B	C	D
26–50	A	B	B	C	C	D	E
51–90	B	B	C	C	C	E	F
91–150	B	B	C	D	D	F	G
151–280	B	C	D	E	E	G	H
281–500	B	C	D	E	F	H	J
501–1200	C	C	E	F	G	J	K
1201–3200	C	D	E	G	H	K	L
3201–10,000	C	D	F	G	J	L	M
10,001–35,000	C	D	F	H	K	M	N
35,001–150,000	D	E	G	J	L	N	P
150,001–500,000	D	E	G	J	M	P	Q
500,001 and over	D	E	H	K	N	Q	R

EXAMPLE 15.9. Find the MIL-STD-105D plan which suits a lot of 800 items with $AQL = 4.0$.

From Table 15-4, the sample size code letter is J. Table 15-5 gives a sampling plan with $n = 80$, $c = 7$, $r = 8$. *Ans.*

These plans may be further modified to provide for *tightened* and *reduced* inspection. The nominal AQL is changed to—compare (*15.12*)—

$$AQL \mp 3\sigma_{AQL} = AQL \mp 3\sqrt{\frac{AQL(1 - AQL)}{n}}$$

where the upper sign is used for tightened, and the lower for reduced, inspection.

Table 15-5

Acceptable Quality Levels (Normal Inspection)

(Each cell shows Ac Re, where Ac = acceptance number and Re = rejection number.)

Sample Size Code Letter	Sample Size	0.010	0.015	0.025	0.040	0.065	0.10	0.15	0.25	0.40	0.65	1.0	1.5	2.5	4.0	6.5	10	15	25	40	65	100	150	250	400	650	1000
A	2	↓	↓	↓	↓	↓	↓	↓	↓	↓	↓	↓	↓	↓	↓	↓	↓	0 1	1 2	2 3	3 4	5 6	7 8	10 11	14 15	21 22	30 31
B	3	↓	↓	↓	↓	↓	↓	↓	↓	↓	↓	↓	↓	↓	↓	↓	0 1	1 2	2 3	3 4	5 6	7 8	10 11	14 15	21 22	30 31	44 45
C	5	↓	↓	↓	↓	↓	↓	↓	↓	↓	↓	↓	↓	↓	↓	0 1	1 2	2 3	3 4	5 6	7 8	10 11	14 15	21 22	30 31	44 45	↑
D	8	↓	↓	↓	↓	↓	↓	↓	↓	↓	↓	↓	↓	↓	0 1	1 2	2 3	3 4	5 6	7 8	10 11	14 15	21 22	30 31	44 45	↑	↑
E	13	↓	↓	↓	↓	↓	↓	↓	↓	↓	↓	↓	↓	0 1	1 2	2 3	3 4	5 6	7 8	10 11	14 15	21 22	30 31	44 45	↑	↑	↑
F	20	↓	↓	↓	↓	↓	↓	↓	↓	↓	↓	↓	0 1	1 2	2 3	3 4	5 6	7 8	10 11	14 15	21 22	30 31	44 45	↑	↑	↑	↑
G	32	↓	↓	↓	↓	↓	↓	↓	↓	↓	↓	0 1	1 2	2 3	3 4	5 6	7 8	10 11	14 15	21 22	30 31	44 45	↑	↑	↑	↑	↑
H	50	↓	↓	↓	↓	↓	↓	↓	↓	↓	0 1	1 2	2 3	3 4	5 6	7 8	10 11	14 15	21 22	30 31	44 45	↑	↑	↑	↑	↑	↑
J	80	↓	↓	↓	↓	↓	↓	↓	↓	0 1	1 2	2 3	3 4	5 6	7 8	10 11	14 15	21 22	30 31	44 45	↑	↑	↑	↑	↑	↑	↑
K	125	↓	↓	↓	↓	↓	↓	↓	0 1	1 2	2 3	3 4	5 6	7 8	10 11	14 15	21 22	30 31	44 45	↑	↑	↑	↑	↑	↑	↑	↑
L	200	↓	↓	↓	↓	↓	↓	0 1	1 2	2 3	3 4	5 6	7 8	10 11	14 15	21 22	30 31	44 45	↑	↑	↑	↑	↑	↑	↑	↑	↑
M	315	↓	↓	↓	↓	↓	0 1	1 2	2 3	3 4	5 6	7 8	10 11	14 15	21 22	30 31	44 45	↑	↑	↑	↑	↑	↑	↑	↑	↑	↑
N	500	↓	↓	↓	↓	0 1	1 2	2 3	3 4	5 6	7 8	10 11	14 15	21 22	30 31	44 45	↑	↑	↑	↑	↑	↑	↑	↑	↑	↑	↑
P	800	↓	↓	↓	0 1	1 2	2 3	3 4	5 6	7 8	10 11	14 15	21 22	30 31	44 45	↑	↑	↑	↑	↑	↑	↑	↑	↑	↑	↑	↑
Q	1250	↓	↓	0 1	1 2	2 3	3 4	5 6	7 8	10 11	14 15	21 22	30 31	44 45	↑	↑	↑	↑	↑	↑	↑	↑	↑	↑	↑	↑	↑
R	2000	↓	0 1	1 2	2 3	3 4	5 6	7 8	10 11	14 15	21 22	30 31	44 45	↑	↑	↑	↑	↑	↑	↑	↑	↑	↑	↑	↑	↑	↑

↓ = use first sampling plan below arrow. If sample size equals, or exceeds, lot or batch size, do 100% inspection.

↑ = use first sampling plan above arrow.

Ac = acceptance number.

Re = rejection number.

Table 15-6

Acceptable Quality Levels (Tightened Inspection)

Sample Size Code Letter	Sample Size	0.010		0.015		0.025		0.040		0.065		0.10		0.15		0.25		0.40		0.65		1.0		1.5		2.5		4.0		6.5		10		15		25		40		65		100		150		250		400		650		1000	
		Ac	Re	Ac	Re	Ac	Re	Ac	Re	Ac	Re	Ac	Re	Ac	Re	Ac	Re	Ac	Re	Ac	Re	Ac	Re	Ac	Re	Ac	Re	Ac	Re	Ac	Re	Ac	Re	Ac	Re	Ac	Re	Ac	Re	Ac	Re	Ac	Re	Ac	Re	Ac	Re	Ac	Re	Ac	Re
A	2	↓		↓		↓		↓		↓		↓		↓		↓		↓		↓		↓		↓		↓		↓		↓		↓		↓		0	1	1	2	2	3	3	4	5	6	8	9	12	13	18	19	27	28
B	3	↓		↓		↓		↓		↓		↓		↓		↓		↓		↓		↓		↓		↓		↓		↓		↓		0	1	1	2	2	3	3	4	5	6	8	9	12	13	18	19	27	28	41	42
C	5	↓		↓		↓		↓		↓		↓		↓		↓		↓		↓		↓		↓		↓		↓		↓		0	1	1	2	2	3	3	4	5	6	8	9	12	13	18	19	27	28	41	42	↑	
D	8	↓		↓		↓		↓		↓		↓		↓		↓		↓		↓		↓		↓		↓		↓		0	1	1	2	2	3	3	4	5	6	8	9	12	13	18	19	27	28	41	42	↑		↑	
E	13	↓		↓		↓		↓		↓		↓		↓		↓		↓		↓		↓		↓		↓		0	1	1	2	2	3	3	4	5	6	8	9	12	13	18	19	27	28	41	42	↑		↑		↑	
F	20	↓		↓		↓		↓		↓		↓		↓		↓		↓		↓		↓		↓		0	1	1	2	2	3	3	4	5	6	8	9	12	13	18	19	27	28	41	42	↑		↑		↑		↑	
G	32	↓		↓		↓		↓		↓		↓		↓		↓		↓		↓		↓		0	1	1	2	2	3	3	4	5	6	8	9	12	13	18	19	27	28	41	42	↑		↑		↑		↑		↑	
H	50	↓		↓		↓		↓		↓		↓		↓		↓		↓		↓		0	1	1	2	2	3	3	4	5	6	8	9	12	13	18	19	27	28	41	42	↑		↑		↑		↑		↑		↑	
J	80	↓		↓		↓		↓		↓		↓		↓		↓		↓		0	1	1	2	2	3	3	4	5	6	8	9	12	13	18	19	27	28	41	42	↑		↑		↑		↑		↑		↑		↑	
K	125	↓		↓		↓		↓		↓		↓		↓		↓		0	1	1	2	2	3	3	4	5	6	8	9	12	13	18	19	27	28	41	42	↑		↑		↑		↑		↑		↑		↑		↑	
L	200	↓		↓		↓		↓		↓		↓		↓		0	1	1	2	2	3	3	4	5	6	8	9	12	13	18	19	27	28	41	42	↑		↑		↑		↑		↑		↑		↑		↑		↑	
M	315	↓		↓		↓		↓		↓		↓		0	1	1	2	2	3	3	4	5	6	8	9	12	13	18	19	27	28	41	42	↑		↑		↑		↑		↑		↑		↑		↑		↑		↑	
N	500	↓		↓		↓		↓		↓		0	1	1	2	2	3	3	4	5	6	8	9	12	13	18	19	27	28	41	42	↑		↑		↑		↑		↑		↑		↑		↑		↑		↑		↑	
P	800	↓		↓		↓		↓		0	1	1	2	2	3	3	4	5	6	8	9	12	13	18	19	27	28	41	42	↑		↑		↑		↑		↑		↑		↑		↑		↑		↑		↑		↑	
Q	1250	↓		↓		↓		0	1	1	2	2	3	3	4	5	6	8	9	12	13	18	19	27	28	41	42	↑		↑		↑		↑		↑		↑		↑		↑		↑		↑		↑		↑		↑	
R	2000	↓		↓		0	1	1	2	2	3	3	4	5	6	8	9	12	13	18	19	27	28	41	42	↑		↑		↑		↑		↑		↑		↑		↑		↑		↑		↑		↑		↑		↑	
S	3150	↓		0	1	1	2	2	3	3	4	5	6	8	9	12	13	18	19	27	28	41	42	↑		↑		↑		↑		↑		↑		↑		↑		↑		↑		↑		↑		↑		↑		↑	

↓ = use first sampling plan below arrow. If sample size equals, or exceeds, lot or batch size, do 100% inspection.

↑ = use first sampling plan above arrow.

Ac = acceptance number.

Re = rejection number.

Table 15-7

Acceptable Quality Levels (Reduced Inspection)†

Each cell shows the acceptance number (Ac) and rejection number (Re) as "Ac Re". An arrow (↓ or ↑) means use the first sampling plan below / above the arrow.

Sample Size Code Letter	Sample Size	0.010	0.015	0.025	0.040	0.065	0.10	0.15	0.25	0.40	0.65	1.0	1.5	2.5	4.0	6.5	10	15	25	40	65	100	150	250	400	650	1000
A	2	↓	↓	↓	↓	↓	↓	↓	↓	↓	↓	↓	↓	↓	↓	↓	↓	0 1	1 2	2 3	3 4	5 6	7 8	10 11	14 15	21 22	30 31
B	2	↓	↓	↓	↓	↓	↓	↓	↓	↓	↓	↓	↓	↓	↓	↓	0 1	0 2	1 3	2 4	3 5	5 6	7 8	10 11	14 15	21 22	30 31
C	2	↓	↓	↓	↓	↓	↓	↓	↓	↓	↓	↓	↓	↓	↓	0 1	0 2	1 3	1 4	2 5	3 6	5 8	7 10	10 13	14 17	21 24	↑
D	3	↓	↓	↓	↓	↓	↓	↓	↓	↓	↓	↓	↓	↓	0 1	0 2	1 3	1 4	2 5	3 6	5 8	7 10	10 13	14 17	21 24	↑	↑
E	5	↓	↓	↓	↓	↓	↓	↓	↓	↓	↓	↓	↓	0 1	0 2	1 3	1 4	2 5	3 6	5 8	7 10	10 13	14 17	21 24	↑	↑	↑
F	8	↓	↓	↓	↓	↓	↓	↓	↓	↓	↓	↓	0 1	0 2	1 3	1 4	2 5	3 6	5 8	7 10	10 13	↑	↑	↑	↑	↑	↑
G	13	↓	↓	↓	↓	↓	↓	↓	↓	↓	↓	0 1	0 2	1 3	1 4	2 5	3 6	5 8	7 10	10 13	↑	↑	↑	↑	↑	↑	↑
H	20	↓	↓	↓	↓	↓	↓	↓	↓	↓	0 1	0 2	1 3	1 4	2 5	3 6	5 8	7 10	10 13	↑	↑	↑	↑	↑	↑	↑	↑
J	32	↓	↓	↓	↓	↓	↓	↓	↓	0 1	0 2	1 3	1 4	2 5	3 6	5 8	7 10	10 13	↑	↑	↑	↑	↑	↑	↑	↑	↑
K	50	↓	↓	↓	↓	↓	↓	↓	0 1	0 2	1 3	1 4	2 5	3 6	5 8	7 10	10 13	↑	↑	↑	↑	↑	↑	↑	↑	↑	↑
L	80	↓	↓	↓	↓	↓	↓	0 1	0 2	1 3	1 4	2 5	3 6	5 8	7 10	10 13	↑	↑	↑	↑	↑	↑	↑	↑	↑	↑	↑
M	125	↓	↓	↓	↓	↓	0 1	0 2	1 3	1 4	2 5	3 6	5 8	7 10	10 13	↑	↑	↑	↑	↑	↑	↑	↑	↑	↑	↑	↑
N	200	↓	↓	↓	↓	0 1	0 2	1 3	1 4	2 5	3 6	5 8	7 10	10 13	↑	↑	↑	↑	↑	↑	↑	↑	↑	↑	↑	↑	↑
P	315	↓	↓	↓	0 1	0 2	1 3	1 4	2 5	3 6	5 8	7 10	10 13	↑	↑	↑	↑	↑	↑	↑	↑	↑	↑	↑	↑	↑	↑
Q	500	↓	↓	0 1	0 2	1 3	1 4	2 5	3 6	5 8	7 10	10 13	↑	↑	↑	↑	↑	↑	↑	↑	↑	↑	↑	↑	↑	↑	↑
R	800	↓	0 1	0 2	1 3	1 4	2 5	3 6	5 8	7 10	10 13	↑	↑	↑	↑	↑	↑	↑	↑	↑	↑	↑	↑	↑	↑	↑	↑

↓ = use first sampling plan below arrow. If sample size equals, or exceeds, lot or batch size, do 100% inspection.

↑ = use first sampling plan above arrow.

Ac = acceptance number.

Re = rejection number.

† If the acceptance number has been exceeded but the rejection number has not been reached, accept the lot but reinstate normal inspection.

Table 15-6 shows that in tightened inspection the sample size is kept the same, but the acceptance number c is reduced; by the rules of MIL-STD-105D tightened inspection must be adopted when 2 out of 5 consecutive batches are rejected; after 5 more pass tightened inspection, normal inspection may be resumed.

Reduced inspection uses smaller sample sizes, thus providing a cost incentive. It is adopted whenever 10 consecutive lots are accepted under normal inspection and when the client's representative approves it. As shown in Table 15-7, in reduced inspection, c and r may differ by more than 1. If the number of defectives falls between c and r, the lot is accepted but normal inspection must be resumed. Indeed, normal inspection must be resumed immediately whenever a lot is rejected.

EXAMPLE 15.10. Find the corresponding tightened and reduced MIL-STD-105D single sampling plans corresponding to the plan of Example 15.9.

For tightened inspection, Table 15-6, with code letter J and AQL $= 4.0$, gives $n = 80$, $c = 5$, $r = 6$.   *Ans.*

For reduced inspection, Table 15-7, with code letter J and AQL $= 4.0$, gives $n = 32$, $c = 3$, $r = 6$.   *Ans.*

MIL-STD-105D also gives double sampling and multiple sampling plans, again for normal, tightened and reduced standards, as well as the OC curves for all plans. For the double and multiple plans, they also give the *average sample number*. See Problems 15.3 and 15.4.

Solved Problems

CONTROL CHARTS

15.1. A certain account shows the following deviations from budget in 14 months: -620, 1058, 5, 722, -1150, 522, -150, 1091, 94, 1453, -771, -327, 236, 426. (Such deviations make up a *variance account*; the word "variance" is used in an accounting and not in a statistical sense.) Find suitable control limits for this variance account.

The first task is to see if the variances from expected costs show significant rising or falling trends over time. Plotting them on a time basis usually allows a judgment to be made on this point; otherwise the correlation methods of Chapter 17 must be used. We shall assume here that the above variances are values of a random variable X. The problem is an application of control charts, with the important difference that the monthly variances are *single* readings, rather than means of samples, so that the control limits are on X directly, i.e.

$$\mu \pm z_{(1-\alpha)/2}\sigma_X$$

and not on the sample means $\overline{X}$. Because the central-limit theorem does not automatically apply, we must check whether or not the population variable X is itself approximately normally distributed. We shall use normal probability paper (Fig. 15-6) for the purpose, which has a scale of $F(z)$ vertically and the variable X horizontally. The use of this paper requires us to find a value of $F(z)$ for each value of the variance X. This follows the procedures of *order statistics*. First, order the X's from small to large, irrespective of their time sequence. Then

$$F(z) = \frac{m}{n+1} \tag{15.15}$$

on the vertical scale, where m is the *order* of the reading and n is the total number of readings. The cumulative probabilities $F(z)$ are, beginning with the smallest X, 1/15, 2/15, 3/15, ..., 14/15. The plotting positions are given in the following table:

X	−1150	−771	−620	−327	−150	5	94	236	426	522	722	1058	1091	1453
$F(z)$	0.067	0.133	0.200	0.267	0.333	0.400	0.467	0.533	0.600	0.667	0.733	0.800	0.867	0.933

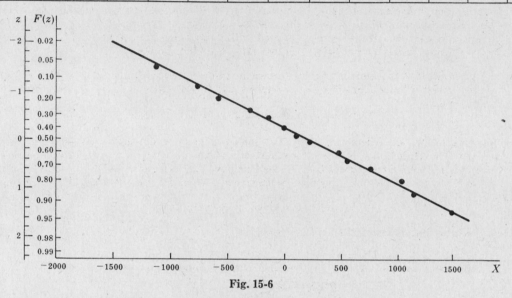

Fig. 15-6

The result shows a reasonably straight line and we may therefore consider the data to be a sample of size $n = 14$ from a normal population with mean μ and standard deviation σ. (Actually, a fair degree of divergence might be tolerated in view of our discussion in Chapter 9.) The limits used for costs are 2-sigma rather than 3-sigma, because, for costs, a Type I error would merely lead to a study of the process and of its *past* cost structure and would not typically lead to the kind of stoppage and waste which it might in process control. Warning limits are set at 1 sigma. Thus two points falling between the 1- and 2-sigma limits do so with probability $(0.4772 - 0.3413)^2 = 0.0185$, which calls for action.

The tabulation gives $\Sigma X = 2589$ and $\Sigma X^2 = 7,871,175$, from which

$$\overline{X} = \frac{2589}{14} = 185 \qquad s = \sqrt{\frac{7,871,175}{14} - (185)^2} = 727$$

Using these as estimates of μ and σ respectively, we obtain

$$\text{UCL}_X = 185 + 2(727) = 1639 \qquad \text{UWL}_X = 185 + 727 = 912$$
$$\text{LCL}_X = 185 - 2(727) = -1269 \qquad \text{LWL}_X = 185 - 727 = -542 \quad Ans.$$

From these results charts may be prepared which can serve as controls for subsequent financial periods. Such charts are superior to fixed percentage limits on deviations from budget, which may be too rigid a standard for highly variable costs and too lax a one for costs with little variability.

ACCEPTANCE SAMPLING

15.2. Consider the family of single sampling plans on page 248 the OC curves of which pass near $(0.02, 0.90)$. Find LTPD for $\beta = 0.10$ for each plan listed in Table 15-8.

Table 15-8

n	5	26	55	87	122	158	195	233	
c	0	1	2	3	4	5	6	7	
m	2.1	3.9	5.33	6.72	8.0	9.3	10.5	11.8	
LTPD	0.42	0.15	0.097	0.077	0.066	0.059	0.054	0.051	*Ans.*

In the table, m is the value for which $P(A) = 0.10$ in the appropriate c column of Appendix D. LTPD is obtained as $np_2/n = m/n$.

15.3. The following sampling scheme is proposed: Take a sample of 50 items, with $c = 3$, $r = 7$. If 4, 5 or 6 defectives are found, take a second sample of 50; then, accept with *total* $c = 8$ and reject with $r = 9$. Draw the OC curve for this plan.

This is a double sampling plan. We will compute the points on the OC curve for $p = 0.04$, 0.08 and 0.12, which, since both samples are of 50 items, correspond to $m = 2$, 4 and 6 respectively. A double sampling plan has three OC curves (Fig. 15-7). The lowest one is the plan ($n = 50$, $c = 3$), which gives the probability of accepting the lot after the first sample. The middle one gives $P(A)$ for the case when the second sample is used. The upper one is the plan ($n = 50$, $c = 6$), i.e. it gives the probability of the lot *not* being rejected after the first sample.

In Table 15-9 the plotting points (shown in italics) for the lowest and highest OC curves are obtained directly from Appendix D, as well as the probabilities $f_P(c \mid m)$ of exactly 4, 5 or 6 defectives, e.g.

$$f_P(5 \mid 2) = F_P(5 \mid 2) - F_P(4 \mid 2) = 0.983 - 0.947 = 0.036$$

The probabilities of acceptance when the second sample is taken are computed in Table 15-10. As shown on the left side of the table, there are 4 ways in which a lot can be accepted on the first *or* second sample. The probabilities in the third column are given by the product rule, since the first and second samples are assumed independent. Thus, for $m = 2$ and the second line,

$$f_P(4 \mid m) \, F_P(4 \mid m) = (0.090)(0.947) = 0.085$$

etc. Figure 15-7 presents the final results.

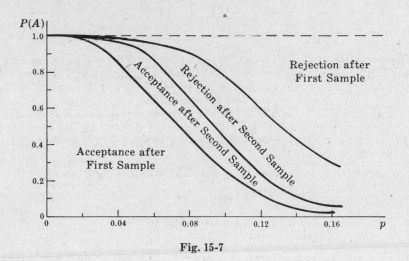

Fig. 15-7

MIL-STD-105D gives double sampling plans as well; the above example is, in fact, that for AQL = 4.0 and sample size code letter J. The standard also gives multiple sampling plans with 7 samples; for the first six samples, the decision must be made to accept, reject or take another sample. The plan for AQL = 4.0 and code letter J is shown in Table 15-11. The 7th sample has $r = c + 1$, as usual when a final decision is to be made.

Table 15-9

	$m = 2$		$m = 4$		$m = 6$		$m = 8$	
	$F_P(c \mid m)$	$f_P(c \mid m)$	$F_P(c \mid m)$	$f_P(c \mid m]$	$F_P(c \mid m)$	$f_P(c \mid m]$	$F_P(c \mid m)$	$f_P(c \mid m]$
$c = 2$	0.677	..	0.238	..	0.062	..	0.014	..
3	*0.857*	..	*0.433*	..	*0.151*	..	*0.042*	..
4	0.947	0.090	0.629	0.196	0.285	0.134	0.100	0.058
5	0.983	0.036	0.785	0.156	0.446	0.161	0.191	0.091
6	*0.995*	0.012	*0.889*	0.104	*0.606*	0.160	*0.313*	0.122

Table 15-10

Defectives in Sample 1	Defectives in Sample 2	Probability	$m = 2$	$m = 4$	$m = 6$	$m = 8$
3	(not taken)	$F_P(3 \mid m)$	0.857	0.433	0.151	0.042
4	0, 1, 2, 3, 4	$f_P(4 \mid m) F_P(4 \mid m)$	0.085	0.123	0.038	0.006
5	0, 1, 2, 3	$f_P(5 \mid m) F_P(3 \mid m)$	0.031	0.068	0.024	0.004
6	0, 1, 2	$f_P(6 \mid m) F_P(2 \mid m)$	0.008	0.025	0.010	0.002
		TOTALS = $P(A)$	0.981	0.649	0.223	0.054

Table 15-11

Sample No.	Sample Size	Ac (c)	Re (r)
1	20	0	4
2	20	1	6
3	20	3	8
4	20	5	10
5	20	7	11
6	20	10	12
7	20	13	14

15.4. Find the average sample number for the plan in Problem 15.3, using $p = 0.04, 0.08, 0.12, 0.16, 0.20$.

In double sampling plans the second sample will be used only part of the time; the probability of needing it is

$$1 - [P(\text{acceptance after 1st sample}) + P(\text{rejection after 1st sample})]$$

Substituting $F_P(c \mid m)$ for $P(A)$ and $1 - F_P(r-1 \mid m)$ for the probability of rejection, as in the upper OC curve of Fig. 15-7, the *average sample number* is

$$
\begin{aligned}
\text{ASN} &= n_1 + n_2[1 - P(A) - P(R)] \\
&= n_1 + n_2\{1 - F_P(c \mid m) - [1 - F_P(r-1 \mid m)]\} \\
&= n_1 + n_2[F_P(r-1 \mid m) - F_P(c \mid m)]
\end{aligned}
$$

$$(15.16)$$

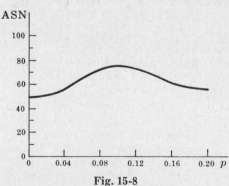

Fig. 15-8

where n_1 and n_2 are the sizes of the first and second samples respectively. In the present example, this reduces to $\text{ASN} = 50[1 + F_P(6 \mid m) - F_P(3 \mid m)]$. The calculations are shown in Table 15-12 and the ASN is plotted in Fig. 15-8. It starts at 50 when $p = 0$, rises to a peak at about $p = 0.10$ and then declines, eventually becoming asymptotic to $\text{ASN} = 50$ again.

Table 15-12

p	$m = 50p$	$F(6 \mid m)$	$F(3 \mid m)$	ASN
0.04	2	0.995	0.857	56.9
0.08	4	0.889	0.433	72.8
0.10	5	0.762	0.265	74.9
0.12	6	0.606	0.151	72.8
0.16	8	0.313	0.042	63.6
0.20	10	0.130	0.010	56.0

Supplementary Problems

15.5. The data in Table 15-13 pertain to a series of 10 tests. Find the control limits for mean, range and standard deviation.

Table 15-13

#1	#2	#3	#4	#5	#6	#7	#8	#9	#10
34	46	24	92	64	80	82	10	52	44
62	40	54	104	44	66	46	22	70	88
20	38	94	84	44	76	28	46	60	42
32	60	44	44	48	54	84	70	74	38

Ans. $\overline{X}$: 87.2, 23.0; R: 97.6, 0; s: 37.7, 0

15.6. In Problem 15.5, find σ' from (a) $\overline{R}$ and (b) $\overline{s}$.   *Ans.* (a) 20.805; (b) 20.787

15.7. Use Appendix C (binomial distribution) to check out Table 15-3.

15.8. Check that the family of plans in Table 15-8 passes close to $[p = 0.02, P(A) = 0.90]$.

15.9. Find the ordinates at $p = 0.06$ on the OC curves for the double sampling plan of Problem 15.3.
Ans.   0.647; 0.870; 0.966

15.10. Find the average sample number for $p = 0.06$ in the plan of Problem 15.9.   *Ans.* 67

15.11. For the single sampling plan ($n = 80, c = 3$), find the ordinates of the OC curve at intervals of 0.01 up to 0.09.
Ans.   1; 0.991; 0.921; 0.779; 0.603; 0.433; 0.294; 0.191; 0.119; 0.072

15.12. Find the average outgoing quality limit for the plan of Problem 15.11 given $\alpha = 0.05$ and the LTPD given $\beta = 0.05$.   *Ans.* 0.0238; 0.0968

15.13. A double sampling plan has a first sample of 35 with $c_1 = 1$ and $r_1 = 5$, followed, if necessary, by a second sample of 70, with cumulative $c_2 = 4$ and $r_2 = 5$. Find the points on the OC curves for $p = 0.02, 0.04, 0.08, 0.12$.   *Ans.* See Table 15-14

Table 15-14

	p			
	0.02	0.04	0.08	0.12
lower	0.844	0.592	0.231	0.078
middle	0.963	0.733	0.256	0.080
upper	0.999	0.986	0.848	0.590

15.14. Find the ASN for the same plan and values of p as in Problem 15.13.
Ans.   40.5; 48.8; 56.7; 53.0

15.15. By inspection of the middle (two-sample) OC curve in Fig. 15-7, find the AQL for a producer's risk of 0.05 and the LTPD for a consumer's risk of 0.10. Then show that a *single* sampling plan with $n = 85$ and $c = 7$ passes approximately through the points (AQL, 0.95) and (LTPD, 0.10) on the OC curve. This single sampling plan is thus the equivalent of a two-sample plan; now, however, we need a sample of 85 at all times rather than an ASN of about 75 in the worst case, as shown in Problem 15.4.

15.16. The following numbers of defectives were obtained in a series of tests on samples of 80 items: 3, 4, 2, 1, 0, 0, 2, 3, 5, 2, 1, 1, 0, 2, 1. Establish control limits for (a) fraction defective, (b) number defective.

   Ans.   (a) 0.0722, 0;   (b) 5.82, 0

15.17. In the single sampling plan $(n = 60, c = 3)$ find the points on the OC curve for $p = 0.01, 0.05, 0.10$ and the corresponding AOQ.   Take $N = 1000$.

   Ans. $P(A)$: 0.997, 0.647, 0.151;   AOQ: 0.009372, 0.03041, 0.01419

15.18. In the sampling plan $(n = 60, c = 3)$ find the AQL for a producer's risk of 0.05 and the LTPD for a consumer's risk of 0.10.   *Ans.*   0.0227; 0.111

Chapter 16

Analysis of Variance and Allied Methods

PURPOSE

In statistical analysis it often happens that the data are or can be classified in several categories. It is then necessary to determine whether or not there is a statistically significant difference between one category and another. In *enumeration statistics*, which forms the first part of this chapter, it is simply a matter of testing whether the actual and expected numbers of items in a category differ significantly from each other. The *analysis of variance* makes use of the actual variables; specifically it tests for differences between the means of the categories. The practical applications range over most of industrial experimentation that cannot be analyzed by the methods of Chapters 11 and 15.

ENUMERATION STATISTICS

Whenever it is possible in an experiment to count the numbers of items falling into k categories and also possible to obtain information on how many items *should be* in that category, we have for each category i an actual number of members A_i and expected number E_i. Then it can be shown that, provided the E_i are not less than 5,

$$(\chi^2)_c = \sum_{i=1}^{k} \frac{(A_i - E_i)^2}{E_i} \qquad (16.1)$$

has approximately a χ^2 distribution with degrees of freedom ν depending on the arrangement of the categories.

The null hypothesis is that there are no significant differences between the actual and expected numbers. This null hypothesis is accepted if $(\chi^2)_c < \chi^2_{1-\alpha,\nu}$, i.e. it is rejected because of a chance event only with probability α (which is very small).

EXAMPLE 16.1. A group of 200 firms is distributed with respect to credit rating as shown in column (2) of Table 16-1. From other sources it is known what proportion of the population (of firms) falls into each of the categories [column (3)]. At a significance level of 0.05, does this group differ significantly from the general population?

Table 16-1

Credit Rating	Number in Category, A	Proportion of Population, p	Expected Number in Category, E	$(\chi^2)_c$
(1)	(2)	(3)	(4)	(5)
High	38	0.12	24	8.167
Good	118	0.60	120	0.033
Fair	42	0.25	50	1.280
Limited	2	0.03	6	2.667
TOTALS	200	1.00	200	12.147

Column (4) gives the expected numbers, $E_i = np_i$. Thus, $E_1 = 200(0.12) = 24$, etc. Column (5) gives the contributions to $(\chi^2)_c$, e.g. for the "high" rating the contribution is

$$\frac{(38-24)^2}{24} = 8.167$$

This example is an $r \times 1$ array, i.e. a single column of data with r rows. The expected values must be provided from outside information. For this case, the degrees of freedom are

$$\nu = r - 1 \tag{16.2}$$

The rationale (though not formal proof) for (16.2) is that if r numbers total to a given n, then $r-1$ of these numbers can be selected in any way desired, but the rth is determined by the total. Thus there are $r-1$ "degrees of freedom."

There are $r = 4$ categories; thus $\nu = 4 - 1 = 3$. The tabular value to which the calculated $(\chi^2)_c$ must be compared is, by Appendix E, $\chi^2_{0.95, 3} = 7.81$. From Table 16-1, $(\chi^2)_c = 12.147 > 7.81$; so reject the null hypothesis. There *is* a difference between the sample and the population; by inspection, the sample is seen to have, on balance, a higher credit rating.

A more complex case is that of the *contingency table*, in which the enumerations are classified in two directions, with r rows and c columns. The expected values are here generated from the row, column and grand totals. The method is best shown by an example.

EXAMPLE 16.2. Table 16-2(a) gives the number of pieces produced by each of 5 operators on each of 3 machines. Within $\alpha = 0.05$, is there a relationship between operators and machines?

First, it is useful to establish the notation A_{ij}, where i is the row and j the column. A typical entry has row, column and grand totals denoted as follows:

$$\text{TOTALS}$$
$$A_{ij} \quad \ldots \quad A_{i.}$$
$$\ldots \quad\quad \ldots$$
$$\text{TOTALS} \quad A_{.j} \quad \ldots \quad A_{..}$$

This "dot" notation is simpler than using summation signs.

Under the null hypothesis that operators and machines are independent of one another, we would expect the 45 pieces produced by Operator A to be distributed among the three machines in the ratio $82 : 77 : 83$, i.e.

$$E_{11} = \frac{(45)(82)}{242} \qquad E_{12} = \frac{(45)(77)}{242} \qquad E_{13} = \frac{(45)(83)}{242}$$

and in general

$$E_{ij} = \frac{A_{i.}A_{.j}}{A_{..}} = \frac{\text{row total} \times \text{column total}}{\text{grand total}} \tag{16.3}$$

The E_{ij} are computed in Table 16-2(b). Finally, in Table 16-2(c), the $(\chi^2)_c$ contributions are calculated cell by cell from (16.1). For example, for the cell (C, II) the contribution is

$$\frac{(12-16.2)^2}{16.2} = 1.09$$

The grand total is $(\chi^2)_c = 20.36$.

In contingency tables, each column and row loses a degree of freedom if the row and column totals are to be maintained, as noted above. Therefore the degrees of freedom are

$$\nu = (r-1)(c-1) \tag{16.4}$$

i.e. $\nu = (5-1)(3-1) = 8$. From Appendix E, $\chi^2_{0.95, 8} = 15.5 < (\chi^2)_c$. Therefore reject the null hypothesis. *Ans.*

In looking over the cells of Table 16-2(a), (E, I) and (B, III) have unusually low, and (A, II) and (E, III) unusually high, actual outputs. These would have to be investigated in a real-life test of this kind.

Table 16-2

(a) Actual Outputs, A_{ij}

Operator	Machine			TOTALS
	I	II	III	
A	10	20	15	45
B	21	17	10	48
C	22	12	17	51
D	19	9	15	43
E	10	19	26	55
TOTALS	82	77	83	242

(b) Expected Values, E_{ij}

A	15.2	14.3	15.5	45
B	16.3	15.3	16.4	48
C	17.3	16.2	17.5	51
D	14.6	13.7	14.7	43
E	18.6	17.5	18.9	55
	82	77	83	242

(c) $(\chi^2)_c$ Contributions

A	1.78	2.27	0.02
B	1.36	0.19	2.50
C	1.28	1.09	0.14
D	1.33	1.61	0.01
E	3.98	0.13	2.67

TOTAL   20.36

ONE-WAY ANALYSIS OF VARIANCE

In this technique, c samples of r each are taken. Each sample may possibly come from a different normal population; however, all the populations are assumed to have the same variance, σ^2. It is required to test whether all samples in fact come from the same normal population, i.e. the null hypothesis is

$$(H_0: \ \mu_1 = \mu_2 = \cdots = \mu_c = \mu)$$

Such a problem arises frequently; for instance, a public utility receives a unit coal train. It wishes to test whether the coal in each of the cars is from the same mine run, i.e. of consistent quality. Or, samples are taken in each of several communities and the income of each respondent is ascertained. Do the populations differ significantly from each other?

The underlying model is

$$X_{ij} \ = \ \mu + \eta_j + \epsilon_{ij} \qquad\qquad (16.5)$$

where X_{ij} is the reading in row i and column j, μ is the grand mean of the underlying populations, η_j is a term pertaining to sample j ($j = 1, 2, \ldots, c$) and ϵ_{ij} is an unexplained error term which is normally distributed with mean 0 and variance σ^2. The procedure is to derive two estimates of the variance σ^2 by partitioning the *variation* of X, which is defined as

$$V = \Sigma\Sigma(X_{ij} - \overline{X})^2$$

where $\overline{X} = (\Sigma\Sigma X_{ij})/rc$ is the grand mean of the readings. The partitioning is $V = V_c + V_e$, where V_c relates to the differences between the sample means (actually, we work with the sample totals) and V_e is the residual variation. It can be shown that

$$E(\hat{s}_c^2) = E\left(\frac{V_c}{c-1}\right) = \frac{r}{c-1}\Sigma\eta_j^2 + \sigma^2$$

$$E(\hat{s}_e^2) = E\left(\frac{V_e}{rc-c}\right) = \sigma^2$$

The null hypothesis is equivalent to $\eta_1 = \eta_2 = \cdots = \eta_c = 0$. We therefore conduct an F-test (as in Chapter 11) on $\hat{s}_c^2/\hat{s}_e^2$; if this ratio turns out to be too large, we reject the null hypothesis.

A summary of the F-test is presented in Table 16-3 or, in simplified computational form, in Table 16-4. In Table 16-3 the "dot" notation is used (see Example 16.2), and also the *correction factor*

$$C = \frac{(\Sigma\Sigma X_{ij})^2}{rc} = \frac{X_{..}^2}{rc} \tag{16.6}$$

In Table 16-4 the terminology *column sum of squares* (CSS) and *residual sum of squares* (RSS) is used for V_c and V_e respectively. (The terms *between sum of squares* and *within sum of squares* are often used; these apply whether the sample data are arranged as columns or as rows.)

Table 16-3

Source	Sum of Squares	Degrees of Freedom	Mean Square	$(F)_c$	$(F)_{\text{table}}$	Verdict
Column	$V_c = \dfrac{1}{r}\sum_{j=1}^{c} X_{.j}^2 - C$	$\nu_c = c - 1$	$\hat{s}_c^2 = \dfrac{V_c}{\nu_c}$	$\dfrac{\hat{s}_c^2}{\hat{s}_e^2}$	$F_{1-\alpha,\,\nu_c,\,\nu_e}$	Accept if $(F)_c < (F)_{\text{table}}$
Residual	$V_e = \sum_{i=1}^{r}\sum_{j=1}^{c} X_{ij}^2 - \dfrac{1}{r}\sum_{j=1}^{c} X_{.j}^2$	$\nu_e = rc - c$	$\hat{s}_e^2 = \dfrac{V_e}{\nu_e}$			
Total	$V = \sum_{i=1}^{r}\sum_{j=1}^{c} X_{ij}^2 - C$	$\nu_t = rc - 1$				

Table 16-4

Source	Sum of Squares	Degrees of Freedom	Mean Square	$(F)_c$	$(F)_{\text{table}}$	Verdict
Column	$\dfrac{\Sigma(\text{Column sum})^2}{\text{No. in a column}} - \dfrac{(\text{Grand total})^2}{\text{Total no.}}$	$c - 1$	CSS/df	$\dfrac{\text{CSS/df}}{\text{RSS/df}}$	$F_{1-\alpha,\,c-1,\,rc-c}$	Accept if $(F)_c < (F)_{\text{table}}$
Residual	(By difference)	(By difference)	RSS/df			
Total	$\Sigma\Sigma\,\text{Squares} - \dfrac{(\text{Grand total})^2}{\text{Total no.}}$	$rc - 1$				

EXAMPLE 16.3. A chemical firm has three plants, A, B and C, turning out the same product. It wishes to determine whether the average yield per batch is the same in all three plants. It takes a sample of four batches in each plant, with the results shown in Table 16-5(a). Given that $\alpha = 0.05$, test the null hypothesis.

Since only variances are involved, a constant may be subtracted from each given result. The coded data in Table 16-5(b) are easier to use in the calculations. The next step is to square every number, producing Table 16-5(c); note particularly that the bottom line is the *squares of the totals* and *not* the totals of the squares. This is a highly useful step because it gives all the numbers required to complete the analysis and, further, each entry in Table 16-5(b) is used only *once* (if desired, the entries can be crossed off as used).

Table 16-5

(a) Raw Data

Yield, lb per batch		
A	B	C
118.5	116.5	121.0
118.5	120.5	119.0
120.0	121.5	121.0
119.5	122.5	121.5

(b) Raw Data Minus 119

	A	B	C	TOTAL
	−0.5	−2.5	2.0	
	−0.5	1.5	0.0	
	1.0	2.5	2.0	
	0.5	3.5	2.5	
TOTALS	0.5	5.0	6.5	12

(c) Squares of Coded Data

	A	B	C	SQUARE OF TOTAL
	0.25	6.25	4.00	
	0.25	2.25	0.00	
	1.00	6.25	4.00	
	0.25	12.25	6.25	
SQUARES OF TOTALS	0.25	25.00	42.25	144

Table 16-6

Source	Sum of Squares	d.f.	Mean Square	$(F)_c$	$(F)_{\text{table}}$	Verdict
Column	$\dfrac{0.25 + 25 + 42.25}{4} - \dfrac{144}{(3)(4)} = \;\; 4.875$	2	2.4375	0.84	4.26	Accept H_0
Residual	26.125	9	2.9027			
Total	$(0.25 + \cdots + 6.25) - 12 \;=\; 31.000$	11				

The analysis of variance, based on the model of Table 16-4, is carried out in Table 16-6, with Appendix G being used to provide $F_{0.95, 2, 9} = 4.26$. Actually, whenever $(F)_c < 1$, H_0 can be accepted without looking up $(F)_{\text{table}}$, which is always greater than 1.

TWO-WAY ANALYSIS OF VARIANCE

The basic two-way model is

$$X_{ij} = \mu + \theta_i + \eta_j + \epsilon_{ij} \tag{16.7}$$

where θ_i is the row effect.   There are now two null hypotheses:

$$(H_{0c}:\ \eta_1 = \eta_2 = \cdots = \eta_c = 0),\ \text{ i.e. the column means are all equal}$$

$$(H_{0r}:\ \theta_1 = \theta_2 = \cdots = \theta_r = 0),\ \text{ i.e. the row means are all equal}$$

In Table 16-7, Tables 16-3 and 16-4 are extended to include the row analysis.

Table 16-7

Source	Sum of Squares	Degrees of Freedom	Mean Square	$(F)_c$	$(F)_{table}$	Verdict
Row	$\dfrac{\Sigma(\text{Row sum})^2}{\text{No. in a row}} - C$	$r - 1$	$\hat{s}_r^2$	$\dfrac{\hat{s}_r^2}{\hat{s}_e^2}$	$F_{1-\alpha,\, r-1,\, (r-1)(c-1)}$	Accept H_{0r} if $(F)_c < (F)_{table}$
Column	$\dfrac{\Sigma(\text{Column sum})^2}{\text{No. in a column}} - C$	$c - 1$	$\hat{s}_c^2$	$\dfrac{\hat{s}_c^2}{\hat{s}_e^2}$	$F_{1-\alpha,\, c-1,\, (r-1)(c-1)}$	Accept H_{0c} if $(F)_c < (F)_{table}$
Residual	(By difference)	$(r-1)(c-1)$	$\hat{s}_e^2$			
Total	$\Sigma\Sigma X^2 - C$	$rc - 1$				

EXAMPLE 16.4. Suppose in Example 16.3 that the raw material for the first batch in each sample came from supplier I; for the second, from II; etc. With $\alpha = 0.05$, is there a difference among suppliers, as well as among plants?

The data (coded) must now be arranged as in Table 16-8(a), including the row totals. In Table 16-8(b), the squares are again worked out, also subject to the rule that each cell of Table 16-8(a) is used only once. The analysis of variance proper appears in Table 16-9. Since the data have not changed, the total sum of squares and its d.f., and the column sum of squares, d.f. and mean square, are the same as in Table 16-6. Here, both hypotheses are accepted; in other cases, one might be accepted and the other rejected (see Problem 16.11). It would also be possible to choose different α's for the two hypotheses.

Table 16-8

(a) Raw Data Minus 119

	A	B	C	TOTALS
I	−0.5	−2.5	2.0	−1.0
II	−0.5	1.5	0.0	1.0
III	1.0	2.5	2.0	5.5
IV	0.5	3.5	2.5	6.5
TOTALS	0.5	5.0	6.5	12.0

(b) Squares of Coded Data

	A	B	C	SQUARES OF TOTALS
I	0.25	6.25	4.00	1.00
II	0.25	2.25	0.00	1.00
III	1.00	6.25	4.00	30.25
IV	0.25	12.25	6.25	42.25
SQUARES OF TOTALS	0.25	25.00	42.25	144.00

Table 16-9

Source	Sum of Squares	d.f.	Mean Square	$(F)_c$	$(F)_{\text{table}}$	Verdict
Row	$\dfrac{1 + 1 + 30.25 + 42.25}{3} - 12 = 12.833$	3	4.2778	1.931	4.76	Accept H_{0r}
Column	4.875	2	2.4375	1.100	5.14	Accept H_{0c}
Residual	13.292	6	2.2153			
Total	31.000	11				

LATIN SQUARES

A *Latin square* makes possible the analysis of three effects in an economical manner, providing the data can be gathered in a way suitable for the model. A Latin square is a square array of $n \times n$ numbers, i.e. $r = c = n$. In addition, a third effect or *treatment*, categorized n ways, is superimposed on the square, such that each treatment category occurs once only in each row and column. If these treatment categories are denoted $A, B, C, \ldots$, then two Latin squares for $n = 4$ are shown in Fig. 16-1.

	Rows		Columns					Rows		Columns		
		C_1	C_2	C_3	C_4				C_1	C_2	C_3	C_4
	R_1	A	B	C	D			R_1	A	B	C	D
	R_2	B	A	D	C			R_2	B	C	D	A
	R_3	C	D	B	A			R_3	C	D	A	B
	R_4	D	C	A	B			R_4	D	A	B	C

Fig. 16-1

For $n = 4$, there are 576 different Latin squares; for $n = 5$, there are 161,280 and for $n = 6$, there are 812,851,200. Extensive listings have been published and a scheme should be chosen at random for each experiment. The preliminary calculations, i.e. coding and the squares table, are arranged as before, with the treatment data added. The analysis itself takes place according to the scheme in Table 16-10. The main difference between this and the two-way analysis is the treatment line.

Table 16-10

Source	Sum of Squares	Degrees of Freedom	Mean Square	$(F)_c$	$(F)_{\text{table}}$	Verdict
Row	$\dfrac{\Sigma(\text{Row sum})^2}{n} - C$	$n-1$	$\hat{s}_r^2$	$\hat{s}_r^2/\hat{s}_e^2$	$F_{1-\alpha,\, n-1,\, (n-1)(n-2)}$	Accept H_{0r} if $(F)_c < (F)_{\text{table}}$
Column	$\dfrac{\Sigma(\text{Column sum})^2}{n} - C$	$n-1$	$\hat{s}_c^2$	$\hat{s}_c^2/\hat{s}_e^2$	$F_{1-\alpha,\, n-1,\, (n-1)(n-2)}$	Accept H_{0c} if $(F)_c < (F)_{\text{table}}$
Treatment	$\dfrac{\Sigma(\text{Treatment sum})^2}{n} - C$	$n-1$	$\hat{s}_t^2$	$\hat{s}_t^2/\hat{s}_e^2$	$F_{1-\alpha,\, n-1,\, (n-1)(n-2)}$	Accept H_{0t} if $(F)_c < (F)_{\text{table}}$
Residual	(By difference)	$(n-1)(n-2)$	$\hat{s}_e^2$			
Total	$\Sigma\Sigma X^2 - C$	$n^2 - 1$				

Note: $C = X_{..}^2/n^2$

EXAMPLE 16.5. Four operators (#1, #2, #3 and #4) on 4 machines (I, II, III and IV) are given 4 different materials for their cutting tools (considered as treatments A, B, C and D). Table 16-11(a) shows coded average production times for a set workpiece. With $\alpha = 0.05$, analyze the Latin square.

Note the inclusion of the treatment totals and the manner in which everything is again squared [Table 16-11(b)]. The analysis itself appears in Table 16-12. We conclude that it does not matter what operator or machine is used, but that there is a difference among the tool materials.

Table 16-11

(a) Coded Data

	#1	#2	#3	#4	TOTALS
I	7A	4B	5C	3D	19
II	6D	9A	4B	2C	21
III	5C	1D	6A	1B	13
IV	6B	3C	4D	10A	23
TOTALS	24	17	19	16	76

A	B	C	D	TOTAL
32	15	15	14	76

(b) Squares

49A	16B	25C	9D	361
36D	81A	16B	4C	441
25C	1D	36A	1B	169
36B	9C	16D	100A	529
SQUARES OF TOTALS 576	289	361	256	5776

A	B	C	D	SQUARE OF TOTAL
1024	225	225	196	5776

$C = 5776/16 = 361$

Table 16-12

Source	Sum of Squares	d.f.	Mean Square	$(F)_c$	$F_{0.95, 3, 6}$	Verdict
Row	$\dfrac{361 + 441 + 169 + 529}{4} - 361 = 14.0$	3	4.67	1.474	4.76	Accept
Column	$\dfrac{576 + 289 + 361 + 256}{4} - 361 = 9.5$	3	3.17	1.000	4.76	Accept
Treatment	$\dfrac{1024 + 225 + 225 + 196}{4} - 361 = 56.5$	3	18.83	5.946	4.76	Reject
Residual	19.0	6	3.17			
Total	$(49 + \cdots + 100) - 361 = 99.0$	15				

RANKING METHODS

Ranking methods may be used to analyze problems similar to the one-way analysis of variance and they may also be used to demonstrate whether a group of judges of a set of products agree with one another to a statistically significant extent. The principal methods for both purposes are given.

Rank Sum Tests.

Rather than deal with the actual values of the variable in each of several samples (i.e. a one-way analysis of variance), the readings for *all* samples are ranked in descending order and then the ranks for each sample take the place of the original data. For instance, sample #2 may consist of the 2nd, 3rd, 7th, 11th and 15th largest reading out of the 25 in the whole array. The ranks 2, 3, 7, 11 and 15 then take the place of sample #2. Information is lost thereby and the test becomes less sensitive; but the arithmetic is simpler and the test is *nonparametric*, i.e. it does not require assumptions about the form of the underlying statistical distribution (such as the assumption of normality in the population for the analysis of variance).

If N items are subdivided into k samples of size n_i, where $i = 1, 2, \ldots, k$ and $\Sigma n_i = N$, and if R_i is the sum of the ranks in the ith sample, then the statistic of Kruskal and Wallis,

$$H = \frac{12}{N(N+1)} \sum_{i=1}^{k} \frac{R_i^2}{n_i} - 3(N+1) \tag{16.8}$$

has the χ^2 distribution with $k - 1$ degrees of freedom. If $H < \chi^2_{1-\alpha, \, k-1}$, accept the null hypothesis that $\mu_1 = \mu_2 = \cdots = \mu_k$.

EXAMPLE 16.6. The following are annual expenditures for entertainment in three samples of families from communities A, B and C. Use the H-test to see if there is a significant ($\alpha = 0.05$) difference between the mean expenses in the three towns.

> A: 967, 917, 895, 835, 802, 783, 770, 713, 692, 656, 648, 648, 463
>
> B: 690, 534, 511, 388, 368, 349, 327, 321, 321, 236, 156
>
> C: 941, 915, 820, 742, 681, 458, 361, 236

Each sample happens to be listed in descending order, but that is only to facilitate the ranking in Table 16-13.

Table 16-13

Sample	Ranks	R_i	n_i	R_i^2/n_i
A	1, 3, 5, 6, 8, 9, 10, 12, 13, 16, 17.5, 17.5, 21	139	13	1486.23
B	14, 19, 20, 23, 24, 26, 27, 28.5, 28.5, 30.5, 32	272.5	11	6750.57
C	2, 4, 7, 11, 15, 22, 25, 30.5	116.5	8	1696.53
		TOTALS	32	9933.33

By (16.8)

$$H = \frac{12}{(32)(33)} (9933.33) - 3(33) = 13.879$$

From Appendix E, $\chi^2_{0.95, 2} = 5.99$. The null hypothesis is rejected; the difference in expenditures among the communities is significant. *Ans.*

Ties may be treated as having their mean ranks, as in Table 16-13, unless they are more than a quarter of all readings. If they are, there are ways of adjusting for them, but little accuracy is lost by simply choosing between the ranks by lot. If the ties are that numerous, it is in any event questionable whether ranking methods give sufficient discrimination.

Concordance.

The extent of agreement between m judges, each of whom ranks n objects, is called *concordance*. It can be quantified and tested for significance, as shown in the following example.

EXAMPLE 16.7. There are 4 members of a test panel and each of them judges 5 products. The rankings are shown in Table 16-14. Find the coefficient of concordance and test it at the 5 percent level.

Table 16-14

Observer	Product				
	A	B	C	D	E
1	1	2	3	4	5
2	3	1	4	2	5
3	2	1	3	5	4
4	3	2	4	1	5

The sum of the ranks given by each observer is $1 + 2 + \cdots + n = \frac{1}{2}n(n+1)$. There are m observers, so that the sum for all observers is $\frac{1}{2}mn(n+1)$. The mean sum of all the ranks for each *object* is therefore

$$\bar{S} = \frac{\frac{1}{2}mn(n+1)}{n} = \frac{1}{2}m(n+1) \tag{16.9}$$

The actual S_i for each object will generally be different from this, and we define $\Sigma s^2 = \Sigma (S - \bar{S})^2$, which is the sum of the squares of the deviations of the *actual* rank sums for each object from the mean rank sum. By looking at the differences between the actual and mean rank sums in the case in which all judges agree, it is possible to show that the maximum value of Σs^2 is $m^2(n^3 - n)/12$, see (*17.18*). We then define the *coefficient of concordance W* as

$$W = \frac{\Sigma s^2}{\max (\Sigma s^2)} = \frac{12 \Sigma s^2}{m^2(n^3 - n)} \tag{16.10}$$

[Writing $n^3 - n$ as $n(n-1)(n+1)$ or $n(n^2 - 1)$ may simplify the arithmetic.]

To test its significance, we calculate the value of

$$(F)_c = \frac{(m-1)W}{1-W} \tag{16.11}$$

The null hypothesis is that there is no concordance, i.e. (H_0: $W = 0$). It is rejected if $(F)_c > F_{1-\alpha, \nu_1, \nu_2}$, where the degrees of freedom are given by

$$\nu_1 = n - 1 - \frac{2}{m} \qquad \nu_2 = (m-1)\nu_1 \tag{16.12}$$

The F-test is an approximation but is suitable in practice.

To solve the problem at hand, first find Σs^2. From (*16.9*), $\bar{S} = \frac{1}{2}(4)(5+1) = 12$ and the calculation proceeds as in Table 16-15.

Table 16-15

	A	B	C	D	E	TOTAL
S	9	6	14	12	19	
$S - \bar{S}$	−3	−6	2	0	7	
$(S - \bar{S})^2$	9	36	4	0	49	$\Sigma s^2 = 98$

From (*16.10*)

$$W = \frac{12(98)}{16(125 - 5)} = 0.6125 \quad Ans.$$

From (*16.11*)

$$(F)_c = \frac{(4-1)(0.6125)}{1 - 0.6125} = 4.742$$

From (*16.12*)

$$\nu_1 = 5 - 1 - \frac{2}{4} = 3.5 \qquad \nu_2 = (4-1)(3.5) = 10.5$$

These are not whole numbers.   In Appendix G the relevant entries are

ν_2 \ ν_1	3	4
10	3.71	3.48
11	3.59	3.36

However one chooses to interpolate, W is significant.   *Ans.*

Solved Problems

ENUMERATION STATISTICS

16.1. It is necessary to show whether or not output is of the same quality on all the days of the week.   This is done by picking a given day's output n_i and counting the number of defectives A_i in it.   These results are given in Cols. 2 and 3 of Table 16-16. Given that $\alpha = 0.05$, test whether or not there is such a difference.

This is a 5×2 contingency table which requires an additional step, because the $(\chi^2)_c$ contributions must be based not only on comparing the defectives but the good parts as well.   Column 4 therefore gives $n_i - A_i$.   The total defectives number 60 out of a weekly total of 550; thus the pooled fraction defective is $\bar{p} = 60/550 = 0.1091$.   Under the null hypothesis, $\bar{p}$ applies to all five days. Thus the expected number of defectives is $E_i = n_i\bar{p}$ (Col. 5) and the expected number of good parts is $n_i - E_i$ (Col. 6).   The $(\chi^2)_c$ contributions are computed separately by matching the A_i and E_i (Col. 7) and the $n_i - A_i$ and $n_i - E_i$ (Col. 8).   For example, for Wednesday, in Col. 7,

$$\chi^2 = \frac{(8 - 10.9)^2}{10.9} = 0.772$$

and, in Col. 8

$$\chi^2 = \frac{(92 - 89.1)^2}{89.1} = 0.094$$

The total of both Cols. 7 and 8 is $(\chi^2)_c$.   In the tabular value $\chi^2_{1-\alpha,\nu}$, ν is given by *(16.14)* as

$$\nu = (5-1)(2-1) = 4$$

From Appendix E, $\chi^2_{0.95,4} = 9.49 > (\chi^2)_c$.   Hence, accept the null hypothesis; there is no significant difference in output quality.   *Ans.*

Table 16-16

Day	Actual Total, n_i	Actual Defective, A_i	Actual Good, $n_i - A_i$	Expected Defective, $E_i = n_i\bar{p}$	Expected Good, $n_i - E_i$	$(\chi^2)_c$ Contributions Defective	$(\chi^2)_c$ Contributions Good
Monday	106	13	93	11.6	94.4	0.169	0.021
Tuesday	110	10	100	12.0	98.0	0.333	0.041
Wednesday	100	8	92	10.9	89.1	0.772	0.094
Thursday	108	13	95	11.8	96.2	0.122	0.015
Friday	126	16	110	13.7	112.3	0.386	0.047
TOTALS	550	60	490	60.0	490.0	$(\chi^2)_c = 2.000$	

ANALYSIS OF VARIANCE

16.2. The following are coded test results obtained by measuring the output of electronic components. Two samples are taken and it is required to test whether or not they come from the same population ($\alpha = 0.05$).

$$\text{Sample 1:} \quad 12 \quad 10 \quad 8 \quad 11 \quad 6$$

$$\text{Sample 2:} \quad 4 \quad 7 \quad 2 \quad 4 \quad 2 \quad 6 \quad 1 \quad 3$$

This example introduces two additional points to our discussion of one-way analysis of variance. Here the sizes of the samples differ and there are only two samples. This latter problem is often treated separately in statistics texts, resulting in rather awkward formulas. It is, however, exactly solvable by the analysis of variance methods. As to the differences in sample size, the size of a sample is now r_j (here, $j = 1, 2$). The column sum of squares is then transformed into

$$\text{CSS} = \sum_{j=1}^{c} \frac{X_{.j}^2}{r_j} - C$$

i.e. each square of a column total now has to be divided by its own sample size. The total degrees of freedom are now $\sum_{j=1}^{c} r_j - 1$, which is again 1 less than the total number of readings taken.

The calculations appear in Tables 16-17 and 16-18. Reject the null hypothesis. *Ans.*

Here, $F_{0.95, 1, 11}$ was used as the table value. Whenever $\nu_1 = 1$, $F_{1-\alpha, 1, \nu_2} = t_{(1-\alpha)/2, \nu_2}^2$; thus we could have looked up $t_{0.475, 11} = 2.20$ in Appendix F, from which $t^2 = 4.84$.

Table 16-17

Data			Squares of Data	
X_1	X_2		X_1^2	X_2^2
12	4		144	16
10	7		100	49
8	2		64	4
11	4		121	16
6	2		36	4
	6			36
	1			1
	3			9

$$X_{.1} = 47 \quad X_{.2} = 29 \quad X_{..} = 76$$

$$C = 76^2/(5+8) = 444.3$$

$$47^2 = 2209 \quad 29^2 = 841$$

$$\Sigma X_1^2 = 465 \quad \Sigma X_2^2 = 135 \quad \Sigma\Sigma X^2 = 600$$

Table 16-18

Source	Sum of Squares	d.f.	Mean Square	$(F)_c$	$(F)_{\text{table}}$	Verdict
Column	$\dfrac{2209}{5} + \dfrac{841}{8} - 444.3 = 102.6$	1	102.6	21.2	4.84	Reject
Residual	(By difference) 53.1	11	4.8			
Total	$600 - 444.3 = 155.7$	12				

RANKING METHODS

16.3. A panel of 7 judges is asked to rank 7 brands of whiskey. To preserve acuity of judgment, each one is to taste only 3 brands. Table 16-19 gives the brands A, ..., G tasted by each judge and the rank given to each. Find the coefficient of concordance and test it for significance at the 0.05 level.

Table 16-19

Judge	1	2	3	4	5	6	7
	Brand and Rank						
	A1	B2	C1	D3	E2	F1	G3
	B2	C1	D3	E2	F3	G3	A1
	D3	E3	F2	G1	A1	B2	C2

The 3×7 array in Table 16-19 is called an *incomplete Latin square* or *Youden square*. As in a Latin square, (1) each brand appears only once in a row; moreover, (2) each brand appears an equal number of times (3 times) and (3) each brand is compared an equal number of times (once) to each of the other brands. The calculations call for a similar procedure to Example 16.7, but with different formulas. First, collect all the ranks by brand, noting that $\bar{S} = 1 + 2 + 3 = 6$:

Table 16-20

	A	B	C	D	E	F	G	
	1	2	1	3	3	2	3	
	1	2	1	3	2	3	3	
	1	2	2	3	2	1	1	
TOTAL: S	3	6	4	9	7	6	7	TOTAL
$S - \bar{S}$	-3	0	-2	3	1	0	1	
$s^2 = (S - \bar{S})^2$	9	0	4	9	1	0	1	$\Sigma s^2 = 24$

In the incomplete case, n objects are presented to n judges k at a time and are each ranked m times. We now define λ, the number of judges who make a given comparison, as

$$\lambda = \frac{m(k-1)}{n-1} \tag{16.13}$$

and the coefficient of concordance

$$W = \frac{12 \Sigma s^2}{\lambda^2(n^3 - n)} = \frac{12 \Sigma s^2}{\lambda^2 n(n^2 - 1)} \tag{16.14}$$

To test its significance, the F-test is approximately correct:

$$(F)_c = \frac{W\{[\lambda(n+1)/(k+1)] - 1\}}{1 - W} \tag{16.15}$$

which is tested against $F_{1-\alpha, \nu_1, \nu_2}$ in Appendix G, where

$$\nu_1 = \frac{nm\{1 - [(k+1)/\lambda(n+1)]\}}{[nm/(n-1)] - [k/(k-1)]} - \frac{2(k+1)}{\lambda(n+1)}$$

$$\nu_2 = \nu_1 \left[\frac{\lambda(n+1)}{k+1} - 1 \right] \tag{16.16}$$

For the present example, $n = 7$, $m = k = 3$; from (16.13)

$$\lambda = \frac{3(3-1)}{7-1} = 1$$

From (16.14)

$$W = \frac{12(24)}{(1)(7)(49-1)} = 0.8571 \quad Ans.$$

From (16.15)

$$(F)_c = \frac{(0.8571)\{[(7+1)/(3+1)] - 1\}}{1 - 0.8571} = 6.00$$

From (16.16)

$$\nu_1 = \frac{7(3)\{1 - [(3+1)/(7+1)]\}}{[7(3)/(7-1)] - [3/(3-1)]} - \frac{2(3+1)}{7+1} = 4.25$$

$$\nu_2 = (4.25)\left(\frac{7+1}{3+1} - 1\right) = 4.25$$

This requires interpolation in Appendix G, which, in view of the nature of the F-function, must be done using the reciprocals of the degrees of freedom. Here we deal first with ν_2, then with ν_1, but either order is acceptable:

	$\nu_1 =$	4	4.25	5
$1/\nu_1$ $\diagdown$ $1/\nu_2$		0.25	0.235	0.2
$\nu_2 = 4$	0.25	6.39		6.26
4.25	0.235	6.03	6.00	5.90
5	0.2	5.19		5.05

In each case, the multiplier for interpolation is

$$\frac{0.235 - 0.2}{0.25 - 0.2} = 0.7$$

e.g. for ν_2,

$$F_{0.95, 4, 4.25} = 5.19 + (0.7)(6.39 - 5.19) = 6.03$$

Completing the interpolations, we obtain $F_{0.95, 4.25, 4.25} = 6.00$, which is the same as $(F)_c$. This is therefore a borderline case and no decisive judgment is possible. Such problems sometimes arise in statistical tests and introduce an area of doubt into the analysis. In this case, the test might perhaps be repeated to obtain a more certain verdict.

Incomplete Latin squares can be devised only for certain dimensions of rows and columns. For example, they may be derived from any 4×4, 5×5, 6×6 or 8×8 Latin square by omitting the last row. Certain other designs are also available; a 4×7 design is shown in Table 16-23. Further flexibility is obtained by repeating the ranking, e.g. by getting a second panel of 7 judges, or using the first panel a second time. The rankings awarded the second time are simply added to the S-table for the first judging. Then $n = 7$ and $k = 3$, as before, but $m = 6$. The rest of the work is as above.

Supplementary Problems

16.4. A bag of mixed nuts is supposed to come from a mixture with the ingredients in proportions listed below. The actual composition is also given. (a) Find, with $\alpha = 0.05$, the calculated and tabular values of χ^2. (b) State whether this sample differs significantly from the population and if so, in what respects?

	Almonds	Hazelnuts	Pecans	Brazil Nuts	Peanuts
No. in Sample	18	28	40	34	100
Population p	0.11	0.16	0.20	0.18	0.35

Ans.   (a) $(\chi^2)_c = 11.08$; $(\chi^2)_{table} = 9.49$. (b) Yes; large $(\chi^2)_c$ contributions indicate too many peanuts, too few hazelnuts and almonds.

16.5. There are three dominant brands in a certain product. It is necessary to determine whether market shares differ significantly among four communities. A set of 240 sales is examined and found to be allocated among communities and brands as in Table 16-21. With $\alpha = 0.05$, is there any significant difference in brand preference? What is $(\chi^2)_c$?   *Ans.* no; 10.01

Table 16-21

Brands	Communities			
	A	B	C	D
I	10	14	18	25
II	15	18	23	16
III	28	29	21	23

16.6. A general 2×2 contingency table has the following form:

		TOTALS
a	b	R_1
c	d	R_2
TOTALS C_1	C_2	T

Show that

$$(\chi^2)_c = \frac{T(ad - bc)^2}{R_1 R_2 C_1 C_2}$$

16.7. A 2×3 contingency table has the general form:

			TOTALS
a	b	c	R_1
d	e	f	R_2
TOTALS C_1	C_2	C_3	T

Show that

$$(\chi^2)_c = \frac{T}{R_1}\left(\frac{a^2}{C_1} + \frac{b^2}{C_2} + \frac{c^2}{C_3}\right) + \frac{T}{R_2}\left(\frac{d^2}{C_1} + \frac{e^2}{C_2} + \frac{f^2}{C_3}\right) - T$$

16.8. A group of 500 unemployed is classified as follows:

Location	Clerical	Manufacturing	Professional
Central City	120	60	40
Suburbs	50	200	30

Within $\alpha = 0.05$, find whether the composition of the unemployed population is related to location; state $(\chi^2)_c$.   *Ans.* yes; 99.8

16.9. A fourth sample is added to the three in Example 16.3. Its coded results are -3.0, -2.0, -4.0 and -3.0. Repeat the analysis of variance ($\alpha = 0.05$).   *Ans.* $(F)_c = 7.525$, reject H_0

16.10. Two samples, one of 13 and the other of 10 families, are taken and their annual supermarket purchases are measured. Use an analysis of variance to find out if the two samples come from populations having equal mean purchases, with $\alpha = 0.05$. (Data are coded by deducting $8000 from each.)

$$X_1: \quad 1200, 900, 800, 700, 200, 0, -100, \ -500, \ -600, \ -1000, -1200, -1400, -2000$$

$$X_2: \quad 2500, 1900, 1500, 700, 500, 300, 0, -200, -700, -1200$$

Ans. $(F)_c = 2.88$,   accept H_0

16.11.   Table 16-22 gives the (coded) yield per acre from 5 grades of seed planted in 5 different locations. Perform an analysis of variance at the 5 percent significance level.

Ans.   Location: reject H_0;   Seed: accept H_0

Table 16-22

Location	Seed Grade				
	1	2	3	4	5
1	5	3	7	4	5
2	3	5	4	5	0
3	0	2	0	2	0
4	3	2	1	3	4
5	2	0	5	0	2

16.12.   In Problem 16.11, 5 different grades of fertilizer are added to the experimental plots. They are applied in accordance with the Latin square shown in Fig. 16-2.

A	B	C	D	E
E	A	B	C	D
D	E	A	B	C
C	D	E	A	B
B	C	D	E	A

Fig. 16-2

Perform the analysis of variance; comment on the difference from the results of Problem 16.11.

Ans.   Accept H_0 for all effects. The addition of fertilizer has explained a significant part of the variation due to location; hence the latter is no longer significant. Also, lower degrees of freedom for the residual variation decrease the sensitivity of the analysis.

16.13.   Suppose there are only two samples in an H-test (i.e. $k = 2$). Using Chapter 11, show that the H-test statistic may be reduced to the normal variable

$$z = \frac{2R - n(N+1)}{[n(N+1)(N-n)/3]^{1/2}}$$

where R is the rank sum of one of the samples, which is of size n. (The other sample size is $N - n$.) The test is now: When $z < z_{(1/2)-\alpha}$ (e.g. $z < 1.645$ when $\alpha = 0.05$), accept $(H_0: \mu_1 = \mu_2)$. This test is called the *Wilcoxon Two-Sample Rank Test*.

16.14.   Use the Wilcoxon Two-Sample Rank Test to compare the mean expenditures in A and B only, in Example 16.6. What is the rank sum of A? Check your result by using the H-test.

Ans.   97; reject H_0

16.15.   In Example 16.7, suppose observer 4 had given the ranks as

A	B	C	D	E
5	3	4	2	1

Recompute W and test its significance at the 5 percent level.   *Ans.*   0.25; not significant

16.16. Show that when ranking is complete, i.e. $k = n$ and hence $\lambda = m$, (16.14), (16.15) and (16.16) become identical to (16.10), (16.11) and (16.12), respectively.

16.17. A second panel of judges tastes the whiskeys of Problem 16.3, with the following result:

A1	B3	C1	D2	E3	F1	G2
B2	C2	D2	E1	F1	G2	A1
D3	E1	F3	G3	A2	B3	C3

Find W and test it for significance at the 0.05 level.   *Ans.*   0.4286; not significant

16.18. Combine the rankings of Problems 16.3 and 16.17 and rework W for this double panel; test its significance at the 0.05 level.   *Ans.*   0.4821; not significant

16.19. Table 16-23 is a 4×7 incomplete ranking scheme, together with the ranks awarded by the judges. Find W and test it at 0.05 significance.

Table 16-23

A1	B2	C3	D4	E3	F4	G1
C3	D4	E1	F3	G4	A1	B2
D4	E1	F4	G2	A1	B2	C3
E2	F3	G2	A1	B2	C3	D4

Ans. $W = 53/56 = 0.9464$; significant

16.20. The following ranks were awarded by the judges in a 3×7 design. Show that $W = 1$.

A1	B2	C2	D3	E2	F1	G3
B2	C3	D3	E1	F3	G3	A1
D3	E1	F1	G2	A1	B2	C2

16.21. Figure 16-3 is a Latin square. Test it at the 0.05 level.

3A	−1B	1C	4D
2B	0C	4D	1A
4D	1A	−1B	2C
3C	4D	2A	3B

Fig. 16-3

Ans.   Accept H_0 for rows and columns; reject for treatments.

16.22. Table 16-24 shows the rankings given to 6 brands by 3 observers. Find the coefficient of concordance; test it at $\alpha = 0.05$.   *Ans.* $W = 0.822$; significant

Table 16-24

Observer	A	B	C	D	E	F
1	1	2	3	4	5	6
2	1	4	2	3	6	5
3	2	3	1	5	6	4

Chapter 17

Forecasting

INTRODUCTION

This chapter concentrates on several mathematical methods of forecasting for various planning and other analytical purposes in business. In one way or another, they are all based on an interpretation of past performance and on the assumption that the causal system which determined outcomes in the past will continue to do so. This may or may not be true; it cannot be emphasized too strongly that there is no substitute for careful and searching study of what really makes things happen in a business situation. Without it, what follows is an exercise in misplaced mathematics.

It is also important to establish two procedures:

1. All time trends or scatter diagrams should actually be plotted to scale.

2. Any straight lines or curves fitted to the data should be superimposed on the plotted points. In this way it is easy to detect at least gross errors in the functions chosen or in the computations.

In some of the examples of this chapter, several methods are used to arrive at different forecasts from the same set of data. This is done to illustrate the variety of approaches possible. In an actual case, however, one would usually choose just the one method which best fits the prior trend of the data.

EXPONENTIAL SMOOTHING

This is a useful method for forecasting one period ahead.

Notation

$$d_1' = \text{the forecast for the next period}$$

$$d_0 = \text{actual consumption for the period just ending}$$

$$d_0' = \text{forecast for the period just ending}$$

$$d_{-1} = \text{actual consumption for the first preceding period}$$

$$d_{-1}' = \text{forecast for first preceding period}$$

$$d_{-n}', d_{-n} = \text{forecast and actual consumption for the } n\text{th preceding period}$$

Then
$$d_1' = ad_0 + (1-a)d_0' \qquad (17.1)$$

where a is a smoothing constant or weighting factor, with $0 < a < 1$. This equation means that the forecast for the next period is a times the consumption for the period just ending plus $(1-a)$ times the forecast made *for* the period just ending, i.e. the forecast made at the *beginning* of the last period. Its effect is to compensate, depending on the value of a, for any discrepancies in the prior forecast. If the latter was 100 percent accurate, then $d_1' = d_0$ and current consumption is projected one period ahead.

By substituting in (17.1),

$$d_0' = ad_{-1} + (1-a)d_{-1}'$$

and, continuing, we can write

$$d_1' = ad_0 + a(1-a)d_{-1} + a(1-a)^2 d_{-2} + \cdots + a(1-a)^n d_{-n} + \cdots \qquad (17.2)$$

The coefficients of $d_0, d_{-1}, \ldots$ are a geometric progression with first term a and common factor $(1-a)$. Its sum to infinity is therefore

$$S_\infty = \frac{a}{1-(1-a)} = 1$$

The effect of (17.2) is thus to take into account all the events of the past with more or less rapidly diminishing weights (depending on a) for the more remote data. If $a = 1$, the consumption in the last period is the forecast for the next; if a is near 0, the result is to give almost equal weights to all past results, i.e. the forecast tends to the arithmetic mean of many past periods.

EXAMPLE 17.1. The following is the usage of a certain part by month for the year 1974:

Month	J	F	M	A	M	J	J	A	S	O	N	D
Usage	43	55	62	71	73	73	62	54	49	41	47	48

The forecast for January 1974 was 52 units. Prepare a schedule of forecasts as they would have been made for every month of 1974, using exponential smoothing with $a = 0.2, 0.5$ and 0.8. Forecast usage for January 1975. Plot the results together with the data.

The calculations appear in Table 17-1. For instance, for February 1974 and $a = 0.2$:

$$d_1' = (0.2)(43) + (1-0.2)(52) = 50.2$$

Table 17-1

Month	Actual Usage, d_n	Forecast, d_n'		
		$a = 0.2$	$a = 0.5$	$a = 0.8$
1974 January	43	52.0	52.0	52.0
February	55	50.2	47.5	44.8
March	62	51.2	51.3	53.0
April	71	53.4	56.7	60.2
May	73	56.9	63.9	70.4
June	73	60.1	68.5	72.5
July	62	70.4	70.8	72.9
August	54	68.7	66.4	64.2
September	49	65.8	60.2	56.0
October	41	62.4	54.6	50.4
November	47	58.1	47.8	42.9
December	48	55.6	47.4	46.2
1975 January	..	54.1	47.7	47.6

The results are plotted in Fig. 17-1. The choice $a = 0.2$ gives a more damped response than $a = 0.5$ or $a = 0.8$; $a = 0.2$ would result in more uniform employment but higher inventory, whereas $a = 0.8$ would have the opposite effect. Indeed, $a = 0.8$ closely resembles the original data, one month late. The choice depends on whether inventory costs are greater than the costs due to increased unemployment insurance, training of new employees, etc. (Compare the deterministic Problem 6.4.)

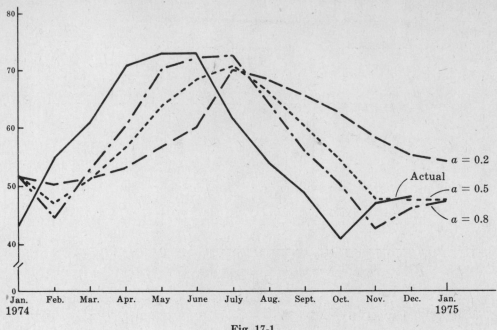

Fig. 17-1

SIMPLE REGRESSION

In many forecasting and allied problems, it happens that the variable to be determined or forecast (called the *dependent variable*) is a function of one or more other variables, called *independent*. Before undertaking an analysis of this kind it is essential that a physical mechanism be identified by which it can be shown that X really does something to Y.

In *simple regression* there is one independent variable. The process of analysis consists in finding a "best" straight line through a scatter of n points. The line itself has the equation

$$Y_{\text{calc}} = \alpha + \beta X$$

while the points have coordinates given by

$$Y_i = \alpha + \beta X_i + \epsilon_i \qquad i = 1, 2, \dots, n \tag{17.3}$$

Thus $\epsilon_i = Y_i - Y_{\text{calc}}$ is the error between the actual and the calculated ordinates at X_i, see Fig. 17-2. At any value of X, the total deviation of Y from its mean is $Y - \bar{Y}$, of which $Y_{\text{calc}} - \bar{Y}$ is "explained" by having the line pass through or near the points. By definition of $\bar{Y}$, $\Sigma(Y - \bar{Y}) = 0$; furthermore, since each positive value of $Y_{\text{calc}} - \bar{Y}$ has an equal and opposite negative one, $\Sigma(Y_{\text{calc}} - \bar{Y}) = 0$. Hence

$$\Sigma(Y - Y_{\text{calc}}) = \Sigma \epsilon_i = 0$$

We are thus led to suppose that each ϵ_i is a random variable with mean zero; moreover, we assume that all the ϵ_i have the same variance $\sigma_{Y \cdot X}^2$, called the square of the *standard error of the regression*. The distribution of each ϵ_i is assumed to be normal, just as in the analysis of variance.

To estimate values of α and β so as to produce the "best" line, we write $Y_{\text{calc}} = a + bX$ and require that the sum of the squares of the deviations, $\Sigma \epsilon^2$, be minimized. This yields a and b as unbiased estimates of α and β; they are called the *least-squares coefficients*.

$$\Sigma \epsilon^2 = \Sigma(Y - Y_{\text{calc}})^2 = \Sigma(Y - a - bX)^2$$

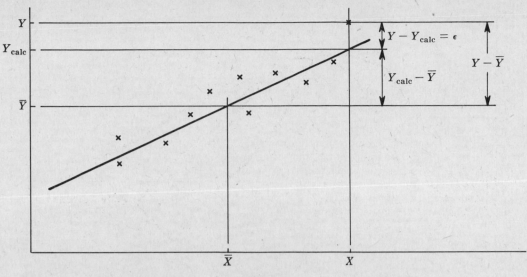

Fig. 17-2

Differentiating with respect to a and to b,

$$\frac{\partial(\Sigma \epsilon^2)}{\partial a} = -2\,\Sigma(Y - a - bX) = 0 \qquad \frac{\partial(\Sigma \epsilon^2)}{\partial b} = -2\,\Sigma X(Y - a - bX) = 0$$

from which
$$\Sigma Y = na + b\Sigma X \tag{17.4}$$

$$\Sigma XY = a\Sigma X + b\Sigma X^2 \tag{17.5}$$

From (17.4), dividing by n and rearranging,

$$a = \bar{Y} - b\bar{X} \tag{17.6}$$

and, substituting in (17.5),

$$b = \frac{\Sigma XY - n\bar{X}\bar{Y}}{\Sigma X^2 - n\bar{X}^2} \tag{17.7}$$

Thus, the best estimate is

$$Y_{\text{calc}} = a + bX \tag{17.8}$$

where a and b are given by (17.6) and (17.7). Note that, because $\bar{Y} = a + b\bar{X}$, the least-squares line always passes through the point $(\bar{X}, \bar{Y})$.

EXAMPLE 17.2. Corresponding values of two variables, X and Y, are listed in Table 17-2. In a practical case their significance and purpose might be as indicated in Table 17-3. Find the regression equation.

Table 17-2

Y	53.42	84.53	80.87	52.45	25.60	87.12	72.93	76.50
X	53	91	87	49	14	98	78	82
Y	55.14	41.00	49.51	53.16	26.22	66.04	59.26	
X	53	33	45	52	16	68	61	

Table 17-3

Y	X	Objective
costs of a job	number of items produced	budgeting for other quantities; finding the fixed cost ($= a$)
costs of a job	inputs (e.g. manhours, quantity of materials, etc.)	budgeting; efficiency studies
sales	an economic indicator (e.g. spending for plant and equipment; spending for consumer durables, housing starts, etc.)	sales forecasting

The means, squares and cross products are found by use of the cumulative feature of a calculator. With $n = 15$:

$$\Sigma Y = 883.84 \qquad\qquad \Sigma X = 880$$

$$\bar{Y} = \frac{883.84}{15} = 58.923 \qquad\qquad \bar{X} = \frac{880}{15} = 58.667$$

$$\Sigma Y^2 = 57,280.69 \qquad\qquad \Sigma X^2 = 60,869$$

$$\Sigma XY = 58,787.88$$

From (17.7) and (17.6),

$$b = \frac{58,787.88 - 15(58.667)(58.923)}{60,869 - 15(58.667)^2} = \frac{6935.31}{9269.33} = 0.7482$$

$$a = 58.923 - (0.7482)(58.667) = 15.028$$

whence $Y_{\text{calc}} = 15.028 + (0.7482)X$ *Ans.*

The scatter diagram with its fitted line is shown in Fig. 17-3.

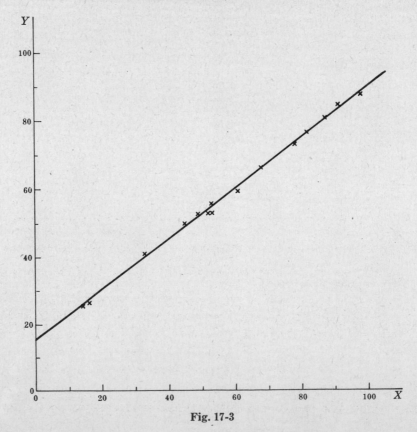

Fig. 17-3

EXAMPLE 17.3. In Example 17.2 find the estimated value of Y when (a) $X = 41$, (b) $X = 53$.

(a)
$$Y_{calc} = 15.028 + (0.7482)(41) = 45.70 \quad Ans.$$

(b)
$$Y_{calc} = 15.028 + (0.7482)(53) = 54.68 \quad Ans.$$

Result (b) differs from the actual value by $55.14 - 54.68 = 0.46$.

The expression for b (and, also, later work) is simplified by the change of variables
$$x = X - \bar{X} \qquad y = Y - \bar{Y}$$

which gives

$$\Sigma X^2 - n\bar{X}^2 = \Sigma x^2 \tag{17.9}$$

$$\Sigma XY - n\bar{X}\bar{Y} = \Sigma xy \tag{17.10}$$

$$\Sigma Y^2 - n\bar{Y}^2 = \Sigma y^2 \tag{17.11}$$

Equation (17.7) becomes

$$b = \frac{\Sigma xy}{\Sigma x^2} \tag{17.12}$$

SIMPLE CORRELATION

Simple correlation is an extension of simple regression. It measures the "quality" of the fit of the line, i.e. it tests whether or not a significant portion of the variation of Y has been explained by the regression equation. The process is best visualized in an analysis of variance table. The second column in Table 17-4 shows the total variation of Y partitioned into explained and unexplained components; the formulas follow directly from the partitioning of the total deviation $Y - \bar{Y}$ into $Y - Y_{calc}$ (unexplained) and $Y_{calc} - \bar{Y}$ (explained), and from (17.8)–(17.11). In the fourth column we have set

$$r^2 = \frac{\text{explained variation}}{\text{total variation}}$$

Table 17-4

Source	Sum of Squares	d.f.	Mean Square	$(F)_c$	$(F)_{table}$
Explained	$\Sigma(Y_{calc} - \bar{Y})^2 = b^2\Sigma x^2$	1	r^2	$\frac{r^2(n-2)}{1-r^2}$	$F_{1-\alpha,\,1,\,n-2}$
Unexplained	$\Sigma(Y - Y_{calc})^2 = \Sigma y^2 - b^2\Sigma x^2$	$n-2$	$\frac{1-r^2}{n-2}$		
Total	$\Sigma(Y - \bar{Y})^2 = \Sigma y^2$	$n-1$			

where r^2 is the *coefficient of determination*. Its square root r is the *coefficient of correlation*. From Table 17-4 and (17.12),

$$r^2 = \frac{b^2\Sigma x^2}{\Sigma y^2} = \frac{(\Sigma xy)^2}{(\Sigma x^2)(\Sigma y^2)} \tag{17.13}$$

The right-hand version does not require the computation of b and is therefore convenient when only r^2 is needed. It is called the *product moment formula*.

Table 17-4 also shows that $0 \le r^2 \le 1$. Equation (17.13) also leads to

$$r = b\sqrt{\frac{\Sigma x^2}{\Sigma y^2}}$$

so that r takes on the same sign as b, which may be positive or negative. Thus $-1 \le r \le 1$, with $r = 1$ and $r = -1$ denoting perfect direct and perfect inverse correlation, respectively, and $r = 0$ demonstrating independence of X and Y (provided their joint distribution is normal). The regression lines for these cases are shown in Fig. 17-4.

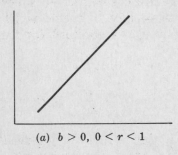 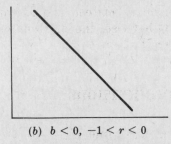 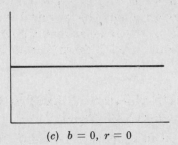

(a) $b > 0,\ 0 < r < 1$ (b) $b < 0,\ -1 < r < 0$ (c) $b = 0,\ r = 0$

Fig. 17-4

For the general test of significance of r, we establish the null hypothesis $(H_0\colon r = 0)$ and test it by following the same analysis of variance procedure as in the one-way model of Chapter 16. The third column of Table 17-4 gives the degrees of freedom. For the explained variation it is

$$(\text{number of variables} - 1) = 2 - 1 = 1$$

and the total is $n - 1$, as before. The mean squares are worked out in the next column, followed by $(F)_c$. We can test this value against the tabular one and accept H_0 if $(F)_c < F_{1-\alpha,\,1,\,n-2}$. Alternatively, the numerator degrees of freedom is $\nu_1 = 1$, so that, recalling the limiting values of F defined in Chapter 11,

$$(F)_c = (t)_c^2 = \frac{r^2(n-2)}{1-r^2}$$

or
$$(t)_c = |r|\sqrt{\frac{n-2}{1-r^2}} \qquad\qquad (17.14)$$

The null hypothesis $(H_0\colon r = 0)$ is accepted when $(t)_c < t_{(1-\alpha)/2,\,n-2}$.

EXAMPLE 17.4. Find the coefficients of determination and correlation for the data of Example 17.2. Test r at a level of $\alpha = 0.05$.

Using the data in (17.9) and (17.11) gives

$$\Sigma x^2 = 60{,}896 - 15(58.667)^2 = 9269.33$$

$$\Sigma y^2 = 57{,}280.69 - 15(58.923)^2 = 5201.38$$

Then, since $b = +0.7482$, (17.13) gives

$$r^2 = \frac{(0.7482)^2(9269.33)}{5201.38} = 0.99763 \quad Ans.$$

and
$$r = +0.99881 \quad Ans.$$

From (17.14)
$$(t)_c = (0.99881)\sqrt{\frac{15 - 2}{1 - 0.99763}} = 74.13$$

From Appendix F, $t_{0.475,\,13} = 2.16$; reject $(H_0\colon r = 0)$. $\quad Ans.$

The product moment formula, (17.13), can be partitioned into

$$r^2 = \frac{\Sigma xy}{\Sigma x^2} \frac{\Sigma xy}{\Sigma y^2}$$

The left fraction is b; the right fraction is an expression for the slope if X and Y were to be interchanged. If we denote this as b', then

$$r^2 = bb' \qquad\qquad (17.15)$$

When $|r| = 1$, $b = 1/b'$; in all other cases $b \neq 1/b'$. It is therefore essential to know enough about the physical relationships between the variables to be able to decide which one is the independent variable. Otherwise, inconsistent values would be obtained for the estimates of Y from X and X from Y.

TIME SERIES: LEAST-SQUARES METHODS
Straight-Line Trend.

The simplest time trend is the straight line $Y_{\text{calc}} = a + bX$. It means that every period Y_{calc} increases by a constant absolute amount b. The parameters a and b are fitted by the least-squares methods of the last section, where, for ease of computation, n is chosen as an odd number and the time periods are coded so that the middle one is zero and the other X's are chosen so as to make $\Sigma X = 0$. (Such a coding defines a *centered time series*. If a series is not centered, we can make it so by changing from the variable X to the variable $x = X - \bar{X}$.)

With $\Sigma X = 0$, (17.6) and (17.7) become

$$a = \bar{Y} \qquad\qquad (17.16)$$

$$b = \frac{\Sigma XY}{\Sigma X^2} \qquad\qquad (17.17)$$

When n is odd, it can be shown that, with X running from $-(n-1)/2$ to $(n-1)/2$,

$$\Sigma X^2 = \frac{n(n^2-1)}{12} = \frac{(n-1)n(n+1)}{12} \qquad\qquad (17.18)$$

This formula is especially helpful when n is large.

Table 17-5

(1)	(2)	(3)	(4)	(5)	(6)
	X	Y	XY	$V = \log Y$	XV
1964	-4	4.94	-19.76	0.6937	-2.7748
1965	-3	6.21	-18.63	0.7931	-2.3793
1966	-2	7.18	-14.36	0.8561	-1.7122
1967	-1	7.74	-7.74	0.8887	-0.8887
1968	0	8.38	0	0.9232	0
1969	1	8.45	8.45	0.9269	0.9269
1970	2	8.73	17.46	0.9410	1.8820
1971	3	9.42	28.26	0.9741	2.9223
1972	4	10.24	40.96	1.0103	4.0412
TOTALS	0 $= \Sigma X$	71.29 $= \Sigma Y$	34.64 $= \Sigma XY$	8.0071 $= \Sigma V$	2.0174 $= \Sigma XV$

EXAMPLE 17.5. Column (3) of Table 17-5 gives sales figures (in $ billion) for the General Electric Co. for the years indicated. Find a straight-line equation for the sales and estimate sales for 1973. (Actual 1973 sales were $11.58 billion.)

Column (4) shows the computation of ΣXY. From (17.18), with $n = 9$,

$$\Sigma X^2 = \frac{(8)(9)(10)}{12} = 60$$

From (17.17) and (17.16),

$$b = \frac{34.64}{60} = 0.5773 \qquad a = \frac{71.29}{9} = 7.921$$

The equation is

$$Y_{\text{calc}} = 7.921 + (0.5773)X \quad Ans.$$

For 1973, $X = 5$; therefore

$$Y_{\text{calc}} = 7.921 + (0.5773)(5) = \$10.81 \text{ billion} \quad Ans.$$

which is in error by 6.6 percent. The actual and calculated sales figures are shown in Fig. 17-5.

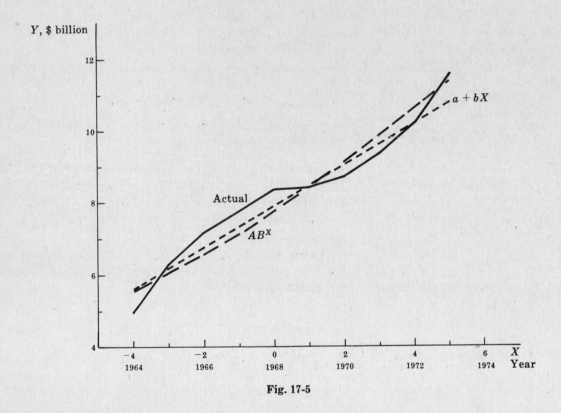

Fig. 17-5

Logarithmic Transforms.

When the straight-line model gives poor answers, it may be advisable to try a model based on constant *rates* of growth rather than constant increments. Such a model is given by

$$Y_{\text{calc}} = AB^X \tag{17.19}$$

The relationship (17.19) is also called the *exponential curve*. A and B must be positive; $0 < B < 1$ is the equivalent of $b < 0$, i.e. the curve has a negative slope, like Fig. 17-4(b), and represents a negative growth rate. $B > 1$ means a positive slope and growth rate. (If we set $B = 1 + i$, this model becomes the compound amount Y_{calc} of an initial investment A compounded at the end of each of X periods.)

To apply standard least-squares methods, take logarithms of both sides of (17.19):

$$\log Y_{\text{calc}} = \log A + X \log B$$

Writing $V = \log Y$; $a = \log A$; $b = \log B$, this transforms into

$$V_{\text{calc}} = a + bX \tag{17.20}$$

Now it is only necessary to replace Y by V in (17.16) and (17.17) to obtain:

$$a = \bar{V} \tag{17.21}$$

$$b = \frac{\Sigma XV}{\Sigma X^2} \tag{17.22}$$

EXAMPLE 17.6. Recompute Example 17.5, using the logarithmic transform for sales.

The required preliminary calculations are shown in Table 17-5, Cols. (5) and (6). From (17.21) and (17.22)

$$a = \frac{8.0071}{9} = 0.8897 \qquad A = \text{antilog } 0.8897 = 7.757$$

$$b = \frac{2.0174}{60} = 0.0336 \qquad B = \text{antilog } 0.0336 = 1.08$$

Therefore
$$Y_{\text{calc}} = (7.757)(1.08)^X \quad Ans.$$

As noted earlier, this is equivalent to an average annual growth rate of 8 percent. Equation (17.20) gives for the year 1973

$$V_{\text{calc}} = 0.8897 + (0.0336)(5) = 1.0578 \quad \text{or} \quad Y_{\text{calc}} = \text{antilog } V_{\text{calc}} = 11.42 \quad Ans.$$

This is within 1.4 percent of the value actually realized. The curve is plotted on the arithmetic grid in Fig. 17-5. It would appear as a straight line on semilogarithmic paper.

Example 17.6 gives a better result than Example 17.5 but that does not mean that the logarithmic transform always gives better results. It just happens to do so here; actually, over a large range in Fig. 17-5, the straight line gives the better result.

Confidence Limits.

A least-squares fit is the "best" obtainable, but, as noted in the discussion on correlation, a fraction $1 - r^2$ of the variation remains unexplained. This permits us, after some further analysis, to establish confidence limits for forecasts of individual points made from the given data.

We first define the *standard error of estimate*, $s_{\text{Y.X}}$, which is given by

$$s_{\text{Y.X}}^2 = \frac{\Sigma(Y - Y_{\text{calc}})^2}{n} = \frac{1}{n}(\Sigma y^2 - b^2 \Sigma x^2) \tag{17.23}$$

This is the sample result equivalent to the population standard error, $\sigma_{\text{Y.X}}$, which was introduced on page 278.

The confidence limits for an individual ordinate Y_e, given X_e, are

$$C_{1-\alpha}(Y_e) = a + bX_e \pm t_{(1-\alpha)/2,\, n-2}\, s_{\text{Y.X}} \left(1 + \frac{1}{n} + \frac{(X_e - \bar{X})^2}{\Sigma x^2}\right)^{1/2} \tag{17.24}$$

While this is the general formula, it is again possible to simplify operations when the X's are part of a centered time series and $\Sigma X = 0$. Let h be the number of periods *beyond the last observation* which it is desired to forecast. Then the square root term in (17.24) may be rewritten, using (17.18), as

$$U(n, h) = \left\{1 + \frac{1}{n} + \frac{12[\frac{1}{2}(n-1) + h]^2}{(n-1)n(n+1)}\right\}^{1/2} \tag{17.25}$$

Appendix K tabulates $U(n, h)$ for n (odd numbers only) up to 35 and for h up to 15 periods. The function $U(n, h)$ is greatest when n is small relative to h; i.e. trying to forecast for a long period on the basis of few original observations leads to confidence limits likely to prove impractically large. Additionally, a small n also has large t-values, as shown in Appendix F. If $s_{Y.X}$ is large, that further helps to produce a wide spread.

The quick formula for the confidence limits is therefore

$$C_{1-\alpha}(Y_e) = Y_e \pm t_{(1-\alpha)/2,\, n-2}\, s_{Y.X}\, U(n, h) \tag{17.26}$$

where $Y_e = a + bX_e$.

EXAMPLE 17.7. Find 95 percent confidence limits for the 1973 forecast in Example 17.5.

First find $s_{Y.X}$; this requires the computation of Σy^2, which in turn needs ΣY^2. From Table 17-5, Col. (3),

$$\Sigma Y^2 = (4.94)^2 + (6.21)^2 + \cdots + (10.24)^2 = 585.86$$

From (17.11):

$$\Sigma y^2 = 585.86 - 9(7.921)^2 = 21.18$$

From (17.23):

$$s_{Y.X}^2 = \frac{1}{9}[21.18 - (0.5773)^2(60)] = 0.1315$$

whence $s_{Y.X} = 0.3626$. For $\alpha = 0.05$ and $\nu = 9 - 2 = 7$ degrees of freedom, $t_{0.475,7} = 2.36$. From Appendix K, $U(n, h)$ for $n = 9$, $h = 1$ (i.e. 1 year beyond the last given year 1972) is $U(9, 1) = 1.23603$. We also have $Y_e = 10.81$ (Example 17.5). From (17.26)

$$C_{0.95}(Y_e) = 10.81 \pm (2.36)(0.3626)(1.23603) = 11.87,\ 9.75 \quad Ans.$$

When the Y's have been transformed into logarithms, the method is exactly the same, except for working with V's rather than Y's. The final results are in the form of V's, however, and so antilogs must be taken to bring the results into units of Y.

EXAMPLE 17.8. Find 95 percent confidence limits for the 1973 forecast in Example 17.6.

From Table 17-5, Col. (5),

$$\Sigma V^2 = (0.6937)^2 + (0.7931)^2 + \cdots + (1.0103)^2 = 7.19943$$

and $\bar{V} = 8.0071/9 = 0.8897$. The reduced sum of squares is denoted Σv^2 and is given by

$$\Sigma v^2 = \Sigma V^2 - n\bar{V}^2 = 7.19943 - 9(0.8897)^2 = 0.075336$$

From Example 17.6, $b = 0.0336$, so that (17.23) gives

$$s_{V.X}^2 = \frac{1}{9}[0.075336 - (0.0336)^2(60)] = 0.0008353 \quad \text{or} \quad s_{V.X} = 0.0289$$

The values of t and $U(n, h)$ are the same as in Example 17.7. Therefore, with $V_e = 1.0578$ (Example 17.6),

$$C_{0.95}(V_e) = 1.0578 \pm (2.36)(0.0289)(1.23603) = 1.1423,\ 0.9733$$

Taking antilogs, $C_{0.95}(Y_e) = 13.88,\ 9.40.$ *Ans.*

These are wider limits than in Example 17.7; the reason is that $s_{Y.X}$ appears to be relatively larger. As we noted before in discussing Fig. 17-5, the exponential curve gives a better current fit but in the past had larger deviations than the straight line. Again, other data might yield quite different results.

THE MEAN GROWTH RATE

Given the time series $Y_1, Y_2, \ldots, Y_n$, a quick but crude alternative to (17.19) is to compute

$$r_g = (Y_n/Y_1)^{1/(n-1)} \tag{17.27}$$

Then Y_n may be multiplied by r_g to give next year's forecast, and so on.

Because r_g is the *geometric mean* of the $n-1$ year-to-year growth ratios, it will approximate the growth rate for data that actually can be fitted by an exponential curve.

EXAMPLE 17.9. Derive a forecast for 1973 from the sales data in Table 17-5.

From Col. (3)

$$r_g = (10.24/4.94)^{1/8} = 1.095$$

and the forecast for 1973 is

$$(1.095)(10.24) = 11.21 \quad Ans.$$

Compare Example 17.6.

THE GOMPERTZ CURVE

The Gompertz curve is the most generally used *growth curve*. Its formula is

$$Y_{\text{calc}} = ka^{b^X} \tag{17.28}$$

Depending on the value of the parameters k, a and b (or their logarithms) it may take on any one of a variety of shapes (Fig. 17-6). Form (a) is of special interest in that it has an upper asymptote which, in a business context, means market saturation.

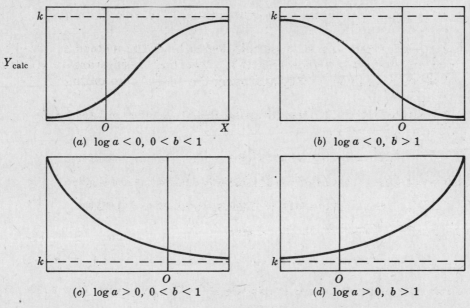

(a) $\log a < 0,\ 0 < b < 1$ (b) $\log a < 0,\ b > 1$

(c) $\log a > 0,\ 0 < b < 1$ (d) $\log a > 0,\ b > 1$

Fig. 17-6

The parameters k, a and b are obtained as follows:

1. The number of observations must be divisible by 3, i.e. there are $3n$ periods of base data.

2. Convert the Y's to logs.

3. Add the first n log-Y's to obtain $\Sigma_1 \log Y$; then the second n data points to obtain $\Sigma_2 \log Y$; and the last n points to obtain $\Sigma_3 \log Y$.

4. Note that $X = 0$ for the first year.

5. Substitute in the following formulas:

$$b^n = \frac{\Sigma_3 \log Y - \Sigma_2 \log Y}{\Sigma_2 \log Y - \Sigma_1 \log Y} \qquad (17.29)$$

$$\log a = (\Sigma_2 \log Y - \Sigma_1 \log Y)\frac{b-1}{(b^n-1)^2} \qquad (17.30)$$

$$\log k = \frac{1}{n}\left[\Sigma_1 \log Y - \frac{b^n - 1}{b - 1}\log a\right] \qquad (17.31)$$

6. A formula for obtaining the asymptote k directly is

$$\log k = \frac{1}{n}\left[\frac{(\Sigma_1 \log Y)(\Sigma_3 \log Y) - (\Sigma_2 \log Y)^2}{\Sigma_1 \log Y + \Sigma_3 \log Y - 2\,\Sigma_2 \log Y}\right] \qquad (17.32)$$

EXAMPLE 17.10. Make a forecast of 1973 sales, using the data of Table 17-5, Col. (3), and the Gompertz curve.

Here we happen to have a column of log Y's. Thus, from Col. (5),

$$\Sigma_1 \log Y = 0.6937 + 0.7931 + 0.8561 = 2.3429$$

$$\Sigma_2 \log Y = 0.8887 + 0.9232 + 0.9269 = 2.7388$$

$$\Sigma_3 \log Y = 0.9410 + 0.9741 + 1.0103 = 2.9254$$

From (17.29), with $n = 3$,

$$b^3 = \frac{2.9254 - 2.7388}{2.7388 - 2.3429} = 0.4713 \qquad b = 0.7782$$

From (17.30)

$$\log a = (2.7388 - 2.3429)\frac{0.7782 - 1}{(0.4713 - 1)^2} = -0.3141 = \overline{1}.6859$$

$$a = 0.4852$$

These results show the curve to be of type (a) in Fig. 17-6. From (17.31)

$$\log k = \frac{1}{3}\left[2.3429 - \frac{0.4713 - 1}{0.7782 - 1}(-0.3141)\right] = 1.0306$$

$$k = 10.73$$

Check, using (17.32):

$$\log k = \frac{1}{3}\left[\frac{(2.3429)(2.9254) - (2.7388)^2}{2.3429 + 2.9254 - 2(2.7388)}\right] = 1.0306$$

To find the estimate for 1973, we recode to make $X = 0$ for the year 1964; for 1973, $X = 9$. Taking logs of (17.28),

$$\log Y_{\text{calc}} = \log k + b^X \log a \qquad (17.33)$$

which is the most convenient form for obtaining Y_{calc}'s. From (17.33)

$$\log Y_{\text{calc}} = 1.0306 + (0.7782)^9(-0.3141) = 0.9977$$

$$Y_{\text{calc}} = \text{antilog } 0.9977 = 9.947 \quad Ans.$$

Again, this is a worse result than the exponential one in Example 17.6, but this is due to the fact that the data indeed appeared headed for an asymptote, only to turn sharply upwards in 1973. Gompertz curves actually fit many practical cases rather well.

Solved Problems

17.1. Using the data of Examples 17.2, 17.3 and 17.4, find 95 percent confidence limits for Y_e when $X_e = 41$.

The problem is to find confidence limits for the result of Example 17.3(*a*), in which Y_e was found to be 45.70. We use (*17.24*) for the purpose (if we wished to center the X's, we could then use (*17.25*) or Appendix K, as well). From (*17.23*) and Examples 17.2 and 17.4,

$$s^2_{Y.X} = \frac{1}{15}[5201.38 - (0.7482)^2(9269.33)] = 0.8253 \quad \text{or} \quad s_{Y.X} = 0.9085$$

From Appendix F, $t_{0.475,\,15-2} = 2.16$; substituting this and the other results in (*17.24*),

$$C_{0.95}(Y_e) = 45.70 \pm (2.16)(0.9085)\left[1 + \frac{1}{15} + \frac{(41 - 58.667)^2}{9269.33}\right]^{1/2}$$

$$= 45.70 \pm 2.159 = 47.86,\ 43.54 \quad \textit{Ans.}$$

17.2. In Table 17-6, Cols. (1) and (2) show horsepower and price respectively of a piece of electrical equipment. Find (*a*) a function expressing price in terms of horsepower and (*b*) the coefficient of correlation. (*c*) Test r at $\alpha = 0.05$. (*d*) What is the estimated price of a 100-hp machine?

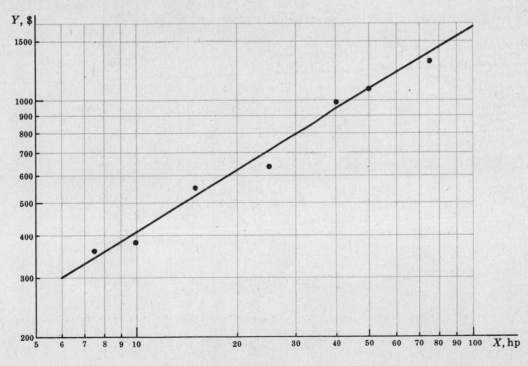

Fig. 17-7

(*a*) This appears to be an economy of scale problem. From (*1.8*), the desired function has the form

$$Y_{\text{calc}} = AX^b \qquad\qquad (17.34)$$

This is tentatively confirmed by the appearance of the data points on log-log graph paper (Fig. 17-7). Taking logarithms of (*17.34*),

$$\log Y_{\text{calc}} = \log A + b \log X$$

Writing $V = \log Y$, $a = \log A$ and $W = \log X$, this becomes

$$V_{\text{calc}} = a + bW \qquad (17.35)$$

which is a straight line. Denoting v and w the equivalents of y and x respectively, we can work out the problem exactly as in Example 17.2, taking antilogs at the end as required for the final answers; V, W, the squares and cross products appear in the other columns of Table 17-6.

$$\bar{W} = \frac{9.6253}{7} = 1.3750 \qquad \bar{V} = \frac{19.8347}{7} = 2.8335$$

From (17.9), (17.10) and (17.11)

$$\Sigma w^2 = 14.0724 - 7(1.3750)^2 = 0.8380$$

$$\Sigma wv = 27.7745 - 7(1.3750)(2.8335) = 0.5021$$

$$\Sigma w^2 = 56.5090 - 7(2.8335)^2 = 0.3079$$

From (17.12) and (17.6)

$$b = \frac{0.5021}{0.8380} = 0.5992$$

$$a = 2.8335 - (0.5992)(1.3750) = 2.0096 \qquad \text{and} \qquad A = \text{antilog}\, 2.0096 = 102.20$$

The equation is therefore

$$Y_{\text{calc}} = (102.20)X^{0.5992} \qquad Ans.$$

Table 17-6

X	Y	W	V	W²	V²	WV
7.5	360	0.8751	2.5563	0.7658	6.5347	2.2370
10	380	1.0000	2.5798	1.0000	6.6554	2.5798
15	550	1.1761	2.7404	1.3832	7.5098	3.2230
25	620	1.3979	2.7924	1.9541	7.7975	3.9035
40	980	1.6021	2.9912	2.5667	8.9473	4.7922
50	1150	1.6990	3.0607	2.8866	9.3679	5.2001
75	1300	1.8751	3.1139	3.5160	9.6964	5.8389
TOTALS		9.6253	19.8347	14.0724	56.5090	27.7745

(b) Using (17.13),

$$r^2 = \frac{(0.5021)^2}{(0.8380)(0.3079)} = 0.9771 \qquad \text{and} \qquad r = +0.9885 \quad Ans.$$

(c) From (17.14)

$$(t)_c = (0.9885)\sqrt{\frac{7-2}{1-0.9771}} = 14.6$$

The tabular value is $t_{0.475,5} = 2.57 < 14.6$; therefore reject ($H_0$: $r = 0$), i.e. there is significant correlation.

(d) From (17.35), with $W = \log 100 = 2$,

$$V_{\text{calc}} = 2.0096 + (0.5992)(2) = 3.2080 \qquad Y_{\text{calc}} = \text{antilog}\, 3.2080 = \$1614 \quad Ans.$$

This result is confirmed by Fig. 17-8.

17.3. For the last 15 periods, inventory requirements in units for a certain item were: 54, 37, 65, 72, 45, 58, 78, 63, 49, 40, 59, 76, 62, 55, 69. Forecast the requirements for the next three periods, using exponential smoothing with $a = 0.7$.

Here we use (17.2) directly, first computing the weights $a(1-a)^n$ ($n = 0, 1, 2, \ldots$) until these are no longer significant. This task is facilitated by Table 17-7, which gives the values of $a(1-a)^n$ for selected values of a until they are no longer significant to the third decimal place. Table 17-8 then shows the successive weighting of the past few periods. With $a = 0.7$, only six periods need be considered when using Table 17-7; note that the result quickly converges to a "steady state" value. Numbers in italics are the forecasts for the next three periods. This example also demonstrates that exponential smoothing cannot be used when there are grounds for the view that the data show a continuing upward or downward trend. In such cases, the forecast can never be higher than the last known result for rising trends, nor lower than the last known result for falling trends, and thus always gives a wrong result if the trends continue.

Table 17-7. Values of $a(1-a)^n$

n	a							
	0.2	0.3	0.4	0.5	0.6	0.7	0.8	0.9
0	0.200	0.300	0.400	0.500	0.600	0.700	0.800	0.900
1	0.160	0.210	0.240	0.250	0.240	0.210	0.160	0.090
2	0.128	0.147	0.144	0.125	0.096	0.063	0.032	0.009
3	0.102	0.103	0.086	0.063	0.038	0.019	0.006	0.001
4	0.082	0.072	0.052	0.031	0.015	0.006	0.001	
5	0.066	0.050	0.031	0.016	0.006	0.002		
6	0.052	0.035	0.019	0.008	0.002			
7	0.042	0.025	0.011	0.004	0.001			
8	0.034	0.017	0.007	0.002				
9	0.027	0.012	0.004	0.001				
10	0.021	0.008	0.002					
11	0.017	0.006	0.001					
12	0.014	0.004	0.001					
13	0.011	0.003	0.001					
14	0.009	0.002						
15	0.007	0.001						
16	0.006	0.001						
17	0.005	0.001						
18	0.004							
19	0.003							
20	0.002							
21	0.002							
22	0.001							
23	0.001							
24	0.001							
25	0.001							
26	0.001							

Table 17-8

Data	Weights	Products	Weights	Products	Weights	Products
40	0.002	0.08				
59	0.006	0.35	0.002	0.12		
76	0.019	1.44	0.006	0.46	0.002	0.15
62	0.063	3.91	0.019	1.18	0.006	0.37
55	0.210	11.55	0.063	3.47	0.019	1.05
69	0.700	48.30	0.210	14.49	0.063	4.35
		65.63	0.700	45.94	0.210	13.78
				65.66	0.700	45.96
						65.66

Supplementary Problems

17.4. Assume that, in Example 17.2, the roles of X and Y are interchanged. Find the regression equation for this changed situation. Plot it together with the regression line in Fig. 17-3.

Ans. $X_{\text{calc}} = 19.9001 + (1.3334)Y$

17.5. Compute the values of Y_{calc} for all the points in Example 17.6.

Ans. 5.702, 6.158, 6.650, 7.182, 7.757, 8.378, 9.048, 9.772, 10.553 (in \$ billion)

17.6. The following sales data are presented for a certain firm:

Year	1966	1967	1968	1969	1970	1971	1972	1973	1974
\$ mill.	48	55	63	65	72	84	90	87	82

Find (a) the regression equation for sales as a function of time, based on the exponential curve; (b) the forecast for 1975.   *Ans.* (a) $Y_{\text{calc}} = (70.3)(1.0777)^X$; (b) 102.19

17.7. Repeat Problem 17.6, using the geometric mean of the growth rate. State (a) the mean growth rate, (b) the 1975 forecast.   *Ans.* (a) 6.9 percent; (b) 87.66

17.8. Repeat Problem 17.6, using the straight-line relationship. Give (a) the regression equation, (b) the 1975 forecast.   *Ans.* (a) $Y_{\text{calc}} = 71.778 + (5.083)X$; (b) 97.19

17.9. Following are sales data for R. H. Macy & Co. Provide forecasts for 1972, 1973, 1974 and 1975 and state the regression equation for sales as a function of time, using the straight-line projection.

Year	1961	1962	1963	1964	1965	1966	1967	1968	1969	1970	1971
\$ mill.	520.1	541.5	582.9	623.5	668.9	719.2	758.6	824.8	878.4	907.0	957.0

Ans. $Y_{\text{calc}} = 725.6 + (45.7)X$; 999.8, 1045.5, 1091.2, 1136.9

17.10. Repeat Problem 17.9, using the exponential curve.

> *Ans.* $Y_{calc} = (711.0)(1.066)^X$; 1043, 1112, 1185, 1264

17.11. Using the data of Problem 17.9, find the geometric mean growth rate and forecast sales for 1972, 1973, 1974 and 1975.   *Ans.*   6.3 percent; 1017.3, 1081.4, 1149.5, 1221.9

17.12. Given that in Problem 17.9 actual sales for 1972 were \$999.7 million, fit a Gompertz curve and use it to forecast sales for 1973, 1974 and 1975.

> *Ans.* $Y_{calc} = 3888(0.1303)^{(0.963)^X}$; 1064, 1116, 1169

17.13. Sales Y of a firm were correlated with an economic indicator X (the independent variable) and the following preliminary results were obtained: $n = 10$; $\Sigma X = 120$; $\Sigma Y = 30$; $\Sigma X^2 = 1600$; $\Sigma XY = 310$; $\Sigma Y^2 = 110$.   Find the regression equation and the coefficient of correlation, and test the latter at the 5 percent significance level.

> *Ans.* $Y_{calc} = 6.75 - (0.3125)X$; $r = -0.884$; r is significant

17.14. The following table shows the serial numbers and the cumulative average time taken in manufacturing a certain production run of a product:

Serial Number	10	20	40	80	160	320
Average Time per Item, min	200	175	150	120	107	86

Find the index k of the learning curve and translate this into a learning percentage. (*Hint:* Use methods of Chapter 1 and Problem 17.2.)   *Ans.* $k = 0.244$; $p = 84.4$ percent

17.15. Table 17-9 gives sales of a company and consumer spending in a corresponding market sector, which is used as an economic indicator for predicting sales.   (*a*) Compute an arithmetical time series for

Table 17-9

Year	Sales, $ million	Spending, $ billion
1969	8	1.1
1970	10	1.3
1971	11	1.3
1972	14	1.7
1973	14	1.8
1974	16	2.0
1975	18	2.0

sales and forecast 1976 sales.   (*b*) Compute a logarithmic time series for sales and forecast 1976 sales.   (*c*) Compute a regression equation for the sales of the company, using spending as the independent variable.   (*d*) Find r for (*c*) and test it at a significance level of 5 percent.

> *Ans.*   (*a*) $Y_{calc} = 13 + (1.6071)X$, 19.4   (*c*) $Y_{calc} = (9.375)X - 2$, $r = 0.975$ (significant)
> (*b*) $Y_{calc} = (12.57)(1.138)^X$, 21.08

Chapter 18

Reliability and Allied Phenomena

INTRODUCTION

The theory of reliability is part of the so-called *theory of extremes*. It can be applied to a variety of natural events such as the biggest flood, highest wind gusts, gravest droughts, etc.; to human survival and other actuarial phenomena; and to the reliability and life to failure of machinery and its components. The simple examples presented in this chapter cover several important applications to business problems. The reliability of production equipment is obviously one of them and we also relate the standard life table to the general theory.

RELIABILITY ATTRIBUTES

A reliability attribute is a statement about whether or not a system is operative during the time it is required to function (i.e. its "mission"). Let element i in a system have a probability p_i of functioning at a given time. If k elements are connected *in series*, and if they function independently of each other, the probability R_s of the system functioning is the product of all the p's:

$$R_s = p_1 p_2 \cdots p_k \qquad (18.1)$$

EXAMPLE 18.1. Figure 18-1(*a*) shows four elements connected in series, with their corresponding values of p. Find the reliability of the system.

$$R_s = 0.8 \times 0.7 \times 0.9 \times 0.7 = 0.3528 \quad Ans.$$

Note that if one component in a series system does not function, the whole system is inoperative.

If the elements are arranged *in parallel*, so that the load can be taken by any one of them, system failure takes place only when all elements are inoperative at once. The probability of element i failing is $1 - p_i$ and the probability of all k elements failing is, assuming independence,

$$F_p = (1 - p_1)(1 - p_2) \cdots (1 - p_k)$$

The probability of the system functioning is

$$R_p = 1 - F_p = 1 - (1 - p_1)(1 - p_2) \cdots (1 - p_k) \qquad (18.2)$$

EXAMPLE 18.2. The three components in Fig. 18-1(*b*) are connected in parallel. Their individual probabilities of functioning are as listed. Find the reliability of the system.

$$R_p = 1 - (1 - 0.9)(1 - 0.7)(1 - 0.8) = 0.994 \quad Ans.$$

Note that R_p is much higher than the p_i of any component; in the case of a series system, $R_s < p_i$. This prompts the introduction of parallel circuitry whenever it is desired to improve reliability. A special case is the one in which k identical elements are connected in parallel, each with the same p. Equation (18.2) for such redundant elements becomes

$$R_p = 1 - (1 - p)^k \qquad (18.3)$$

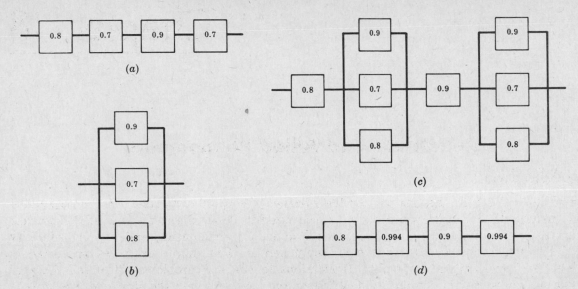

Fig. 18-1

Systems incorporating both series and parallel elements are analyzed by first reducing the parallel subsystems to equivalent series components and then treating the system as one consisting only of series elements.

EXAMPLE 18.3.   Find the reliability of the system of Fig. 18-1(c).

Note that the two parallel portions are the same as those of Example 18.2.   The system may thus be converted into the one shown in Fig. 18-1(d) and, from (18.1),

$$R_s = 0.8 \times 0.994 \times 0.9 \times 0.994 = 0.71 \quad Ans.$$

In essence, what has been done is to replace the two "weak links" of the series circuit of Example 18.1 by parallel subsystems, with great improvement in overall reliability.   Instead of being $0.7 \times 0.7 = 0.49$ reliable, they are now $0.994 \times 0.994 = 0.988$ reliable.

RELIABILITY AND SURVIVAL TIMES

The simplest way of predicting survival times of a part or system is to assume an exponential survival function $R_e(t \mid T)$; see (9.18).   We now recall from Chapter 14 the definition of the *hazard rate,* also called the *intensity function* and *instantaneous failure rate* (IFR), as the coefficient of δt in the probability of failure between t and $t + \delta t$, given that the part has lasted until t.   In Problem 14.4 we showed the hazard rate for the exponential distribution to be

$$Z(t) = \frac{f_e(t \mid T)}{R_e(t \mid T)} = \frac{1}{T}$$

This means that when failures are exponentially distributed, the probability of failing in the next small time interval remains constant at the reciprocal of the mean time to failure, for the whole life of the part or system.   Thus, the chance of an old part failing in the next interval is no different from that of a young part.   While many items (e.g. electronic components) have such characteristics, or approximate them closely, it is also often found, especially in mechanical as well as complex electronic systems, that the older a system gets, the more likely is it to fail in the next time interval.

It has been found through theoretical analysis, and confirmed in practice, that a superior correspondence to reality results from working with t^k rather than t, where k is a parameter. Replacing T with another parameter θ (so as to avoid confusion with the mean of the distribution), we define the *Weibull distribution* by its reliability or survival function

$$R(t) = e^{-(t/\theta)^k} \qquad (18.4)$$

from which

$$F(t) = 1 - e^{-(t/\theta)^k} \qquad (18.5)$$

and, differentiating,

$$f(t) = k\theta^{-k}t^{k-1}e^{-(t/\theta)^k} \qquad (18.6)$$

This gives a hazard rate of

$$Z(t) = \frac{f(t)}{R(t)} = k\theta^{-k}t^{k-1} \qquad (18.7)$$

which, depending on the value of k, can take on a variety of shapes. When $k = 1$, the distribution is exponential and $Z(t) = 1/\theta$ is constant, as before (Fig. 18-2). The case $k < 1$ is the one in which failure is *less* likely, the longer the part has been in service. It occurs rarely in practice in failure profiles, but the Weibull model for $k < 1$ was used in the obsolescence model for inventory (Example 14.3), where the longer an item has remained unsold, the less likely is it to be sold in the next small time interval.

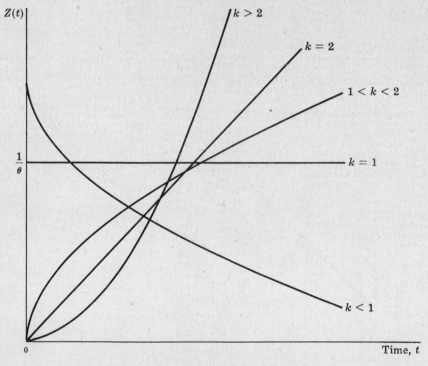

Fig. 18-2

In practice, there are often some initial failures, followed by an increasing rate of *degradation* failures, with $k > 1$. The following deals with the degradation phase. Note also that when $k \approx 3.2$, the Weibull distribution approximates the normal.

When there is a substantial time period before any degradation failures occur, a simple two-parameter Weibull distribution may not give a satisfactory fit. In that case, it is useful to add a third parameter γ and change $R(t)$ to

$$R(t) = \exp\left[-\left(\frac{t - \gamma}{\theta - \gamma}\right)^k\right] \qquad (18.8)$$

from which

$$F(t) = 1 - \exp\left[-\left(\frac{t-\gamma}{\theta-\gamma}\right)^k\right] \tag{18.9}$$

$$f(t) = k(\theta-\gamma)^{-k}(t-\gamma)^{k-1}\exp\left[-\left(\frac{t-\gamma}{\theta-\gamma}\right)^k\right] \tag{18.10}$$

Although more precise methods exist, a useful approximation is to take $\gamma \approx (0.75)t_1$, where t_1 is the time of the first degradation failure. Then all other t's in the original data are adjusted by subtracting γ from each and the rest of the work proceeds just as in the two-parameter case. We then obtain a parameter $\theta' = \theta - \gamma \approx \theta - (0.75)t_1$ from which θ can be computed.

The Weibull parameter k is called the *shape parameter*, θ the *scale parameter* or *characteristic value*, and γ the *location parameter*. For the two-parameter case, the values of k and θ may be readily determined by using *Weibull probability paper* or simple charts which are all derived from the theory of the Weibull distribution. In Fig. 18-3, which illustrates the probability paper, percentage scales for $F(t)$ and $R(t)$ are given on the left side and the reduced or standardized variable y has an arithmetical scale on the right (see Problem 18.4 for the theory). The age t at failure or survival is given in the logarithmic scale at the bottom, with a further scale of the natural logs, $\ln t$, on the top; that too is an arithmetical scale.

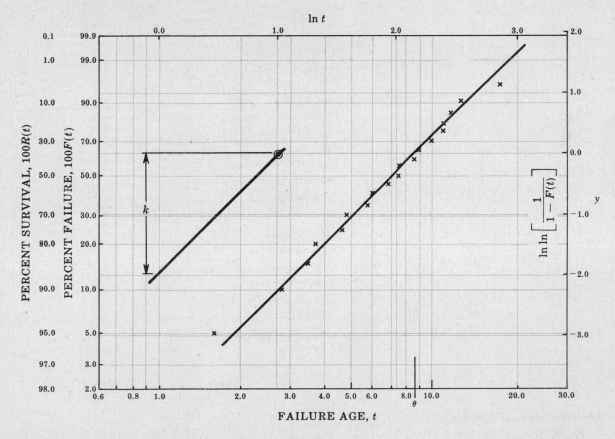

Fig. 18-3

Survival data are plotted by using the coordinates

$$\left(t, R(t) = 1 - \frac{m}{n+1}\right)$$

Here, m is the counting order of the failure at t, and n is the total number of failures. If the points lie sufficiently well on a straight line for it to be drawn by inspection, the parameters may be read off the graph paper as follows:

1. Where the line crosses $y = 0$, $t = \theta$.

2. From the point $(y = 0, \ln t = 1)$, which is circled on the graph paper, draw a line parallel to the fitted line to intersect $\ln t = 0$. Then k is read off the y-scale, as shown.

This method is especially convenient when it is not desired to wait till all test objects in a group have failed but rather the test is terminated after a small number of components have failed. After plotting the first few points, it may be possible to estimate a failure profile for the remaining ones, and k and θ may then be read off the graph; this is called a *censored* test.

When the points are too widely scattered for an easy line fit by hand or when it is known that a Weibull fit exists but it is desired only to get a survival profile without plotting it, a method is available for the calculation of the parameters based on the mean $\bar{t}$ and estimated standard deviation $\hat{s}$:

1. Calculate $\bar{t} = \Sigma t/n$, and $\hat{s}$ from $\hat{s}^2 = \dfrac{\Sigma t^2 - n\bar{t}^2}{n-1}$.

2. Enter Fig. 18.4 at left with the ratio $\bar{t}/\hat{s}$; drop down to the horizontal scale to obtain k^{-1} and thus k.

3. Proceed upwards along the vertical line through k^{-1} to the curve of $\Gamma(1+k^{-1})$ (see Problem 18.5), then go across to the left scale to find its value. Calculate θ from $\theta = \bar{t}/\Gamma(1+k^{-1})$.

EXAMPLE 18.4. Table 18-1 gives the points of failure, t, measured in cycles $\times 10^4$, for a group of 19 components. Plot them on Weibull probability paper and find the two parameters.

The values of $R(t)$, also shown in Table 18-1, were derived from

$$R(t) = 1 - \frac{m}{n+1} = 1 - \frac{m}{20}$$

where $m = 1$ for $t = 1.6$, ..., $m = 19$ for $t = 17.5$. From the table,

$$\Sigma t = 147.78 \qquad \Sigma t^2 = 1451.48$$

so that

$$\bar{t} = \frac{147.78}{19} = 7.78 \qquad \hat{s}^2 = \frac{1451.48 - 19(7.78)^2}{18} = 16.76 \qquad \hat{s} = 4.09$$

The points are plotted in Fig. 18-3; the parameters appear where shown.

To obtain them more precisely, we calculate $\bar{t}/\hat{s} = 1.9$. Entering Fig. 18-4 at $\bar{t}/\hat{s} = 1.9$ and following the dashed line downwards, $k^{-1} \approx 0.5$; $k \approx 2$. *Ans.*

Proceeding upwards, $\Gamma(1+k^{-1}) = 0.89$; $\theta = 7.78/0.89 = 8.742$. *Ans.*

Note that the approximate results from Fig. 18-3 are the same.

Table 18-1

t	1.6	2.8	3.5	3.7	4.7	4.9	5.7	6.0	6.8	7.5
$R(t)$	0.95	0.90	0.85	0.80	0.75	0.70	0.65	0.60	0.55	0.50
t	7.6	8.6	9.0	10.2	10.9	11.0	11.8	14.0	17.5	
$R(t)$	0.45	0.40	0.35	0.30	0.25	0.20	0.15	0.10	0.05	

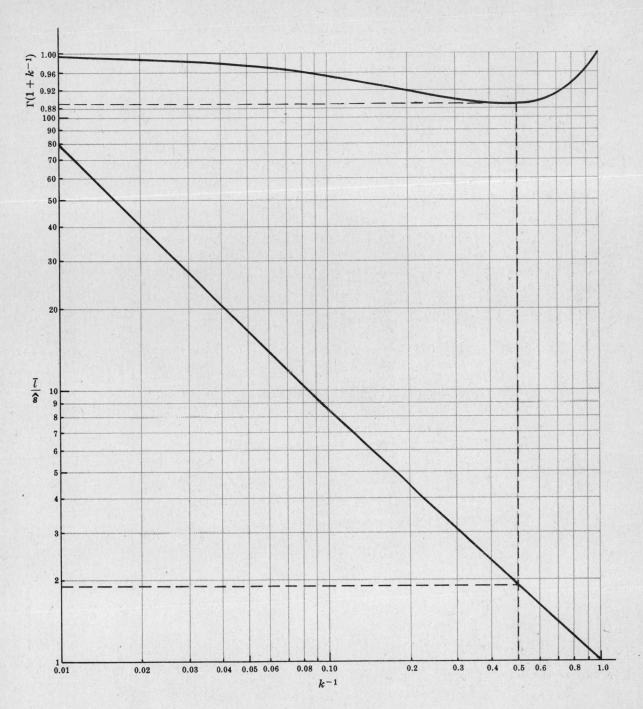

Fig. 18-4

It is also often useful to find the time which a given proportion of the parts may be expected to survive.   Figure 18-5 gives the ratio t/θ as a function of k^{-1}.

EXAMPLE 18.5.   Use the results of Example 18.4 to find the number of cycles which 99, 95, 80, 50, 25, 10 and 1 percent of the components may be expected to survive.

Enter Fig. 18-5 at $k^{-1} = 0.5$.   A dashed line is drawn to facilitate this example.   Read off each t/θ and multiply by $\theta = 8.742$ to obtain t (in cycles $\times$ 10^4).

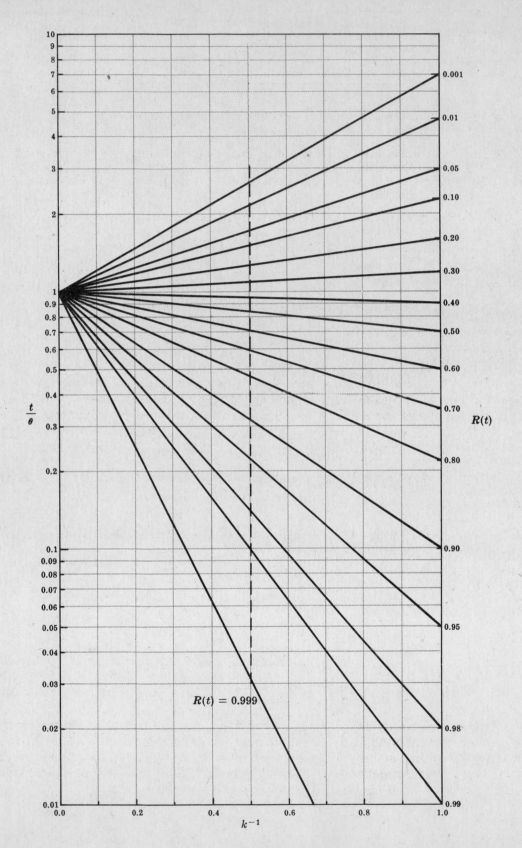

Fig. 18-5

$R(t)$	0.99	0.95	0.80	0.50	0.25	0.10	0.01
t/θ	0.099	0.22	0.48	0.83	1.18	1.50	2.16
t	0.865	1.923	4.196	7.256	10.316	13.113	18.883

EXAMPLE 18.6. The survival profile of a certain part is exponential, with MTBF = 2000 hours. (a) What is the median life of the part? (b) What proportion will survive 1000 hours?

(a) By definition, the median is the life exceeded by one-half of the parts, i.e. with probability 0.5. For $k = 1$, the Weibull distribution is exponential. Enter Fig. 18-5 at extreme right, where $k^{-1} = 1$, with probability $R(t) = 0.50$ and read horizontally to $t/\theta = 0.693$ on the left scale. Since $\theta =$ MTBF for the exponential distribution, the median life is $2000(0.693) = 1386$ hours. *Ans.*

This result can also be obtained from the formula for $R_e(t \mid \theta)$ and Appendix A; by looking up X for which $e^{-X} = 0.5$; or from

$$-\frac{t}{\theta} = \ln 0.5 = 0.6931$$

(b) For $t/\theta = 0.5$, $R(t) = 0.607$.   *Ans.*

This also agrees with Appendix A, where $e^{-0.5} = (1.6487)^{-1} = 0.6065$.

THE ORDINARY MORTALITY TABLE

The ordinary mortality table (Table 18-2) is an empirical survival or failure (death) tabulation which incorporates all the elements hitherto presented for the Weibull distribution. The table shows the notation usual in the life insurance field, but this can be converted as follows:

$$lx \to 10^7 R(t) \quad dx \to 10^7 f(t) \quad qx \to Z(t) \quad px \to 1 - Z(t)$$

The table may be readily used for calculations similar to those carried out for equipment failures.

EXAMPLE 18.7. If you are now 22 years old, what is the probability of your (a) living another year, (b) living another 22 years, (c) living another 45 years, (d) dying by age 50?

(a)
$$p(22) = 1 - Z(22) = 0.99814 \quad Ans.$$

(b)
$$\frac{l(44)}{l(22)} = \frac{9,093,740}{9,630,039} = 0.944 \quad Ans.$$

(c)
$$\frac{l(67)}{l(22)} = \frac{6,355,865}{9,630,039} = 0.660 \quad Ans.$$

(d)
$$1 - \frac{l(50)}{l(22)} = 1 - \frac{8,762,306}{9,630,039} = 0.0901 \quad Ans.$$

The ordinary mortality table shows a poor fit on Weibull paper, but if the logarithmic scale for the data on Weibull paper is replaced by an arithmetical scale, the fit is very much better, deviating mainly at the beginning of life (it will be noted that qx declines until the ages 9 and 10 and then increases). This fit shows that the relevant distribution is the *double exponential* or *Gumbel distribution* (see Problem 18.4).

Table 18-2.   Commissioners 1958 Standard Ordinary (CSO) Mortality Table

Age	Number Living at Beginning of Designated Year (lx)	Number Dying During Designated Year (dx)	Yearly Probability of Dying (qx)	Yearly Probability of Surviving (px)
0	10,000,000	70,800	0.00708	0.99292
1	9,929,200	17,475	0.00176	0.99824
2	9,911,725	15,066	0.00152	0.99848
3	9,896,659	14,449	0.00146	0.99854
4	9,882,210	13,835	0.00140	0.99860
5	9,868,375	13,322	0.00135	0.99865
6	9,855,053	12,812	0.00130	0.99870
7	9,842,241	12,401	0.00126	0.99874
8	9,829,840	12,091	0.00123	0.99877
9	9,817,749	11,879	0.00121	0.99879
10	9,805,870	11,865	0.00121	0.99879
11	9,794,005	12,047	0.00123	0.99877
12	9,781,958	12,325	0.00126	0.99874
13	9,769,633	12,896	0.00132	0.99868
14	9,756,737	13,562	0.00139	0.99861
15	9,743,175	14,225	0.00146	0.99854
16	9,728,950	14,983	0.00154	0.99846
17	9,713,967	15,737	0.00162	0.99838
18	9,698,230	16,390	0.00169	0.99831
19	9,681,840	16,846	0.00174	0.99826
20	9,664,994	17,300	0.00179	0.99821
21	9,647,694	17,655	0.00183	0.99817
22	9,630,039	17,912	0.00186	0.99814
23	9,612,127	18,167	0.00189	0.99811
24	9,593,960	18,324	0.00191	0.99809
25	9,575,636	18,481	0.00193	0.99807
26	9,557,155	18,732	0.00196	0.99804
27	9,538,423	18,981	0.00199	0.99801
28	9,519,442	19,324	0.00203	0.99797
29	9,500,118	19,760	0.00208	0.99792
30	9,480,358	20,193	0.00213	0.99787
31	9,460,165	20,718	0.00219	0.99781
32	9,439,447	21,239	0.00225	0.99775
33	9,418,208	21,850	0.00232	0.99768
34	9,396,358	22,551	0.00240	0.99760
35	9,373,807	23,528	0.00251	0.99749
36	9,350,279	24,685	0.00264	0.99736
37	9,325,594	26,112	0.00280	0.99720
38	9,299,482	27,991	0.00301	0.99699
39	9,271,491	30,132	0.00325	0.99675
40	9,241,359	32,622	0.00353	0.99647
41	9,208,737	35,362	0.00384	0.99616
42	9,173,375	38,253	0.00417	0.99583
43	9,135,122	41,382	0.00453	0.99547
44	9,093,740	44,741	0.00492	0.99508
45	9,048,999	48,412	0.00535	0.99465
46	9,000,587	52,473	0.00583	0.99417
47	8,948,114	56,910	0.00636	0.99364
48	8,891,204	61,794	0.00695	0.99305
49	8,829,410	67,104	0.00760	0.99240

Table 18-2.   Commissioners 1958 Standard Ordinary (CSO) Mortality Table (Cont.)

Age	Number Living at Beginning of Designated Year (lx)	Number Dying During Designated Year (dx)	Yearly Probability of Dying (qx)	Yearly Probability of Surviving (px)
50	8,762,306	72,902	0.00832	0.99168
51	8,689,404	79,160	0.00911	0.99089
52	8,610,244	85,758	0.00996	0.99004
53	8,524,486	92,832	0.01089	0.98911
54	8,431,654	100,337	0.01190	0.98810
55	8,331,317	108,307	0.01300	0.98700
56	8,223,010	116,849	0.01421	0.98579
57	8,106,161	125,970	0.01554	0.98446
58	7,980,191	135,663	0.01700	0.98330
59	7,844,528	145,830	0.01859	0.98141
60	7,698,698	156,592	0.02034	0.97966
61	7,542,106	167,736	0.02224	0.97776
62	7,374,370	179,271	0.02431	0.97569
63	7,195,099	191,174	0.02657	0.97343
64	7,003,925	203,394	0.02904	0.97096
65	6,800,531	215,917	0.03175	0.96825
66	6,584,614	228,749	0.03474	0.96526
67	6,355,865	241,777	0.03804	0.96196
68	6,114,088	254,835	0.04168	0.95832
69	5,859,253	267,241	0.04561	0.95439
70	5,592,012	278,426	0.04979	0.95021
71	5,313,586	287,731	0.05415	0.94585
72	5,025,855	294,766	0.05865	0.94135
73	4,731,089	299,289	0.06326	0.93674
74	4,431,800	301,894	0.06812	0.93188
75	4,129,906	303,011	0.07337	0.92663
76	3,826,895	303,014	0.07918	0.92082
77	3,523,881	301,997	0.08570	0.91430
78	3,221,884	299,829	0.09306	0.90694
79	2,922,055	295,683	0.10119	0.89881
80	2,626,372	288,848	0.10998	0.89002
81	2,337,524	278,983	0.11935	0.88065
82	2,058,541	265,902	0.12917	0.87083
83	1,792,639	249,858	0.13938	0.86062
84	1,542,781	231,433	0.15001	0.84999
85	1,311,348	211,311	0.16114	0.83886
86	1,100,037	190,108	0.17282	0.82718
87	909,929	168,455	0.18513	0.81487
88	741,474	146,997	0.19825	0.80175
89	594,477	126,303	0.21246	0.78754
90	468,174	106,809	0.22814	0.77186
91	361,365	88,813	0.24577	0.75423
92	272,552	72,480	0.26593	0.73407
93	200,072	57,881	0.28930	0.71070
94	142,191	45,026	0.31666	0.68334
95	97,165	34,128	0.35124	0.64876
96	63,037	25,250	0.40056	0.59944
97	37,787	18,456	0.48842	0.51158
98	19,331	12,916	0.66815	0.33185
99	6,415	6,415	1.00000	......

Solved Problems

RELIABILITY ATTRIBUTES

18.1. A system is designed such that it operates whenever 3 or more out of 5 elements operate, where each of them has reliability 0.82. Find the system reliability.

In the general case there are k elements, each with reliability p, out of which X must operate if the system is to function. The probability $R(X, k)$ that X or more out of k will function is the cumulative binomial distribution (cf. Example 9.9)

$$R(X, k) = R_B(X \mid k, p) \tag{18.11}$$

Substituting in (18.11), and using the right side of Appendix C,

$$R(3, 5) = R_B(3 \mid 5, 0.82) = 1 - F_B(2 \mid 5, 0.82) = 1 - 0.0437 = 0.9563 \quad Ans.$$

18.2. A certain number of components, each with reliability 0.75, are to be connected in parallel. Each one costs \$20; if the system fails altogether, the damage is \$3500. Find the optimal number of components in parallel and the optimal cost; establish a general procedure in developing the solution.

The probability of failure of k components in parallel was shown to be

$$F_p = (1 - p)^k$$

The expected cost of failure is the probability of failure times the conditional cost, C_f, i.e. it is $C_f F_p$. The cost of k components is kC_c, where C_c is the unit cost. The total cost C is given by

$$C = kC_c + C_f(1 - p)^k$$

To find k^* which will make C a minimum, solve $dC/dk = 0$. Recalling the general formula

$$\frac{d}{dx}(a^x) = a^x \ln a$$

we have

$$\frac{dC}{dk} = C_c + C_f(1 - p)^k \ln(1 - p) = 0$$

which can be rearranged as

$$\left(\frac{1}{1 - p}\right)^k = \frac{C_f \ln\left(\dfrac{1}{1 - p}\right)}{C_c}$$

Taking natural logarithms and solving,

$$k \ln\left(\frac{1}{1 - p}\right) = \ln C_f + \ln \ln\left(\frac{1}{1 - p}\right) - \ln C_c$$

$$k^* = \frac{\ln C_f + \ln \ln\left(\dfrac{1}{1 - p}\right) - \ln C_c}{\ln\left(\dfrac{1}{1 - p}\right)}$$

In the present case

$$\ln C_f = \ln 3500 = \ln 3.5 + \ln 1000 = 1.2528 + 6.9077 = 8.1605$$
$$\ln C_c = \ln 20 = 2.9957$$
$$\ln\left(\frac{1}{1 - p}\right) = \ln 4 = 1.3863$$
$$\ln \ln 4 = \ln 1.3863 = 0.3267$$

$$k^* = \frac{8.1605 + 0.3267 - 2.9957}{1.3863} \approx 3.96 \approx 4 \quad Ans.$$

$$C^* = 4(20) + 3500(0.25)^4 = \$93.67 \quad Ans.$$

18.3. A system operates properly when 5 components in parallel function. It is desired to include *redundant components* in order to improve the overall reliability. How many components should be provided, given that each one is 0.92 reliable and costs $50, and that a malfunction of the whole system costs $2500? What is the expected cost?

Because the minimum number of Bernoulli trials needed to produce 5 "successes" is governed by the Pascal distribution, this problem is essentially the same as Problem 13.11, with C_c and C_f in place of v and S, p and X as before, and n instead of Q as the number of components installed. Thus $C_c = 50$, $C_f = 2500$, $p = 0.92$, $X = 5$. The critical ratio is

$$\frac{C_c}{C_f} = \frac{50}{2500} = 0.02$$

Table 18-3

n	$F_{Pa}(n \mid 5, 0.92)$	$f_{Pa}(n \mid 5, 0.92)$	$\dfrac{f_{Pa}(n \mid 5, 0.92)}{F_{Pa}(n \mid 5, 0.92)}$
5	0.6591	0.6591	1.0000
6	0.9227	0.2636	0.2857
7	0.9860	0.0633	0.0632
8	0.9978	0.0128	0.0128*

Using the relationship

$$F_{Pa}(n \mid 5, \ 0.92) = 1 - F_B(4 \mid n, 0.92)$$

and Appendix C, we compile Table 18-3. It is seen that $n^* = 8$ gives a result nearest to the critical ratio 0.02. *Ans.*

As before, the optimal cost (= EVPI in Problem 13.11) is

$$C^* = C_c\{n^* F_{Pa}(n^* \mid X, p) - \frac{X}{p}[1 - F_B(X \mid n^* + 1, p)]\} + C_f[1 - F_{Pa}(n^* \mid X, p)]$$

$$= 50\{8(0.9978) - \frac{5}{0.92}[1 - F_B(5 \mid 9, 0.92)]\} + 2500(1 - 0.9978)$$

$$= 128.39 + 5.50 = \$133.89 \quad Ans.$$

SURVIVAL PROFILES

18.4. Show why a Weibull-distributed survival profile gives a straight line on Weibull probability paper (Fig. 18-3).

Recall from *(18.4)* that $R(t) = e^{-(t/\theta)^k}$. Take natural logarithms twice:

$$\ln R(t) = -\left(\frac{t}{\theta}\right)^k$$

$$\ln[-\ln R(t)] = k \ln \frac{t}{\theta} \tag{18.12}$$

The probability scale of Weibull paper is actually not based on the Weibull distribution itself (which would be impossible without knowing the parameters) but on the *double exponential* or *Gumbel distribution*

$$R(t) = e^{-e^y} \tag{18.13}$$

The linear scale is y and the probability scale gives the corresponding values of $R(t)$, computed from *(18.13)*. Now take natural logarithms of *(18.13)* twice:

$$\ln R(t) = -e^y$$

$$\ln[-\ln R(t)] = y \tag{18.14}$$

Substituting (*18.14*) in (*18.12*),

$$y = k \ln \frac{t}{\theta}$$

$$\ln \frac{t}{\theta} = \frac{y}{k} \quad \text{or} \quad \log \frac{t}{\theta} = (0.434)\frac{y}{k} \tag{18.15}$$

which is a straight line on semilog paper. From (*18.15*) it follows that when $y = 0$, $\ln(t/\theta) = 0$ and therefore $t = \theta$, i.e. θ can be read off the t scale. Also, the line parallel to (*18.15*) through the circled point is

$$y = k(\ln t - 1)$$

so that when $\ln t = 0$, $y = -k$.

Equation (*18.15*) may also be represented by plotting $\ln(t/\theta)$ against $1/k$ for different values of y. This also results in straight lines and is the basis for Fig. 18-5.

18.5. Give the derivation of Fig. 18-4.

The mth moment of the Weibull distribution is, from (*18.6*),

$$E(t^m) = \int_0^\infty t^m f(t)\, dt = k\theta^{-k} \int_0^\infty t^{m+k-1} e^{-(t/\theta)^k}\, dt$$

$$= \theta^m \int_0^\infty u^{mk-1} e^{-u}\, du$$

where $u = (t/\theta)^k$. Comparing this with the definition of the *gamma function*,

$$\Gamma(v) = \int_0^\infty w^{v-1} e^{-w}\, dw$$

we see that $E(t^m) = \theta^m \Gamma(1 + mk^{-1})$. Thus, the mean and variance are

$$E(t) = \theta\, \Gamma(1 + k^{-1}) \tag{18.16}$$

$$\sigma^2 = E(t^2) - [E(t)]^2 = \theta^2[\Gamma(1 + 2k^{-1}) - \Gamma^2(1 + k^{-1})] \tag{18.17}$$

By replacing σ^2 and $E(t)$ by their unbiased estimates $\hat{s}^2$ and $\bar{t}$ respectively, we obtain the ratio

$$\frac{\bar{t}}{\hat{s}} = \frac{\Gamma(1 + k^{-1})}{\sqrt{\Gamma(1 + 2k^{-1}) - \Gamma^2(1 + k^{-1})}} \tag{18.18}$$

This is a function of k^{-1} only. It can be shown that, for integral values of v, $\Gamma(v) = (v-1)!$. Thus $\Gamma(1) = \Gamma(2) = 1$, i.e. at the limits $k^{-1} = 0$ and $k^{-1} = 1$, $\Gamma(1 + k^{-1}) = 1$. In between, tables of the gamma function for nonintegral values show a minimum value for $\Gamma(1 + k^{-1})$ of 0.885 at $k^{-1} \approx 0.45$ ($k \approx 2.2$). The values of $\Gamma(1 + k^{-1})$ may thus be plotted as shown at the top of Fig. 18-4 and used to find θ, as in (*18.16*) and page 298, once k is known. The value of k is determined by plotting (*18.18*) against k^{-1}. The result is very nearly a straight line on log-log paper, as shown in the lower portion of Fig. 18-4.

18.6. A reliability test on 100 components is conducted by having them all operate and checking how many are still working after 500, 1500, 2500, etc., hours until 10,500 hours have elapsed. The number surviving under these conditions is given in Col. (2) of Table 18-4. (*a*) Find the parameters of the underlying Weibull distribution. (*b*) Find the times at which 10 and 90 percent of the components are likely to be found operative. (*c*) What proportion of the components is likely to be found working after 4000 hours?

(*a*) Here the failure data are given in the form of grouped data. The data may be plotted on Weibull paper by taking the midpoints t [Col. (3)] and converting the number surviving into $R(t)$. This is done by dividing Col. (2) by 100, obtaining 0.99, 0.94, ... The points turn out to lie approximately on a straight line, indicating a Weibull survival profile.

Table 18-4

Checkpoint, hours	Number Operative	Midpoints t	u	f	uf	u^2f
500	100	..	..	..	..	..
1500	99	1000	−4	1	−4	16
2500	94	2000	−3	5	−15	45
3500	82	3000	−2	12	−24	48
4500	67	4000	−1	15	−15	15
5500	49	5000	0	18	0	0
6500	30	6000	1	19	19	19
7500	17	7000	2	13	26	52
8500	8	8000	3	9	27	81
9500	4	9000	4	4	16	64
10,500	1	10,000	5	1	5	25
			TOTALS	99	45	415

To find θ and k, $\bar{t}$ and $\hat{s}$ must be computed. It is most convenient to use the coding method of (9.9) and (9.10) for this purpose. In Table 18-4, the life is first reduced to midpoints of class intervals (with width 1000 hours) from which the codes u are derived. The frequencies f are then the numbers of failures in the intervals, obtained as the differences of Col. (2). Note that, since at the end of the period 1 item is still functioning, the analysis is based on 99 failures. From (9.9)

$$\bar{t} = 5000 + \frac{1000(45)}{99} = 5454.5$$

From (9.10)

$$s^2 = (1000)^2\left[\frac{415}{99} - \left(\frac{45}{99}\right)^2\right] = 3,985,307.6$$

To obtain $\hat{s}^2$, s^2 must be multiplied by $n/(n-1)$, i.e. by 99/98.   Thus

$$\hat{s}^2 = \frac{99}{98}(3,985,307.6) = 4,025,973.9 \qquad \hat{s} = 2006.5$$

$$\frac{\bar{t}}{\hat{s}} = \frac{5454.5}{2006.5} = 2.718$$

From Fig. 18-4, $k^{-1} = 0.34$ and $k = 2.94$.   *Ans.*

Also $\Gamma(1 + 0.34) = 0.9$, obtained from upper part of Fig. 18-4.   Thus

$$\theta = \frac{5454.5}{0.9} = 6060.6 \quad Ans.$$

(b) From Fig. 18-5, for $k^{-1} = 0.34$ and $R(t) = 0.10$, $t/\theta = 1.31$; hence

$$t = (1.31)(6060.6) = 7939 \text{ hours} \quad Ans.$$

From Fig. 18-5, for $k^{-1} = 0.34$ and $R(t) = 0.90$, $t/\theta = 0.46$; hence

$$t = (0.46)(6060.6) = 2788 \text{ hours} \quad Ans.$$

(c) $t/\theta = 4000/6060.6 = 0.66$.   Enter Fig. 18-5 at $t/\theta = 0.66$, go across to $k^{-1} = 0.34$ and interpolate the probability as approximately 0.74.   *Ans.*

THE ORDINARY MORTALITY TABLE

18.7. To what age may a person expect to live with probability $p' = 0.5$, if the present age is (a) 22, (b) 51, (c) 75?

If a is the sought age and a_0 the present age,

$$P(t > a \mid t > a_0) = p'$$

$$\frac{P(t > a \cap t > a_0)}{P(t > a_0)} = p'$$

$$\frac{R(a)}{R(a_0)} = p'$$

$$R(a) = p' R(a_0)$$

Thus, in terms of Table 18-2, the solution involves multiplying the number living at the present age by the probability of survival p' and then looking up the nearest age to the revised lx. See Table 18-5.

Table 18-5

Present Age	Number Living (lx)	$p'(lx) = (0.5)(lx)$	Corresponding Age (approx.)
22	9,630,039	4,815,019	73
51	8,689,404	4,344,702	74
75	4,129,906	2,064,953	82

Supplementary Problems

18.8. Find the total reliability of the system shown in Fig. 18-6.

Ans. 0.556

18.9. In order to improve the overall reliability of the system in Fig. 18-6 to 0.75, a parallel element is to be added to the one with reliability 0.7. What reliability would this have to have?   *Ans.* 0.817

18.10. Suppose it were only possible to parallel the 0.7 component in Fig. 18-6 with one or more others like it. How many would be needed for the most economical way of getting a system reliability of at least 0.75? What would be the actual reliability of the system?   *Ans.* 3 in parallel; 0.772

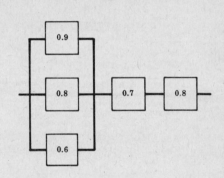

Fig. 18-6

18.11. By considering (*18.1*), (*18.3*) and (*18.11*) show that when p is the same for all elements, the series case is the special case when $X = k$ and the parallel case is $X = 1$.

18.12. In Fig. 18-7 at least two of the four elements with $p = 0.75$ must function. Find the reliability of the whole system.   *Ans.* 0.8254

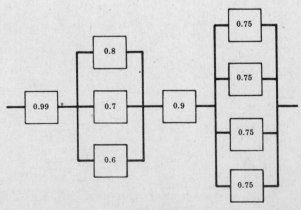

Fig. 18-7

18.13. Let the mean time to failure equal 6000 hours, with $\hat{s}$, based on a test, equal to 1000 hours. Find (a) the Weibull parameters; (b) the approximate time when (i) 95%, (ii) 50%, (iii) 5% of the components may be expected to be still functioning; (c) the proportion of components working after 7000 hours.   *Ans.* (a) $k = 7.14$, $\theta = 6452$;   (b) (i) 4190, (ii) 6130, (iii) 7420;   (c) 0.15

18.14. Review Problem 3.3. Given a reliability of each machine of 0.95, find the probability of the system functioning when (a) 1 out of 2, (b) 2 out of 3, (c) 3 out of 4, (d) 4 out of 5, (e) 5 out of 6 machines have to function.   *Ans.* (a) 0.9975; (b) 0.9927; (c) 0.9860; (d) 0.9774; (e) 0.9672

18.15. A set of 25 components is tested for reliability and gives a mean time to failure of 100 hours, with a variance of 144. Find (a) the parameter k, (b) the characteristic time θ, (c) the time to failure of the first 25 percent of the population, (d) the proportion of the population likely to have failed by 80 hours.   *Ans.* (a) 10; (b) 105.3 hr; (c) 88 hr; (d) 8 percent

18.16. A group of 600 items is subjected to a reliability test which results in a mean time to failure of 400 hours, with a standard deviation of 20 hours. (a) Find the Weibull shape and scale parameters. (b) After how many hours can we expect that (i) 99 and (ii) 1 percent of the parts are still operating?   *Ans.* (a) $k = 25$, $\theta = 409$;   (b) (i) 340 hours, (ii) 435 hours

18.17. A person is 50 years old and intends to retire at 65. What are the probabilities of living (a) 1, (b) 5, (c) 10, (d) 15, (e) 20 years beyond retirement?

   Ans.   (a) 0.751; (b) 0.638; (c) 0.471; (d) 0.300; (e) 0.150

Chapter 19

Waiting Lines

INTRODUCTION

Waiting lines (or *queues*) occur whenever arriving customers must seek service at one or more stations (*channels, servers*), each of which performs one or more tasks (i.e. there are one or more *stages*). Various assumptions can be made concerning the customers' arrival rate, the order of service (e.g. "first come, first served"; service at random; priorities; line switching allowed; etc.), and the distribution of service times. In this chapter it will be assumed that the *steady state* has been attained, in which the characteristics of the queue no longer change with time. We shall consider selected kinds of steady-state queues for which computations are not excessively burdensome or for which convenient analytical aids exist. The kinds of models discussed do, however, have wide applicability.

The results we seek are mainly: (1) the probability of being delayed, (2) the average number of people who will be kept waiting, and (3) the average waiting time. Sometimes additional useful results are available. All these can then serve as inputs to economic analysis, leading to optimal design of service facilities.

In what follows, the order of service will be taken as "first come, first served" unless stated otherwise.

NOTATION AND SOME GENERAL RELATIONSHIPS

λ = mean number of customers arriving per unit of time (*mean arrival rate*)

U = mean interval between arrivals = $1/\lambda$

μ = mean number of customers served per unit of time (*mean service rate*)

V = mean service time = $1/\mu$

M = number of channels

k = number of stages

P_0 = probability of nobody in the system (i.e., of nobody being served)

P_n = probability of n customers in the system (i.e., of a total of n customers waiting and being served)

D = probability of delay

L = average (expected) number of those waiting and being served

L_q = average (expected) number of those waiting only

W = average (expected) time spent in the system (including waiting and being served)

W_q = average (expected) time spent waiting before being served

N = number of possible customers (if finite)

c = maximum permitted number in system before *balking* (refusal to join queue) takes place

The quantities W and W_q are averages over all arriving customers. We also define

$$\rho = \frac{\lambda}{\mu} \quad \text{for one channel } (M = 1) \qquad\qquad (19.1)$$

$$\rho = \frac{\lambda}{M\mu} \quad \text{for } M \text{ channels } (M > 1) \qquad\qquad (19.2)$$

The parameter ρ is called the *channel utilization factor* or *traffic intensity ratio* and must be less than 1 for a finite queue (one with L_q finite).

Before discussing specific models, we note four relationships that hold for every type of steady-state queue.

$$L = \lambda W \quad \text{or} \quad W = \frac{L}{\lambda} \qquad\qquad (19.3)$$

$$L_q = \lambda W_q \quad \text{or} \quad W_q = \frac{L_q}{\lambda} \qquad\qquad (19.4)$$

$$W = W_q + \frac{1}{\mu} \qquad\qquad (19.5)$$

Equation (19.3) states that the expected number of people in the system is given by the expected time spent in the system times the expected number of arrivals per unit of time. Equation (19.4) is the analogous relationship for those customers waiting before service. Equation (19.5) links the other two by stating that the average time spent in the system is the average waiting time before service plus the average service time. Substituting in (19.5) from (19.3) and (19.4),

$$L = L_q + \frac{\lambda}{\mu} \qquad\qquad (19.6)$$

When customers arrive at random, the fraction who have to wait for service is equal to the probability that M or more people are in the system. Thus,

$$D = P_M + P_{M+1} + \cdots = 1 - (P_0 + P_1 + \cdots + P_{M-1}) \qquad\qquad (19.7)$$

The expected length of queue, L_q, and the expected number in the system (waiting and being served), L, are given as the first moments of the relevant probabilities, i.e.

$$L = \sum_{n=0}^{\infty} nP_n \qquad\qquad (19.8)$$

$$L_q = \sum_{n=M+1}^{\infty} (n-M)P_n \qquad\qquad (19.9)$$

These are useful results only if expressions for the P_n are available. However, if any one of the four parameters L, L_q, W, W_q can be calculated by other means, then (19.3)–(19.5) furnish the other three.

THE ROLE OF THE POISSON AND EXPONENTIAL DISTRIBUTIONS

Suppose that the number of customer arrivals in *any* time interval of length t has a Poisson distribution. From Table 9-6, with $m = \lambda t$, the density function is

$$f_P(X \mid \lambda t) = \frac{e^{-\lambda t}(\lambda t)^X}{X!} \qquad X = 0, 1, 2, \ldots$$

If time is measured from the instant of the last arrival, then the probability that the next arrival occurs later than time t is

$$f_P(0 \mid \lambda t) = e^{-\lambda t} = R_e(t \mid 1/\lambda)$$

Table 19-1. Single-Server Models

(1)	(2)	(3)	(4)	(5)	(6)	(7)
Arrival Rate Distribution	Poisson	Poisson	Poisson	Poisson	Poisson	Poisson
Population (Number of Potential Customers)	∞	∞	∞	∞	N	∞
Nature of Queue	finite	finite	finite	finite	finite	number in system is truncated to a maximum of c
Number of Service Stages	$k=1$	$k>1$	$k=1$	$k=1$	$k=1$	$k=1$
Service Time Distribution	exponential	Erlang (gamma)	constant	arbitrary, with mean $1/\mu$ and variance σ^2	exponential	exponential
P_0	$1-\rho$	$1-\rho$	$1-\rho$	$1-\rho$	$\left(\sum_{n=0}^{N}\dfrac{N!}{(N-n)!}\rho^n\right)^{-1}$	$\dfrac{1-\rho}{1-\rho^{c+1}}$
P_n	$(1-\rho)\rho^n$	n.a.	n.a.	n.a.	$\dfrac{N!}{(N-n)!}\rho^n P_0$	$\dfrac{1-\rho}{1-\rho^{c+1}}\rho^n$ $(n\le c)$
L	$\dfrac{\rho}{1-\rho}$	$\dfrac{k+1}{2k}\dfrac{\rho^2}{1-\rho}+\rho$	$L_q+\rho$	$L_q+\rho$	$N-\dfrac{1-P_0}{\rho}$	$\dfrac{\rho}{1-\rho}-\dfrac{(c+1)\rho^{c+1}}{1-\rho^{c+1}}$
L_q	$\dfrac{\rho^2}{1-\rho}$	$\dfrac{k+1}{2k}\dfrac{\rho^2}{1-\rho}$	$\dfrac{\rho^2}{2(1-\rho)}$	$\dfrac{\lambda^2\sigma^2+\rho^2}{2(1-\rho)}$	$N-\dfrac{\rho+1}{\rho}(1-P_0)$	$\dfrac{\rho^2}{1-\rho}-\dfrac{(c+1)\rho^{c+1}}{1-\rho^{c+1}}$
W	$\dfrac{1}{\mu-\lambda}$	$\dfrac{k+1}{2k}\dfrac{\rho}{\mu-\lambda}+\dfrac{1}{\mu}$	$\dfrac{L}{\lambda}$	$\dfrac{L}{\lambda}$	$\dfrac{L}{\lambda}$	$\dfrac{L}{\lambda}$
W_q	$\dfrac{\rho}{\mu-\lambda}$	$\dfrac{k+1}{2k}\dfrac{\rho}{\mu-\lambda}$	$\dfrac{\rho}{2(\mu-\lambda)}$	$\dfrac{L_q}{\lambda}$	$\dfrac{L_q}{\lambda}$	$\dfrac{L_q}{\lambda}$

see (9.18). We have thus shown that if the *number of* arrivals has a Poisson distribution (with mean arrival rate λ), the times *between* arrivals are exponentially distributed (with mean $U = 1/\lambda$). Conversely, when the interarrival times are known to have an exponential distribution, the number of arrivals must have a Poisson distribution.

Similarly, if the time which it takes to serve a customer is exponentially distributed, the number of completions of service has a Poisson distribution (in the periods in which the system is not empty). The exponential and Poisson distributions thus play an important part in waiting line theory, and several widely useful models are based on them.

SINGLE-SERVER MODELS

A variety of waiting line problems involving only one service channel can be solved by means of the formulas in Table 19-1. The six different models cover a wide array of practical situations, as the examples below will show. Where direct formulas are convenient, they are included; otherwise they follow from the simple basic relationships defined in the first part of the chapter. We note the following additional formulas:

Column (2) presents the simplest of all waiting lines—one channel, Poisson arrivals and exponential service times. The results shown there can be extended quite readily to certain other models. First, from (19.7) with $M = 1$,

$$D = 1 - (1 - \rho) = \rho \tag{19.10}$$

Second, we can derive the probability that the time spent in the system exceeds a particular value W_0. If the service time and interarrival interval are both exponentially distributed, then so is the time in the system, w. From (9.18), w has the cumulative distribution function

$$F_e(w \,|\, W) = 1 - e^{-w/W} \quad \text{or} \quad R_e(w \,|\, W) = e^{-w/W}$$

Substituting for W from Table 19-1,

$$R_e(W_0) = e^{-(\mu - \lambda)W_0} \tag{19.11}$$

EXAMPLE 19.1. A repair shop attended by a single mechanic has an average of four customers an hour who bring small appliances for repair. The mechanic inspects them for defects and quite often can fix them right away or otherwise render a diagnosis. This takes him six minutes, on the average. Arrivals are Poisson and service time has the exponential distribution. Find (a) the proportion of time during which the shop is empty (during which the mechanic can work on the items left with him); (b) the probability of three customers being in the shop; (c) the probability of finding at least 1 customer in the shop; (d) the average number of customers in the system; (e) the average time spent, including service; (f) the average number of customers waiting to be served; (g) the average time spent, excluding service; (h) the probability of having to spend more than 15 minutes in the shop.

Here, $\lambda = 4$ per hour, $\mu = 10$ per hour, and $\rho = \lambda/\mu = 0.4$. Then, from Col. (2) of Table 19-1 (except as noted):

(a) $$P_0 = 1 - 0.4 = 0.6 \quad Ans.$$

(b) $$P_3 = (0.6)(0.4)^3 = 0.0384 \quad Ans.$$

(c) $$D = \rho = 0.4 \quad Ans.$$

(d) $$L = \frac{0.4}{1 - 0.4} = 0.67 \text{ customers} \quad Ans.$$

(e) $$W = \frac{1}{10 - 4} = \frac{1}{6} \text{ hour or 10 minutes} \quad Ans.$$

(f) $$L_q = \frac{0.16}{1 - 0.4} = 0.267 \text{ customers} \quad Ans.$$

(g) $$W_q = \frac{0.4}{10 - 4} = 0.067 \text{ hours or 4 minutes} \quad Ans.$$

(h) From (19.11) and Appendix A, $R_e(1/4) = e^{-(10-4)(1/4)} = e^{-1.5} = 0.2231$ *Ans.*

Columns (3), (4) and (5) in Table 19-1 show the formulas for service time distributions other than the exponential. For these cases a general formula for P_n is not available; a few rather complex special cases have been partially solved. However, the formulas listed are highly useful. They all derive from the general formula for L_q given in Col. (5). [Thus, substituting the exponential variance, $\sigma^2 = 1/\mu^2$, gives the results in Col. (2).]

EXAMPLE 19.2. Suppose in Example 19.1 that the service time is normally distributed with mean 6 minutes and variance $\sigma^2 = 1/8$. Find the expected number of people waiting before service.

$$L_q = \frac{4^2(1/8) + (0.4)^2}{2(1 - 0.4)} = 1.8 \text{ customers} \quad Ans.$$

There is actually no independent physical reason why service times should be normally distributed; such a relationship would have to be confirmed empirically.

EXAMPLE 19.3. In many cases service times are constant; for example in machines with automatic cycles, like vending machines. In Col. (4) of Table 19-1, L_q is derived from the general case by setting $\sigma^2 = 0$. A comparison with Col. (2) reveals that L_q is half that for exponentially distributed service time; W for the constant case is likewise half that of the exponential. In Example 19.1, suppose the service rendered consists in testing the appliances in a special machine with a six-minute operating cycle. Find (a) the expected number of people waiting for service; (b) the expected number of people in the shop; (c) the expected waiting time before service; (d) the expected total time in the system.

As before, $\lambda = 4$ per hour; $\mu = 10$ per hour (constant); $\rho = 0.4$.

(a) $$L_q = \frac{(0.4)^2}{2(1 - 0.4)} = 0.133 \text{ customers} \quad Ans.$$

(b) $$L = 0.133 + 0.4 = 0.533 \text{ customers} \quad Ans.$$

(c) $$W_q = \frac{0.4}{2(10 - 4)} = 0.033 \text{ hours or 2 minutes} \quad Ans.$$

(d) $$W = \frac{0.533}{4} = 0.133 \text{ hours or 8 minutes} \quad Ans.$$

Alternatively, we can simply add the six-minute cycle to W_q: $W = 2 + 6 = 8$ minutes.

Column (3) of Table 19-1 deals with the case in which k jobs must be performed, each of which has an exponentially distributed service time with mean $1/k\mu$. The mean of the total service time is then

$$V = k(1/k\mu) = 1/\mu \qquad (19.12)$$

as usual. The total service time has the *Erlang distribution*, which is the gamma with parameters $X = k$, $T = 1/k\mu$ (see Table 9-6). Thus the variance of the service time is

$$\sigma^2 = XT^2 = 1/k\mu^2 \qquad (19.13)$$

and the mode is, from (13.18),

$$V_0 = XT - T = (k-1)/k\mu \qquad (19.14)$$

Selected Erlang p.d.f.'s are shown in Fig. 19-1. Equation (19.13) indicates that when $k = 1$, the exponential distribution results; and when $k = \infty$, the service time is constant.

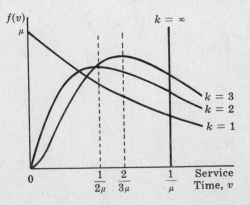

Fig. 19-1

EXAMPLE 19.4. A clerk checking registration applications has to examine 8 forms which take an average of 1 minute each to check. Customers arrive at the rate of 6 per hour. The service times for each operation and the arrival intervals are exponentially distributed. Find (a) the probability that the clerk is idle; (b) the average number of people waiting before being served; (c) the average number in the system; (d) the average waiting time before service; (e) the average time in the system.

Here, $k = 8$; $1/8\mu = 1$ minute; $V = 1/\mu = 1 \times 8 = 8$ minutes; $\mu = 60/8 = 7.5$ per hour; $\rho = 6/7.5 = 0.8$.

(a)
$$P_0 = 1 - 0.8 = 0.2 \quad Ans.$$

(b)
$$L_q = \frac{8+1}{2(8)} \frac{(0.8)^2}{1-0.8} = 1.8 \text{ customers} \quad Ans.$$

(c)
$$L = 1.8 + 0.8 = 2.6 \text{ customers} \quad Ans.$$

(d)
$$W_q = \frac{8+1}{2(8)} \frac{0.8}{7.5-6} = 0.3 \text{ hour} = 18 \text{ minutes} \quad Ans.$$

(e)
$$W = 18 + 8 = 26 \text{ minutes} \quad Ans.$$

In Column (6) of Table 19-1 we have the standard formulas for the case in which the number of possible customers is limited to N.

EXAMPLE 19.5. A tool crib is in considerable disorder so that it takes an average of 12 minutes to serve a machinist who comes for service. There are five such machinists and, on the average, one of them comes for a new set of tools every 15 minutes. Arrivals are Poisson and service times exponential. Find (a) the probability that the crib attendant is idle; (b) the probability that all 5 mechanics are at the crib; (c) the average number waiting, including the one being served; (d) the average number waiting before service; (e) the average time spent waiting and being served; (f) the average time spent waiting before service; (g) Comment on the results.

Here $N = 5$ and
$$\rho = \frac{\lambda}{\mu} = \frac{V}{U} = \frac{12}{15} = 0.8$$

(a)
$$P_0 = \left[\frac{5!}{5!}(0.8)^0 + \frac{5!}{4!}(0.8)^1 + \frac{5!}{3!}(0.8)^2 + \frac{5!}{2!}(0.8)^3 + \frac{5!}{1!}(0.8)^4 + \frac{5!}{0!}(0.8)^5 \right]^{-1}$$
$$= [0.8 + 5(0.8) + 20(0.8)^2 + 60(0.8)^3 + 120(0.8)^4 + 120(0.8)^5]^{-1}$$
$$= (0.8 + 4.0 + 12.8 + 30.72 + 49.15 + 39.32)^{-1} = 1/136.8 = 0.00731 \quad Ans.$$

(b)
$$P_5 = \frac{5!}{0!}(0.8)^5 P_0 = (39.32)(0.00731) = 0.287 \quad Ans.$$

(c)
$$1 - P_0 = 1 - 0.00731 = 0.9927$$
$$L = 5 - \frac{0.9927}{0.8} = 3.76 \quad Ans.$$

(d) From (19.6)
$$L_q = 3.76 - 0.8 = 2.96 \quad Ans.$$

(e)
$$\lambda = \frac{60}{15} = 4 \text{ per hour}$$
$$W = \frac{3.76}{4} = 0.94 \text{ hour} \quad Ans.$$

(f)
$$W_q = \frac{2.96}{4} = 0.74 \text{ hour} \quad Ans.$$

(g) The long lines and high waiting times (close to 1 hour in the system) make it almost impossible to get any work done. It would therefore be necessary either to clean up the tool crib so that the mean service time can be cut or to get more than one attendant—or possibly both.

Finally, Col. (7) of Table 19-1 gives the case in which, whenever c customers are in the system, new arrivals balk and will not join the queue. This refusal can be *voluntary* or *involuntary*, the latter case being the one where a limit to the number of people permitted to wait is imposed by fire regulations or traffic restrictions (as in a crowded entrance to a parking lot, where waiting cars might block the street).

EXAMPLE 19.6. Consider again Example 19.1. All the previous assumptions hold, except that if three customers are in the shop, any other arriving will not join the queue. Find (a) the proportion of time during which the shop is empty; (b) the average number of customers in the system; (c) the average number of customers waiting for service; (d) the average time spent, including service; (e) the average time spent, excluding service. (f) Verify that there are never more than three people in the shop.

Here, $c = 3$ and, as before, $\lambda = 4$, $\mu = 10$, $\rho = 0.4$.

(a)
$$P_0 = \frac{1 - 0.4}{1 - (0.4)^4} = \frac{0.6}{0.9744} = 0.6158 \quad Ans.$$

(b)
$$L = \frac{0.4}{1 - 0.4} - \frac{(3+1)(0.4)^4}{1 - (0.4)^4} = 0.6667 - 0.1051 = 0.5616 \quad Ans.$$

(c)
$$L_q = \frac{0.16}{1 - 0.4} - \frac{4(0.4)^4}{1 - (0.4)^4} = 0.2667 - 0.1051 = 0.1616 \quad Ans.$$

(d)
$$W = \frac{0.5616}{4} = 0.1404 \text{ hr} = 8.424 \text{ min} \quad Ans.$$

(e)
$$W_q = \frac{0.1616}{4} = 0.0404 \text{ hr} = 2.424 \text{ min} \quad Ans.$$

(f) From the formula for P_n in Table 19-1,

$$P(n \leq c) = \frac{1 - \rho}{1 - \rho^{c+1}} \sum_{n=0}^{c} \rho^n = \frac{1 - \rho}{1 - \rho^{c+1}} \frac{1 - \rho^{c+1}}{1 - \rho} = 1$$

so that $P(n > c) = 0$.

For queues with balking, the channel utilization factor ρ can be greater than 1 because the limit on queue length is set by the truncation rather than by having $\rho < 1$.

MULTIPLE CHANNELS

The analysis of multiple channels is much more complicated than that of single servers. Formulas are available for several important models, but they are usually awkward for routine computations. In what follows we shall introduce four selected models, together with charts and tables which simplify the work very considerably.

1. Poisson arrivals, exponential service times, infinite population.
The principal relationships are:

$$\rho = \frac{\lambda}{M\mu} \quad \text{or} \quad \frac{\lambda}{\mu} = M\rho \tag{19.15}$$

$$P_0 = \left[\sum_{n=0}^{M-1} \frac{(M\rho)^n}{n!} + \frac{(M\rho)^M}{M!} \frac{1}{1 - \rho} \right]^{-1} \tag{19.16}$$

$$P_n = \begin{cases} \dfrac{(M\rho)^n}{n!} P_0 & 0 \leq n \leq M \\[3mm] \dfrac{M^M \rho^n}{M!} P_0 & n > M \end{cases} \tag{19.17}$$

$$L_q = \frac{M^M \rho^{M+1}}{M!(1 - \rho)^2} P_0 \tag{19.18}$$

$$W_q = \frac{L_q}{\lambda} \tag{19.19}$$

$$W = W_q + \frac{1}{\mu} \tag{19.20}$$

$$L = \lambda W \tag{19.21}$$

Formulas (19.19), (19.20) and (19.21) repeat the universally valid (19.4), (19.5) and (19.3).

EXAMPLE 19.7. In the repair shop of Example 19.1 there is an increase in business so that customers now arrive (Poisson) at a rate of 12 per hour. Each service still takes an average of 6 minutes and is exponentially distributed. Since

$$\frac{\lambda}{\mu} = \frac{12}{60/6} = 1.2 > 1$$

the job is now obviously beyond the capacity of one mechanic, and a second one has been employed. Find (a) the probability of nobody in the shop, i.e. the proportion of idle time during which repairs can be carried out; (b) the probability of two or more customers in the shop; (c) the probability of three customers in the shop; (d) the average length of queue; (e) the average waiting time before service; (f) the average time spent waiting; (g) the average number of customers in the shop.

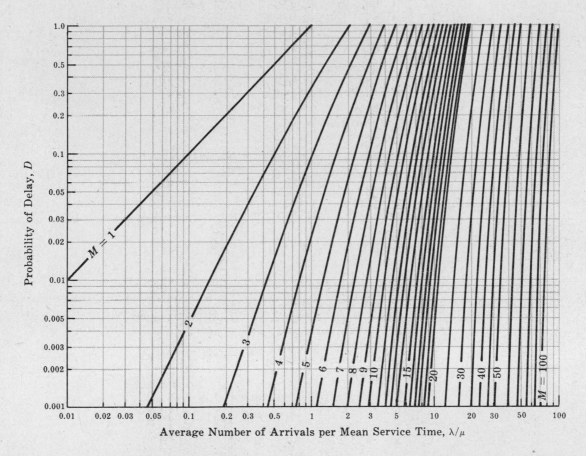

Fig. 19-2　(reprinted by permission from J. R. Shelton, "Solution Methods for Waiting Line Problems," *J. Indust. Eng.* IX, No. 4, 1960)

(a) From (19.15), $\rho = 12/2(10) = 0.6$; from (19.16),

$$P_0 = \left[\frac{(1.2)^0}{0!} + \frac{(1.2)^1}{1!} + \frac{(1.2)^2}{2!} \frac{1}{1-0.6} \right]^{-1} = 4^{-1} = 0.25 \quad Ans.$$

(b) From (19.17)

$$D = \sum_{n=M}^{\infty} P_n = \frac{M^M \rho^M}{M!\,(1-\rho)} P_0 = \frac{2^2(0.6)^2}{2!\,(1-0.6)}(0.25) = 0.45 \quad Ans.$$

(c)
$$P_3 = \frac{2^2(0.6)^3}{2!}(0.25) = 0.054 \quad Ans.$$

(d) $$L_q = \frac{2^2(0.6)^3}{2!\,(1-0.6)^2}(0.25) = (2.7)(0.25) = 0.675 \text{ customers} \quad Ans.$$

(e) $$W_q = \frac{0.675}{12} = 0.05625 \text{ hours} = 3.375 \text{ minutes} \quad Ans.$$

(f) $$W = 3.375 + 6 = 9.375 \text{ minutes} \quad Ans.$$

(g) $$L = \frac{12}{60}(9.375) = 1.875 \text{ customers} \quad Ans.$$

These results may be obtained more simply by use of Figs. 19-2 and 19-3. Figure 19-2 gives the probability of M or more customers, i.e. D, plotted against the ratio of the arrival rate to the service rate, λ/μ. The family of curves is labeled according to the number of channels. One enters the graph with the appropriate ratio λ/μ, moves vertically upward to meet the appropriate curve for the channel number and then goes horizontally to the value of D. To obtain W_q, enter Fig. 19-3 at M, proceed upward to the appropriate ρ curve and then travel horizontally to the value of μW_q. Dividing this result by μ gives W_q.

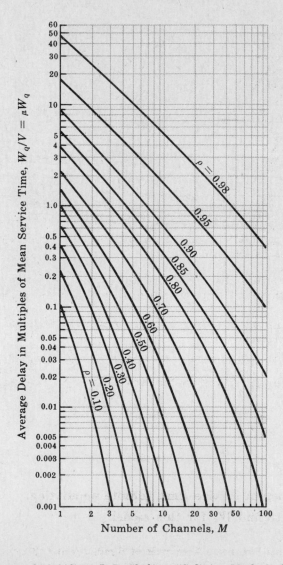

Fig. 19-3   (reprinted by permission from J. R. Shelton, "Solution Methods for Waiting Line Problems," *J. Indust. Eng.* IX, No. 4, 1960)

Let w_q denote the time spent waiting before being served. Figure 19-4 may be used to compute the probability that $w_q > W_m$. The figure provides $P(w_q > W_m \mid w_q > 0)$, while Fig. 19-2 gives $P(w_q > 0) = D$. Then, by the multiplication rule,

$$P(w_q > W_m) = P(w_q > W_m \mid w_q > 0) \times D \qquad (19.22)$$

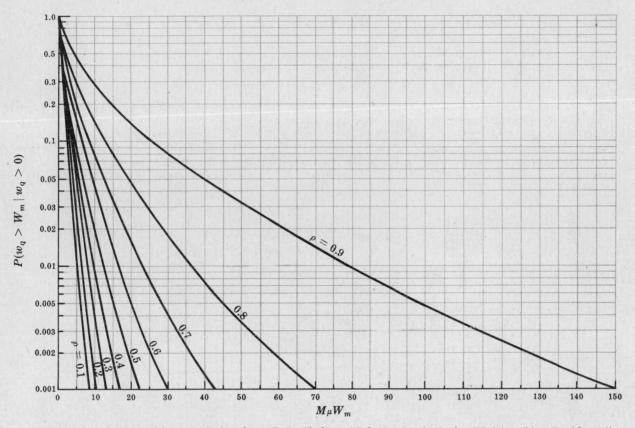

Fig. 19-4   (reprinted by permission from J. R. Shelton, "Solution Methods for Waiting Line Problems," *J. Indust. Eng.* IX, No. 4, 1960)

EXAMPLE 19.8. There are 3 channels, arrivals are Poisson at a rate of 21 per hour and service time is exponentially distributed with mean 6 minutes. Find the probability of a customer having to wait more than 12 minutes for service.

First, enter Fig. 19-2 with $\lambda/\mu = 21/10 = 2.1$, go vertically to the curve for $M = 3$, then horizontally to $D = 0.48$. Second, compute

$$\rho = 21/3(10) = 0.7 \qquad M\mu W_m = 3(10)(1/5) = 6$$

Enter Fig. 19-4 at $M\mu W_m = 6$, go vertically to the curve for $\rho = 0.7$, then horizontally to

$$P\left(w_q > \frac{1}{5} \,\middle|\, w_q > 0\right) = 0.18$$

Then, from (*19.22*),

$$P\left(w_q > \frac{1}{5}\right) = (0.18)(0.48) = 0.0864 \quad Ans.$$

2. Poisson arrivals, constant service time, infinite population.

Figure 19-5 is used to find W_q for this model.

EXAMPLE 19.9. A testing machine has a fixed cycle of 6 minutes and there are 3 machines. Arrivals are Poisson at the rate of 21 per hour. How long is the average wait before service?

Here, $\rho = 21/3(10) = 0.7$ (as in Example 19.8). Entering Fig. 19-5 at $M = 3$, go upwards to the

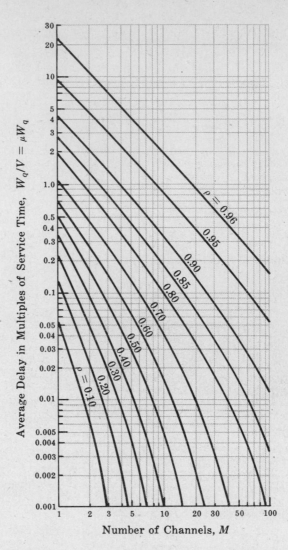

Fig. 19-5 (reprinted by permission from J. R. Shelton, "Solution Methods for Waiting Line Problems," *J. Indust. Eng.* IX, No. 4, 1960)

curve for $\rho = 0.7$, then horizontally to $\mu W_q = 0.27$; hence, $W_q = 0.27/10 = 0.027$ hr $= 1.62$ min   *Ans.*

3. Poisson arrivals, exponential service times, finite population.

Formulas corresponding to the ones for infinite population are available when the population is finite, but they are not convenient for practical use. Rather, models of this kind are analyzed by using tables of their characteristics. A complete set takes up a whole book, but a typical sample page is shown as Table 19-2. It applies to the case $N = 10$; the complete tables are indexed by the population size N, and within each N by a service factor X and the number of channels M. The service factor X is given by

$$X = \frac{V}{V + U} = \frac{1}{1 + (\mu/\lambda)} \tag{19.23}$$

For each combination of N, X and M, the table gives D, the probability of delay, and an efficiency factor F which is used in the subsequent calculations. The important results are:

1. The mean number of customers being served is given by

$$H = L - L_q = NFX \tag{19.24}$$

2. The mean number of customers waiting for service is given by

$$L_q = N(1 - F) \tag{19.25}$$

3. The mean number of customers not in the system is given by

$$J = N - L = NF(1 - X) \tag{19.26}$$

Note that $H + L_q + J = N$.

EXAMPLE 19.10. A group of 10 machines needs setups every half hour, on the average. Each setup takes an average of 10 minutes, both times being exponentially distributed. There are 4 mechanics. Find H, L_q and J, and the probability of delay. Also find W_q and W.

From Table 19-2, for $X = 10/(10 + 30) = 0.25$ and $M = 4$, $D = 0.183$ (*Ans.*) and $F = 0.983$. Then

$$H = 10(0.983)(0.25) = 2.46, \quad L_q = 10(1 - 0.983) = 0.17, \quad J = 10(0.983)(1 - 0.25) = 7.37 \quad Ans.$$

$$\textbf{Check:} \quad H + L_q + J = 2.46 + 0.17 + 7.37 = 10.00$$

From (*19.4*)

$$W_q = \frac{L_q}{\lambda} = \frac{0.17}{2} = 0.085 \text{ hr} = 5.1 \text{ min} \quad Ans.$$

From (*19.5*)

$$W = 5.1 + 10 = 15.1 \text{ min} \quad Ans.$$

4. Poisson arrivals, exponential service times, absolute truncation.

Absolute truncation is the special case where arriving customers enter the system so long as there is an empty channel and do not enter if the system is full. The maximum value of L is thus restricted as in balking to c, but here $c = M$. The two important formulas for such a model are

$$P_n = \frac{(\lambda/\mu)^n/n!}{\sum\limits_{n=0}^{M} (\lambda/\mu)^n/n!} \tag{19.27}$$

$$L = (\lambda/\mu) \frac{\sum\limits_{n=0}^{M-1} (\lambda/\mu)^n/n!}{\sum\limits_{n=0}^{M} (\lambda/\mu)^n/n!} \tag{19.28}$$

The other leading characteristics again follow from (*19.3*)–(*19.5*).

EXAMPLE 19.11. It is proposed to build a motel in an area where, due to a local scenic attraction, stays have a mean of two days and are exponentially distributed. There are an average of six Poisson arrivals per day. Construct a table showing the average occupancy of the motel and the probability of being full, given that there are 1, 2, 3, ..., 8 rooms.

The arrangement of Table 19-3 is helpful in solving problems of this kind.

Col. (1):   Self-explanatory; as we compute the other columns, we successively assume that $n = M$.

Col. (2): $\lambda/\mu = 6/\frac{1}{2} = 12$, therefore entries are 12^n.

Col. (3): $n!$.

Col. (4):   Col. (2) / Col. (3).

Col. (5):   Running total of Col. (4).

Col. (6):   The probability of being full, P_M, is simply Col. (4) / Col. (5), i.e. we work out the ratio as if, on each line, $n = M$. Note how the probability declines as the number of rooms goes up.

Table 19-2. Finite Queueing Table for $N = 10$ (adapted with permission from L. G. Peck and R. N. Hazlewood, *Finite Queueing Tables*, John Wiley & Sons, Inc., 1958)

X	M	D	F	X	M	D	F	X	M	D	F
0.008	1	0.072	0.999		2	0.177	0.990		3	0.182	0.986
0.013	1	0.117	0.998		1	0.660	0.899		2	0.528	0.921
0.016	1	0.144	0.997	0.085	3	0.037	0.999		1	0.954	0.610
0.019	1	0.170	0.996		2	0.196	0.988	0.165	4	0.049	0.997
0.021	1	0.188	0.995		1	0.692	0.883		3	0.195	0.984
0.023	1	0.206	0.994	0.090	3	0.043	0.998		2	0.550	0.914
0.025	1	0.224	0.993		2	0.216	0.986		1	0.961	0.594
0.026	1	0.232	0.992		1	0.722	0.867	0.170	4	0.054	0.997
0.028	1	0.250	0.991	0.095	3	0.049	0.998		3	0.209	0.982
0.030	1	0.268	0.990		2	0.237	0.984		2	0.571	0.906
0.032	2	0.033	0.999		1	0.750	0.850		1	0.966	0.579
	1	0.285	0.988	0.100	3	0.056	0.998	0.180	5	0.013	0.999
0.034	2	0.037	0.999		2	0.258	0.981		4	0.066	0.996
	1	0.302	0.986		1	0.776	0.832		3	0.238	0.978
0.036	2	0.041	0.999	0.105	3	0.064	0.997		2	0.614	0.890
	1	0.320	0.984		2	0.279	0.978		1	0.975	0.549
0.038	2	0.046	0.999		1	0.800	0.814	0.190	5	0.016	0.999
	1	0.337	0.982	0.110	3	0.072	0.997		4	0.078	0.995
0.040	2	0.050	0.999		2	0.301	0.974		3	0.269	0.973
	1	0.354	0.980		1	0.822	0.795		2	0.654	0.873
0.042	2	0.055	0.999	0.115	3	0.081	0.996		1	0.982	0.522
	1	0.371	0.978		2	0.324	0.971	0.200	5	0.020	0.999
0.044	2	0.060	0.998		1	0.843	0.776		4	0.092	0.994
	1	0.388	0.975	0.120	4	0.016	0.999		3	0.300	0.968
0.046	2	0.065	0.998		3	0.090	0.995		2	0.692	0.854
	1	0.404	0.973		2	0.346	0.967		1	0.987	0.497
0.048	2	0.071	0.998		1	0.861	0.756	0.210	5	0.025	0.999
	1	0.421	0.970	0.125	4	0.019	0.999		4	0.108	0.992
0.050	2	0.076	0.998		3	0.100	0.994		3	0.333	0.961
	1	0.437	0.967		2	0.369	0.962		2	0.728	0.835
0.052	2	0.082	0.997		1	0.878	0.737		1	0.990	0.474
	1	0.454	0.963	0.130	4	0.022	0.999	0.220	5	0.030	0.998
0.054	2	0.088	0.997		3	0.110	0.994		4	0.124	0.990
	1	0.470	0.960		2	0.392	0.958		3	0.366	0.954
0.056	2	0.094	0.997		1	0.893	0.718		2	0.761	0.815
	1	0.486	0.956	0.135	4	0.025	0.999		1	0.993	0.453
0.058	2	0.100	0.996		3	0.121	0.993	0.230	5	0.037	0.998
	1	0.501	0.953		2	0.415	0.952		4	0.142	0.988
0.060	2	0.106	0.996		1	0.907	0.699		3	0.400	0.947
	1	0.517	0.949	0.140	4	0.028	0.999		2	0.791	0.794
0.062	2	0.113	0.996		3	0.132	0.991		1	0.995	0.434
	1	0.532	0.945		2	0.437	0.947	0.240	5	0.044	0.997
0.064	2	0.119	0.995		1	0.919	0.680		4	0.162	0.986
	1	0.547	0.940	0.145	4	0.032	0.999		3	0.434	0.938
0.066	2	0.126	0.995		3	0.144	0.990		2	0.819	0.774
	1	0.562	0.936		2	0.460	0.941		1	0.996	0.416
0.068	3	0.020	0.999		1	0.929	0.662	0.250	6	0.010	0.999
	2	0.133	0.994	0.150	4	0.036	0.998		5	0.052	0.997
	1	0.577	0.931		3	0.156	0.989		4	0.183	0.983
0.070	3	0.022	0.999		2	0.483	0.935		3	0.469	0.929
	2	0.140	0.994		1	0.939	0.644		2	0.844	0.753
	1	0.591	0.926	0.155	4	0.040	0.998		1	0.997	0.400
0.075	3	0.026	0.999		3	0.169	0.987	0.260	6	0.013	0.999
	2	0.158	0.992		2	0.505	0.928		5	0.060	0.996
	1	0.627	0.913		1	0.947	0.627		4	0.205	0.980
0.080	3	0.031	0.999	0.160	4	0.044	0.998		3	0.503	0.919

Table 19-2　(Cont.)

X	M	D	F	X	M	D	F	X	M	D	F
	2	0.866	0.732		4	0.533	0.906		7	0.171	0.982
	1	0.998	0.384		3	0.840	0.758		6	0.413	0.939
0.270	6	0.015	0.999		2	0.986	0.525		5	0.707	0.848
	5	0.070	0.995	0.400	7	0.026	0.998		4	0.917	0.706
	4	0.228	0.976		6	0.105	0.991		3	0.991	0.535
	3	0.537	0.908		5	0.292	0.963	0.580	8	0.057	0.995
	2	0.886	0.712		4	0.591	0.887		7	0.204	0.977
	1	0.999	0.370		3	0.875	0.728		6	0.465	0.927
0.280	6	0.018	0.999		2	0.991	0.499		5	0.753	0.829
	5	0.081	0.994	0.420	7	0.034	0.998		4	0.937	0.684
	4	0.252	0.972		6	0.130	0.987		3	0.994	0.517
	3	0.571	0.896		5	0.341	0.954	0.600	9	0.010	0.999
	2	0.903	0.692		4	0.646	0.866		8	0.072	0.994
	1	0.999	0.357		3	0.905	0.700		7	0.242	0.972
0.290	6	0.022	0.999		2	0.994	0.476		6	0.518	0.915
	5	0.093	0.993	0.440	7	0.045	0.997		5	0.795	0.809
	4	0.278	0.968		6	0.160	0.984		4	0.953	0.663
	3	0.603	0.884		5	0.392	0.943		3	0.996	0.500
	2	0.918	0.672		4	0.698	0.845	0.650	9	0.021	0.999
	1	0.999	0.345		3	0.928	0.672		8	0.123	0.988
0.300	6	0.026	0.998		2	0.996	0.454		7	0.353	0.954
	5	0.106	0.991	0.460	8	0.011	0.999		6	0.651	0.878
	4	0.304	0.963		7	0.058	0.995		5	0.882	0.759
	3	0.635	0.872		6	0.193	0.979		4	0.980	0.614
	2	0.932	0.653		5	0.445	0.930		3	0.999	0.461
	1	0.999	0.333		4	0.747	0.822	0.700	9	0.040	0.997
0.310	6	0.031	0.998		3	0.947	0.646		8	0.200	0.979
	5	0.120	0.990		2	0.998	0.435		7	0.484	0.929
	4	0.331	0.957	0.480	8	0.015	0.999		6	0.772	0.836
	3	0.666	0.858		7	0.074	0.994		5	0.940	0.711
	2	0.943	0.635		6	0.230	0.973		4	0.992	0.571
0.320	6	0.036	0.998		5	0.499	0.916	0.750	9	0.075	0.994
	5	0.135	0.988		4	0.791	0.799		8	0.307	0.965
	4	0.359	0.952		3	0.961	0.621		7	0.626	0.897
	3	0.695	0.845		2	0.998	0.417		6	0.870	0.792
	2	0.952	0.617	0.500	8	0.020	0.999		5	0.975	0.666
0.330	6	0.042	0.997		7	0.093	0.992		4	0.998	0.533
	5	0.151	0.986		6	0.271	0.966	0.800	9	0.134	0.988
	4	0.387	0.945		5	0.553	0.901		8	0.446	0.944
	3	0.723	0.831		4	0.830	0.775		7	0.763	0.859
	2	0.961	0.600		3	0.972	0.598		6	0.939	0.747
0.340	7	0.010	0.999		2	0.999	0.400		5	0.991	0.625
	6	0.049	0.997	0.520	8	0.026	0.998		4	0.999	0.500
	5	0.168	0.983		7	0.115	0.989	0.850	9	0.232	0.979
	4	0.416	0.938		6	0.316	0.958		8	0.611	0.916
	3	0.750	0.816		5	0.606	0.884		7	0.879	0.818
	2	0.968	0.584		4	0.864	0.752		6	0.978	0.705
0.360	7	0.014	0.999		3	0.980	0.575		5	0.998	0.588
	6	0.064	0.995		2	0.999	0.385	0.900	9	0.387	0.963
	5	0.205	0.978	0.540	8	0.034	0.997		8	0.785	0.881
	4	0.474	0.923		7	0.141	0.986		7	0.957	0.777
	3	0.798	0.787		6	0.363	0.949		6	0.995	0.667
	2	0.978	0.553		5	0.658	0.867	0.950	9	0.630	0.938
0.380	7	0.019	0.999		4	0.893	0.729		8	0.934	0.841
	6	0.083	0.993		3	0.986	0.555		7	0.994	0.737
	5	0.247	0.971	0.560	8	0.044	0.996				

Col. (7):   This is the first step in computing L.   The entry at n is the ratio of the Col. (5) entry at $n-1$ to the Col. (5) entry at n.

Col. (8):   This completes the computation of L by multiplying Col. (7) by $\lambda/\mu = 12$; L is the average daily occupancy.

The foregoing method is convenient when Cols. (2) and (3) are small enough for reasonable computation.   For higher numbers, the use of a computer is advisable.

Table 19-3

(1)	(2)	(3)	(4)	(5)	(6)	(7)	(8)
n	$(\lambda/\mu)^n$	$n!$	$\dfrac{(\lambda/\mu)^n}{n!}$	$\displaystyle\sum_{n=0}^{M}\dfrac{(\lambda/\mu)^n}{n!}$	P_M (Ans.)	$\displaystyle\sum_{n=0}^{M-1}\Big/\sum_{n=0}^{M}$	L (Ans.)
0	1	1	1	1	1	..	..
1	12	1	12	13	0.923	0.0769	0.9228
2	144	2	72	85	0.847	0.1529	1.8348
3	1,728	6	288	373	0.772	0.2279	2.7348
4	20,736	24	864	1237	0.698	0.3015	3.6180
5	248,832	120	2073.6	3310.6	0.625	0.3736	4.4832
6	2,985,984	720	4147.2	7457.8	0.556	0.4439	5.3268
7	35,831,808	5040	7109.5	14,567.3	0.488	0.5120	6.1440
8	429,981,696	40,320	10,664.2	25,231.5	0.423	0.5773	6.9276

ECONOMIC OPTIMIZATION

The most generally useful example is the determination of the optimal number of channels.   Let

C_2 = cost per unit of customer waiting time

C_3 = cost of one channel per unit of time (whether actually working or not)

The total expected cost of the system per unit of time is

$$C = C_3 M + C_2 \lambda W_q \qquad (19.29)$$

The second term is C_2 times the expected number of people entering per unit of time times the average wait *before service* of each.   Only W_q can be reduced by adding more channels; the service itself still takes an average of $V = 1/\mu$.

EXAMPLE 19.12.   Given that a channel costs \$3 per hour to run and that waiting time costs \$10 per man-hour, find the optimal number of channels for a Poisson arrival rate of 16 per hour and a Poisson service rate of 4 per hour.

The minimum number of channels which will make $\rho = \lambda/M\mu < 1$ is 5.   The function (*19.29*) must then be minimized, subject to the constraint $M \geq 5$.   This is done by trial, using Fig. 19-3.   The solution is given in Table 19-4; 7 channels at a cost of \$22.89 per hour is the best arrangement.

Table 19-4

	$M = 5$	6	7	8	9
$\rho = \lambda/M\mu$	0.8	0.67	0.57	0.5	0.44
μW_q (from Fig. 19-3)	0.57	0.16	0.047	0.016	0.0058
W_q	0.1425	0.0400	0.0118	0.004	0.0015
λW_q	2.38	0.64	0.1888	0.064	0.024
$C_2\lambda W_q$	23.80	6.40	1.89	0.64	0.24
$C_3 M$	15.00	18.00	21.00	24.00	27.00
C	38.80	24.40	22.89*	24.64	27.24

Solved Problems

19.1. Patients arrive at a doctor's office at mean intervals of 20 minutes, and spend a mean of 15 minutes in consultation, both times exponentially distributed. The doctor wishes to have enough seats in the waiting room so that no more than about 1 percent of arriving patients will have to stand. How many seats should be provided?

Let c be the number of seats required. Then the probability of c or fewer patients in the system should be about 0.99, i.e.

$$\sum_{n=0}^{c} P_n = 0.99$$

From the formula for P_n in Table 19-1, Col. (2),

$$\sum_{n=0}^{c} P_n = (1-\rho) \sum_{n=0}^{c} \rho^n = 1 - \rho^{c+1}$$

Hence,
$$1 - \rho^{c+1} = 0.99$$

$$\rho^{c+1} = 0.01$$

$$(c+1) \log \rho = \log 0.01 = -2$$

Substituting $\rho = 15/20 = 0.75$, $\log 0.75 = \bar{1}.8751 = -0.1249$,

$$c = \frac{-2}{-0.1249} - 1 \approx 16 \quad Ans.$$

19.2. Trucks arrive at a terminal at a mean rate of 12 per hour and are serviced at a mean rate of 4 per hour (Poisson distributions). How many docks should be provided so that the probability of delay is no more than 5 percent?

Here, $\lambda/\mu = 12/4 = 3$. Enter Fig. 19-2 at $D = 0.05$ and $\lambda/\mu = 3$. The coordinate lines intersect near the curve for $M = 7$, which actually gives $D = 0.042$. Thus 7 docks should be provided. *Ans.*

19.3. A bank has M tellers; it may be assumed that customers choose one lane at random and stay in it until served. Arrivals and service are Poisson, with mean rates λ and μ respectively. Find L and W.

If the arrival stream is allocated at random among the M tellers, each may expect to receive λ/M arrivals per unit of time. Each teller, therefore, is a single-channel system with $\rho = \lambda/M\mu$. From Table 19-1, Col. (2),

$$L = \frac{\rho}{1-\rho}. \qquad W = \frac{1}{\mu - (\lambda/M)}$$

and, for the whole bank,

$$L_T = ML = \frac{M\rho}{1-\rho} \quad Ans. \qquad W_T = W \quad Ans.$$

19.4. A bank has been conforming to the model of Problem 19.3 with 5 tellers. Arrivals are Poisson at a rate of 40 per hour. Service time is exponential with a mean of 5 minutes. The bank considers the advisability of changing to a single-queue system with each customer taking the first available teller. What are the expected effects of the change on the probability of delay and on W_q?

For the model of Problem 19.3:

$$M = 5, \quad \lambda = 40, \quad \mu = \frac{60}{5} = 12, \quad \rho = \frac{40}{5(12)} = 0.67$$

From (*19.10*)

$$D = \rho = 0.67 \quad Ans.$$

From Table 19-1, Col. (2),

$$W_q = \frac{\rho}{\mu - (\lambda/M)} = \frac{0.67}{12 - (40/5)} = \frac{1}{6} \text{ hr} = 10 \text{ min}$$

for each lane and therefore for the entire bank.   *Ans.*

For a single queue with 5 tellers, we have, using Fig. 19-2,

$$\frac{\lambda}{\mu} = \frac{40}{12} = 3.33 \quad \text{and} \quad D = 0.33 \quad Ans.$$

Using Fig. 19-3, $\rho = 0.67$, $\mu W_q = 0.2$, whence

$$W_q = \frac{0.2}{12} \text{ hr} = 1.0 \text{ min} \quad Ans.$$

Figures 19-2 and 19-3 may also be used to obtain the results for the first model.

19.5. Given that each setup mechanic is paid \$8 per hour and that each machine, when running, earns a gross profit of \$50 per hour, show that, for the set of machines considered in Example 19.10, it is optimal to provide 4 mechanics.

For M mechanics, the expected number of machines running is obtained from (*19.26*) with $X = 0.25$ and $N = 10$, i.e.

$$J = 10F(1 - 0.25) = (7.5)F$$

The expected profit per hour is then $50(7.5)F = 375F$. We now tabulate this as a function of M, using Table 19-2. To obtain the net profit, we subtract the cost of the mechanics, i.e. $8M$. The computations are shown in Table 19-5. Four mechanics maximizes net profit.

Table 19-5

M	F	Gross Profit, $375F$	$8M$	Net Profit, $375F - 8M$
6	0.999	374.63	48	326.63
5	0.997	373.88	40	333.88
4	0.983	368.63	32	336.63*
3	0.929	348.38	24	324.38
2	0.753	282.38	16	266.38
1	0.400	150.00	8	142.00

19.6. A service is rendered in a one-channel system (exponential service times). It is possible to adjust the mean service rate; the expected cost per unit of time of providing a service rate of 1 is C_1. Arrivals are at a mean rate λ (Poisson) and the clients' time in the system is worth C_2 per man per unit of time. Find the optimal value μ^* of the service rate.

The expected cost of operating the channel at service rate μ is $C_1\mu$ per unit of time. The expected cost of waiting and being served is C_2L per unit of time. The total expected cost C is thus (cf. Table 19-1)

$$C = C_1\mu + C_2L = C_1\mu + C_2\frac{\lambda}{\mu - \lambda}$$

To find μ^*, set

$$\frac{dC}{d\mu} = C_1 - \frac{C_2\lambda}{(\mu - \lambda)^2} = 0$$

from which

$$\mu^* = \lambda + \sqrt{\frac{C_2\lambda}{C_1}} \quad Ans.$$

Note that $\mu^* > \lambda$, as it must be.

19.7. In the model of Problem 19.6, C_1 is redefined as the *cost per service*. Is there now an optimal service rate?

> Per unit of time, an average of λ clients enter the system and so, in the steady state, an average of λ clients leave the system. The cost of running the channel is then $C_1\lambda$ per unit of time, and

$$C = C_1\lambda + C_2\frac{\lambda}{\mu - \lambda}$$

> This cost function is asymptotic to $C_1\lambda$ from above; there is no optimal value of μ.   *Ans.*

19.8. A machine does a certain job at a mean rate of 15 per week. Jobs arrive at a mean rate of 12 a week and are divided into three categories: (1) back orders, which must be done as soon as the machine is free; (2) work to order, which is next in line; and (3) work for future inventory, which can wait. Each week there are, on the average, 2.5 back orders, 4 regular work orders and 5.5 orders for inventory. Arrivals are Poisson and service times are exponential. Find W, W_q, L and L_q for this system.

> This is a system in which the queue discipline is one of *nonpreemptive priorities*. We first list the formulas for the general case of M service channels, with the subscript g referring to the gth class of priority $(g = 1, 2, \ldots, G)$; λ_g is the mean rate of arrival for the gth class. All classes add up to the total arrivals, i.e.

$$\sum_{i=1}^{G} \lambda_i = \lambda$$

> The expected time in the system for arrivals in the gth class is given by

$$W_g = \frac{1}{AB_{g-1}B_g} + \frac{1}{\mu} \qquad\qquad (19.30)$$

> where

$$A = \frac{M!\,(M\mu - \lambda)}{(\lambda/\mu)^M} \sum_{j=0}^{M-1} \frac{(\lambda/\mu)^j}{j!} + M\mu$$

$$B_g = 1 - \frac{1}{M\mu}\sum_{i=1}^{g} \lambda_i \qquad\qquad B_0 = 1$$

> In the present case $M = 1$, which yields

$$A = \frac{\mu^2}{\lambda} = \frac{(15)^2}{12} = 18.75$$

$$B_1 = 1 - \frac{\lambda_1}{\mu} = 1 - \frac{2.5}{15} = 0.833$$

$$B_2 = 1 - \frac{\lambda_1 + \lambda_2}{\mu} = 1 - \frac{2.5 + 4}{15} = 0.567$$

$$B_3 = 1 - \frac{\lambda_1 + \lambda_2 + \lambda_3}{\mu} = 1 - \frac{\lambda}{\mu} = 1 - \frac{12}{15} = 0.2$$

$$W_1 = \frac{1}{AB_0B_1} + \frac{1}{\mu} = \frac{1}{(18.75)(1)(0.833)} + \frac{1}{15} = 0.064 + 0.067 = 0.131 \text{ week} \quad Ans.$$

$$W_2 = \frac{1}{AB_1B_2} + \frac{1}{\mu} = \frac{1}{(18.75)(0.833)(0.567)} + 0.067 = 0.113 + 0.067 = 0.180 \text{ week} \quad Ans.$$

$$W_3 = \frac{1}{AB_2B_3} + \frac{1}{\mu} = \frac{1}{(18.75)(0.567)(0.2)} + 0.067 = 0.470 + 0.067 = 0.537 \text{ week} \quad Ans.$$

From (*19.5*) it follows that the first term on the right-hand side of (*19.30*) is W_{qg}. Thus

$$W_{q1} = 0.064 \text{ week} \qquad W_{q2} = 0.113 \text{ week} \qquad W_{q3} = 0.470 \text{ week} \quad Ans.$$

We can now compute L_g and L_{qg} from the general relations $L_g = \lambda_g W_g$ and $L_{qg} = \lambda_g W_{qg}$ (see Table 19-6).

Table 19-6

	Priority Class, g			TOTALS
	1	2	3	
λ_g	2.5	4	5.5	12
L_g	0.328	0.720	2.954	4.002
L_{qg}	0.165	0.452	2.585	3.202

Note that for the equivalent system without priorities, Table 19-1 gives

$$L = \frac{0.8}{1 - 0.8} = 4 \qquad L_q = \frac{(0.8)^2}{1 - 0.8} = 3.2$$

The L_g and L_{qg} add to these totals, within rounding errors.

19.9. In Problem 19.8, the workload is quadrupled and 4 machines are installed. They receive a mean of 10 back orders, 16 regular orders and 22 inventory orders each week. Each machine can still handle a mean of 15 jobs per week. Find W, W_q, L and L_q for this system, assuming that priorities are nonpreemptive.

Here $M = 4$; otherwise we proceed as in Problem 19.8. Now

$$\lambda = 10 + 16 + 22 = 48 \qquad \frac{\lambda}{\mu} = \frac{48}{15} = 3.2$$

$$A = \frac{4! \, [4(15) - 48]}{(3.2)^4} \left[1 + 3.2 + \frac{(3.2)^2}{2!} + \frac{(3.2)^3}{3!} \right] = 40.59$$

$$B_0 = 1 \qquad\qquad B_1 = 1 - \frac{10}{4(15)} = 0.833$$

$$B_2 = 1 - \frac{10 + 16}{4(15)} = 0.567 \qquad B_3 = 1 - \frac{48}{4(15)} = 0.200$$

(Note that the B's are the same as in Problem 19.8 because both workload and number of machines were increased equally.)

$$W_1 = \frac{1}{(40.59)(1)(0.833)} + \frac{1}{15} = 0.030 + 0.067 = 0.097 \text{ week} \quad Ans.$$

$$W_2 = \frac{1}{(40.59)(0.833)(0.567)} + \frac{1}{15} = 0.052 + 0.067 = 0.119 \text{ week} \quad Ans.$$

$$W_3 = \frac{1}{(40.59)(0.567)(0.200)} + \frac{1}{15} = 0.217 + 0.067 = 0.284 \text{ week} \quad Ans.$$

From these, $W_{q1} = 0.030$ week; $W_{q2} = 0.052$ week; $W_{q3} = 0.217$ week. *Ans.* The L_g and L_{qg} are computed in Table 19-7.

Table 19-7

	Priority Class, g		
	1	2	3
λ_g	10	16	22
L_g	0.963	1.902	6.250
L_{qg}	0.296	0.835	4.783

19.10. In Problem 19.8, all data are left the same, except that the queue discipline is one of *preemptive* priorities, i.e. when a higher-priority job comes along, service is interrupted and the lower-priority job is returned to the waiting line. (For an exponential service time distribution, it is immaterial whether service to the preempted job resumes where it left off or starts again at the beginning.)

Here the formula for W_g is

$$W_g \;=\; \frac{1}{\mu B_{g-1} B_g} \tag{19.31}$$

where B_{g-1} and B_g are as before.   Therefore,

$$W_1 \;=\; \frac{1}{15(1)(0.833)} \;=\; 0.080 \text{ week}$$

$$W_2 \;=\; \frac{1}{15(0.833)(0.567)} \;=\; 0.141 \text{ week}$$

$$W_3 \;=\; \frac{1}{15(0.567)(0.200)} \;=\; 0.588 \text{ week}$$

The W_{qg}, L_g and L_{qg} are obtained as before (see Table 19-8).   Again the L_g and L_{qg} add to the equivalent nonpriority L and L_q, within rounding errors.

Table 19-8

	Priority Class, g			
	1	2	3	
W_{qg}	0.013	0.074	0.521	TOTALS
λ_g	2.5	4	5.5	12
L_g	0.200	0.564	3.234	3.008
L_{qg}	0.033	0.297	2.867	3.197

19.11. Rework Example 19.12, where all the data remain the same except that the mean arrival rate is not known to be 16 per hour but is estimated according to the distribution

λ	16	20	24
$P(\lambda)$	0.2	0.5	0.3

It is first necessary to find the costs for $\lambda = 20$ and 24, using the method of Example 19.12. The results appear in the upper part of Table 19-9, which is thus a table of the conditional costs C_λ for the various values of λ.   The expected cost is then obtained as

$$E(C) \;=\; \sum_\lambda P(\lambda) C_\lambda$$

(This is the same approach as in Chapter 10.)

The lowest cost in Table 19-9 is that for 8 channels, although 9 channels gives almost the same result. A decision would have to take other factors into account, like prospects for growth or downside risks.

Table 19-9

$P(\lambda)$	λ	$M = 7$	$M = 8$	$M = 9$
		C_λ (\$/hr)		
..	16	22.89	24.64	27.24
..	20	29.00	26.50	28.00
..	24	61.80	34.80	31.00
		$P(\lambda)C_\lambda$ (\$/hr)		
0.2	16	4.58	4.93	5.45
0.5	20	14.50	13.25	14.00
0.3	24	18.54	10.44	9.30
TOTALS, $E(C)$ (\$/hr)		37.62	28.62*	28.70

19.12. In a *deterministic* waiting line, arrivals are at equal intervals of $U = 1/\lambda$ and service takes a constant time $V = 1/\mu$. Consider a single-channel deterministic system for which $\lambda > \mu$, i.e. $\rho > 1$ and thus the queue increases as long as there are admissions. These go on for a time t_a, after which they are stopped; however, service continues until, at time T, all customers have been served. (*a*) Find T, L and W. (*b*) Find T, L and W for a system in which arrivals are every 20 minutes and each service takes 30 minutes. Admissions are stopped after 5 hr 20 min.

(*a*) Since $\rho > 1$, the server is continuously busy from the moment of the first arrival, at time 0, until time T. Thus, exactly μT customers pass through the system. Consider the jth customer to enter the system $(j = 1, 2, \ldots, \mu T)$.

$$\text{Arrival time:} \quad (j-1)\frac{1}{\lambda}$$

$$\text{Departure time:} \quad j\frac{1}{\mu}$$

$$\text{Time spent in system:} \quad j\frac{1}{\mu} - (j-1)\frac{1}{\lambda} = \frac{1}{\lambda} + \left(\frac{1}{\mu} - \frac{1}{\lambda}\right)j$$

Because the times spent in the system are in arithmetic progression, their average is just the time of the "middle man," i.e.

$$W = \frac{1}{\lambda} + \left(\frac{1}{\mu} - \frac{1}{\lambda}\right)\frac{\mu T + 1}{2} \quad Ans.$$

The arrival time of the last customer is t_a, hence

$$(\mu T - 1)\frac{1}{\lambda} = t_a \quad \text{or} \quad T = \frac{\lambda t_a + 1}{\mu} = \rho t_a + \frac{1}{\mu} \quad Ans.$$

To find L for this nonsteady queue we cannot apply the basic formula $L = \lambda W$, because here the arrivals are at the rate λ for only part of the time interval 0 to T. However, imagine that a movie of the entire process were run backwards. It is obvious that the reversed process would have the same L and W as the actual process; moreover, it would have the arrival rate μ over the whole interval 0 to T. Therefore, by the basic formula,

$$L = \mu W \quad Ans.$$

This result can also be obtained by a direct calculation (Problem 19.20).

(*b*) For $\lambda = 3$ per hour, $\mu = 2$ per hour and $t_a = 5\frac{1}{3}$ hours, part (*a*) gives:

$$T = \frac{3(5\frac{1}{3}) + 1}{2} = \frac{17}{2}\,\text{hr} = 8\,\text{hr } 30\,\text{min} \quad Ans.$$

$$W = \frac{1}{3} + \left(\frac{1}{2} - \frac{1}{3}\right)\frac{2(17/2) + 1}{2} = \frac{11}{6}\,\text{hr} = 1\,\text{hr } 50\,\text{min} \quad Ans.$$

$$L = 2\left(\frac{11}{6}\right) = 3\frac{2}{3}\,\text{customers} \quad Ans.$$

Supplementary Problems

19.13. In Problem 19.1, it is found that there is space for only 9 seats in the waiting room. All other conditions are the same. What is the probability that an arriving patient will not find a seat?

Ans.   0.0564

19.14. The model of Problem 19.6 is changed so that the expected cost of operation per unit of time is now $C_1\mu + C_3\mu^2$. All other conditions are the same. Find the optimal service rate and cost, and the corresponding expected time in the system, given that $C_1 = 2$, $C_2 = 9$, $C_3 = 2.5$, $\lambda = 4$ (the basic units being dollars and hours).

Ans. $\mu^* = 5.14$ per hr; $W = 0.877$ hr; $C^* = \$107.90$ per hr

19.15. Six clerks operate six customer windows. Each has a mean arrival rate of 12 per hour and each clerk is able to serve customers at a mean rate of 16 per hour (Poisson distributions). Assume that customers pick clerks at random. There are the following ways of arranging the job:

(a) Individual lines.

(b) The clerks work in twos, with a common customer line for each set.

(c) The clerks work in threes, with a common customer line for each set.

(d) The clerks work in one group of six, with a single customer line.

Find the average waiting time for each arrangement and the average times in system.

Ans. W_q: (a) 11.3; (b) 5.6; (c) 3.1; (d) 1.1 (in minutes) W: (a) 15.0; (b) 9.4; (c) 6.9; (d) 4.9

19.16. Assume that in the model of Problem 19.15 the four arrangements refer to (a) 6, (b) 3, (c) 2 and (d) 1 different office locations. Rates of arrival and service are as before, but now it is necessary to consider travel time as well. The mean round trip travel time for customers corresponding to the above is (a) 4, (b) 6, (c) 8, (d) 12 minutes. Which arrangement will minimize total expected time in system and what is the minimum expected time?

Ans.   (c) 2 locations; 14.9 minutes

19.17. In Example 19.11 the annual costs (in dollars) of running the motel are $20,000 + 1400n$, where n is the number of rooms. Room rates are $20 a day and the motel is open all year. (a) What is the smallest number of rooms which would yield a profit if such a motel were built? (b) If the motel has 8 rooms, what is the expected profit?   *Ans.* (a) 4; (b) $19,371

19.18. In Example 19.11 suppose the mean rate of arrival were reduced to 4 a day (Poisson), with costs as in Problem 19.17. Find (a) the smallest size of motel that would be profitable and (b) the expected profit.   *Ans.* (a) 5 rooms; (b) $3396.

19.19. Suppose the motel in Problem 19.18 had been built with 8 rooms. What would be (a) the average number of rooms occupied, (b) the probability of being full and (c) the expected profit?

Ans.   (a) 6.15; (b) 0.237; (c) $13,666

19.20. Determine L in Problem 19.12 by graphing cumulative arrivals and cumulative departures against time and computing the difference in areas ($= LT$) under the two graphs.

Appendix A

Values of e^x

x	0	1	2	3	4	5	6	7	8	9
.0	1.0000	1.0101	1.0202	1.0305	1.0408	1.0513	1.0618	1.0725	1.0833	1.0942
.1	1.1052	1.1163	1.1275	1.1388	1.1503	1.1618	1.1735	1.1853	1.1972	1.2092
.2	1.2214	1.2337	1.2461	1.2586	1.2712	1.2840	1.2969	1.3100	1.3231	1.3364
.3	1.3499	1.3634	1.3771	1.3910	1.4049	1.4191	1.4333	1.4477	1.4623	1.4770
.4	1.4918	1.5068	1.5220	1.5373	1.5527	1.5683	1.5841	1.6000	1.6161	1.6323
.5	1.6487	1.6653	1.6820	1.6989	1.7160	1.7333	1.7507	1.7683	1.7860	1.8040
.6	1.8221	1.8404	1.8589	1.8776	1.8965	1.9155	1.9348	1.9542	1.9739	1.9937
.7	2.0138	2.0340	2.0544	2.0751	2.0959	2.1170	2.1383	2.1598	2.1815	2.2034
.8	2.2255	2.2479	2.2705	2.2933	2.3164	2.3396	2.3632	2.3869	2.4109	2.4351
.9	2.4596	2.4843	2.5093	2.5345	2.5600	2.5857	2.6117	2.6379	2.6645	2.6912
1.0	2.7183	2.7456	2.7732	2.8011	2.8292	2.8577	2.8864	2.9154	2.9447	2.9743
1.1	3.0042	3.0344	3.0649	3.0957	3.1268	3.1582	3.1899	3.2220	3.2544	3.2871
1.2	3.3201	3.3535	3.3872	3.4212	3.4556	3.4903	3.5254	3.5609	3.5966	3.6328
1.3	3.6693	3.7062	3.7434	3.7810	3.8190	3.8574	3.8962	3.9354	3.9749	4.0149
1.4	4.0552	4.0960	4.1371	4.1787	4.2207	4.2631	4.3060	4.3492	4.3929	4.4371
1.5	4.4817	4.5267	4.5722	4.6182	4.6646	4.7115	4.7588	4.8066	4.8550	4.9037
1.6	4.9530	5.0028	5.0531	5.1039	5.1552	5.2070	5.2593	5.3122	5.3656	5.4195
1.7	5.4739	5.5290	5.5845	5.6407	5.6973	5.7546	5.8124	5.8709	5.9299	5.9895
1.8	6.0496	6.1104	6.1719	6.2339	6.2965	6.3598	6.4237	6.4883	6.5535	6.6194
1.9	6.6859	6.7531	6.8210	6.8895	6.9588	7.0287	7.0993	7.1707	7.2427	7.3155
2.0	7.3891	7.4633	7.5383	7.6141	7.6906	7.7679	7.8460	7.9248	8.0045	8.0849
2.1	8.1662	8.2482	8.3311	8.4149	8.4994	8.5849	8.6711	8.7583	8.8463	8.9352
2.2	9.0250	9.1157	9.2073	9.2999	9.3933	9.4877	9.5831	9.6794	9.7767	9.8749
2.3	9.9742	10.074	10.176	10.278	10.381	10.486	10.591	10.697	10.805	10.913
2.4	11.023	11.134	11.246	11.359	11.473	11.588	11.705	11.822	11.941	12.061
2.5	12.182	12.305	12.429	12.554	12.680	12.807	12.936	13.066	13.197	13.330
2.6	13.464	13.599	13.736	13.874	14.013	14.154	14.296	14.440	14.585	14.732
2.7	14.880	15.029	15.180	15.333	15.487	15.643	15.800	15.959	16.119	16.281
2.8	16.445	16.610	16.777	16.945	17.116	17.288	17.462	17.637	17.814	17.993
2.9	18.174	18.357	18.541	18.728	18.916	19.106	19.298	19.492	19.688	19.886
3.0	20.086	20.287	20.491	20.697	20.905	21.115	21.328	21.542	21.758	21.977
3.1	22.198	22.421	22.646	22.874	23.104	23.336	23.571	23.807	24.047	24.288
3.2	24.533	24.779	25.028	25.280	25.534	25.790	26.050	26.311	26.576	26.843
3.3	27.113	27.385	27.660	27.938	28.219	28.503	28.789	29.079	29.371	29.666
3.4	29.964	30.265	30.569	30.877	31.187	31.500	31.817	32.137	32.460	32.786
3.5	33.115	33.448	33.784	34.124	34.467	34.813	35.163	35.517	35.874	36.234
3.6	36.598	36.966	37.338	37.713	38.092	38.475	38.861	39.252	39.646	40.045
3.7	40.447	40.854	41.264	41.679	42.098	42.521	42.948	43.380	43.816	44.256
3.8	44.701	45.150	45.604	46.063	46.525	46.993	47.465	47.942	48.424	48.911
3.9	49.402	49.899	50.400	50.907	51.419	51.935	52.457	52.985	53.517	54.055
4.	54.598	60.340	66.686	73.700	81.451	90.017	99.484	109.95	121.51	134.29
5.	148.41	164.02	181.27	200.34	221.41	244.69	270.43	298.87	330.30	365.04
6.	403.43	445.86	492.75	544.57	601.85	665.14	735.10	812.41	897.85	992.27
7.	1096.6	1212.0	1339.4	1480.3	1636.0	1808.0	1998.2	2208.3	2440.6	2697.3
8.	2981.0	3294.5	3641.0	4023.9	4447.1	4914.8	5431.7	6002.9	6634.2	7332.0
9.	8103.1	8955.3	9897.1	10938	12088	13360	14765	16318	18034	19930
10.	22026									

Appendix B

Areas
under the
Standard
Normal Curve
from 0 to z

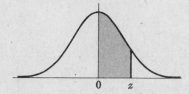

z	0	1	2	3	4	5	6	7	8	9
0.0	.0000	.0040	.0080	.0120	.0160	.0199	.0239	.0279	.0319	.0359
0.1	.0398	.0438	.0478	.0517	.0557	.0596	.0636	.0675	.0714	.0753
0.2	.0793	.0832	.0871	.0910	.0948	.0987	.1026	.1064	.1103	.1141
0.3	.1179	.1217	.1255	.1293	.1331	.1368	.1406	.1443	.1480	.1517
0.4	.1554	.1591	.1628	.1664	.1700	.1736	.1772	.1808	.1844	.1879
0.5	.1915	.1950	.1985	.2019	.2054	.2088	.2123	.2157	.2190	.2224
0.6	.2258	.2291	.2324	.2357	.2389	.2422	.2454	.2486	.2518	.2549
0.7	.2580	.2612	.2642	.2673	.2704	.2734	.2764	.2794	.2823	.2852
0.8	.2881	.2910	.2939	.2967	.2996	.3023	.3051	.3078	.3106	.3133
0.9	.3159	.3186	.3212	.3238	.3264	.3289	.3315	.3340	.3365	.3389
1.0	.3413	.3438	.3461	.3485	.3508	.3531	.3554	.3577	.3599	.3621
1.1	.3643	.3665	.3686	.3708	.3729	.3749	.3770	.3790	.3810	.3830
1.2	.3849	.3869	.3888	.3907	.3925	.3944	.3962	.3980	.3997	.4015
1.3	.4032	.4049	.4066	.4082	.4099	.4115	.4131	.4147	.4162	.4177
1.4	.4192	.4207	.4222	.4236	.4251	.4265	.4279	.4292	.4306	.4319
1.5	.4332	.4345	.4357	.4370	.4382	.4394	.4406	.4418	.4429	.4441
1.6	.4452	.4463	.4474	.4484	.4495	.4505	.4515	.4525	.4535	.4545
1.7	.4554	.4564	.4573	.4582	.4591	.4599	.4608	.4616	.4625	.4633
1.8	.4641	.4649	.4656	.4664	.4671	.4678	.4686	.4693	.4699	.4706
1.9	.4713	.4719	.4726	.4732	.4738	.4744	.4750	.4756	.4761	.4767
2.0	.4772	.4778	.4783	.4788	.4793	.4798	.4803	.4808	.4812	.4817
2.1	.4821	.4826	.4830	.4834	.4838	.4842	.4846	.4850	.4854	.4857
2.2	.4861	.4864	.4868	.4871	.4875	.4878	.4881	.4884	.4887	.4890
2.3	.4893	.4896	.4898	.4901	.4904	.4906	.4909	.4911	.4913	.4916
2.4	.4918	.4920	.4922	.4925	.4027	.4929	.4931	.4932	.4934	.4936
2.5	.4938	.4940	.4941	.4943	.4945	.4946	.4948	.4949	.4951	.4952
2.6	.4953	.4955	.4956	.4957	.4959	.4960	.4961	.4962	.4963	.4964
2.7	.4965	.4966	.4967	.4968	.4969	.4970	.4971	.4972	.4973	.4974
2.8	.4974	.4975	.4976	.4977	.4977	.4978	.4979	.4979	.4980	.4981
2.9	.4981	.4982	.4982	.4983	.4984	.4984	.4985	.4985	.4986	.4986
3.0	.4987	.4987	.4987	.4988	.4988	.4989	.4989	.4989	.4990	.4990
3.1	.4990	.4991	.4991	.4991	.4992	.4992	.4992	.4992	.4993	.4993
3.2	.4993	.4993	.4994	.4994	.4994	.4994	.4994	.4995	.4995	.4995
3.3	.4995	.4995	.4995	.4996	.4996	.4996	.4996	.4996	.4996	.4997
3.4	.4997	.4997	.4997	.4997	.4997	.4997	.4997	.4997	.4997	.4998
3.5	.4998	.4998	.4998	.4998	.4998	.4998	.4998	.4998	.4998	.4998
3.6	.4998	.4998	.4999	.4999	.4999	.4999	.4999	.4999	.4999	.4999
3.7	.4999	.4999	.4999	.4999	.4999	.4999	.4999	.4999	.4999	.4900
3.8	.4999	.4999	.4999	.4999	.4999	.4999	.4999	.4999	.4999	.4999
3.9	.5000	.5000	.5000	.5000	.5000	.5000	.5000	.5000	.5000	.5000

Appendix C

Cumulative Binomial Distribution*

$$R_B(X \mid n, p) \qquad\qquad F_B(X \mid n, p)$$
$$(p \leq 0.5) \qquad\qquad\qquad (p \geq 0.5)$$

X					$n = 1$						X
	p = 01	02	03	04	05	06	07	08	09	10 = (1 − p)	
1	0100	0200	0300	0400	0500	0600	0700	0800	0900	1000	0
	p = 11	12	13	14	15	16	17	18	19	20 = (1 − p)	
1	1100	1200	1300	1400	1500	1600	1700	1800	1900	2000	0
	p = 21	22	23	24	25	26	27	28	29	30 = (1 − p)	
1	2100	2200	2300	2400	2500	2600	2700	2800	2900	3000	0
	p = 31	32	33	34	35	36	37	38	39	40 = (1 − p)	
1	3100	3200	3300	3400	3500	3600	3700	3800	3900	4000	0
	p = 41	42	43	44	45	46	47	48	49	50 = (1 − p)	
1	4100	4200	4300	4400	4500	4600	4700	4800	4900	5000	0

X					$n = 2$						X
	p = 01	02	03	04	05	06	07	08	09	10 = (1 − p)	
1	0199	0396	0591	0784	0975	1164	1351	1536	1719	1900	1
2	0001	0004	0009	0016	0025	0036	0049	0064	0081	0100	0
	p = 11	12	13	14	15	16	17	18	19	20 = (1 − p)	
1	2079	2256	2431	2604	2775	2944	3111	3276	3439	3600	1
2	0121	0144	0169	0196	0225	0256	0289	0324	0361	0400	0
	p = 21	22	23	24	25	26	27	28	29	30 = (1 − p)	
1	3759	3916	4071	4224	4375	4524	4671	4816	4959	5100	1
2	0441	0484	0529	0576	0625	0676	0729	0784	0841	0900	0
	p = 31	32	33	34	35	36	37	38	39	40 = (1 − p)	
1	5239	5376	5511	5644	5775	5904	6031	6156	6279	6400	1
2	0961	1024	1089	1156	1225	1296	1369	1444	1521	1600	0
	p = 41	42	43	44	45	46	47	48	49	50 = (1 − p)	
1	6519	6636	6751	6864	6975	7084	7191	7296	7399	7500	1
2	1681	1764	1849	1936	2025	2116	2209	2304	2401	2500	0

X					$n = 3$						X
	p = 01	02	03	04	05	06	07	08	09	10 = (1 − p)	
1	0297	0588	0873	1153	1426	1694	1956	2213	2464	2710	2
2	0003	0012	0026	0047	0073	0104	0140	0182	0228	0280	1
3				0001	0001	0002	0003	0005	0007	0010	0
	p = 11	12	13	14	15	16	17	18	19	20 = (1 − p)	
1	2950	3185	3415	3639	3859	4073	4282	4486	4686	4880	2
2	0336	0397	0463	0533	0608	0686	0769	0855	0946	1040	1
3	0013	0017	0022	0027	0034	0041	0049	0058	0069	0080	0
	p = 21	22	23	24	25	26	27	28	29	30 = (1 − p)	
1	5070	5254	5435	5610	5781	5948	6110	6268	6421	6570	2
2	1138	1239	1344	1452	1563	1676	1793	1913	2035	2160	1
3	0093	0106	0122	0138	0156	0176	0197	0220	0244	0270	0
	p = 31	32	33	34	35	36	37	38	39	40 = (1 − p)	
1	6715	6856	6992	7125	7254	7379	7500	7617	7730	7840	2
2	2287	2417	2548	2682	2818	2955	3094	3235	3377	3520	1
3	0298	0328	0359	0393	0429	0467	0507	0549	0593	0640	0
	p = 41	42	43	44	45	46	47	48	49	50 = (1 − p)	
1	7946	8049	8148	8244	8336	8425	8511	8594	8673	8750	2
2	3665	3810	3957	4104	4253	4401	4551	4700	4850	5000	1
3	0689	0741	0795	0852	0911	0973	1038	1106	1176	1250	0

X					$n = 4$						X
	p = 01	02	03	04	05	06	07	08	09	10 = (1 − p)	
1	0394	0776	1147	1507	1855	2193	2519	2836	3143	3439	3
2	0006	0023	0052	0091	0140	0199	0267	0344	0430	0523	2
3			0001	0002	0005	0008	0013	0019	0027	0037	1
4								0001	0001		0
	p = 11	12	13	14	15	16	17	18	19	20 = (1 − p)	
1	3726	4003	4271	4530	4780	5021	5254	5479	5695	5904	3
2	0624	0732	0847	0968	1095	1228	1366	1509	1656	1808	2
3	0049	0063	0079	0098	0120	0144	0171	0202	0235	0272	1
4	0001	0002	0003	0004	0005	0007	0008	0010	0013	0016	0
	p = 21	22	23	24	25	26	27	28	29	30 = (1 − p)	
1	6105	6298	6485	6664	6836	7001	7160	7313	7459	7599	3
2	1963	2122	2285	2450	2617	2787	2959	3132	3307	3483	2
3	0312	0356	0403	0453	0508	0566	0628	0694	0763	0837	1
4	0019	0023	0028	0033	0039	0046	0053	0061	0071	0081	0

X					$n = 4$ (Continued)						X
	p = 31	32	33	34	35	36	37	38	39	40 = (1 − p)	
1	7733	7862	7985	8103	8215	8322	8425	8522	8615	8704	3
2	3660	3837	4015	4193	4370	4547	4724	4900	5075	5248	2
3	0915	0996	1082	1171	1265	1362	1464	1569	1679	1792	1
4	0092	0105	0119	0134	0150	0168	0187	0209	0231	0256	0
	p = 41	42	43	44	45	46	47	48	49	50 = (1 − p)	
1	8788	8868	8944	9017	9085	9150	9211	9269	9323	9375	3
2	5420	5590	5759	5926	6090	6252	6412	6569	6724	6875	2
3	1909	2030	2155	2283	2415	2550	2689	2831	2977	3125	1
4	0283	0311	0342	0375	0410	0448	0488	0531	0576	0625	0

X					$n = 5$						X
	p = 01	02	03	04	05	06	07	08	09	10 = (1 − p)	
1	0490	0961	1413	1846	2262	2661	3043	3409	3760	4095	4
2	0010	0038	0085	0148	0226	0319	0425	0544	0674	0815	3
3		0001	0003	0006	0012	0020	0031	0045	0063	0086	2
4						0001	0002	0003	0005		1
	p = 11	12	13	14	15	16	17	18	19	20 = (1 − p)	
1	4416	4723	5016	5296	5563	5818	6061	6293	6513	6723	4
2	0965	1125	1292	1467	1648	1835	2027	2224	2424	2627	3
3	0112	0143	0179	0220	0266	0318	0375	0437	0505	0579	2
4	0007	0009	0013	0017	0022	0029	0036	0045	0055	0067	1
5					0001	0001	0001	0001	0002	0003	0
	p = 21	22	23	24	25	26	27	28	29	30 = (1 − p)	
1	6923	7113	7293	7464	7627	7781	7927	8065	8196	8319	4
2	2833	3041	3251	3461	3672	3883	4093	4303	4511	4718	3
3	0659	0744	0836	0933	1035	1143	1257	1376	1501	1631	2
4	0081	0097	0114	0134	0156	0181	0208	0238	0272	0308	1
5	0004	0005	0006	0008	0010	0012	0014	0017	0021	0024	0
	p = 31	32	33	34	35	36	37	38	39	40 = (1 − p)	
1	8436	8546	8650	8748	8840	8926	9008	9084	9155	9222	4
2	4923	5125	5325	5522	5716	5906	6093	6276	6455	6630	3
3	1766	1905	2050	2199	2352	2509	2670	2835	3003	3174	2
4	0347	0390	0436	0486	0540	0598	0660	0726	0796	0870	1
5	0029	0034	0039	0045	0053	0060	0069	0079	0090	0102	0
	p = 41	42	43	44	45	46	47	48	49	50 = (1 − p)	
1	9285	9344	9398	9449	9497	9541	9582	9620	9655	9688	4
2	6801	6967	7129	7286	7438	7585	7728	7865	7998	8125	3
3	3349	3525	3705	3886	4069	4253	4439	4625	4813	5000	2
4	0949	1033	1121	1214	1312	1415	1522	1635	1753	1875	1
5	0116	0131	0147	0165	0185	0206	0229	0255	0282	0313	0

X					$n = 6$						X
	p = 01	02	03	04	05	06	07	08	09	10 = (1 − p)	
1	0585	1142	1670	2172	2649	3101	3530	3936	4321	4686	5
2	0015	0057	0125	0216	0328	0459	0608	0773	0952	1143	4
3		0002	0005	0012	0022	0038	0058	0085	0118	0159	3
4				0001	0002	0003	0005	0008	0013		2
5									0001		1
	p = 11	12	13	14	15	16	17	18	19	20 = (1 − p)	
1	5030	5356	5664	5954	6229	6487	6731	6960	7176	7379	5
2	1345	1556	1776	2003	2235	2472	2713	2956	3201	3446	4
3	0206	0261	0324	0395	0473	0560	0655	0759	0870	0989	3
4	0018	0025	0034	0045	0059	0075	0094	0116	0141	0170	2
5	0001	0001	0002	0003	0004	0005	0007	0010	0013	0016	1
6										0001	0
	p = 21	22	23	24	25	26	27	28	29	30 = (1 − p)	
1	7569	7748	7916	8073	8220	8358	8487	8607	8719	8824	5
2	3692	3937	4180	4422	4661	4896	5128	5356	5580	5798	4
3	1115	1250	1391	1539	1694	1856	2023	2196	2374	2557	3
4	0202	0239	0280	0326	0376	0431	0492	0557	0628	0705	2
5	0020	0025	0031	0038	0046	0056	0067	0079	0093	0109	1
6	0001	0001	0001	0002	0002	0003	0004	0005	0006	0007	0
	p = 31	32	33	34	35	36	37	38	39	40 = (1 − p)	
1	8921	9011	9095	9173	9246	9313	9375	9432	9485	9533	5
2	6012	6220	6422	6619	6809	6994	7172	7343	7508	7667	4
3	2744	2936	3130	3328	3529	3732	3937	4143	4350	4557	3
4	0787	0875	0969	1069	1174	1286	1404	1527	1657	1792	2
5	0127	0148	0170	0195	0223	0254	0288	0325	0365	0410	1
6	0009	0011	0013	0015	0018	0022	0026	0030	0035	0041	0

*Adapted from Appendix A of P. Jedamus and R. Frame, *Business Decision Theory*, McGraw-Hill, New York, 1969.

X	n = 6 (Continued)										X
	p = 41	42	43	44	45	46	47	48	49	50 = (1 − p)	
1	9578	9619	9657	9692	9723	9752	9778	9802	9824	9844	5
2	7819	7965	8105	8238	8364	8485	8599	8707	8810	8906	4
3	4764	4971	5177	5382	5585	5786	5985	6180	6373	6563	3
4	1933	2080	2232	2390	2553	2721	2893	3070	3252	3438	2
5	0458	0510	0566	0627	0692	0762	0837	0917	1003	1094	1
6	0048	0055	0063	0073	0083	0095	0108	0122	0138	0156	0

X	n = 7										X
	p = 01	02	03	04	05	06	07	08	09	10 = (1 − p)	
1	0679	1319	1920	2486	3017	3515	3983	4422	4832	5217	6
2	0020	0079	0171	0294	0444	0618	0813	1026	1255	1497	5
3		0003	0009	0020	0038	0063	0097	0140	0193	0257	4
4				0001	0002	0004	0007	0012	0018	0027	3
5								0001	0001	0002	2
	p = 11	12	13	14	15	16	17	18	19	20 = (1 − p)	
1	5577	5913	6227	6521	6794	7049	7286	7507	7712	7903	6
2	1750	2012	2281	2556	2834	3115	3396	3677	3956	4233	5
3	0331	0416	0513	0620	0738	0866	1005	1154	1313	1480	4
4	0039	0054	0072	0094	0121	0153	0189	0231	0279	0333	3
5	0003	0004	0006	0009	0012	0017	0022	0029	0037	0047	2
6					0001	0001	0001	0002	0003	0004	1
	p = 21	22	23	24	25	26	27	28	29	30 = (1 − p)	
1	8080	8243	8395	8535	8665	8785	8895	8997	9090	9176	6
2	4506	4775	5040	5298	5551	5796	6035	6266	6490	6706	5
3	1657	1841	2033	2231	2436	2646	2861	3081	3304	3529	4
4	0394	0461	0536	0617	0706	0802	0905	1016	1134	1260	3
5	0058	0072	0088	0107	0129	0153	0181	0213	0248	0288	2
6	0005	0006	0008	0011	0013	0017	0021	0026	0031	0038	1
7					0001	0001	0001	0001	0002	0002	0
	p = 31	32	33	34	35	36	37	38	39	40 = (1 − p)	
1	9255	9328	9394	9454	9510	9560	9606	9648	9686	9720	6
2	6914	7113	7304	7487	7662	7828	7987	8137	8279	8414	5
3	3757	3987	4217	4447	4677	4906	5134	5359	5581	5801	4
4	1394	1534	1682	1837	1998	2167	2341	2521	2707	2898	3
5	0332	0380	0434	0492	0556	0625	0701	0782	0869	0963	2
6	0046	0055	0065	0077	0090	0105	0123	0142	0164	0188	1
7	0003	0003	0004	0005	0006	0008	0009	0011	0014	0016	0
	p = 41	42	43	44	45	46	47	48	49	50 = (1 − p)	
1	9751	9779	9805	9827	9848	9866	9883	9897	9910	9922	0
2	8541	8660	8772	8877	8976	0068	9153	9233	9307	9375	5
3	0017	6229	6436	6638	6836	7027	7213	7393	7567	7734	4
4	3094	3294	3498	3706	3917	4131	4346	4563	4781	5000	3
5	1063	1169	1282	1402	1529	1663	1803	1951	2105	2266	2
6	0216	0246	0279	0316	0357	0402	0451	0504	0562	0625	1
7	0019	0023	0027	0032	0037	0044	0051	0059	0068	0078	0

X	n = 8										X
	p = 01	02	03	04	05	06	07	08	09	10 = (1 − p)	
1	0773	1492	2163	2786	3366	3904	4404	4868	5297	5695	7
2	0027	0103	0223	0381	0572	0792	1035	1298	1577	1869	6
3	0001	0004	0013	0031	0058	0096	0147	0211	0289	0381	5
4			0001	0002	0004	0007	0013	0022	0034	0050	4
5							0001	0001	0003	0004	3
	p = 11	12	13	14	15	16	17	18	19	20 = (1 − p)	
1	6063	6404	6718	7008	7275	7521	7718	7956	8147	8322	7
2	2171	2480	2794	3111	3428	3744	4057	4366	4670	4967	6
3	0487	0608	0743	0891	1052	1226	1412	1608	1815	2031	5
4	0071	0097	0129	0168	0214	0267	0328	0397	0476	0563	4
5	0007	0010	0015	0021	0029	0038	0050	0065	0083	0104	3
6		0001	0001	0002	0002	0003	0005	0007	0009	0012	2
7									0001	0001	1
	p = 21	22	23	24	25	26	27	28	29	30 = (1 − p)	
1	8483	8630	8764	8887	8999	9101	9194	9278	9354	9424	7
2	5257	5538	5811	6075	6329	6573	6807	7031	7244	7447	6
3	2255	2486	2724	2967	3215	3465	3718	3973	4228	4482	5
4	0659	0765	0880	1004	1138	1281	1433	1594	1763	1941	4
5	0129	0158	0191	0230	0273	0322	0377	0438	0505	0580	3
6	0016	0021	0027	0034	0042	0052	0064	0078	0094	0113	2
7	0001	0002	0002	0003	0004	0005	0006	0008	0010	0013	1
8									0001	0001	0
	p = 31	32	33	34	35	36	37	38	39	40 = (1 − p)	
1	9486	9543	9594	9640	9681	9719	9752	9782	9808	9832	7
2	7640	7822	7994	8156	8309	8452	8586	8711	8828	8936	6
3	4736	4987	5236	5481	5722	5958	6189	6415	6634	6846	5
4	2126	2319	2519	2724	2936	3153	3374	3599	3828	4059	4
5	0661	0750	0846	0949	1061	1180	1307	1443	1586	1737	3
6	0134	0159	0187	0218	0253	0293	0336	0385	0439	0498	2
7	0016	0020	0024	0030	0036	0043	0051	0061	0072	0085	1
8	0001	0001	0001	0002	0002	0003	0004	0004	0005	0007	0
	p = 41	42	43	44	45	46	47	48	49	50 = (1 − p)	
1	9853	9872	9889	9903	9916	9928	9938	9947	9954	9961	7
2	9037	9130	9216	9295	9368	9435	9496	9552	9602	9648	6
3	7052	7250	7440	7624	7799	7966	8125	8276	8419	8555	5
4	4292	4527	4762	4996	5230	5463	5694	5922	6146	6367	4
5	1895	2062	2235	2416	2604	2798	2999	3205	3416	3633	3
6	0563	0634	0711	0794	0885	0982	1086	1198	1318	1445	2
7	0100	0117	0136	0157	0181	0208	0239	0272	0310	0352	1
8	0008	0010	0012	0014	0017	0020	0024	0028	0033	0039	0

X	n = 9										X
	p = 01	02	03	04	05	06	07	08	09	10 = (1 − p)	
1	0865	1663	2398	3075	3698	4270	4796	5278	5721	6126	8
2	0034	0131	0282	0478	0712	0978	1271	1583	1912	2252	7
3	0001	0006	0020	0045	0084	0138	0209	0298	0405	0530	6
4			0001	0003	0006	0013	0023	0037	0057	0083	5
5						0001	0002	0003	0005	0009	4
6										0001	3
	p = 11	12	13	14	15	16	17	18	19	20 = (1 − p)	
1	6496	6835	7145	7427	7684	7918	8131	8324	8499	8658	8
2	2599	2951	3304	3657	4005	4348	4685	5012	5330	5638	7
3	0672	0833	1009	1202	1409	1629	1861	2105	2357	2618	6
4	0117	0158	0209	0269	0339	0420	0512	0615	0730	0856	5
5	0014	0021	0030	0041	0056	0075	0098	0125	0158	0196	4
6	0001	0002	0003	0004	0006	0009	0013	0017	0023	0031	3
7						0001	0001	0002	0002	0003	2
	p = 21	22	23	24	25	26	27	28	29	30 = (1 − p)	
1	8801	8931	9048	9154	9249	9335	9411	9480	9542	9596	8
2	5934	6218	6491	6750	6997	7230	7452	7660	7856	8040	7
3	2885	3158	3434	3713	3993	4273	4552	4829	5102	5372	6
4	0994	1144	1304	1475	1657	1849	2050	2260	2478	2703	5
5	0240	0291	0350	0416	0489	0571	0662	0762	0870	0988	4
6	0040	0051	0065	0081	0100	0122	0149	0179	0213	0253	3
7	0004	0006	0008	0010	0013	0017	0022	0028	0035	0043	2
8			0001	0001	0001	0001	0002	0003	0003	0004	1
	p = 31	32	33	34	35	36	37	38	39	40 = (1 − p)	
1	9645	9689	9728	9762	9793	9820	9844	9865	9883	9899	8
2	8212	8372	8522	8661	8789	8908	9017	9118	9210	9295	7
3	5636	5894	6146	6390	6627	6856	7076	7287	7489	7682	6
4	2935	3173	3415	3662	3911	4163	4416	4669	4922	5174	5
5	1115	1252	1398	1553	1717	1890	2072	2262	2460	2666	4
6	0298	0348	0404	0467	0536	0612	0696	0787	0886	0994	3
7	0053	0064	0078	0094	0112	0133	0157	0184	0215	0250	2
8	0006	0007	0009	0011	0014	0017	0021	0026	0031	0038	1
9				0001	0001	0001	0001	0002	0002	0003	0
	p = 41	42	43	44	45	46	47	48	49	50 = (1 − p)	
1	9913	9926	9936	9946	9954	9961	9967	9972	9977	9980	8
2	9372	9442	9505	9563	9615	9662	9704	9741	9775	9805	7
3	7866	8039	8204	8359	8505	8642	8769	8889	8999	9102	6
4	5424	5670	5913	6152	6386	6614	6836	7052	7260	7461	5
5	2878	3097	3322	3551	3786	4024	4265	4509	4754	5000	4
0	1109	1233	1366	1508	1658	1817	1985	2161	2346	2539	3
7	0290	0334	0383	0437	0498	0564	0637	0717	0804	0898	2
8	0046	0055	0065	0077	0091	0107	0125	0145	0169	0195	1
9	0003	0004	0005	0006	0008	0009	0011	0014	0016	0020	0

X	n = 10										X
	p = 01	02	03	04	05	06	07	08	09	10 = (1 − p)	
1	0956	1829	2626	3352	4013	4614	5160	5656	6106	6513	9
2	0043	0162	0345	0582	0861	1176	1517	1879	2254	2639	8
3	0001	0009	0028	0062	0115	0188	0283	0401	0540	0702	7
4			0001	0004	0010	0020	0036	0058	0088	0128	6
5					0001	0002	0003	0006	0010	0016	5
6									0001	0001	4
	p = 11	12	13	14	15	16	17	18	19	20 = (1 − p)	
1	6882	7215	7516	7787	8031	8251	8448	8626	8784	8926	9
2	3028	3417	3804	4184	4557	4920	5270	5608	5932	6242	8
3	0884	1087	1308	1545	1798	2064	2341	2628	2922	3222	7
4	0178	0239	0313	0400	0500	0614	0741	0883	1039	1209	6
5	0025	0037	0053	0073	0099	0130	0168	0213	0266	0328	5
6	0003	0004	0006	0010	0014	0020	0027	0037	0049	0064	4
7			0001	0001	0001	0002	0003	0004	0006	0009	3
8									0001	0001	2
	p = 21	22	23	24	25	26	27	28	29	30 = (1 − p)	
1	9053	9166	9267	9357	9437	9508	9570	9626	9674	9718	9
2	6536	6815	7079	7327	7560	7778	7981	8170	8345	8507	8
3	3526	3831	4137	4442	4744	5042	5335	5622	5901	6172	7
4	1391	1587	1794	2012	2241	2479	2726	2979	3239	3504	6
5	0399	0479	0569	0670	0781	0904	1037	1181	1337	1503	5
6	0082	0104	0130	0161	0197	0239	0287	0342	0404	0473	4
7	0012	0016	0021	0027	0035	0045	0056	0070	0087	0106	3
8	0001	0002	0002	0003	0004	0006	0007	0010	0012	0016	2
9							0001	0001	0001	0001	1
	p = 31	32	33	34	35	36	37	38	39	40 = (1 − p)	
1	9755	9789	9818	9843	9865	9885	9902	9916	9929	9940	9
2	8656	8794	8920	9035	9140	9236	9323	9402	9473	9536	8
3	6434	6687	6930	7162	7384	7595	7794	7983	8160	8327	7
4	3772	4044	4316	4589	4862	5132	5400	5664	5923	6177	6
5	1679	1867	2064	2270	2485	2708	2939	3177	3420	3669	5
6	0551	0637	0732	0836	0949	1072	1205	1348	1500	1662	4
7	0129	0155	0185	0220	0260	0305	0356	0413	0477	0548	3
8	0020	0025	0032	0039	0048	0059	0071	0086	0103	0123	2
9	0002	0003	0003	0004	0005	0007	0009	0011	0014	0017	1
10								0001	0001	0001	0

n = 10 (Continued)

X	p = 41	42	43	44	45	46	47	48	49	50 = (1 − p)	X
1	9949	9957	9964	9970	9975	9979	9983	9986	9988	9990	9
2	9594	9645	9691	9731	9767	9799	9827	9852	9874	9893	8
3	8483	8628	8764	8889	9004	9111	9209	9298	9379	9453	7
4	6425	6665	6898	7123	7340	7547	7745	7933	8112	8281	6
5	3922	4178	4436	4696	4956	5216	5474	5730	5982	6230	5
6	1834	2016	2207	2407	2616	2832	3057	3288	3526	3770	4
7	0626	0712	0806	0908	1020	1141	1271	1410	1560	1719	3
8	0146	0172	0202	0236	0274	0317	0366	0420	0480	0547	2
9	0021	0025	0031	0037	0045	0054	0065	0077	0091	0107	1
10	0001	0002	0002	0003	0003	0004	0005	0006	0008	0010	0

n = 11

X	p = 01	02	03	04	05	06	07	08	09	10 = (1 − p)	X
1	1047	1993	2847	3618	4312	4937	5499	6004	6456	6862	10
2	0052	0195	0413	0692	1019	1382	1772	2181	2601	3026	9
3	0002	0012	0037	0083	0152	0248	0370	0519	0695	0896	8
4			0002	0007	0016	0030	0053	0085	0129	0185	7
5					0001	0003	0005	0010	0017	0028	6
6								0001	0002	0003	5

X	p = 11	12	13	14	15	16	17	18	19	20 = (1 − p)	X
1	7225	7549	7839	8097	8327	8531	8712	8873	9015	9141	10
2	3452	3873	4286	4689	5078	5453	5811	6151	6474	6779	9
3	1120	1366	1632	1915	2212	2521	2839	3164	3494	3826	8
4	0256	0341	0442	0560	0694	0846	1013	1197	1397	1611	7
5	0042	0061	0087	0119	0159	0207	0266	0334	0413	0504	6
6	0005	0008	0012	0018	0027	0037	0051	0068	0090	0117	5
7		0001	0001	0002	0003	0005	0007	0010	0014	0020	4
8							0001	0001	0002	0002	3

X	p = 21	22	23	24	25	26	27	28	29	30 = (1 − p)	X
1	9252	9350	9436	9511	9578	9636	9686	9730	9769	9802	10
2	7065	7333	7582	7814	8029	8227	8410	8577	8730	8870	9
3	4158	4488	4814	5134	5448	5753	6049	6335	6610	6873	8
4	1840	2081	2333	2596	2867	3146	3430	3719	4011	4304	7
5	0607	0723	0851	0992	1146	1313	1493	1685	1888	2103	6
6	0148	0186	0231	0283	0343	0412	0490	0577	0674	0782	5
7	0027	0035	0046	0059	0076	0095	0119	0146	0179	0216	4
8	0003	0005	0007	0009	0012	0016	0021	0027	0034	0043	3
9			0001	0001	0001	0002	0002	0003	0004	0006	2

X	p = 31	32	33	34	35	36	37	38	39	40 = (1 − p)	X
1	9831	9856	9878	9896	9912	9926	9938	9948	9956	9964	10
2	8997	9112	9216	9310	9394	9470	9537	9597	9650	9698	9
3	7123	7361	7587	7799	7999	8186	8360	8522	8672	8811	8
4	4598	4890	5179	5464	5744	6019	6286	6545	6796	7037	7
5	2328	2563	2807	3059	3317	3581	3850	4122	4397	4672	6
6	0901	1031	1171	1324	1487	1661	1847	2043	2249	2465	5
7	0260	0309	0366	0430	0501	0581	0670	0768	0876	0994	4
8	0054	0067	0082	0101	0122	0148	0177	0210	0249	0293	3
9	0008	0010	0013	0016	0020	0026	0032	0039	0048	0059	2
10	0001	0001	0001	0002	0002	0003	0004	0005	0006	0007	1

X	p = 41	42	43	44	45	46	47	48	49	50 = (1 − p)	X
1	9970	9975	9979	9983	9986	9989	9991	9992	9994	9995	10
2	9739	9776	9808	9836	9861	9882	9900	9916	9930	9941	9
3	8938	9055	9162	9260	9348	9428	9499	9564	9622	9673	8
4	7269	7490	7700	7900	8089	8266	8433	8588	8733	8867	7
5	4948	5223	5495	5764	6029	6288	6541	6787	7026	7256	6
6	2690	2924	3166	3414	3669	3929	4193	4460	4729	5000	5
7	1121	1260	1408	1568	1738	1919	2110	2312	2523	2744	4
8	0343	0399	0461	0532	0610	0696	0791	0895	1009	1133	3
9	0072	0087	0104	0125	0148	0175	0206	0241	0282	0327	2
10	0009	0012	0014	0018	0022	0027	0033	0040	0049	0059	1
11	0001	0001	0001	0001	0002	0002	0002	0003	0004	0005	0

n = 12

X	p = 01	02	03	04	05	06	07	08	09	10 = (1 − p)	X
1	1136	2153	3062	3873	4596	5241	5814	6323	6775	7176	11
2	0062	0231	0486	0809	1184	1595	2033	2487	2948	3410	10
3	0002	0015	0048	0107	0196	0316	0468	0652	0866	1109	9
4		0001	0003	0010	0022	0043	0075	0120	0180	0256	8
5				0001	0002	0004	0009	0016	0027	0043	7
6							0001	0002	0003	0005	6
7										0001	5

X	p = 11	12	13	14	15	16	17	18	19	20 = (1 − p)	X
1	7530	7843	8120	8363	8578	8766	8931	9076	9202	9313	11
2	3867	4314	4748	5166	5565	5945	6304	6641	6957	7251	10
3	1377	1667	1977	2303	2642	2990	3344	3702	4060	4417	9
4	0351	0464	0597	0750	0922	1114	1324	1552	1795	2054	8
5	0065	0095	0133	0181	0239	0310	0393	0489	0600	0726	7
6	0009	0014	0022	0033	0046	0065	0088	0116	0151	0194	6
7	0001	0002	0003	0004	0007	0010	0015	0021	0029	0039	5
8					0001	0001	0002	0003	0004	0006	4
9										0001	3

n = 12 (Continued)

X	p = 21	22	23	24	25	26	27	28	29	30 = (1 − p)	X
1	9409	9493	9566	9629	9683	9730	9771	9806	9836	9862	11
2	7524	7776	8009	8222	8416	8594	8755	8900	9032	9150	10
3	4768	5114	5450	5778	6093	6397	6687	6963	7225	7472	9
4	2326	2610	2904	3205	3512	3824	4137	4452	4765	5075	8
5	0866	1021	1192	1377	1576	1790	2016	2254	2504	2763	7
6	0245	0304	0374	0453	0544	0646	0760	0887	1026	1178	6
7	0052	0068	0089	0113	0143	0178	0219	0267	0322	0386	5
8	0008	0011	0016	0021	0028	0036	0047	0060	0076	0095	4
9	0001	0001	0002	0003	0004	0005	0007	0010	0013	0017	3
10						0001	0001	0001	0002	0002	2

X	p = 31	32	33	34	35	36	37	38	39	40 = (1 − p)	X
1	9884	9902	9918	9932	9943	9953	9961	9968	9973	9978	11
2	9256	9350	9435	9509	9576	9634	9685	9730	9770	9804	10
3	7704	7922	8124	8313	8487	8648	8795	8931	9054	9166	9
4	5381	5681	5973	6258	6533	6799	7053	7296	7528	7747	8
5	3032	3308	3590	3876	4167	4459	4751	5043	5332	5618	7
6	1343	1521	1711	1913	2127	2352	2588	2833	3087	3348	6
7	0458	0540	0632	0734	0846	0970	1106	1253	1411	1582	5
8	0118	0144	0176	0213	0255	0304	0359	0422	0493	0573	4
9	0022	0028	0036	0045	0056	0070	0086	0104	0127	0153	3
10	0003	0004	0005	0007	0008	0011	0014	0018	0022	0028	2
11				0001	0001	0001	0001	0002	0002	0003	1

X	p = 41	42	43	44	45	46	47	48	49	50 = (1 − p)	X
1	9982	9986	9988	9990	9992	9994	9995	9996	9997	9998	11
2	9834	9860	9882	9901	9917	9931	9943	9953	9961	9968	10
3	9267	9358	9440	9513	9579	9637	9688	9733	9773	9807	9
4	7953	8147	8329	8498	8655	8801	8934	9057	9168	9270	8
5	5899	6175	6443	6704	6956	7198	7430	7652	7862	8062	7
6	3616	3889	4167	4448	4731	5014	5297	5577	5855	6128	6
7	1765	1959	2164	2380	2607	2843	3089	3343	3604	3872	5
8	0662	0760	0869	0988	1117	1258	1411	1575	1751	1938	4
9	0183	0218	0258	0304	0356	0415	0481	0555	0638	0730	3
10	0035	0043	0053	0065	0079	0095	0114	0137	0163	0193	2
11	0004	0005	0007	0009	0011	0014	0017	0021	0026	0032	1
12				0001	0001	0001	0001	0001	0002	0002	0

n = 13

X	p = 01	02	03	04	05	06	07	08	09	10 = (1 − p)	X
1	1225	2310	3270	4118	4867	5526	6107	6617	7065	7458	12
2	0072	0270	0564	0932	1354	1814	2298	2794	3293	3787	11
3	0003	0020	0062	0135	0245	0392	0578	0799	1054	1339	10
4		0001	0005	0014	0031	0060	0103	0163	0242	0342	9
5				0001	0003	0007	0013	0024	0041	0065	8
6						0001	0001	0003	0005	0009	7
7									0001	0001	6

X	p = 11	12	13	14	15	16	17	18	19	20 = (1 − p)	X
1	7802	8102	8364	8592	8791	8963	9113	9242	9354	9450	12
2	4270	4738	5186	5614	6017	6396	6751	7080	7384	7664	11
3	1651	1985	2337	2704	3080	3463	3848	4231	4611	4983	10
4	0464	0609	0776	0967	1180	1414	1667	1939	2226	2527	9
5	0097	0139	0193	0260	0342	0438	0551	0681	0827	0991	8
6	0015	0024	0036	0053	0075	0104	0139	0183	0237	0300	7
7	0002	0003	0005	0008	0013	0019	0027	0038	0052	0070	6
8			0001	0001	0002	0003	0004	0006	0009	0012	5
9								0001	0001	0002	4

X	p = 21	22	23	24	25	26	27	28	29	30 = (1 − p)	X
1	9533	9604	9666	9718	9762	9800	9833	9860	9883	9903	12
2	7920	8154	8367	8559	8733	8889	9029	9154	9265	9363	11
3	5347	5699	6039	6364	6674	6968	7245	7505	7749	7975	10
4	2839	3161	3489	3822	4157	4493	4826	5155	5478	5794	9
5	1173	1371	1585	1816	2060	2319	2589	2870	3160	3457	8
6	0375	0462	0562	0675	0802	0944	1099	1270	1455	1654	7
7	0093	0120	0154	0195	0243	0299	0365	0440	0527	0624	6
8	0017	0024	0032	0043	0056	0073	0093	0118	0147	0182	5
9	0002	0004	0005	0007	0010	0013	0018	0024	0031	0040	4
10			0001	0001	0001	0002	0003	0004	0005	0007	3
11									0001	0001	2

X	p = 31	32	33	34	35	36	37	38	39	40 = (1 − p)	X
1	9920	9934	9945	9955	9963	9970	9975	9980	9984	9987	12
2	9450	9527	9594	9653	9704	9749	9787	9821	9849	9874	11
3	8185	8379	8557	8720	8868	9003	9125	9235	9333	9421	10
4	6101	6398	6683	6957	7217	7464	7698	7917	8123	8314	9
5	3760	4067	4376	4686	4995	5301	5603	5899	6188	6470	8
6	1867	2093	2331	2581	2841	3111	3388	3673	3962	4256	7
7	0733	0854	0988	1135	1295	1468	1654	1853	2065	2288	6
8	0223	0271	0326	0390	0462	0544	0635	0738	0851	0977	5
9	0052	0065	0082	0102	0126	0154	0187	0225	0270	0321	4
10	0009	0012	0015	0020	0025	0032	0040	0051	0063	0078	3
11	0001	0001	0002	0003	0003	0005	0006	0008	0010	0013	2
12						0001	0001	0001	0001		1

X	n = 13 (Continued)										X
	p = 41	42	43	44	45	46	47	48	49	50 = (1 − p)	
1	9990	9992	9993	9995	9996	9997	9997	9998	9998	9999	12
2	9895	9912	9928	9940	9951	9960	9967	9974	9979	9983	11
3	9499	9569	9630	9684	9731	9772	9808	9838	9865	9888	10
4	8492	8656	8807	8945	9071	9185	9288	9381	9464	9539	9
5	6742	7003	7254	7493	7721	7935	8137	8326	8502	8666	8
6	4552	4849	5146	5441	5732	6019	6299	6573	6838	7095	7
7	2524	2770	3025	3290	3563	3842	4127	4415	4707	5000	6
8	1114	1264	1426	1600	1788	1988	2200	2424	2659	2905	5
9	0379	0446	0520	0605	0698	0803	0918	1045	1183	1334	4
10	0096	0117	0141	0170	0203	0242	0287	0338	0396	0461	3
11	0017	0021	0027	0033	0041	0051	0063	0077	0093	0112	2
12	0002	0002	0003	0004	0005	0007	0009	0011	0014	0017	1
13							0001	0001	0001	0001	0

X	n = 14										X
	p = 01	02	03	04	05	06	07	08	09	10 = (1 − p)	
1	1313	2464	3472	4353	5123	5795	6380	6888	7330	7712	13
2	0084	0310	0645	1059	1530	2037	2564	3100	3632	4154	12
3	0003	0025	0077	0167	0301	0478	0698	0958	1255	1584	11
4		0001	0006	0019	0042	0080	0136	0214	0315	0441	10
5				0002	0004	0010	0020	0035	0059	0092	9
6						0001	0002	0004	0008	0015	8
7									0001	0002	7
	p = 11	12	13	14	15	16	17	18	19	20 = (1 − p)	
1	8044	8330	8577	8789	8972	9129	9264	9379	9477	9560	13
2	4658	5141	5599	6031	6433	6807	7152	7469	7758	8021	12
3	1939	2315	2708	3111	3521	3932	4341	4744	5138	5519	11
4	0594	0774	0979	1210	1465	1742	2038	2351	2679	3018	10
5	0137	0196	0269	0359	0467	0594	0741	0907	1093	1298	9
6	0024	0038	0057	0082	0115	0157	0209	0273	0349	0439	8
7	0003	0006	0009	0015	0022	0032	0046	0064	0087	0116	7
8		0001	0001	0002	0003	0005	0008	0012	0017	0024	6
9						0001	0001	0002	0003	0004	5
	p = 21	22	23	24	25	26	27	28	29	30 = (1 − p)	
1	9631	9691	9742	9786	9822	9852	9878	9899	9917	9932	13
2	8259	8473	8665	8837	8990	9126	9246	9352	9444	9525	12
3	5887	6239	0574	6891	7189	7467	7727	7967	8188	8392	11
4	3366	3719	4076	4432	4787	5136	5479	5813	6137	6448	10
5	1523	1765	2023	2297	2585	2884	3193	3509	3832	4158	9
6	0543	0662	0797	0949	1117	1301	1502	1718	1949	2195	8
7	0152	0196	0248	0310	0383	0467	0563	0673	0796	0933	7
8	0033	0045	0060	0079	0103	0132	0167	0208	0257	0315	6
9	0006	0008	0011	0016	0022	0029	0038	0050	0065	0083	5
10	0001	0001	0002	0002	0003	0005	0007	0009	0012	0017	4
11						0001	0001	0001	0002	0002	3
	p = 31	32	33	34	35	36	37	38	39	40 = (1 − p)	
1	9945	9955	9963	9970	9976	9981	9984	9988	9990	9992	13
2	9596	9657	9710	9756	9795	9828	9857	9881	9902	9919	12
3	8577	8746	8899	9037	9161	9271	9370	9457	9534	9602	11
4	6747	7032	7301	7556	7795	8018	8226	8418	8595	8757	10
5	4486	4813	5138	5458	5773	6080	6378	6666	6943	7207	9
6	2454	2724	3006	3297	3595	3899	4208	4519	4831	5141	8
7	1084	1250	1431	1626	1836	2059	2296	2545	2805	3075	7
8	0381	0458	0545	0643	0753	0876	1012	1162	1325	1501	6
9	0105	0131	0163	0200	0243	0294	0353	0420	0497	0583	5
10	0022	0029	0037	0048	0060	0076	0095	0117	0144	0175	4
11	0003	0005	0006	0008	0011	0014	0019	0024	0031	0039	3
12		0001	0001	0001	0001	0002	0003	0003	0005	0006	2
13										0001	1
	p = 41	42	43	44	45	46	47	48	49	50 = (1 − p)	
1	9994	9995	9996	9997	9998	9998	9999	9999	9999	9999	13
2	9934	9946	9956	9964	9971	9977	9981	9985	9988	9991	12
3	9661	9713	9758	9797	9830	9858	9883	9903	9921	9935	11
4	8905	9039	9161	9270	9368	9455	9532	9601	9661	9713	10
5	7459	7697	7922	8132	8328	8510	8678	8833	8974	9102	9
6	5450	5754	6052	6344	6627	6900	7163	7415	7654	7880	8
7	3355	3643	3937	4236	4539	4843	5148	5451	5751	6047	7
8	1692	1896	2113	2344	2586	2840	3105	3380	3663	3953	6
9	0680	0789	0910	1043	1189	1348	1520	1707	1906	2120	5
10	0212	0255	0304	0361	0426	0500	0583	0677	0782	0898	4
11	0049	0061	0076	0093	0114	0139	0168	0202	0241	0287	3
12	0008	0010	0013	0017	0022	0027	0034	0042	0053	0065	2
13	0001	0001	0001	0002	0003	0003	0004	0006	0007	0009	1
14										0001	0

X	n = 15										X
	p = 01	02	03	04	05	06	07	08	09	10 = (1 − p)	
1	1399	2614	3667	4579	5367	6047	6633	7137	7570	7941	14
2	0096	0353	0730	1191	1710	2262	2832	3403	3965	4510	13
3	0004	0030	0094	0203	0362	0571	0829	1130	1469	1841	12
4		0002	0008	0024	0055	0104	0175	0273	0399	0556	11
5			0001	0002	0006	0014	0028	0050	0082	0127	10
6					0001	0001	0003	0007	0013	0022	9
7								0001	0002	0003	8

X	n = 15 (Continued)										X
	p = 11	12	13	14	15	16	17	18	19	20 = (1 − p)	
1	8259	8530	8762	8959	9126	9269	9389	9490	9576	9648	14
2	5031	5524	5987	6417	6814	7179	7511	7813	8085	8329	13
3	2238	2654	3084	3520	3958	4392	4819	5234	5635	6020	12
4	0742	0959	1204	1476	1773	2092	2429	2782	3146	3518	11
5	0187	0265	0361	0478	0617	0778	0961	1167	1394	1642	10
6	0037	0057	0084	0121	0168	0227	0300	0387	0490	0611	9
7	0006	0010	0015	0024	0036	0052	0074	0102	0137	0181	8
8	0001	0001	0002	0004	0006	0010	0014	0021	0030	0042	7
9					0001	0001	0002	0003	0005	0008	6
10									0001	0001	5
	p = 21	22	23	24	25	26	27	28	29	30 = (1 − p)	
1	9709	9759	9802	9837	9866	9891	9911	9928	9941	9953	14
2	8547	8741	8913	9065	9198	9315	9417	9505	9581	9647	13
3	6385	6731	7055	7358	7639	7899	8137	8355	8553	8732	12
4	3895	4274	4650	5022	5387	5742	6086	6416	6732	7031	11
5	1910	2195	2495	2810	3135	3469	3810	4154	4500	4845	10
6	0748	0905	1079	1272	1484	1713	1958	2220	2495	2784	9
7	0234	0298	0374	0463	0566	0684	0817	0965	1130	1311	8
8	0058	0078	0104	0135	0173	0219	0274	0338	0413	0500	7
9	0011	0016	0023	0031	0042	0056	0073	0094	0121	0152	6
10	0002	0003	0004	0006	0008	0011	0015	0021	0028	0037	5
11			0001	0001	0001	0002	0002	0003	0005	0007	4
12									0001	0001	3
	p = 31	32	33	34	35	36	37	38	39	40 = (1 − p)	
1	9962	9969	9975	9980	9984	9988	9990	9992	9994	9995	14
2	9704	9752	9794	9829	9858	9883	9904	9922	9936	9948	13
3	8893	9038	9167	9281	9383	9472	9550	9618	9678	9729	12
4	7314	7580	7829	8060	8273	8469	8649	8813	8961	9095	11
5	5187	5523	5852	6171	6481	6778	7062	7332	7587	7827	10
6	3084	3393	3709	4032	4357	4684	5011	5335	5654	5968	9
7	1509	1722	1951	2194	2452	2722	3003	3295	3595	3902	8
8	0599	0711	0837	0977	1132	1302	1487	1687	1902	2131	7
9	0190	0236	0289	0351	0422	0504	0597	0702	0820	0950	6
10	0048	0062	0079	0099	0124	0154	0190	0232	0281	0338	5
11	0009	0012	0016	0022	0028	0037	0047	0059	0075	0003	4
12	0001	0002	0003	0004	0005	0006	0009	0011	0015	0019	3
13					0001	0001	0001	0002	0002	0003	2
	p = 41	42	43	44	45	46	47	48	49	50 = (1 − p)	
1	9996	9997	9998	9998	9999	9999	9999	9999	10000	10000	14
2	9958	9966	9073	9979	9983	9987	9990	9992	9994	9995	13
3	9773	9811	9843	9870	9893	9913	9929	9943	9954	9963	12
4	9215	9322	9417	9502	9576	9641	9697	9746	9788	9824	11
5	8052	8261	8454	8633	8796	8945	9080	9201	9310	9408	10
6	6274	6570	6856	7131	7392	7641	7875	8095	8301	8491	9
7	4214	4530	4847	5164	5478	5789	6095	6394	6684	6964	8
8	2374	2630	2898	3176	3465	3762	4065	4374	4686	5000	7
9	1095	1254	1427	1615	1818	2034	2265	2510	2767	3036	6
10	0404	0479	0565	0661	0769	0890	1024	1171	1333	1509	5
11	0116	0143	0174	0211	0255	0305	0363	0430	0506	0592	4
12	0025	0032	0040	0051	0063	0079	0097	0119	0145	0176	3
13	0004	0005	0007	0009	0011	0014	0018	0023	0029	0037	2
14			0001	0001	0001	0002	0002	0003	0004	0005	1

X	n = 16										X
	p = 01	02	03	04	05	06	07	08	09	10 = (1 − p)	
1	1485	2762	3857	4796	5599	6284	6869	7366	7789	8147	15
2	0109	0399	0818	1327	1892	2489	3098	3701	4289	4853	14
3	0005	0037	0113	0242	0429	0673	0969	1311	1694	2108	13
4		0002	0011	0032	0070	0132	0221	0342	0496	0684	12
5			0001	0003	0009	0019	0038	0068	0111	0170	11
6					0001	0002	0005	0010	0019	0033	10
7							0001	0001	0003	0005	9
8										0001	8
	p = 11	12	13	14	15	16	17	18	19	20 = (1 − p)	
1	8450	8707	8923	9105	9257	9386	9493	9582	9657	9719	15
2	5386	5885	6347	6773	7161	7513	7830	8115	8368	8593	14
3	2545	2999	3461	3926	4386	4838	5277	5698	6101	6482	13
4	0907	1162	1448	1763	2101	2460	2836	3223	3619	4019	12
5	0248	0348	0471	0618	0791	0988	1211	1458	1727	2018	11
6	0053	0082	0120	0171	0235	0315	0412	0527	0662	0817	10
7	0009	0015	0024	0038	0056	0080	0112	0153	0204	0267	9
8	0001	0002	0004	0007	0011	0016	0024	0036	0051	0070	8
9			0001	0001	0002	0003	0004	0007	0010	0015	7
10							0001	0001	0002	0002	6
	p = 21	22	23	24	25	26	27	28	29	30 = (1 − p)	
1	9770	9812	9847	9876	9900	9919	9935	9948	9958	9967	15
2	8791	8965	9117	9250	9365	9465	9550	9623	9686	9739	14
3	6839	7173	7483	7768	8029	8267	8482	8677	8851	9006	13
4	4418	4814	5203	5583	5950	6303	6640	6959	7260	7541	12
5	2327	2652	2991	3341	3698	4060	4425	4788	5147	5501	11
6	0992	1188	1405	1641	1897	2169	2458	2761	3077	3402	10
7	0342	0432	0536	0657	0796	0951	1125	1317	1526	1753	9
8	0095	0127	0166	0214	0271	0340	0420	0514	0621	0744	8
9	0021	0030	0041	0056	0075	0098	0127	0163	0206	0257	7
10	0004	0006	0008	0012	0016	0023	0031	0041	0055	0071	6
11	0001	0001	0001	0002	0003	0004	0006	0008	0011	0016	5
12						0001	0001	0001	0002	0003	4

n = 16 (*Continued*)

X	p = 31	32	33	34	35	36	37	38	39	40 = (1 − p)	X
1	9974	9979	9984	9987	9990	9992	9994	9995	9996	9997	15
2	9784	9822	9854	9880	9902	9921	9936	9948	9959	9967	14
3	9144	9266	9374	9467	9549	9620	9681	9734	9778	9817	13
4	7804	8047	8270	8475	8661	8830	8982	9119	9241	9349	12
5	5846	6181	6504	6813	7108	7387	7649	7895	8123	8334	11
6	3736	4074	4416	4759	5100	5438	5770	6094	6408	6712	10
7	1997	2257	2531	2819	3119	3428	3746	4070	4398	4728	9
8	0881	1035	1205	1391	1594	1813	2048	2298	2562	2839	8
9	0317	0388	0470	0564	0671	0791	0926	1076	1242	1423	7
10	0092	0117	0148	0185	0229	0280	0341	0411	0491	0583	6
11	0021	0028	0037	0048	0062	0079	0100	0125	0155	0191	5
12	0004	0005	0007	0010	0013	0017	0023	0030	0038	0049	4
13		0001	0001	0001	0002	0003	0004	0005	0007	0009	3
14								0001	0001	0001	2

X	p = 41	42	43	44	45	46	47	48	49	50 = (1 − p)	X
1	9998	9998	9999	9999	9999	9999	10000	10000	10000	10000	15
2	9974	9979	9984	9987	9990	9992	9994	9995	9997	9997	14
3	9849	9876	9899	9918	9934	9947	9958	9966	9973	9979	13
4	9444	9527	9600	9664	9719	9766	9806	9840	9869	9894	12
5	8529	8707	8869	9015	9147	9265	9370	9463	9544	9616	11
6	7003	7280	7543	7792	8024	8241	8441	8626	8795	8949	10
7	5058	5387	5711	6029	6340	6641	6932	7210	7476	7728	9
8	3128	3428	3736	4051	4371	4694	5019	5343	5665	5982	8
9	1619	1832	2060	2302	2559	2829	3111	3405	3707	4018	7
10	0687	0805	0936	1081	1241	1416	1607	1814	2036	2272	6
11	0234	0284	0342	0409	0486	0574	0674	0786	0911	1051	5
12	0062	0078	0098	0121	0149	0183	0222	0268	0322	0384	4
13	0012	0016	0021	0027	0035	0044	0055	0069	0086	0106	3
14	0002	0002	0003	0004	0006	0007	0010	0013	0016	0021	2
15					0001	0001	0001	0001	0002	0003	1

n = 17

X	p = 01	02	03	04	05	06	07	08	09	10 = (1 − p)	X
1	1571	2907	4042	5004	5819	6507	7088	7577	7988	8332	16
2	0123	0446	0909	1465	2078	2717	3362	3995	4604	5182	15
3	0006	0044	0134	0286	0503	0782	1118	1503	1927	2382	14
4		0003	0014	0040	0088	0164	0273	0419	0603	0826	13
5			0001	0004	0012	0026	0051	0089	0145	0221	12
6					0001	0003	0007	0015	0027	0047	11
7							0001	0002	0004	0008	10
8										0001	9

X	p = 11	12	13	14	15	16	17	18	19	20 = (1 − p)	X
1	8621	8862	9063	9230	9369	9484	9579	9657	9722	9775	16
2	5723	6223	6682	7099	7475	7813	8113	8379	8613	8818	15
3	2858	3345	3836	4324	4802	5266	5711	6133	6532	6904	14
4	1087	1383	1710	2065	2444	2841	3251	3669	4091	4511	13
5	0321	0446	0598	0778	0987	1224	1487	1775	2087	2418	12
6	0075	0114	0166	0234	0319	0423	0548	0695	0864	1057	11
7	0014	0023	0037	0056	0083	0118	0163	0220	0291	0377	10
8	0002	0004	0007	0011	0017	0027	0039	0057	0080	0109	9
9		0001	0001	0002	0003	0005	0008	0012	0018	0026	8
10						0001	0001	0002	0003	0005	7
11										0001	6

X	p = 21	22	23	24	25	26	27	28	29	30 = (1 − p)	X
1	9818	9854	9882	9906	9925	9940	9953	9962	9970	9977	16
2	8996	9152	9285	9400	9499	9583	9654	9714	9765	9807	15
3	7249	7567	7859	8123	8363	8578	8771	8942	9093	9226	14
4	4927	5333	5728	6107	6470	6814	7137	7440	7721	7981	13
5	2766	3128	3500	3879	4261	4643	5023	5396	5760	6113	12
6	1273	1510	1770	2049	2347	2661	2989	3329	3677	4032	11
7	0479	0598	0736	0894	1071	1268	1485	1721	1976	2248	10
8	0147	0194	0251	0320	0402	0499	0611	0739	0884	1046	9
9	0037	0051	0070	0094	0124	0161	0206	0261	0326	0403	8
10	0007	0011	0016	0022	0031	0042	0057	0075	0098	0127	7
11	0001	0002	0003	0004	0006	0009	0013	0018	0024	0032	6
12				0001	0001	0002	0002	0003	0005	0007	5
13									0001	0001	4

X	p = 31	32	33	34	35	36	37	38	39	40 = (1 − p)	X
1	9982	9986	9989	9991	9993	9995	9996	9997	9998	9998	16
2	9843	9872	9896	9917	9933	9946	9957	9966	9973	9979	15
3	9343	9444	9532	9608	9673	9728	9775	9815	9849	9877	14
4	8219	8437	8634	8812	8972	9115	9241	9353	9450	9536	13
5	6453	6778	7087	7378	7652	7906	8142	8360	8559	8740	12
6	4390	4749	5105	5458	5803	6139	6465	6778	7077	7361	11
7	2536	2838	3153	3479	3812	4152	4495	4839	5182	5522	10
8	1227	1426	1642	1877	2128	2395	2676	2971	3278	3595	9
9	0492	0595	0712	0845	0994	1159	1341	1541	1757	1989	8
10	0162	0204	0254	0314	0383	0464	0557	0664	0784	0919	7
11	0043	0057	0074	0095	0120	0151	0189	0234	0286	0348	6
12	0009	0013	0017	0023	0030	0040	0051	0066	0084	0106	5
13	0002	0002	0003	0004	0006	0008	0011	0015	0019	0025	4
14				0001	0001	0001	0002	0002	0003	0005	3
15										0001	2

n = 17 (*Continued*)

X	p = 41	42	43	44	45	46	47	48	49	50 = (1 − p)	X
1	9999	9999	9999	9999	10000	10000	10000	10000	10000	10000	16
2	9984	9987	9990	9992	9994	9996	9997	9998	9998	9999	15
3	9900	9920	9935	9948	9959	9968	9975	9980	9985	9988	14
4	9610	9674	9729	9776	9816	9849	9877	9901	9920	9936	13
5	8904	9051	9183	9301	9404	9495	9575	9644	9704	9755	12
6	7628	7879	8113	8330	8529	8712	8878	9028	9162	9283	11
7	5856	6182	6499	6805	7098	7377	7641	7890	8122	8338	10
8	3920	4250	4585	4921	5257	5590	5918	6239	6552	6855	9
9	2238	2502	2780	3072	3374	3687	4008	4335	4667	5000	8
10	1070	1236	1419	1618	1834	2066	2314	2577	2855	3145	7
11	0420	0503	0597	0705	0826	0962	1112	1279	1462	1662	6
12	0133	0165	0203	0248	0301	0363	0434	0517	0611	0717	5
13	0033	0042	0054	0069	0086	0108	0134	0165	0202	0245	4
14	0006	0008	0011	0014	0019	0024	0031	0040	0050	0064	3
15	0001	0001	0002	0002	0003	0004	0005	0007	0009	0012	2
16							0001	0001	0001	0001	1

n = 18

X	p = 01	02	03	04	05	06	07	08	09	10 = (1 − p)	X
1	1655	3049	4220	5204	6028	6717	7292	7771	8169	8499	17
2	0138	0495	1003	1607	2265	2945	3622	4281	4909	5497	16
3	0007	0052	0157	0333	0581	0898	1275	1702	2168	2662	15
4		0004	0018	0050	0109	0201	0333	0506	0723	0982	14
5			0002	0006	0015	0034	0067	0116	0186	0282	13
6				0001	0002	0005	0010	0021	0038	0064	12
7							0001	0003	0006	0012	11
8									0001	0002	10

X	p = 11	12	13	14	15	16	17	18	19	20 = (1 − p)	X
1	8773	8998	9185	9338	9464	9566	9651	9719	9775	9820	17
2	6042	6540	6992	7398	7759	8080	8362	8609	8824	9009	16
3	3173	3690	4206	4713	5203	5673	6119	6538	6927	7287	15
4	1282	1618	1986	2382	2798	3229	3669	4112	4554	4990	14
5	0405	0558	0743	0959	1206	1482	1787	2116	2467	2836	13
6	0102	0154	0222	0310	0419	0551	0708	0889	1097	1329	12
7	0021	0034	0054	0081	0118	0167	0229	0306	0400	0513	11
8	0003	0006	0011	0017	0027	0041	0060	0086	0120	0163	10
9		0001	0002	0003	0005	0008	0013	0020	0029	0043	9
10					0001	0001	0002	0004	0006	0009	8
11								0001	0001	0002	7

X	p = 21	22	23	24	25	26	27	28	29	30 = (1 − p)	X
1	9856	9886	9909	9928	9944	9956	9965	9973	9979	9984	17
2	9169	9306	9423	9522	9605	9676	9735	9784	9824	9858	16
3	7616	7916	8187	8430	8647	8839	9009	9158	9288	9400	15
4	5414	5825	6218	6591	6943	7272	7578	7860	8119	8354	14
5	3220	3613	4012	4414	4813	5208	5594	5968	6329	6673	13
6	1586	1866	2168	2488	2825	3176	3538	3907	4281	4656	12
7	0645	0799	0974	1171	1390	1630	1891	2171	2469	2783	11
8	0217	0283	0363	0458	0569	0699	0847	1014	1200	1407	10
9	0060	0083	0112	0148	0193	0249	0316	0395	0488	0596	9
10	0014	0020	0028	0039	0054	0073	0097	0127	0164	0210	8
11	0003	0004	0006	0009	0012	0018	0025	0034	0046	0061	7
12		0001	0001	0002	0002	0003	0005	0007	0010	0014	6
13						0001	0001	0001	0002	0003	5

X	p = 31	32	33	34	35	36	37	38	39	40 = (1 − p)	X
1	9987	9990	9993	9994	9996	9997	9998	9998	9999	9999	17
2	9886	9908	9927	9942	9954	9964	9972	9978	9983	9987	16
3	9498	9581	9652	9713	9764	9807	9843	9873	9897	9918	15
4	8568	8759	8931	9083	9217	9335	9439	9528	9606	9672	14
5	7001	7309	7598	7866	8114	8341	8549	8737	8907	9058	13
6	5029	5398	5759	6111	6450	6776	7086	7379	7655	7912	12
7	3111	3450	3797	4151	4509	4867	5224	5576	5921	6257	11
8	1633	1878	2141	2421	2717	3027	3349	3681	4021	4366	10
9	0720	0861	1019	1196	1391	1604	1835	2084	2350	2632	9
10	0264	0329	0405	0494	0597	0714	0847	0997	1163	1347	8
11	0080	0104	0133	0169	0212	0264	0325	0397	0480	0576	7
12	0020	0027	0036	0047	0062	0080	0102	0130	0163	0203	6
13	0004	0005	0008	0011	0014	0019	0026	0034	0044	0058	5
14	0001	0001	0001	0002	0003	0004	0005	0007	0010	0013	4
15						0001	0001	0001	0002	0002	3

X	p = 41	42	43	44	45	46	47	48	49	50 = (1 − p)	X
1	9999	9999	10000	10000	10000	10000	10000	10000	10000	10000	17
2	9990	9992	9994	9996	9997	9998	9998	9999	9999	9999	16
3	9934	9948	9959	9968	9975	9981	9985	9989	9991	9993	15
4	9729	9777	9818	9852	9880	9904	9923	9939	9952	9962	14
5	9193	9313	9418	9510	9589	9658	9717	9767	9810	9846	13
6	8151	8372	8573	8757	8923	9072	9205	9324	9428	9519	12
7	6582	6895	7193	7476	7742	7991	8222	8436	8632	8811	11
8	4713	5062	5408	5750	6085	6412	6728	7032	7322	7597	10
9	2928	3236	3556	3885	4222	4562	4906	5249	5591	5927	9
10	1549	1768	2004	2258	2527	2812	3110	3421	3742	4073	8
11	0686	0811	0951	1107	1280	1470	1677	1902	2144	2403	7
12	0250	0307	0372	0449	0537	0638	0753	0883	1028	1189	6
13	0074	0094	0118	0147	0183	0225	0275	0334	0402	0481	5
14	0017	0022	0029	0038	0049	0063	0079	0100	0125	0154	4
15	0003	0004	0006	0007	0010	0013	0017	0023	0029	0038	3
16		0001	0001	0001	0001	0002	0003	0004	0005	0007	2
17									0001	0001	1

X	n = 19										X
	p = 01	02	03	04	05	06	07	08	09	10 = (1 − p)	
1	1738	3188	4394	5396	6226	6914	7481	7949	8334	8649	18
2	0153	0546	1100	1751	2453	3171	3879	4560	5202	5797	17
3	0009	0061	0183	0384	0665	1021	1439	1908	2415	2946	16
4		0005	0022	0061	0132	0243	0398	0602	0853	1150	15
5			0002	0007	0020	0044	0085	0147	0235	0352	14
6				0001	0002	0006	0014	0029	0051	0086	13
7						0001	0002	0004	0009	0017	12
8								0001	0001	0003	11
	p = 11	12	13	14	15	16	17	18	19	20 = (1 − p)	
1	8908	9119	9291	9431	9544	9636	9710	9770	9818	9856	18
2	6342	6835	7277	7669	8015	8318	8581	8809	9004	9171	17
3	3488	4032	4568	5089	5587	6059	6500	6910	7287	7631	16
4	1490	1867	2275	2708	3159	3620	4085	4549	5005	5449	15
5	0502	0685	0904	1158	1444	1762	2107	2476	2864	3267	14
6	0135	0202	0290	0401	0537	0700	0891	1110	1357	1631	13
7	0030	0048	0076	0113	0163	0228	0310	0411	0532	0676	12
8	0005	0009	0016	0026	0041	0061	0089	0126	0173	0233	11
9	0001	0002	0003	0005	0008	0014	0021	0032	0047	0067	10
10				0001	0001	0002	0004	0007	0010	0016	9
11							0001	0001	0002	0003	8
	p = 21	22	23	24	25	26	27	28	29	30 = (1 − p)	
1	9887	9911	9930	9946	9958	9967	9975	9981	9985	9989	18
2	9313	9434	9535	9619	9690	9749	9797	9837	9869	9896	17
3	7942	8222	8471	8692	8887	9057	9205	9333	9443	9538	16
4	5877	6285	6671	7032	7369	7680	7965	8224	8458	8668	15
5	3681	4100	4520	4936	5346	5744	6129	6498	6848	7178	14
6	1929	2251	2592	2950	3322	3705	4093	4484	4875	5261	13
7	0843	1034	1248	1487	1749	2032	2336	2657	2995	3345	12
8	0307	0396	0503	0629	0775	0941	1129	1338	1568	1820	11
9	0093	0127	0169	0222	0287	0366	0459	0568	0694	0839	10
10	0023	0034	0047	0066	0089	0119	0156	0202	0258	0326	9
11	0005	0007	0011	0016	0023	0032	0044	0060	0080	0105	8
12	0001	0001	0002	0003	0005	0007	0010	0015	0021	0028	7
13				0001	0001	0001	0002	0003	0004	0006	6
14									0001	0001	5
	p = 31	32	33	34	35	36	37	38	39	40 = (1 − p)	
1	9991	9993	9995	9996	9997	9998	9998	9999	9999	9999	18
2	9917	9935	9949	9960	9969	9976	9981	9986	9989	9992	17
3	9618	9686	9743	9791	9830	9863	9890	9913	9931	9945	16
4	8856	9022	9169	9297	9409	9505	9588	9659	9719	9770	15
5	7486	7773	8037	8280	8500	8699	8878	9038	9179	9304	14
6	5641	6010	6366	6707	7032	7339	7627	7895	8143	8371	13
7	3705	4073	4445	4818	5188	5554	5913	6261	6597	6919	12
8	2091	2381	2688	3010	3344	3690	4043	4401	4762	5122	11
9	1003	1186	1389	1612	1855	2116	2395	2691	3002	3325	10
10	0405	0499	0608	0733	0875	1035	1213	1410	1626	1861	9
11	0137	0176	0223	0280	0347	0426	0518	0625	0747	0885	8
12	0038	0051	0068	0089	0114	0146	0185	0231	0287	0352	7
13	0009	0012	0017	0023	0031	0041	0054	0070	0091	0116	6
14	0002	0002	0003	0005	0007	0009	0013	0017	0023	0031	5
15			0001	0001	0001	0002	0002	0003	0005	0006	4
16									0001	0001	3
	p = 41	42	43	44	45	46	47	48	49	50 = (1 − p)	
1	10000	10000	10000	10000	10000	10000	10000	10000	10000	10000	18
2	9994	9995	9996	9997	9998	9999	9999	9999	9999	10000	17
3	9957	9967	9974	9980	9985	9988	9991	9993	9995	9996	16
4	9813	9849	9878	9903	9023	9939	9952	9963	9971	9978	15
5	9413	9508	9590	9660	9720	9771	9814	9850	9879	9904	14
6	8579	8767	8937	9088	9223	9342	9446	9537	9615	9682	13
7	7226	7515	7787	8039	8273	8488	8684	8862	9022	9165	12
8	5480	5832	6176	6509	6831	7138	7430	7706	7964	8204	11
9	3660	4003	4353	4706	5060	5413	5762	6105	6439	6762	10
10	2114	2385	2672	2974	3290	3617	3954	4299	4648	5000	9
11	1040	1213	1404	1613	1841	2087	2351	2631	2928	3238	8
12	0429	0518	0621	0738	0871	1021	1187	1372	1575	1796	7
13	0146	0183	0227	0280	0342	0415	0500	0597	0709	0835	6
14	0040	0052	0067	0086	0109	0137	0171	0212	0261	0318	5
15	0009	0012	0016	0021	0028	0036	0046	0060	0076	0096	4
16	0001	0002	0003	0004	0005	0007	0010	0013	0017	0022	3
17				0001	0001	0001	0001	0002	0003	0004	2

X	n = 20										X
	p = 01	02	03	04	05	06	07	08	09	10 = (1 − p)	
1	1821	3324	4562	5580	6415	7099	7658	8113	8484	8784	19
2	0169	0599	1198	1897	2642	3395	4131	4831	5484	6083	18
3	0010	0071	0210	0439	0755	1150	1610	2121	2666	3231	17
4		0006	0027	0074	0159	0290	0471	0706	0993	1330	16
5			0003	0010	0026	0056	0107	0183	0290	0432	15
6				0001	0003	0009	0019	0038	0068	0113	14
7						0001	0003	0006	0013	0024	13
8								0001	0002	0004	12
9										0001	11

X	n = 20 (*Continued*)										X
	p = 11	12	13	14	15	16	17	18	19	20 = (1 − p)	
1	9028	9224	9383	9510	9612	9694	9759	9811	9852	9885	19
2	6624	7109	7539	7916	8244	8529	8773	8982	9159	9308	18
3	3802	4369	4920	5450	5951	6420	6854	7252	7614	7939	17
4	1710	2127	2573	3041	3523	4010	4496	4974	5439	5886	16
5	0610	0827	1083	1375	1702	2059	2443	2849	3271	3704	15
6	0175	0260	0370	0507	0673	0870	1098	1356	1643	1958	14
7	0041	0067	0103	0153	0219	0304	0409	0537	0689	0867	13
8	0008	0014	0024	0038	0059	0088	0127	0177	0241	0321	12
9	0001	0002	0005	0008	0013	0021	0033	0049	0071	0100	11
10			0001	0001	0002	0004	0007	0011	0017	0026	10
11						0001	0001	0002	0004	0006	9
12									0001	0001	8
	p = 21	22	23	24	25	26	27	28	29	30 = (1 − p)	
1	9910	9931	9946	9959	9968	9976	9982	9986	9989	9992	19
2	9434	9539	9626	9698	9757	9805	9845	9877	9903	9924	18
3	8230	8488	8716	8915	9087	9237	9365	9474	9567	9645	17
4	6310	6711	7085	7431	7748	8038	8300	8534	8744	8929	16
5	4142	4580	5014	5439	5852	6248	6625	6981	7315	7625	15
6	2297	2657	3035	3427	3828	4235	4643	5048	5447	5836	14
7	1071	1301	1557	1838	2142	2467	2810	3169	3540	3920	13
8	0419	0536	0675	0835	1018	1225	1455	1707	1982	2277	12
9	0138	0186	0246	0320	0409	0515	0640	0784	0948	1133	11
10	0038	0054	0075	0103	0139	0183	0238	0305	0385	0480	10
11	0009	0013	0019	0028	0039	0055	0074	0100	0132	0171	9
12	0002	0003	0004	0006	0009	0014	0019	0027	0038	0051	8
13			0001	0001	0002	0003	0004	0006	0009	0013	7
14							0001	0001	0002	0003	6
	p = 31	32	33	34	35	36	37	38	39	40 = (1 − p)	
1	9994	9996	9997	9998	9998	9999	9999	9999	9999	10000	19
2	9940	9953	9964	9972	9979	9984	9988	9991	9993	9995	18
3	9711	9765	9811	9848	9879	9904	9924	9940	9953	9964	17
4	9092	9235	9358	9465	9556	9634	0700	9755	9802	9840	16
5	7911	8173	8411	8626	8818	8989	9141	9274	9390	9490	15
6	6213	6574	6917	7242	7546	7829	8090	8329	8547	8744	14
7	4305	4693	5079	5460	5834	6197	6547	6882	7200	7500	13
8	2591	2922	3268	3624	3990	4361	4735	5108	5478	5841	12
9	1340	1568	1818	2087	2376	2683	3005	3341	3688	4044	11
10	0591	0719	0866	1032	1218	1424	1650	1897	2163	2447	10
11	0220	0279	0350	0434	0532	0645	0775	0923	1090	1275	9
12	0069	0001	0119	0154	0196	0247	0308	0381	0466	0565	8
13	0018	0025	0034	0045	0060	0079	0102	0132	0167	0210	7
14	0004	0006	0008	0011	0015	0021	0028	0037	0049	0065	6
15	0001	0001	0001	0002	0003	0004	0006	0009	0012	0016	5
16						0001	0001	0002	0002	0003	4
	p = 41	42	43	44	45	46	47	48	49	50 = (1 − p)	
1	10000	10000	10000	10000	10000	10000	10000	10000	10000	10000	19
2	9996	9997	9998	9998	9999	9999	9999	10000	10000	10000	18
3	9972	9979	9984	9988	9991	9993	9995	9996	9997	9998	17
4	9872	9898	9920	9937	9951	9962	9971	9977	9983	9987	16
5	9577	9651	9714	9767	9811	9848	9879	9904	9924	9941	15
6	8921	9078	9217	9340	9447	9539	9619	9687	9745	9793	14
7	7780	8041	8281	8501	8701	8861	9042	9186	9312	9423	13
8	6196	6539	6868	7183	7480	7759	8020	8261	8482	8684	12
9	4406	4771	5136	5499	5857	6207	6546	6873	7186	7483	11
10	2748	3064	3394	3736	4086	4443	4804	5166	5525	5881	10
11	1480	1705	1949	2212	2493	2791	3104	3432	3771	4119	9
12	0679	0810	0958	1123	1308	1511	1734	1977	2238	2517	8
13	0262	0324	0397	0482	0580	0694	0823	0969	1133	1316	7
14	0084	0107	0136	0172	0214	0265	0326	0397	0480	0577	6
15	0022	0029	0038	0050	0064	0083	0105	0133	0166	0207	5
16	0004	0006	0008	0011	0015	0020	0027	0035	0046	0059	4
17	0001	0001	0001	0002	0003	0004	0005	0007	0010	0013	3
18						0001	0001	0001	0001	0002	2

X	n = 50										X
	p = 01	02	03	04	05	06	07	08	09	10 = (1 − p)	
1	3950	6358	7819	8701	9231	9547	9734	9845	9910	9948	49
2	0894	2642	4447	5995	7206	8100	8735	9173	9468	9662	48
3	0138	0784	1892	3233	4595	5838	6892	7740	8395	8883	47
4	0016	0178	0628	1391	2396	3527	4673	5747	6697	7497	46
5	0001	0032	0168	0490	1036	1794	2710	3710	4723	5688	45
6		0005	0037	0144	0378	0776	1350	2081	2928	3839	44
7		0001	0007	0036	0118	0289	0583	1019	1596	2298	43
8			0001	0008	0032	0094	0220	0438	0768	1221	42
9				0001	0008	0027	0073	0167	0328	0579	41
10					0002	0007	0022	0056	0125	0245	40
11						0002	0006	0017	0043	0094	39
12							0001	0005	0013	0032	38
13								0001	0004	0010	37
14									0001	0003	36
15										0001	35

n = 50 (Continued)

X	p = 11	12	13	14	15	16	17	18	19	20 = (1 − p)	X
1	9971	9983	9991	9995	9997	9998	9999	10000	10000	10000	49
2	9788	9869	9920	9951	9971	9983	9990	9994	9997	9998	48
3	9237	9487	9661	9779	9858	9910	9944	9965	9979	9987	47
4	8146	8655	9042	9330	9540	9688	9792	9863	9912	9943	46
5	6562	7320	7956	8472	8879	9192	9428	9601	9726	9815	45
6	4760	5647	6463	7186	7806	8323	8741	9071	9327	9520	44
7	3091	3935	4789	5616	6387	7081	7686	8199	8624	8966	43
8	1793	2467	3217	4010	4812	5594	6328	6996	7587	8096	42
9	0932	1392	1955	2605	3319	4071	4832	5576	6280	6927	41
10	0435	0708	1074	1537	2089	2718	3403	4122	4849	5563	40
11	0183	0325	0535	0824	1199	1661	2203	2813	3473	4164	39
12	0069	0135	0242	0402	0628	0929	1309	1768	2300	2893	38
13	0024	0051	0100	0179	0301	0475	0714	1022	1405	1861	37
14	0008	0018	0037	0073	0132	0223	0357	0544	0791	1106	36
15	0002	0006	0013	0027	0053	0096	0164	0266	0411	0607	35
16	0001	0002	0004	0009	0019	0038	0070	0120	0197	0308	34
17			0001	0003	0007	0014	0027	0050	0087	0144	33
18				0001	0002	0005	0010	0019	0036	0063	32
19					0001	0001	0003	0007	0013	0025	31
20							0001	0002	0005	0009	30
21								0001	0002	0003	29
22										0001	28

X	p = 21	22	23	24	25	26	27	28	29	30 = (1 − p)	X
1	10000	10000	10000	10000	10000	10000	10000	10000	10000	10000	49
2	9999	9999	10000	10000	10000	10000	10000	10000	10000	10000	48
3	9992	9995	9997	9998	9999	10000	10000	10000	10000	10000	47
4	9964	9978	9986	9992	9995	9997	9998	9999	9999	10000	46
5	9877	9919	9948	9967	9979	9987	9992	9995	9997	9998	45
6	9663	9767	9841	9893	9930	9954	9970	9981	9988	9993	44
7	9236	9445	9603	9720	9806	9868	9911	9941	9961	9975	43
8	8523	8874	9156	9377	9547	9676	9772	9842	9892	9927	42
9	7505	8009	8437	8794	9084	9316	9497	9635	9740	9817	41
10	6241	6870	7436	7934	8363	8724	9021	9260	9450	9598	40
11	4864	5552	6210	6822	7378	7871	8299	8663	8965	9211	39
12	3533	4201	4878	5544	6184	6782	7329	7817	8244	8610	38
13	2383	2963	3585	4233	4890	5539	6163	6749	7287	7771	37
14	1490	1942	2456	3023	3630	4261	4901	5534	6145	6721	36
15	0862	1181	1565	2013	2519	3075	3669	4286	4912	5532	35
16	0462	0665	0926	1247	1631	2075	2575	3121	3703	4308	34
17	0229	0347	0508	0718	0983	1306	1689	2130	2623	3161	33
18	0105	0168	0259	0384	0551	0766	1034	1359	1741	2178	32
19	0045	0075	0122	0191	0287	0418	0590	0809	1080	1406	31
20	0018	0031	0054	0088	0139	0212	0314	0449	0626	0848	30
21	0006	0012	0022	0038	0063	0100	0155	0232	0338	0478	29
22	0002	0004	0008	0015	0026	0044	0071	0112	0170	0251	28
23	0001	0001	0003	0006	0010	0018	0031	0050	0080	0123	27
24			0001	0002	0004	0007	0012	0021	0035	0056	26
25				0001	0001	0002	0004	0008	0014	0024	25
26						0001	0002	0003	0005	0009	24
27								0001	0002	0003	23
28									0001	0001	22

X	p = 31	32	33	34	35	36	37	38	39	40 = (1 − p)	X
1	10000	10000	10000	10000	10000	10000	10000	10000	10000	10000	49
2	10000	10000	10000	10000	10000	10000	10000	10000	10000	10000	48
3	10000	10000	10000	10000	10000	10000	10000	10000	10000	10000	47
4	10000	10000	10000	10000	10000	10000	10000	10000	10000	10000	46
5	9999	9999	10000	10000	10000	10000	10000	10000	10000	10000	45
6	9996	9997	9998	9999	9999	10000	10000	10000	10000	10000	44
7	9984	9990	9994	9996	9998	9999	9999	10000	10000	10000	43
8	9952	9969	9980	9987	9992	9995	9997	9998	9999	9999	42
9	9874	9914	9942	9962	9975	9984	9990	9994	9996	9998	41
10	9710	9794	9856	9901	9933	9955	9971	9981	9988	9992	40
11	9409	9563	9683	9773	9840	9889	9924	9949	9966	9978	39
12	8916	9168	9371	9533	9658	9753	9825	9878	9916	9943	38
13	8197	8564	8873	9130	9339	9505	9635	9736	9811	9867	37
14	7253	7732	8157	8524	8837	9097	9310	9481	9616	9720	36
15	6131	6698	7223	7699	8122	8491	8805	9069	9286	9460	35
16	4922	5530	6120	6679	7199	7672	8094	8462	8779	9045	34
17	3734	4328	4931	5530	6111	6664	7179	7649	8070	8439	33
18	2666	3197	3760	4346	4940	5531	6105	6653	7164	7631	32
19	1786	2220	2703	3227	3784	4362	4949	5533	6101	6644	31
20	1121	1447	1826	2257	2736	3255	3805	4376	4957	5535	30
21	0657	0882	1156	1482	1861	2289	2764	3278	3824	4390	29
22	0360	0503	0685	0912	1187	1513	1890	2317	2788	3299	28
23	0184	0267	0379	0525	0710	0938	1214	1540	1916	2340	27
24	0087	0133	0196	0282	0396	0544	0730	0960	1236	1562	26
25	0039	0061	0094	0141	0207	0295	0411	0560	0748	0978	25
26	0016	0026	0042	0066	0100	0149	0216	0305	0423	0573	24
27	0006	0011	0018	0029	0045	0070	0106	0155	0223	0314	23
28	0002	0004	0007	0012	0019	0031	0048	0074	0110	0160	22
29	0001	0001	0002	0004	0007	0012	0020	0032	0050	0076	21
30			0001	0002	0003	0005	0008	0013	0021	0034	20
31					0001	0002	0003	0005	0008	0014	19
32						0001	0001	0002	0003	0005	18
33								0001	0001	0002	17
34										0001	16

n = 50 (Continued)

X	p = 41	42	43	44	45	46	47	48	49	50 = (1 − p)	X
1	10000	10000	10000	10000	10000	10000	10000	10000	10000	10000	49
2	10000	10000	10000	10000	10000	10000	10000	10000	10000	10000	48
3	10000	10000	10000	10000	10000	10000	10000	10000	10000	10000	47
4	10000	10000	10000	10000	10000	10000	10000	10000	10000	10000	46
5	10000	10000	10000	10000	10000	10000	10000	10000	10000	10000	45
6	10000	10000	10000	10000	10000	10000	10000	10000	10000	10000	44
7	10000	10000	10000	10000	10000	10000	10000	10000	10000	10000	43
8	10000	10000	10000	10000	10000	10000	10000	10000	10000	10000	42
9	9999	9999	10000	10000	10000	10000	10000	10000	10000	10000	41
10	9995	9997	9998	9999	9999	10000	10000	10000	10000	10000	40
11	9986	9991	9994	9997	9998	9999	9999	10000	10000	10000	39
12	9962	9975	9984	9990	9994	9996	9998	9999	9999	10000	38
13	9908	9938	9958	9973	9982	9989	9993	9996	9997	9998	37
14	9799	9858	9902	9933	9955	9970	9981	9988	9992	9995	36
15	9599	9707	9789	9851	9896	9929	9952	9968	9980	9987	35
16	9265	9443	9585	9696	9780	9844	9892	9926	9950	9967	34
17	8757	9025	9248	9429	9573	9687	9774	9839	9888	9923	33
18	8051	8421	8740	9010	9235	9418	9565	9680	9769	9836	32
19	7152	7617	8037	8406	8727	8998	9225	9410	9559	9675	31
20	6099	6638	7143	7608	8026	8396	8718	8991	9219	9405	30
21	4965	5539	6099	6635	7138	7602	8020	8391	8713	8987	29
22	3840	4402	4973	5543	6100	6634	7137	7599	8018	8389	28
23	2809	3316	3854	4412	4981	5548	6104	6636	7138	7601	27
24	1936	2359	2826	3331	3866	4422	4989	5554	6109	6641	26
25	1255	1580	1953	2375	2840	3343	3876	4431	4996	5561	25
26	0762	0992	1269	1593	1966	2386	2850	3352	3885	4439	24
27	0432	0584	0772	1003	1279	1603	1975	2395	2858	3359	23
28	0229	0320	0439	0591	0780	1010	1286	1609	1981	2399	22
29	0113	0164	0233	0325	0444	0595	0784	1013	1289	1611	21
30	0052	0078	0115	0166	0235	0327	0446	0596	0784	1013	20
31	0022	0034	0053	0079	0116	0167	0236	0327	0445	0595	19
32	0009	0014	0022	0035	0053	0079	0116	0166	0234	0325	18
33	0003	0005	0009	0014	0022	0035	0053	0078	0114	0164	17
34	0001	0002	0003	0005	0009	0014	0022	0034	0052	0077	16
35		0001	0001	0002	0003	0005	0008	0014	0021	0033	15
36				0001	0001	0002	0003	0005	0008	0013	14
37						0001	0001	0002	0003	0005	13
38								0001	0001	0002	12

n = 100

X	p = 01	02	03	04	05	06	07	08	09	10 = (1 − p)	X
1	6340	8674	9524	9831	9941	9979	9993	9998	9999	10000	99
2	2642	5967	8054	9128	9629	9848	9940	9977	9991	9997	98
3	0794	3233	5802	7679	8817	9434	9742	9887	9952	9981	97
4	0184	1410	3528	5705	7422	8570	9256	9633	9827	9922	96
5	0034	0508	1821	3711	5640	7232	8368	9097	9526	9763	95
6	0005	0155	0808	2116	3840	5593	7086	8201	8955	9424	94
7	0001	0041	0312	1064	2340	3936	5557	6968	8060	8828	93
8		0009	0106	0475	1280	2517	4012	5529	6872	7939	92
9		0002	0032	0190	0631	1463	2660	4074	5506	6791	91
10			0009	0068	0282	0775	1620	2780	4125	5487	90
11			0002	0022	0115	0376	0908	1757	2882	4168	89
12				0007	0043	0168	0469	1028	1876	2970	88
13				0002	0015	0069	0224	0559	1138	1982	87
14					0005	0026	0099	0282	0645	1239	86
15					0001	0009	0041	0133	0341	0726	85
16						0003	0016	0058	0169	0399	84
17						0001	0006	0024	0078	0206	83
18							0002	0009	0034	0100	82
19							0001	0003	0014	0046	81
20								0001	0005	0020	80
21									0002	0008	79
22									0001	0003	78
23										0001	77

X	p = 11	12	13	14	15	16	17	18	19	20 = (1 − p)	X
1	10000	10000	10000	10000	10000	10000	10000	10000	10000	10000	99
2	9999	10000	10000	10000	10000	10000	10000	10000	10000	10000	98
3	9992	9997	9999	10000	10000	10000	10000	10000	10000	10000	97
4	9966	9985	9994	9998	9999	10000	10000	10000	10000	10000	96
5	9886	9947	9977	9990	9996	9998	9999	10000	10000	10000	95
6	9698	9848	9926	9966	9984	9993	9997	9999	10000	10000	94
7	9328	9633	9808	9903	9953	9978	9990	9996	9998	9999	93
8	8715	9239	9569	9766	9878	9939	9970	9986	9994	9997	92
9	7835	8614	9155	9508	9725	9853	9924	9962	9982	9991	91
10	6722	7743	8523	9078	9449	9684	9826	9908	9953	9977	90
11	5471	6663	7663	8440	9006	9393	9644	9800	9891	9943	89
12	4206	5458	6611	7591	8365	8939	9340	9605	9773	9874	88
13	3046	4239	5446	6566	7527	8297	8876	9289	9567	9747	87
14	2076	3114	4268	5436	6526	7469	8234	8819	9241	9531	86
15	1330	2160	3173	4294	5428	6490	7417	8177	8765	9196	85
16	0802	1414	2236	3227	4317	5420	6458	7370	8125	8715	84
17	0456	0874	1492	2305	3275	4338	5414	6429	7327	8077	83
18	0244	0511	0942	1563	2367	3319	4357	5408	6403	7288	82
19	0123	0282	0564	1006	1628	2424	3359	4374	5403	6379	81
20	0059	0147	0319	0614	1065	1689	2477	3395	4391	5398	80

X	n = 100 (Continued)										X
	p = 11	12	13	14	15	16	17	18	19	20 = (1 − p)	
21	0026	0073	0172	0356	0663	1121	1745	2525	3429	4405	79
22	0011	0034	0088	0196	0393	0710	1174	1797	2570	3460	78
23	0005	0015	0042	0103	0221	0428	0754	1223	1846	2611	77
24	0002	0006	0020	0051	0119	0246	0462	0796	1270	1891	76
25	0001	0003	0009	0024	0061	0135	0271	0496	0837	1314	75
26		0001	0004	0011	0030	0071	0151	0295	0528	0875	74
27			0001	0005	0014	0035	0081	0168	0318	0558	73
28			0001	0002	0006	0017	0041	0091	0184	0342	72
29				0001	0003	0008	0020	0048	0102	0200	71
30					0001	0003	0009	0024	0054	0112	70
31						0001	0004	0011	0027	0061	69
32						0001	0002	0005	0013	0031	68
33							0001	0002	0006	0016	67
34								0001	0003	0007	66
35									0001	0003	65
36										0001	64
37										0001	63

X	p = 21	22	23	24	25	26	27	28	29	30 = (1 − p)	X
1	10000	10000	10000	10000	10000	10000	10000	10000	10000	10000	99
2	10000	10000	10000	10000	10000	10000	10000	10000	10000	10000	98
3	10000	10000	10000	10000	10000	10000	10000	10000	10000	10000	97
4	10000	10000	10000	10000	10000	10000	10000	10000	10000	10000	96
5	10000	10000	10000	10000	10000	10000	10000	10000	10000	10000	95
6	10000	10000	10000	10000	10000	10000	10000	10000	10000	10000	94
7	10000	10000	10000	10000	10000	10000	10000	10000	10000	10000	93
8	9999	10000	10000	10000	10000	10000	10000	10000	10000	10000	92
9	9996	9998	9999	10000	10000	10000	10000	10000	10000	10000	91
10	9989	9995	9998	9999	10000	10000	10000	10000	10000	10000	90
11	9971	9986	9993	9997	9999	9999	10000	10000	10000	10000	89
12	9933	9965	9983	9992	9996	9998	9999	10000	10000	10000	88
13	9857	9922	9959	9979	9990	9995	9998	9999	10000	10000	87
14	9721	9840	9911	9953	9975	9988	9994	9997	9999	9999	86
15	9496	9695	9823	9900	9946	9972	9986	9993	9997	9998	85
16	9153	9462	9671	9806	9889	9939	9967	9983	9992	9996	84
17	8668	9112	9430	9647	9789	9878	9932	9963	9981	9990	83
18	8032	8625	9074	9399	9624	9773	9867	9925	9959	9978	82
19	7252	7991	8585	9038	9370	9601	9757	9850	9918	9955	81
20	0358	7220	7953	8547	9005	9342	9580	9741	9846	9911	80
21	5394	6338	7189	7918	8512	8973	9316	9560	9726	9835	79
22	4419	5391	6320	7162	7886	8479	8943	9291	9540	9712	78
23	3488	4432	5388	6304	7136	7856	8448	8915	9267	9521	77
24	2649	3514	4444	5386	6289	7113	7828	8420	8889	9245	76
25	1933	2684	3539	4455	5383	6276	7091	7802	8393	8864	75
26	1355	1972	2717	3561	4465	5381	6263	7071	7778	8369	74
27	0911	1393	2009	2748	3583	4475	5380	6252	7053	7756	73
28	0588	0945	1429	2043	2776	3602	4484	5378	6242	7036	72
29	0364	0616	0978	1463	2075	2803	3621	4493	5377	6232	71
30	0216	0386	0643	1009	1495	2105	2828	3638	4501	5377	70
31	0123	0232	0406	0669	1038	1526	2134	2851	3654	4509	69
32	0067	0134	0247	0427	0693	1065	1554	2160	2873	3669	68
33	0035	0074	0144	0262	0446	0717	1091	1580	2184	2893	67
34	0018	0039	0081	0154	0276	0465	0739	1116	1605	2207	66
35	0009	0020	0044	0087	0164	0290	0482	0760	1139	1629	65
36	0004	0010	0023	0048	0094	0174	0303	0499	0780	1161	64
37	0002	0005	0011	0025	0052	0101	0183	0316	0515	0799	63
38	0001	0002	0005	0013	0027	0056	0107	0193	0328	0530	62
39		0001	0002	0006	0014	0030	0060	0113	0201	0340	61
40			0001	0003	0007	0015	0032	0064	0119	0210	60
41				0001	0003	0008	0017	0035	0068	0125	59
42				0001	0001	0004	0008	0018	0037	0072	58
43					0001	0002	0004	0009	0020	0040	57
44						0001	0002	0005	0010	0021	56
45							0001	0002	0005	0011	55
46								0001	0002	0005	54
47									0001	0003	53
48										0001	52
49										0001	51

X	p = 31	32	33	34	35	36	37	38	39	40 = (1 − p)	X
1	10000	10000	10000	10000	10000	10000	10000	10000	10000	10000	99
2	10000	10000	10000	10000	10000	10000	10000	10000	10000	10000	98
3	10000	10000	10000	10000	10000	10000	10000	10000	10000	10000	97
4	10000	10000	10000	10000	10000	10000	10000	10000	10000	10000	96
5	10000	10000	10000	10000	10000	10000	10000	10000	10000	10000	95
6	10000	10000	10000	10000	10000	10000	10000	10000	10000	10000	94
7	10000	10000	10000	10000	10000	10000	10000	10000	10000	10000	93
8	10000	10000	10000	10000	10000	10000	10000	10000	10000	10000	92
9	10000	10000	10000	10000	10000	10000	10000	10000	10000	10000	91
10	10000	10000	10000	10000	10000	10000	10000	10000	10000	10000	90
11	10000	10000	10000	10000	10000	10000	10000	10000	10000	10000	89
12	10000	10000	10000	10000	10000	10000	10000	10000	10000	10000	88
13	10000	10000	10000	10000	10000	10000	10000	10000	10000	10000	87
14	10000	10000	10000	10000	10000	10000	10000	10000	10000	10000	86
15	9999	10000	10000	10000	10000	10000	10000	10000	10000	10000	85
16	0000	9999	10000	10000	10000	10000	10000	10000	10000	10000	84
17	9995	9998	0009	10000	10000	10000	10000	10000	10000	10000	83
18	9989	9995	9997	9999	9999	10000	10000	10000	10000	10000	82
19	9076	9988	9994	9997	9999	9999	10000	10000	10000	10000	81
20	9950	9973	9986	9993	9997	9998	9999	10000	10000	10000	80

X	n = 100 (Continued)										X
	p = 31	32	33	34	35	36	37	38	39	40 = (1 − p)	
21	9904	9946	9971	9985	9992	9996	9998	9999	10000	10000	79
22	9825	9898	9942	9968	9983	9991	9996	9998	9999	10000	78
23	9698	9816	9891	9938	9966	9982	9991	9995	9998	9999	77
24	9504	9685	9806	9885	9934	9963	9980	9990	9995	9997	76
25	9224	9487	9672	9797	9879	9930	9961	9979	9989	9994	75
26	8841	9204	9471	9660	9789	9873	9926	9958	9977	9988	74
27	8346	8820	9185	9456	9649	9780	9867	9922	9956	9976	73
28	7736	8325	8800	9168	9442	9638	9773	9862	9919	9954	72
29	7021	7717	8305	8781	9152	9429	9628	9765	9857	9916	71
30	6224	7007	7699	8287	8764	9137	9417	9618	9759	9852	70
31	5376	6216	6994	7684	8270	8748	9123	9405	9610	9752	69
32	4516	5376	6209	6982	7669	8254	8733	9110	9395	9602	68
33	3683	4523	5375	6203	6971	7656	8240	8720	9098	9385	67
34	2912	3696	4530	5375	6197	6961	7643	8227	8708	9087	66
35	2229	2929	3708	4536	5376	6192	6953	7632	8216	8697	65
36	1650	2249	2946	3720	4542	5376	6188	6945	7623	8205	64
37	1181	1671	2268	2961	3731	4547	5377	6184	6938	7614	63
38	0816	1200	1690	2285	2976	3741	4553	5377	6181	6932	62
39	0545	0833	1218	1708	2301	2989	3750	4558	5378	6178	61
40	0351	0558	0849	1235	1724	2316	3001	3759	4562	5379	60
41	0218	0361	0571	0863	1250	1739	2330	3012	3767	4567	59
42	0131	0226	0371	0583	0877	1265	1753	2343	3023	3775	58
43	0075	0136	0233	0380	0594	0889	1278	1766	2355	3033	57
44	0042	0079	0141	0240	0389	0605	0901	1290	1778	2365	56
45	0023	0044	0082	0146	0246	0397	0614	0911	1301	1789	55
46	0012	0024	0046	0085	0150	0252	0405	0623	0921	1311	54
47	0006	0012	0025	0048	0088	0154	0257	0411	0631	0930	53
48	0003	0006	0013	0026	0050	0091	0158	0262	0417	0638	52
49	0001	0003	0007	0014	0027	0052	0094	0162	0267	0423	51
50	0001	0001	0003	0007	0015	0029	0054	0096	0165	0271	50
51		0001	0002	0003	0007	0015	0030	0055	0098	0168	49
52			0001	0002	0004	0008	0016	0030	0056	0100	48
53				0001	0002	0004	0008	0016	0031	0058	47
54					0001	0002	0004	0008	0017	0032	46
55						0001	0002	0004	0009	0017	45
56							0001	0002	0004	0009	44
57								0001	0002	0004	43
58									0001	0002	42
59										0001	41

X	p = 41	42	43	44	45	46	47	18	49	50 = (1 − p)	X
1	10000	10000	10000	10000	10000	10000	10000	10000	10000	10000	99
⋮	⋮	⋮	⋮	⋮	⋮	⋮	⋮	⋮	⋮	⋮	⋮
23	10000	10000	10000	10000	10000	10000	10000	10000	10000	10000	77
24	9999	9999	10000	10000	10000	10000	10000	10000	10000	10000	76
25	9997	9999	9999	10000	10000	10000	10000	10000	10000	10000	75
26	9994	9997	9999	9999	10000	10000	10000	10000	10000	10000	74
27	9987	9994	9997	9998	9999	10000	10000	10000	10000	10000	73
28	9975	9987	9993	9997	9998	9999	10000	10000	10000	10000	72
29	9952	9974	9986	9993	9996	9998	9999	10000	10000	10000	71
30	9913	9950	9972	9985	9992	9996	9998	9999	10000	10000	70
31	9848	9910	9848	9971	9985	9992	9996	9998	9999	10000	69
32	9746	9844	0907	9947	9970	9984	9992	9996	9998	9999	68
33	9594	9741	9840	9905	9945	9969	9984	9991	9996	9998	67
34	9376	9587	9736	9837	9902	9944	9969	9983	9991	9996	66
35	9078	9368	9581	9732	9834	9900	9942	9968	9983	9991	65
36	8687	9069	9361	9576	9728	9831	9899	9941	9967	9982	64
37	8196	8678	9061	9355	9571	9724	9829	9897	9941	9967	63
38	7606	8188	8670	9054	9349	9567	9721	9827	9896	9940	62
39	6927	7599	8181	8663	9049	9345	9563	9719	9825	9895	61
40	6176	6922	7594	8174	8657	9044	9341	9561	9717	9824	60
41	5380	6174	6919	7589	8169	8653	9040	9338	9558	9716	59
42	4571	5382	6173	6916	7585	8165	8649	9037	9335	9557	58
43	3782	4576	5383	6173	6913	7582	8162	8646	9035	9334	57
44	3041	3788	4580	5385	6172	6912	7580	8160	8645	9033	56
45	2375	3049	3794	4583	5387	6173	6911	7579	8159	8644	55
46	1799	2384	3057	3799	4587	5389	6173	6911	7579	8159	54
47	1320	1807	2391	3063	3804	4590	5391	6174	6912	7579	53
48	0938	1328	1815	2398	3069	3809	4593	5393	6176	6914	52
49	0644	0944	1335	1822	2404	3074	3813	4596	5395	6178	51
50	0428	0650	0950	1341	1827	2409	3078	3816	4599	5398	50
51	0275	0432	0655	0955	1346	1832	2413	3082	3819	4602	49
52	0170	0278	0436	0659	0960	1350	1836	2417	3084	3822	48
53	0102	0172	0280	0439	0662	0963	1353	1838	2419	3086	47
54	0059	0103	0174	0282	0441	0664	0965	1355	1840	2421	46
55	0033	0059	0104	0175	0284	0443	0666	0967	1356	1841	45
56	0017	0033	0060	0105	0176	0285	0444	0667	0967	1356	44
57	0009	0018	0034	0061	0106	0177	0286	0444	0667	0967	43
58	0004	0009	0018	0034	0061	0106	0177	0286	0444	0666	42
59	0002	0005	0009	0018	0034	0061	0106	0177	0285	0443	41
60	0001	0002	0005	0009	0018	0034	0061	0106	0177	0284	40
61		0001	0002	0005	0000	0018	0034	0061	0106	0176	39
62			0001	0002	0005	0009	0018	0034	0061	0105	38
63				0001	0002	0005	0009	0018	0034	0060	37
64					0001	0002	0005	0009	0018	0033	36
65						0001	0002	0005	0009	0018	35
66							0001	0002	0004	0009	34
67								0001	0002	0004	33
68									0001	0002	32
69										0001	31

Appendix D

Cumulative Poisson Distribution, $F_P(X \mid m)$

m \ X	0	1	2	3	4	5	6	7	8	9	10	11	12	13	14	15	16
0.02	.980	1.000															
0.04	.961	.999	1.000														
0.06	.942	.998	1.000														
0.08	.923	.997	1.000														
0.10	.905	.995	1.000														
0.15	.861	.990	.999	1.000													
0.20	.819	.982	.999	1.000													
0.25	.779	.974	.998	1.000													
0.30	.741	.963	.996	1.000													
0.35	.705	.951	.994	1.000													
0.40	.670	.938	.992	.999	1.000												
0.45	.638	.925	.989	.999	1.000												
0.50	.607	.910	.986	.998	1.000												
0.55	.577	.894	.982	.998	1.000												
0.60	.549	.878	.977	.997	1.000												
0.65	.522	.861	.972	.996	.999	1.000											
0.70	.497	.844	.966	.994	.999	1.000											
0.75	.472	.827	.959	.993	.999	1.000											
0.80	.449	.809	.953	.991	.999	1.000											
0.85	.427	.791	.945	.989	.998	1.000											
0.90	.407	.772	.937	.987	.998	1.000											
0.95	.387	.754	.929	.984	.997	1.000											
1.00	.368	.736	.920	.981	.996	.999	1.000										
1.1	.333	.699	.900	.974	.995	.999	1.000										
1.2	.301	.663	.879	.966	.992	.998	1.000										
1.3	.273	.627	.857	.957	.989	.998	1.000										
1.4	.247	.592	.833	.946	.986	.997	.999	1.000									
1.5	.223	.558	.809	.934	.981	.996	.999	1.000									
1.6	.202	.525	.783	.921	.976	.994	.999	1.000									
1.7	.183	.493	.757	.907	.970	.992	.998	1.000									
1.8	.165	.463	.731	.891	.964	.990	.997	.999	1.000								
1.9	.150	.434	.704	.875	.956	.987	.997	.999	1.000								
2.0	.135	.406	.677	.857	.947	.983	.995	.999	1.000								
2.2	.111	.355	.623	.819	.928	.975	.993	.998	1.000								
2.4	.091	.308	.570	.779	.904	.964	.988	.997	.999	1.000							
2.6	.074	.267	.518	.736	.877	.951	.983	.995	.999	1.000							
2.8	.061	.231	.469	.692	.848	.935	.976	.992	.998	.999	1.000						
3.0	.050	.199	.423	.647	.815	.916	.966	.998	.996	.999	1.000						
3.2	.041	.171	.380	.603	.781	.895	.955	.983	.994	.998	1.000						
3.4	.033	.147	.340	.558	.744	.871	.942	.977	.992	.997	.999	1.000					
3.6	.027	.126	.303	.515	.706	.844	.927	.969	.988	.996	.999	1.000					
3.8	.022	.107	.269	.473	.668	.816	.909	.960	.984	.994	.998	.999	1.000				
4.0	.018	.092	.238	.433	.629	.785	.889	.949	.979	.992	.997	.999	1.000				
4.2	.015	.078	.210	.395	.590	.753	.867	.936	.972	.989	.996	.999	1.000				
4.4	.012	.066	.185	.359	.551	.720	.844	.921	.964	.985	.994	.998	.999	1.000			
4.6	.010	.056	.163	.326	.513	.686	.818	.905	.955	.980	.992	.997	.999	1.000			
4.8	.008	.048	.143	.294	.476	.651	.791	.887	.944	.975	.990	.996	.999	1.000			
5.0	.007	.040	.125	.265	.440	.616	.762	.867	.932	.968	.986	.995	.998	.999	1.000		
5.2	.006	.034	.109	.238	.406	.581	.732	.845	.918	.960	.982	.993	.997	.999	1.000		
5.4	.005	.029	.095	.213	.373	.546	.702	.822	.903	.951	.977	.990	.996	.999	1.000		
5.6	.004	.024	.082	.191	.342	.512	.670	.797	.886	.941	.972	.988	.995	.998	.999	1.000	
5.8	.003	.021	.072	.170	.313	.478	.638	.771	.867	.929	.965	.984	.993	.997	.999	1.000	
6.0	.002	.017	.062	.151	.285	.446	.606	.744	.847	.916	.957	.980	.991	.996	.999	.999	1.000

X / m	0	1	2	3	4	5	6	7	8	9	10
6.2	.002	.015	.054	.134	.259	.414	.574	.716	.826	.902	.949
6.4	.002	.012	.046	.119	.235	.384	.542	.687	.803	.886	.939
6.6	.001	.010.	040	.105	.213	.355	.511	.658	.780	.869	.927
6.8	.001	.009	.034	.093	.192	.327	.480	.628	.755	.850	.915
7.0	.001	.007	.030	.082	.173	.301	.450	.599	.729	.830	.901
7.2	.001	.006	.025	.072	.156	.276	.420	.569	.703	.810	.887
7.4	.001	.005	.022	.063	.140	.253	.392	.539	.676	.788	.871
7.6	.001	.004	.019	.055	.125	.231	.365	.510	.648	.765	.854
7.8	.000	.004	.016	.048	.112	.210	.338	.481	.620	.741	.835
8.0	.000	.003	.014	.042	.100	.191	.313	.453	.593	.717	.816
8.5	.000	.002	.009	.030	.074	.150	.256	.386	.523	.653	.763
9.0	.000	.001	.006	.021	.055	.116	.207	.324	.456	.587	.706
9.5	.000	.001	.004	.015	.040	.089	.165	.269	.392	.522	.645
10.0	.000	.000	.003	.010	.029	.067	.130	.220	.333	.458	.583

X / m	11	12	13	14	15	16	17	18	19	20	21	22
6.2	.975	.989	.995	.998	.999	1.000						
6.4	.969	.986	.994	.997	.999	1.000						
6.6	.963	.982	.992	.997	.999	.999	1.000					
6.8	.955	.978	.990	.996	.998	.999	1.000					
7.0	.947	.973	.987	.994	.998	.999	1.000					
7.2	.937	.967	.984	.993	.997	.999	.999	1.000				
7.4	.926	.961	.980	.991	.996	.998	.999	1.000				
7.6	.915	.954	.976	.989	.995	.998	.999	1.000				
7.8	.902	.945	.971	.986	.993	.997	.999	1.000				
8.0	.888	.936	.966	.983	.992	.996	.998	.999	1.000			
8.5	.849	.909	.949	.973	.986	.993	.997	.999	.999	1.000		
9.0	.803	.876	.926	.959	.978	.989	.995	.998	.999	1.000		
9.5	.752	.836	.898	.940	.967	.982	.991	.996	.998	.999	1.000	
10.0	.697	.792	.864	.917	.951	.973	.986	.993	.997	.998	.999	1.000

X / m	0	1	2	3	4	5	6	7	8	9	10	11	12	13
10.5	.000	.000	.002	.007	.021	.050	.102	.179	.279	.397	.521	.639	.742	.825
11.0	.000	.000	.001	.005	.015	.038	.079	.143	.232	.341	.460	.579	.689	.781
11.5	.000	.000	.001	.003	.011	.028	.060	.114	.191	.289	.402	.520	.633	.733
12.0	.000	.000	.001	.002	.008	.020	.046	.090	.155	.242	.347	.462	.576	.682
12.5	.000	.000	.000	.002	.005	.015	.035	.070	.125	.201	.297	.406	.519	.628
13.0	.000	.000	.000	.001	.004	.011	.026	.054	.100	.166	.252	.353	.463	.573
13.5	.000	.000	.000	.001	.003	.008	.019	.041	.079	.135	.211	.304	.409	.518
14.0	.000	.000	.000	.000	.002	.006	.014	.032	.062	.109	.176	.260	.358	.464
14.5	.000	.000	.000	.000	.001	.004	.010	.024	.048	.088	.145	.220	.311	.413
15.0	.000	.000	.000	.000	.001	.003	.008	.018	.037	.070	.118	.185	.268	.363

X / m	14	15	16	17	18	19	20	21	22	23	24	25	26	27	28	29
10.5	.888	.932	.960	.978	.988	.994	.997	.999	.999	1.000						
11.0	.854	.907	.944	.968	.982	.991	.995	.998	.999	1.000						
11.5	.815	.878	.924	.954	.974	.986	.992	.996	.998	.999	1.000					
12.0	.772	.844	.899	.937	.963	.979	.988	.994	.997	.999	.999	1.000				
12.5	.725	.806	.869	.916	.948	.969	.983	.991	.995	.998	.999	.999	1.000			
13.0	.675	.764	.835	.890	.930	.957	.975	.986	.992	.996	.998	.999	1.000			
13.5	.623	.718	.798	.861	.908	.942	.965	.980	.989	.994	.997	.998	.999	1.000		
14.0	.570	.669	.756	.827	.883	.923	.952	.971	.983	.991	.995	.997	.999	.999	1.000	
14.5	.518	.619	.711	.790	.853	.901	.936	.960	.976	.986	.992	.996	.998	.999	.999	1.000
15.0	.466	.568	.664	.749	.819	.875	.917	.947	.967	.981	.989	.994	.997	.998	.999	1.000

Appendix E

Percentile Values , $\chi^2_{g,\nu}$,
for the
Chi-Square Distribution
with ν Degrees of Freedom

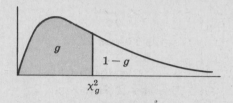

ν	$\chi^2_{.005}$	$\chi^2_{.01}$	$\chi^2_{.025}$	$\chi^2_{.05}$	$\chi^2_{.10}$	$\chi^2_{.25}$	$\chi^2_{.50}$	$\chi^2_{.75}$	$\chi^2_{.90}$	$\chi^2_{.95}$	$\chi^2_{.975}$	$\chi^2_{.99}$	$\chi^2_{.995}$	$\chi^2_{.999}$
1	.0000	.0002	.0010	.0039	.0158	.102	.455	1.32	2.71	3.84	5.02	6.63	7.88	10.8
2	.0100	.0201	.0506	.103	.211	.575	1.39	2.77	4.61	5.99	7.38	9.21	10.6	13.8
3	.0717	.115	.216	.352	.584	1.21	2.37	4.11	6.25	7.81	9.35	11.3	12.8	16.3
4	.207	.297	.484	.711	1.06	1.92	3.36	5.39	7.78	9.49	11.1	13.3	14.9	18.5
5	.412	.554	.831	1.15	1.61	2.67	4.35	6.63	9.24	11.1	12.8	15.1	16.7	20.5
6	.676	.872	1.24	1.64	2.20	3.45	5.35	7.84	10.6	12.6	14.4	16.8	18.5	22.5
7	.989	1.24	1.69	2.17	2.83	4.25	6.35	9.04	12.0	14.1	16.0	18.5	20.3	24.3
8	1.34	1.65	2.18	2.73	3.49	5.07	7.34	10.2	13.4	15.5	17.5	20.1	22.0	26.1
9	1.73	2.09	2.70	3.33	4.17	5.90	8.34	11.4	14.7	16.9	19.0	21.7	23.6	27.9
10	2.16	2.56	3.25	3.94	4.87	6.74	9.34	12.5	16.0	18.3	20.5	23.2	25.2	29.6
11	2.60	3.05	3.82	4.57	5.58	7.58	10.3	13.7	17.3	19.7	21.9	24.7	26.8	31.3
12	3.07	3.57	4.40	5.23	6.30	8.44	11.3	14.8	18.5	21.0	23.3	26.2	28.3	32.9
13	3.57	4.11	5.01	5.89	7.04	9.30	12.3	16.0	19.8	22.4	24.7	27.7	29.8	34.5
14	4.07	4.66	5.63	6.57	7.79	10.2	13.3	17.1	21.1	23.7	26.1	29.1	31.3	36.1
15	4.60	5.23	6.26	7.26	8.55	11.0	14.3	18.2	22.3	25.0	27.5	30.6	32.8	37.7
16	5.14	5.81	6.91	7.96	9.31	11.9	15.3	19.4	23.5	26.3	28.8	32.0	34.3	39.3
17	5.70	6.41	7.56	8.67	10.1	12.8	16.3	20.5	24.8	27.6	30.2	33.4	35.7	40.8
18	6.26	7.01	8.23	9.39	10.9	13.7	17.3	21.6	26.0	28.9	31.5	34.8	37.2	42.3
19	6.84	7.63	8.91	10.1	11.7	14.6	18.3	22.7	27.2	30.1	32.9	36.2	38.6	43.8
20	7.43	8.26	9.59	10.9	12.4	15.5	19.3	23.8	28.4	31.4	34.2	37.6	40.0	45.3
21	8.03	8.90	10.3	11.6	13.2	16.3	20.3	24.9	29.6	32.7	35.5	38.9	41.4	46.8
22	8.64	9.54	11.0	12.3	14.0	17.2	21.3	26.0	30.8	33.9	36.8	40.3	42.8	48.3
23	9.26	10.2	11.7	13.1	14.8	18.1	22.3	27.1	32.0	35.2	38.1	41.6	44.2	49.7
24	9.89	10.9	12.4	13.8	15.7	19.0	23.3	28.2	33.2	36.4	39.4	43.0	45.6	51.2
25	10.5	11.5	13.1	14.6	16.5	19.9	24.3	29.3	34.4	37.7	40.6	44.3	46.9	52.6
26	11.2	12.2	13.8	15.4	17.3	20.8	25.3	30.4	35.6	38.9	41.9	45.6	48.3	54.1
27	11.8	12.9	14.6	16.2	18.1	21.7	26.3	31.5	36.7	40.1	43.2	47.0	49.6	55.5
28	12.5	13.6	15.3	16.9	18.9	22.7	27.3	32.6	37.9	41.3	44.5	48.3	51.0	56.9
29	13.1	14.3	16.0	17.7	19.8	23.6	28.3	33.7	39.1	42.6	45.7	49.6	52.3	58.3
30	13.8	15.0	16.8	18.5	20.6	24.5	29.3	34.8	40.3	43.8	47.0	50.9	53.7	59.7
40	20.7	22.2	24.4	26.5	29.1	33.7	39.3	45.6	51.8	55.8	59.3	63.7	66.8	73.4
50	28.0	29.7	32.4	34.8	37.7	42.9	49.3	56.3	63.2	67.5	71.4	76.2	79.5	86.7
60	35.5	37.5	40.5	43.2	46.5	52.3	59.3	67.0	74.4	79.1	83.3	88.4	92.0	99.6
70	43.3	45.4	48.8	51.7	55.3	61.7	69.3	77.6	85.5	90.5	95.0	100	104	112
80	51.2	53.5	57.2	60.4	64.3	71.1	79.3	88.1	96.6	102	107	112	116	125
90	59.2	61.8	65.6	69.1	73.3	80.6	89.3	98.6	108	113	118	124	128	137
100	67.3	70.1	74.2	77.9	82.4	90.1	99.3	109	118	124	130	136	140	149

Source: E. S. Pearson and H. O. Hartley, *Biometrika Tables for Statisticians*, Vol. 1 (1966), Table 8, pages 137 and 138, by permission.

344

Appendix F

Percentile Values , $t_{g,\nu}$,
for
Student's t Distribution
with ν Degrees of Freedom

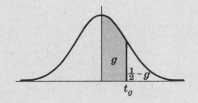

ν	$t_{0.05}$	$t_{0.10}$	$t_{0.20}$	$t_{0.25}$	$t_{0.30}$	$t_{0.40}$	$t_{0.45}$	$t_{0.475}$	$t_{0.49}$	$t_{0.495}$
1	.158	.325	.727	1.000	1.376	3.08	6.31	12.71	31.82	63.66
2	.142	.289	.617	.816	1.061	1.89	2.92	4.30	6.96	9.92
3	.137	.277	.584	.765	.978	1.64	2.35	3.18	4.54	5.84
4	.134	.271	.569	.741	.941	1.53	2.13	2.78	3.75	4.60
5	.132	.267	.559	.727	.920	1.48	2.02	2.57	3.36	4.03
6	.131	.265	.553	.718	.906	1.44	1.94	2.45	3.14	3.71
7	.130	.263	.549	.711	.896	1.42	1.90	2.36	3.00	3.50
8	.130	.262	.546	.706	.889	1.40	1.86	2.31	2.90	3.36
9	.129	.261	.543	.703	.883	1.38	1.83	2.26	2.82	3.25
10	.129	.260	.542	.700	.879	1.37	1.81	2.23	2.76	3.17
11	.129	.260	.540	.697	.876	1.36	1.80	2.20	2.72	3.11
12	.128	.259	.539	.695	.873	1.36	1.78	2.18	2.68	3.06
13	.128	.259	.538	.694	.870	1.35	1.77	2.16	2.65	3.01
14	.128	.258	.537	.692	.868	1.34	1.76	2.14	2.62	2.98
15	.128	.258	.536	.691	.866	1.34	1.75	2.13	2.60	2.95
16	.128	.258	.535	.690	.865	1.34	1.75	2.12	2.58	2.92
17	.128	.257	.534	.689	.863	1.33	1.74	2.11	2.57	2.90
18	.127	.257	.534	.688	.862	1.33	1.73	2.10	2.55	2.88
19	.127	.257	.533	.688	.861	1.33	1.73	2.09	2.54	2.86
20	.127	.257	.533	.687	.860	1.32	1.72	2.09	2.53	2.84
21	.127	.257	.532	.686	.859	1.32	1.72	2.08	2.52	2.83
22	.127	.256	.532	.686	.858	1.32	1.72	2.07	2.51	2.82
23	.127	.256	.532	.685	.858	1.32	1.71	2.07	2.50	2.81
24	.127	.256	.531	.685	.857	1.32	1.71	2.06	2.49	2.80
25	.127	.256	.531	.684	.856	1.32	1.71	2.06	2.48	2.79
26	.127	.256	.531	.684	.856	1.32	1.71	2.06	2.48	2.78
27	.127	.256	.531	.684	.855	1.31	1.70	2.05	2.47	2.77
28	.127	.256	.530	.683	.855	1.31	1.70	2.05	2.47	2.76
29	.127	.256	.530	.683	.854	1.31	1.70	2.04	2.46	2.76
30	.127	.256	.530	.683	.854	1.31	1.70	2.04	2.46	2.75
40	.126	.255	.529	.681	.851	1.30	1.68	2.02	2.42	2.70
60	.126	.254	.527	.679	.848	1.30	1.67	2.00	2.39	2.66
120	.126	.254	.526	.677	.845	1.29	1.66	1.98	2.36	2.62
∞	.126	.253	.524	.674	.842	1.28	1.645	1.96	2.33	2.58

Source: R. A. Fisher and F. Yates, *Statistical Tables for Biological, Agricultural and Medical Research*, published by Longman Group Ltd., London (previously published by Oliver and Boyd, Edinburgh), and by permission of the authors and publishers.

Appendix G

95th Percentile Values (0.05 Levels), $F_{0.95, \nu_1, \nu_2}$, for the F Distribution

ν_1 degrees of freedom in numerator

ν_2 degrees of freedom in denominator

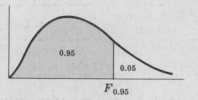

ν_2 \ ν_1	1	2	3	4	5	6	7	8	9	10	12	15	20	24	30	40	60	120	∞
1	161	200	216	225	230	234	237	239	241	242	244	246	248	249	250	251	252	253	254
2	18.5	19.0	19.2	19.2	19.3	19.3	19.4	19.4	19.4	19.4	19.4	19.4	19.4	19.5	19.5	19.5	19.5	19.5	19.5
3	10.1	9.55	9.28	9.12	9.01	8.94	8.89	8.85	8.81	8.79	8.74	8.70	8.66	8.64	8.62	8.59	8.57	8.55	8.53
4	7.71	6.94	6.59	6.39	6.26	6.16	6.09	6.04	6.00	5.96	5.91	5.86	5.80	5.77	5.75	5.72	5.69	5.66	5.63
5	6.61	5.79	5.41	5.19	5.05	4.95	4.88	4.82	4.77	4.74	4.68	4.62	4.56	4.53	4.50	4.46	4.43	4.40	4.37
6	5.99	5.14	4.76	4.53	4.39	4.28	4.21	4.15	4.10	4.06	4.00	3.94	3.87	3.84	3.81	3.77	3.74	3.70	3.67
7	5.59	4.74	4.35	4.12	3.97	3.87	3.79	3.73	3.68	3.64	3.57	3.51	3.44	3.41	3.38	3.34	3.30	3.27	3.23
8	5.32	4.46	4.07	3.84	3.69	3.58	3.50	3.44	3.39	3.35	3.28	3.22	3.15	3.12	3.08	3.04	3.01	2.97	2.93
9	5.12	4.26	3.86	3.63	3.48	3.37	3.29	3.23	3.18	3.14	3.07	3.01	2.94	2.90	2.86	2.83	2.79	2.75	2.71
10	4.96	4.10	3.71	3.48	3.33	3.22	3.14	3.07	3.02	2.98	2.91	2.85	2.77	2.74	2.70	2.66	2.62	2.58	2.54
11	4.84	3.98	3.59	3.36	3.20	3.09	3.01	2.95	2.90	2.85	2.79	2.72	2.65	2.61	2.57	2.53	2.49	2.45	2.40
12	4.75	3.89	3.49	3.26	3.11	3.00	2.91	2.85	2.80	2.75	2.69	2.62	2.54	2.51	2.47	2.43	2.38	2.34	2.30
13	4.67	3.81	3.41	3.18	3.03	2.92	2.83	2.77	2.71	2.67	2.60	2.53	2.46	2.42	2.38	2.34	2.30	2.25	2.21
14	4.60	3.74	3.34	3.11	2.96	2.85	2.76	2.70	2.65	2.60	2.53	2.46	2.39	2.35	2.31	2.27	2.22	2.18	2.13
15	4.54	3.68	3.29	3.06	2.90	2.79	2.71	2.64	2.59	2.54	2.48	2.40	2.33	2.29	2.25	2.20	2.16	2.11	2.07
16	4.49	3.63	3.24	3.01	2.85	2.74	2.66	2.59	2.54	2.49	2.42	2.35	2.28	2.24	2.19	2.15	2.11	2.06	2.01
17	4.45	3.59	3.20	2.96	2.81	2.70	2.61	2.55	2.49	2.45	2.38	2.31	2.23	2.19	2.15	2.10	2.06	2.01	1.96
18	4.41	3.55	3.16	2.93	2.77	2.66	2.58	2.51	2.46	2.41	2.34	2.27	2.19	2.15	2.11	2.06	2.02	1.97	1.92
19	4.38	3.52	3.13	2.90	2.74	2.63	2.54	2.48	2.42	2.38	2.31	2.23	2.16	2.11	2.07	2.03	1.98	1.93	1.88
20	4.35	3.49	3.10	2.87	2.71	2.60	2.51	2.45	2.39	2.35	2.28	2.20	2.12	2.08	2.04	1.99	1.95	1.90	1.84
21	4.32	3.47	3.07	2.84	2.68	2.57	2.49	2.42	2.37	2.32	2.25	2.18	2.10	2.05	2.01	1.96	1.92	1.87	1.81
22	4.30	3.44	3.05	2.82	2.66	2.55	2.46	2.40	2.34	2.30	2.23	2.15	2.07	2.03	1.98	1.94	1.89	1.84	1.78
23	4.28	3.42	3.03	2.80	2.64	2.53	2.44	2.37	2.32	2.27	2.20	2.13	2.05	2.01	1.96	1.91	1.86	1.81	1.76
24	4.26	3.40	3.01	2.78	2.62	2.51	2.42	2.36	2.30	2.25	2.18	2.11	2.03	1.98	1.94	1.89	1.84	1.79	1.73
25	4.24	3.39	2.99	2.76	2.60	2.49	2.40	2.34	2.28	2.24	2.16	2.09	2.01	1.96	1.92	1.87	1.82	1.77	1.71
26	4.23	3.37	2.98	2.74	2.59	2.47	2.39	2.32	2.27	2.22	2.15	2.07	1.99	1.95	1.90	1.85	1.80	1.75	1.69
27	4.21	3.35	2.96	2.73	2.57	2.46	2.37	2.31	2.25	2.20	2.13	2.06	1.97	1.93	1.88	1.84	1.79	1.73	1.67
28	4.20	3.34	2.95	2.71	2.56	2.45	2.36	2.29	2.24	2.19	2.12	2.04	1.96	1.91	1.87	1.82	1.77	1.71	1.65
29	4.18	3.33	2.93	2.70	2.55	2.43	2.35	2.28	2.22	2.18	2.10	2.03	1.94	1.90	1.85	1.81	1.75	1.70	1.64
30	4.17	3.32	2.92	2.69	2.53	2.42	2.33	2.27	2.21	2.16	2.09	2.01	1.93	1.89	1.84	1.79	1.74	1.68	1.62
40	4.08	3.23	2.84	2.61	2.45	2.34	2.25	2.18	2.12	2.08	2.00	1.92	1.84	1.79	1.74	1.69	1.64	1.58	1.51
60	4.00	3.15	2.76	2.53	2.37	2.25	2.17	2.10	2.04	1.99	1.92	1.84	1.75	1.70	1.65	1.59	1.53	1.47	1.39
120	3.92	3.07	2.68	2.45	2.29	2.18	2.09	2.02	1.96	1.91	1.83	1.75	1.66	1.61	1.55	1.50	1.43	1.35	1.25
∞	3.84	3.00	2.60	2.37	2.21	2.10	2.01	1.94	1.88	1.83	1.75	1.67	1.57	1.52	1.46	1.39	1.32	1.22	1.00

Source: E. S. Pearson and H. O. Hartley, *Biometrika Tables for Statisticians*, Vol. 2 (1972), Table 5, page 178, by permission.

Appendix H

Factors Useful in the Construction of Control Charts

| Sample Size | Chart for Averages | | | Chart for Standard Deviations | | | | | | Chart for Ranges | | | | | | |
| | Factors for Control Limits | | | Factors for Central Line | | Factors for Control Limits | | | | Factors for Central Line | | Factors for Control Limits | | | | |
n	A	A_1	A_2	c_2	$1/c_2$	B_1	B_2	B_3	B_4	d_2	$1/d_2$	d_3	D_1	D_2	D_3	D_4
2	2.121	3.760	1.880	0.5642	1.7725	0	1.843	0	3.267	1.128	0.8865	0.853	0	3.686	0	3.267
3	1.732	2.394	1.023	0.7236	1.3820	0	1.858	0	2.568	1.693	0.5907	0.888	0	4.358	0	2.575
4	1.500	1.880	0.729	0.7979	1.2533	0	1.808	0	2.266	2.059	0.4857	0.880	0	4.698	0	2.282
5	1.342	1.596	0.577	0.8407	1.1894	0	1.756	0	2.089	2.326	0.4299	0.864	0	4.918	0	2.115
6	1.225	1.410	0.483	0.8686	1.1512	0.026	1.711	0.030	1.970	2.534	0.3946	0.848	0	5.078	0	2.004
7	1.134	1.277	0.419	0.8882	1.1259	0.105	1.672	0.118	1.882	2.704	0.3698	0.833	0.205	5.203	0.076	1.924
8	1.061	1.175	0.373	0.9027	1.1078	0.167	1.638	0.185	1.815	2.847	0.3512	0.820	0.387	5.307	0.136	1.864
9	1.000	1.094	0.337	0.9139	1.0942	0.219	1.609	0.239	1.761	2.970	0.3367	0.808	0.546	5.394	0.184	1.816
10	0.949	1.028	0.308	0.9227	1.0837	0.262	1.584	0.284	1.716	3.078	0.3249	0.797	0.687	5.469	0.223	1.777
11	0.905	0.973	0.285	0.9300	1.0753	0.299	1.561	0.321	1.679	3.173	0.3152	0.787	0.812	5.534	0.256	1.744
12	0.866	0.925	0.266	0.9359	1.0684	0.331	1.541	0.354	1.646	3.258	0.3069	0.778	0.924	5.592	0.284	1.716
13	0.832	0.884	0.249	0.9410	1.0627	0.359	1.523	0.382	1.618	3.336	0.2998	0.770	1.026	5.646	0.308	1.692
14	0.802	0.848	0.235	0.9453	1.0579	0.384	1.507	0.406	1.594	3.407	0.2935	0.762	1.121	5.693	0.329	1.671
15	0.775	0.816	0.223	0.9490	1.0537	0.406	1.492	0.428	1.572	3.472	0.2880	0.755	1.207	5.737	0.348	1.652
16	0.750	0.788	0.212	0.9523	1.0501	0.427	1.478	0.448	1.552	3.532	0.2831	0.749	1.285	5.779	0.364	1.636
17	0.728	0.762	0.203	0.9551	1.0470	0.445	1.465	0.466	1.534	3.588	0.2787	0.743	1.359	5.817	0.379	1.621
18	0.707	0.738	0.194	0.9576	1.0442	0.461	1.454	0.482	1.518	3.640	0.2747	0.738	1.426	5.854	0.392	1.608
19	0.688	0.717	0.187	0.9599	1.0418	0.477	1.443	0.497	1.503	3.689	0.2711	0.733	1.490	5.888	0.404	1.596
20	0.671	0.697	0.180	0.9619	1.0396	0.491	1.433	0.510	1.490	3.735	0.2677	0.729	1.548	5.922	0.414	1.586
21	0.655	0.679	0.173	0.9638	1.0376	0.504	1.424	0.523	1.477	3.778	0.2647	0.724	1.606	5.950	0.425	1.575
22	0.640	0.662	0.167	0.9655	1.0358	0.516	1.415	0.534	1.466	3.819	0.2618	0.720	1.659	5.979	0.434	1.566
23	0.626	0.647	0.162	0.9670	1.0342	0.527	1.407	0.545	1.455	3.858	0.2592	0.716	1.710	6.006	0.443	1.557
24	0.612	0.632	0.157	0.9684	1.0327	0.538	1.399	0.555	1.445	3.895	0.2567	0.712	1.759	6.031	0.452	1.548
25	0.600	0.619	0.153	0.9696	1.0313	0.548	1.392	0.565	1.435	3.931	0.2544	0.709	1.804	6.058	0.459	1.541
>25	$\frac{3}{\sqrt{n}}$	$\frac{3}{\sqrt{n}}$	..	..	..	*	**	*	**	..	..	..	..	..	..	..

$*1 - \dfrac{3}{\sqrt{2n}}$ $**1 + \dfrac{3}{\sqrt{2n}}$

Reproduced with permission from Table B2 of the *ASTM Manual on Quality Control of Materials*, p. 115.

347

Appendix I

Unit Normal Loss Integral,*
$$L(z) = f_N(z) - zR_N(z)$$

z	.00	.01	.02	.03	.04	.05	.06	.07	.08	.09
.0	.3989	.3940	.3890	.3841	.3793	.3744	.3697	.3649	.3602	.3556
.1	.3509	.3464	.3418	.3373	.3328	.3284	.3240	.3197	.3154	.3111
.2	.3069	.3027	.2986	.2944	.2904	.2863	.2824	.2784	.2745	.2706
.3	.2668	.2630	.2592	.2555	.2518	.2481	.2445	.2409	.2374	.2339
.4	.2304	.2270	.2236	.2203	.2169	.2137	.2104	.2072	.2040	.2009
.5	.1978	.1947	.1917	.1887	.1857	.1828	.1799	.1771	.1742	.1714
.6	.1687	.1659	.1633	.1606	.1580	.1554	.1528	.1503	.1478	.1453
.7	.1429	.1405	.1381	.1358	.1334	.1312	.1289	.1267	.1245	.1223
.8	.1202	.1181	.1160	.1140	.1120	.1100	.1080	.1061	.1042	.1023
.9	.1004	.09860	.09680	.09503	.09328	.09156	.08986	.08819	.08654	.08491
1.0	.08332	.08174	.08019	.07866	.07716	.07568	.07422	.07279	.07138	.06999
1.1	.06862	.06727	.06595	.06465	.06336	.06210	.06086	.05964	.05844	.05726
1.2	.05610	.05496	.05384	.05274	.05165	.05059	.04954	.04851	.04750	.04650
1.3	.04553	.04457	.04363	.04270	.04179	.04090	.04002	.03916	.03831	.03748
1.4	.03667	.03587	.03508	.03431	.03356	.03281	.03208	.03137	.03067	.02998
1.5	.02931	.02865	.02800	.02736	.02674	.02612	.02552	.02494	.02436	.02380
1.6	.02324	.02270	.02217	.02165	.02114	.02064	.02015	.01967	.01920	.01874
1.7	.01829	.01785	.01742	.01699	.01658	.01617	.01578	.01539	.01501	.01464
1.8	.01428	.01392	.01357	.01323	.01290	.01257	.01226	.01195	.01164	.01134
1 9	.01105	.01077	.01049	.01022	$.0^2$9957	$.0^2$9698	$.0^2$9445	$.0^2$9198	$.0^2$8957	$.0^2$8721
2.0	$.0^2$8491	$.0^2$8266	$.0^2$8046	$.0^2$7832	$.0^2$7623	$.0^2$7418	$.0^2$7219	$.0^2$7024	$.0^2$6835	$.0^2$6649
2.1	$.0^2$6468	$.0^2$6292	$.0^2$6120	$.0^2$5952	$.0^2$5788	$.0^2$5628	$.0^2$5472	$.0^2$5320	$.0^2$5172	$.0^2$5028
2.2	$.0^2$4887	$.0^2$4750	$.0^2$4616	$.0^2$4486	$.0^2$4358	$.0^2$4235	$.0^2$4114	$.0^2$3996	$.0^2$3882	$.0^2$3770
2.3	$.0^2$3662	$.0^2$3556	$.0^2$3453	$.0^2$3352	$.0^2$3255	$.0^2$3159	$.0^2$3067	$.0^2$2977	$.0^2$2889	$.0^2$2804
2.4	$.0^2$2720	$.0^2$2640	$.0^2$2561	$.0^2$2484	$.0^2$2410	$.0^2$2337	$.0^2$2267	$.0^2$2199	$.0^2$2132	$.0^2$2067
2.5	$.0^2$2004	$.0^2$1943	$.0^2$1883	$.0^2$1826	$.0^2$1769	$.0^2$1715	$.0^2$1662	$.0^2$1610	$.0^2$1560	$.0^2$1511
2.6	$.0^2$1464	$.0^2$1418	$.0^2$1373	$.0^2$1330	$.0^2$1288	$.0^2$1247	$.0^2$1207	$.0^2$1169	$.0^2$1132	$.0^2$1095
2.7	$.0^2$1060	$.0^2$1026	$.0^3$9928	$.0^3$9607	$.0^3$9295	$.0^3$8992	$.0^3$8699	$.0^3$8414	$.0^3$8138	$.0^3$7870
2.8	$.0^3$7611	$.0^3$7359	$.0^3$7115	$.0^3$6879	$.0^3$6650	$.0^3$6428	$.0^3$6213	$.0^3$6004	$.0^3$5802	$.0^3$5606
2.9	$.0^3$5417	$.0^3$5233	$.0^3$5055	$.0^3$4883	$.0^3$4716	$.0^3$4555	$.0^3$4398	$.0^3$4247	$.0^3$4101	$.0^3$3959
3.0	$.0^3$3822	$.0^3$3689	$.0^3$3560	$.0^3$3436	$.0^3$3316	$.0^3$3199	$.0^3$3087	$.0^3$2978	$.0^3$2873	$.0^3$2771
3.1	$.0^3$2673	$.0^3$2577	$.0^3$2485	$.0^3$2396	$.0^3$2311	$.0^3$2227	$.0^3$2147	$.0^3$2070	$.0^3$1995	$.0^3$1922
3.2	$.0^3$1852	$.0^3$1785	$.0^3$1720	$.0^3$1657	$.0^3$1596	$.0^3$1537	$.0^3$1480	$.0^3$1426	$.0^3$1373	$.0^3$1322
3.3	$.0^3$1273	$.0^3$1225	$.0^3$1179	$.0^3$1135	$.0^3$1093	$.0^3$1051	$.0^3$1012	$.0^4$9734	$.0^4$9365	$.0^4$9009
3.4	$.0^4$8666	$.0^4$8335	$.0^4$8016	$.0^4$7709	$.0^4$7413	$.0^4$7127	$.0^4$6852	$.0^4$6587	$.0^4$6331	$.0^4$6085
3.5	$.0^4$5848	$.0^4$5620	$.0^4$5400	$.0^4$5188	$.0^4$4984	$.0^4$4788	$.0^4$4599	$.0^4$4417	$.0^4$4242	$.0^4$4073
3.6	$.0^4$3911	$.0^4$3755	$.0^4$3605	$.0^4$3460	$.0^4$3321	$.0^4$3188	$.0^4$3059	$.0^4$2935	$.0^4$2816	$.0^4$2702
3.7	$.0^4$2592	$.0^4$2486	$.0^4$2385	$.0^4$2287	$.0^4$2193	$.0^4$2103	$.0^4$2016	$.0^4$1933	$.0^4$1853	$.0^4$1776
3.8	$.0^4$1702	$.0^4$1632	$.0^4$1563	$.0^4$1498	$.0^4$1435	$.0^4$1375	$.0^4$1317	$.0^4$1262	$.0^4$1208	$.0^4$1157
3.9	$.0^4$1108	$.0^4$1061	$.0^4$1016	$.0^5$9723	$.0^5$9307	$.0^5$8908	$.0^5$8525	$.0^5$8158	$.0^5$7806	$.0^5$7469

* Source: R. Schlaifer, *Probability and Statistics for Business Decisions*,
McGraw-Hill, New York, 1959, pp. 706, 707.

Appendix J

Values of $\log N!$

N	0	1	2	3	4	5	6	7	8	9
00	0.0000	0.0000	0.3010	0.7782	1.3802	2.0792	2.8573	3.7024	4.6055	5.5598
10	6.5598	7.6012	8.6803	9.7943	10.9404	12.1165	13.3206	14.5511	15.8063	17.0851
20	18.3861	19.7083	21.0508	22.4125	23.7927	25.1906	26.6056	28.0370	29.4841	30.9465
30	32.4237	33.9150	35.4202	36.9387	38.4702	40.0142	41.5705	43.1387	44.7185	46.3096
40	47.9116	49.5244	51.1477	52.7811	54.4246	56.0778	57.7406	59.4127	61.0939	62.7841
50	64.4831	66.1906	67.9066	69.6309	71.3633	73.1037	74.8519	76.6077	78.3712	80.1420
60	81.9202	83.7055	85.4979	87.2972	89.1034	90.9163	92.7359	94.5619	96.3945	98.2333
70	100.0784	101.9297	103.7870	105.6503	107.5196	109.3946	111.2754	113.1619	115.0540	116.9516
80	118.8547	120.7632	122.6770	124.5961	126.5204	128.4498	130.3843	132.3238	134.2683	136.2177
90	138.1719	140.1310	143.0948	144.0632	146.0364	148.0141	149.9964	151.9831	153.9744	155.9700
100	157.9700	159.9743	161.9829	163.9958	166.0128	168.0340	170.0593	172.0887	174.1221	176.1595
110	178.2009	180.2462	182.2955	184.3485	186.4054	188.4661	190.5306	192.5988	194.6707	196.7462
120	198.8254	200.9082	202.9945	205.0844	207.1779	209.2748	211.3751	213.4790	215.5862	217.6967
130	219.8107	221.9280	224.0485	226.1724	228.2995	230.4298	232.5634	234.7001	236.8400	238.9830
140	241.1291	243.2783	245.4306	247.5860	249.7443	251.9057	254.0700	256.2374	258.4076	260.5808
150	262.7569	264.9359	267.1177	269.3024	271.4899	273.6803	275.8734	278.0693	280.2679	282.4693
160	284.6735	286.8803	289.0898	291.3020	293.5168	295.7343	297.9544	300.1771	302.4024	304.6303
170	306.8608	309.0938	311.3293	313.5674	315.8079	318.0509	320.2965	322.5444	324.7948	327.0477
180	329.3030	331.5606	333.8207	336.0832	338.3480	340.6152	342.8847	345.1565	347.4307	349.7071
190	351.9859	354.2669	356.5502	358.8358	361.1236	363.4136	365.7059	368.0003	370.2970	372.5959

Appendix K

Values of $U(n,h) = \left\{ 1 + \dfrac{1}{n} + \dfrac{12[\frac{1}{2}(n-1)+h]^2}{(n-1)n(n+1)} \right\}^{1/2}$ **for Centered Time Series**

h / n	1	2	3	4	5	6	7
3	1.82574	2.41522	3.05505	3.71931	4.39696	5.08265	5.77350
5	1.44913	1.67332	1.92353	2.19089	2.46981	2.75680	3.04959
7	1.30930	1.42678	1.55838	1.70084	1.85164	2.00890	2.17124
9	1.23603	1.30809	1.38844	1.47572	1.56879	1.66666	1.76855
11	1.19087	1.23950	1.29333	1.35176	1.41421	1.48017	1.54919
13	1.16023	1.19522	1.23368	1.27529	1.31975	1.36679	1.41615
15	1.13808	1.16445	1.19323	1.22425	1.25735	1.29237	1.32916
17	1.12131	1.14189	1.16421	1.18817	1.21368	1.24065	1.26897
19	1.10818	1.12468	1.14248	1.16151	1.18173	1.20306	1.22546
21	1.09761	1.11113	1.12565	1.14112	1.15750	1.17477	1.19287
23	1.08893	1.10021	1.11227	1.12508	1.13861	1.15284	1.16774
25	1.08166	1.09122	1.10139	1.11217	1.12352	1.13544	1.14790
27	1.07549	1.08369	1.09239	1.10157	1.11123	1.12135	1.13191
29	1.07019	1.07730	1.08482	1.09274	1.10105	1.10974	1.11880
31	1.06559	1.07181	1.07837	1.08527	1.09249	1.10003	1.10788
33	1.06155	1.06704	1.07282	1.07888	1.08521	1.09181	1.09868
35	1.05798	1.06286	1.06799	1.07335	1.07895	1.08478	1.09083

h / n	8	9	10	11	12	13	14	15
3	6.46786	7.16472	7.86341	8.56348	9.26462	9.96661	10.66927	11.37248
5	3.34664	3.64691	3.94968	4.25440	4.56070	4.86826	5.17687	5.48634
7	2.33758	2.50713	2.67928	2.85356	3.02961	3.20713	3.38589	3.56570
9	1.87379	1.98186	2.09231	2.20479	2.31900	2.43470	2.55168	2.66978
11	1.62088	1.69491	1.77097	1.84883	1.92825	2.00907	2.09110	2.17422
13	1.46759	1.52091	1.57591	1.63243	1.69030	1.74941	1.80962	1.87082
15	1.36756	1.40746	1.44872	1.49124	1.53491	1.57963	1.62532	1.67189
17	1.29856	1.32934	1.36122	1.39414	1.42801	1.46277	1.49836	1.53472
19	1.24885	1.27320	1.29844	1.32453	1.35141	1.37904	1.40737	1.43636
21	1.21177	1.23144	1.25183	1.27292	1.29467	1.31705	1.34002	1.36356
23	1.18329	1.19947	1.21624	1.23358	1.25148	1.26990	1.28882	1.30822
25	1.16090	1.17440	1.18840	1.20288	1.21781	1.23319	1.24899	1.26521
27	1.14292	1.15434	1.16618	1.17842	1.19104	1.20404	1.21741	1.23112
29	1.12823	1.13801	1.14814	1.15860	1.16939	1.18050	1.19192	1.20364
31	1.11604	1.12450	1.13325	1.14229	1.15161	1.16120	1.17105	1.18116
33	1.10581	1.11319	1.12082	1.12869	1.13680	1.14515	1.15373	1.16253
35	1.09710	1.10359	1.11030	1.11721	1.12434	1.13166	1.13919	1.14691

Appendix L

Values of the Present Worth Factor

for Uniform Flow, $f_u = \dfrac{1 - e^{-x}}{x}$

x	.00	.01	.02	.03	.04	.05	.06	.07	.08	.09
0	1.00000	.99502	.99007	.98515	.98026	.97541	.97059	.96580	.96105	.95632
.1	.95163	.94696	.94233	.93773	.93316	.92861	.92410	.91962	.91517	.91074
.2	.90635	.90198	.89764	.89333	.88905	.88480	.88057	.87637	.87220	.86806
.3	.86394	.85985	.85578	.85175	.84773	.84375	.83979	.83585	.83194	.82806
.4	.82420	.82037	.81656	.81277	.80901	.80527	.80156	.79787	.79420	.79056
.5	.78694	.78334	.77977	.77622	.77269	.76918	.76570	.76224	.75880	.75538
.6	.75198	.74861	.74525	.74192	.73861	.73531	.73204	.72879	.72556	.72235
.7	.71916	.71599	.71284	.70971	.70660	.70351	.70044	.69739	.69435	.69134
.8	.68834	.68536	.68240	.67946	.67654	.67363	.67074	.66787	.66502	.66218
.9	.65937	.65657	.65378	.65102	.64827	.64554	.64282	.64012	.63744	.63477
1.0	.63212	.62949	.62687	.62427	.62168	.61911	.61655	.61401	.61149	.60898
1.1	.60648	.60400	.60154	.59909	.59665	.59423	.59182	.58943	.58705	.58469
1.2	.58234	.58000	.57768	.57537	.57308	.57080	.56853	.56627	.56403	.56181
1.3	.55959	.55739	.55520	.55302	.55086	.54871	.54657	.54445	.54233	.54023
1.4	.53815	.53607	.53400	.53195	.52991	.52788	.52587	.52386	.52187	.51988
1.5	.51791	.51595	.51401	.51207	.51014	.50823	.50632	.50443	.50255	.50068
1.6	.49881	.49696	.49512	.49329	.49148	.48967	.48787	.48608	.48430	.48253
1.7	.48077	.47903	.47729	.47556	.47384	.47213	.47043	.46874	.46706	.46539
1.8	.46372	.46207	.46043	.45879	.45716	.45555	.45394	.45234	.45075	.44917
1.9	.44760	.44603	.44448	.44293	.44139	.43986	.43834	.43682	.43532	.43382
2.0	.43233	.43085	.42938	.42791	.42646	.42501	.42357	.42213	.42071	.41929
2.1	.41788	.41647	.41508	.41369	.41231	.41094	.40957	.40821	.40686	.40552
2.2	.40418	.40285	.40153	.40021	.39890	.39760	.39631	.39502	.39373	.39246
2.3	.39119	.38993	.38868	.38743	.38618	.38495	.38372	.38250	.38128	.38007
2.4	.37887	.37767	.37648	.37529	.37411	.37294	.37177	.37061	.36946	.36831
2.5	.36717	.36603	.36490	.36377	.36265	.36154	.36043	.35932	.35823	.35714
2.6	.35605	.35497	.35389	.35282	.35176	.35070	.34964	.34859	.34755	.34651
2.7	.34548	.34445	.34343	.34241	.34140	.34039	.33939	.33839	.33740	.33641
2.8	.33542	.33445	.33347	.33250	.33154	.33058	.32963	.32868	.32773	.32679
2.9	.32585	.32492	.32400	.32307	.32215	.32124	.32033	.31943	.31853	.31763
3.0	.31674	.31585	.31497	.31409	.31321	.31234	.31147	.31061	.30975	.30890
3.1	.30805	.30720	.30636	.30552	.30469	.30386	.30303	.30221	.30139	.30057
3.2	.29976	.29895	.29815	.29735	.29655	.29576	.29497	.29419	.29341	.29263
3.3	.29185	.29108	.29032	.28955	.28879	.28803	.28728	.28653	.28578	.28504
3.4	.28430	.28357	.28283	.28210	.28138	.28065	.27993	.27922	.27850	.27779
3.5	.27709	.27638	.27568	.27498	.27429	.27360	.27291	.27223	.27154	.27086
3.6	.27019	.26951	.26884	.26818	.26751	.26685	.26619	.26554	.26489	.26424
3.7	.26359	.26294	.26230	.26166	.26103	.26040	.25976	.25914	.25851	.25789
3.8	.25727	.25665	.25604	.25543	.25482	.25421	.25361	.25301	.25241	.25181
3.9	.25122	.25063	.25004	.24945	.24887	.24829	.24771	.24714	.24656	.24599
4.0	.24542	.24485	.24429	.24373	.24317	.24261	.24206	.24150	.24095	.24041

INDEX

Catalog

If you are interested in a list of SCHAUM'S
OUTLINE SERIES send your name
and address, requesting your free catalog, to:

SCHAUM'S OUTLINE SERIES, Dept. C
McGRAW-HILL BOOK COMPANY
1221 Avenue of Americas
New York, N.Y. 10020